Dictionary
of
Cultural Theorists

ARNOLD STUDENT REFERENCE

Dictionary
of
Cultural Theorists

Edited by

Ellis Cashmore
Professor of Sociology, Staffordshire University

and

Chris Rojek
Professor of Sociology and Culture, Nottingham Trent University

Foreword by Douglas Kellner
Professor of Education and Philosophy, University of California,
Los Angeles

A member of the Hodder Headline Group
LONDON • NEW YORK • SYDNEY • AUCKLAND

First published in Great Britain in 1999 by
Arnold, a member of the Hodder Headline Group,
338 Euston Road, London NW1 3BH

http://www.arnoldpublishers.com

Co-published in the United States of America by
Oxford University Press Inc.
198 Madison Avenue, New York, NY 10016

© 1999 Edward Arnold (Publishers) Ltd
Foreword © 1998 Douglas Kellner

All rights reserved. No part of this publication may be reproduced or
transmitted in any form or by any means, electronically or mechanically,
including photocopying, recording or any information storage or retrieval
system, without either prior permission in writing from the publisher or a
licence permitting restricted copying. In the United Kingdom such licences
are issued by the Copyright Licensing Agency: 90 Tottenham Court Road,
London W1P 9HE.

The advice and information in this book are believed to be true and accurate at
the date of going to press; neither the author[s] nor the publisher can accept any
legal responsibility or liability for any errors or omissions that may be made.

British Library Cataloguing in Publication Data
A catalogue record for this book is available from the British Library

Library of Congress Cataloging-in-Publication Data
A catalog record for this book is available from the Library of Congress

ISBN 0 340 64549 0 (hb)
ISBN 0 340 64548 2 (pb)

1 2 3 4 5 6 7 8 9 10

Production Editor: Wendy Rooke
Production Controller: Sarah Kett
Cover Design: Terry Griffiths

Typeset in 10/12.5pt Times by J&L Composition Ltd, Filey, North Yorkshire
Printed and bound in Great Britain by MPG Books Ltd, Bodmin, Cornwall

What do you think about this book? Or any other Arnold title?
Please send your comments to feedback.arnold@hodder.co.uk

CONTENTS

List of Contributors

This list includes contributors' initials as they appear in the text.

Editors

Ellis Cashmore, Staffordshire University, UK (E.C.)
Chris Rojek, Nottingham Trent University, UK (C.R.)

Editorial Assistant

Ray Guins, University of Leeds, UK (R.G.)

Consultants and Contributors

Jennifer Craik, Griffiths University, Australia (J.C.)
Mike Gane, Loughborough University, UK (M.G.)
Timothy J Lukes, Santa Clara University, USA (T.J.L.)
Jim McGuigan, Loughborough University, UK (J.McG.)
George Paton, Aston University, UK (G.P.)

Contributors

John Armitage, University of Northumbria, UK (J.A.)
Bob Ashey, Nottingham Trent University, UK (B.A.)
David Bell, Staffordshire University, UK (D.B.)
Peter Beilharz, La Trobe University, Australia (P.Be.)
Paul Bowman, University of Leeds, UK (P.B.)
Carl Bromley, University of Massachusetts, USA (C.B.)
Mary Bryden, University of Reading, UK (M.B.)
David Buehrer, Valdosta State University, USA (D.B.)
Hugo de Burgh, Nottingham Trent University, UK (H.d.B.)
Glenda Carrière, Griffith University, Australia (G.C.)
Chris Carter, Aston University, UK (C.C.)
Stephen Chan, Nottingham Trent University, UK (S.C.)
Stuart Cooper, Aston University, UK (S.M.C.)
Joanne Crawford, University of Leeds, UK (J.S.C.)
David Crowther, Aston University, UK (D.E.A.C.)
Omayra Cruz, University of California, San Diego, USA (O.C.)
Guy Cumberbatch, University College Worcester, UK (G.Cu.)
David Ames Curtis, Paris, France (D.A.C.)

Glyn Daly, Essex University, UK (G.D.)
Ioan Davies, York University, Canada (I.D.)
Matt Davies, Aston University, UK (M.D.)
Kay Dickinson, Exeter University, UK (K.D.)
Richard Ellis, Nottingham Trent University, UK (R.J.E.)
Carole Fleming, Nottingham Trent University, UK (C.F.)
David Gabbard, East Carolina University, USA (D.A.G.)
Nicholas Gane, Loughborough University of Technology, UK (N.G.)
John Goodridge, Nottingham Trent University, UK (J.G.)
Ian Inkster, Nottingham Trent University, UK (I.I.)
Julian Ives, Nottingham Trent University, UK (J.I.)
David Jary, Staffordshire University, UK (D.J.)
Oswald Jones, Aston University, UK (O.J.)
Barbara Kennedy, Staffordshire University, UK (B.K.)
Amy Kenyon, University of Leeds, UK (A.K.)
Maria Lauret, University of Sussex, UK (M.L.)
Nigel Liddell, University of Leeds, UK (N.L.)
Ray Loveridge, Aston University, UK (R.L.)
Patrick McGovern, London School of Economics, UK (P.McG.)
Peter McLaren, University of California, Los Angeles, USA (P.McL.)
Eugene McLaughlin, The Open University, UK (E.McL.)
Betsan Martin, University of Auckland, New Zealand (B.M.)
Christopher May, University of the West of England, UK (C.M.)
Stjepan Mestrovic, Texas A & M University, USA (S.M.)
Gill Moore, Nottingham Trent University, UK (G.B.M.)
Joanne Morra, University of Leeds, UK (J.M.)
Peter Murphy, La Trobe University, Australia (P.M.)
Simon O'Sullivan, University of Leeds, UK (S.O'S.)
William Pawlett, Loughborough University of Technology, UK (W.P.)
Michael Peters, University of Auckland, New Zealand (M.P.)
Georges Salemohammed, Loughborough University of Technology, UK (G.S.)
Valerie Scatamburlo, York University, Canada (V.S.)
Dennis Smith, Aston University, UK (D.S.)
John Smith, Aston University, UK (J.H.S.)
Marq Smith, University of Leeds, UK (M.S.)
Tony Spybey, Staffordshire University, UK (T.S.)
Rob Stone, University of Newcastle, UK (R.S.)
Theresa Thompson, Valdosta State University, USA (T.T.)
John Tomlinson, Nottingham Trent University, UK (J.T.)
Paolo Tripodi, Nottingham Trent University, UK (P.T.)
David Utterson, London, UK (D.U.)
Joost Van Loon, Nottingham Trent University, UK (J.V.L.)
Patrick Williams, Nottingham Trent University, UK (P.W.)
Gregory Woods, Nottingham Trent University, UK (G.W.)

Foreword

Douglas Kellner

FOR MANY CONTEMPORARY critics and social theorists, culture is central to understanding the current configurations of the economy, polis, society and everyday life. Computers and new technologies are revolutionising the economy, creating what many label an information society, while generating a new cyberculture. Politics has been increasingly colonised by the media and now the Internet, in which image and style are more important to electoral choices and public opinion than substance and more traditional political virtues, and in which rumours, gossip and tabloid sensationalism increasingly permeate public discourse. Mass-mediated cultural forms infiltrate our social and everyday life, influencing how we dress, present ourselves, make love, engage in leisure activities, and work. Even personal identity is becoming more and more constructed from the material of cultural images, styles and models, while computer-mediated communication (CMC) enables us to try out new identities, unencumbered by the constraints of gender, race, class and other real-life (RL) identity markers.

Classical social theory, on the whole, neglected culture, making it an epiphenomenon of the economy (Marx), contingent on the organisation of society (Comte and Durkheim), of derivative importance to bureaucracy, instrumental rationality and political organisation (Weber) or, with Freud, a mere mask for the vicissitudes of instincts. Yet the centrality of culture to contemporary life requires sociological analysis and reflection to capture the manifold effects of contemporary culture on every realm of life. Hence, major social theorists are focusing ever more intently on culture, and debates over its role, nature and effects are becoming central to contemporary social theory.

In this constellation, it is necessary to understand the new configurations of culture and society and to be able critically to discuss and dissect their multifarious dimensions. Consequently, a primer on the variety and diversity of discourses on culture in contemporary social theory provides a welcome aid to coming to terms with the overwhelming heterogeneity of contemporary social theory and its discourses on culture, which are often of a bewildering complexity, enmeshed in jargon and elusive webs of discourse. Readers of this volume should thus find helpful introductory material that provides an overview of the more important theorists of culture and society in the present age, a discussion of their major ideas, and an introduction to the texts in which their ideas are embedded.

The Editors' introduction signals the context in which one should read and study contemporary writings on culture and society. Whereas classical social theory discussed the nature, novelties, conflicts and possible futures of the modern era, contemporary social theory is deeply engaged in debates over the postmodern turn, concerning whether modernity is over and we are in a new postmodern age, and what sort of economy, culture, polity and society we are living in. Consequently, while classical and some current theorists presented in this book focus primarily on the modern age, others claim that we are in a new, postmodern era and that previous modern theories and discourses are obsolete. Contemporary social theory is thus engaged in a contentious and exciting drama of sorting out these issues and helping to clarify what sort of a world we are currently living in and moving towards.

Social theory can help generate the contextual and holistic understanding to grasp the centrality of culture in the present, and can also provide resources to engage its more fragmentary and heterogeneous moments, in which some phenomena, for instance, resist assimilation in habitual frames of thought. Such modes of analysis and inquiry thus help us to understand the present, perceive its novelties and come to terms with its problems and crises, as well as its possibilities and opportunities. We are living in a particularly turbulent era, subject to perhaps unparalleled social change, and need all the theoretical and practical guides that the best minds of the past and present era can provide.

Thus, to understand the vicissitudes and trajectory of our present moment, we must learn to envisage the imbrications of culture and society, to understand the ways in which they are interwoven and mutually effect each other, and to grasp, in turn, how these configurations influence the other domains of contemporary life. A first step in the arduous task of understanding the present is engaging the thought of those who have most illuminated it. A social theory is an optic or perspective on social life, it illuminates the area of its focus, and in turn has its blind spots, requiring multiple theories to grasp the complexities of the present moment. Thus, theories, at their best, provide instruments to help understand and engage contemporary reality. The more powerful theories one has at their disposal, the better able one is to make sense of social life today and to act intelligently within it.

Thus, the theorists described in this collection enable us to make sense of our present moment, to understand its constituents and to move forward into a better future. Understanding is a prerequisite to action, and if we want to think and act intelligently we must make use of the most helpful and provocative theories which give us the tools to comprehend and transform our contemporary world. Thus, theory, rather than being a dispensable luxury, or unnecessary encumbrance to empirical research, provides those tools and that mode of vision that make understanding, research and social action possible. Each of the theorists discussed in this book provides his or her own unique way of seeing and tools for analysis and research. Students and those who would like to understand better our current situation can therefore benefit from serious study of the major theorists introduced in this book. Gaining an overview of each thinker is of assistance in the admittedly arduous task of coming to terms with contemporary social and cultural theory. Thus, readers of this book are encouraged to move from the introductory overview to serious engagement with the thinkers and texts presented, in order to produce their own understanding of the social world we inhabit.

Douglas Kellner
Los Angeles

Editors' Introduction

THIS BOOK IS a primer. In no sense is our intention to be exhaustive, nor even comprehensive, in our coverage of the field. It is a preparatory guide intended to lead students through what sometimes seems like the torments of the damned. The idea stole on us when we were working together teaching a Master's degree class in contemporary social theory at Staffordshire University in the mid-1990s. Our students wanted a route map through the complicated, intricate and labyrinthine field of social and cultural theory, a field where boundaries constantly change. So, our task was to produce a book about a subject while that subject was – and is – changing rapidly. Secondary surveys were of some help, but they tended to be written from the standpoint of either sociology or cultural studies.

These books assume a high level of commitment on the part of the student to the outlook and vocabulary of the field. The vocabulary is frequently daunting. Cross-referencing is rare. Most textbooks written by people in cultural studies departments give the impression that sociology doesn't exist, and vice versa. It is a classical problem. Disciplines are organised within boundaries, but, of course, the human mind is not.

Clearly, there is no substitute for reading the original texts and delving into the secondary literature. But just as clearly, nowadays, undergraduate and Master's courses do not provide unlimited resources for reading, debating or thinking. Students are being encouraged to relate to the ideas and arguments of more and more theorists, but they are given less and less time to get to grips with the issues involved. Moreover, independent learning strategies encourage them to find out for themselves, a practice which we know can be as strenuous as it is frustrating.

We decided that there is a need for an introductory text which enables students to get started on a theorist almost as quickly as they can click on a window on a computer screen. We are aware that hackles will rise at this comparison. It suggests immediacy, cutting corners and a McDonaldised rubric. For this reason, we need to state plainly that we are not advocating a pedagogy in this book. Rather, we are attempting a practical solution to a practical problem: How can educators today help students to assimilate the complex traces, twists and turns of recent social and cultural theory in a quick and effective way, wasting the least possible time?

The organisation of the book

We have opted for an approach that concentrates on the ideas associated with flesh-and-blood theorists. This gives a concreteness to the issues involved, a concreteness often absent in works which operate solely, or mainly, at the level of abstract ideas or themes. All the same, we do not subscribe to the 'Great Man' and, increasingly, 'Great Woman' approach to social and cultural theory. All thinkers and indeed – as Merton once observed – all of us, stand on the shoulders of the men and women who precede us. Our response to the practical and theoretical problems that we face are bound up with the responses and solutions they made in their own time, to their own circumstances. The approach taken in this book is to treat theorists as participants in an elaborate, deeply rooted and developing project. We will elaborate on this in more detail later.

Conveying the sense of participation and dialogue can be cumbersome and repetitive. To get around these difficulties we decided to use a standardised method of organising entries which is designed to help students, to facilitate comprehension and make cross-referencing links. Each of the entries includes:

• key works by the theorists under discussion;
• the concepts and terms with which they are associated;
• pivotal influences on their work;
• other theorists with whom they share intellectual concerns;
• a brief biographical sketch;
• a summary of their main contributions to the understanding of aspects of culture;
• a short series of further readings either on or by the theorist.

We make no apology for producing a shamelessly user-friendly book intended for people seeking elementary principles, rather than advanced scholars.

To the left of each entry is a designation: philosopher, sociologist, historian, literary critic, and so on. In many senses these are arbitrary. What will become obvious is that one of the few hallmarks of contemporary social and cultural theory is that its practice does not neatly follow the formal subject distinctions to which most university faculties are attached. If, as we advise, social and cultural theory is regarded as fluid, and disciplinary boundaries as porous, then the titles of philosopher, sociologist, etc., might be usefully seen as membranes through which the fluid passes – from one to another and back again.

The project of modernity

Social and cultural theory comes in all shapes and sizes; but, we propose that there are three basic questions to the enterprise: What is our situation? How did we reach it? What are the prospects for change? Of course, these questions are not exhaustive. A variety of methodological and policy-oriented questions derive from them. For example, what are our criteria of knowledge? How can we test our propositions? What defences do we have to prevent our policies becoming dominated by values? How can we ensure that our solutions remain relevant in changing circumstances? But the three basic questions relating to present, past and future are common to all varieties of social and cultural theory.

There are several ways of contextualising these questions. One might situate them in relation to the rise of industrial society, or the conditions in a specific nation-state; or one might pursue them in relation to the circumstances of particular social strata, such as élite groups, classes, the masses, or gender, race and ethnic criteria. In recent years, the most common practice has been to locate the matter in the context of the debate around modernity and postmodernity.

Since this has been a debate conducted largely by academics working in the social sciences and humanities, it has become ferociously complex, loaded with definitional clauses and sub-clauses, preconditions, caveats, counterfactual arguments and all of the customary paraphernalia of scholarly debate. But, the heart of the matter is that modernity is understood as an attempt to discover secular, rational principles of order in the physical social world. There is some disagreement about when this attempt began. Some commentators place it in the fifteenth century with the voyages of discovery to find the limits of the world; others point to a technological basis, with the invention of the printing press which made the shapeless complexity of physical and human experience subject to the rule of the written word; still others enumerate different contenders such as the rise of the nation-state, the development of clocks and timekeeping in monasteries to regulate prayer which gradually spread to regulate labour and other aspects of life, and the emergence of accounting systems.

What no one disagrees with is that the momentous scientific revolutions instigated by Copernicus, Newton and Darwin were a crucial catalyst. Methods of collecting data and modes of analysing them that had proved successful for Copernicus and Newton in particular, were adopted and refined by, among many others, Descartes and Hobbes, both of whom were instrumental in changing the intellectual milieu of the seventeenth century.

The 'quest for certainty' began in earnest. No longer content to accept religious doctrine or metaphysical thought-systems, philosophers and soi-disant sociologists found a new resource in human consciousness. By centralising the role of the human mind in the process of discovery, they came to understand the world as potentially comprehensible and subject to the rule of human will. If the physical world was within the grasp of natural sciences, why not social sciences?

All of the thinkers discussed in this book have been influenced by the issues surrounding the modernity vs. postmodernity debate. It is the primary context in which their ideas were formulated and developed. In so far as Western thought has been bound up with a project, it is the project of modernising the world and the postmodern reactions to it that occupy centre stage. For this reason it is important to set out some of the main issues involved in the debate. Students will not fully understand the precise themes and arguments of the key thinkers discussed later if the primary context of thought is not elucidated. At the same time, in the last few years, the modernity vs. postmodernity debate has been like a gigantic mega-corporation in the academic world: it has all but monopolised consciousness. So, it is important to reveal some of the origins of the debate in the arguments. The following subsections will give readers an introduction to the debate and a framework inside which they might locate the work of the theorists covered in the dictionary.

Progress?

Modernity refers to the categorisation of the world in terms of a post-traditional cosmology, and the creation of post-traditional, rational–bureaucratic institutions, such as the state, the education system, the medical profession, the legal profession, and so on, to manage physical and human relations. Human arrangements are governed by ostensibly efficient rules, each geared to the attainment of specified goals or end-products. Modernism is the term usually given to the project of obtaining a secular, scientific understanding of natural and human reality.

Social and cultural theory was born in the throes of this massive upheaval and continual change in the ordinary, accustomed ways of understanding and managing human affairs. Such were the early successes of modernity, notably in the fields of economic production, health care, transport, education, warfare and colonisation, that modernism became infused with evangelical zeal. For a time, it was believed that there was nothing that the scientific mind could not accomplish. The modernising world was regarded to be *progressing* to an ever - higher state. Secular humanism was the power-driver behind this optimism. Human beings were redefined as having the power to mobilise rather than simply react to the physical environment. There was nothing that Man – and these were pre-feminist times – could not accomplish.

Classical Newtonian physics teaches that for every action there is a reaction. So it was in the growing field of social and cultural theory. Causes have effects; so achieving the desired effects was a question of locating the appropriate causes. Optimism about progress was soon met by critics who pointed to the costs of transforming the world. These costs were first expressed in human terms: in the uprooting of populations, the erosion of community life, the growth of alienation, the physical dangers of the new machine age and the coarsening of cultural values. But they were soon enlarged to encompass broader criticisms concerning the one-sidedness of industrial civilisation, the hazards posed to the environment by industrial and economic exploitation, the dubious character of collectivist concepts such as class, gender, nation and race and the dehumanisation involved in colonialism.

In the twentieth century, the two world wars, the Holocaust, the Stalinist Gulag, the atomic bombs dropped on Hiroshima and Nagasaki and the American war in Vietnam stand as symbols of the carnage and destruction that the modernist rhetoric of progress is capable of creating. Humanist defenders of modernity will counter with the argument that these historical cases represent deformations of modernism which spring from a concatenation of specific and unrepeatable events. Yet, as Arendt and Bauman have argued so persuasively, the logic that made the trains to Auschwitz run on time is indistinguishable from the logic of the clock that monitors work time and the use of the police to prevent agitation and disturbance. Integral to modernism is the possibility that rational means will displace moral ends. This is something that Weber realised in his prediction that the rationalisation process would bring about the disenchantment of the world.

This lack of confidence in the archetype of modernity as a force for unmitigated progress has gathered momentum in the last 30 years. The 1968 Paris spring stalled the revolutionary appeal of Marxism. The workers and students who took to the streets and appeared to be on the brink of taking over the country backed down and settled for a mixture of higher wages and better conditions. But this was nothing compared to the collapse of the Soviet empire – the so-called 'presently existing alternative' to capitalism – in the late 1980s and early 1990s. With these historic failures, the dream of a momentous, rational, all-encompassing change in the human condition, achieved through the revolutionary transformation of society, dimmed.

The 1990s were marked by a resurgence of market principles in the allocation of resources and the replacement of *grands projets* of total collective transformation with the patchwork of what some called identity politics. Nominally left-wing governments come to power, with a commitment to control taxes and cap borrowing and so reduce the size of the pot available for socialist change. Class revolution and even gender revolution seem to be things from the past. Classes and the sexes may not have achieved equality. But there is now a deep scepticism about whether the collective concepts of class and gender refer to unitary categories of experience. Throughout the West the dominant ethos today is one of living with capitalism and accepting difference. It is a far cry from the revolutionary politics espoused among the New Left and the counter-culture in the 1950s and 1960s.

The last 30 years have witnessed a decline in the concept of *society* and a rise in the concept of *culture*. Today, we are less certain about what we hold in common. We are more aware of the differences that divide us, and the lack of stability in our own values and outlook. 'There is no such thing as society', Baroness (then just Mrs) Thatcher trumpeted in the 1980s. While many would reject the Thatcherite picture of possessive, atomised individuals pursuing their own interests and the interests of their families without reference to 'society', there is no doubt that we are less confident in the modernist concept of 'society' as an entity to which we all belong and which shapes our destiny. Nowadays, we think of our destiny as being shaped by our immediate families, big business corporations, style gurus and the juggernaut of constant technical innovation, new risks and uncertainties. Society seems to have broken up into different fragments, and we commit to the islands of humanity those who best represent our personal mix of prejudices and desires.

The many meanings of postmodernity

Postmodernity describes a condition in which fixed, universal categories and certainty are replaced by difference, process and anomaly; it is the orientation to social and cultural life which proposes that there are no longer any collective subjects, no agreed cultural boundaries and no certainties. Postmodernists argue that there is no longer an embracing belief in 'scientific' rationality or unitary theories of truth or progress. Instead, they emphasise the ambivalence and indeterminacy or 'undecidability' of things. The theory and method of *deconstruction* takes the apparent solids of human life and exposes their insubstantiality. It peels layer upon layer of 'purity' from the modernist illusion of conceptual unity and institutional integrity, to reveal eclecticism and hybridity. Everything exists only in its relationship to everything else; in isolation they have no meaning, no sense, no *actualité*. As analysts, our attention is directed to the relations rather than the things: the rules, codes, customs, conventions and agreements – i.e. discourses – that allow us to recognise that something exists at all.

Depthlessness, not solidity, is the presiding metaphor of postmodernist analysis. The modernist faith in the gridlike order of social hierarchy and high and low culture is attacked as a myth. Postmodernism pointedly presents human relations as fragmentary, changeable and elastic. It questions whether there is any longer a meaningful basis for collective agreement or collective action. Indeed, it questions the status of 'self', 'identity' and 'agency' in the postmodern world of simulation and intertextuality.

Simulation is the process through which real, original objects are replaced by copies and 'treatments', which psychologically cause us to dismiss the concept of what Berger (following Schutz) called paramount reality. Intertextuality refers to the connections between the construction and representation of individual texts and objects. We should point out that *text*, in this sense, refers not just to written documents, but to *all* aspects of social reality, such as speech, actions, historical archives, TV shows, and so on – statements of experience. Culture, on this view, becomes an assembly of texts, none of which has meaning in itself, but which gain meaning through their intricate connections with other texts.

The effect of simulation and intertextuality is to undermine our traditional certainty in the concepts of originality and the real world. Intertextuality suggests that nothing is comprehensible save in relations to other texts: a rock concert may have no obvious connection with, say, postage stamps or agricultural policy, but they all derive their meaning from the lattice of relationships through which they are bound into particular discourses. Intertextuality makes us more aware of the hybrid, eclectic and contingent character of human practice and the products of these practices. 'We' are all living through texts, all reading, all transforming our experiences into texts that we can relate to other texts. In this way, 'we' make sense of experiences: nothing has meaning in itself; we give it meaning. This opens up the possibility of many meanings and many voices. For every text there is an infinity of meanings and none of them is 'better' than any other. The term favoured to capture this is polysemy – literally 'many meanings'.

To some extent, the thoroughgoing questioning of modernist categories was anticipated in the structuralist and post-structuralist debates that spanned the period from the Second World War to the end of the 1960s. Before there was a cultural turn there was a linguistic turn. Linguistic structuralists were dissatisfied with theories of language that either saw language as a mirror of the external world or, as in some way, a determinant of what we thought about the world. They offered an alternative. Language must be a social phenomenon; to talk in terms of a language of one person is an absurdity as there must be a structural basis for agreement over terms and meanings. So there are rules by which we must abide if we are to make sense to each other. Of course, the rules do not exist in some abstract way; they are what we might call today 'virtual' – they only come to life when they are activated through our speech. Saussure called the structure of rules of codes *langue* and the way that we operationalise them *parole*. He also observed that one without the other is literally senseless: we need to take stock of the interactions between the whole system.

Saussure also added the important point that language is a system of signs, each one of which comprises two parts. The signifier is the sound or image given off; the signified is the way in which the signifier is interpreted, heard or read. There is no automatic or mechanical relationship between the two and the link between them is a matter of cultural investigation. The principle of not studying individual acts (in Saussure's case, speech acts) in isolation has been widely observed. Not that Saussure was the first to recognise this. Yet, his stress on the structure of language, the primacy of the cultural domain and the moving patterns of links between signifiers and signified suggest areas of works that have been extended by more contemporary theorists and called semiology or semiotics, Barthes being one of its foremost exponents.

The strains of thought engendered by such approaches ignored the traditional dichotomy of knowledge based on reason and knowledge based on persuasion. All knowledge was seen as located in particular discourses and, as such, was politically constituted – 'made' through communicative action. Realistic representation became Truth not by some correspondence to what Kant would have called *noumena* (objects that exist independently of our thought), but by convention, agreement and consensus. In other words, if our readings of something coincide, then it passes as truth. Whereas social theory was traditionally thought to represent an exterior reality, its newer variants made no such pretence. Contemporary social and, particularly, cultural theory became the practices through which things take on meaning and value. And that was all.

Cognitive authority was banished by new cultural theory and its many tendencies: there were no privileged positions from where one could pronounce his or her theory as 'fact'. The Enlightenment's hallowed distinction between, on the one hand, scientific knowledge which could be tested against an empirical reality and, on the other, mere description, impression or rhetoric was thrown into confusion as the focus shifted. The new turn in theory spurned universal claims or grand theories that purported to have a direct line to real knowledge. In contrast, it set Truth adrift in a sea of epistemological relativism. Statements can only be 'true' in their specific discourse.

The discourse both constitutes Truth and is constituted by it. 'Constitute' is an apposite verb here: it suggests establishing, framing or giving form to; and this is precisely what the discourse involves. We create it and are created by it. In contrast to the project kick-started by modernity, cultural theory in the second half of the twentieth century entertained the possibility that consciousness and thought were not so much resources as objects of study. The questions shifted from: 'What can consciousness tell us about the world?' to 'How is it possible for us to talk in terms of consciousness as the fundamental element of Western social thought?' From: 'What is Truth?' to 'What makes it possible for us to recognise something as True?' The emphasis that post-structuralists and postmodernists placed on power and discourse undermined modernist faith in scientific impartiality. It paved the way to what some see as the baroque excesses of postmodernism.

Our knowledge of Truth is based not on some reality that our consciousness makes available to us via the application of logic and rationality, and which has no relation to the language we use to speak about the world. That is pure modernism. The preferred conception of Truth is as a linguistic projection; something which is decided on by agreement, not by reference to empirical testing. Knowledge is a creative activity: it becomes a matter of persuasion rather than an appeal to facts. The reader will notice that a great many theorists who work in this orbit pay scant respect to the obligation to provide illustration and instance, still less hard facts.

This gives contemporary cultural theory what is, for some, too much licence with the Truth. Critics see in postmodernism an 'anything-goes' approach to social and cultural analysis. The endless destabilising, de-essentialising or decentring of orthodoxies creates a power-vacuum in which resistance is spurned, because its effect will simply be to install new orders of power. Critics regard this as tantamount to siding with modernity. For while postmodernists deconstruct and despoil the central categories of modernist thought, global corporations continue to exploit, oppress and brutalise; ethnic groups continue to commit genocide in the name of purity, as the recent tragedies in Bosnia and Rwanda revealed so poignantly in the 1980s and 1990s; and men continue to oppress women in many parts of the world.

But postmodernist arguments cannot be swept aside so easily. They highlight the obduracy of modernist orthodoxy, which attempted to lay down a rational order for the whole world, irrespective of local conditions and local reactions. The totalitarian strands in modernism are expressed variously, in the sovereign freedom of individuals to pursue their own interests within the limits of the law which the powerful ordain and control; in the Fascist desire to produce a neat and tidy world of purity and order by physically eliminating 'polluting' peoples, practices and institutions; and in the action of the state to speak for the abstract collectivity against the individual, and particularly against individual difference.

Postmodernism runs the gauntlet against all of this. It has reinforced the turn towards culture by constantly stressing difference and fragmentation. In addition, it compels us to rethink the relationships between the core and the periphery and the real and the imaginary. Since these relations intrude upon so many human processes and practices, it would be unwise to announce the death of postmodernism just yet. By the same token, it would be hyperbole to claim that the age of postmodernity has arrived.

This in no sense captures the full range of concerns, expressions or analyses that make up cultural theory. In this book, readers will meet theorists who have opted for the grand totalising theories that are anathema to those of post-modernist persuasion. They will meet critics who have no time for linguistic minutiae as well as those for whom it was, and is, a virtual obsession. There are critics of today's culture; champions of it – those who focus on aspects of it; those who look only at the big picture.

Cultural theory has a fluidlike ungraspability: it consists of particles that move freely among themselves and yield, or so it seems, to the slightest pressure that we cynically call fashions (or, even more cynically, fads). In other words, it is never solid or rigid, but moving, changing shape, ebbing and flowing. In the time it takes to turn the manuscript we are now preparing into a book, the shape will have changed some more. And it has to: theory doesn't purport to provide us with universal truths and, even if it did, we should regard them sceptically. Theory moves in response to changing times: as contexts change, so we need theories that are appropriate to the new contexts.

But this is only a partial view of theory. Yes, it enlightens and liberates; it should also inform. The initial idea behind early social theory in the last century was to offer an analysis of a rapidly changing and perhaps perplexing world, and a *warning* of what might happen if those changes were left unchecked. In the twentieth century, particularly the second half, theories are more cautious in their warnings, more limited in their demands. We have no equivalents to Freud, Marx or Weber, though contemporary critical theory is arguably as wide-ranging and as admonishing in its tone, seeking, as it does, to reinsert the emancipatory dimension into theory by separating science from the restrictive technologies that now surround and infiltrate us.

While it a useful starting point to understand cultural theory as a product of the change ushered in by postmodernity, closer examination reveals far more overlap between various theories. If anything, cultural theory should be characterised by its egregious eclecticism and diffusion. In this book, the reader will discover theorists from a diversity of disciplines, all of whom have enriched our interpretation of culture in some way: the issues raised by the debates around structuralism and post-structuralism, modernity and postmodernity, have and will continue to influence us all. Even the great movements of sexual and ethnic liberation in this century have clearly been touched by the ripples of these debates. For example, the feminist movement between the 1940s and 1970s operated with a concept of the oppressed subject (women) and the dominant force (men). The strategy of women's liberation was founded on the project of releasing women from the unitary concept of patriarchy. Nowadays, post-feminist writers are openly querulous about concepts like collective subject, oppressed subject and patriarchy. Their accounts of sexual exploitation allow for a shifting power-balance between the sexes and internal divisions within the so-called 'common worlds' of women and men.

Similarly, the civil rights movement of the 1950s and 1960s spawned the movement of black power. This worked with crude binary oppositions between blacks and whites that reproduced the most mechanical features of structuralist thought. Today, post-colonial writers are more comfortable with the concepts of shifting signifiers, hybridity and Diaspora. Typically, they accept much of Derrida's work. His famed method of deconstruction leads to an investigation of the nature of Western traditions and their assumptions of permanent identities. This is coupled with his concept of difference, or *différance*. In everyday life, we talk of the difference between things, tea, for example, having different features to coffee. In doing so, we impute identities to both tea and coffee. But, for Derrida, *différance* (which, in French, is both to differ and to defer) suggests words are defined by what they are not, i.e. what other things are. Meaning is split; it is both present and absent. Analogously, *différance* enjoins that full and fixed meaning is never achieved but always deferred. It can only be elucidated by examining other concepts whose meanings are similarly deferred in an endless slippage and circularity of meaning. This approach encourages theorists to deconstruct culturally pervasive shibboleths about both 'race' and ethnicity, blackness and whiteness and the whole baggage of suppositions they bring with them.

But it is not only the symmetries of race and ethnicity that are disturbed by this type of approach to contemporary culture. Distinctive identities of gender, sexuality and nationality have changed under the patina of postmodernity. Newer and often unfamiliar forms of identification have surfaced, making even the modern unified individual subject prone to volatility and fragmentation. This has consequences on all our lives.

Mixing cultural theory with everyday life

An understanding of social and cultural theories and debates which confines them to the lecture theatre or the seminar room is profoundly unsatisfactory. In everyday life we see issues of structuralism/post-structuralism, modernity/postmodernity, expressed in advertising which mixes various styles and symbols to achieve an effect; the films of Jim Jarmusch, Atom Egoyan and David Lynch, which return again and again to question our notions of the discreteness of social and cultural categories and the order of narrative space and time. Today's music consciously recycles styles and simulates through sampling methods; in many cases, it owes more to production and mixing skills than to instrumentalism, as the examples of the Chemical Brothers, Sven Vath, Leftfield and countless others show.

Fashion, as essayed by the likes of John Galliano and Alexander McQueen, parodies the idea of stylistic purity by mixing incongruous elements from different times and cultures in a single design. The tribal divisions of youth that inspired countless subcultural studies in the 1970s and 1980s have now dissolved and, in their place, a sort of youth culture emporium has emerged, selling essential, commodified products, many of them incarnations from youth subcultures of previous decades.

Even the seemingly least flexible of bifurcations, the male–female distinction, has lost its firmness. Sexuality, it seems, is a matter of choice rather than destiny; and dozens of thousands of people not only feel trapped in the 'wrong' body but try to do something about it, women often travelling to Holland in search of transexual surgery, men opting for the surgeon's knife to relieve them of their encumbrances. Quite apart from this, untold numbers of transvestites (who may or may not be gay) add to the, for many, agreeable confusion over sexual identities.

Architecture borrows design references from the high and low cultures of modernity and fuses them to create design values that transcend modernism; and even in the construction and appearance of our own bodies, in which rings, chains, studs, tattoos, wigs, dyes, coloured contact lenses and cosmetic surgery are routinely used to challenge concepts of natural purity and enlarge the scope of bodily representation. Art spurns the approval of connoisseurs: witness the work of Damien Hirst, which seems to conflate fantasy with butchery as much to repel as to attract. Other conceptualist artists confound traditional critics.

How have cultural theorists helped us explain these changes? At times, it appears that they have contributed more to puzzlement than enlightenment. Yet this book has been prepared in the belief that theory is meant to enrich our understanding, promote our appreciation and release us with new wisdom. The entries in the dictionary were commissioned and prepared with a simple conviction: that the consequences of social and cultural theory for social and cultural practice in everyday life should be conveyed to the reader.

This is why we have included entries, for example, on the French existentialist philosopher Sartre, the critic and novelist Sontag, the architect Le Corbusier and the critic, dramatist and film-maker Debord, with the work of professional academic theorists like Gadamer, Bourdieu and Chomsky, policy-makers such as Fukuyama and scholars whose influence has reached the highest political levels, Galbraith and Etzioni being obvious examples. The reader will find odd pairings. Next door to Burnham, author of the seminal *The Managerial Revolution*, is Breton, the French surrealist writer and Dadaist architect. Kristeva, the feminist semiotician whose work has become almost synonymous with the avant-garde literary journal *Tel Quel*, is next to Kuhn, whose philosophy of science can lay every legitimate claim to have changed conceptions of truth and knowledge.

We have been deliberately sparing in our choices, because to represent fully the impact of social and cultural theory on cultural practitioners who have influenced everyday life would require a quite different and appreciably larger book than this. In any case, given the nature of the exercise, the weight has to be on the side of the contribution of the professional academic thinkers in the field. Even so, it is important to our sense of how the book should be seen and used, to insist that one of the best ways of determining the value of the ideas and propositions set out in the entries is to test them practically – in trying to make sense of our own lives and social and cultural discourses that surround and inhabit us.

We will close this introduction by revealing the devices that we employed to select our theorists, as we already anticipate upsetting disciples of certain writers who might have been excluded. A list of names was drawn up and circulated to an editorial board, comprising our publisher's commissioning editor and a panel of scholars from Australia, the UK and the USA. We made revisions in the light of feedback and arrived at our list of key theorists. In compiling a book on contemporary social and cultural theory, we focus on writers whose main contribution has been in the twentieth century. Yet, on occasion, we were persuaded to include thinkers from the nineteenth century because their intellectual impact has been so profound.

The bulk of the entries were written by ourselves and members of the editorial panel, all of whom work in the fields of cultural studies, literary criticism, political theory and sociology. Where we felt that the contribution of specialised scholars would be particularly appropriate, we approached them. The other contributions are by friends and colleagues from various academic institutions, but mainly from Aston, Leeds and Nottingham Trent universities.

Finally, in thinking about the book and commissioning and preparing the entries, we kept thinking of the metaphor of 'the open text' that semioticians use in writing about culture. This is also how we see culture. Our attempt to put lines around it in this volume is, no doubt, prone to errors of exclusion and maybe a few of inclusion. We thank in advance those readers who will write to us with recommendations of who, in future, we should leave in and take out. While every effort has been made to include dates of birth and death, one of the theorists covered in this book prefers not to disclose her birth date.

E.C./C.R.

ADORNO, Theodor

Philosopher/musicologist	born Germany 1903–1969
Associated with	THE FRANKFURT SCHOOL
Influences include	HEGEL ■ KANT ■ MARX
Shares common ground with	BENJAMIN ■ HORKHEIMER ■ MARCUSE
Main works	DIALEKTIK DER AUFKLÄRUNG (WITH MAX HORKHEIMER, 1944, TRANS. DIALECTIC OF ENLIGHTENMENT, 1972) MINIMA MORALIA: REFLEXIONEN AUS DEM BESCHÄDIGTEN LEBEN (1951, TRANS. MINIMA MORALIA: REFLECTIONS ON A DAMAGED LIFE, 1974) PRISMEN (1955, TRANS. PRISMS, 1967)

THEODOR ADORNO WAS born in Frankfurt am Main on 11 September 1903. At the age of 18, having already published two scholarly articles, he enrolled at the University of Frankfurt, where he would eventually co-direct, with Max Horkheimer, the Institute for Social Research, later known as the Frankfurt School. In the meantime, he not only completed his dissertation on Kierkegaard (a first on Freud had been rejected), but he also spent two years in Vienna studying music with Alban Berg, the most famous pupil of the composer Arnold Schoenberg. Adorno himself was a gifted musician and composer, and his writings betray a breadth of genius and experience rare in modern scholarship. Among the most famous of the Frankfurt School, which included Max Horkheimer, Walter Benjamin and Herbert Marcuse, Adorno not surprisingly concentrated more on aesthetic issues. Yet he also could be considered the most 'scientific' amongst his colleagues, participating in Paul Lazarsfeld's Office of Radio Research at Columbia, and later contributing to the famous quantitative study of Fascism and its psychic roots, *The Authoritarian Personality*.

It may be puzzling why a Marxist, even of Adorno's versatility, would be included in a volume on cultural theory. After all, conventional Marxism holds that culture (both 'high culture' and culture in the more generic sense of the constellation of social morays and practices) is a secondary phenomenon, and that it derives from more powerful economic, material forces. Culture, in this view, is ideology, and as such it serves to mitigate the barbarous practices of the dominant class, or it serves to glorify the achievements of that class. Scholars should focus, then, on economic structures, not their cultural by-products.

Adorno, whilst retaining Marxist methodology, is less inclined to relegate culture to this secondary role. He fears that modern society has reached a stage where material forces alone cannot be trusted to galvanise revolutionary practice. He is aghast at the proficiency with which the 'culture industry' neutralises and displaces the most heinous material obscenities with mindless cultural enterprises. Bourgeois culture is a narcotic, and it seduces its targets into a false sense of reconciliation and tranquillity. The bourgeois ideal, in which an autonomous individual or subject finds peace and harmony amidst a heretofore antagonistic environment, is disfigured by an insidious effort to subvert autonomy completely. When Adorno makes his famous declaration, 'to write poetry after Auschwitz is barbaric', he betrays a concern that the aftermath of Fascism might be just as abominable as its notorious precedent. He alludes to a population of happy automatons who blissfully revel in poetry and song amidst a backdrop of grotesque inhumanity.

Adorno's project is to break through the manipulative cultural enterprises, and his interest and expertise in music prompted him to suggest particular composers whom he felt capable of disrupting the stupor of mass culture. Igor Stravinsky, however, was not among those suggested. Adorno savages Stravinsky's affinity for melody and dance, not because Adorno is unreservedly opposed to the communalism and consonance that dance portrays, but because he believes that unity is not a rational position when the unification reinforces a society of manufactured desires and needs. Instead, Adorno endorses Arnold Schoenberg, whose atonal, serialistic motif allows no form of premature reconciliation or unity. The 12-tone row, invented by Schoenberg, prohibits the repetition of any one note until all 11 others have been played. By avoiding premature 'conciliation', Schoenberg's music not only reveals the dissonance of the present system, but does so with an opposing system. Schoenberg's art is a 'catalyst for change' because it reveals a contradiction (in this case, between bourgeois utility and a rational society) and thus reveals the contingency of the given. But perhaps more importantly, Schoenberg's reorganisation (the 12-tone technique) of the damaged elements reveals a commitment to a more legitimate alternative.

True to his modernist convictions, Adorno scrupulously avoided simplicity and conciliation. He often employed a cryptic, aphoristic motif, and he admitted that his writings were akin to notes in a bottle, tossed into the sea with hopes of discovery by a more exotic, receptive audience. His refusal to endorse the naïve counter-cultural exertions of the 1960s ensured his isolation and his philosophical integrity; yet his cumulative cynicism regarding the efficacy of any liberative mechanism leads one to wonder if his work does not culminate in a dead end.

Further reading

Benjamin, A. (ed.) THE PROBLEMS OF MODERNITY: ADORNO AND BENJAMIN, Routledge, 1989.
Jameson, F. LATE MARXISM: ADORNO, OR, THE PERSISTENCE OF THE DIALECTIC, Verso, 1990.
Jay, M. ADORNO, Harvard University Press, 1984.

T.J.L.

ALLPORT, Gordon W.

Psychologist	born USA 1897–1967
Associated with	FUNCTIONAL AUTONOMY ▪ PROPRIUM
Influences include	CATTELL ▪ JAMES ▪ STERN ▪ MCDOUGALL
Shares common ground with	CATTELL ▪ LEWIN ▪ ROGERS ▪ MASLOW
Main works	THE NATURE OF PREJUDICE (1954)
	PERSONALITY AND SOCIAL ENCOUNTER (1953)
	PATTERN AND GROWTH IN PERSONALITY (1961)

INDIANA-BORN ALLPORT studied at Harvard, gaining his BA in 1919, MA in 1921 and Ph.D. in 1922. He worked briefly as an English instructor in Istanbul and at Dartmouth College, New Hampshire, but spent most of his intellectually fertile years at Harvard. There he was Director of the National Opinion Research Council from 1942. In 1966, a year before his death, he was appointed Professor of Social Ethics. Between 1937 and 1949, he edited the influential *Journal of Abnormal and Social Psychology*.

Allport's research and theories were designed to avoid the *tabula rasa* assumptions of behavioursim and the biological reductionsim of Freudian analysis. Both, he contended, obscure the unique character and qualities of the human personality and, in the process, eliminate the possibility of free will. His alternative was to propose a model which allowed for the possibility of basic needs, or drives, but allowed the possibility of an active human agency that could function independently of those drives. His task was complicated by his insistence that he saw no role for an homunculus, or 'inner being' that exercises choice. Given the scale of Allport's enterprise, it was perhaps inevitable that his theory was flawed.

Like his fellow-humanist, Rogers, Allport was at pains to establish what was distinct about the human being. He concluded that his concept of the *functional autonomy of motives* supplied an answer. The motives behind our actions are not vestiges of past events, or deeply embedded tendencies that are not available to our senses: they are anticipations of the future. We discover more about motives from the conscious present than from repressed memories *à la Freud* or innate drives (as suggested by countless others). For example, to find out why a person shops at Toys 'Я' Us rather than Funfayre, we might analyse some set of rewards that leads to a gratification, or perhaps some past incident that unconsciously deters us from shopping at one place rather than another. Neither account was satisfactory for Allport; instead he advocated an approach based on the obvious fact that the person just enjoys shopping at their favourite toy shop – they have a good time there. His or her original motives *may* have origins in primal needs or in some other area, but Allport believes that human experiences takes on a status quite independent of its sources. It functions autonomously.

While he criticised peers for generalising from animal to human experience, Allport demonstrated his point with an oft-quoted experiment involving hungry rats which ran along a runway. Even after the hunger drive was removed, the rats continued to race at high speed. A human example might involve a hunter who hunts because of the need to procure food. Even after a food supply is made available, he or she may continue to hunt just for the sake of it. The activity becomes the aim or the goal itself, in spite of the fact that it was engaged in for an entirely different reason. We might argue that sport is an example of such mimetic activity.

This conception is rooted in Allport's conception of the human personality. Like his contemporaries, Allport situated this at the centre of his analysis, though he defined it rather interestingly: 'Personality is the dynamic [i.e. changing] organization within the individual of those psychophysical systems that determine his unique adjustments to his environment.' A later amendment switched 'characteristic behavior' for 'unique adjustments'. The amendment permitted Allport to conceive of the personality not only as a response to the environment, but as an entity that can reflect and act back on the environment. In other words, the personality is the organisational basis of our ability to change our social world. In fact, the personality cannot exist in isolation: it is developed in reaction, or response to other people and things.

The dynamic in Allport's model of personality is the *trait*, 'a neuropsychic structure having the capacity to render many stimuli functionally equivalent and to initiate and guide equivalent (meaningfully consistent) forms of adaptive and expressive behavior'. So, the traits are not items as such, but rather the way in which our capacities are organised into unitary systems. There are cardinal traits and central traits. The former plays an overriding role in a person's life; the latter are less enduring and constitute the basic units that are organised into the personality. There is a third category of secondary traits which equate to mental attitudes: no two constellations of traits are ever exactly the same, so every human has a unique personality.

In his attempt to avoid the homunculus as the force that fosters this unity of personality, Allport emphasised consistency of attitudes, intentions and evaluations and his term to capture this is *proprium*. The personality has propriate functions, he argued: these handle vital regions such as self-identity, a sense of selfhood and rational thinking. There is no ego, self or other motivating force that is distinct from the personality. Behaviourist principles of learning may work perfectly well for non-humans, children and elementary types of opportunistic learning. But not for propriate learning, which involves, for example, self-image, cognitive insight, identification, and so on.

While Allport criticised some of the limitations of early behaviourist theories of learning, his own model posed no meaningful alternative beyond a humanist conception of personality and a way to understand the relationship between the mind of the social environment. His work on prejudice was widely quoted as an example of how what were once considered personality traits relate to particular types of environments, though much of his *oeuvre* has not worn especially well.

Further reading

Costa, P. and Maddi, S. Humanism and Personality: Allport, Maslow and Murray, Aldine Atherton, 1972.
Evans, Robert I. Gordon Allport: The Man and His Ideas, Dutton, 1970.
Scroggs, J. Key Ideas in Personality Theory, West Publishing, 1985.

E.C.

ALTHUSSER, Louis

Philosopher	born Algeria 1918–1990
Associated with	INTERPELLATION ▪ ISAS ▪ RELATIVE AUTONOMY ▪ STRUCTURAL MARXISM
Influences include	HEGEL ▪ MARX ▪ SPINOZA
Shares common ground with	BARTHES ▪ FOUCAULT ▪ ZIZEK
Main works	FOR MARX (1965) READING CAPITAL (1968) LENIN AND PHILOSOPHY AND OTHER ESSAYS (1971)

LOUIS ALTHUSSER WAS educated in Lyons (Lycée du Parc), where he was also active in the Catholic youth movement. He was about to enter the École Normale Supérieure (ENS), Paris, in 1939 when he was mobilized into the French army. He was captured by the Germans and was a prisoner of war in Schleswig-Holstein until 1945. He then resumed his studies at the ENS where, after graduating in 1948, he spent the rest of his teaching career. His account of the event which ended his career and the history of his depressive illnesses appeared in his autobiography *The Future Lasts a Long Time* (1993).

Althusser's strategy was to reveal the weaknesses of the humanist theories of social praxis and class-consciousness (true and false) which were fashionable and influential in the 1950s and 1960s by appealing to the ideas of Marx and Lenin. For Althusser Marx abandoned his youthful flirtation with humanism and, in his mature writings, tried to establish a science of social formations. Althusser attempted to give the concept of materialism a new critical edge. His appeal to Marx was one which was to reassert the primacy of production, or even social reproduction, over ideological or cultural practices. Althusser was one of the first of recent philosophers to pose the question: How should a theoretical text be read? His reply launched a fundamental attack on hermeneutic understanding, for he tried to show, with particular reference to Marxist texts, that theory is governed by its epistemological frame, not the conscious intention of the author. Marx installed a scientific theory of society in which culture was a dependent element of the social superstructure, ultimately determined in its content by the configuration of the mode of economic production and the class struggle arising from it. This meant that culture in class-divided societies was intimately connected with the power of the state, and the dominant class. Specifically, his theory rejected any formal structural homologies between base and superstructure, indeed his conception of the complexity of the social formation recognised the necessary contingency of heterogeneous sociocultural elements which were held in place by overdetermination by the economy 'in the last instance'. According to Althusser, the way to analyse a social or cultural process is to see it as a practice. He developed the concept of theoretical practice, an idea which has had wide ramifications in all approaches which examine cultural practices. He also introduced the concept of interpellation, which sought to provide, by uniting Marxian and Freudian theory, an analysis of how individuals are as subjects. Interpellation is not a simple process of calling the subject into existence. The term implies a legal accusation to be responded to, a challenge which prompts and requires self-identification.

In a very radical attempt to develop Gramsci's theory of cultural hegemony, Althusser introduced a theory of the Ideological State Apparatuses (ISAs). Instead of a notion of culture as a more or less successful avoidance of the 'false class-conscious', Althusser suggested that ideology was to be contrasted with well-founded scientific knowledge, and therefore could be said to be a necessary illusion or first form of consciousness which recognised objects only as metaphor or metonymy, in a relation similar to that described by Freud for dreamwork. The state organised an apparatus of repression, one which Marxists previously concentrated on almost exclusively. But it also relied on a set of ideological apparatuses which functioned to create social subjects by calling them (interpellation) into existence as subjects of a greater Subject (the state). In the transition from feudalism to capitalism, the dominant ISAs shifted from the church-family 'couple' to that of the education-family 'couple.' This led Althusser to argue that the transition to a post capitalist society would inevitably mean a form of cultural revolution, just as the capitalist revolution had required a religious revolution. He argued that the problems of communism in the Soviet Union had largely arisen as a result of the failure of the revolutionary movement to complete the economic and political transitions with a profound cultural revolution. Without this third revolution, restoration of capitalism remained a strong possibility.

The main criticisms of Althusser's arguments have been that, although he tried to rescue Marxism as a science, his relation to Marx was essentially dogmatic. His attempt to develop a new theory of the state with specific emphasis on culture was widely seen as resting on functionalist presuppositions, a methodological flaw which was ironic in a writer who gave great weight to epistemology.

Further reading

Benton, T. The Rise and Fall of Structural Marxism, Macmillan, 1984.
Elliott, G.A. The Detour of History, Verso, 1987.
Gane, M. 'On the ISAs Episode', Economy and Society, 12: 4, pp. 431–67.

M.G.

ANDERSON, Perry

Historian/social theorist	born China 1938—
Associated with	WESTERN MARXISM
Influences include	MARX ■ GRAMSCI ■ LÉVI-STRAUSS
Shares common ground with	ALTHUSSER ■ THOMPSON ■ HALL
Main works	ENGLISH QUESTIONS (1992)
	IN THE TRACKS OF HISTORICAL MATERIALISM (1983)
	ARGUMENTS WITHIN ENGLISH MARXISM (1980)

PERRY ANDERSON, BROTHER of Benedict Anderson (who provides an account of the family in his *Language and Power* (Ithaca, 1990)), was educated at Eton and the University of Cambridge. He took over from Stuart Hall as editor of the *New Left Review* (*NLR*) in the early 1960s, and his involvement with this journal led to an important shift in its political and theoretical orientation. *NLR* played a significant formative intellectual role for a generation of Marxist intellectuals in the UK. With Anderson the journal developed a strategy of translating and introducing the main currents of European Marxism, particularly the theoretical traditions in Germany, Italy and France. A gifted linguist, Anderson had a working knowledge of texts from these traditions in the original languages and was able, in the publishing programme undertaken not only in *NLR* but also by New Left Books, to make a major impact not only on Marxist thinking but on theory in a wide spectrum of disciplines, not least cultural studies. Anderson now teaches history at the University of California, Los Angeles (UCLA), USA.

Anderson developed a wide-ranging historical account of the evolution of European societies within a Marxist framework, decisively modified by the influences of Weber and Gramsci. In studies such as *Passages from Antiquity to Feudalism* (1974) and *Lineages of the Absolutist State* (1974) Anderson seemed to be working towards a detailed analysis of the background to the split in the tactics of communist parties (Western versus Eastern models). But Anderson also worked with Tom Nairn on an analysis of English history and culture which led to a number of theses: the English case was unique for the prematurity and complexity of the capitalist revolution in the seventeenth century, and the climax of the Industrial Revolution at a time of political counter-revolution against France. And in the nineteenth century, the socialist movement grew within the framework of a triumphant British imperialism, a process of profound structural transition which occurred without a break in the political institutional forms of political power. Anderson concentrated on the cultural dimensions of these changes by taking up the suggestion that the relative backwardness of Marxism, and sociology as a discipline, in the UK could be explained by the absence of a revolutionary theoretical culture. Because of the way this transition had occurred, bourgeois intellectuals had incorporated themselves within the hegemony of an already established aristocratic culture. The newly emerging industrial working classes thus sought to incorporate themselves within a culture to which the bourgeoisie had already accommodated itself, by adopting a narrowly empirical philosophical and reformist political agenda, and socialists adopted this agenda themselves. Anderson's problem was how to escape this historically constituted frame.

In his essay 'Components of the National Culture' ([1968] 1992) Anderson provided a detailed analysis of the intellectual disciplines across the range: history, sociology, anthropology, economics, political theory, philosophy, aesthetics, literary criticism, psychology and psychoanalysis. He adopted a structural approach for the analysis which was thus embedded in an historical analysis of the incorporatist strategies of intellectuals – in fact, he concluded that in each of these disciplines the predominant intellectual had come from Austria (Wittgenstein, Popper, Klein), Poland (Malinowski, Namier, Deutscher), Russia (Berlin) or Germany (Eysenck). He called this 'the white emigration' since it seemed that, in the main, these intellectuals were particularly attracted to the conservatism of British culture. In the absence of a general theoretical account of British history or culture in the form of a sociology, there was a void in the intellectual landscape that was filled by a pervasive psychologism.

In 1992 Anderson returned to analyse what had happened in the intervening years in an essay called 'A Culture in Contraflow'. He noted that remarkable shifts had occurred. In particular, where sociology had been conspicuously absent, it had now grown to an overarching prominence. There had been a reordering of boundaries, an expansion of the social base of the intelligentsia, but, most significantly, a new academic hierarchy. In the intervening period there had also been Thatcherite neo-liberal radicalism, reacting to the new radical cultural developments. At the end of the essay Anderson suggests that a new period of cultural development is beginning, with the further weakening of the traditional and insular framework. Many of his observations in this essay are self-critical and reflect the response of critics who have suggested an over-evaluation of purely cultural factors in his account.

Further reading

Elliot, G. The Merciless Laboratory of History, University of Minnesota Press, 1998.
Hoch, P. 'No Utopia: Refugee Scholars in Britain', History Today, November 1985, pp. 53–6.
M.G.

ARENDT, Hannah

Political scientist/philosopher	born Germany 1906–1975
Associated with	Humanism
Influences include	Heidegger ■ Jaspers ■ Kant
Shares common ground with	Benjamin ■ Dwight Macdonald ■ Rorty
Main works	The Origins of Totalitarianism (1951)
	Eichmann in Jerusalem: A Report on the Banality of Evil (1963)
	On Revolution (1965)

Born in 1906, Hannah Arendt grew up in Königsberg, the home of Immanuel Kant, whose influence she felt throughout her life, in a well established, non-religious German-Jewish family. In her early life she had few connections with Jewish religious or cultural traditions, and displayed no interest in politics, studying philosophy, theology and classical Greek literature at Marburg under Martin Heidegger, and completing her doctoral thesis, 'The Concept of Love in St. Augustine' (1929), at Heidelberg, where she studied with Karl Jaspers. The rise of Nazism, and in particular the act of many German intellectuals – including Heidegger – backing Hitler in 1933, spurred her to abandon pure academia to work in the Zionist movement. This led to her being detained in German police custody for a short spell, before fleeing to France as a refugee. In 1941, after internment in a French camp, she was able to go to the USA where she continued to play a part within Jewish politics, writing in the New York German-Jewish paper, *Aufbau*, campaigning for a Jewish army to be formed to fight alongside the Allies, and after the war for a bi-national state in Palestine. She became an American citizen in 1951.

Arendt's first major work – *The Origins of Totalitarianism* – came out of a study of anti-Semitism and the antecedents of Nazism. In it she looked at the conditions that allowed a totalitarian state to be formed, taking Nazi Germany and the Stalinist Soviet Union as examples, how it perpetuated itself through the use of ideology, and how it differed from tyranny through its use of violence – 'terror is the essence of totalitarian domination'. Acclaimed by some critics as a profound analysis of Nazism and Stalinism, others viewed it as Cold War propaganda, and condemned her analysis of the still largely unknown Soviet system as inadequate.

Nonetheless, the issue of the responsibility we all have for our political condition, first raised in *The Origins of Totalitarianism*, was one that Arendt repeatedly returned to in her later work. She believed it was the duty of everyone to face up to political realities and take action rather than allow events to overcome them, and she condemned both a retreat to philosophical solitude and surrendering to supposedly inevitable trends as an abdication of responsibility.

Arendt expanded her notion of action in *The Human Condition* (1958), arguing for a Socratian position where thought and action, or philosophy and politics, are not opposed, and where plural opinions are not overthrown by a single truth. She also argued that each action must be judged on its own without reference to a general rule or external standard, and this concept of rising above moral standards to form independent judgements is apparent throughout her most controversial work, *Eichmann in Jerusalem: A Report on the Banality of Evil*. In it she portrayed Eichmann as an ordinary man who failed to rise above the prevailing moral standards of Nazi Germany to form an independent judgement about his actions. 'He did not need to 'close his ears to the voice of conscience', as the judgement had it, not because he had none, but because his conscience spoke with a 'respectable voice', with the voice of respectable society around him' (*Eichmann in Jerusalem*, p. 126). This work was seen by many as an act of disloyalty to the Jewish community, many of whom failed to see that her point was that the failure to take responsibility for the political conditions of the time affected both persecutors and victims.

Her advocacy of participatory politics was reaffirmed in *On Revolution*, a comparative study of revolutions, and in particular of the American and French revolutions. This again had a mixed reception, with her distinction between social and political revolutions baffling many critics, who objected to her rejection of the traditional opposition between socialism and capitalism, and saw it as an attack on the social concerns of modern politics.

Throughout her life Hannah Arendt struggled with the connection between philosophy and politics, and although it was one she never fully resolved, her concern for the freedom to participate in action as a possibility for achieving 'public happiness' makes her work as relevant today as it was when it was written. As Margaret Canovan (1992) points out, the fall of communism in Eastern Europe and subsequent revolutions there also seem to confirm her claim that power is less a matter of weapons and resources than of people acting in concert.

Further reading

Canovan, M. Hannah Arendt: A Reinterpretation of her Political Thought, Cambridge University Press, 1992.
Hill, M. (ed.) Hannah Arendt: The Recovery of the Public World, St Martin's Press, 1979.
May, L. and Kohn, J. (eds.) Hannah Arendt: Twenty Years Later, MIT Press, 1996.

C.F.

BACHELARD, Gaston

Philosopher of science	born France 1884–1962
Associated with	Discontinuity ■ Surrationalisme
Influences include	Descartes
Shares common ground with	Althusser ■ Jung ■ Kuhn
Main works	The New Scientific Spirit (1934)
	The Philosophy of No: A Philosophy of the New Scientific Mind (1940)
	The Poetics of Space (1957)

 AFTER COMPLETING HIS degree in mathematics, Bachelard taught physics and chemistry at a college in his birthplace, Bar-sur-Aube, France, while studying for his doctorate in philosophy. His scientific background affected his entire approach to the philosophy of science, which was to influence such theorists as Althusser and Foucault. His doctoral thesis was published as *Essay on Approximate Knowledge* and the recognition of this enabled Bachelard to take up a Chair of History and Philosophy of Science at the Sorbonne, a position he held until 1954.

The premise of Bachelard's theories is that any philosophy concerned with knowledge must learn from science: specifically, it must take into account the unique features of twentieth-century science. In particular, the disjuncture occasioned by the replacement of Newtonian physics by Einstein's theory of relativity and quantum mechanics suggested a 'discontinuity', a term later translated by Althusser as 'epistemological rupture'.

Historically, discontinuity is in evidence in the shift from Euclidean to non-Euclidean geometry and in the veritable revolution in conceptions of time and space of the late nineteenth and twentieth centuries. Heisenberg and Einstein advanced new definitions of mass as a function of velocity; previously it was regarded as the reverse, i.e. velocity as a function of mass – so the greater the matter, the greater the force needed to oppose it. Old theories were not inadequate, but the new theories entirely transcended existing explanations. They were not comparable on the same level. No knowledge, for Bachelard, was immutable. To use one of his metaphors, the stability of the contents (of knowledge) is not due to the stability of the container: forms of rationality cannot be permanent. This issued a strong challenge to empiricist conceptions of science, a challenge that was further strengthened in 1962 with the publication of Kuhn's *The Structure of Scientific Revolutions*.

Bachelard's observation that the subject-matter of science is not matter, but relations, suggests a point later elaborated by structuralists. All science is involved in what Bachelard called 'objectification': it is oriented to observing phenomena as things. But Bachelard ventured that the phenomena under investigation are not substantive but relational: in other words, the subject of science is the relations of properties, not properties themselves. Science, like thought itself, is always in the process of objectifying, but is never complete or whole.

In his most famous book, *The New Scientific Spirit*, Bachelard wrote of two metaphysical bases. 'Rationalism' is the area of interpretation and reason, while 'realism' provides rationalism with the raw material to be interpreted. Any science that engages with the material world by collecting facts and making observations will remain at a naïve, experimental level and will stagnate. Rationalism provides frameworks for interpretation by posing theories, abstractions or an underlying philosophical system. One cannot be privileged over the other: 'Experimentation must give way to argument, and argument must have recourse to experimentation', Bachelard insisted. While the inextricability of theory and empirical research is nowadays taken for granted, Bachelard was boldly fusing the concerns of pragmatic science with philosophy, arguing to scientists that they were reliant on philosophical frames of reference, even if they were not aware of it. He cited Einstein as an example of a rational theorist, who needed experimentation in order to develop his theories.

In this sense, Bachelard's work emphasises the role of human imagination, especially the image related to matter, movement, forces and dreams linked to his theories of science. Imagination is not a reflection of the observable world, but a creative force that enables us to build interpretative frames of reference. Bachelard introduces the concept of *surrationalisme*: this describes the way in which we enrich rationalism by a combination of observation of the material world and creative, non-rational imagination. Imagination has an autonomy that resists predictive science. But it is not an imagination that has its source in the unconscious, as in Freud; but emerges from semi-conscious states, such as daydreaming. It is this inviolable human quality that feeds into science and revivifies it. In this sense, Bachelard's conception of imagination is close to Jung's.

Effectively, the imagination so vital to science is a product of human will, but which is made possible by its relation with the material world. Hence we see the importance of relational properties: humans imagine in frameworks of knowledge made possible by science, which is itself subject to both rationalism and experimentation. It is this emphasis that resurfaced in structuralism and post-structuralism.

Further reading

McEllester Jones, M. GASTON BACHELARD: SUBVERSIVE HUMANIST: TEXTS AND READINGS, University of Winsconsin Press, 1991.
Smith, R.C. GASTON BACHELARD, Twayne, 1982.
Tiles, M. BACHELARD, SCIENCE AND OBJECTIVITY, Cambridge University Press, 1984.

E.C.

BAGEHOT, Walter

Economist/political historian	born England 1826–1877
Associated with	DIFFERENCE ■ SCIENTISM
Influences include	SPENCER ■ COMTE ■ DARWIN
Shares common ground with	RICARDO ■ MICHELS ■ SMITH
Main works	THE ENGLISH CONSTITUTION (1867) PHYSICS AND POLITICS (1869) LOMBARD STREET (1873)

AFTER GRADUATION FROM London University in 1846, Bagehot managed the family banking business in Somerset, at the same time editing
The Economist (from 1860), becoming a prospective (but several
times failed) Member of Parliament, activist of the Political Economy Club
and *éminence grise* of the City of London and civil service. His posthumous
volumes of *Literary Studies* (1879) and *Economic Studies* (1880) are refresh-
ingly witty and incisive, but his present importance is based almost entirely on
the three works listed above, particularly the first of 1867. To students of
cultural dynamics, Bagehot is of especial importance as a representative but
brilliant example of later nineteenth-century scientism, i.e. the application of
dispassionate and detailed analysis to matters hitherto considered emotional
and ideational. To this extent, his work on political economy is comparable to
that of Francis Gaton (1822–1911) in natural science.

Lombard Street is a view of the money markets of 1850–70 and is based on a
series of articles in *The Economist*. It has been considered as performing for the
complexities of the banking and financial sectors that which Adam Smith
achieved for the economy more generally. The subsequent conduct of British
banking was greatly influenced by Bagehot's theory of a one-reserve system
and the principles applied to the level below which such a reserve should not
fall.

Although *Physics and Politics* is nominally a description of the evolution of
communities of men on approximately Darwinian grounds, it also represents a
basis for his more overtly political work, if only because 'unconscious imita-
tion' was 'the main force which moulds and fashions men in society'. Britain's
advantage lay in the size and vigour of the educated intellectual and moral
élite: 'nobility is the symbol of the mind'.

The English Constitution was dated on completion, more so on publication,
if only because of the disappearance from the political scene of the Lords
Palmerston, Derby and Russell, the last great aristocratic representatives of the

pre-1832 politics, the living cement which bound Bagehot's society to its constitution. There is little in Bagehot's first edition which foresaw the tumults of the latter 1860s and the coming of the Second Reform Bill; nothing which predicted the great debate and problematical character of the Gladstone–Disraeli tussles. Still less did *The English Constitution* lay any initial ground-work for understanding collectivism or socialism, of the Third Reform Bill (1885) or of the politics which would come with Lloyd George and Chamberlain. As G.M. Young always believed, Bagehot might well have been analysing a political system which represented at best an uneasy compromise between the 1830s culture of the bourgeoisie and the 1840s reassertion of tradition, a compromise which possessed no ultimate principle of stability. So why was *The English Constitution* so significant?

Bagehot's point was that the limited freedoms of the 1860s and the hegemony of 'the better educated classes' just sufficed to prevent a descent into Coleridge's feared democracy of 'fools and knaves'. The ignorance of the masses might be feared, but it could also be used, and it was upon this element that he settled in his book of 1867. Free discussion and social change served to crumble 'the cake of custom', necessary for progress, but institutional and cultural hegemony were then required in order to maintain a stable Victorian democracy: 'The principle of popular government is that the supreme power, the determining efficiency in matters political, resides with the people, not necessarily or commonly in the whole people but in a chosen people, a picked and selected people.' A deep-rooted defence, combined with 'removable qualities' (through income mobility), sustained a delicate equipoise. Recently, *Chapter 88* and the work of the Institute of Public Policy Research in Britain (1989) have once more brought constitutional matters to the fore, and all sides of the debate now ponder the significance of Bagehot's conception of the British political system as 'a living institution'.

Further reading

Guttsman, W.L. THE BRITISH POLITICAL ELITE, McGibbon & Kee, 1968.
Harrison, B. THE TRANSFORMATION OF BRITISH POLITICS 1860–1995, Oxford University Press, 1996.
I.I.

BAHRO, Rudolph

Philosopher	born Germany 1935–1997
Associated with	PERESTROIKA ■ ECOLOGY ■ ACTUALLY EXISTING SOCIALISM
Influences include	MARX ■ LUKÁCS ■ HEGEL
Shares common ground with	GORZ ■ HABERMAS ■ BECK
Main works	THE ALTERNATIVE IN EASTERN EUROPE (1978) SOCIALISM AND SURVIVAL (1982) BUILDING THE GREEN MOVEMENT (1986)

'PRESENTLY EXISTING SOCIALISM' was not a phrase in common parlance until Bahro invented it. Born in Silesia, and only 10 at the end of the Second World War, he followed others in his generation and became a committed Communist. He read philosophy at Greifswald University and, throughout his undergraduate days, toed the party line. After graduating he worked on a communist youth magazine. In his early thirties he published a text of a dramatic work that subjected communism to criticism. He was dismissed, and a year later, in 1968, he protested against the Soviet clampdown in Prague.

Deprived of a place in the official intelligentsia, Bahro spent the 1970s working in a rubber factory in East Berlin. But by night he worked on a full-length critique of the communist 'achievement' in Eastern Europe. His argument followed that of the Yugoslav communist apostate, Milovan Djilas, in condemning the party for evacuating communist principles in favour of bureaucratic rationality. In the heart of one of the most developed economies in the Eastern European bloc, he maintained communism was not working. He subjected the centralisation of state power in the hands of the party élite, the mismanagement of resources, and the abuses of human rights, to principled comprehensive attack. Bahro argued from within the Marxist tradition. He did not wish to replace state society with market society. Rather, he wanted to recover the promise of communism in Marx's original writings. Ultimately this is what made him so threatening to party ideologues. Bahro held that the application of Marxist–Leninist propositions in Eastern Europe had produced a travesty of Marxism. 'Presently existing socialism' negated the free and full development of individuals and policed popular culture in order to neutralise difference and dissent. Individuals were subject to the tyranny of the party. The operation of Marxist–Leninist theory had created the reverse of the intentions of Marx and Lenin.

This was music to the ears of critics based in the safe haven of the capitalist West. The German newspaper *Der Spiegel* serialised Bahro's arguments and the response of the East German authorities was predictable. Bahro was arrested and condemned as a Western spy. He later discovered that his first wife had supplied information to the authorities throughout the writing of his critique. He was tried and sentenced to eight years' imprisonment. An outcry in the West lead to his early release in 1977.

The precondition of his release was that Bahro should relocate to the West. Bahro migrated to West Berlin, where he was fêted as a hero. He embraced Green politics, and between 1982 and 1984 he sat on the federal board of the Green Party. During these years he developed his concept of sustainable economics. Bahro sought to replace obedience to the capitalist work ethic and the doctrine of exponential economic growth with a more balanced system of economic, cultural and ecological relations designed to fulfil human need. But he became disenchanted with what he took to be a failure of nerve in the Green movement. He argued that the Greens symbolised mere superficial resistance to the rule of capital. The Green alternative stopped well short of dismantling the logic of capitalism, which is to remorselessly transform nature into the service of multiplying monetary wealth. In his most acerbic moments, he maintained that if the Green Party did not exist, the capitalist system would have invented it. Not surprisingly, he left the party in 1985.

Barho's philosophy now took a turn to the East. He studied Buddhism as an alternative to the dehumanisation of both capitalist and socialist *realpolitik.* After the collapse of the Berlin Wall in 1989 Bahro returned to East Berlin, and from 1990 he ran the Institute for Social Ecology at the Humboldt University. Here he attempted to fuse an alloy of humanist socialism and ecological politics. Bahro became interested in building socialism from below. He set up an organic farming project in Pommeritz and experimented with 'basic communes'. These were in part designed to recover the egalitarianism, liberation and ethic of mutual care inherent in Marx's original concept of communism.

Bahro is a notable cultural theorist because he did not merely confine himself to cultural analysis, but also endeavoured to test his ideas in practice. His brave and magisterial critique of command economies was an important catalyst in the liberalisation and eventual transformation of the Soviet-type system. But like many disillusioned Communists of his generation, he was naïve about the capacity of capitalism to reform from within. The basic commune was no more than a peripheral critical counterpoint to the progress of capitalism. He was unable to find an answer to the replacement of monetary values with transcendent values that would deliver acceptable economic standards with the satisfaction of human needs.

Further reading

Dobson, R. GREEN POLITICAL THOUGHT, Routledge, 1990.
Doherty, B. and De Geus, M. DEMOCRACY AND GREEN POLITICAL THOUGHT, Routledge, 1996.
Hayward, T. ECOLOGICAL THOUGHT, Polity, 1994.

C.R.

BAKHTIN, Mikhail

Literary theorist/philosopher	born Russia 1895–1975
Associated with	CARNIVALESQUE ■ DIALOGISM ■ HETEROGLOSSIA
Influences include	FISCHER ■ KANT ■ VOSSLER
Shares common ground with	GRAMSCI ■ LUKÁCS ■ VOLOSHINOVA
Main works	RABELAIS AND HIS WORLD (1968) PROBLEMS OF DOSTOEVSKY'S POETICS (1973) THE DIALOGIC IMAGINATION (1981)

BORN IN TSARIST Russia, Bakhtin studied philosophy and religion at St Petersburg University during the First World War. Upon graduation he moved to a small town in western Russia, where he worked irregularly as a schoolteacher. He participated in study circles of friends (later known as 'The Bakhtin Circle'), discussing broad questions known in Russia as 'Culturology'. There he started his book on Dostoevsky and early unpublished essays, notably his critique of Formalism. On his return to Leningrad in 1924 he lectured regularly on religious ethics and neo-Kantian philosophy and published many works under the names of his Marxist friends, Medvedev and Voloshinov.

Following the intercession of influential friends on his arrest in 1929 by the Soviet authorities, Bakhtin's death sentence was commuted to internal exile in Kazakhstan. In 1936 he resumed his academic career as Professor of Russian and World Literature in the remote town of Saransk, where he taught until

1961. The rediscovery of his work on Dostoevsky by young Moscow scholars led to the publication of a second, reworked edition of *Problems of Dostoevsky's Poetics*, to be rapidly followed by other long-delayed seminal essays and subsequent translations of all his major works into English. Bakhtin's earliest essays reflected concerns with the crisis in culture and philosophy associated with modernism in the early twentieth century. His neo-Kantianism and philosophical stoicism led to his central concerns with ethical and aesthetic acts, as well as the potential of the word in language and the novel.

His influential redefinition of languages, anticipating much later developments in linguistics and literary theory in the West, derived from his attack on Russian Formalists and a questioning of the privileging of *langue* over *parole* in Saussurian linguistics. Thus Bakhtin perceived language as a living, diversified construct in use, which also took into account the non-linguistic components of any speech act arising out of the dialogue between the speaker and his interlocutor. Bakhtin's most influential and frequently adopted motif is the seminal idea of the 'carnivalesque', which he explores extensively in *Rabelais and his World*.

Of all the major Renaissance figures, Rabelais is for Bakhtin the most radically democratic and humanistic in revealing the heterogeneity and grotesque realism of medieval popular culture, his masterpiece, *Gargantua and Pantagruel*, representing an encyclopaedia of folk culture. In celebrating Carnival as the cultural mode expressing the collective human impulse towards freedom and equality in which the principle of differences prevails over domination, Bakhtin points up the tradition of subversive medieval popular culture and folk humour as a preliterate, and even pre-verbal, social fact *sui generis*. Through the liberating 'permanent collective' of laughter, merriment and foolery and the central carnivalised genres of parody and Menippean satire, Bakhtin argues, different ways of talking about the world are unmasked and defamiliarised in the dialogue between heteroglot, as opposed to the monoglot official, language users of different professions, classes, interests, ideologies or points of view.

In *Problems of Dostoevsky's Poetics* Bakhtin sets out a radically new way of examining language and intertextuality in both everyday life and literature. In this work he introduces his concepts of 'heteroglossia' and 'dialogism' which remained central to his philosophical project until his death in 1975. For Bakhtin, Dostoevsky was the first genuine exponent of the 'fully polyphonic novel', representing the interaction of his characters' consciousnesses and ideological worlds in a radically different way from the accepted monologic tradition of the eighteenth- and nineteenth-century, fully-fledged novel, poetry and drama. Heteroglossia is Bakhtin's term for the internal stratification of a unitary national language divided historically and normatively at the level of style. Such multi-voiced and double-voiced discursive forces are at work in whole cultural systems as well as in the workings of language, enriching meaning and the creative tension between heteroglot linguistic diversity and the hegemonic monoglot social authority prescribing unity. In the literary discourse of the novel the tension is between the actually different functions of author and hero which, in Bakhtin's version of literary history, leads him to conclude that 'A certain latitude for heteroglossia exists only in the 'low' poetic genres in the satiric and comic genres and others.'

From the 1930s onwards Bakhtin embarked on a general research programme in the politics of culture, with particular stress on the tensile 'struggle over the sign', from which, only with free dialogic interaction between 'speaking men', could real or practical truth emerge and be interpreted. Central to all his work and underpinning polyphony and heteroglossia is the rich, if polysemic, Bakhtinian concept of 'dialogism', where dialogue articulates a genuine 'sociology of consciousness' and the creation of meaningful utterances. Dialogism is the very principle of binary thinking about language and literature as well as the defining characteristic of linguistic structuring, which is realised most evocatively for Bakhtin as the action of the polyphonic, avant-garde Dostoevskian novel and, historically, the earlier comic and satiric writing of the classical period, as well as the carnival tradition of popular culture.

Bakhtin's rich and polysemic concepts heralded postmodernism in not only coinciding with the questioning of cultural history and recasting of hierarchical notions of aesthetics associated with the role of the author and reader since the 1970s, but also in revolutionising linguistics and literary studies traditionally associated exclusively with so-called learned or high culture. His major works have stimulated and been instrumental in pioneering reappraisals and new intellectual analyses of myriad forms of popular culture, inspiring sociolinguistic and semiotic studies of film, television, popular music, and joke-telling, etc., as well as modern literature, drama and painting. In addition to providing a monumental rethinking of what constitutes discourse in its interpersonal and wider social and cultural contexts, Bakhtin's most fundamental contribution lies in his breaking-away from one-dimensional models of literary communication, and providing methods of analysis which take into account the multi-layered nature of human language, and, consequently, of literary works of art (Wales, 1988: 177).

Further reading

Clark, K. and Holquist, M. MIKHAIL BAKHTIN, Harvard University Press, 1984.
Gardiner, M. THE DIALOGICS OF CRITIQUE: M.M. BAKHTIN AND THE THEORY OF IDEOLOGY, Routledge, 1992.
Wales, K. 'Back to the Future: Bakhtin, stylistics and discourse', in W. Van Peer (ed.), THE TAMING OF THE TEXT: EXPLORATIONS IN LANGUAGE, LITERATURE AND CULTURE (Routledge, 1988).

G.P.

BARTHES, Roland

Cultural critic	born France, 1915–1980
Associated with	CULTURAL STUDIES ■ LITERARY CRITICISM ■ SEMIOTICS ■ STRUCTURALISM
Influences include	BAUDELAIRE ■ SAUSSURE ■ PEIRCE
Shares common ground with	BAUDRILLARD ■ BOURDIEU ■ ECO ■ WILLIAMS
Main works	ELEMENTS OF SEMIOLOGY (1964, trans. 1967) MYTHOLOGIES (1957, trans. 1972) THE PLEASURE OF THE TEXT (1973)

ROLAND BARTHES WAS perhaps the most influential cultural critic of the postwar generation. Despite being quintessentially French, his writings shaped the development of new modes of cultural criticism (associated with structuralism, deconstructionism and postmodernism) worldwide. He taught French in Romania, Egypt and at the École Pratique des Hautes Études in Paris before being elected to a chair in literary semiology in 1976 at the Collège de France.

While he wrote on a wide range of topics – his foci and approach constantly shifting – he revolutionised the way in which the role of the cultural critic and the objects of cultural analysis could be seen. Drawing on the work of linguist, Ferdinand de Saussure, and semiotician, Charles Sanders Peirce, Barthes applied the techniques of semiology, the study of signs and signifying systems to reconsider how literary texts operated as sites of production as well as meaning; moreover, he also investigated interrelationships with contiguous cultural phenomena.

Above all, Barthes's work questioned the conditions under which cultural objects (or texts) produced meaning. Central to this approach was the role of language in producing systems of meaning which framed the multiple ways in which texts could be 'read'. He argued that texts were not given but written in the act of reading, a view expounded in his oft-cited controversial essay, 'Death of the Author' (reprinted in *Image–Music–Text*, 1977). In questioning the fixed nature of texts, Barthes explored the shifting, unstable and interrogative dimensions of understanding and negotiating all cultural forms.

As well as reinterpreting literary works, Barthes was among the first cultural critics (excluding anthropologists) to explore and expose aspects of everyday culture (or interrogate the obvious). He challenged the assumption that cultural products seem to be natural and are therefore taken for granted. In so doing, Barthes questioned the apparent innocence of cultural production. His book, *Mythologies* – perhaps his best-known work – brought together provocative analyses of cultural phenomena as diverse as wrestling, soap-powder advertisements, wine and milk, the face of Garbo, striptease, and photography. By taking on an apparently random array of cultural forms drawn from consumer culture, high culture and popular culture, Barthes not only introduced new techniques of cultural analysis but imbued them with an explicitly political and historical dimension. This inquisitive and innovative approach became a linchpin of cultural studies and postmodern literary criticism.

Central to Barthes's approach was the argument that meanings were generated through systems of signs (languages of words, images and sounds) that are historically variable and culturally specific. The process of signification, of composing messages through combinations of signifiers, involves the production of messages with two layers of meaning: transparent or intended meaning (denotation) and contextual meaning that is socially inflected and culturally embedded (connotations). This produces a discursive norm, or consensus, about what reality is and what matters, and which makes up the yardstick by which societies measure conformity and deviation. One detailed example of a signifying system was the fashion system, which, for Barthes, explored how systems of clothes produced a complex 'world' of meaning defining style, fashionability, implicit dress codes, and a fashion language (*The Fashion System* (1967; English translation 1983)).

Like Brecht, Barthes emphasised the specifically bourgeois inflections that patterned French cultural forms, including influences of consumerism, imperialism, and issues of race and gender. In this light, identity – such as national identity – are a composite of a complex system of different sign systems (linguistic, coded iconic and non-coded iconic) that anchor and relay a series of messages and meanings from which a reader/viewer/listener distils an essential meaning. One frequently cited example of Barthes is his discussion of how an advertisement depicting a mesh shopping bag containing a packet of pasta and fresh vegetables connotes an image of 'Italianicity' by relaying familiar messages (a consensus) of what being Italian means (see 'Rhetoric of the image' in *Image–Music–Text*).

For Barthes, cultural processes of producing meaning were explicitly political and politicised; hence also were the products of culture. He explicated this position in an essay, 'Myth today', at the end of *Mythologies*, where he showed that myths were semiological systems that produced ideology as 'ideas-in-form'. There is no such thing as an 'innocent' image or sign, because the process of signification depoliticises speech, giving it a 'natural and eternal justification' as a 'statement of fact'. Barthes was concerned not just to expose such semiological workings but to 'liberate' cultural forms from their depoliticised yokes. For Barthes, this liberation oscillated between a political act, the experience of *jouissance* (or sexual pleasure), and abandonment to the pleasure of the signifiers themselves.

Through his writings on a number of interrelated topics, Barthes revitalised the role of the intellectual as a critic, teacher, theorist, and popular writer. Above all, his many writings have become seminal texts which retain the freshness of their time of writing and continue to explode the complacency of contemporary cultural norms.

Further reading

Culler, J. ROLAND BARTHES, Fontana, 1984.
Lavers, A. ROLAND BARTHES: STRUCTURALISM AND AFTER, Macmillan, 1982.
Moriarty, M. ROLAND BARTHES, Polity, 1991.
J.C.

BATAILLE, Georges

Philosopher/social theorist	born France 1897–1962
Associated with	SURREALISM ■ PORNOGRAPHY
Influences include	NIETZSCHE ■ HEGEL ■ DURKHEIM
Shares common ground with	NIETZSCHE ■ FOUCAULT ■ BAUDRILLARD
Main works	THE STORY OF THE EYE (1928)
	THE ACCURSED SHARE (1949)
	EROTICISM (1957)

BATAILLE CONSIDERED HIMSELF to have suffered a painful and disturbed childhood and youth. His earliest academic interests were in numismatics, religion and history and his first published work was a pious and devout invocation of the cathedral, *Notre-Dame de Rheims*, in 1918. In 1922 he graduated from the École des Chartres in Paris as a medievalist and then attended the École des Hautes Études Hispaniques in Madrid. During this time Bataille claimed to have witnessed the horrific death of a matador whose skull was penetrated through the eye, an event that reappears in his fictional work *The Story of the Eye*. He also began reading Nietzsche and Freud, shattering his Christian faith and exacerbating his preoccupations with death, obscenity and revolution. In 1927 Bataille underwent psychoanalysis, believed himself to have been saved from insanity and embarked on a career as a writer, academic and librarian at the Bibliothèque Nationale in Paris. A dissident Surrealist and Marxist, Bataille set up a number of short-lived radical political and intellectual societies during the 1930s and attended Alexandre Kojève's influential lectures on Hegel. In 1946 Bataille established the important academic journal, *Critique*, which presented the early work of Blanchot, Foucault and Derrida. His later years were spent systematising and developing earlier, often fragmentary, material. Bataille died in Paris in 1962.

Until quite recently Bataille's work was not well known outside the French academic world. Both Foucault and Derrida published influential essays on Bataille shortly after his death and Bataille's work was known largely through their mediation. However, during the last 10 years, most of Bataille's work has been translated into English and Bataille is recognised widely as one of the founders of post-structuralism.

Bataille's early writings exhibit a fundamental concern with excess, that which lies at or beyond various cultural limits, in particular with death, eroticism, waste, expenditure and sacrifice. *The Story of the Eye* is a semi-autobiographical rendering of many of these themes. During the 1930s Bataille was preoccupied increasingly with revolutionary politics. Dissatisfied with the humanist and progressive assumptions of Marxism and Surrealism, he sought to oppose Fascism by setting up a dissident group called *Contre-Attaque*. This attempted to subvert Fascism by seizing its own tactics, the rediscovery of myth and the sacred, and turning them against it. Bataille was accused of being a Fascist himself, disbanding the group but replacing it with other collective projects, the *Collège de Sociologie* and *Acéphale*, all of them short-lived.

Disillusioned with political activism, Bataille turned, during the 1940s, to an introspective literary contemplation of similar recurrent themes, an atheological, sacred mysticism, the nature of intimacy and communication. *Inner Experience* (1943) and *Guilty* (1954) record this difficult process in a fragmentary and elliptical style.

From the late 1940s up to his death, Bataille was engaged in a systematic and even scientific reappraisal and summary of his earlier work. *The Accursed Share* explicates Bataille's central concept, that of an excess of biochemical energy (the accursed share) that exists in all living matter. In the human or cultural world, Bataille argued, this excess must be expended, not stored or accumulated, as occurs in classical economy. Bataille traces sacrificial religion amongst the Aztecs and the *Potlach* of North American Indians as examples of profitless expenditure. For modern industrial societies Bataille advocated a planned relocation of wealth, without return, from West to East. *Eroticism* (1957) and *The Tears of Eros* (1959) offer an idiosyncratic history of human sexuality, Bataille focusing on the intimate relationship between sexuality, violence and death.

Critical evaluations of Bataille's merits are conflicting. Some quarters of feminism have denounced his work, while others have embraced its destabilising effects. Bataille may be read as sociologist, literary theorist, philosopher or pornographer; however, recognition of his influence on Foucault, Derrida and others is growing, as is the perception of his contemporary influence.

Further reading

Hollier, D. AGAINST ARCHITECTURE: THE WRITINGS OF GEORGES BATAILLE, MIT Press, 1992.
Land, N. THE THIRST FOR ANNIHILATION: GEORGES BATAILLE AND VIRULENT NIHILISM, Routledge, 1992.
Pawlett, W. 'Utility and Excess: The Radical Sociology of Bataille and Baudrillard', ECONOMY AND SOCIETY, 26: 1 (February 1997), pp. 92–125.
W.P.

BAUDRILLARD, Jean

Cultural theorist	born France 1929—
Associated with	POSTMODERNITY ■ HYPERREALITY
Influences include	NIETZSCHE ■ BATAILLE ■ BARTHES
Shares common ground with	BATAILLE ■ McLUHAN ■ CANETTI
Main works	SYMBOLIC EXCHANGE AND DEATH (1976)
	SIMULACRA AND SIMULATIONS (1981)
	THE TRANSPARENCY OF EVIL: ESSAYS ON EXTREME PHENOMENA (1990)

R ELATIVELY LITTLE BIOGRAPHICAL information on Baudrillard's early life is available. He was born into humble circumstances, referring to his grandparents as 'peasants' and his parents as 'very lowly petit bourgeois'. Baudrillard struggled through the Lycée but failed to gain access to the élite *École Normale Supériere*. He taught German for several years before becoming an academic sociologist in 1966. Baudrillard considers himself, clearly, to be an outsider, both on a personal and academic level. After early political involvements with Marxism, anarchism and situationism, Baudrillard rejected political engagement and delivered a stunning attack on the underpinnings of Marxist thought. Equally disillusioned with the university system, Baudrillard retired early, and continues to write difficult and provocative texts which are often rejected outright by the intellectual establishment.

Baudrillard's earliest full-length studies criticised the functional and utilitarian basis of both classical and Marxist economics by focusing on the nature of the object in consumer culture. Drawing on Mauss's *The Gift* and Bataille's *Notion of Expenditure*, Baudrillard argued that the use-value/exchange-value pairing was inadequate. He argued that contemporary society involved the acceleration of sign-value, the mechanism of conspicuous consumption; and, in addition, continued to be influenced by symbolic value, associated with pre-capitalist forms of cultural organisation.

Symbolic Exchange and Death marks an important shift in Baudrillard's work, away from structuralism, semiotics and materialism. Here, the symbolic order becomes a crucial form of resistance or antagonism with the semiotic or sign-dominated form of contemporary culture. The symbolic is characterised, according to Baudrillard, by enchantment, seduction, expenditure, cruelty and reversibility, whereas semiotic culture is marked by disenchantment, production, accumulation, human rights and irreversible acceleration.

In the late 1970s Baudrillard demonstrated a penchant for political critique, issuing *Forget Foucault* (1977), critical of the latter's conception of power, and *Seduction* (1979), widely, but hastily, perceived as an affront to feminism. *Simulacra and Simulations* expands on the notion of hyperreality, focusing on culture, the media, science and technology. Baudrillard argues that these institutions operate as an integrated code, and the code 'precedes' and structures modern culture, generating a hyperreality, based not on referents but on simulations; images, models and signs. At this stage Baudrillard depicts simulations as destructive of the vestiges of the symbolic order. However, in *Fatal Strategies* (1983) and *The Transparency of Evil* Baudrillard describes the exorbitation and fragmentation of the code, and the mutation and re-emergence of the symbolic in the form of irony, fatality, catastrophe and evil. In these works Baudrillard seeks to show the reduction of human subjectivity to the periphery of modern culture which is then dominated by the object; of technology, science and sexuality which assert a fundamentally elusive or illusory character beyond subjective control and understanding.

Baudrillard's latest works, *The Illusion of the End* (1992) and *The Perfect Crime* (1995), portray the modern technological age as pathological, 'whitewashed' and at the mercy of any object, event or system that is alien or 'other' to its functioning (Islamic fundamentalism, the Gulf War, ethnic 'cleansing').

Technological culture attempts the 'perfect crime' of the reduction of otherness to homogeneity. Fortunately, according to Baudrillard, this is impossible. Otherness and radical alterity will continue to undermine the systems of homogeneity because the strategies, devices and concepts of homogeneity are themselves, ultimately illusory.

There have been many critical assaults on Baudrillard's work, particularly from mainstream sociology and feminism, many of them ill-judged and reductive. Lyotard, more plausibly, has questioned the meaning of the symbolic, which, like many of Baudrillard's notions, remains somewhat sketchy, polemical and elusive. Nevertheless Baudrillard continues to challenge and provoke, unsettling orthodoxies and often appearing able to offer insights into contemporary events that make conventional academic enquiry look tame and outdated.

Further reading

Gane, M. (ed.) BAUDRILLARD LIVE: SELECTED INTERVIEWS, Routledge, 1993.
Genosko, G. BAUDRILLARD AND SIGNS: SIGNIFICATION ABLAZE, Routledge, 1994.
Kellner, D. (ed.) BAUDRILLARD: A CRITICAL READER, Polity Press, 1994.
W.P.

BAUMAN, Zygmunt

Sociologist/cultural theorist	born Poland 1925—
Associated with	POSTMODERNITY ▪ AMBIVALENCE
Influences include	FOUCAULT ▪ LEVINAS ▪ KOLAKOWSKI
Shares common ground with	FOUCAULT ▪ BAUDRILLARD
Main works	FREEDOM (1988)
	MODERNITY AND THE HOLOCAUST (1989)
	POSTMODERN ETHICS (1993)

Z YGMUNT BAUMAN BEGAN his academic career at Warsaw University, where he was a professor of sociology. After the political upheavals of 1968 he left Poland and eventually settled down in England, where he was Dean of the Department of Sociology at Leeds University. Now retired, he lectures and publishes books on the shift from the modern to postmodern society. For Bauman, culture is the 'ordering' device, driven by the fear of chaos and death. However, mastering the chaos, modern culture organises both order and institutionalised crime – the tragedy of the Holocaust is the most infamous example of the managing skills it is able to produce. Bauman sees the Holocaust as an outcome, not a result, of the lack of modern reason. In general, ordering endeavours ('gardening' society, planning, caring and eradicating 'weeds') prove to be ambivalent themselves. The dream of order is never accomplished and reproduces itself in the continuous effort.

The difference between modern and postmodern culture is grounded in social structures. Postmodern societies depend more on consumption than on the production of goods, which puts the traditional normative discourses in crisis. The cultural patterns of control and identity undergo fundamental changes. As far as control is concerned, in consumer societies it is no longer necessary to subjugate individuals to produce their subjectivities (which was the key thesis in Michel Foucault): the contemporary state can do without surveillance in relation to the majority of its society and *seduce* people to the desired patterns of behaviour instead. Those who cannot afford the freedom of self-creation through consumption, however, are still subject to modern techniques of subjugation. As to the models of identity, their change includes a shift from the type of *pilgrim* (someone living his life purposefully, as a laborious journey to the given end) in favour of those of the *flâneur*, the *tourist*, the *vagabond*, and the *game-player*. The demands concerning the body change, too. Disciplined bodies of 'soldier-workers' are no longer important for postmodern society. For the social system based on unnecessary consumption, it is crucial that the bodies are open to the permanent influx of new sensations, ready to 'collect impressions'. The production of such subjectivities demands that social bonds are temporary and loose. One of the instruments to implement this change is the new discourse of sexuality, stressing risk, fun, harassment and abuse. We are getting distrustful in building close personal relations, free to move and to invest our desires in the market. Also, the patterns of coping with death change: we 'rehearse death' in daily experiences of separation, of the temporality of all bonds and obligations (which in turn makes us desire communities most of all), rather than try to overcome it in a craving for immortality in other people's memory and 'eternal values'.

Contemporary culture, and the freedom it boasts about, is then, also ambivalent: its pleasures are seductive, loaded with coercion and control. This time, though, there are no solutions in sight to the problem of ambivalence.

In spite of his acute understanding of the new technologies of seduction and control, Bauman sees postmodernity as a situation of particular openness. For instance, the crisis of traditional normative narratives paradoxically brings about the possibility of a renaissance of morality. As Bauman says, morality is built in discursive exchange between people in their responsible 'being together'; it is not a product of ethics imposed by 'philosophers, preachers and teachers'. In contemporary society, the ethical, legislating role of intellectuals loses its importance and is being replaced by that of *interpreters* helping others in their attempts at understanding their lives. This is where Bauman's refined sociological hermeneutic, challenging the traditional sociology with its 'ordering' functions, is grounded. Zygmunt Bauman, with his disbelief in modern promises and with his nomadic positioning between cultures, is himself one of the most ingenious interpreters.

Further reading

Bauman, Z. LEGISLATORS AND INTERPRETERS, Polity Press, 1987.
Bauman, Z. MODERNITY AND AMBIVALENCE, Polity Press, 1991.
Bauman, Z. INTIMATIONS OF POSTMODERNITY, Routledge 1992.
Bauman, Z. MORTALITY, IMMORTALITY, AND OTHER LIFE STRATEGIES, Polity Press, 1992.

J.McG.

BECK, Ulrich

Sociologist	born Germany 1944—
Associated with	RISK SOCIETY ■ REFLEXIVITY ■ ECOLOGICAL CRISIS
Influences include	WEBER ■ LUHMANN ■ HABERMAS
Shares common ground with	GIDDENS ■ LASH ■ LATOUR
Main works	RISK SOCIETY (1992) REFLEXIVE MODERNIZATION (WITH A. GIDDENS AND S. LASH, 1994a) ECOLOGICAL ENLIGHTENMENT (1994b)

R ISK SOCIETY IS a landmark in the social sciences and sociology in particular. It has made Beck one of the world's most well known contemporary sociologists. In the book, Beck argues that the developments of science and technology, which have taken off in a big way with industrialisation, have come to pose a set of problems for industrial society. Industrial society is treated as synonymous with 'modernity'. Whereas the organisation of industrial society is primarily based on the production and distribution of goods, for which scarcity functions as the main regulatory principle, its institutions have not been designed to handle and process the production and distribution of 'bads' – which he predominantly conceptualises as the risks and hazards that emerge with industrial production. Too often this argument has been turned into one of periodisation. It is as if at one time we had low-risk industrial society, and now we have risk-society. But this is a gross misconception of the actual argument made by Beck. The misconception is due to a one-sided interpretation of the risk-society thesis as a social theory in which the dynamics of social groups and institutions are conceived as the main agents of social change, albeit overdetermined by the political–economic forces of late-capitalist production.

What this interpretation misses is a sense of the cultural dynamics that Beck stresses as being central to the risk-society thesis. Understanding the full extent of the risk-society thesis in the context of reflexive modernisation requires a detailed, nuanced and qualified incorporation of the ethos of Beck's thinking as a cultural theorist. Although generally linked with the works of Giddens and Lash, Beck's initial theoretical framework was cultivated largely outside the Anglo-Saxon tradition. Instead, the two main German theorists, Luhmann and Habermas, provided a large part of the necessary ammunition for Beck to conceptualise, in his own original and eclectic way, risk society as more than merely a type of social formation. Furthermore, Beck's more recent work allows for some interesting comparisons with, for example, Latour's approach to science and technology.

There is more than a hint of Luhmann's system theory in Beck's notion of social (dis)organisation. Like Luhmann, Beck does not project 'integration' accompanying the effective 'differentiation' produced by modernisation. In other words, his concept of the social is engendered from an idea of complexity and instability – social organisation is an accomplishment not a matter of fact.

Related to this idea of complexity is Beck's sophisticated use of the notion of 'agency'. Here, links with Latour's actor-network theory, which were not explicit in *Risk Society* but developed more recently, are apparent. Sociologists working within the Anglo-Saxon tradition are perhaps ill-equipped to understand agency as anything but human; but this is exactly what is required if one wants to understand the full dynamics of risk society. The agents in risk society are not only social groups and institutions, but 'risks' and 'risk technologies' as well.

Although they are inherently contradictory, Beck's theoretical apparatuses can be seen as a clever combination of system theory and actor-network theory. Whereas he recognises that one could analytically differentiate between different 'domains' of social organisation, each with their own systematic logic (rationality or cognitive structure), he does not resort to autopoiesis to explain the emergence of these systematic differences, but adopts instead a notion of open systems, which are connected via a range of media such as money (capital), goods, laws, signs and people. In other words, rather than a model of the social as a conglomerate of autonomising spheres, he projects an image of interconnected webs.

What makes the production and distribution of 'bads' so potent in the contemporary world is the impossibility of evading their implications. Systematic closure is no longer an option, as we are all located in this worldwide web of risk technologies. Science and its technologies of visualisation have fundamentally transformed the 'see no evil/hear no evil' principle that accompanied the focus of the visible and quantifiable aspects of risks and dangers commonly associated with industrial production. As invisibility is no longer an excuse for non-decision and non-action, the full implications of the catastrophic potential of industrial production are increasingly becoming part of everyone's 'being-in-the-world'. This catastrophic potential is engendered by the indeterminable character of risks and hazards, which has eroded the politics of security of the capital–finance and insurance complex, upon which so much of contemporary capitalism depends.

Beck's relation with the work of Habermas is rather ambivalent. Like Habermas, Beck has not exclusively concerned himself with social analysis. Instead he has placed his concept of risk in relation to environmental issues. Although Beck's politics are more eclectic and pragmatic than the philosophically based ideas of Habermas, the latter's thought has clearly influenced that of Beck. Without this connection it becomes virtually impossible to understand the intricate mechanisms of the arguments developed in *Risk Society*. His emphasis on 'another modernity', which he later – and in close connection with Giddens and Lash – termed 'reflexive modernity', must be seen in this light. He is not proposing that an alternative to industrial society is inevitable because it is determined by politico-social and economic forces. Rather, his concern is with uncovering a new ethical grounding of our being in the world (Beck, 1994a). The particular 'making sense' of our being in the world, which he developed in *Risk Society* and which is part of our cultural theory, becomes further appropriated in a more ethically oriented discussion of 'how' to live in a society whose catastrophic potential has already deconstructed the political–institutional basis upon which social organisation was founded. Beck develops these arguments in his *Politics in an Age of Risk* (1995) and *The Reinvention of Politics* (1997).

Beck's cultural theory extends beyond the limitations of the realist–constructivist and structure–agency debates that have dominated social theory for decades. It sets itself the task of reconnecting the making-sense of our 'being-in-the-world', with the ethical sensibilities that enable us to continue our existence with a concern for the future.

Further reading

Adam, B., Beck, U. and Van Loon, J. (eds.) REPOSITIONING RISK: CRITICAL ISSUES FOR SOCIAL THEORY, Sage, 1999.
Beck, U. RISK SOCIETY, Sage, 1992.
Beck, U. THE REINVENTION OF POLITICS, Polity, 1997.

J.V.L.

BELL, Daniel

Sociologist	born USA 1919—
Associated with	IDEOLOGY ■ POST-INDUSTRIALIST SOCIETY ■ ANATOMIAN CULTURE
Influences include	WEBER ■ SCHUMPETER ■ ROUSSEAU ■ SAINT-SIMON
Shares common ground with	TOURAINE ■ GIDDENS ■ BECK
Main works	THE END OF IDEOLOGY: ON THE EXHAUSTION OF POLITICAL IDEAS IN THE FIFTIES (1965) THE COMING OF POST-INDUSTRIAL SOCIETY: A VENTURE IN SOCIAL FORECASTING (1974) THE CULTURAL CONTRADICTIONS OF CAPITALISM (1976)

AT THE AGE OF 15 Bell rejected his Jewish heritage by declaring himself an atheist, and was for a while 'tempted' by communism, but Trotsky's brutality encouraged him to become a democratic socialist. In 1935 he went to the City College of New York, and after graduation, worked as a journalist, eventually becoming managing editor of a social democratic magazine known as the *New Leader*. For three years following the war he was employed by the University of Chicago as a lecturer in social science. In 1948 he returned to journalism as a staff writer and then labour editor on the US business journal *Fortune*, where he remained for 10 years.

During his time at *Fortune* he worked as an adjunct lecturer in sociology at Columbia University and, in 1958, took up a full-time post as an Associate Professor. Bell's Ph.D., based on a compilation of his published work, was awarded in 1960 and he was made full professor in 1962. He moved to Harvard in 1969, was appointed Henry Ford II Professor of Social Sciences in 1980, and retired in 1990. According to Waters (1996), Bell's approach to theorising social transformations fits between 'the sterilities of grand theory and empiricism'. His published output was prodigious, with fourteen books (authored or edited) and over two hundred 'scholarly articles'. Perhaps surprisingly, Bell published very little in mainstream sociology journals as his preferred outlets were 'non-refereed, general intellectual journals', which were often associated with the New York Jewish community. Because much of his published output appeared in these 'friendly' journals there is considerable inconsistency which Waters (1996: 24) describes as a mixture of 'good social science, anecdote, personal philosophy and exegesis'. Bell's three big ideas are summarised in the titles of his most influential books: *The End Of Ideology*, *The Coming of Post-Industrial Society*, and *The Cultural Contradictions of Capitalism*.

Bell rejected holistic views of society represented by the grand theories of Parsons and Marx in favour of an approach which encompassed contradiction and divergent historical trends. His first big idea, the end of ideology, was to some extent an attempt to come to terms with his early political radicalism. The book analysed why, in contrast with Europe, American political parties eschewed ideology in favour of pragmatism. Even the trade unions, which at one time represented 30 per cent of workers, separated themselves from politics. For example, there were no institutional links between the labour movement and political parties such as those connecting UK unions to the Labour Party. Bell was also concerned about the rise of the extreme Right, represented by McCarthyism in the 1950s and militia groups such as the Minutemen in the 1960s. Having rejected politics of the Left and Right, Bell concentrates on the centre by utilising the phrase 'the end of ideology', first used by Albert Camus in 1946. The secularisation of industrial states created a vacuum which was filled by political ideologies such as Marxism, Liberalism and Nationalism (Fascism). Bell (1965: 402) argued that the Left and Right were gradually converging: 'There is today a rough consensus among intellectuals on political issues: the acceptance of the Welfare State; the desirability of decentralised power; a system of mixed economy and of political pluralism. In that sense too the ideological age has ended.'

Bell's second, and possibly his most influential, big idea was that of post-industrial society. The main thesis was outlined in an unpublished paper written in 1962, 'The Post-Industrial Society: A Speculative View of the United States and Beyond'. Several papers on this theme were written in the late 1960s and these were eventually published in 1973 as *The Coming of Post-Industrial Society*. Post-industrial society is a theory of social change which distinguishes pre-industrial and post-industrial societies. The concept is constructed as a Weberian ideal-type which comprises five dimensions:

1 *A service-based economy* – the majority of labour is no longer employed in agriculture or manufacturing, but in services such as trade, finance, health, education, recreation, research and government.
2 *Pre-eminence of professionals* – the most influential groups in society are those occupations requiring a tertiary level of education and broadly defined as professional and technical, such as scientists and engineers.
3 *Primacy of theoretical knowledge* – the axial principle of post-industrial society is that theoretical knowledge replaces traditional or practical knowledges as the basis for social control.
4 *Planning of technology* – the advance of theoretical knowledge allows more accurate assessment of the risks, costs and advantages of new technologies.
5 *Emergence of a new intellectual technology* –replaces the concept of technology as an artefact with the idea of an intellectual technology which can be represented by abstract symbols and algorithms.

One of the most contentious issues relating to post-industrial society is Bell's view that knowledge will replace property as the main source of social inequality. Despite criticism of Bell's thesis, the concept of post-industrial society continues to be an important analytical device for those studying societal change.

Bell (1976: x) defined his values thus: 'I am a socialist in economics, a liberal in politics and a conservative in culture.' This view is certainly confirmed by his writing on contemporary culture, which he regards as 'antinomian'. *The Cultural Contradiction of Capitalism* rebuts some of the ideas that Bell expounded in his post-industrial thesis. Instead of new technologies freeing society from the drudgery of industrial work, they are perceived to lead to rampant consumerism, self-indulgence and disintegrating value systems. Until industrial maturity, the Techno Economic Structure (TES) had been the main driver of societal change; the shift from agrarian to urban societies, increased work – time discipline and capital accumulation. However, Bell argues that around the middle of the twentieth century, culture began to dominate the TES. as the main agency of societal change. While traditional cultures had been strongly influenced by religion and were the main source of morality, secularisation meant that culture became the site of new and titillating sensations. A key element in the change was the emergence and influence of technologies associated with the mass media. The bourgeois morality of early capitalism was based on the Protestant ethics of work as an end in itself and an ascetic lifestyle. For Bell this was symbolised by the life and character of small-town America, however, modernity increasingly permeated this isolation. First radio and then TV advertising encouraged materialism and consumerism, while cinema created a fantasy world of instant gratification. Bell regards postmodernism as a continuation of the modernist logic by a constant emphasis on the instinctive and the erotic. While bemoaning the decline of high culture and the democratisation of individual genius, typical of postmodernism, Bell remains optimistic about society's ability to 'recover the sacred'. Secularisation, which has loosened moral restraint, leading to increased violence and overt expression of sexuality, will gradually be displaced through the restoration of religion as a central feature of culture. The obvious distaste for postmodern hedonism and his laments for lost cultural traditions have led to Bell being described as a neo-conservative. Despite embracing anti-communism and anti-populism, to Waters (1996: 167) he remains an 'old-fashioned, traditional, élitist conservative'.

Further reading

Brick, H. DANIEL BELL AND THE DECLINE OF INTELLECTUAL RADICALISM, Wisconsin University Press, 1986.

Kumar, K. PROPHESY AND PROGRESS: THE SOCIOLOGY OF INDUSTRIAL AND POST-INDUSTRIAL SOCIETY, Penguin, 1978.
Leibowitz, N. DANIEL BELL AND THE AGONY OF MODERN LIBERALISM, Greenwood Press, 1985.
Waters, M. DANIEL BELL, Routledge, 1996.

O.J.

BENEDICT, Ruth F.

Cultural anthropologist	born USA, 1887–1948
Associated with	CULTURAL RELATIVISM ■ SYNERGY ■ CULTURE AND PERSONALITY
Influences include	BOAS ■ PARSONS ■ SAPIR
Shares common ground with	MEAD ■ HUXLEY
Main works	PATTERNS OF CULTURE (1934) ZUNI MYTHOLOGY (2 vols., 1935) THE CHRYSANTHEMUM AND THE SWORD: PATTERNS OF JAPANESE CULTURE (1946)

RUTH BENEDICT WAS born in 1887 and came to anthropology late in life. Her approach to this subject was influenced by unhappy childhood experiences. The premature death of her father led to a family life of struggle and hard work, and produced an outlook that was pessimistic and cynical yet stressed self-reliance and the overcoming of adversity. Her background also shaped her disillusionment with the conventions expected of contemporary women. Benedict graduated from Vassar College in 1909 and continued her studies in anthropology at the New School for Social Research, where her mentor was Elsie Clews Parsons. The latter introduced her to Franz Boas at Columbia University, where she completed her Ph.D. in 1923.

Benedict undertook extensive fieldwork studies of American first peoples, in particular the Pueblos and Zuni. She joined the staff of Columbia (where she taught and befriended Margaret Mead) and became a full professor belatedly in 1948. During the Second World War she worked at the Office of War Information. Her contribution to anthropology was her concept of patterns of culture, which was developed to understand how particular cultures systematically selected certain human potentialities. These traits were transmitted over time across generations. Individuals within any given culture were shaped by the designated potentialities. This resulted in distinctive personality styles within different cultures.

While Benedict was not a prolific writer, two of her works became best-sellers: *Patterns of Culture* and *The Chrysanthemum and the Sword: Patterns of Japanese Culture* the former becoming the classic introduction to anthropology and the latter the template not only for understanding Japanese culture but for studies of national culture in general. Other significant publications included her two-volume study of Zuni culture, in which she contrasted four first peoples in terms of psychological types: the Pueblo as extrovert and Apollonian, the Plains Indians as introvert and Dionysian, the Kwakiutl as megalomaniac and the Dobuans as paranoid. This typecasting led to controversy which overshadowed Benedict's other work. Benedict took a strong interest in applying the lessons of anthropology to other issues and her social concern not only led to her work during the war on national character but also to her book *Race: Science and Politics* (1940).

Benedict's contribution to anthropology was marked by her previous training in the humanities, which enabled her to combine different approaches and insights and to communicate anthropological findings to a wide readership. Her works were also shaped by her belief in the ability of individuals to learn from experience and to reassess situations and respond appropriately, with the goal of improving their circumstances. She also believed in acknowledging the 'passionate experience of living' in anthropological work, especially acknowledging the implications of 'maleness' and femaleness' in culture and anthropological endeavour.

Above all, she believed that culture could only be appreciated as a whole in which different elements fitted like a jigsaw, but, individually, may be inconsistent and even contradictory. While seeking to explain the whole of culture, she did not believe in a grand theory which could explain all. Instead, Benedict adopted a configurationalist approach and proposed the concept of synergy which stated that 'any society that is compatible with human advancements is a good one, but a society that works against basic human goals is antihuman and evil, and can be judged as such'. Benedict has often been accused of endorsing cultural relativism and cultural determinism, but supporters have defended her, arguing that the criticism stems from 'ill-informed interpretations of her earlier work' (Mead, 1968: 51) and that 'she never implied either that inborn temperament was negligible or that the individual had no control over her surroundings' (Modell, 1988: 5). Rather, she was well aware of temperamental differences and the social consequences of cultural predispositions, and hence preached tolerance. In this respect, Benedict's anthropology went well beyond the bounds of traditional anthropology and gave it a personalised and politicised edge that made many in the discipline nervous.

As a result, the major achievements and insights of Benedict have been less well recognised than was warranted even though her classic, *Patterns of Culture*, remains arguably the single best explanation of the potential of anthropological method.

Further reading

Caffrey, M. RUTH BENEDICT: STRANGER IN THIS LAND, University of Austin at Texas Press, 1989.
Mead, M. 'Benedict, Ruth', in D. Sills (ed.) INTERNATIONAL ENCYCLOPAEDIA OF THE SOCIAL SCIENCES (Macmillan Co. and Free Press, 1968), pp. 48–52.
Mead, M. RUTH BENEDICT, Columbia University Press, 1974.
Modell, J. 'Ruth Fulton Benedict', in U. Gacs, A. Khan, J. McIntyre and R. Weinberg (eds.) WOMEN ANTHROPOLOGISTS. A BIOGRAPHICAL DICTIONARY (Greenwood Press, 1988), pp. 1–7.

J.C.

BENJAMIN, Walter

Essayist	born Germany 1892–1940
Associated with	THE FRANKFURT SCHOOL
Influences include	SCHLEGEL ■ MARX ■ SOREL
Shares common ground with	SCHOLEM ■ KAFKA ■ ADORNO
Main works	BRIEFE (1966 TRANS. THE CORRESPONDENCE OF WALTER BENJAMIN, 1910–1940, 1994)
	SCHRIFTEN (1955 PARTIAL TRANS. ILLUMINATIONS, 1968, and BENJAMIN: PHILOSOPHY, HISTORY, AESTHETICS, 1989)

T HERE WAS A time, early in his adult life, when Walter Benjamin considered himself a scholar. He could certify that he had read every book in his modest library. He described an interesting metamorphosis, however, which turned him from a scholar into a 'collector'. He claimed that just touching a treasured book became more rewarding than actually reading it. Liberated from the obligation to read, Benjamin's collection multiplied profusely, blessing him with the exquisite disarray he describes in his essay, 'Unpacking My Library'.

It was not laziness or greed that promoted Benjamin's aversion to reading. Instead, he characterised the reading of a book as a potential liability, drawing the patron into the systematic, ordered milieu ('aura') of the book's origin. Benjamin felt uncomfortable and superfluous in this order, preferring instead to extract his books out of their world and into his, allowing him to dabble in an eclectic pluralism of genuine and rare influences.

This preference for collecting over specialising characterises Benjamin's intellectual demeanour. He collected influences as he collected books, arranging his mentors in an eclectic collage. He contemplated the spiritual tributaries of Judaism, with a special affinity for mystical treatments such as the Kabbalah. He accepted a grant to study Hebrew, in preparation for a teaching position in Jerusalem (which he never assumed). And some of his essays betrayed a conviction in a cosmic consistency amongst all that is spoken, written and signified (see 'On the Mimetic Faculty', 1936).

Benjamin seemed to suspend all metaphysics, however, while indulging his allegiance to Bertolt Brecht and the tendentiousness of 'epic theatre'. Benjamin travelled to the Soviet Union in 1926 and met Mayakovsky. Yet he also read Lukács, and was eventually inducted into the Frankfurt circle of critical theory by founders Adorno and Horkheimer. Indeed, Benjamin produced essays that appealed to the more subtle and ambiguous Marxism of this group, four of which appeared in the Institute's *Journal of Social Research*. Benjamin was attracted also to Kafka, whose emphasis on human folly compromised dialectical materialism as well as metaphysics.

It is not surprising, then, that Benjamin was drawn to Baudelaire's depiction of the *flâneur*, the leisurely stroller who haphazardly samples Parisian neighbourhoods and cafés. To be sure, the sampling is hardly an immersion, as Benjamin is quick to amend Baudelaire's contention that the *flâneur* is of the masses, insisting instead on a certain distance from that being observed.

In his monumental essay, 'Art in the Age of Mechanical Reproduction' (in *Illuminations* [Fontana, 1968]), Benjamin demonstrated that the collector mentality was hardly a self-indulgent idiosyncrasy. Instead, he argued that unprecedented reproduction was liberating art from its 'aura', and thus from its rootedness in tradition. Before easy reproduction, art's value was connected to ritual, and to the cult that celebrated the work's aura. Now deprived of its aura, and thus of its cult value, the art object is valued as an exhibit, the interpretation of which is open to manipulation. Thus, art in the age of reproduction is political. Stripped of its tradition, it can be used as 'evidence' (p. 228) in a political indictment.

Thus, we can see the source of Benjamin's attachment to Bertolt Brecht. For Brecht and Benjamin, there is no tension between authentic and tendentious art. All art is now tendentious, and so the appropriate question becomes: 'What sort of tendentiousness ought to be pursued?' For Benjamin, Brecht's epic theatre provided the appropriate model.

Epic theatre shuns the linearity and organisation that characterise capitalist industry. Benjamin connects epic theatre to the daily newspaper. A newspaper does not 'end', and it can be read in various orders and with various levels of attention, all according to the whim of the reader. Sitting passively while absorbing a predetermined meaning is not only a trait of bourgeois art, but it is also an aspect of capitalist manipulation of human productivity. Art, like labour, ought properly to be an aspect of communal interchange. Thus, the relationship of art and its audience ought to be such that the distinction itself is continually diminishing.

Just as the library needs a catalogue, so the life of a collector needs some semblance of order. In the summer of 1940, the Gestapo seized Benjamin's Paris apartment and his books. His friends arranged visas for emigration to America, but after a bureaucratic snag on the Franco-Spanish border, Benjamin took his own life. From what was perhaps a too orderly childhood in a wealthy neighbourhood of West Berlin, Benjamin's lifelong adjustment to disorder had reached intolerable proportions.

Further reading

Brodersen, Momme WALTER BENJAMIN: A BIOGRAPHY, trans. Malcolm R. Green and Ingrida Ligers, Verso, 1996.
Knizek, I. 'Walter Benjamin and the Mechanical Reproducibility of Art Works Revisited', BRITISH JOURNAL OF AESTHETICS, 33: 4 (Oct. 1993), pp. 357–67.
Smith, G. (ed.) ON WALTER BENJAMIN, MIT Press, 1988.
Wolin, R. WALTER BENJAMIN: AN AESTHETIC OF REDEMPTION, University of California Press, 1994.

T.J.L.

BENTLEY, Eric

Drama critic/essayist	born England 1916—
Associated with	DRAMATURGY ■ SOCIAL DRAMA
Influences include	HEBBEL ■ NIETZSCHE ■ SHAW
Shares common ground with	ESSLIN ■ LUKÁCS ■ YOUNG
Main works	THE PLAYWRIGHT AS THINKER (1946)
	WHAT IS THEATRE? (1956)
	THE LIFE OF THE DRAMA (1964)

B ORN AND EDUCATED in England, after completing his literary education at Oxford, Bentley moved to the USA in 1939, obtained his doctorate at Yale in 1942 and became an American citizen in 1948. From 1948 to 1951 he was guest director at various prestigious theatres in Europe, notably assisting Brecht in one of his own productions. Aside from his Professorship of Dramatic Literature at Columbia University from 1952 to 1969 he was drama critic for *New Republic* from 1952 to 1956, during which time he was an outspoken critic of the melodramatic school of American playwriting. In translating and adapting over one hundred plays, he introduced new and more polemical drama (à la Brecht and Pirandello).

Bentley's first major work was *The Playwright as Thinker*. His central concern is with interpreting the rise of naturalism in relation to the dominant mode of realism in the nineteenth century, and the shifting fortunes of tragedy and comedy in modern drama as a high art form. His arguments tend to be historical, seeing drama as only a portion of a complex historical and cultural whole, rather than theoretical. Thus Zola is seen as the official spokesperson of naturalism without whom, as Bentley argues, there would be no Ibsen, Strindberg, Chekhov or Shaw, who are particularly important as playwrights of ideas which are questioned and thereby become dramatic. He contrasts with relevant examples the two traditions of modern drama as realistic and anti-realistic, using a typology of critical terms (political vs religious, prosaic vs poetic, etc.). Whilst 'modern' drama, for Bentley, may be said to have made three fresh starts around 1730, 1830 or 1880, it has essentially meant plays of tragedy and comedy which are post-classical, post-industrial and products of the New Theatre movement beginning in the 1880s.

Bentley sees the nineteenth century as witnessing the ascendancy of the middle-class mind. This is reflected artistically in the 'bourgeois tragedy' as the most direct expression of a middle-class epoch as realised in the 'dialectic of dramaturgy'. Never is there drama and an epoch without conflicts, for the great minds of the modern age, Bentley argues, are the great fighters or socially radical propagandists against the modern age: 'An age can and must fight itself.' Thus, in revolutionary modernist periods, the artistry, dynamic and subversive power of the real dramatist finds and portrays socioanalytically, in his plays, the dramaturgical contradictions in the society around him.

Bentley also heralds the much later explosion of postmodernism as reflected in dramatic works, which Esslin later calls the Theatre of the Absurd. Thus his pioneering championing and exposition of Pirandello's innovative and revolutionary plays established the proper critical course in the history of contemporary theatre in seeing this playwright as the 'Father of the Absurd': the human condition is portrayed dramatically as cyclical, circular and open-ended as well as linguistically fragmented.

Bentley's theatrical criticism brought together in *What is Theatre?* essentially inveighs against the escapism of the Broadway stage in New York and the lack of concern for political affairs by American playwrights in the McCarthy era. These 'periodic soundings' of the drama, coupled with his championing of the dormant power of subversive masters such as Brecht, mark him out as a strong proponent of the 'theatre of commitment', the title of his book of essays published in 1968. For him, the theatre is essentially a society within a society which, at certain moments in history, with political crises begetting artistic crises (fifth-century Athens or seventeenth-century Spain), has been more reflective of the life of the people in its drama of committed 'counter-playwrights'.

Thus, unlike most music and painting, which is inaccessible except to people of certain training, he sees great drama in the self-contained, human transaction of the theatrical event as more accessible to new, untrained audiences in that cultural barriers between it and the 'great public' can often be broken down by the 'fact of theatre, the act of performance', in which the dramatist's ideas are brought into the audience's consciousness. Bentley designates as 'social drama' plays which are, in their main emphasis, political and socio-logical, e.g. Brecht's *Mother Courage*. Alongside him, Sartre, Osborne and the new generation of German playwrights such as Hochhuth are committed playwrights in the cultural revolution of the 1960s. This form of modern drama, however, differs from the traditional patterns of tragedy and comedy in being associated with tragicomedy and its heroic failures, which puts the onus on to the audience's understanding of the dramatic event. *The Life Of the Drama* represents his attempt at a comprehensive theory of the roots and bases of dramatic art in general and the continuing psychological appeal of its five basic genres – tragedy, melodrama, comedy, farce and tragicomedy – differ-entiated according to the play's proper subject-matter and its differing power to move us in distinct and definable ways. Bentley's dialectical argument is Aristotelian in spirit, art being imitative and giving pleasure in the act of personal recognition and identification in pursuit of the 'insatiable appetite for knowledge'. We demand that our own lives be dramatic. To this end Bentley devises kindred categories of plot, character, thought, dialogue and enactment (the psychological mechanisms of role-playing, substitution and identification). Thus, if tragedy is perceived existentially and forces the audience to reflect on the 'nonsensical life we lead', comedy, like tragedy, is a way of trying to cope with despair, mental suffering, guilt and anxiety in assuring us that happy endings are possible. Unlike melodrama, which acts as a 'modest catharsis' to purge us of fear, the motor and 'comic dialectic' of farce is the impulse to attack. In positing tragicomedy as a form of comic disap-proval, he anticipates the postmodernist condition of contemporary life in propounding it as our characteristic mode of artistic challenge to human despair.

Further reading

Bertin, M. (ed.) THE PLAY AND ITS CRITICS, University Press of America, 1986.
Borklund, E. 'Eric Bentley', in CONTEMPORARY LITERARY CRITICS, Macmillan, 1982.
Kolin, P. and Kullman, C. (eds.) SPEAKING ON STAGE: INTERVIEWS WITH CON-TEMPORARY AMERICAN PLAYWRIGHTS, University of Alabama Press, 1996.

G.P.

BERGER, Peter L.

Sociologist	born USA 1929—
Associated with	Objectification ■ Humanistic Sociology
Influences include	Schutz ■ James ■ Mannheim ■ Mead ■ Weber
Shares common ground with	Bellah ■ Fromm ■ Riesman
Main works	Invitation to Sociology: A Humanistic Perspective (1963) The Social Construction of Reality (with T. Luckmann, 1966) The Sacred Canopy (1967) Pyramids of Sacrifice (1974)

Until 1970, Berger was Professor of Sociology at the New School for Social Research in New York; he moved to Rutgers University and, from there, to Boston University. Over three decades from 1960, Berger produced work that could be fairly said to have influenced a generation of sociologists, with his own particular synthesis of a 'humanistic sociology'.

Berger's theoretical approach is best gleaned from three books: his primer, *Invitation to Sociology: A Humanistic Perspective*, his treatise on the role of religion in modernity, *The Sacred Canopy* (*The Social Reality of Religion* for the British market) and his syncretism of Marx, Weber, Durkheim and Mead, *The Social Construction of Reality* (with Thomas Luckman). These provide evidence of the eclectic *par excellence*, a theorist able to pull together the various contributions of four classical theorists and, with the addition of Schutz's phenomenology, suggest a way of understanding the origins of society, our subjective apprehension of it and our captivation by it.

Starting with Mead's and James's observations on how children acquire the ability to view themselves as objects as well as subjects ('I' and 'me'), Berger builds a conception of society in which the human agent, specifically his or her consciousness, is central to a process whereby society takes on the appearance and facticity of an objective phenomenon. As we objectify ourselves, we objectify the contents of the world that both surrounds us and, simultaneously, enters us. We act volitionally, but in a way that observes that there are such things as social structures, themselves composed of institutions. In a memorable simile, Berger likens society's members to prisoners who build the walls that imprison them. This Berger takes to be an instance of what Weber called an unintended consequence of social action – an irony. The objectively-real structure that seems to surround us bears resemblance to the social facts written of by Durkheim.

Social life is possible only because we are able to make objectifications, and we do this through language. Here Berger marshals the insights of Schutz to show how we make society real through language, a medium that typifies and anonymises; we share intersubjectively the meanings that our language conveys. Without such sharedness, there would be no agreement as to the status of phenomena and so no society. Society is 'a human product, and nothing but a human product, that yet continuously acts back upon its producer'. Critics have noted that this is a fragile conception of society, one which is always precarious and conditional on shared intersubjectivities.

Religion's role in the meaning–construction process is in providing a link between the reality we build and an 'ultimate reality': religion is one source of legitimacy for the social order we create, observe and support. Berger argues that we erect overarching *nomos*, or laws, which need legitimate backing for them to remain stable. Modernity weakens the power of religion to provide that legitimacy by catalysing the process of secularisation. Religious institutions and symbols lose potency; religion itself becomes a private matter, since the proliferation of forms of belief opened up by the questing impulse of modernity means that no single religion is credible to enough people in society.

Much, if not all, of Berger's work might be seen as an attempt to resist all forms of determinism and to centralise consciousness as the source of sociological knowledge. While he uses the concept of structure, he means it phenomenologically – as a description of how packages, or constellations of consciousness are carried, or transmitted at an institutional level. Modernity describes a shift in packages of consciousness, according to Berger. Several of his books of the 1970s (e.g. *The Homeless Mind,* 1974; *Facing Up To Modernity,* 1979 and *Pyramids of Sacrifice*) were concerned with rehumanising experience in the face of the multiplying bureaucracies brought by modernity.

In *The War over the Family* (1983) Berger (with Brigitte Berger) turned his attention to what he called 'capturing the middle ground' between the two competing 'visions of the family': one depicts it as 'a natural unit . . . united by love, mutual respect, trust and fidelity', the other as 'a narrowly constraining cage'. In a sense, Berger's arguments about the family can be applied to the general conditions in which families exist. Like any other institution, the nuclear family has developed with rationalism, that is, the mind-set oriented to control via calculation, rather than freedom of expression. The modern family has provided a context for the formation of highly individuated persons with autonomy; the irony is that they use that autonomy to conform.

Further reading

Berger, P.L. and Kellner, H. SOCIOLOGY REINTERPRETED, Anchor Doubleday, 1981.
Hunter, J.D. and Ainlay, S.C. (eds.) MAKING SENSE OF MODERN TIMES, Routledge, 1986.

E.C.

BERGSON, Henri

Philosopher/essayist	born France 1859–1941
Associated with	EVOLUTIONISM ■ INTUITION ■ VITALISM
Influences include	DARWIN ■ LUCRETIUS ■ SPENCER
Shares common ground with	HEIDEGGER ■ PROUST ■ WHITEHEAD
Main works	CREATIVE EVOLUTION (1911)
	MATTER AND MEMORY (1911)
	THE TWO SOURCES OF MORALITY AND RELIGION
	(1935)

BERGSON WAS BORN in Paris and, after an early childhood in London, moved to Paris, where he taught philosophy at various *lycées* before becoming Professor of Philosophy, first at the École Normale Supériere in 1897, then at the Collège de France, where his public lectures became a fashionable Parisian cult. He was elected to the Académie Française in 1914, and took an active part in international affairs on several government missions to Spain and the USA during the First World War. He received the Nobel Prize for Literature in 1928 and the French Legion of Honour in 1930.

Whilst, in *Matter and Memory*, Bergson critically examined and challenged the Kantian notion of science and mathematical physics, the theme of his contemporaneous work *Creative Evolution* centred on an investigation of the non-mathematical sciences (biology, physiology and psychology). His endeavour at the turn of the twentieth century was to present a fresh and novel non-mechanistic approach to metaphysical problems in philosophy and science, not least to counter the latter's positivism. His comprehensive survey of the field of biology to that date had exposed the theoretical weaknesses of the mechanical and materialistic tenets of various theories of evolution, principally Darwinism and Lamarckism.

Bergson's dynamic world-view constituted an emergence theory of cosmic evolution – propounding the grandiose vision of all biological forms as 'pure mobility' and 'endlessly continued creation' – which invented its human biological forms through the tools of instinct and intelligence, in their intense and continued effort of creation and successive victories over inert matter. Thus 'creative evolution', which was the holistic principle central to Bergson's whole philosophy, and which he ascribed to an original, though immaterial, prime impulse of psychical life – the *élan vital* or 'life force' – which in evolutionary terms accounted for the emergence of new species and the ever-increasing complexity of organisms. Bergsonism, as it came to be known, is a totalising philosophical doctrine synonymous with the more holistic aspects of vitalism. The existence of this *élan vital* cannot be verified scientifically, Bergson describing it as qualitative, continuous, and in foregoing intentionality, permitting of free human intervention.

Both instinct and intelligence, however, have severe limitations in man's understanding of reality, searching for knowledge and discovery of things so that only a third function – intuition – as proposed by Bergson is capable of simultaneously apprehending the true nature of things, especially the unknown. Intuition, allied to reflection, is in turn a manifestation of the creative energy of human self-consciousness and creative freedom or diversity in shaping the future, which cannot be separated from time and being and is synonymous with what he distinguishes as two radically different kinds of memory: 'pure memory' (the awareness of past experience as psychical function) and 'habit memory' (remembering how to play a musical instrument).

Making perception the fundamental mode of man's relation to being is one of Bergson's most significant contributions to modern philosophical thinking. He viewed perception as the active searching, selective outreach of human organisms which conditions our experience of and grasp of reality, enabling us to cope with being and to appraise the field of matter. The autonomy of the mind, independently of the brain, for Bergson, both directed and accessed life through perception, which, coupled with the creative energy of consciousness, were, for him, irrefutable arguments that freedom was real and not an illusion.

Bergson propounded a distinctive theory of time as real (*durée réelle*, or 'real duration') and a form of being which could never be grasped through the then common scientific methods. In relation to the time-flux as the basic quality of life processes, he proposed a dualism of real duration, or 'inner time', as we experience it self-consciously, in contrast to 'outer time' as divisible and measurable. In pursuit of the new task of modern philosophy to investigate our living, qualitative apprehension of real duration, Bergson set out to substitute inner 'pure' durational for external non-temporal and static scientific representations.

Bergson's last major work was *The Two Sources of Morality and Religion* in which, in keeping with his vitalism and delineation of polar opposites of static and dynamic principles, he presented religion as essentially the worship of the life-force God, conceived as a singular and qualitative infinite being, as divine creative principle and source of all change.

Despite the nuances given to him by each of his key concepts (intelligence, intuition, memory), they have all subsequently largely been improved upon and superseded, if not contradicted, weakening much of his argumentation. Bergson's further limitation was that, in restricting the notions of duration and evolution to organic life, the opposition of physical scientists in the twentieth century has meant that his fate as a thinker has largely been determined by them rather than philosophers, despite some rehabilitation of his central ideas by the American scientist and metaphysician Alfred Whitehead. Despite this, his non-analytical philosophy exerted a central influence on modern thought, not least existentialism, in the first half of the twentieth century, notably on Heidegger and especially Marcel Proust.

Finally, as a key pioneering modernist thinker, Bergson's influence, direct or indirect, on modern literature as a cultural artefact cannot be de-emphasised, as is clearly shown by important figures such as George Bernard Shaw and D.H. Lawrence. Bergsonism also anticipated postmodernism, directly influencing Deleuze, for example, whilst post-structuralism represents a genuine extension of the vitalist urge to find universals, and shares with Bergson a strong streak of irrationalism and relativism, if not the latter's optimism.

Further reading

Barwick, F. and Douglas, P. (eds.) THE CRISIS IN MODERNISM: BERGSON AND THE VITALIST CONTROVERSY, Cambridge University Press, 1992.
Kolakowski, L. BERGSON, Oxford University Press, 1985.
Panicolaou, A. and Gunter, P. (eds.) BERGSON AND MODERN THOUGHT: TOWARDS A UNITED SCIENCE, Harwood, 1987.

G.P.

BERLIN, Isaiah

Historian of ideas	born Latvia 1909–1997
Associated with	LIBERTY ■ ETHICAL PLURALISM
Influences include	HERZEN ■ VICO
Shares common ground with	DWORKIN ■ FROMM ■ POPPER
Main works	TWO CONCEPTS OF LIBERTY (1958)
	FOUR ESSAYS ON LIBERTY (1969)
	AGAINST THE CURRENT (1979)

AFTER HIS EARLY childhood in Russia, Berlin settled in England where he was educated at St Pauls', London, and Oxford University, becoming a philosophy lecturer there in 1932 and a founding member of Austin's linguistic philosophy group. During the Second World War he worked as First Secretary to the British Embassy in Washington and later, briefly, in Moscow. On his return to Oxford in 1949 he became Chichele Professor of Social and Political Theory from 1957 to 1967 and first President of Wolfson College from 1966 to 1975. Knighted in 1957, he was later elected President of the British Academy from 1974 to 1978. From 1949 he also was visiting professor at a number of American universities.

Berlin's writings rest on a concrete historical study of the major intellectual developments in Western culture since the eighteenth century, some largely ignored and unrecognised by his predecessors. Berlin rejects the historical determinist view that laws or social processes exist over and above individuals and dictate what must inevitably take place. He also rejects logical positivism – the idea that temporal mechanistic laws or social processes can be discovered.

Berlin's concern for the moral, as opposed to the technical, dimension in the writing of history predicates indeterminacy in history. He confirms that history 'does not move in straight lines': in this, he is influenced by such unorthodox thinkers of the 'Counter-Enlightenment' as Vico and Herder. He affirms their central idea of cultural diversity as intrinsic to human history. Berlin first spelt out his influential views on one such central idea, namely freedom, in his *Two Concepts of Liberty*, further elaborated in *Four Essays on Liberty*, where he is at pains to distinguish between the concept of liberty and the conditions for it. For Berlin, *negative liberty* means the removal or absence of the obstacles to individual conduct and actions, which are not needed for the purpose of satisfying other ultimate human values.

Positive liberty, by contrast, relates psychologically to freedoms under the control of our 'real' or 'higher' selves, and sociologically to the exercising of control by others over one's life and actions to realise human values and ends – what Bobbio prefers to call 'social liberalism'. There are clearly discernible theories defining freedom exclusively in terms of the independence of the individual from interference by others, be these governments, corporations or private persons (what Charles Taylor subsequently terms an 'opportunity-concept'); equally clearly, these theories are challenged by those who believe that freedom enshrined in rights resides at least in part in collective control over the common life, an 'exercise-concept' (Taylor, Charles: *Sources of the Self: The Making of the Modern Identity*. Cambridge University Press, 1989).

Berlin's powerful defence of negative liberty is based on a complex notion of the psychological roots of humanity as well as the nature of a liberal society in which they are nurtured and realised, albeit in a balanced way. Implicit in his writings is a developmental account of three levels of human nature, permitting the attainment of the higher potentialities and cultural accomplishments of civilisations, although these values can be in conflict and involve human choices. Thus, at the quasi-Kantian level, Berlin sees individuals possessing the universal attributes of choosers and purpose-seekers as one of the 'inescapable characteristics' of the human situation. At the second (tragic) level he sees human agents as sundered by opposing tendencies ('hedgehogs' or 'foxes') .

At the third (Herderian) level of psychological pluralism, the empirical diversity of cultures in history demonstrates human beings as capable of living in any one of a number of ways and for a variety of purposes, none demonstrably superior to others. In affirming his ethical pluralism, Berlin rejects humans' proneness to historical agoraphobia (dread of open spaces), with its attendant doctrine of monism, redefining all competing values in terms of 'rational freedom' redolent of dictatorships and totalitarianism, and prevalent in European thought from Plato to Hegel, and Marx's deterministic social doctrines. His profound interpretation of pluralism and the Counter-Enlightenment thinkers' response to historical claustrophobia (intellectual and social stagnation) centres on the open issues on which men's moral conduct depends revolving principally around the social and moral questions raised by and lived through solutions to often conflicting desirable ends of equality and freedom in society. Thus Berlin's valuation of the paramountcy of negative liberty means that there is a variety of equal 'goods', ends or values to which the individual can subscribe as opposed to any rationally discoverable hierarchic structure of absolute values determining the preference of one end (not even liberty) to another.

Following Herder, Berlin discusses the other two major doctrines still vitally alive today, namely populism and expressivism, to which can be added nationalism, which Berlin examines presciently in *Against the Current*, well before its recent resurgence. Such views resonate respectively with Popper's contemporaneous concern to contrast closed and open *societies*. The latter are associated with negative liberty, classical liberalism and the political regimes of democratic societies. However, in a liberal society of a participatory pluralist kind which demands consultation, says Berlin, one cannot avoid compromises and trade-offs, within narrow limits, between desirable but incompatible values or ends in the absence of universal criteria; rarely can the individual have more of one without surrendering some part of the other.

Further reading

Jahanbegloo, Ramin CONVERSATIONS WITH ISAIAH BERLIN, Peter Halban, 1992.
Kocis, Robert A CRITICAL APPRAISAL OF SIR ISAIAH BERLIN'S POLITICAL PHILOSOPHY, Edwin Mellor Press, 1989.
Ryan, Alan (ed.) THE IDEA OF FREEDOM: ESSAYS IN HONOUR OF ISAIAH BERLIN, Oxford University Press, 1979.

G.P.

BERNSTEIN, Basil

Sociologist	born England 1924—
Associated with	CLASS ■ SYMBOLIC CONTROL ■ LANGUAGE
Influences include	DURKHEIM ■ MARX ■ HYMES
Shares common ground with	APPLE ■ BOURDIEU ■ DOUGLAS
Main works	CLASS, CODES AND CONTROL (4 vols., 1971–90)
	PEDAGOGY, SYMBOLIC CONTROL AND IDENTITY THEORY: RESEARCH, CRITIQUE (1996)

BERNSTEIN WAS EDUCATED at London University and was, until 1990, the Karl Mannheim Professor of the Sociology of Education at the University of London, when he became Emeritus Professor of Sociology Education. He is also Distinguished Research Fellow at the University of Wales, Cardiff.

Bernstein's work is a tightly woven series of encounters with the relationships between symbolic codes and the class structures and power mechanisms within which they seem to be embedded. As such, it stands in opposition to most of contemporary postmodern theory ('The privileging of discourse in these analyses tends to abstract the analysis of discourse from the detailed empirical analysis of its base in social structure').

If, on the one hand, 'education cannot compensate for society', on the other hand, education is a system of knowing, with its own social and cultural processes, which helps determine the lives of those who are brought into its living structure. Thus much of Bernstein's work is a struggle against the inherent fatalism of his initial underlying thesis – that the linguistic codes inherited from class and the power nexus within society at large are replicated within the education system. (Or, why bother to even think about the school system except as a replication of the social?)

The early Bernstein was concerned with the language of schoolchildren, a series of theoretical/empirical writings (in Vols. 1 and 2 of *Class, Codes and Control*) which teased out the various languages employed by children as they tried to cope with the experience of schooling, based on his own research in London schools. Much of this hinged on the definition of elaborated and restricted codes. While middle-class children were able to think, act and converse in different linguistic codes (and therefore play different roles), working-class children were more restricted in their abilities to adopt other codes. The implications of this work were twofold. For educationalists it meant that the schools were presented with a challenge: if social relations provided a pattern which permanently disadvantaged students, then the task of pedagogues and school administrators was to provide a creative environment which assisted the disadvantaged.

In the mid-1960s, Bernstein's work provided the theoretical and empirical ballast for the development of comprehensive schools, which implied integrated curricula and the non-segregation of students by ability. But for sociologists of knowledge, the issue was directly related to the organisational basis of how knowledge is produced. As if to answer both sets of concerns, Bernstein immediately turned his attention to issues of curriculum reform and the social organisation of knowledge. In a classic essay 'On the Classification and Framing of Educational Knowledge' (published in 1971 and reprinted at the end of Vol. 1 of *Class, Codes and Control*), drawing in part from Durkheim and Mary Douglas for theoretical inspiration, Bernstein spelt out his approach to pedagogy and curriculum (though the 'open' and 'closed' definition of content may have owed something to Karl Popper, whom Bernstein encountered when he was a student at the London School of Economics). In his analysis of curriculum and knowledge, Bernstein provided a set of reticulated dichotomies between collection and integrated codes and types of power, which, with the elaborated and restricted definitions of linguistic competence, became the central preoccupations of his work for the next three decades, but with one addition. At the end of 'Classification and Framing' he argued that 'integrated codes are symptoms of a moral crisis rather than the terminal state of an educational system'. That moral crisis became the topic for much of Bernstein's subsequent work.

In the late 1970s and through to the early 1990s, Bernstein published work on visible and invisible pedagogies which explored institutionalisation and change. By the mid-1990s, this work took on a sharper focus in developing the applicability of performance and competence models, themselves reaching back to the socio-structural linguistic modes of Bernstein's work in the 1960s, but also building on 'Classification and Framing'. The clearest and most concise version of this work is in the article 'Pedagogizing Knowledge: Studies in Recontextualizing' (in *Pedagogy, Symbolic Control and Identity*), in which the notion of field position with distinguishing levels of author, actor and identity is explored in relation to the recontextualising levels of field, state and identity. This is, perhaps, Bernstein's most carefully thought-out response to his critics, in that he confronts them on their own ground (this last volume contains many direct discussions with Edwards, A.D., Harker, R. and May, S.A., Bourdieu and on sociolinguistics in general), and the confrontation is at once discursive and rigidly programmatic. If the sociology of knowledge and the various sociologies of education are to recover from abstract empiricism on the one hand and the *mitrailleuse*, random shots of postmodernism on the other, this article by Bernstein offers an agenda. 'We have produced for the first time a virtually secular pedagogic discourse and culture, and at the same time a revival of the sacred' (1996). What we need is to think about how knowledge is now being pedagogised, how pedagogic consciousness is being managed and regulated and how identity is being constructed through visible and invisible pedagogies. In this last volume, the tension between the social and the culturally symbolic is brought together in a dialectic of creative intelligence. Bernstein is one of the few contemporary sociologists who takes the task of theory construction – and therefore understanding the present empirically – seriously enough not to write any one book but to go on writing and rewriting the same essay until he has produced a finely-tuned masterpiece. 'Pedagogizing Knowledge' is that essay.

Further reading

Atkinson, P.A. LANGUAGE, STRUCTURE AND REPRODUCTION: AN INTRODUCTION TO THE SOCIOLOGY OF BASIL BERNSTEIN, Methuen, 1985.
Atkinson, P.A., Davies, B. and Delamont, S. (eds.) DISCOURSE AND REPRODUCTION: ESSAYS IN HONOR OF BASIL BERNSTEIN, Hampton Press, 1995.
Sadovnik, A.R. KNOWLEDGE AND PEDAGOGY: THE SOCIOLOGY OF BASIL BERNSTEIN, Ablex, 1995.

I.D.

BLOCH, Ernst

Philosopher	born Germany 1885–1977
Associated with	UTOPIAN MARXISM
Influences include	MORE ∎ FOURIER ∎ MARX
Shares common ground with	WEBER ∎ LUKÁCS ∎ BENJAMIN
Main works	DAS PRINZIP HOFFNUNG (3 VOLS., 1954–59, TRANS. THE PRINCIPLE OF HOPE, 1986)
	ATHEISMUS IM CHRISTENTUM (1968, TRANS. ATHEISM IN CHRISTIANITY, 1972)
	NATURRECHT UND MENSCHLICHE WÜRDE (1961, TRANS. NATURAL LAW AND HUMAN DIGNITY, 1986)

I N 1949, ERNST BLOCH accepted a Chair in Philosophy at the University of Leipzig, in what was then East Germany, the most loyal of the Soviet satellites. At 64 years of age, this was his first formal academic appointment. Theretofore, he had been at odds with establishment politics. He had vigorously opposed the German adventurism of the First World War. By the 1920s he was considered a 'hard-line' communist, excusing Stalinist excess and excoriating Western democracies. He fled fascist Germany in 1933 and a year later was expelled from Switzerland for having affiliated with resistance groups. From 1938 until 1949 he lived in the USA, but his reputation as a Soviet zealot raised suspicions on the left and right of the American intelligentsia, thus reinforcing his itinerant status.

However, Bloch's scholarly pedigree, along with the complexity of his scholarship, defies the simplicity with which he was caricatured by his political opponents. In 1908, he went to Berlin to study with Georg Simmel, in whose seminar he met Georg Lukács, who was to become a close friend. In 1913, he moved to Heidelberg to study with Max Weber. In exile in Switzerland during the First World War, he exchanged ideas with Hugo Ball. He deeply admired the work of Walter Benjamin and Bertolt Brecht. These influences predicated Bloch's distaste for a dogmatic and mechanistic Marxism. Bloch argued that Marx had intentionally skewed his presentation towards economic forces in order to shock naïve intellectuals from their fantasies of pervasive altruism. Bloch complicated Marxism by discussing the critical and revolutionary potential of art, and he began to detect an environment which no longer demanded the harshness of the hardliners.

Thus, it is no surprise that Bloch's appointment in Leipzig was not a smooth one. He became increasingly disillusioned with the crudity and barbarity of

Soviet communism and he began to promote a more humanistic form for Germany. In 1956 he was conveniently linked to an unsuccessful attempt to oust Walter Ulbricht, and he was relieved of his academic duties. His more vocal students were imprisoned and harassed. In 1961, hearing of the imminent construction of the Berlin Wall, Bloch decided to prolong a vacation in West Germany. Not surprisingly, his reception there was a cool one, but he was able to obtain a position at the University of Tubingen. His long personal struggle to balance Marxist expediency with Marxist humanism prepared him well, however, as a resource in the development of alternatives to the Soviet model. He vigorously opposed the Soviet invasion of Prague, while he just as strongly opposed American intervention in Vietnam.

When Friedrich Engels examined the concepts of utopian and scientific socialism, in *Socialism: Utopian and Scientific*, his conclusion was that the two concepts were mutually exclusive. Bloch, on the other hand, consistently argued for their compatibility. While faulting the likes of Fourier and Saint-Simon for naïvely underestimating the self-interest of the mercantilist class, Bloch maintained an appreciation for utopian thinking, and thus entertained the idea that the science of Marx was compatible with daydreaming, story-telling, hoping and imagining. Bloch was quick to recognise the subjective, emotive attractiveness of fascism, and he was critical of the lifeless, mechanistic approach of many strains of Marxism. In his masterpiece, *The Spirit of Utopia*, Bloch compared scientific Marxism to Kant's *Critique of Pure Reason*. Marx had been understood to have discovered the hidden but unavoidable forces of social evolution. Yet there remained the need for a Marxian equivalent of the *Critique of Pure Reason*, an explanation and focus on human energy and action.

For Bloch, action and energy are derived from utopian contemplation. More's brilliant treatment of the concept was somewhat deficient. Utopia for More was a spatial entity, a distant yet existing entity. Bloch, who is more interested in the spirit rather than the reality of utopia, prefers to focus on the temporal issue. For Bloch, utopia is not only spatially distant but temporally distant. It is, in his famous phrase, an expression of the 'not yet'. It is the cultivation and the celebration of that which has yet to occur, but of that for which we still have some inkling (*vor-schien*). Great works of art and literature, but also mythology, and even detective novels, carry the promise of a future conciliation. Utopia, far from a mollifying distraction, inspires hope, and hope provides the practical motivation for human subjects to participate in what would otherwise be a dreary and oppressive existence.

Further reading

Hudson, W. THE MARXIST PHILOSOPHY OF ERNST BLOCH, Macmillan, 1982.
Kellner, D. and O'Hara, H. 'Utopia and Marxism in Ernst Bloch', NEW GERMAN CRITIQUE, 9 (Fall 1976), pp. 11–34.

Solomon, M. 'Marx and Bloch: Reflections on Utopia and Art', TELOS, 13 (Fall 1972), pp. 68–85.

T.J.L.

BLOOM, Allan

Political philosopher/popular culture analyst	born USA 1930—
Associated with	CONSERVATISM
Influences include	PLATO ■ ROUSSEAU ■ NIETZSCHE
Shares common ground with	STRAUSS ■ BELLOW
Main works	THE CLOSING OF THE AMERICAN MIND: HOW HIGHER EDUCATION HAS FAILED DEMOCRACY AND IMPOVERISHED THE SOULS OF TODAY'S STUDENTS (1987) LOVE AND FRIENDSHIP (1993)

ALLAN BLOOM, a student of political philosopher Leo Strauss, first gained scholarly notoriety as a translator of Plato's *The Republic*. His was distinguished from other such endeavours by its uncompromising literalness. Bloom was disappointed by the extent to which translators had taken liberty with the original in their attempts to make Plato more 'accessible' to a modern audience. For Bloom, accessibility meant adulteration.

Preserving the integrity of classical political thought is indeed the core of Bloom's entire scholarship. As a student, and finally as a teacher in the University of Chicago's Committee on Social Thought, he was steeped in the classical Western canon, and he agitated to protect it. His most important work, *The Closing of the American Mind*, is an adaptation of Plato's general critique of democracy to the specifics of contemporary American society. In *The Republic*, Plato ironically describes democracy as the 'fairest' of regimes, refusing to privilege one pursuit over another. For Bloom, this indiscriminateness has reached intolerable proportions in America; and the university, as the last bastion of considering the truly good, has succumbed without as much as a whimper.

Bloom endorses the Platonic division of the soul. Most of American society is preoccupied with appetite and cannot be expected to engage in much else. The university in today's society ought to be the repository for spirit and its attendant virtue, courage, protecting wisdom and the very few individuals capable of its appreciation. Unfortunately, the courage is not there and wisdom is thus threatened. Students are preoccupied with their animal functions, accompanied by the unsublimated, coital beat of rock music. They run in packs, pairing up intermittently for libidinal relief.

And their professors, rather than transforming the beast, cater to it. Once in a while, the beast resists training, as in the 1960s, and easily overpowers the feeble and cowardly keepers. Bloom recounts his experiences at Cornell with colleagues who capitulated to all the selfish and simplistic demands of student protesters. The students thought they knew what they wanted, but they had no respect for the scholarly tradition which demanded contemplative scrutiny of their interests. The 'stinging drones' were taking over, and only Bloom and a handful of colleagues were prepared to defend philosophy over expediency.

Bloom traces the ascension of expediency and the attendant abandonment of considering the good. The likes of Machiavelli and Locke lowered the sights of philosophy, settling for self-interest as the guiding principle for human behaviour, thereby locking out courage and wisdom in favour of the more common appetite. Bloom argues that Rousseau was the first to articulate the deficiencies of this society, and that Nietzsche's 'last man' was the most devastating critique of this self-interested wimp, who is so thoroughly preoccupied with creature comforts that he finds it impossible to see the values implicit in a natural science that has been devised to provide those comforts.

Socrates, of course, recognises the value-ladenness of science, and bemoans the vanity and conceit of the geometrists who do not question their original hypothesis – that geometry is inherently and unquestionably important. Bloom, like Socrates, recognises the need to discuss the purpose of human pursuits – technical or theoretical – in terms of the whole, and in terms of how the pursuits contribute to human existence in general. Nietzsche's solution was courageous, but not wise. He counselled action and creation – of any kind – to disrupt the last man's interest in sleeping well. Bloom, instead, remains committed to creativity for the sake not of the exciting life, but of the good life. He finds that university culture, and culture in general, unfortunately promote neither.

Further reading

Berube, M. 'Winning Hearts and Minds', YALE JOURNAL OF CRITICISM, 5: 2 (Spring 1992), pp. 1–25.
Hayes, F. 'Politics and Education in America's Multicultural Society: An African-American Studies' Response to Allan Bloom', JOURNAL OF ETHNIC STUDIES, 17: 2 (Summer 1989), pp. 71–89.

T.J.L.

BLUMER, Herbert

Sociologist	born USA 1900–1987
Associated with	SYMBOLIC INTERACTIONISM ▪ CHICAGO SCHOOL
Influences include	MEAD ▪ PARK ▪ FARIS ▪ DEWEY
Shares common ground with	BECKER ▪ STRAUSS ▪ GOFFMAN
Main works	MOVIES AND CONDUCT (1933) SYMBOLIC INTERACTIONISM: PERSPECTIVES AND METHOD (1969)

HERBERT BLUMER WAS born in St Louis, Missouri, and studied at the University of Missouri (1918–22) and University of Chicago (1925–28). He taught at the Universities of Missouri (1922–25), Chicago (1925–52) and California, Berkeley (1952–72). He was especially influenced by the work of the so-called Chicago School, namely the work of Robert Park, William Thomas and Ellsworth Faris.

The name of Herbert Blumer is synonymous with the qualitative approach in sociology called symbolic interactionism. His book of that title was published in 1969. It remains the definitive explanation and elaboration of George Mead's proposition that human interaction is mediated by the use of symbols which become the means by which others interpret, make sense of, and respond to, the actions of individuals. Blumer coined the term 'symbolic interactionism' in 1937.

Blumer emphasised the interpretative component of how people respond to situations as critical in understanding the dynamics of human behaviour. While some have assumed from this that Blumer was overplaying the role of the individual and downplaying the role of social organisations and institutions, more sympathetic commentators have argued that his position was more complex and that he recognised the collective context in which individual negotiations of situations occur. In particular, Blumer acknowledged three key aspects of the structural framework of social formations: recurrent patterns of collective activity; complex networks and institutional relations; and historical processes and forces (David Maines and Thomas Morrione, 'On the breadth and relevance of Blumer's perspective: introduction to his analysis of industrialisation', in *Industrialisation as an Agent of Social Change: A Critical Analysis*, edited with an introduction by David Maines and Thomas Morrione, Aldine de Gruyter, 1990, p. xv). In other words, he incorporated a dual focus on social processes and outcomes which acknowledge individual and collective actions, as well as stability and change in social structures.

Blumer's approach to social analysis was shaped by the naturalistic emphasis of the case-study fieldwork of the Chicago School which employed qualitative methods, such as participant observation and other ethnographic techniques, to explore aspects of everyday life in the city (e.g. in studies of slum life, dance halls and street people). Blumer, for example, was especially interested in Robert Park's work which framed Blumer's study into the effects of films on audiences, especially young people. Blumer published *Movies and Conduct* (Macmillan, 1933) and a co-authored book, with Philip Hauser, *Movies, Delinquency and Crime* (Macmillan, 1933). Their conclusions pre-empted subsequent studies by arguing that, although films could have a significant effect on audience members, it depended on the propensities of the individual and the social milieu in which the individual was located.

Despite his prodigious reputation, Blumer published only three books (one of which was co-authored), most of his ideas appearing as journal articles. He was an inspiring teacher, energetic university colleague, and very active in promoting the profession of sociology (for example as editor of the *American Journal of Sociology* from 1941 to 1952, and editor of the Sociology Series from Prentice-Hall from 1934). Less well-known was his career in professional football, work in labour arbitration (from both the union and corporate side), and connections with Chicago's underworld.

After his death, a collection of his writings on the processes of industrialisation was published as *Industrialisation as an Agent of Social Change*, 1990. Its editors, David Maines and Thomas Morrione, argue that Blumer's approach has been systematically misrepresented and that this lesser-known body of work provides a more realistic sense of the distinctiveness of his approach.

The legacy of Blumer has been enshrined in the qualitative methodologies of a number of social sciences, in particular, sociology and social psychology. In fact, his perspective was much broader and more politicised than usual interpretations allow. He recognised only too clearly the complex interactions between individuals and organisations and the mutual dynamics of social interactions. Perhaps the best short account of his position can be found in his chapter, 'Society as Symbolic Interaction' 1962.

Further reading

Baugh, K. THE METHODOLOGY OF HERBERT BLUMER: CRITICAL INTERPRETATION AND REPAIR, Cambridge University Press, 1990.

Blumer, H. 'Society as symbolic interaction', in A. Rose (ed.), HUMAN BEHAVIOUR AND SOCIAL PROCESSES (Houghton-Mifflin, 1962), pp. 179–92.

Hammersley, M. AN ANALYSIS AND INTERPRETATION OF THE WORK OF HERBERT BLUMER, University of Arkansas Press, 1988.

Hammersley, M. THE DILEMMA OF QUALITATIVE METHOD, Routledge, 1989.

Shibutani, T. HUMAN NATURE AND COLLECTIVE BEHAVIOUR: PAPERS IN HONOUR OF HERBERT BLUMER, Prentice-Hall, 1970.

J.C.

BLUMLER, Jay

Communication Theorist	Born USA 1924—
Associated with	USES AND GRATIFICATIONS ■ POLITICAL COMMUNICATION ■ CULTURAL CONSUMERS
Influences include	LASKI ■ POPPER ■ MILL
Shares common ground with	GUREVITCH ■ KATZ ■ MCQUAIL
Main works	TELEVISION IN POLITICS: ITS USES AND INFLUENCE (WITH D. MCQUAIL, 1968) THE USES OF MASS COMMUNICATIONS (WITH E. KATZ, 1974) THE CRISIS OF PUBLIC COMMUNICATION WITH M. GUREVITCH, 1995).

B LUMER GRADUATED IN political science from Antioch College in Ohio before travelling to the London School of Economics in 1947 as a doctoral student. He spent the 1950s teaching sociology to mature students at Ruskin College, Oxford University, before moving to Leeds in 1963 as the Granada Television Research Fellow. It was here that he developed a new way of studying and theorising communications which steered a fresh course between the two extremes of Marxist historicism and American behavioural empiricism.

Working with a series of collaborators – particularly Denis McQuail, Jack McLeoad and Tom Nossiter – as Research Director of the Centre for Television Research at the University of Leeds, Blumler led a succession of influential studies which covered different aspects of political television and its audiences. He is currently Emeritus Professor of the University of Leeds and Emeritus Professor of Journalism at the University of Maryland and he is also the founding editor of the *European Journal of Communication*, as well as being Research Adviser to the Broadcasting Standards Council.

Blumler's approach to empirical work calls on the academic media observer to adopt a formative, as opposed to a confrontational, role in relation to media production. This is a controversial position which has led to criticism on the grounds that engaging with programme-makers' problems necessarily inhibits the researcher's independence.

However, Blumler's 'institutional perspective' of mass communication argues that in the realm of television, the viewer (who at election times becomes, in a democracy, the voter) should be sovereign. He calls upon the researcher to explore how the viewer/voter's information and other needs must be satisfied. In practice, this may well mean engaging with the problems facing the professional

journalist who seeks to provide more effective and probing factual programmes, usually in the face of criticism and 'patterns of collusive conflict'
at close quarters, academic independence can be assured. Blumler believes,
well short of having to assume that programme-makers are the researcher's
enemy.

His groundbreaking theoretical work on 'Uses and Gratifications' has also
concerned itself with viewers, not as passive victims, but as active players who
are capable of making choices for themselves. Blumler's work emphasises the
skill of TV viewers in making sense of the information and points of view
broadcast on television. This is in marked contrast with the 'culturalist' tradition in media and communication studies, which has tended to emphasise the
determining power of the media in shaping opinions. Blumler's work reaffirms
the insistence on viewers as skilled and accomplished agents. Implicit in
Blumler's work is an ideal of viewers as consumers assisted by increasingly
conscientious programme-makers to become, one day, controllers of their own
cultural and political destiny.

Further reading

Asard, E. and Bennett, W.L. DEMOCRACY IN THE MARKET PLACE OF IDEAS,
Cambridge University Press, 1997.
Livingstone, S.M. MAKING SENSE OF TELEVISION: THE PSYCHOLOGY OF AUDIENCE
INTERPRETATION, Routledge, 1998.
Rosengren, K.-E., Wenner, L.A. and Palmgreen, P. MEDIA GRATICATIONS
RESEARCH: CURRENT PERSPECTIVES, Sage, 1985.

J.I.

BOURDIEU, Pierre

Sociologist/cultural anthropologist	born France 1930—
Associated with	EXISTENTIALISM ▪ MARXISM ▪ STRUCTURALISM
Influences include	DURKHEIM ▪ LÉVI-STRAUSS ▪ SARTRE
Shares common ground with	GARNHAM ▪ GIDDENS ▪ GOFFMAN ▪ WILLIAMS
Main works	REPRODUCTION IN EDUCATION, CULTURE AND SOCIETY (WITH JEAN-CLAUDE PASSERON, 1970) DISTINCTION: A SOCIAL CRITIQUE OF THE JUDGEMENT OF TASTE (1979) THE LOGIC OF PRACTICE (1980) THE FIELD OF CULTURAL PRODUCTION (1993)

BOURDIEU WAS BORN at Béarn in rural south-east France. He studied philosophy in Paris and, at the end of his period of conscription in the French Army in Algeria (1956–58), he wrote a sociology of Algeria and remained there for a further two years to conduct anthropological fieldwork (see his study, 'The Kabyle House or the World Reversed' in *The Logic of Practice*). He has spent most of his working life in Paris, where he is Professor of Sociology at the College de France and Director of the Centre for European Sociology. Like many young French intellectuals during the 1950s, Bourdieu experienced the sometimes mutual and frequently contervailing influences of Sartrean existentialism, Lévi-Straussian structuralism and the Marxissant culture of the post-Second World War French Left. Unusually, however, amongst major French cultural theorists, much of his work is grounded in empirical sociology and makes elaborate use, on occasion, of statistical method. Yet his thinking is complex philosophically and diverse in its applications.

Throughout his work Bourdieu has sought to combine agency and structure analytically in what he has called a 'genetic structuralism', a term which he uses in a rather different sense from Lucien Goldmann's use of the same term to describe his theoretical perspective. At the heart of Bourdieu's work is a preoccupation with class as both a determinant of life trajectory and a key feature of social structure. In the 1960s Bourdieu directed research on educational attainment and class background, and also on cultural consumption and class, in the latter case, for instance, concerning attendance at art museums. He analysed processes of familial and educational disadvantage and how working-class people typically become complicit with their exclusion from 'legitimate culture'. Bourdieu's concept of *habitus* signifies the lived reality of social positioning and is used to contrast the lifestyles and expectations of the working, middle and upper classes. From this perspective, dominant groups have the symbolic power to define what counts culturally in ways which sustain and reproduce their commanding positions in society.

It is characteristic of Bourdieu to use economic analogies to theorise social and cultural power. His notion of symbolic capital refers particularly to linguistic power, and the idea of cultural capital refers to the possession and use of cultural competencies, such as the appreciation of classical music as a sign of social distinction. In addition, he uses 'market' not only to refer to the buying and selling of commodities, but with reference to operations of judgement in artistic and literary fields. More generally, culture is seen as a force field structured by the poles of social power.

Bourdieu's developed position is best known with regard to his most famous book, *Distinction*, which reports on a series of empirical studies of cultural consumption and taste conducted in Bordeaux and Paris during the 1960s and 1970s. *Distinction* is a challenge to the Kantian aesthetic tradition which assumes that disinterested judgements can be made about the cultural value and quality of art works. For Bourdieu, no judgement is disinterested, although he himself deploys an objectivist mode of social analysis. Taste is entirely a social construct in Bourdieu's perspective. He was no longer principally concerned with the social disadvantage and cultural exclusion of the working class in general. In fact, his concept of the 'popular' aesthetic, which stresses immediacy and pleasure, is compared favourably with the 'pure' aesthetic of the bourgeoisie in which detachment is valued. However, Bourdieu is not a populist. He casts a rather jaundiced eye over all levels of social practice. Most notably in *Distinction*, Bourdieu identifies the social locale of postmodern sensibility in the tastes of the new petite bourgeoisie, 'agents of presentation and representation', who in scrambling traditional categories of culture by picking and mixing tastes high and low, establish their own distinction against older and competing groups. They also, in their work, individualism and political vacuity, contribute to the 'ethical re-tooling' required by the new bourgeoisie of post-industrialist and consumer capitalism.

Bourdieu's analyses tend to debunk common-sense wisdoms and pomposity through what is, in effect, a kind of sociological reductionism. So, academics, for example, do not rise to prominence so much because of their intellectual brilliance but, rather, because of their social connections and ability to market their wares. It would be mistaken, however, to permit a disinterestedness to Bourdieu that he denies others. His point of view is that of the upwardly mobile cynic who has seen it all and is kidded by no one.

Further reading

Bourdieu, P. and Haacke, H. Free Exchange, Polity, 1995.
Calhoun, C., LiPuma, E. and Postone, M. (eds.) Bourdieu: Critical Perspectives, Polity, 1993.
Fowler, B. Pierre Bourdieu and Cultural Theory, Sage, 1997.
Jenkins, R. Pierre Bourdieu, Routledge, 1992.

J.McG.

BRAUDEL, Fernand P.

Historian	born France 1902–1985
Associated with	Longue Durée ▪ Annales School of History
Influences include	Febvre ▪ Bloch ▪ Gurvitch
Shares common ground with	Ladurie ▪ Wallerstein ▪ Tilly
Main works	The Mediterranean and the Mediterranean World in the Age of Philip II (1972)
	Civilization and Capitalism 15th – 18th Centuries (1981–84)
	The Identity of France (1986–90)

ERNAND BRAUDEL WAS a highly individualistic craftsman who worked on a very large scale. His themes included the Mediterranean world, the material civilisation of the early modern world from the fifteenth to the eighteenth centuries, and the historical development of France. In each case, he tried to capture, in the compass of a single, multi-volumed work, the impact of geographical structures and demographic processes on the collective destinies of nations and civilisations over the long term (or *longue durée*). Braudel's attention was fixed on massive, slow-moving structures embodied in climate, custom, culture, patterns of trade and migration, and the buffeting of civilisation against civilisation across long-established frontiers. His energy and dedication were prodigious. He researched for over a quarter of a century to produce his classic work on the Mediterranean world, photographing archival documents, he later recalled, at a rate of over two thousand a day.

Braudel's particular approach to history was shaped by the influence of Lucien Febvre and Marc Bloch, who in 1929 founded the *Annales d'histoire économique et social*. This journal was dedicated to a new kind of 'total' history with an openness to other disciplines, especially historical geography and demography. However, the key experience of Braudel's early life was being confined in a German prisoner-of-war camp from 1940 to 1945. During these years, without any of his notes, he composed the first draft of *The Mediterranean and the Mediterranean World in the Age of Philip II* (henceforth *The Mediterranean*). He later wrote that his concern with the long term was a psychological response to being trapped and helpless at a time when momentous events were happening almost every day. He took refuge in the belief that history was written at a more profound level and on a much longer time-scale.

Apart from the examples provided by Bloch and Febvre, and the impact of being a prisoner of war, a third influence on Braudel was the work of the sociologist George Gurvitch, his colleague during the 1950s and 1960s at the École des Hautes Études in Paris (where Braudel became head of the Sixth Section in 1956, succeeding Febvre). Gurvitch argued that social phenomena underwent constant processes of 'structuration', 'de-structuration' and 're-structuration', in the course of which social groups and whole societies were created and then changed. In practical terms this meant that sociologists and historians should be alert to the complex tensions and conflicts found below the surface of every type of society, giving pattern and meaning to the events of political, military, diplomatic and economic life. Braudel found this idea useful but did not adopt Gurvitch's theoretical approach as a whole. In fact, Braudel was less interested in theoretical constructs than in getting to grips with the empirical reality, as he saw it, of historical structures and historical change.

The Mediterranean and his second major work, *Civilization and Capitalism 15th–18th Centuries* (henceforth *Civilization and Capitalism*), are both organised in three sections: the first concerned with large-scale and long-term *structures*, the second with the way medium- and short-term *conjunctures* (historical events or trends) were shaped by these *structures*, and the third with the particular patterns traced by specific *conjunctures*. For example, the first part of *The Mediterranean* deals with humankind and its environment, especially the dynamic relations between land and sea, mountains and plains, cities and countryside, East and West and North and South, within 'geographical' time or the *longue durée*. In a similar way, the first volume of *Civilization and Capitalism* considers choices and strategies within the market economy and market capitalism, and deals with relations between economics, social hierarchies, states and civilisations. The third part of *The Mediterranean* deals with political and military events in 'individual' time, while the final volume of *Civilization and Capitalism* is about specific economic and cultural conjectures, including the rise and fall of particular world economies. In his last major work, *The Identity of France*, Braudel planned to follow a similar pattern. His first two volumes, which reached back from the present to Roman Gaul, were subtitled 'history and environment' (inspired by geography) and 'people and production' (concerned with demography and political economy). A third volume was planned on French politics, culture and society, and even a fourth on the international influence of the French nation. However, this was prevented by Braudel's death in 1985 at the age of 83. By that time he had become the defining figure of the *Annales* school of history.

Further reading

Braudel, F. Afterthoughts on Material Civilization and Capitalism, Johns Hopkins University Press, 1977.
Hughes, H.S. The Obstructed Path: French Social Thought in the Years of Desperation 1930–1960, Harper & Row, 1966.
Stoianovich, T. French Historical Method: The 'Annales' Paradigm, Cornell University Press, 1976.

D.S.

BRECHT, Bertolt

Playwright/poet	born Germany 1898–1956
Associated with	EXPRESSIONISM ▪ FORMALISM ▪ MARXISM
Influences include	BENJAMIN ▪ MARX ▪ WEDEKIND
Shares common ground with	BAKHTIN ▪ VOLOSINOV ▪ BARTHES ▪ EAGLETON ▪ WILLIAMS
Main works	BRECHT ON THEATRE (ED. J. WILLETT, 1957/1964) THE MESSINGKAUF DIALOGUES (1963) 'AGAINST GEORG LUKÁCS' (1974) POEMS (3 VOLS. 1976)

THE PLAYWRIGHT AND poet Bertolt Brecht became a leading exponent of modern aesthetics and a proponent of communist politics during the Weimar Republic in the 1920s. On Hitler's rise to power in 1933 he went into exile, first in Denmark and subsequently the USA. He returned to Germany after the Second World War and shortly before the setting-up of the German Democratic Republic which is where Brecht was to live for the rest of his life, although in possession of a Western passport and a Swiss bank account. He established the world-famous Berliner Ensemble Theatre to put on his plays according to his own dramaturgical precepts. His attitude to the Stalinist regime in East Germany was critically ironic in private but apparently loyal in public. He was awarded the Stalin Peace Prize in 1955.

Brecht is not, of course, a cultural theorist in the conventional sense, but rather an artist who theorised his own practice and influenced other practices not only in theatre but also, for instance, in cinema. The Marxism to which he owed allegiance took art very seriously indeed, both for its propaganda value against capitalism and as fundamentally important to the would-be socialist transformation of culture and society. Marxist aesthetics typically favoured realism in order to show what capitalist society was like and, after the Bolshevik Revolution in 1917, to celebrate the building of socialism. Thus twentieth-century Marxism had a problematical relationship with modernist trends in art and cultural practice, which were frequently denounced as decadent and formalist (meaning form with no politically serious content).

In his dramaturgy, Brecht challenged Aristotelian mimesis and Stanislavski's naturalistic code of acting, insisting, alternatively, that the play should be seen as a performance, an artificial construct, 'revealing the device', in the Russian formalist term. *Verfremdung* (alienation device) is meant to make events strange to the audience in Brecht's 'epic theatre'. Narrative suspense is disrupted by the narrator recounting events in advance of their occurrence, actors 'gesture' their parts rather than mimicking 'natural' action, and so forth. Brecht's intention was to invoke an active audience response, to foster in the audience a 'complex seeing'. It was crucial, for him, that the problems posed by his plays are not to be solved merely theatrically: the audience should, rather, leave the theatre contemplating the contradictions of real life, appreciating that politics not art must be the site of transformative action. This, according to Brecht, was 'true realism'.

Brecht's dramaturgy (and his equally didactic but entertaining poetry), which is just one instance of a wider twentieth-century aesthetic that has been opposed to nineteenth-century modes of representation, is frequently contrasted with Georg Lukács's Marxist defence of the nineteenth-century realist novel. What is sometimes called the Brecht/Lukács debate, however, never really occurred and was, in effect, reconstructed several years after Brecht died, when his critical esays on Lukácsian aesthetics were eventually published. Lukács did, however, criticise Brecht during his lifetime. Lukács believed that characters should typify social forces, for instance the nouveaux riches of the nineteenth century, and they should also be credible individuals with whom to identify. Brecht was hostile to this kind of empathic art. In his view, empathising with characters merely allows the reader/audience member to wallow in emotions and, in consequence, eliminates critical thought. Characters should be seen, instead, as demonstrations of social contradictions and political struggle. Brecht later qualified these schematic views by synthesising them with more naturalistic theatrical conventions, which is particularly evident in the revised versions of his *The Life of Galileo* (1947). Galileo's dilemma concerning science and religion is presented as a parable of the nuclear scientist's role in the age of the atom bomb.

Although Brecht is best known as a dramatist and poet, he was himself enthusiastic about working in radio and cinema; and shared with his friend Walter Benjamin a commitment to exploring their democratising potential. Brecht anticipated the possibilities of interactive communications media by stressing radio's talkback capacity and, like Benjamin, he saw cinema as the major entertainment medium of the masses in the mid-twentieth century. His influence is discernible, however, on Jean-Luc Godard and other avant-garde film-makers and theorists. In the 1970s, Colin MacCabe drew upon Brecht's ideas to criticise the 'classic realist text' of mainstream Hollywood cinema and naturalistic television. It is an irony now, however, that estrangement devices recommended by Brecht and other left-wing theorists, which were intended to subvert bourgeois culture, should have become such routinely 'postmodernist' tricks of latter-day capitalist media, including advertising.

Further reading

Benjamin, W. UNDERSTANDING BRECHT, New Left Books, 1973.
Lunn, E. MODERNISM AND MARXISM, Verso, 1985.
Wright, E. POSTMODERN BRECHT, Routledge, 1989.

J.McG.

BRETON, André

Psychologist	born France 1896–1966
Associated with	SURREALISM
Influences include	RIMBAUD ■ MALLARMÉ ■ MOREAU
Shares common ground with	ARAGON ■ TZARA ■ ERNST
Main works	MANIFESTE DU SURRÉALISME, POISSON SOLUBLE (1924, TRANS. MANIFESTOS OF SURREALISM, 1969) NADJA (1928, TRANS. NADJA, 1960) L'AMOUR FOU (1937, TRANS. MAD LOVE, 1937)

IN HIS 1924 *Manifestos of Surrealism*, André Breton describes a drowsy encounter with a puzzling apparition. He sees a man with a window cleaving his own body in half, in a fashion perpendicular to the vertical axis. In fact, the spectre came to be a metaphor of surrealism, which holds that indeed human existence is artificially but powerfully divided into spiritual and practical concerns, into dream and reality. Surrealism embraces and transcends both universes. Unlike Christianity, surrealism does not give up on the profane. And unlike vulgar science, surrealism does not eschew the ambiguities of the soul. Techniques developed by Breton and his surrealist colleagues were intended to shatter the window and allow the parts to circulate together.

There is no doubt that Breton had the inclination and the tools to look through the window separating pragmatism and imagination. In 1913, he undertook medical studies at the Sorbonne, and from 1915 to 1919, he was a medical assistant in the army, including a tour of duty, in 1917, as a psychiatric assistant at the psychiatric centre at Saint-Dizier. Unlike Freud, however (to whom Breton frequently expressed intellectual gratitude), Breton was not content with the idea that certain subconscious inclinations would have to be repressed for the sake of civilisation. Rather, in his numerous attempts to 'open the window', he became increasingly confident in the ultimate compatibility of dream and reality.

One means of integrating the antinomies of experience was 'automatic writing', a practice of the earlier Dadaists, with whom Breton was at times associated. Breton was impressed with the work of Professor Pierre Janet, who used the technique in psychoanalysis. Whereas the Dadaists hoped only to mock the seriousness of their bourgeois colleagues with random utterances, Breton believed that language unmediated by the grammar of rationality could tap human essence which was untainted by the routine, efficiency and instrumentality of modern life. What had been partitioned and labelled as 'mysterious' could emerge in automatic writing as 'marvellous' – beautiful and puzzling, yet accessible in a way that Christian mystery was not. Perhaps the quintessential expression of automatic writing is 'Soluble Fish', a fantastic, erotic, fractured account of encounters with giant, speaking wasps and phosphorescent, suffering crates. Yet the encounters transpired amidst the decidedly familiar streets and neighbourhoods of Paris.

Breton also conducted experiments with hypnosis, arguing that the induced dream state, like automatic writing, bypassed the debilitating impositions and inhibitions of practical life. His 'diary', *Nadja*, records his curious relationship with a woman whose life is a blending of dream and reality. She is ultimately locked away in an insane asylum, inspiring simultaneous inspiration to the possibilities of imaginative bliss, along with disgust for the banality and restrictiveness of the status quo. Breton was harshly critical of the psychiatry of his day, claiming that it represented the status quo, and that its pronouncements of insanity were nothing more than an insidious discrimination against dream and subjectivity. For Breton, Baudelaire, Nietzsche and Nadja, along with countless others, succumbed to the brutality of this 'scientific' discrimination.

Further reading

Balakian, A. ANDRÉ BRETON: MAGUS OF SURREALISM, Oxford University Press, 1971.
Caws, M.A. THE POETRY OF DADA AND SURREALISM, Princeton University Press, 1970.
Matthews, J.H. ANDRÉ BRETON, Columbia University Press, 1967.

T.J.L.

BURKE, Kenneth

Literary theorist	born USA 1897–1993
Associated with	DRAMATISM ▪ NEW CRITICISM ▪ SYMBOLIC ACTION
Influences include	ARISTOTLE ▪ FREUD ▪ MARX
Shares common ground with	DUNCAN ▪ GOFFMAN ▪ JAMESON
Main works	PERMANENCE AND CHANGE: AN ANATOMY OF PURPOSE (1935) THE PHILOSOPHY OF LITERARY FORMS (1941) A GRAMMAR OF MOTIVES (1947)

KENNETH BURKE WAS born in Pittsburgh where, after attending high school and developing an interest in language and literature, he entered Ohio State University, followed by enrolment at Columbia University in 1917 to study philosophy, which he abandoned after a year. He then began a rigorous self-education, reading widely in classical and European literature, as well as philosophy, in addition to writing plays, short stories and translating literary works from German. Although he held visiting positions at various universities, including Chicago, his main work was in music and literary criticism; in fact, he became a leading proponent of what became known as New Criticism.

Burke's first major work, *Permanence and Change: An Anatomy of Purpose* was a diverse and eclectic study of humans as symbol-making animals. The book extends the analysis of motive begun earlier in *Counterstatement*, with its literary and critical concerns, to a more general analysis of human motivation in the context of his historical change. As the title of his book signifies, he is centrally interested in the tension between states of permanence and change in extending his initial programme with its social vision and oppositional stance rather than an interest in aesthetics and literary art for art's sake. In surveying and dissecting historical periods to display parallels and affinities in systems of thought and language which had been neglected, Burke employed the modernist method of what he terms 'perspectives by incongruity' or 'planned incongruity'. Whilst showing the influence of Marx, Burke, in his formulations, reverses base and superstructure and critiques Marx's materialism, arguing that changes in consciousness must necessarily precede material and economic ones, and insisting that forms of human experience exist prior to their material embodiment.

A similarly unorthodox approach via incongruity, displaying what the noted literary critic Fredric Jameson calls Burke's 'Freudo-Marxism', is a feature of

Attitudes Towards History, with its psychological interpretations of historical events and characters, marking his first sustained attempt to apply his dramatic method and terminology of critical analysis and interpretation of historical change. Akin to Marx's stages of socio-economic development, Burke employs what he calls 'poetic categories' as literary genres and historical tempers (of tragedy, comedy, the grotesque, etc.), which act as frames of acceptance and rejection by individuals and communities to characterise the collective ideological transitions and synthesis in organised social systems of each of the five eras of Western history. He presents a comparative cultural structure of basic dramatic plots (the return of the prodigal son, the death of a king, etc.), corresponding to a set of conventional literary critical terms that are enacted and re-enacted throughout history, representing for Burke major psychological devices by which the human mind equips itself to name and confront its situations.

In *The Philosophy of Literary Forms*, Burke switches his attention from the earlier emphases on the psychology of form to the study of the philosophy or ideology of form as an internal structure. He insists on distinguishing his concept of the symbolic as act or praxis to reinforce his contention that all discursive action is symbolic action serving as 'equipment for living', as distinct from 'symbolism', the late nineteenth century movement in poetry, with its connotations of unreality and irrationality as well as an external 'pool' of symbols.

Burke's notion of the symbolic act, as an anticipation of current notions of the primacy of language, also marks his change from a social psychological to a language-based understanding of the social order, albeit here he only hints at his theory of social order. He further anticipates the later transformational structuralism of Lévi-Strauss, the semiological analysis of Barthes and the New Criticism of structuralist-oriented literary criticism as it developed in the 1960s. His more ambitious explanatory project of a theory of literature as symbolic action with its meaning as a response to, not a mirror of, a determinate human or social situation was to unconventionally propose a 'sociological' literary criticism, leading one critic to refer to Burke as the 'Bakhtin of the New Criticism'.

Burke's next major work, *A Grammar of Motives*, expands his earlier ideas about our experience of, in contrast to our *knowledge* of, reality, which he metaphorically terms 'dramatism'. His treatment of the relationship of language and action in human motivation consists of five fundamental terms which collectively form a modal typology (a 'Pentad') of act, scene, agent, agency and purpose. These basic co-ordinates involved in the organisation of all symbolic action serve as a critical vocabulary for humans as symbol-using animals for measuring their intricate 'ratios' or connections (e.g. the relation of scene to act is the scene–act ratio) animating any given narrative or verbal statement. Burke regards words and their connective links as their 'grammar', equipping us to analyse and criticise our lived experience of reality and thereby constituting the form and content of the mental process.

Burke's sociological literary criticism and linguistic realism are recognised in his acknowledgement of the early ideas of Talcott Parsons on units of social systems. His exposition of dramatism has clear affinities with symbolic interactionism (termed 'dramaturgy' in sociology as exemplified by Goffman). In terms of linguistic realism (as opposed to linguistic science) and the centrality of language in human orientations and motivations, G.H. Mead's earlier stress on gestures and conversation as crucial features of socialisation in symbolic interaction between actors – especially in formulating the 'generalised other' and 'significant other' – clearly resonate with Burke's sociological perspective.

Further reading

Bygrave, S. KENNETH BURKE: RHETORIC AND IDEOLOGY, Routledge, 1993.
Cheesbro, J.W. EXTENSION OF THE BURKEAN SYSTEM, University of Alabama Press, 1993.
Frank, A. KENNETH BURKE, Twayne, 1969.

G.P.

BURNHAM, James

Political theorist	born USA 1905—
Associated with	MANAGERIAL CAPITALISM ■ TECHNOCRATS
Influences include	MARX ■ MICHELS ■ MOSCA ■ PARETO ■ MANNHEIM
Shares common ground with	SCHUMPETER ■ DJILAS ■ DAHRENDORF
Main works	THE MANAGERIAL REVOLUTION OR WHAT IS HAPPENING IN THE WORLD NOW (1941) THE MACHIAVELLIANS (1942)

BURNHAM WAS BORN of English immigrant parents in Chicago in 1905. After studying at Princeton he obtained a scholarship to Balliol College, Oxford, where he graduated in 1929. Over the next four years he studied for his doctorate at New York University before obtaining a faculty position there. While doing so he edited a quarterly journal, *Symposium*, designed to introduce European political writers to an American audience. Shortly afterwards he joined the American Socialist Workers' Party and became editor of the leading Trotskyite journal, *The New International*. In 1940, he resigned after Trotsky announced his support for the 1939 German–Soviet pact. In a published letter to the exiled Trotsky, he suggested that the party leaders had abandoned moral principle for bureaucratic domination.

Burnham accepted much of Marx's view of history as being made up of cycles or epochs in which a simple class gains dominance over the prevailing mode of production and, hence, over the structures and processes of governance. However, its ascendancy is by no means as assured as was suggested by the then prevalent Marxian, mechanistic view of history. (Burnham's work on the metaphorical use of class struggle is particularly important in its similarity to the criticism of the Frankfurt School.) This contingent view of history leads Burnham to the crux of his thesis. The crisis of unemployment in the 1930s and the Second World War were symptoms of the inability of owner-capitalism to cope, as were the rise of fascism and communism. But it was not the proletariat that would usurp control within post-war society: it was a managerial class. They, and not the workers, had developed both a coherent identity and the means and opportunity to assume class control. The means were to be found in the very reins of bureaucratic governance by which managerial roles in the production process had been created and legitimated by owners. The opportunity to assume control had, again, grown out of the previous mode of capitalist domination. Here Burnham makes use of the findings of an extremely influential study of US share-owners that had been published in 1932 by Berle and Means, *The Modern Corporation and Property*. In this book, the authors had demonstrated the dominance of the 200 largest non-banking corporations within the US economy. Yet the majority were found to have such dispersed share ownership that they were effectively management-controlled enterprises. Burnham also describes the way in which the totalitarian regimes of the USSR and Germany had become dependent on what he describes as 'technocrats'. In both liberal and totalitarian states, then, management class and management discourse would dominate by the late twentieth century.

The publication of *The Modern Corporation and Property* at the moment of America's entry into a total war between these latter regimes might have been expected to guarantee its notoriety. However, its impact on Marxist dialogues was, and still is, relatively slight. The most significant reference is to be found in the work of Djilas's *The New Class*, published in 1957. Djilas was a member of the Yugoslav communist élite and biographer of Tito. In *The New Class*, the party is seen to have become the effective controller of all property rights in communist countries. *It*, therefore, rather than capitalist bureaucracies, provides entrance to the new managerial class. Like Burnham's writing, Djilas's thesis presented the culmination of a long period of disaffection with orthodox communism. In his case, it led to imprisonment for most of his remaining life.

The same was experienced by Voslensky, where similar analysis contributed to political dialogue within the final phase of the existence of the Soviet Union.

A much greater impact can be observed among liberal theorists in the West. As with all works of scholarly significance, the strands of Burnham's thesis can be traced to the earlier influences, particularly those of élite theorists such as Michels, Mosca and Pareto. However, Burnham's partisanal style evidently triggered at least three trajectories in structural modernist debate. The first was that of convergence in political structures brought about by what Kerr and others were later to describe as 'the web of rules' stretching across national boundaries.

The second might be seen in the shift in the analysis of class control from emphasis on the ownership of property to sources of authority developed within and through bureaucratic procedures and, more especially, to the basis of consent within organised society. This focus was one already accepted in Weberian critiques of Marxist materialism. Dahrendorf refocused the wider structural debate down to the 'command situation' and to the uncertainty surrounding the exercise of authority in micro-events in his *Class and Class Conflict in Industrial Societies.*

A third trajectory was driven by a liberal-democratic concern over the regulation of managerial authority unconstrained by ownership control. The American economist John K. Galbraith was, perhaps, the best-known articulator of this concern. In *The New Industrial State* he revived Burnham's views on the emergence of a 'technocracy' within the large corporation. Other institutional economists explored the concept of 'managerial capitalism' in a more technical way or, more often, of management as the subordinate but largely autonomous agent of capital owners. On one side Ehrenreich and Ehrenreich spoke of a shared professional–managerial class position. On the other, Wright sought to demonstrate contradictory class locations within these occupations, whilst advocating a movement from market exploitation to bureaucratic domination in analytical emphasis.

The indifference shown to Burnham's work by Marxist sociologists indicates their rejection of his belief in and evidence of a distinctive and dominant management class. Maurice Zeitlin concludes that 'news of the demise of the capitalist classes is . . . somewhat premature' (1974: 1107). A number of studies have been undertaken in the last 20 years that suggest the existence of networks of corporate élites with ownership interests in the organisations for which they hold responsibility. Postmodern theorists have suggested that these groups of financial capitalists cannot, once more, cope with the problems of 'disorganised capitalism'.

Further reading

Dahrendorf, R. CLASS AND CLASS CONFLICT IN INDUSTRIAL SOCIETIES, Stanford University Press, 1959.
Djilas, M. THE NEW CLASS, Praeger, 1957.
Scott, J. STRATIFICATION POWER: STRUCTURE OF CLASS, STATUS AND COMMAND, Polity, 1997.
Zeitlin, M. 'Corporate Ownership and Control: The Large Corporation and Capitalist Class', AMERICAN JOURNAL OF SOCIOLOGY, 79: 5 (1974), pp. 1073–119.
R.L.

BUTLER, Judith

Philosopher/feminist theorist	born USA 1960—
Associated with	POST-STRUCTURALISM ■ DECONSTRUCTION ■ PERFORMATIVITY
Influences include	DERRIDA ■ FOUCAULT ■ LACAN
Shares common ground with	HARAWAY ■ SEDGEWICK ■ SCOTT
Main works	SUBJECTS OF DESIRE (1987) GENDER TROUBLE (1990) BODIES THAT MATTER (1993)

I
N THE LAST decade, Judith Butler has established herself as one of the foremost feminist scholars, theorising categories of sex, gender, identity and the subject. Profoundly influenced by Michel Foucault's view of power and Jacques Derrida's deconstructive techniques, Butler's most significant contributions to contemporary theory lie in her relentless efforts to 'denaturalise' the categories of sex/gender; destabilise rigid categories of identity politics; and disrupt the 'heterosexual matrix' in the conceptualisation of desire. She has shown how heterosexuality, masculine dominance and oppressive metaphysical notions of gender are interwoven and naturalised in the discursive fabrics of structural anthropology, the psychoanalytic theories

of Sigmund Freud and Jacques Lacan and the scholarship of several feminist thinkers, most notably Luce Irigaray and Julia Kristeva.

In general, Butler's *modus operandi* possesses a dual quality – consisting of both 'deconstructive' and 'constructive' dimensions. The deconstructive aspect of her work is most explicitly manifest in her genealogical critique, influenced largely by Foucault's reformulation of Nietzsche, of the foundational categories of sex and gender. Provocatively wreaking havoc with the sex/gender distinction typical of most feminist trajectories, Butler demonstrates how 'sex', commonly understood as the material foundation which exists prior to the cultural inscription of gender, is not a bodily given with ontological status but rather a cultural norm which governs the materialisation of bodies. The 'body' is given its boundaries, fixity and surface through the citationality of discourse, through the reiteration of hegemonic norms which act as regulatory ideals and which conform to the logic of the heterosexual symbolic. Hence, the category of sex is as culturally constructed as that of gender – an insight which enables Butler to claim that these categories are actually effects of a specific formation of power. Butler therefore argues for the necessity of defining all such identifactory classifications as *effects* of institutions, practices and discourses rather than the natural grounds, causes or origins of identity. Quite simply Butler rejects those that would place identity categories 'before', 'outside' or 'beyond' existing power relations and discursive practices.

The 'constructive' facet of Butler's work is reflected in her theory of gender. Echoing Nietzsche's claim in *On the Genealogy of Morals* that there is no 'being' behind the 'doing', and drawing upon Foucault's work on discursive formation, Derrida's speech-act theory and Eve Sedgewick's reflections on queer performativity, Butler claims that gender is performative – a persistent impersonation that passes as the real. For Butler, identities, gendered or otherwise, are the dramatic effects of our performances, rather than expressions of some inner, authentic core. This, however, is not the equivalent of suggesting that gender is a matter of mere choice or of performance in the sense of theatrical role-playing, as many of her critics have assumed. Rather, gender performativity is a citational, discursive practice which produces or enacts that which it names, and a phenomenon which cannot be considered, apart from the forcible and reiterative practice of regulatory sexual regimes.

Butler maintains that the notion of 'performativity' enables a mode of inquiry into the construction of the subject which avoids the essentialism/constructivism dichotomy that has plagued theoretical investigations of the subject and identity formation, since it seeks to explore the ways in which particular social and historical interpellations give rise to specific subjectivities. Butler's political project therefore entails the radical, even parodic deconstruction of the compulsory gendered matrix that supports the 'order of things' and the subversional reinscription of citationally constructed identities. The loss of gender norms generated by such a practice would, according to Butler, have the effect of destabilising substantive identity and depriving the 'naturalising narratives' of 'compulsory heterosexuality' of the fixed categories of 'man' and 'woman'. For Butler, then, the use of parody and/or resignification practices to subvert established conventions provides a basis for a form of liberatory politics.

Despite her provocative ideas and sophisticated philosophical analyses, Butler has been roundly criticised for her extreme 'linguistic foundationalism'; her uncritical embrace of Foucault's theory of power; her advocacy of parody as an adequate political strategy and her rejection of any feminist politics which relies on the category of 'women'. These critiques notwithstanding, Butler's inquiries into the construction of identities and subjectivities have provided a fresh and astute critique of several of the problems inherent in current forms of identity-based politics.

Further reading

Benhabib, S. *et al.* FEMINIST CONTENTIONS: A PHILOSOPHICAL EXCHANGE, Routledge, 1995.
Bordo, S. 'Postmodern Subjects, Postmodern Bodies', FEMINIST STUDIES (Spring 1992), pp. 159–75.
Butler, J. and Scott, J. (eds.) FEMINISTS THEORIZE THE POLITICAL, Routledge, 1992.
P.McL.

CAMPBELL, Joseph

Anthropologist	born USA 1904–1987
Associated with	CULTURAL ANTHROPOLOGY
Influences include	JUNG ■ FREUD
Shares common ground with	LÉVI-STRAUSS ■ HUXLEY ■ BETTELHEIM
Main works	THE HERO WITH A THOUSAND FACES (1949)
	THE MASKS OF GOD, 4 VOLS. (1959–68)
	MYTHS TO LIVE BY (1972)

B ORN AND RAISED in New York State, Joseph Campbell graduated from high school with the 'Head Boy' award before studying humanities at Columbia University. After a spell travelling in Europe, made possible by a fellowship award, he studied Sanskrit at the University of Munich, where he discovered the work of Freud and Jung. Returning to the USA in 1928, he dropped his Ph.D work and retired to the woods near Woodstock to pursue his studies and attempt to write. Five years later he sold his first (and last) story and, when offered a job at Sarah Lawrence College in 1934, financial pressures forced his acceptance. He remained there until his retirement in 1972 and was Emeritus Professor until his death in 1987. The many awards he received included honorary doctorates and the Medal of Honour for Literature from the National Arts Club of New York. He was featured in a six-part television series entitled 'Joseph Campbell and the Power of Myth' and in a film entitled 'The Hero's Journey'. He worked with George Lucas and the Grateful Dead, amongst others.

Campbell described his work as an attempt to tell the story of humankind as the 'One Great Story'. By this he meant the saga of the spiritual awakening of mankind and the subsequent development of society. He believed that the many differing mythical and religious beliefs which are present throughout the world and throughout history, while seeming to be disparate, are neither discrete nor unique. Instead, each is simply a cultural or ethnic manifestation of the elemental ideals which have forever transfixed the human psyche. Campbell adopted a comparative historical approach to mythology, religion and literature but, unlike most scholars, rather than concentrating upon differences he concentrated upon similarities. He was convinced that common themes and images could reveal mankind's common psychological roots. He argued that the recognition we have of images from primal cultures, contemporary work and from different societies reflects the common spiritual ground from which all human life springs.

Although old myths were a way of explaining the origins of the world and of humanity, they also played a vital role in uniting a society. Campbell argued that this cohesive role remains crucial today and so myths remain relevant to us. Indeed, he demonstrates that these myths continue to be reinvented in modern form. For individuals these myths provide a source of strength and a sense of roots and values; they offer a mirror to reveal the source of our anxieties and the means by which they might be resolved. In this respect his work parallels that of Jung and of Bruno Bettelheim on fairy stories. Among his many publications include edited works by Jung as well as edited works of his mentor, Heinrich Zimmer.

Campbell argues that the function of ritual is to give a form to human life and to mark the passage from one part of that life to the next. He states that the reservation of such ritual for exceptional occasions in modern society is one source of neuroticism, and contrasts the present with the way ritual was embedded in all social occasions in older, more stable societies. He also identifies the common archetypes prevalent in myth and compares them to the archetypes revealed in psychoanalytic writings and in dreams. His concern, however, is with the relevance of all of this to present-day life.

Although relatively unknown in British cultural theory, Campbell's work has been enormously influential. Many of his ideas have emerged recently in New Age philosophy, spirituality and religion and overlap considerably with the influence of Jung. Equally, George Lucas acknowledges Campbell's work as the basis for all of the characters in his *Star Wars* trilogy, while many other writers acknowledge his influence on their work. In many respects, his work addresses the kinds of metaphysical question addressed by many other philosophers and, as such, can be expected to have a timeless appeal.

Further reading

Cousineau, P. and Brown, S. (eds.) THE HERO'S JOURNEY: THE WORLD OF JOSEPH CAMPBELL, Harper & Row, 1990.
Lefkowitz, M. 'The Myth of Joseph Campbell', AMERICAN SCHOLAR, 59: 3 (1990), pp. 429–34.
May, R. THE CRY OF MYTH, Souvenir Press, 1991.

D.E.A.C.

CASTORIADIS, Cornelius

Philosopher	born Turkey 1922–1997
Associated with	PROJECT OF AUTONOMY ■ SOCIAL IMAGINARY SIGNIFICATIONS ■ PSYCHICAL MONAD
Influences include	MARX ■ WEBER ■ FREUD
Shares common ground with	ARENDT ■ MORIN ■ LEFORT
Main works	POLITICAL AND SOCIAL WRITINGS (3 vols. [1946–79]; 1988, 1988, 1993) THE IMAGINARY INSTITUTION OF SOCIETY ([1964–65, 1975]; 1987) WORLD IN FRAGMENTS ([1978–93]; 1997)

ASTORIADIS WORKED AS a professional economist at the OECD between 1948 and 1970. He studied first-hand the changes wrought by 'modern capitalism'. In particular, he focused on the destruction of meaning in work and everyday life and the depoliticisation and privatisation of individuals. Upon retirement he took up French citizenship and began to practise psychoanalysis. In 1979 he was elected Professor at the École des Hautes Études en Sciences Sociales in Paris.

Castoriadis is the philosopher of the social imagination. He co-founded Socialisme ou Barbarie (1948–67), the now-legendary post-war revolutionary group of workers and intellectuals. Advocating 'workers' management', the group broke with Trotskyism to develop a radical critique of 'bureaucratic capitalism' in both its 'total and totalitarian' (Russian) and 'fragmented' (Western) forms. Attacking head-on the fellow-travelling of Sartre and others, this critique greatly influenced the May 1968 student–worker rebellion in France, which demanded 'self-management' in the universities and factories. In the journal's final issue (reprinted in *The Imaginary Institution of Society*), Castoriadis posed the question whether to remain Marxist or revolutionary. He chose the latter. In this work and in subsequent writings (*Crossroads in the Labyrinth* 1984 and *Philosophy, Politics, Autonomy* 1991), he drew on insights from Freud and cultural anthropology to create a thoroughgoing critique of economic reductionism, historical determinism, functionalism, structuralism (both Lévi-Straussian and Althusserian) and the 'French ideology' of Lacan, Foucault, and so on. He thereby revitalised the role of the imagination for art, philosophy, politics, psychoanalysis, linguistics and social thought.

Castoriadis argued that the cultural and sexual functions are as important as the economic one for understanding and transforming society. This distinctive approach to culture derives from his political concerns and his interest in the ontological status of society. What makes a society one? How is it capable of change? He contends that the 'social-historical' has its own mode of being-for-itself which is irreducible to physical, biological or psychocorporeal existence. Society institutes itself, instead of being a product of Nature, Reason, God, etc. It creates its own world – though usually without knowledge that it is doing so by incorporating a religious (heteronomous) 'occultation' of this very creation.

Society is embodied in its institutions. These are composed of – are – its 'social imaginary significations'. Castoriadis describes these as 'social' because they are shared by all; 'imaginary' because they are neither reducible to nor deducible from 'real' or 'rational' referents; and 'significations' because they are not just 'ideas' or 'representations' but the cement of social life. Things, ideas, subjects, norms, values, orientations, tools, fetishes, gods, God, *polis*, citizen, nation, party, contract, enterprise, wealth, are a few examples of social imaginary significations. While some of them may have physical correlates ('automobile' as physical correlate of 'commodity'), other ones, God *par excellence*, do not. They possess a *sui generis* mode of being: 'the immanent unperceivable'.

Yet these social significations must not be confused with psychical meaning. The true opposition is not 'individual versus society', mediated by 'intersubjectivity', but psyche and society as mutually irreducible poles. This is because the psychical monad cannot, by itself, produce social signification. The work of the radical social instituting imaginary is to create, reproduce and alter itself by instrumenting itself in fabricated social individuals that, in turn, socialize the radical imagination of the singular psyche via an imposed internalisation of the society's imaginary significations.

Difficult to grasp at first and far removed from current fads (post-structuralism, deconstructionism, etc.), Castoriadis's radical theoretical renewal offers a wealth of conceptual tools to any student interested in doing cultural theory with a global political relevance. He does not wade through the detritus of a consumer society to find micro(counter)powers, interpret real social events as (timeless) expressions of a Lacanian unconscious, or become bogged down in identity politics. Modernity is understood as a divided whole whose main contending social imaginary significations are the project of autonomy (expressed in revolutions, workers', women's and students' movements, and liberation movements of racial and cultural minorities, as well as in philosophy, politics, psychoanalysis and a transformative civic pedagogy) and a capitalist project for the unlimited expansion of (pseudo)-rational mastery over nature and humanity. This view of the dual institution of modernity offers a more complex and conflictual cultural account of the West than, for example, Habermas's communicative rationality theory of an 'unfinished project of the Enlightenment' or former Socialisme on Barbarie member

Jean-François Lyotard's 'postmodern condition' (which, Castoriadis says, is the theoretical expression of today's 'generalised conformism').

For Castoriadis, the present crisis of culture is the crisis of our society. Through privatisation, depoliticisation and withdrawal, a destruction of meaning and emptying of value, society is rapidly desocialising itself even as it experiences a hypersocialisation through ubiquitous mediatisation. Castoriadis anticipates that, 'just as the current evolution of culture is not wholly unrelated to the inertia and the social and political passivity characteristic of our world today, so a renaissance of its vitality, should it take place, will be indissociable from a great new social-historical movement which will reactivate democracy and will give it at once the form and the contents the project of autonomy requires' (*The Castoriadis Reader* 1997).

Further reading

Busino, G. (ed.) special issue of REVUE EUROPÉEN DES SCIENCES SOCIALES, 86 (1989) (special issue devoted to Castoriadis).
Curtis, D. A. 'Cornelius Castoriadis', in P. Beilharz (ed.), SOCIAL THEORY: A GUIDE TO THE CENTRAL THINKERS, Allen & Unwin, 1991, pp. 46–53.
Curtis, D. A. (ed.) THESIS ELEVEN, 49 (May 1997 special issue devoted to Castoriadis).

D.A.C.

CHOMSKY, Noam

Linguistic theorist/political and media critic	born USA 1928—
Associated with	RATIONALISM ▪ STRUCTURALISM ▪ ANARCHISM
Influences include	DESCARTES ▪ ROUSSEAU ▪ MARX ▪ ORWELL
Shares common ground with	SAUSSURE ▪ LÉVI-STRAUSS ▪ SCHILLER
Main works	SYNTACTIC STRUCTURES (1957) CARTESIAN LINGUISTICS (1966) THE CHOMSKY READER (ED. JAMES PECK, 1987). NECESSARY ILLUSIONS (1989)

C HOMSKY WAS BORN into a Jewish family in a mainly Roman Catholic and anti-Semitic neighbourhood of Philadelphia. Both parents were teachers of Hebrew and his father was a published scholar of Hebrew. During childhood visits to his uncle in New York he came into contact with a Jewish working-class milieu where libertarian–socialist and anarchistic values flourished. Inspired by Zellig Harris at the University of Pennsylvania, Chomsky first studied linguistics and then also mathematics and philosophy. In his early twenties he was appointed to a fellowship at Harvard and shortly afterwards he moved to the Massachusetts Institute of Technology, where he has remained on the faculty ever since, conducting scientific research into language.

Although Chomsky's scientific work and political convictions are related and they derive from his youth, his career can be divided into two broad phases. Between the mid-1950s and the mid-1960s he brought about a theoretical revolution in linguistics for which he is still regarded as 'arguably the most important intellectual alive', according to the *New York Times*. Since his involvement in the anti-Vietnam War movement of the 1960s he has also come to be seen as the leading left-wing critic of US geopolitics and its news media.

The Western study of language can be traced back to ancient Greek rhetoric and subsequently it developed in various ways, most notably with the work of the medieval grammarians and in the study of language and logic at Port-Royal in the seventeenth and eighteenth centuries. 'Scientific' linguistics is generally said to have begun in earnest, however, with the historical and comparative work of nineteenth century philologists. In the twentieth century there has been a further shift from this empiricist approach to a rationalist perspective on linguistics, heralded by Saussure, Peirce and the Prague School; what, in effect, came to be known as 'structural linguistics'. Similarly, Chomsky has sought to produce a general account of language which breaks with the routines of historical and comparative classification. He aimed to give mathematical precision to the structural operations of language, and challenged the blank-slate conception of the mind propounded by behavioural psychology. Chomsky's 'generative grammar' is a theory of how the innate structures of the human mind facilitate the acquisition and use of language. That children learn to speak with syntactical intelligibility without necessarily understanding the formal rules of grammar indicates that language is universally structured, according to Chomsky, irrespective of the enormous diversity of languages spoken in the world.

Chomsky, then, claims that his scientific model explains how language works in general: moreover, he sees this as evidence of the sheer creativity and ingenuity of the human mind, a view which underpins his libertarian beliefs and, simultaneously, provides scientific legitimation for his critique of the mind-shackling media. While his linguistic theory is extremely complex and technical, his account of how the dominant media, especially the US news media, represent the world is disarmingly simple and straightforward. It rests upon two basic assumptions: first, that the USA is the paramount power in the world and, like other great powers in history, will stop at almost nothing to serve its own prevailing interests; second, that the powerful do not trust popular judgement and, in consequence, seek to manipulate public opinion for their own purposes.

In many heavily documented studies, Chomsky has traced how American power has been served by intervening in parts of the world such as Vietnam and, when it suits, casting a blind eye to atrocities such as the genocide conducted in East Timor, Indonesia. The news media reflect powerful interests and ignore issues that run counter to them. Chomsky's co-author of *Manufacturing Consent* (1968), Edward Herman, formulated the 'propaganda model' to explain how this is done. Herman and Chomsky circumvent the charge of 'conspiracy theory' by arguing that direct governmental manipulation of the media is unnecessary in order to serve the interests of the 'free market'. The capitalist media are at one with the interests of American capital. Their main source of revenue is advertising and, after all, they are themselves profit-making firms. Manipulative public relations and the construction of necessary enemies (communism in the past, resurgent Islam more recently) ensure that the view of the world presented to the American public fosters ignorance of what is really going on.

An indefatigable campaigner on behalf of human rights and against abuse of democracy, Chomsky's critical writings on the media and politics are denied mainstream publication in the USA, although they circulate widely through oppositional publishing and distribution networks. His arguments are usually ignored or occasionally denigrated in mainstream reviewing and the media, thereby confirming Chomsky's one-sided critique of how the media function ideologically. It has to be said that he does not offer a satisfactory general theory and comprehensive analysis of media culture. For example, at times he seems to suggest that pleasure in media consumption is merely a means of public manipulation. Yet Chomsky's standing as both 'the most important intellectual alive' and political pariah in his own country is an uncomfortable and revealing paradox for the USA.

Further reading

Achbor, M. (ed.) MANUFACTURING CONSENT: NOAM CHOMSKY AND THE MEDIA, Black Rose Books, 1994.
Cogswell, D. and Gordon, P. CHOMSKY FOR BEGINNERS, Writers & Readers, 1996.
Salkie, R. THE CHOMSKY UPDATE: LINGUISTICS AND POLITICS, Unwin Hyman, 1990.

J.McG.

CIXOUS, Hélène

Philosopher	born Algeria 1937—
Associated with	ECOCENTRISM ■ PHALLOGOCENTRISM
Influences include	DE BEAUVOIR ■ LACAN ■ BARTHES ■ DERRIDA
Shares common ground with	KRISTEVA ■ IRIGARAY
Main works	DEDANS (1969, TRANS. INSIDE, 1986)
	THE LAUGH OF THE MEDUSA (1975, TRANS. 1980)
	THE NEWLY BORN WOMAN (1975, TRANS. WITH CATHERINE CLÉMENT, 1986)
	'COMING TO WRITING' AND OTHER ESSAYS (TRANS. 1991)

HÉLÈNE CIXOUS IS A dedicated feminist writer who is among the most influential French intellectuals today. She is Professor of Literature, and co-founder, of the experimental University of Paris VIII

Vincennes, and has lectured at many universities throughout the world. Yet she disdains theory, and the bulk of her writing has been fiction in the form of novels, plays, short stories and poetry. Her writing is characterised by a constant slippage between these literary forms, and philosophy, literary and theoretical criticism, with the result that her work refuses any neat categorisation.

Since the 1970s, Cixous has explicitly championed women's issues and the women's movement, initiated women's studies programmes and has had a central involvement in the exploration of women's issues through her literary and theoretical work. She has refused to be categorised as a feminist because of the misunderstood and misrepresented associations of the term. She has also questioned the bourgeois goals of feminism which strive for equality within the patriarchal order. Cixous is best known for advocating the possibility of a feminine writing (*l'écriture féminine*), a project which she has pursued with Julia Kristeva, Luce Irigaray and Monique Wittig.

For Cixous, the need for *l'écriture féminine* stems from patriarchy's exclusion of women's experience from the symbolic order (language). Her essay, *The Laugh of the Medusa*, one of her most important works, outlines her arguments about the historical repression of women's differences and calls for *l'écriture féminine* to combat the 'phallogocentric' nature of Western writing. Cixous's neologism combines the term phallocentrism (denoting the phallic structure of language) with logocentrism (denoting the privilege of spoken over written language in Western culture).

A feminine writing develops a female discourse which is based on female experience and is not phallogocentric. Women must journey back to the pre-Oedipal, specifically the mother/child relationship, before the feminine is crushed by socialisation into a male symbolic order. They must rediscover their drives, their psyches, the diverse nature of female desire and the specificities of the female body. Cixous believes that this enables women to 'write the body' and discover a new rhetoric of difference which will produce *l'écriture féminine*, thereby subverting the male symbolic order. Through writing their bodies and their selves, women can forge new identities and break free from the phallogocentric order. Cixous believes that new social institutions will evolve from this.

Cixous also argues (from an anti-essentialist position) that men can produce feminine writing. She broadens the concept of *l'écriture féminine* to address the suppressed bisexuality of all humans, exhorting us all to express in our writing our repressed Other; the femininity of men, the masculinity of women. Her own writing style indicates what *l'écriture féminine* could be. Cixous embraces a poetic and unconventional writing style. She refuses to abide by grammatical rules or conform to set genres. Her style is central to her desire to subvert patriarchal language, with its linear logic and binary hierarchical oppositions which position women as the Other, powerless and passive. She nonetheless aruges that 'it is impossible to define a feminine practice of writing, and this is an impossibility that will remain, for this practice can never be theorised, enclosed, coded – which doesn't mean that it doesn't exist' (*The Newly Born Woman*).

As with contemporary French feminism in general, Cixous's work builds upon Lacan's rereading of Freud (see *Castration or Decapitation*). From Derrida, she extrapolates the notion of *différance* (that meaning is produced through a continual deferral of signifiers, as opposed to the structuralist view that meaning is produced through binary oppositions), which she applies to writing. She identifies multiple, heterogenous difference as the source of *l'écriture féminine* and extends Barthes's notion of *jouissance* to encompass a feminine possibility of pleasure stemming from multiple sources, including the pleasure of 'creating' the female body through writing.

Cixous has always been considered radical and controversial. In English-speaking countries, she has also been misunderstood due to the complexity of her writing, her unorthodox theoretical position, and because much of her work is not available in English. One of the highest accolades for her work comes from Jacques Derrida, who has called her the greatest French writer ever.

Further reading

Jones, A.R. 'Writing the Body: Toward an Understanding of L'écriture Féminine', FEMINIST STUDIES, 7: 2 (1981), pp. 247–63.
Moi, T. SEXUAL/TEXTUAL POLITICS: FEMINIST LITERARY THEORY, Routledge, 1985.
Shiach, M. HÉLÈNE CIXOUS: A POLITICS OF WRITING, Routledge, 1991.

G.C.

COLEMAN, James S.

Sociologist	born USA 1926–1995
Associated with	ADOLESCENCE ■ CORPORATE ACTION ■ RATIONAL CHOICE
Influences include	MERTON ■ LAZARSFELD ■ BURNHAM
Shares common ground with	BLAU ■ BELL ■ LIPSET
Main works	THE ADOLESCENT SOCIETY (1961)
	YOUTH: TRANSITION TO ADULTHOOD (1974)
	FOUNDATIONS OF SOCIAL THEORY (1990)

COLEMAN TRAINED AS a chemical engineer at Purdue University, from which he graduated in 1949. In 1952 he quit his job as a chemist with Eastman Kodak and enrolled in graduate school at Columbia University. He quickly attracted the interest of Robert Merton and Paul Lazarsfeld. Both identified him as a promising figure in the somewhat contrasting fields of social theory and mathematical sociology.

Coleman gained his Ph.D. in Sociology in 1955, and participated in Seymour Lipset's influential Columbia study of *Union Democracy* (1956). He accepted an Assistant Professorship at Chicago University, from whence his early reputation was forged. His research into adolescent subcultures in 10 Illinois high schools was published as *The Adolescent Society* (1961). Coleman was gaining a reputation as an expert on youth and schooling.

In 1959 he moved to Johns Hopkins University. Here he embarked on a research programme into the effects of academic games on educational achievement. As a result, he was approached by the National Center for Education Statistics to conduct intensive research into unequal educational opportunities and performance on the basis of race, colour, national origin and religion. The research involved 3000 schools and covered over 600,000 school children, and its findings were published as *Equality of Educational Opportunity* (1966). The 'Coleman Report', as it soon became known, carved out the benchmark of US educational policy for a generation. Coleman argued that the key to educational achievement was home background. This flew in the face of the conventional wisdom of the day which held that generous public resourcing of schools would, in itself, raise standards.

In 1973 Coleman was appointed to a Professorship at Chicago University. In the following year he published *Youth: Transition to Adulthood* which enlarged his research on inequality and educational achievement. The study earned him the wrath of many liberals and left-wingers. Coleman argued that the policies

of school desegregation in the inner cities had the unintended effect of exacerbating inequality because of the 'white flight' to the suburbs. Coleman became
the subject of attacks and endured an unsuccessful attempt by senior figures in
the American Sociological Association to censure him. Unbowed, Coleman
continued to conduct a series of major empirical studies into educational
privilege and inequality. His findings, that private schools did not reinforce
segregation, and that they outperformed state schools in cognitive achievement, sparked renewed criticism from liberal and left-wing sources.

But Coleman's second, and final, term in Chicago also coincided with his
deepening interest in social theory. Perhaps this was related to the hostile
attacks he suffered for his research on inequality and education. In any case,
he became fascinated with the task of finding theoretical solutions to the
question of why people act as they do. As the title of his last major book
indicates, he sought answers to the foundations of social behaviour. He found
these, somewhat controversially, in the rational actions of individuals. *Foundations of Social Theory* works on a number of interrelated levels. First, Coleman
is concerned to make a strategic contribution to sociology by elucidating a
conceptual framework that will reunite theory with empirical research.
Second, he seeks to outline the basis for regarding human actors as rational
beings. Rational actors, he maintains, voluntarily cede power which identifies
rational decision-making in terms of interests and control. For example,
investors cede control over their assets to a company in pursuit of the
maximisation of their returns through the operations of the stock market.
According to Coleman, social life consists of countless exchange and constitution relations which vary the distribution of interest and control between
social actors. Fourth, he aims to bridge the traditional micro–macro divide in
sociology with new conceptual links. Chief among these is his concept of
'corporate actors'. Coleman argues that the conduct of social life involves
'natural persons' (individual actors) and 'corporate actors' (collective units).
The latter are not embodied in physical persons, but nonetheless exert rational
purposive influence in everyday life. Examples of corporate actors include
business corporations, trade unions, voluntary associations and the state.
Coleman believes that corporate actors exert increasing control and interest
in the conduct of social life. Indeed, he claims that, over the last 150 years, the
business corporation has emerged to exert the dominant influence in the
conduct of social life. He argues that business corporations have been effective
in producing economic growth. But because they are detached from natural
persons – a detachment which is symbolised in the concept of limited liability
or the joint-stock company – they are often ineffective in 'person-related' tasks
such as bringing up children, caring for the needy and protecting local
environments.

The main criticisms directed against Coleman are threefold. First, his social
theory is based on a rational-choice model of human behaviour. Coleman is
judged to underestimate the importance of the emotions in the conduct of

social life. Second, his conception of control and interests makes insufficient allowance for the structural influence of class, gender and race. Third, by situating the business corporation in the foreground of social life, Coleman intimates that market capitalism is the inevitable form of industrial society. It is a view which discounts the whole question of the transcendence of capitalism.

Further reading

Clark, J. (ed.) JAMES S. COLEMAN, Falmer, 1996.
Alexander, J. 'Shaky Foundations: The Presuppositions and Internal Contradictions of James Coleman's Foundations of Social Theory', THEORY AND SOCIETY, 21 (1992), pp. 203–17.
Stinchcombe, A. 'Simmel Systematized: James S. Coleman and the Social Forms of Purposive Action in his Foundations of Social Theory', THEORY AND SOCIETY, 21 (1992), pp. 183–202.

C.R.

CROSLAND, Anthony

Political theorist	born England 1918–1977
Associated with	DEMOCRATIC SOCIALISM ▪ REVISIONIST SOCIALISM
Influences include	MARX ▪ MORRIS ▪ KEYNES
Shares common ground with	BERNSTEIN ▪ GALBRAITH
Main works	THE FUTURE OF SOCIALISM (1956) THE CONSERVATIVE ENEMY (1962) SOCIALISM NOW (1974)

C ROSLAND WAS FROM an upper middle-class Plymouth Brethren family. After growing up in Highgate he read Classics at Trinity College, Oxford. His studies were, however, interrupted by the Second World

War, and in 1940 he joined the Royal Welsh Fusiliers, followed by a transfer to the Parachute Regiment. In 1946, he returned to Oxford, switched from Classics to Politics, Philosophy, and Economics and gained a First. In 1947, Crosland became a Fellow of Trinity College and tutored economics, in addition to being active in the Fabian Society. In 1950 he was elected a Member of Parliament. He lost his seat in the 1955 election and it was during his absence from Parliament that he published *The Future of Socialism*, which was to establish him as one of the major thinkers on the left. In 1959 he returned to Parliament, where he was a close confidant of the Labour Party leader Hugh Gaitskell, and a founder member of the Campaign for Democratic Socialism. Crosland held a succession of cabinet positions in Harold Wilson's 1964–70 Labour administration and was to become an increasingly important figure in the Labour Party. In 1976 he became the British Foreign Secretary, a post he was to die in 10 months later.

Although Crosland's political career led him to the very heights of government, it was his role as a left-wing intellectual for which he is best remembered, and indeed it is in this capacity that he made his contribution to cultural theory. His most important work, *The Future of Socialism*, appeared in 1956, shortly after the Labour Party had suffered a second successive General Election defeat. Crosland believed that the Left's problem lay in the obsolescence of its intellectual frameworks for analysing society, in the wake of the profound social changes that had taken place after the Second World War. He argued that the establishment of the Welfare State, achievement of full employment, the acceptance of Keynesianism and a growing economy had reformed society to such an extent that it did not resemble that capitalism chronicled by Marx or the Webbs. Thus, in these changed circumstances, he contended that the socialist prescriptions such as nationalisation and class struggle, which were closely associated with Marx, the Webbs and Laski, were no longer relevant.

In response to these problems Crosland developed a theory of revisionist socialism, the aim of which was to make socialism relevant to the middle of the twentieth century. This endeavour was reminiscent of the question, 'What is socialism about now?' posed by Bernstein, whom Crosland greatly admired, half a century earlier. In formulating an answer to this question Crosland ventured that the future of socialism rested upon a commitment to a set of central values which were separate from the means of reaching them. He argued that while the values or the 'ends' would be an enduring feature of socialism, the means of achieving them would change with societal circumstances. Such an analysis was a rebut to Marxism, which held that taking ownership of the means of production was the key factor in changing society.

Crosland asserted that the core value of socialism was equality, and thus a democratic socialist's aim should be to increase equality. In 1950s Britain, he saw the dismantlement of the rigid, class-based society as being fundamental to the achievement of socialism. He argued that this could be accomplished through the means of taxation, industrial democracy and, most importantly, education. His proposals for education were radical in that he advocated 'comprehensive schools' as an eventual replacement for the existing public, grammar and secondary modern schools. Moreover, he held that such initiatives alone were not sufficient, and proposed to redistribute money from the growing economy in order to fund social welfare policies for the worst-off.

Crosland's theory of Democratic Socialism aimed to eliminate social unfairness, but it also attempted to promote freedom of choice, leisure and personal enjoyment. Indeed, he reviled the austere socialism of the Webbs, arguing that 'Total abstinence and a good filing system are not the right signposts to a socialist utopia: or at least, if they are, some of us will fall by the wayside.'

One of the central assumptions in *The Future of Socialism* was that the economy would continue to expand; the disappointing UK economic performance in the 1960s and early 1970s led Crosland to rethink 'revisionism'. In *Socialism Now*, he lamented that Britain had proved difficult to change, and conceded that a weak economy would make it more difficult to achieve equality, but concluded that, 'whatever the rate of growth, we can, and must, mount a determined attack on specific, social evils and specific inequalities'.

Further reading

Crosland, C.A.R. THE FUTURE OF SOCIALISM, Jonathan Cape, 1956.
Crosland, A. SOCIALISM NOW, Jonathan Cape, 1974.
Crossman, R.H.S. NEW FABIAN ESSAYS, J.M. Dent & Sons, 1970.
Galbraith, J.K. AMERICAN CAPITALISM: THE CONCEPT OF COUNTERVAILING POWER, Pelican, 1963.

C.C.

DAHRENDORF, Ralf

Sociologist	born Germany 1929—
Associated with	CONFLICT THEORY ■ SOCIAL CHANGE
Influences include	MARX ■ POPPER ■ WEBER
Shares common ground with	COSER ■ REX ■ SCHELSKY
Main works	CLASS AND CLASS CONFLICT IN INDUSTRIAL SOCIETY (1959)
	ESSAYS IN THE THEORY OF SOCIETY (1968)
	HOMO SOCIOLOGICUS (1973)

ORN AND EDUCATED in Germany, Dahrendorf completed his under-graduate studies in Classics at Hamburg University. After completing his doctorate in sociology at the London School of Economics in 1954, he returned to Germany where, from 1958, he held a succession of Chairs in Sociology, culminating in Konstanz University in 1969. He joined the Free Democratic Party in 1967 and, after serving on its Executive Committee as well as the Landestag in Baden-Württemberg, he became Junior Foreign Minister in the Federal Government from 1969 to 1970, followed by service as an EEC Commissioner from 1970 to 1974. He then became Director of the London School of Economics from 1974 to 1984 before becoming Warden of St Antony's College, Oxford in 1987, being made a Life Peer in 1993.

Dahrendorf's first major work, *Class and Class Conflict in Industrial Society*, established him as a leading theorist of conflict as well as that of social change in advanced societies. Taking Marx as his exemplar, he examines the major economic and political changes which have taken place in industrial societies (mainly capitalist) from the nineteenth century to contemporary post-capitalist society, as he terms it. Marx's theory of history is grounded in the nineteenth-century connection between private property and authoritative control of the means of production and the class relations and conflicts arising from the social contradictions intrinsic to capitalism. Thus Dahrendorf's two related sets of criticism of Marx centre on conceptual weaknesses in the latter's notion of 'classes' and 'class conflict', as well as his abstract model of capitalist development and its ultimate demise.

Dahrendorf also introduces the conception of 'industrial society', of which capitalism is only one sub-type, thus permitting more macro comparative studies to account for social order and change, including the emergence of communist societies such as the Soviet Union. Two conceptions of social order which have ruled Western social thought are exemplified in industrial societies:

the 'integration theory of society' (consensus or value theory), which conceptualises social structure as a functionally integrated system regulated by normative consensus, as opposed to what Dahrendorf calls the 'coercion theory of society' (conflict theory), which views society as a form of organisation held together by force and constraint in the face of an unending process of change.

A more adequate contemporary theory of class and class conflict, for Dahrendorf, thus requires the relationship between private property and authority to be seen as a special case of a much broader relationship between class and authority, the latter, in the Weberian sense, being defined as the legitimate right to issue commands to others. In contrast to Marx's narrow sense of the legal title to property ownership, he proposes a broad sense of the term as rights of control of the means of production. He argues that Marx was incorrect in stressing property as the basis of class and that, alternatively, classes and social stratification derive from the division of institutionalised authority over such objects between leaders and subordinates.

Dahrendorf proposes a symbolic model of class conflict with authority as the generic form of domination, combined with a strong systematic view of society and the structuration of class relationships. Redefining class in terms of domination and subordination in interest-group terms, class should be taken, in his words, to mean 'conflict groups that are generated by the differential distribution of authority in imperatively co-ordinated associations' (groups which possess a definite authority structure such as the state, an industrial enterprise). In answer to the Marxist problematic of 'class-consciousness' (where interests may not be perceived by those involved), Dahrendorf proposes the notion of the 'quasi-group', which is any social collectivity whose members share latent interests, but who do not organise to further them. In contrast, the interest group, e.g. a trade union, which does organise itself for this purpose, becomes an imperatively co-ordinated association. The resulting class conflict arises from the incompatibility of interests between those who command and those who obey. The ubiquity of conflict in social systems means that such interests tend to be legitimised in terms of some values or images of the 'good society' or the 'rules of the game'. The inevitable outcome of any conflict between groups with diverse interests struggling over the legitimacy of authority relations is social change leading to the establishment of some new system, or the redefinition of the old. Allowing for the transition of industrial society into what he calls 'post-capitalist society', Dahrendorf argues for the retention of certain elements of Marx's conception of industrial society, i.e. there is an inherent connection between social conflict and change and that the former must be understood in terms of a two-party model in which antagonism and struggle devolve on two classes. Thus, for him, post-capitalist society is necessarily a class society which is, however, differentiated from Marx's view of capitalism in terms of the institutional separation of industrial and political conflict, so much so that, according to him, 'the notion of a workers' party has lost its political meaning', and the position of authority occupied by the manager in the economic enterprise yields no political influence.

Since the nineteenth century there has been a decomposition of capital as represented by a process of role differentiation of the 'capitalist' into the executive, manager, entrepreneur, shareholder, etc. This has been complemented by the decomposition of labour and the diversification of the manual working class into skilled, semi-skilled and unskilled, with divided interests which cross-cut the unity of class as a whole. The growth of the 'new middle class' of administrators and non-manual occupations was unanticipated by Marx, and it in turn is bifurcated in post-capitalist society, with bureaucrats as a 'service class' being part of an administrative chain of authority directly linked to that of the dominant group in society, in contrast to lower ranks in service industries (e.g. shop assistants). The increased rate of social mobility evident as a characteristic of post-capitalist society further serves to transpose group conflict into individual competition. In acknowledgement of T.H. Marshall's influence, Dahrendorf further points up the achievement of citizenship rights, embodied in universal suffrage and welfare legislation, by the mass of the population thereby blunting class conflict in the classical Marxist sense. Finally, the institutionalising of class conflict in the form of workers' right to strike and established industrial arbitration procedures prevent the escalation of industrial disputes into wider class conflict.

Further reading

Bryant, C. SOCIOLOGY IN ACTION, George Allen & Unwin, 1976.
Giddens, A. SOCIAL THEORY AND MODERN SOCIOLOGY, Polity, 1987.
Mullan, B. SOCIOLOGISTS ON SOCIOLOGY, Croom Helm, 1987.

G.P.

DEBORD, Guy

Cultural critic/political theorist	born France 1931–1994
Associated with	SPECTACLE ▪ EVERYDAY LIFE ▪ DE TOURNEMENT
Influences include	MARX ▪ LUKÁCS
Shares common ground with	DELEUZE ▪ GUATTARI ▪ ADORNO ▪ BAUDRILLARD
Main works	THE SOCIETY OF THE SPECTACLE (1967) COMMENTS ON THE SOCIETY OF THE SPECTACLE (1988) PANEGYRIC (1989)

DEBORD WAS BORN in Paris in 1931 and it was here that he spent most of his life; the city itself had a major influence on his thought and writings. In 1994, he committed suicide. These meagre personal details belie one of the greatest revolutionary thinkers post-Marx. Debord, unlike other French radicals, shied away from the media and cultivated an enigmatic aura around himself and his work. He wrote little as Guy Debord, though much anonymously as contribution to the Situationist International, the group, or movement, he helped shape. What he did write has been hugely influential, not just theoretically but also in terms of political action.

Debord's most widely known and influential thesis is that of the 'Spectacle'. This term is used in Debord's writing to designate the hegemonic power of capitalism in and through the mechanisms of representation (advertising, for example). Such a view maintains that mainstream culture (and indeed, culture in general) is the culture of the Spectacle, which, as a manifestation of capitalism, is ultimately repressive and alienating, as well as endlessly ingenious in its guises and mutations. The notion of the Spectacle provides a unifying concept under which to subsume the various, often seemingly contradictory, workings of capitalism, particularly as it penetrates and pervades everyday life. One of the central tenets of Debord's writing is that capitalism, or its 'mask', the Spectacle, is not just a force to be fought in the economic realm, but has become the determining factor in almost every area of our lives. As such, Debord's notion has much in common with the Frankfurt School theorists; for example, Adorno's notion of the 'Culture Industry', as well as Lukács's ideas on reification in *History and Class Consciousness*. This latter work exerted a key influence on Debord's own writings. What marks out Debord from the Frankfurt School and, indeed, the Marxist tradition as a whole, is his emphasis on the 'everyday'. The Spectacle's mode of existence is organised around the commodity and the subordination of human life to consumer lifestyle. This results in a kind of unreality or poverty of everday experience and ultimately, for Debord, boredom and banality.

It is in his book *Society of the Spectacle* that Debord conducts his critique on the Spectacle. The book is not easy, and like its 'sequel' (*Comments on the Society of the Spectacle*), is hermetic in nature, designed to fox the agents of the Spectacle. It is Debord's contention that it will only be meaningful to those truly opposed to the Spectacle, 'just as some chemical agents only reveal their hidden properties when they are combined with others'. The later *Comments on the Society of the Spectacle* are even more pessimistic than the earlier volume; here the Spectacle is theorised so completely that there seems to be nothing independent of it, though this lamentation should be understood more as a warning than as a completely accurate picture of how things are; a defining feature of Debord's writing is the desire for, and thus the possibility of, a space 'outside' the Spectacle, that is, the possibility of unalienated living.

Debord's other legacy is of a more active nature. The Situationist International called for a revolution in everyday life, organising creative and disruptive 'Happenings' as well as theoretically critiquing left- and right-wing state politics as stultifyingly bureaucratic and endlessly alienating. The ideas of Debord and of the Situationists in general were influential, if not instrumental, in the Paris uprisings of 1968, especially in terms of the carnivalesque nature of the revolt. The Situationists emphasised the need for pleasure and spontaneity in any revolution against the state and the Spectacle. Perhaps the main legacy of the Situationists can be seen in the history of art; for example with performance/event-orientated art and, of course, avant-garde strategies of *détournement* (parodying and reusing existing artistic materials to produce 'new' meanings). Indeed the Situationists themselves borrowed many of their ideas for 'creative revolution' from the Surrealists and from Dada. Debord was also an experimental film-maker, although none of his films, from *Screams in Favour of De Sade* (1952) to *In Girum Imus Nocte et Consumimur Igni* (1978), are well known, or contain any typical narrative.

Debord's ideas have been immensely influential, however, due to the invisibility of himself as a 'personality', and of the Situationists as a homogenous group, this influence is often eluded. Besides latter-day Situationists, and direct-action anarchists, Debord's writings directly influenced many of the central tenets of postmodernism, particularly as they appear in the writings of Jean Baudrillard (the notions of 'simulation' and 'simulacra' are an extension and development of Debord's concept of the Spectacle). Indeed, it could be argued that the whole tradition of critical writings in France post-1967 harks back to Debord and to the Situationists.

Further reading

Plant, S. THE MOST RADICAL GESTURE: THE SITUATIONIST INTERNATIONAL IN A POSTMODERN AGE, Routledge, 1992.
Vaneigem, R. THE REVOLUTION OF EVERYDAY LIFE, Rising Free Collective, 1979.
Wollen, P. ON THE PASSAGE OF A FEW PEOPLE THROUGH A RATHER BRIEF MOMENT IN TIME: SITUATIONIST INTERNATIONAL 1957–1972, MIT Press, 1989.

S.O'S.

DELEUZE, Gilles

Philosopher/literary theorist	born France 1925–1995
Associated with	SCHIZO-ANALYSIS ■ DETERRITORIALISATION ■ RHIZOME
Influences include	NIETZSCHE ■ SPINOZA ■ LEIBNIZ
Shares common ground with	FOUCAULT ■ GUATTARI ■ CHATELET
Main works	DIFFÉRENCE ET RÉPÉTITION (1969, TRANS. DIFFERENCE AND REPETITION)
CAPITALISME ET SCHIZOPHRÉNIE (WITH FÉLIX GUATTARI, 1972, TRANS. CAPITALISM AND SCHIZOPHRENIA)
VOL. 1: L'ANTI-OEDIPE (1972, TRANS. ANTI-OEDIPUS)
VOL. 2: MILLE PLATEAUX (1980, TRANS. A THOUSAND PLATEAUX)

AFTER TEACHING AT the Sorbonne and in Lyons, Deleuze spent almost the last two decades of his teaching career (until his retirement in 1987) at the University of Paris VIII. He began publishing early in his career, but attained his greatest prominence through his collaborative work with the psychoanalyst and philosopher, Félix Guattari (1930–92), whom he met in 1969. After many years of debilitating respiratory illness, Deleuze took his own life on 4 November 1995.

As a young philosophy student in Paris at the time of the Liberation, Deleuze studied the history of philosophy through such figures as Hume, Husserl and Heidegger. Immersed in what he later described as a constricting scholasticism, Deleuze responded positively to Sartre. Although not attracted by existentialism or phenomenology, he nevertheless found in Sartre 'not a model, method or example, but a little fresh air'.

An early responsiveness to the interface between past and future, between history and potentiality, as well as a detachment from systems and schools of thought, were to characterise the whole of Deleuze's career. Profoundly affected by the Nietzschean model in which presuppositions are cleared away in readiness for the creation of new concepts, Deleuze gravitated to philosophers who seemed to him both to belong to their age and to sidestep it. His first book, on Hume (*Empirisme et subjectivité* (1953), based upon his doctoral thesis) was followed, for example, by others on Nietzsche (1962 and 1965), Kant (1963), Bergson (1966), Spinoza (1968 and 1981), Foucault (1986) and Leibniz (1988).

For Deleuze, whether philosophy proceeds by means of affirmation (Bergson, Spinoza) or by critical negation (Kant, Hume, Hegel), what matters is not the contemplation of latent or eternal verities, but the attempt to conceptualise what is happening, moving, fleeing, becoming. The concept of body is replaced by that of posture, the concept of time by that of moment. As Deleuze argues in his *Différence et Répétition* (1969), there is no stable subject/object relation. One cannot even presume identity between objects, for these can exist only in relation to space and process.

The major outcome of the fertile collaboration between Deleuze and Guattari was the remarkable two-volume *Capitalism and Schizophrenia* (1972 and 1980). The first volume, *L'Anti-Oedipe*, argues strongly against the imposition of triangular, oedipal models ('*papa-maman-moi*') upon patterns of desire. In this and in the following volume, *Mille Plateaux*, Deleuze and Guattari replace the Oedipal patent by a 'schizo-analysis' which foregrounds alternative, deterritorialised flows of energy. Desire is multiple, transcending the pegs of relationship and identity. Within this 'nomadology', which resists the prescriptive power of state or system, a crucial image is that of the rhizome. Unlike the vertical, branching structure of the tree, the rhizome multiplies horizontally and invisibly within the earth.

Deleuze's work is itself an example of multiplicity: in addition to the history of philosophy, it includes books on literary authors (Proust, Sacher-Masoch, Kafka), on painting (Francis Bacon) and a two-volume book on cinema. Aspects of Deleuze's output have caused puzzlement in more rationalist or empiricist circles. Moreover, Deleuze has sometimes been accused of naïvety in appearing to dissociate desire from the specifics of history and identity. Yet his instincts were political as well as philosophical. He lent his support to numerous left-wing causes, and was working towards a book on Marx just before his death. His work does not evade political realities, but resists unexamined ideology and orthopraxis. He did not warm to latter-day conceptualisations (post-structuralism, postmodernism), preferring to remain future-oriented. The privileged mode of being for him is that of *devenir* (becoming), as Foucault acknowledged: 'One day, perhaps, the century will be Deleuzian.'

Further reading

Bogue, R. DELEUZE AND GUATTARI, Routledge, 1989.
Boundas, C.V. and Olkowski, D. (eds.) GILLES DELEUZE AND THE THEATER OF PHILOSOPHY, Routledge, 1994.
Hardt, M. GILLES DELEUZE: AN APPRENTICESHIP IN PHILOSOPHY, University of Minnesota Press, 1993.

M.B.

DER DERIAN, James

Political theorist	born USA 1955—
Associated with	NON-SPACE ■ IMMATERIALITY ■ ANTI-DIPLOMACY
Influences include	BULL ■ HEDLEY ■ NIETZSCHE ■ FOUCAULT
Shares common ground with	VIRILIO ■ BAUDRILLARD ■ CONNOLLY
Main works	ON DIPLOMACY (1987) ANTIDIPLOMACY (1992) VIRTUAL SECURITY (1998)

IN A FIELD noted for scholastic sobriety, James Der Derian's theoretically eclectic and avowedly post-structuralist spin to the study of International Relations (IR) has at various times managed to confuse and outrage a field more inclined to a more social scientific or 'realist' approach to the study of war, statecraft and international institutions. Der Derian has introduced much that is 'foreign' and even 'Frankish' to IR: semiology, deconstruction and discourse analysis are combined with his fascination with the fragmentations and buzz-cuts of contemporary pop culture – to Der Derian, MTV, *The X-Files*, *Blade Runner* and *Radiohead* are subjects just as worthy as the study of the balance of power or international anarchy, and provide us with compasses to chart to the vertigo of contemporary world politics.

For such an *agent provacateur*, Der Derian's intellectual roots are impeccably classical. As important as the work of Foucault, Baudrillard and Virilio are to him, one can detect a continual debt to Hedley Bull and the English School of International Relations. As Rhodes Scholar at Oxford University, Der Derian worked closely with the late Hedley Bull, who was his Ph.D. supervisor. The English School is synonymous with the idea of International Society – this refers to a group of independent but interacting states and other political units who share a common set of values, rules and institutions. The evolution of this society was facilitated by the break-up of a medieval system of suzerain states and the development of an anarchical system of mutually estranged and formally equal states. Importantly, the formation of international society was dependent on the spread of Western cultural values, codes and symbols via an élite international political culture and, importantly, a diplomatic culture – a stock of ideas and beliefs held in common by official representatives of states.

Der Derian's first book, *On Diplomacy*, was an attempt to comprehend the gradual disintegration of this diplomatic culture. The book is a series of historical meditations on the function of diplomacy from the archaic world to late modern times. Traces of the neglected origins of diplomacy are found in the Pentateuch. The tribe of Israel alienated local antagonisms to a single supernatural entity aggregated in the Supreme Covenant of Israel. The legacy for modern diplomacy is how this mytho-diplomacy constructed a mythical response to the ultimate impossibility of fixing a boundary between an adversarial 'sacred' and 'profane'. Metaphysical ritual emerges as a 'non-space' between an estranged world impervious to physical demarcation. Likewise, modern diplomatic culture operates as a discursive and cultural attempt to govern the 'ungovernable' anarchical society.

In *Antidiplomacy*, both a semi-sequel to *On Diplomacy* and a semi-Situationist manifesto, Der Derian suggests that a late modern anti-diplomacy is trying to police and mediate estrangement via new technologies of power and representations of danger. Three forms of power in particular – espionage (intelligence and surveillance); terror (global terror and national security culture) and speed (the acceleration of space in war and diplomacy) – produce a discursive effect more chronopolitical than geopolitical. Though these forces are embedded in both popular culture and national security culture they found their (as yet) highest expression in the Gulf War, a war where 'cyberspace came out of the research labs and into our living rooms . . . reality was reproduced by television cameras equipped with night-vision technology and transmitted in real-time by portable satellite link-ups'.

Simultaneously technostrategic and televisual, these forces made killing more efficient, unreal and more distant to us; they also helped reinscribe a sense of security and sovereignty in a world consisting of highly contested borders of political and human identity. National securityspeak and the cinematic certainties of such films as *Patriot Games* and *Air Force One* suggest that 'someone under the table, in the highest corporate or government office, someone is pulling the strings – or at the very least, is willing with the best technology, fastest speed and longest reach to intervene secretly, if not sinisterly, when necessary'.

Antidiplomacy signifies the shift to a more hardboiled prose – Der Derian takes leave from academia and acquires the persona of a Philip Marlowesque international investigator: adventures on the Baltic on a peace ship, and then, in a series of articles, some of which will take final form in his book *Virtual Security*, we find Der Derian eye-witnessing war simulations in the Mojave Desert, at the Hofenfels Combat and Maneuver Training Centre in Germany, and then engulfed in the postmodern phantasmagoria of Disneyland. Using, among others, Virilio, Baudrillard, Bakhtin and Benjamin as a theoretical armoury to guide him through these virtual theatres of war, the terrain he charts is the messy post-Cold War landscape, a place resistant to traditional geopolitics and statecraft: 'Capital, information, technology, drug and refugee flows are supplanting and in some cases subverting the powers of not just international society but of the sovereign states themselves to manage the deleterious effects of global swarming. Contemporary world politics as a hiveless cloud of angry bees remains at best a metaphorical question, not a conclusive answer.'

The task of critical international theorists and those who may wish to make 'discursive repairs' to the effects of 'global swarming' does not require the essentialist truths of traditional and positivist international theory but the construction of counter-myths. Der Derian's prescriptions in this area are thin, and sometimes on his tour of this hyperreal, immaterial epoch, human agency and even hope seem to be lost among the giddying signifiers of a new world disorder, even at the moment when he calls us to 'play peace' and embrace otherness. However, the sheer scandal of Der Derian's iconoclasm and his bold decentring of many of the received wisdoms of two generations of international relations theory suggest that IR will never be the same again.

Further reading

Campbell, D. WRITING SECURITY, Minnesota University Press, 1992.
Constantinou, C.M. ON THE WAY TO DIPLOMACY, Minnesota University Press, 1996.
Tuathail, G.O. CRITICAL GEOPOLITICS, Minnesota University Press, 1997.

C.B.

DERRIDA, Jacques

Philosopher/literary theorist	born Algiers 1930—
Associated with	DECONSTRUCTION ■ LOGOCENTRICITY ■ POLYSEMIA
Influences include	HEIDEGGER ■ SAUSSURE ■ NIETZSCHE ■ DE MAN
Shares common ground with	BLANCHOT ■ LÉVINAS ■ LYOTARD ■ DELEUZE ■ GUATTARI
Main works	OF GRAMMATOLOGY (1967) WRITING AND DIFFERENCE (1967) THE OTHER HEADING (1992)

L IKE MANY OF his contemporaries, including Foucault, Derrida was educated at the École Normale Supériere, where he subsequently took up a teaching post. In the last 20 years or so he has shared his time between France and the USA, where he has his most enthusiastic disciples.

Few thinkers have straddled as many disciplines and subjects as Derrida, one reason for his great popularity with academics all over the world. His writings, encyclopedic in scope, touch on the social sciences, ethics, politics, aesthetics and psychoanalysis, not to mention literature, where his intervention has had a marked influence on literary criticism. The mainspring of his contribution to all these is based on a radical critique of philosophy and linguistics, which goes by the name of deconstruction theory.

Deconstruction involves the dismantling into their constituent features of all types of unities, including culture and cultural specificity: systems, theories, etc. In philosophy, for which Derrida prefers the term 'metaphysics', it seeks to call into question the validity of notions such as truth and reason. In linguistics, primarily in Saussurean linguistics, from which it draws much of its vocabulary, it demonstrates the impossibility of universal meaning. Merging the two, it shows that language, outside which there cannot be thought or meaning, consists of ambivalences. Nothing in thought can therefore be conclusive because every use of language leads to polysemia and aporia. This is because in language there are no positive terms, but only differences such that signs (words) do not capture meanings but merely refer to other signs in an infinite series that permanently defer meaning.

The idea that truth can be attained through thought and meaning controlled in language, so central a feature of the metaphysics of presence, stems, according to Derrida, from its deep-rootedness in subject–object types of dichotomies. These, following Heidegger, he shows as shaping our world-view and the discourses that give expression to it. He characterises the latter as logocentric and shows that their basic impulse lies in the attempt to impose logic (sameness) on differences (otherness).

In the account which Derrida gives of this process one element stands out: violence. Everything to do with identity or unity (self-presence and sameness) results from violence, from forces exerted in the cause of eliminating differences. This is as true of personal identities as it is of totalities such as society and community, as he points out in an essay on Lévi-Strauss, where he also taxes structuralism and the social sciences with ethnocentrism. It is, therefore, also true of the State *qua* organisation and of politics as a process.

Although Derrida's writings are not political in a conventional sense, he has sometimes engaged in institutional criticism, principally of the education system. In addition, his embracing of differences carries with it a condemnation of totalisation, the forging of unities, which has propelled him towards a Messianic vision of political culture. This is clear in his musings on Marx, where he expounds the idea of Marxism as a promise whose fulfilment, like meaning, is always deferred. It is a vision infused with a sense of ethics that sees totalisation – hence also totalitarians – as inherent in the pursuit of defined objectives (projects).

The word 'culture' is difficult to apply to Derrida, who sets it in opposition to 'nature' as one dichotomy alongside others which function as the foundation of metaphysics. It is nevertheless difficult to resist pointing out to what an extent his attacks on philosophy, also characterised as phallogocentrism, have found favour with feminism as a counter-culture and how much his anti-ethnocentrism also denotes an openness towards non-European cultures.

Further reading

Beardsworth, R. DERRIDA AND THE POLITICAL, Routledge, 1996.
Gasché, R. THE TAIN OF THE MIRROR, Harvard University Press, 1986.
Norris, C. DERRIDA, Fontana, 1987.

G.S.

DJILAS, Milovan

Political writer/critic	born Montenegro 1911–1995
Associated with	NEW CLASS ■ CONTEMPORARY COMMUNISM
Influences include	LENIN ■ MARX ■ TROTSKY
Shares common ground with	GEIGER ■ OSSOWSKI ■ WESOLOWSKI ■ BELL
Main works	THE NEW CLASS (1957) CONVERSATIONS WITH STALIN (1962) THE UNPERFECT SOCIETY (1969)

B ORN INTO A poor Serbian–Montenegran family, Djilas graduated in law from Belgrade University in 1933. As an activist in the illegal communist underground, he was imprisoned for three years by Yugoslavia's royalist dictatorship. After meeting Tito in 1937 he became a member of the Jugoslav Party's Politburo. Djilas played a major role in the Partisan resistance to the Germans in the Second World War leading a military mission to Moscow in 1944. With the accession of Tito's Communist government in 1945 he became a leading Cabinet minister, and in 1948 held talks with Stalin in Moscow as the leading exponent of Yugoslavia's position as an 'independent' communist state. In 1953, despite his high office and devotion to Tito, his ideological disagreements with the party leadership and disillusionment with the communist regime began when he published articles critical of the governmental bureaucracy that he later called the 'New Class'. Following expulsion from the party's Central Committee in 1954, he spent nine of the next 10 years in prison, and was only released in 1966 subject to a restriction against making public statements for five years. Despite this, his main writings were translated and published in the West via American publishers.

Djilas's first book, *The New Class*, was published in the West from a smuggled manuscript when he was already in prison. He is at pains to stress that, whilst he is a critic of the social role and ideas of the communist bureaucracy he is, despite Western interpretations, not anti-communist. His primary purpose is to expose the Marxist illusion that the destruction of capitalist ownership in the Soviet Union had resulted in a classless society and that the proletariat was in power in such communist societies.

In equating the then contemporary communism with 'total state capitalism', Djilas points out that because it has so many of its own characteristics it is a special type of new social system. Thus in an unprecedented way contemporary communism, for him, is a type of modern totalitarianism which uniquely has succeeded in incorporating the three basic factors – power, ownership and ideology – for controlling the people. These are monopolised by the bureaucratic oligarchy of the Communist Party forming a New Class (*apparatchiki*), which subordinates both the state and society. Thus, in his words, 'The party is the main force of the communist state and government. It is the motive force of everything. It unites within itself the new class, the government, ownership and ideas.' This leads to inevitable contradictions – a 'form of latent civil war' – between the government and the people in a continuous and lively opposition to the oligarchy, necessitating the communist leaders to treat the state as an instrument to reduce this opposition by naked force. The communist state cannot therefore become a lawful state (i.e. incorporating an independent judiciary and the rule of law) without imperilling the totalitarian authority of the Party's leaders.

Djilas sees power as the central factor for controlling communist societies in two senses. First, power plays a major role in all three phases of the establishment of communism from revolutionary (the usurpation of power), through dogmatic communism (the creation of a new socialist system by means of that power) to non-dogmatic communism (power used to preserve the system). Second, political power has become both the means and the end in itself in order to maintain the special economic privileges and forms of ownership of the New Class of communist officials: 'power is the alpha and omega of contemporary communism'. Whilst Western students of communist societies have utilised ruling-class and élitist theory in sociopolitical analyses, Djilas utilises classical Marxist analysis and postulates in arguing that, concealed in a legal guise, the New Class is the actual owner of the state's resources (distribution of national income, wage setting, etc.). Its members solely enjoy the rights of ownership in the disposal of state property and in exercising exclusive control over its 'surplus revenue'. If ownership is defined as rights over the use and products of collective property, and not simply legal entitlements, then the dominant class of socialist society can be conceived sociologically as the propertied class enjoying special privileges and economic preferences because of the administrative monopoly they hold.

The New Class, at the apex of socialist societies such as the Soviet Union and Yugoslavia, thus use the party parasitically as a basis for their privileged position, thereby strengthening their position at the expense of the party, which grows weaker. Unlike the pattern of recruitment and social mobility into the ruling class of capitalist societies, however, Djilas holds that it is different in the case of the New Class whose social origins lie in the proletariat and cannot accordingly lose its connection with the ranks of the manual workers and non-independent peasantry. Again, whilst the political office of members of the New Class cannot be transferred from father to son in the way that private property can, sociological evidence (Ossowski: *Class Structure in the Social Conscious* Routledge & Kegan Paul, 1963; Wesolowski: *Classes, Strata and Power*. Routledge & Kegan Paul, 1979) increasingly indicates that via higher education especially the privileged position of New Class members is inherited by their offspring, thus resembling the more traditional bourgeois patterns in the West.

Apart from the ideological approach to planning emanating from classical Marxism, what Djilas calls 'ideological economy' (*The Unperfect Society*), he sees communism as predominantly a political ideology in its development phase as 'revolutionary socialism' in well-developed countries. However, in contemporary communist societies in which ideas no longer play the predominant role in controlling the people, he argues that communism as an ideology has mainly run its course, having few new things to reveal to the world. This thesis is further elaborated in *The Unperfect Society* where, in acknowledging that Marxism was the first world ideology (one that has convulsed the whole human race in one way or another), he extensively delineates what he calls 'The Twilight of the Ideologies' thus parallelling Daniel Bell's 'End of Ideology' thesis with regard to Western capitalist societies. In Djilas's words, 'The concepts Communism, capitalism, even socialism – insofar as it does not mean freer personalities, greater rights for social groups, and a more equitable distribution of goods than obtains at present – all belong to earlier ages.'

Further reading

Clissold, S. Djilas: The Progress of a Revolutionary, Universe Books, 1983.
Lustig, M. Trotsky and Djilas: Critics of Communist Bureaucracy, Greenwood Press, 1989.
Ray, L. Social Theory and the Crisis of State Capitalism, Edward Elgar, 1996.

G.P.

DOUGLAS, Mary Tew

Social anthropologist	born England 1921—
Associated with	GROUP/GRID ANALYSIS ■ SYMBOLISM ■ POLLUTION ■ NEO-STRUCTURALISM ■ RISK ANALYSIS
Influences include	LEACH ■ NEEDHAM ■ MAUSS ■ LÉVI-STRAUSS
Shares common ground with	LEACH ■ NEEDHAM ■ TURNER
Main works	PURITY AND DANGER: AN ANALYSIS OF THE CONCEPTS OF POLLUTION AND TABOO (1966) NATURAL SYMBOLS: EXPLORATIONS IN COSMOLOGY (1970) RULES AND MEANINGS: THE ANTHROPOLOGY OF EVERYDAY KNOWLEDGE (1973) THE WORLD OF GOODS: AN ANTHROPOLOGICAL THEORY OF CONSUMPTION (WITH B. ISHERWOOD, 1979)

MARY TEW DOUGLAS was born in Roehampton, England, and graduated in Philosophy, Politics and Economics from Oxford University in 1943. She remained at Oxford where she then completed a Master's degree in anthropology (1947), a Bachelor of Science (1948) and a Ph.D. (1951). As a graduate student, she was heavily influenced by Meyer Fortes, Max Gluckman and Edward Evans-Pritchard. Her dissertation fieldwork was conducted in the then Belgian Congo and explored social accountability through a study of male control of access to younger women (see *The Lele of the Kasai* (1963)). Her ethnographic study became a classic and a model for other women anthropologists entering the field. She taught at the University of London from 1952 to 1978, having become a director of the Russell Sage Foundation in New York (1977–81). Subsequently she taught at Northwestern University (1981–85) and Princeton (1985–88). She is currently Emeritus Professor at Northwestern.

Mary Douglas has had a wide and varied career exploring many aspects of ritual, symbolism, myth and social relations in preliterate and literate societies. While faithful to her training in anthropology and especially influenced by Evans-Pritchard – see *Edward Evans-Pritchard* (1980) – Douglas has developed her own distinctive approach to analysing social relations and their counterparts in cultural patterns. Her contributions are both methodological and theoretical. By tackling topics central to contemporary industrialised societies (e.g. food, risk, drinking) she has brought the techniques of cultural anthropology to a wide audience.

On the methodological side, she is credited with developing a group/grid analytic approach in order to classify and ascertain rules of conduct and forms of social order. Rather than the usual anthropological emphasis on norms and structures, this approach postulates that social relations can be reduced to two independent variables whose combination determines particular social structures. Group refers to the activities of a social unit while grid refers to the rules governing relationships between individuals. Douglas employs this approach to illuminate underlying patterns of social organisation.

While this approach has had more uptake in the sociology of science and technology than anthropology, it underpins Douglas's theoretical and conceptual approach to cultural analysis. This is usually called neo-structuralism, and Douglas was one of its leading British exponents, along with Edmund Leach, Rodney Needham and Victor Turner.

Douglas is most commonly associated with her work on pollution, purity and moral order (see *Purity and Danger* and her entry on 'Pollution' in the 1968 edition of the *International Encyclopaedia of the Social Sciences*, (Free Press/Collier MacMillan, 1979) pp. 336–42). This work explicates her central interest in establishing the rules of social accountability by examining the ways in which confrontations and transgressions are dealt with. Douglas argues that social rules regulate behaviour because they form the basis of processes of human thought which, in turn, classify phenomena, establish codes and conventions, and impose rewards and sanctions for transgressions. For Douglas, these social rules are embedded in every aspect of social life, however mundane; in other words, all social phenomena encode symbolic relations that explain the rules of the social order.

Her analysis of pollution – or purity and impurity – argues that rules about pollution form an accountability system to deal with disorder, and that concern about bodily functions reflects anxieties about group survival. She applied the approach both to the spiritual uses of pollution in preliterate societies and to the hygienic approaches to dirt in contemporary society. Expanding on this interest in how social behaviour relates to symbolic actions, Douglas wrote her best-known books, *Natural Symbols* and *Rules and Meanings*. She expanded her analysis of classification systems in *Implicit Meanings: Essays in Anthropology* (1975) and *In the Active Voice* (1982).

Douglas also tackled other topics, such as studying the meaning of consumption and the role of goods as social markers (*The World of Goods*). The subject of food has also been of interest to her in terms of how food communicates through classificatory systems that determine what is eaten, in what context, and in what order. Her aim has been to establish a grammar of food which accounts for the relationship between eating habits, cultural consumption and social distinctions (her edited volumes, *Food in the Social Order: Studies of Food and Festivities in Three American Communities*) (1984) and *Constructive Drinking: Perspectives on Drink from Anthropology* (1987)).

In recent years, Douglas has become interested in risk, which she analyses in the context of mainstream political practices and contemporary beliefs about pollution (*Risk and Culture: An Essay on the Selection of Technical and Environmental Dangers*, co-authored with Aaron Wildavsky (1982), *Risk Acceptability According to the Social Sciences* (1985); and *Risk and Blame: Essays in Cultural Theory* (1992)).

These examples of Douglas's work indicate her imaginative yet rigorous approach to understanding cultural practices, which have not only had a major impact in reorienting anthropology towards less Eurocentric preoccupations with 'other' people, but also foreshadowed the kinds of inquiry that are conducted within cultural studies.

Further reading

Douglas, M. and Gross, J. 'Food and Culture: Measuring the Intricacy of Rule Systems', SOCIAL SCIENCE INFORMATION, 20: 1 (1981), pp. 1–35.
Kuper, A. ANTHROPOLOGISTS AND ANTHROPOLOGY: THE BRITISH SCHOOL 1922–1972, Allen Lane, 1973.
Wuthnow, R., Hunter, J.D., Bergesen, A. and Kurzweil, E. CULTURAL ANALYSIS: THE WORK OF PETER L. BERGER, MARY DOUGLAS, MICHEL FOUCAULT AND JÜRGEN HABERMAS, Routledge & Kegan Paul, 1984.

J.C./G.C.

DURKHEIM, Emile

Sociologist	born France 1858–1917
Associated with	HOLISM ▪ STRUCTURAL-FUNCTIONALISM
Influences include	KANT ▪ SAINT-SIMON ▪ COMTE
Shares common ground with	MAUSS ▪ LÉVI-STRAUSS ▪ GELLNER
Main works	THE DIVISION OF LABOUR IN SOCIETY (1893) PRIMITIVE CLASSIFICATION (WITH MARCEL MAUSS, 1903) THE ELEMENTARY FORMS OF THE RELIGIOUS LIFE (1912)

E MILE DURKHEIM WAS born into a Jewish family in eastern France and was educated at Epinal and the Lycée Louis-le-Grand (Paris) before entering the École Normale Supériere in 1879. After graduating he taught in Puy and Sens. He then spent a term in Germany from 1885 to 1886, after which he taught in the Lycée at Troyes until his appointment to the first post in sociology at a French university at Bordeaux in 1887. He moved to a post at the Sorbonne in Paris in 1902 where he taught until his death in 1917.

Durkheim tried to establish both the method and the substance of the modern discipline of sociology by examining the relation of cultural representations to social structure. His first major work, in 1893, though nominally about the division of labour, actually concerned the evolution of forms of the *conscience collectif* in law and sanction (from repressive to restitutive) in relation to two types of social structure (segmental to organic). His method was to deal with what he called social facts, that is, a domain of phenomena beyond and external to the sphere of purely individual action. These social facts included what he later called collective representations, and they were to be considered 'as things', and to be explained only in relation to other social facts, never to individual representations. His work sought to reply to that of Comte and Marx: in the first the place of religion and culture had been used in the law of the three states to explain social evolution, while in the second it was economic development. Durkheim tried to develop an approach which was to show that they are mutually dependent. In the end his work tended to develop a complex picture of the relation between culture and social structure in social evolution that was influential on writers as divergent as Parsons and Bataille.

In the later period of his work he wrote a detailed analysis of Australian totemism on the basis of the recent work of ethnographers. In this work, *The Elementary Forms of the Religious Life*, he drastically revised his earlier thesis that primitive cultures were centred on repressive norms, based only on bonds of likeness and uniformity. The evidence suggested that the religions of primitive peoples contained all the elements of the advanced cultures in embryo. In a long analysis he tried to show that the cultures of the aborigines were dependent on elaborate ritual processes and on complex systems of social classification. His argument identified the division between sacred and profane phenomena as a fundamental cultural classification of things. His analysis suggested that the demarcation between the sacred and profane, and indeed the division within the sacred between good and evil, are created in the last resort not by a prior disposition of mind, but in the ritual process itself. He examined the collective process of ritual and the collective effervescence and excitement which accompanied it, as the basis for a distinction with the dispersed and low energy activity of utilitarian or economic activities. A persistent theme of his work was to examine the moral function of religious forms and rituals as providing the basis of group identity and solidarity in a structure of differences. His aim was to be able to provide a scientific answer to the question of whether modern European social and cultural structures are anomalous. Here he advocated a comparative analysis of different forms and levels of social integration. He argued that elevated rates of crime and suicide indicated an exaggerated individualism and an increasing failure of cultural integration. Here he seems to have wanted to find a solution in what he called institutional socialism, particularly a stronger role for occupational or professional corporations on the one hand, and a much stronger role for the social sciences in the process of developing an ethics for a democratic society.

Further reading

Alexander, J. (ed.) DURKHEIMIAN SOCIOLOGY: CULTURAL STUDIES, Cambridge University Press, 1988.
Gane, M. (ed.) THE RADICAL SOCIOLOGY OF DURKHEIM AND MAUSS, Routledge, 1992.
Lukes, S. EMILE DURKHEIM, Penguin, 1973.

M.G.

EAGLETON, Terry

Literary theorist/writer	born England 1943—
Associated with	MARXISM ▪ POST-STRUCTURALISM ▪ DISCOURSE ETHICS
Influences include	ALTHUSSER ▪ BENJAMIN ▪ HABERMAS ▪ MACHEREY ▪ WILLIAMS
Shares common ground with	DERRIDA ▪ HALL ▪ JAMESON
Main works	CRITICISM AND IDEOLOGY (1976) LITERARY THEORY (1983) THE FUNCTION OF CRITICISM (1984) THE IDEOLOGY OF THE AESTHETIC (1990)

TERRY EAGLETON HAILS from an Irish Catholic family in Salford, England. He studied at Cambridge where he came under the influence of Raymond Williams and participated in the writing of *The May Day Manifesto* (1968), a key text of the British New Left. Having turned against Williams in the 1970s he recanted in the 1980s, and edited an appreciative collection of essays on Williams's work following Williams's death in 1988. In his youth, Eagleton was closely associated with the radical Catholic publication, *Slant*. He later became known as an intransigent intellectual of the Far Left in Britain and has never forsworn his Marxist convictions, unlike many of his generation. Eagleton is a Professor at Oxford and has a significant media presence as a reviewer and commentator on cultural and political matters and as a creative writer. He is a novelist, playwright and scriptwriter as well as a critical theorist.

Eagleton has produced a wide range of literary analyses (for instance, on Shakespeare, the Brontës and Samuel Richardson) and has been a leading mediator of European continental theory in Britain. In fact, his role in turning literary study theoretical has been immense. He is adept at combining philosophical, textual and historical modes of analysis and at interpreting complex theoretical ideas, though he has produced little in the way of original theory himself. Once, in response to an interviewer questioning him on this matter, he admitted to not being so much an original theorist as, in his writing, treating theory as a literary genre. This is exactly what traditional literary critics have complained about in the turn towards theory: that students were being asked to read theory but not literature. Eagleton's own *Literary Theory* has been an enormously popular student text, outlining clearly and concisely the basic tenets of a number of theories, including post-structuralism and psychoanalysis, for literary analysis. His genius is that of a populariser of abstruse theory.

In the 1970s Eagleton did, however, set out to be an original theorist inspired by the Althusserian critic, Pierre Macherey. The intention was to produce a scientific model of literature which attended to its own specific determinations (literary mode of production, or LMP) and the general determinations of the social formation (general mode of production, or GMP). He identified various forms of ideology working upon the literary text: general ideology (GI), authorial ideology (AuI) and aesthetic ideology (AI). In the end, however, this elaborate apparatus of concepts amounted to no more, in effect, than a useful set of broad distinctions. In terms of actual literary analysis the model was far too cumbersome and mechanical. Nevertheless, Eagleton was trying to synthesise and codify some important strands of thought and he was attempting to construct a non-reductive kind of Marxist cultural analysis, a not uncommon project of the 1970s.

Eagleton subsequently drifted towards what he later called 'the wilder flights' of post-structuralism, especially the increasingly free play of the text and the Barthesian affectation of the critic as a metawriter. When he finally 're-emerged', in his own word, he became attracted to the work of Habermas who, in a much different and Germanic idiom, has a certain affinity with aspects of Williams's thought, particularly regarding the social conditions of satisfactory communication. Eagleton's short study *The Function of Criticism* picked up on Habermas's concept of the public sphere. The issue then became the role of the critic as a public intellectual, as holding responsibilities concerning the quality of social and political debate, not just operating as a clown of the text.

Eagleton's finest theoretical work to date is *The Ideology of the Aesthetic*, in which he produces scintillating readings of the major contributors to the Western bourgeois tradition of aesthetics, beginning with Baumgarten. He also elaborates upon the role of Habermasian discourse ethics in cultural criticism and abjures the nihilistic aspects of post-structuralism. Again, however, no distinctly Eagletonian theoretical position is enunciated. The failure to develop a distinctive theory of his own should not, however, necessarily be seen as failure. Both Eagleton and his original mentor Raymond Williams wanted not only to write about writing but to write themselves. Williams, in his own quirky way was a more original theorist than Eagleton, yet Eagleton is the better writer. This is evident in his explicatory writing but it is also very much evident in his fiction and dramatic writing, for instance, in the brilliant conceit of the philosophical novel, *Saints and Scholars*, and in his play about Oscar Wilde, *Saint Oscar*, where it becomes difficult to distinguish between the *bons mots* of Oscar and of Terry.

Further reading

Eagleton, T. SAINTS AND SCHOLARS, Futura, 1987.
Eagleton, T. SAINT OSCAR, Field Day, 1989.
Eagleton, T. IDEOLOGY, Verso, 1990.
J.McG.

ECO, Umberto

Historian/philosopher/literary critic/cultural critic	born Italy 1932—
Associated with	SEMIOTICS ∎ IMPERIALISM ∎ POPULAR CULTURE
Influences include	ARISTOTLE ∎ JOYCE ∎ PEIRCE
Shares common ground with	BARTHES ∎ BAUDRILLARD ∎ JAMESON
Main works	A THEORY OF SEMIOTICS (1976) THE NAME OF THE ROSE (1983) TRAVELS IN HYPERREALITY (1986)

UMBERTO ECO WAS born in Piedmont, Italy in 1932. He studied at the University of Turin, and has held the Chair of Semiotics at the University of Bologna since 1971. Although primarily a medieval historian, Eco has long been involved with the 'culture industry', working within Italian television and the weekly magazine *L'Espresso*, as well as having relationships with Italian cultural–political groups, most notably 'Gruppo 63' and 'Gruppo Ufo' (described in *apocalypse postponed* (1994)).

His love of popular culture and commitment to it has enabled Eco to avoid the pessimism of many other Marxist intellectuals, such as Adorno and the Frankfurt School. Indeed, Eco's extensive engagement with the culture industry, his consistent work within TV, publishing and literature, should not be forgotten when reading his academic texts. For Eco's academic work is only one part of his overall 'project' – a project informed by a position that is brilliantly simple, coherent and pragmatic: before decrying culture, Eco maintains, one must first understand it, study it, embrace it. Value judgements can, and must, come into effect in all aspects of life, but such judgements will only be legitimated by a properly rigorous semiotic analysis – one which takes the critic's own position into account.

If, however, after serious analysis, one is still 'pessimistic' (about, say, the culturally repressive, exploitative or impoverishing effects of specific activities of 'capitalism', which Eco does not deny we should always look out for), then the academic can still act in ways other than the 'purely' academic: one way to change culture is to contribute to it, either by gaining power within the mechanisms of cultural decision-making (as Eco demonstrates through his involvement in publishing and TV production), or by enriching it (as Eco does by offering intellectual novels and semiotic essays as a columnist).

Eco was instrumental in constructing the discipline of semiotics after being influenced by the work of Peirce, and even his best-selling works of fiction, *The Name of the Rose* (1983), *Foucault's Pendulum* (1989) and *The Island of the Day Before* (1995), are informed by the complexities of semiotic concerns. It can be said that, just as *The Name of the Rose* is inspired by structuralism as much as the detective novel, so *Foucault's Pendulum* is a detective novel which allegorically criticises such practices of textual 'over-interpretation' which Eco sees as being characteristic of deconstructionists, and *The Island of the Day Before* points out that 'postmodern' ideas can be traced back many centuries.

As such, Eco can be said to be a key practitioner of 'interdisciplinarity', offering works on a vast range of subjects; often traversing the traditional concerns of disciplines such as philosophy, rhetoric, history, anthropology and literary criticism when writing about 'trivial' or 'commonplace' objects and practices of our everyday contemporary world. The works *apocalypse postponed* and *Travels in Hyperreality* include such diverse and dynamic analyses that one and the same light-hearted essay could be accommodated just as well on a history curriculum as on a media studies reading list.

In contrast to some other cultural critics, who seize upon the insights of postmodernism and deconstruction in order to subvert the semiotic systems, ideology and principles of modernity, Eco is, rather, concerned with 'context' (one of the very things that deconstruction has called into question). Eco's formulation of context is that of the 'cultural context' which renders meaning possible at any given point or configuration of time, geography, and the intersecting 'competence' of two or more communicating agents. He uses many of Peirce's and Hjelmslev's categories in order to construct his semiotic theory; most familiarly, the interacting pair of *langue* (the linguistic or other signifying structure) and *parole* (the individual utterances of speech, or other communicative act). Eco's theory gives a compelling account of how meaning is possible, can be produced and reproduced, as well as created and destroyed.

The works of Umberto Eco can be read of and for themselves, as impressive moments of semiotic practice, decoding institutions and messages that constitute instances of the core of our culture(s). But when they are read bearing in mind the extra-academic interventions of Eco into his cultural environment, then it is possible to see that such postmodern or deconstructionist aphorisms as 'there is nothing outside the text' can come to mean more than an imperative to 'read' the world using the tools of literary criticism. Rather, Eco's work in supposedly distinct roles (literary critic, literary producer, editor, columnist, political activist), is exemplary of the advocated part intellectuals might aspire to play within their own cultural contexts.

Further reading

Bondanella, P. Umberto Eco and the Open Text, Cambridge University Press, 1997.
Docherty, T. Postmodernism: A Reader, Harvester Wheatsheaf, 1993.
Lechte, J. Fifty Key Contemporary Thinkers, Routledge, 1994.

P.B.

ELIAS, Norbert

Sociologist	born Germany 1897–1990
Associated with	CIVILISING PROCESS ■ PROCESS/FIGURATIONAL SOCIOLOGY ■ INVOLVEMENT AND DETACHMENT
Influences include	HONINGSWALD ■ MANNHEIM ■ WEBER
Shares common ground with	DUNNING ■ BOURDIEU ■ SENNETT
Main works	THE CIVILIZING PROCESS (2 VOLS., 1939–82) THE COURT SOCIETY (1983) INVOLVEMENT AND DETACHMENT (1987)

ELIAS WAS BORN in Breslau, the only child of Jewish parents who eventually perished in the Holocaust. He fought in the First World War and in 1918 registered at the University of Breslau to study philosophy and medicine. His criticism of the Kantian tradition led him to sociology. He studied in Heidelberg and Frankfurt, although he was never part of the Frankfurt School. With the rise of Hitler, Elias fled Germany, and in 1936, began research in the British Museum library, on the civilising process. The book was first published in 1939 but its significance was missed by reviewers and teachers, owing to the distractions of the war. At the end of the war, Elias worked for 10 years as an extra-mural tutor and occasional lecturer in London. In 1954 he moved to a full-time post in sociology at Leicester University. Here Elias worked on his self-appointed and, by the standards of the day, eccentric, research programme and gained the reputation of being an inspirational teacher. In 1978, the English translation of *The Civilizing Process* was published. The book became a best-seller in France and the second volume was published in 1982. In the last decade of his life Elias enjoyed international acclaim. He relocated to Amsterdam and continued to research and write until his death at the age of 93.

Elias is best known for the theory of the civilising process. He argues that the historical changes in manners and the personality structure can only be correctly understood by examining changes in the social structure. The mono-polisation of physical force and taxation in the hands of the state and the multiplication of 'chains of interdependency' between people through the division of labour form the basis for more 'restrained' and 'polite' interpersonal behaviour. Elias does not intend 'the civilising process' to be understood in evaluative terms. We are not necessarily 'superior' to our ancestors. All that he claims is that certain deep-seated changes in self-constraint can be demonstrated. What is often missed by readers is Elias's methodological originality. He eschews 'static' thinking in favour of what he first called 'figurational sociology', but towards the end of his life, insisted should be known as 'process sociology'. His approach is based in the realisation that all things are in process, including our conceptual and theoretical tools. The fault of much sociology is that it reduces processes to static polarities, such as 'individual and society', 'male and female', 'dominant and subordinate class', 'traditional and modern society'. For Elias these 'false conceptual dichotomies' blur our recognition of the interconnectivity of human life. He developed a variety of 'sociogenetic' methods and concepts to overcome static thinking. The most important is his distinction between 'involvement' and 'detachment'. He argues that human beings are often highly involved in value positions which derive from their position of gender, class, ethicity, etc. One important role of sociology is to bring an attitude of 'detachment' to bear upon our values. Elias defined the sociologist as 'the destroyer of myths'.

Elias has been widely criticised for his alleged 'Eurocentrism', his caricatures of other positions in the sociological tradition, his failure to recognise the real levels of violence and psychological torture in contemporary life and his meliorist belief that the civilising process is a process of human improvement. But critics do not make concessions to the magnitude or originality of Elias's achievement. He constantly worked against the mainstream because he believed that the theoretical approaches and methodologies developed there were fundamentally flawed. This invited voluntary marginalism. His refusal to approve an English translation of *The Civilizing Process* until he was in his eighties prevented the dissemination of his thought and was typical of the fastidious, stubborn streak in his personality. Yet process sociology is a huge achievement and he is the architect of it as well as the author of what is, to date, its most distinguished body of work.

Further reading

Dunning, E. 'Figurational Sociology and its Critics', in E. Dunning and C. Rojek (eds.), Sport and Leisure in the Civilizing Process, Macmillan, 1992.
Goudsblom, J. Sociology in the Balance, Blackwell, 1977.
Mennell, S. Norbert Elias: An Introduction, Blackwell, 1992.

C.R.

EMPSON, William

Literary critic	born England 1906–1984
Associated with	NEW CRITICISM ■ AMBIGUITY ■ PASTORAL
Influences include	RICHARDS ■ GRAVES ■ RIDING
Shares common ground with	HUSSERL ■ DE MAN ■ RICKS
Main works	SEVEN TYPES OF AMBIGUITY (1930)
	SOME VERSIONS OF PASTORAL (1935)
	THE STRUCTURE OF COMPLEX WORDS (1951)

EMPSON WAS EDUCATED at Winchester, and Magdalene College at the University of Cambridge, England. From 1931 to 1934 he took the Chair of English Literature at Bunrika Daigaku, Tokyo, and from 1937 to 1939 was Professor of English Literature at Peking National University. From 1941 to 1946 he was the BBC Chinese Editor, and from 1953 to 1971 he was Professor of English Literature at Sheffield University.

Empson studied both mathematics and literature at Cambridge. He was the most promising pupil of I.A. Richards, who was 'aghast at his pupil's brilliance', and virtually allowed him to go his own way. At the same time, Empson read *A Survey of Modernist Poetry* by Laura Riding and Robert Graves (1927), which influenced him profoundly by helping him towards the method which he used in his first and most famous work, *Seven Types of Ambiguity*.

Originally a dissertation, this strikingly precocious work illustrates by means of deep analysis that many effects in poetry come from conscious or unconscious double meanings. His second volume of criticism, *Some Versions of Pastoral*, continues the notion of ambiguity through further literary structures, such as the double-plot in Elizabethan tragedies, the use of classical imagery in Milton's *Paradise Lost*, burlesque and fantasy. *The Structure of Complex Words*, perhaps the most difficult of his critical works, was a much more technical study of how the use of words like 'wit' and 'sense' – 'There are only about ten uses of the word in the play [*Measure for Measure*], but I think almost all of them carry forward a puzzle which is essential to thought', – can give them a less serious tone which is not implied in their sense. As Frank Kermode (1990: 119) observed, 'Recently Christopher Norris has been meditating . . . the resemblances and differences between the Empson of *The Structure of Complex Words* and the Paul de Man of *Allegories of Reading* – a sign . . . that the most neglected (and the most theoretical) of Empson's books will have something to say even to the young, who may suppose that . . . serious rhetorical analysis only got going in the late sixties.'

Empson was associated with New Criticism, an approach which flourished in the USA and the UK from the 1930s to the 1950s. It was, as Terry Eagleton (1983: 47) has noted, the ideology of a deracinated intelligentsia, who 'reinvented in literature what they could not locate in reality. Poetry was the new religion, a nostalgic haven from the alienations of industrial capitalism.' But although Empson shares their 'lemon-squeezing' analysis, he is, as Eagleton notes (1983: 51) , an opponent of their major doctrines, turning a 'cold douche of very English common sense on [their] fervid pieties'. Empson's breezy, common-sense style insists on treating poetry as a variation of everyday speech and does not shy away from taking the author's intentions into account, 'intention' being a total taboo for the New Critics. Typically Empson devoted an entire book, *Using Biography* (1984), to the idea that the work of writers as diverse as Maxwell and Joyce could be much enhanced by the study of biographical material. Indeed, his reading of T.S. Eliot's *The Waste Land* examines with some brilliance the influence of an obscure countess, whose conversation Eliot used in the early line of the poem, 'I read, much of the night, and go south in the winter.'

Empson published two volumes of poetry, *Poems* (1930) and *The Gathering Storm* (1940). His *Collected Poems* in 1955 added a few more. The strongest influence on his verse was John Donne, though he in no way resembles him. There is undoubtedly an extraordinary cleverness about his poetry, somewhat offset by his own wry notes, but his voice is entirely original, often pitching a hearty muscular tone with the elliptical presence of infinite terror: 'Ripeness is all; her in her cooling planet/Revere; do not presume to think her wasted./Project her no projectile, plan or man it; Gods cool in turn, by the sun long outlasted' (*To an Old Lady*). In old age Empson maintained his maverick status defending such authors as John Donne against impertinences, real and imagined, to a degree bordering on the zany; one of his many essays, for example, was entitled 'Donne the Space Man' (*Essays on Renaissance Literature*, 1 (1993)). But, as Kermode notes (1990: 129), for Empson the attack on Donne was a personal one: 'he reacted like a wicked animal if anybody seemed to disparage his scientist-poet'.

It is difficult to summarise Empson's place in the pattern of culture; any resemblances to other commentators such as Husserl cannot really be proved, but as someone who took an antagonistic view of Christianity and argued the positive features of Buddhism – love over pain – it is clear that he does not sit comfortably in the cosy armchair of post-war liberal life. In an essay significantly titled 'The Critic as Genius', Frank Kermode (1990: 135), whilst alive to his faults, has no doubt that Empson will last, as he concludes: 'He never loses class. And take him for all in all, we shall not look upon his like again.' Whatever the truth of this, it is undeniable that Empson was a creative writer whose talents ran to poetry and criticism rather than fiction, say, and if some of his views appear somewhat over-ingenious they have at least the virtue of humour, a feature which, as another poet put it, is 'like sunlight in the cucumber,/The innermost resource that does not fail' ('A Visit to the Dead' in Norman Cameron's *Collected Poems*, 1957).

Further reading

Kermode, F. 'William Empson: The Critic as Genius', in AN APPETITE FOR POETRY, Fontana, 1990.
Norris, C. and Mapp N. WILLIAM EMPSON: THE CRITICAL ACHIEVEMENT, Cambridge, 1993.
Eagleton, T. LITERARY THEORY: AN INTRODUCTION, Blackwell, 1983.
D.U.

ENGELS, Friedrich

Social theorist	born Germany 1820–1895
Associated with	STRUCTURAL MARXISM
Influences include	SAINT-SIMON ■ FEUERBACH ■ MORGAN
Shares common ground with	MARX ■ FIRESTONE
Main works	THE CONDITION OF THE WORKING CLASS IN ENGLAND (1845)
	THE COMMUNIST MANIFESTO (WITH KARL MARX, 1848)
	SOCIALISM: UTOPIAN AND SCIENTIFIC (1892)
	THE ORIGIN OF THE FAMILY, PRIVATE PROPERTY AND THE STATE: IN THE LIGHT OF THE RESEARCHES OF LEWIS H. MORGAN (1884)

ENGELS WAS BORN into a prosperous commercial family in the pietist community of Barmen, central Westphalia. He attended the local grammar school (gymnasium) in 1834–37, after which he began a career in the family firm, Ermen & Engels. At 17 he worked for over two years in Bremen, a free city of the German Confederation. It was here he started a life of writing, stimulated by the liberal culture he found there. He went through an intense pietist phase before involving himself in radical politics and a fierce critique of religion. He spent a year in Berlin in army service but also had access to the university, where he joined the circles of the young Hegelians. Engels met Marx in Cologne in October 1842 while *en route* to a new position in the family firm in Manchester where he found a milieu of German political exiles. From early on his life was divided between the demands of the family business and political commitment. Between 1844 and 1848 Engels moved between Barmen, Brussels and Paris, engaging with the emerging communist organisations and working with Marx in Brussels. *The Communist Manifesto*, written with Marx, was published in London in 1848. From this period until his retirement in 1869, when he moved to London, Engels lived in Manchester. He died in 1895.

Although Engels is often assimilated to Marx–Engels, his contribution to social analysis is distinctive, particularly in his analysis of gender and culture. This is exemplified in the work published after Marx's death, *The Origin of the Family, Private Property and State: In the Light of the Researches of Lewis H. Morgan*. This work introduces into the framework of the progressive sequence of modes of economic production, the basic theory known as Marxism, another sequence of a more cultural character, the series: savagery, barbarism and civilisation. Engels, following Morgan, underpins this with a further series identifying reorganisations at the level of kinship: the consanguine family, the punaluan family, the pairing family and the monogamian family. The theory reduces this to: savagery-group marriage, barbarism-pairing marriage (in the upper stage of barbarism appears polygamy), civilisation-monogamy, plus adultery. The analysis follows the historical evolution of these series through Greeks, Romans, Celts and Germans to a modern Europe, and becomes a theory which charts technological evolution as a basic aspect of cultural evolution, itself dependent on transformations of social structure (kinship, gender, class and state). There is a shift in this work, therefore, away from a strictly economic determinism based on the ideas of modes of production, to a theory which identifies cultural formations as the key to social classification. It is with civilisation that there appears the state, and class division, the first of which is gender and slavery followed by serfdom, and wage labour. The thesis of the work is that the future of civilisation will entail a political revolution (proletarian), a sexual revolution (feminist) and a cultural revolution (the disappearance of the category of culture itself).

Engels's work was surprisingly influential in the emergence of second-wave feminism, and was given particular attention by Shulamith Firestone, among others. The general basis of its anthropology and sociology have been vigorously criticised on empirical and theoretical grounds, notably its socialist evolutionist assumptions.

Further reading

Arthur, C. (ed.) ENGELS TODAY: A CENTENARY APPRECIATION, Macmillan, 1996.
Firestone, S. THE DIALECTIC OF SEX: THE CASE FOR FEMINIST REVOLUTION, Cape, 1971.

M.G.

ETZIONI, Amitai

Sociologist/communitarian	born Germany 1928—
Associated with	SOCIO-ECONOMICS ▪ COMMUNITARIANISM
Influences include	PARSONS ▪ SIMON ▪ WEBER
Shares common ground with	JOAS ▪ POPENOE ▪ THUROW
Main works	THE ACTIVIST SOCIETY (1968) THE MORAL DIMENSION (1988) THE SPIRIT OF COMMUNITY (1993)

AMITAI ETZIONI, THE first professor of the George Washington University, Washington, DC, is both a prolific sociologist and an influential social activist. As a sociologist, he has made seminal contributions to organisational sociology, sociological theory and to socio-economics – the subject which he helped establish. As a social activist he first came to prominence as an opponent of US involvement in the Vietnam War in the 1960s, before later becoming an adviser to the Carter Administration in the 1970s. He has also managed to found the Centre for Policy Research, a non-profit organisation dedicated to public policy, the Society for Advancement of Socio-economics (SASE), an interdisciplinary scholarly movement and, most recently, the Communitarian Network, which is a new social movement that draws its inspiration from his advocacy of communitarianism. Although he is not, strictly speaking, a cultural theorist, his recent work on communitarianism has, however, marked him out as one of the leading contemporary theorists of moral culture.

Etzioni first came to prominence as the author of *The Comparative Analysis of Complex Organizations* (1961), a path-breaking analysis of the use of power in organisations, which has become one of the most cited books in the sociology of organisations. According to Etzioni, those in superior positions within organisations have three sources of control. These involve the use of force or the threat of force, the allocation of economic assets and the manipulation of normative values. Working from these three types of control, he introduced his influential typology which classified organisations as being coercive, utilitarian or normative in nature.

His next major work, *The Active Society*, was among the first to provide a systematic alternative to the pre-dominant perspective of the post-war era: Talcott Parsons's structural functionalism. In hindsight, this work is of most significance for its anticipation of Etzioni's subsequent contributions to socio-economics. Although he accepted, for instance, the view that the market-based economies were both dependent on and destructive towards communities, he rejected the belief that this would inevitably lead towards economic crisis and the collapse of the market system. Rather, he argued that moral imperatives could be instilled into the market system, which would remove any destructive tendencies, with the result that the relationship between market and community could be transformed into one that was mutually beneficial.

These ideas would re-emerge 20 years later in a much more developed form in *The Moral Dimension*, which is both a critique of, and defensive reaction to, the application of neoclassical economics to areas traditionally covered by sociology. But rather than simply provide another outline of the failings of neoclassical economics, Etzioni forcefully presents the case for a new inter-disciplinary field of socio-economics. He argues that economic behaviour requires a distinct paradigm since rational choice behaviour, of the kind which is found in economic life, is a distinct subject.

His efforts at providing a theoretical basis for a socio-economic alternative to neoclassical economics were instrumental in providing the intellectual stimulus for the establishment of the Society for the Advancement of Socio-economics in 1989. This rapidly expanding group of sociologists and economists meet annually at major international conferences in Europe and North America and publishes an academic journal with the express aim of opening up new directions of enquiry into economic life.

Etzioni's recent work as a social activist led to the establishment of a new social movement, the Communitarian Network in 1990. Communitarians seek to rebuild community, to revive moral voice and civility and to balance the rights of the individual (what Etzioni terms the 'I') with their responsibilities towards the community (the 'We'). Their ultimate goal is to chart new directions for social, economic and political reform. Etzioni's most recent writings, such as his best-selling *The Spirit of Community*, have sought to present the intellectual justification for this rapidly expanding enterprise. Contrary to the claims of some liberal critics, he continues to argue that communitarianism is neither another form of majoritarian neo-puritanism nor a sectarian organisation.

Further reading

Breed, W. THE SELF-GUILDING SOCIETY, Free Press, 1972.
Ritzer, G. 'Socio-economics', WORK AND OCCUPATIONS, 17: 2 (1990), pp. 240–5.
Sciulli, D. (ed.) MACRO SOCIO-ECONOMICS, M.E. Sharpe, 1996.
P.McG.

EVANS-PRITCHARD, Edward

Social anthropologist	born England 1902–1973
Associated with	STRUCTURAL FUNCTIONALISM ■ KINSHIP AND DESCENT THEORY ■ PRIMITIVE RELIGION ■ HISTORY AND ANTHROPOLOGY
Influences include	DURKHEIM ■ SELIGMAN ■ MALINOWSKI
Shares common ground with	FORTES ■ RADCLIFFE-BROWN ■ LÉVI-STRAUSS
Main works	WITCHCRAFT, ORACLES AND MAGIC AMONG THE AZANDE (1937) THE NUER: A DESCRIPTION OF THE MODES OF LIVELIHOOD AND POLITICAL INSTITUTIONS OF A NILOTIC PEOPLE (1940) THEORIES OF PRIMITIVE RELIGION (1965)

BORN IN SUSSEX, England, Evans-Pritchard graduated in Modern History from the University of Oxford in 1924 and pursued graduate studies at the London School of Economics. He studied under C.G. Seligman, who was well known because he had been the first professional anthropologist to carry out fieldwork in Africa; his other mentor was Bronislav

Malinowski, who encouraged Evans-Pritchard to undertake 'intensive and comprehensive field studies of a particular people' (Beidelman 1974: 1). His doctoral work (completed in 1927) on the Azande of Sudan examined the relations between social organisation and religious beliefs and practices. Subsequent fieldwork on the Azande resulted in *Witchcraft, Oracles and Magic Among the Azande, The Azande* (1971) and *Man and Woman among the Azande* (1974). Evans-Pritchard's best-known work was on the Nuer of Sudan, whom he studied during the 1930s amid considerable political difficulties (*The Nuer, Kinship and Marriage among the Nuer* (1951) and *Nuer Religion* (1956)). Evans-Pritchard lectured at the London School of Economics from 1928 to 1931, the Fouad I University in Cairo from 1932 to 1935 and the University of Oxford from 1935 to 1940 and he served in the defence forces during the Second World War. In 1945 he joined Cambridge University, only to accept Radcliffe-Brown's former Chair in Social Anthropology at Oxford in 1946. This remained his primary affiliation until his retirement in 1970, although he held a range of visiting positions during his career. Among his many distinctions, Evans-Pritchard was knighted in 1971.

Evans-Pritchard was among a group of British anthropologists who forged a new approach to social anthropology that was practical and political. Known as the British School of Structural Functionalism, it dominated British anthropology for decades. Other anthropologists associated with this approach include Charles Seligman, A.R. Radcliffe-Brown, Bronislav Malinowski, Meyer Fortes, Raymond Firth, Audrey Richards and Edmund Leach. Evans-Pritchard was best known for his work on the Nuer and Azande peoples of Sudan, although he studied numerous East African peoples during the 1920s and 1930s. Arguably, he was the most important British anthropologist of his generation.

Evans-Pritchard's work emphasised the relation between forms of social organisation and religious rites and beliefs in such a way that eschewed the strictly mechanical kinship connections traced by many anthropologists. He argued that there was no distinction between primitive thought and primitive magic; rather, the latter became a means to achieve certain ends and to resolve conflict. Accordingly, Evans-Pritchard sought to understand social behaviour and cultural patterns on their own terms instead of judging them according to European criteria. For example, he included beliefs and practices of witchcraft, magic, divination and sorcery in his study of religion (or religiosity). As well as understanding cultures in terms of their traditional ways of life, Evans-Pritchard was also concerned with how groups coped with change. Because he was working at a time when British colonial rule in African states was under pressure and exacerbated by tense international politics, he inevitably became embroiled in contemporary political currents and their impact on African peoples and emerging social and political institutions (see, for example, M. Fortes and E. Evans-Pritchard (eds.), *African Political Systems*, Oxford University Press, 1940; Kuklick 1991).

Evans-Pritchard pursued his interest in understanding how primitive peoples thought by extensive and intensive studies of societies examining how thought-patterns related to social behaviour. In so doing, he questioned conventional anthropological ideas about what constituted evidence, opting for a more expansive and less rigorous definition. Above all, he attracted controversy because of his argument that religious beliefs formed a coherent and rational system when considered in their context. This enabled him to understand more comprehensively how a particular people made sense and rationalised phenomena in their everyday lives by drawing selectively on elements of religious and magic belief systems. For example, in relation to the Azande, Evans-Pritchard showed how witchcraft and divination formed a total system which allowed them to contend with misfortune and rationalise sickness and death. At an individual level, witchcraft produced a form of accountability which was then integrated into institutional practices to ensure a self-sustaining community.

His experiences among the Azande contrasted with those among the Nuer, the latter relying on lineage to organise forms of social control. Evans-Pritchard developed segmentary lineage theory, or decent theory, to account for this practice, thus laying the basis for the dominant British anthropological approach of the 1950s and 1960s. Evans-Pritchard argued that the lineage system determined the number of supporters an individual could rely on to press a claim or resolve a conflict, and that, because the system was symmetrical, that two opponents always had about equal numbers of supporters. This meant that conflicts resulted on a stand-off which was resolved by a mediator. While this theory was subsequently questioned (and more pragmatic and transient reasons offered for the mobilisation of supporters), the significance of Evans-Pritchard's work was to illustrate how particular kinship arrangements structured patterns of behaviour and their outcomes. In many ways, this approach shared elements of the structuralist approach of Lévi-Strauss.

In addition to the publications mentioned above, Evans-Pritchard published widely on a range of aspects of African social organisation and political institutions, primitive religion (*Theories of Primitive Religion*), and Islamic and Arabic culture (*The Sansusi of Cyrenaica*, 1949). He also reflected on the development of the field of social anthropology (*Social Anthropology* (the broadcast lectures, 1951; *Essays in Social Anthropology*, 1962 and *The Comparative Method in Social Anthropology*, 1963); and on the relations between anthropology and history (*A History of Anthropological Thought*, published posthumously in 1980). He also showed an interest in gender issues – unusual for a male anthropologist at the time – resulting in two books, *The Position of Women in Primitive Societies and Other Essays* (1965) and *Man and Woman Among the Azande*.

The major contributions of Evans-Pritchard were his emphasis on developing systematic yet responsive anthropological fieldwork techniques, and his application of these as the tools for intensive field studies. He also made profound advances to the use of comparative anthropological method, balancing the focus on 'scientific' approaches (exemplified by his predecessor, Radcliffe-Brown) with historical and phenomenolgical approaches. In theoretical terms, Evans-Pritchard is associated with the development of functionalism, but he was also a forerunner of structuralism; although he later advocated a return to diffusionist approaches.

Further reading

Beidelman, T.O. (ed.) THE TRANSLATION OF CULTURE: ESSAYS TO E. E. EVANS-PRITCHARD, Tavistock Publications, 1971.
Beidelman, T.O. A BIBLIOGRAPHY OF THE WRITINGS OF E. E. EVANS-PRITCHARD, Tavistock Publications, 1974.
Douglas, M. EDWARD EVANS-PRITCHARD, Fontana, 1980.
Kuklick, H. THE SAVAGE WITHIN: THE SOCIAL HISTORY OF BRITISH ANTHROPOLOGY 1885–1945, Cambridge University Press, 1991.

J.C.

EYSENCK, Hans

Psychologist	born Germany 1916–1997
Associated with	INTROVERSION/EXTRAVERSION ■ IQ TESTS ■ BEHAVIOURAL THERAPY
Influences include	PAVLOV ■ GALTON ■ BURT ■ JUNG
Shares common ground with	JENSEN ■ RUSHTON ■ LYNN ■ CATTELL
Main works	CRIME AND PERSONALITY (1964) RACE, INTELLIGENCE AND EDUCATION (1971) GENIUS: THE NATURAL BASIS OF CREATIVITY (1995)

EYSENCK WAS BORN in Berlin and observed the rise of the Nazis with thinly veiled disgust. Eysenck's rejection of the Nazi persecution of Jews earned him the soubriquet of 'white Jew'. The irony cannot have been lost on him in later years, when his work on race and IQ created public disturbances and led to him being denounced as a racist. Eysenck left Germany in 1934, moving first to France, then two years later to London. He studied psychology at the University of London under Sir Cyril Burt and was awarded his Ph.D. in 1940. On graduation he worked as a research psychologist at Mill Hill emergency hospital before returning to academic life at the University of London. He became Professor of Psychology in 1955 and founded the Psychology Department of the Institute of Psychiatry at the Maudsley Hospital.

Eysenck claimed not to have courted controversy. Yet his research findings on race and IQ, the crimogenic personality, nicotine addiction and personality – not to mention his 'conditional belief in the existence of parapsychological phenomena' – were widely seen as controversial. His fame and financial success as an author were partly due to his assiduous choice of subjects that sharply divided public opinion.

Eysenck's work falls into three groups: personality theory and measurement; behavioural genetics; and social attitudes and politics. Underlying these was his commitment to behaviourist principles. He argued that human psychology was a result of genetic predisposition and conditioning. His lifelong antipathy to Freudian psychoanalysis led him to the limits of psychotherapy: he experimented with people who had undergone psychotherapy and people with equally distressing symptoms who had not. He claimed that there was no difference in the rate of cure between the two groups. Linked to this was his argument that criminal behaviour should be understood in classical behaviourist terms. 'Short, sharp shock'-style punishment was ineffective: people with a propensity to violent crime had a personality type which was attracted to the very treatment that was meant to act as a deterrent.

Eysenck posited various dimensions of personality on the basis of his experimental work. He borrowed the terms 'extraversion" and 'introversion' from Jung's *Psychological Types*. These describe the direction of psychological interest. Extraverts are oriented to the outside world and manifest sociability and impulsiveness as dominant behavioural traits; introverts are oriented to the inner world and are characterised by shyness and caution. There is, according to Eysenck, a biological basis for extraversion–introversion in terms of cortical inhibition–excitation. He also developed a distinction between 'stable' and 'neurotic' personality types. Stable types had a low tendency to become anxious and unpredictable; with neurotic types it was the reverse. The Eysenck Personality Inventory (EPI) was devised to enable psychologists to test these traits in people.

Eysenck's research on the relationship between cancer and smoking concluded that the tendency to develop cancer was a result of personality characteristics rather than carcinogens in the cigarettes. He argued that people who smoked were more likely to have emotional problems and were therefore more likely to develop the symptoms of cancer. His findings were heavily criticised when it was discovered that his research was partly funded by a secret US tobacco fund. Eysenck denied that the funding had any bearing on his arguments.

It is the area of race that his work achieved widest notoriety. Following his former colleague Arthur Jensen, Eysenck maintained that, since there is a statistical difference in achievement of some 15 per cent between blacks and whites in IQ tests, there is a genetic difference in IQ between the 'races'. In the aftermath of the civil rights movement it was an incendiary proposition and Eysenck and Jensen were widely condemned as racists. Eysenck was criticised for allegedly misusing a measure of genetic and environmental factors influencing personality development. He later modified this position by arguing that difference may not be genetic and could be changed.

The view was consistent with Eysenck's vision: that humans are biological organisms whose actions are determined by biological (including genetic, psychological and endocrinal) elements and social (historical and interactional) elements in roughly equal measures. This understanding of the human being as a product of evolution, still carrying vestiges of millions of years of development, proved consistently unpopular with all but a small coterie of highly controversial theorists. As well as his obvious affinities with Jensen (famed for his research on the purported 'race–IQ link'), he paved the way for the likes of J. Phillipe Rushton and Richard Lynn, both of whom have proposed a racial hierarchy of intelligence.

Towards the end of his life he became interested in the psychology of genius. He claimed to identify a link between the psychopathological characteristics of creative persons and geniuses. He traced this from DNA through personality, to the special cognitive processes and qualities of genius. Eysenck argued that all geniuses are men and gender differences are genetic.

It is possible that Eysenck's own 'tough'and 'tender' personality theory could shed some light on the *causes célèbres* in which he was frequently involved: tough personalities were on the right, and relied on scientific evidence to inform their reasoning; tender-minded people were on the left, and had personality types which tended to emphasise emotional factors.

Further reading

Eysenck, Hans. REBEL WITH A CAUSE, W.H. Allen, 1990.
Howe, M.J.A. IQ IN QUESTION, Sage, 1997.
Pearson, Roger RACE, INTELLIGENCE AND BIAS IN ACADEME, Scott-Townsend, 1991.

C.R./E.C.

FANON, Frantz

Psychiatrist/social theorist	born Martinique 1925–1961
Associated with	POST-COLONIALISM ■ SOCIAL REVOLUTION
Influences include	NIETZSCHE ■ MARX ■ FREUD ■ SARTRE
Shares common ground with	DAMAS ■ ACHEBE ■ SENGHOR ■ CÉSAIRE
Main works	BLACK SKIN, WHITE MASKS (1952, TRANS. 1967) STUDIES IN A DYING COLONIALISM (1960, TRANS. 1965) THE WRETCHED OF THE EARTH (1961, TRANS. 1965)

BORN ON 20 July 1925 to middle-class parents in Fort-de-France, Martinique, Frantz Fanon was educated both at home and in France, later serving with the French Free forces fighting in Europe and North Africa during the Second World War. Following his war experiences, he trained in France as a psychiatrist and then accepted a post as *chef de service* at the Blida-Joinville Hospital just outside French-controlled Algiers. After being expelled from Algeria because of his political writings and his involvement with the National Liberation Front, Fanon was reassigned to the newly independent nation of Tunisia, where he continued his psychiatric and university teaching duties and intensified his work with the Algerian nationalists. In 1958, Fanon participated in the All-African People's Conference, and served as an ambassador to Ghana for the Algerian Provincial Government in 1960. When he died from leukaemia in 1961, his body was flown back to Tunis and eventually buried inside the then rebel-held Algeria, one year before the country won its independence.

Fanon's chief contribution to cultural theory lies in his books' depictions of the psychological and economic costs of colonisation upon native peoples and his prophetic proposal of a different future for them. In *Black Skin, White Masks*, for instance, Fanon relies on his own experiences with racism while growing up in Martinique – where he saw how the very power structure shaping his education in French language and culture also discriminated against him because he was black – and on his foundations in philosophy and literature to assess the black man's domination by white society and his inability to hide such blackness under a 'white mask' he may try futilely to put on. Like his fellow-countryman Aimé Césaire (the poet who coined the term *négritude* in reference to a resurrection of black values and, with Senghor and Damas, took a strong stance against the cultural assimilation of blacks), Fanon recognised that the acquisition of French customs and ways came at the cost of repressing his Creoleness which, though 'masked'-over, was likely to surface in unexpected, disguised forms.

In two of Fanon's other books, collections of essays translated as *Studies in a Dying Colonialism* and *Toward the African Revolution*, 1967 he reflects on his Algerian experiences and his ambitions for a unified Africa, free of the curse of racism and cultural prejudice. But the culmination of Fanon's social and political philosophy came with *The Wretched of the Earth*, which he completed during his last days while being treated at the National Institute of Health outside Washington, DC. In this book, Fanon advocates violence by the Third World poor against their oppressors, contending that political independence is a prerequisite to true economic and social change and that such violent revolution would even prove purifying to those downtrodden masses enacting it. Of course, Fanon's radical proposal had both its supporters and detractors. His defenders, including the Black Panther Party in the USA and many African nationalists, appreciated the 'shock value' of Fanon's agenda, which ultimately championed violence only as a means to a greater end: the over-throw of oppression in order to regenerate man and society. Fanon's critics, however, viewed his policy of social revolution as excessive and impractical. Some claimed that his notion of pan-African unity was utopian at best, illusory at worst, and that Fanon offered no concrete substitutes for the political and economic systems he rejected.

Nevertheless, Fanon's determination to deliver his message of revolution and regeneration has made him the Messianic prophet of Third World decolonisation. From Africa to Latin American and the Caribbean, Fanon's voice has gained a large number of sympathetic listeners, for such post-colonial peoples, as writer Albert Memmi puts it, face the same fundamental problem Fanon so adamantly expressed in his works: 'that of a confusion of identity and the difficulty of reconstructing a past and a culture with which they can identify' (*New York Times*, 14 March 1971).

Further reading

Bulhan, H. FRANTZ FANON AND THE PSYCHOLOGY OF OPPRESSION, Plenum, 1985.

Gendzier, I. FRANTZ FANON: A CRITICAL STUDY, Pantheon, 1973.

Woddis, J. NEW THEORIES OF REVOLUTION: A COMMENTARY ON THE VIEWS OF FRANTZ FANON, International, 1972.

D.B.

FEYERABEND, Paul K.

Philosopher of science	born Austria 1924–1994
Associated with	ANARCHISTIC METHOD ■ INCOMMENSURABILITY
Influences include	WITTGENSTEIN ■ POPPER ■ LAKATOS
Shares common ground with	KUHN ■ MILL ■ HABERMAS
Main works	AGAINST METHOD (1975)
	SCIENCE IN A FREE SOCIETY (1978)
	REALISM, RATIONALISM AND SCIENTIFIC METHOD. PHILOSOPHICAL PAPERS I (1981)
	PROBLEMS OF EMPIRICISM, PHILOSOPHICAL PAPERS II (1981)

F EYERABEND WAS A philosopher of science who held academic posts in the UK, notably at the London School of Economics, as well as in the USA and Europe. Beginning as a positivist, but especially influenced by Wittgenstein's later philosophy, his main work involved a repudiation of the *falsification* and *critical rationalism* of Karl Popper. In his best known works, *Against Method* and *Science in a Free Society*, he rejects the idea of a universal scientific method.

For Thomas Kuhn, the account of science which emerges is one which places great emphasis on science as a 'flesh and blood activity', and a socially located one, that cannot be understood in formalistic or simple rationalistic terms.

To those 'scientific rationalists' (particularly Karl Popper and Imre Lakatos – Feyerabend's colleagues at the LSE) who claimed to have located a universal scientific method, Feyerabend's answer was that the only universal rule in science is that 'anything goes'.

Among the main reasons why Feyerabend rejects falsificationism as a universal method is the *incommensurability* of the key concepts of competing scientific paradigms and the *theory–relativity*, of the interpretation of any potentially refuting or falsifying empirical data. Under these circumstances, Feyerabend's view is that methodological (and cultural) 'pluralism' and a 'proliferation of theories' – e.g. both Western and Eastern theories of medicine – may often be the best policy, something that is discouraged by falsificationism.

As Benvenuto (1997) suggests, Feyerabend 'sought a double emancipation of science from epistemologies, *and* of citizens from scientists'.

A major part of Feyerabend's objective, especially in his later work, was to debunk the over-rationalistic pretensions of modern science, and its 'church-like' status in modern society, together with the 'rule of experts' to which this often gives rise. His aim was to return scientific judgements to the public domain, an argument stongly based on J.S. Mill's *On Liberty*, and which finds many echoes in modern conceptions of 'counter-expertise' and resistance to a technologically driven, out-of-control society (see Beck 1992).

The frequent charge that Feyerabend's view of science promotes a dangerous 'irrationalism' is one that his frequently polemical and iconoclastic postures encouraged. However, Feyerabend was often deliberately deceptive – and playfully 'Dadaistic' – preparing traps for 'dogmatic rationalists' to mislead them into ever-more dogmatic expressions of their own position. His own general position, however, was explicitly stated by him as not intended to promote a philosophical relativism – since this is simply another form of philosophical dogmatism.

While knowledge claims are sometimes relative to a particular scientific pardadigm or, in Wittgensteinian terms, to particular *forms of life*, on other occasions more general claims to 'realism' may also be mounted. In his 1981 volumes Feyerabend talks of these ever-present contrasted possibilities in terms of 'two argumentative chains', each with benefits and each with disadvantages. Feyerabend's point throughout is that there exist no final rules of method, no single identifiable basis of either scientific or social rationality. 'Critical rationalists' like Popper or Lakatos are simply wrong to suggest otherwise, betraying their own claims to a truly 'critical' philosophy.

There is some similarity between Feyerabend's viewpoint and that of Richard Bernstein (1983), who calls for philosophical and sociological thinking to move 'beyond objectivism or relativism'. There are also similarities, if not direct links, with pragmatism (e.g. Rorty's 'irony') and with the thinking of Jürgen Habermas (especially the conception of a 'consensual' basis of knowledge and Feyerabend's Mill-ism). But, with his 'Dadaism' and his ultimate rejection of *any* system, Feyerabend remained very much his idiosyncratic and iconoclastic 'own man'. While there are resonances with 'postmodernism' in his 'anti-foundationism', there nevertheless remains something more 'traditional' about his respect for Aristotle's mix of 'empiricism' and 'rationalism'.

Further reading

Beck, U. Risk Society, Sage, 1992.
Benvenuto, S. 'Paul K. Feyerabend (1924–92): Search for Abundance', Telos 102 (Winter 1995) 1997.
Bernstein, R. Beyond Objectivism and Relativism, Blackwell, 1983.
Jary, D. 'Beyond Objectivity and Relativism: Feyerabend's "two argumentative chains" and sociology', in P. Buczkowski, The Social Horizon of Knowledge,

POZNÁN STUDIES IN THE PHILOSOPHY OF THE SCIENCES AND HUMANITIES, 22
Rodopi, 1991, pp. 39–58.

D.J.

FIRESTONE, Shulamith

Feminist theorist	born Canada 1945—
Associated with	RADICAL FEMINISM ▪ MARXIST AND UTOPIAN FEMINISM
Influences include	ENGELS ▪ FREUD ▪ DE BEAUVOIR
Shares common ground with	DWORKIN ▪ GREER ▪ ROWBOTHAM
Main work	THE DIALECTIC OF SEX: THE CASE FOR FEMINIST REVOLUTION (1970)

S HULAMITH FIRESTONE WAS involved in the New York Radical Women's Group in the late 1960s, when she edited the radical feminist journal *Notes From the First Year* (1968) and *Notes from the Second Year* (1970). In this period she wrote her key work, *The Dialectic of Sex: The Case for Feminist Revolution*, which has been reprinted a number of times, translated into other languages, and extracted in anthologies and readers of feminist thought.

The Dialectic of Sex: The Case for Feminist Revolution is an ambitious attempt to forge a radical feminist theory of culture and society. Firestone's concern is primarily with gender as a form of class, which she reads as the dynamic underlying all forms of power relationship, including social class and race. Starting from the basic Marxist idea that society is divided into social classes by the processes of economic production, she argues that society is even more fundamentally divided into gender roles in the processes of procreative reproduction. Thus gender is both the deepest division in society, and the most all-pervasive: 'It is everywhere. The division yin and yang pervades all culture, history, economics, nature itself' (p. 11). An analysis of gender accordingly needs to be radical and thoroughgoing: 'feminists have to question, not just all of *Western* culture, but the organisation of culture itself, and further, even the very organisation of nature' (p. 12).

To forge a theoretical framework adequate to this great task Firestone 'expands' or rewrites the historical materialism of Engels, redefining it as 'that view of the course of history which seeks the ultimate cause and the great moving power of all historic events in the dialectic of sex: the division of society into two distinct biological classes for procreative reproduction, and the struggles of these classes with one another' (p. 20). As in classic Marxist theory, there is a 'cultural superstructure' arising from this 'base'; the base itself, however, is necessarily different from that of the Marxist model, since the creation of gender roles in procreative reproduction is not the same as the creation of class roles in economic activity. In order to identify the gender equivalent of the economic imperative, and to measure its manifestation in the creation of gender roles, Firestone brings in a second bold reworking of a classic theory, Freudianism, which she characterises as 'the misguided feminism'. Recognising that 'Freudianism is so charged, so impossible to repudiate because Freud grasped the crucial problem of modern life: sexuality' (p. 48), Firestone nevertheless rejects to a great extent Freud's interpretational models, treating his major theories more as metaphors than literal truths. The 'need for power leading to the development of classes arises from the psychosexual formation of each individual', determined by a basic gender imbalance (p. 17). The Freudian models, read in terms of social rather than sexual power, are utilised to help develop an understanding of how such formations occur.

Alongside these adaptations of Marxist and Freudian models, Firestone draws on the American feminist tradition and de Beauvoir, on American black writers, especially Eldridge Cleaver, and on anecdotal and observed linguistic material, popular and literary sources. With these materials she makes gendered, radical feminist reinterpretations of childhood, race, love, romance, culture and cultural history, especially science (chapters 4 to 9), and concludes with a predictive *tour de force* entitled 'The ultimate revolution: demands and speculations'. Her work in each of these cultural areas repays attention; collectively these rereadings make up a wide-ranging, radical reinterpretation of culture and social formation.

The influence of *The Dialectic of Sex: The Case for Feminist Revolution* has been less extensive than might have been expected, possibly because of its fearless radicalism, more certainly because feminist cultural and political thought moved decisively away from Firestone's position in several key areas, notably ecology and the role of science, motherhood and reproductive technology. Her work, nevertheless, remains a beacon. It showed some of the ways in which familiar bodies of theoretical material might be reread from radical feminist perspectives, to yield valuable new meanings. It helped to pioneer gendered ways of reading and interpreting. And it was an important element in the process Dale Spender has called the 'restructuring of the symbolic order

... to explore and create a new symbolic framework in which women are represented' (*Man Made Language*, Routledge, 1980, pp. 228–9), a development of immeasurable significance in cultural studies and beyond.

Further reading

Delmar, R. 'Introduction' to THE DIALECTIC OF SEX, Women's Press, 1979, pp. 1–10.
Jaggar, A.M. FEMINIST POLITICS AND HUMAN NATURE, Harvester, 1983.
Magner, L.N. 'Women and the Scientific Idiom: Textual Episodes from Wollstonecraft, Fuller and Firestone', SIGNS 4 (1978), pp. 61–80.

J.G.

FISKE, John

Cultural analyst	born England 1939—
Associated with	CULTURALISM ■ POPULISM ■ SEMIOTICS
Influences include	BAKHTIN ■ VOLOSINOV ■ BARTHES ■ BOURDIEU ■ DE CERTEAU ■ FOUCAULT ■ GRAMSCI
Shares common ground with	HALL ■ McROBBIE ■ MORLEY ■ WILLIS
Main works	TELEVISION CULTURE (1987)
	UNDERSTANDING POPULAR CULTURE (1989)
	READING THE POPULAR (1989)
	POWER PLAYS POWER WORKS (1993)

FISKE BEGAN HIS career in British polytechnics (Sheffield and Wales), institutions that pioneered undergraduate cultural studies (and communication and media studies) in the UK. He subsequently worked in Australia (Curtin, Perth) and then in the USA (Wisconsin, Madison). His significance is not that of an original theorist but rather as an influential figure

in the pedagogical and analytical codification of cultural studies and its popu-
larisation as a subject on the university curriculum in mainly anglophone
countries.

The tradition of British cultural studies that was formed in the work of Hall,
Hoggart, Thompson and Williams took popular culture as a key object of
study within a popular education context, at first in adult continuing education
and latterly in 'massified' higher education. This represented a challenge to
Culture with a capital 'C' and an appreciation of popular cultural production.
While the early intentions may have been to recover people's history and to
discriminate between 'good' and 'bad' contemporary popular culture, the
tradition of British cultural studies became increasingly populist and hostile
to any sign of aesthetic and educational elitism. A nodal argument in this
development was that consumption should not be treated as the passive
moment in cultural circulation but should, instead, be regarded as active or
'producerly', in a term used by Fiske.

Fiske's notion of 'producerly' popular culture derives from Barthes's idea of
the 'writerly text', the kind of literary text which the reader is actively engaged
in the production of meaning, typically modernist and experimental forms of
writing as opposed to mainstream realism. The move made by Fiske was to
transpose such an argument from an avant-garde and literary context to a
popular media context whilst also following certain general implications of
semiotics and post-structuralism: the inevitability of differential reading and
the 'death of the author'. This was already implied in Hall's encoding/decoding
model of the television message and was applied in ethnographic audience
research by Morley.

More generally, British cultural studies rejected the 'dominant ideology
thesis' concerning manipulation of mass consciousness in favour of a more
complex and more subtle Gramscian theorisation of cultural hegemony, the
forever-shifting conditions under which social leadership is sought through
processes of negotiation with subordinate forces. To regard television, for
instance, as merely an apparatus of dominant ideology (of class, gender or
race) was too crude and failed to account for sheer popularity. Commercial
television, in particular, aims to maximise audiences. In order to do so, then,
use-values of a popular kind must be supplied. Also, following Eco's argument
on the normality of aberrant decoding, a programme with an audience of
several million has to appeal, of necessity, to a wide range of tastes and desires.

The importance of Fiske is that he took these analytical arguments developed within cultural studies to a logical and extreme conclusion. He also
raided the work of great theorists (Bakhtin, Barthes, Bourdieu, de Certeau,
Foucault) in order to give the logic of cultural populism philosophical authority. He invented something called the 'dominant culture', which is bourgeois,
racist, sexist, and so forth, and that is continually subverted by popular
appreciation of mass-produced commercial products. The folkish idea of popular culture as literally produced by 'the people' and as a residual culture

which is quite different from and more 'authentic' than mass culture is rejected as old-fashioned. In effect, Fiske promoted analytical protocols whereby endless studies could be made of how popular appropriations of mass commercial culture subvert the dominant culture and testify to the mundane creativity of subordinate groups. There is no need, from this perspective, to actually study the cultural industries and criticise the power of media conglomerates, a practice which, in any case, always recalls the pessimism and élitism of the Frankfurt School. Fiske does not, however, defend these capitalist industries and their ideologies. His rhetoric has remained Marxist in flavour. Yet his preferred mode of analysis is curiously consistent with what has been the dominant ideology throughout large parts of the world during the recent period, the neo-liberalism of the 'free market' in which the consumer is held to be sovereign. Fiske's reader or consumer is also sovereign, the agent of a 'semiotic democracy' that routinely facilitates popular resistance to the dominance of capital, patriarchy and racism.

Further reading

McGuigan, J. Cultural Populism, Routledge, 1992.
Storey, J. An Introductory Guide to Cultural Theory and Popular Culture, Harvester-Wheatsheaf, 1993.
Strinati, D. An Introduction to Theories of Popular Culture, Routledge, 1995.
J.McG.

FOUCAULT, Michel

Philosopher	born France, 1926–1984
Associated with	POWER ▪ KNOWLEDGE ▪ DISCOURSE ▪ TEXT ▪ POST-STRUCTURALISM
Influences include	NIETZSCHE ▪ HEIDEGGER ▪ BATAILLE
Shares common ground with	ALTHUSSER ▪ DELEUZE ▪ SAID
Main works	THE ORDER OF THINGS: AN ARCHAEOLOGY OF THE HUMAN SCIENCES (1966) DISCIPLINE AND PUNISH: THE BIRTH OF THE PRISON (1975) THE HISTORY OF SEXUALITY VOLUME ONE: AN INTRODUCTION (1976)

FOUCAULT STUDIED AT the élite École Normale Supériere, gaining a degree in philosophy in 1948. The primary thesis of his doctoral thesis, published in English in abridged form under the title *Madness and Civilization*, (1971) reflects an early interest in psychology, brilliantly connecting the division of madness and reason, and subsequent birth of psychiatry, to the advent of Western rationalism. Following an unhappy experience of the Communist Party (PCF) in the early 1950s, Foucault grew hostile to Marxist thought, turning instead to the philosophy of Nietzsche and Bataille. He lectured and published widely, and in 1970 was appointed Professor of 'History of Systems of Thought' at the illustrious Collège de France, a position he held until his death from AIDS in June 1984.

Foucault's work has had a vast impact on the philosophy and practice of cultural theory. *The Order of Things*, a best-seller within months of publication, charts the development of intellectual culture from the sixteenth century onwards, linking profound changes in the historical foundations of knowledge (the *episteme*) to the emergence of new forms of thought and cultural classification.

Foucault exposes the shifts in the structure of knowledge that enabled the transition from Renaissance and Classical thought to Modern culture, which, through disciplines such as political science and philology, first created Man as both a subject and object of knowledge. He calls this history of the human sciences an archaeology, a term borrowed from Kant in order to define a 'history of that which renders necessary a certain form of thought'. *The Archaeology of Knowledge* (1969) is a complex methodological reflection on this, in which Foucault addresses the theoretical relation of knowledge and history, focusing in particular on the way knowledge is ordered and used in discourse. Foucault here employs the method of archaeology to exhume what he terms 'the archive': the historical law which governs the relation of discourses, their emergence, transformation, and disappearance. This method enables the exposition of the rules which regulate and order statements, and, following this, the conditions under which certain forms of knowledge become possible.

In the early 1970s, Foucault turned from the study of culture as a pure category of thought to the historical analysis of power/knowledge relations. *Discipline and Punish* examines the powers underlying the transition of punishment from the ancient regime of physical torture to the modern micro-politics of discipline and correction. Foucault suggests that this historical separation of pain and punishment, marked by the birth of the prison and the discourse of criminal science, is indicative of a new modality of power that classifies and normalises society through soul rather than body. *The History of Sexuality Volume One* extends this critique of Enlightenment progress by treating the knowledge of sexuality produced by modern medicine, psychiatry, and pedagogy, as a resource of the contemporary power to discipline and control populations. Together these two accounts depict the domination intrinsic to modern culture but also remind us of the difference of the past, and on this basis seek to radically change our understanding of the present. The last two volumes of *The History of Sexuality*, entitled *The Use of Pleasure* and *The Care of the Self* (both 1984), recall the different sexual ethics of ancient Greece and Rome with this intention, both revealing the cultural otherness that lies within Western history.

Criticism of Foucault's work has been pursued along a number of lines. Jürgen Habermas has stressed the conservatism of Foucault's philosophical relativism, arguing that his dismissal of Enlightenment reason removes the rational foundation upon which critique itself may proceed. Historians meanwhile have questioned the accuracy of Foucault's historical documentation, whilst his failure to address the gendering of both power and the subject has been highlighted by feminist critique. These criticisms, however, have largely misunderstood the experimental and oppositional nature of his work, which today continues to direct and inform debates in all areas of cultural theory. Foucault's accounts inspired a post-structuralist approach to literary studies. This involved rereading literary texts in terms of the circuities of power within which they were transacted. Said's work exemplifies this approach. Tennerhouse uses a Foucauldian method in reading Shakespeare's drama as part of a discourse that simultaneously mimics and inscribes sovereign power.

Further reading

Habermas, J. The Philosophical Discourse of Modernity, MIT Press, 1987.
Harootunian, H.D. 'Foucault, Genealogy, History: The Pursuit of Otherness', in J. Arac (ed.), After Foucault: Humanistic Knowledge, Postmodern Challenges, Rutgers University Press, 1988.
Miller, J. The Passion of Michel Foucault, Harper Collins, 1993.

N.G.

FRANK, André Gunder

Development economist	born Germany 1929—
Associated with	Dependence Theory ■ Development
Influences include	Marx ■ Prebisch ■ Myrdal ■ Baran
Shares common ground with	Emmanuel ■ Amin ■ Wallerstein ■ Dos Santos
Main works	The Development of Underdevelopment (1966)
	Capitalism and Underdevelopment in Latin America (1967)
	Crisis: in the World Economy (1980)
	Critique and Anti-Critique (1984)

A ndré Gunder Frank was educated in the USA and at first became a conventional Chicago-trained economist. He taught in America but then went to Latin America where his ideas were changed drastically by the Cuban Revolution. He also met his wife, Marta Fuentes, who he acknowledges as a tremendous influence. Perhaps his most celebrated period was at the University of Chile between 1968 and 1973 when, as he puts it, 'the Revolution still appeared to be advancing in Latin America; and, accompanying it, [he] was still on the offensive'. The fall of Allende's democratically elected Marxist regime forced him to leave Chile in September 1973 and a little while later he took up the Chair in Development Studies at the University of East Anglia in England. He was also successively Visiting Research Fellow at the Max-Planck Institute in Starnberg, Germany and Visiting Professor of Economics at the New School for Social Research in New York. He later became Professor of Development Economics and Social Sciences and Direc- tor of the Institute for Socio-Economic Studies of Developing Regions at the University of Amsterdam.

Frank is most closely associated with dependency theory. The concept of *dependencia* can be traced to Latin American economists during the 1930s; to ECLA, the United Nations Economic Commission for Latin America estab- lished in Chile in 1948; and to the work of Raoul Prebisch, one of the founders and presidents of UNCTAD, the United Nations Council for Trade and Development. In contrast, a major academic influence, Paul Baran, was cri- tical of such institutional affiliations. Frank's own contribution was to inject the dimension of socio-political relationships into existing concerns about economic dependency between nations. Thereby he popularised this approach during the growth period of the social sciences and development studies in the 1960s. The principle of 'modernisation', the prevailing orthodoxy and the basis for post-Second World War economic reconstruction, was rejected and Frank's characteristic phrase 'the development of underdevelopment' may be seen as the contradiction of Rostow's vision of 'take-off' in the economic prospects for 'developing countries'.

Frank's argument was that European colonialism had in the first place rendered much of the world to a subservient economic position, and this position had subsequently been maintained. The purpose was to ensure a cheap supply of raw materials for Western industry from mining and planta- tion agriculture in the European colonies. These commodities were 'demand inelastic' in that their prices did not respond proportionately upwards to economic booms in the West. Additionally, they had become increasingly vulnerable to synthetic (manufactured) substitutes. Frank emphasised the role of local 'comprador élites' in the maintenance of this situation and, in its fullest expression, dependency theory conceptualises a chain of 'metropolis– satellite' relationships linking the 'New York capitalist' to the 'Third World peasant'. The proposition that this chain could only be broken by socialist revolution in the less developed countries reveals once more the influence Frank derived from the Cuban Revolution and also his rejection of Stalinist orthodoxy. It was this that caused orthodox Marxists to criticise him as a 'neo- Marxist' for apparently replacing class analysis with the metropolis–satellite concept and thereby justifying immediate revolution in the 'satellites' rather than the 'metropolis'.

Perhaps the most striking criticism of Frank's work is by Ernesto Laclau, who argues that, by regarding participation in the world economy as sufficient evidence of capitalism, an extraordinary range of exploitative relations become included – Latin American peasants, Manchester textile workers of the Indus- trial Revolution, even serfs in the Middle Ages and slaves on a Roman agricultural estate. In principle, reaction to this probably more than anything else has qualified opinions of Frank's dependency theory.

Further reading

Larrain, J. THEORIES OF DEVELOPMENT, Polity, 1989.
Seers, D. DEPENDENCY THEORY: A CRITICAL REASSESSMENT, Frances Pinter, 1981.

T.S.

FREIRE, Paulo

Philosopher/educator/theorist	born Brazil 1921–1997
Associated with	A PEDAGOGY OF THE OPPRESSED
Influences include	FANON ■ MARX ■ KOSIK
Shares common ground with	VYGOTSKY ■ DEWEY ■ BAKHTIN
Main works	PEDAGOGY OF THE OPPRESSED (1970)
	EDUCATION FOR CRITICAL CONSCIOUSNESS (1974)
	PEDAGOGY IN PROCESS: LETTERS TO GUINEA-BISSAU (1978)

BORN PAULO REGLUS Neves Freire in Recife in north-east Brazil, Freire joined the Faculty of Law at the Universidado do Recife in his early twenties. However, his work at the Social Service of Industry and his participation in the Movement for Popular Culture of Recife helped to motivate him to devote his energies to the area of adult literacy. He abandoned his work as a lawyer shortly after his first case in order to study the relationships among pupils, teachers and parents in working-class communities in north-east Brazil.

As Director of the Extension Service of the University of Recife, Freire began to work with new methods in the teaching of adult literacy. In 1962, in the town of Angicos, in Rio Grande do Norte, Freire's approach to literacy helped 300 rural farm workers learn to read and write in 45 days. By living communally with groups of peasants and workers, the literacy worker was able to identify generative words according to their phonetic value, syllabic length, and social meaning and relevance to the workers. Each word was associated with issues related to existential questions about life and the social factors which determined the economic conditions of everyday existence. Themes were then generated from these words (i.e. words such as 'wages' or 'government') which were then codified and decodified by groups of workers and teachers who worked in groups known as 'cultural circles'. Reading and writing thus became grounded in the lived cultural experiences of peasants and workers and resulted in the process of ideological struggle and revolutionary praxis – or conscientisation. Workers and peasants were able to transform their 'culture of silence' and become collective agents of social and political change. This success marked the beginning of what was to become a legendary approach in education.

Freire's internationally celebrated work with the poor began in the late 1940s and continued unabated until 1964, when a right-wing military coup overthrew João Goulart's democratically elected government. Freire was accused of preaching communism and arrested. He was imprisoned by the military government for 70 days, and exiled for his work in the national literacy campaign, of which he had served as a director. According to Freire's leading biographer, Moacir Gadotti, the Brazilian military considered Freire to be 'an international subversive', 'a traitor to Christ and the Brazilian people' and accused him of developing a teaching method 'similar to that of Stalin, Hitler, Péron, and Mussolini'. He was furthermore accused of trying to turn Brazil into a 'bolshevik country' (Gadotti 1994).

Freire's 16 years of exile were tumultuous and productive times: a five-year stay in Chile as a UNESCO consultant with the Research and Training Institute for Agrarian Reform; an appointment in 1969 to Harvard University's Center of Educational and Developmental Studies associated with the Center for Studies in Developmental and Social Change; a move to Geneva, Switzerland, in 1970 as consultant to the Office of Education of the World Council of Churches, where he developed literacy programmes for Tanzania and Guinea-Bissau that focused on the re-Africanisation of their countries; the development of literacy programmes in some post-revolutionary former Portuguese colonies such as Angola and Mozambique, motivated by personal sympathy for Amilcar Cabral's Movimento Popular Libertaçaõ de Angola (Popular Movement for the Liberation of Angola), Frente de Libertaçaõ de Moçambique (Mozambique Liberation Front) and Partido Africans para Independencia da Guinea-Bissau e Cabo Verde (African Party for the Independence of Guinea-Bissau and Cabo Verde); assisting the governments of Peru and Nicaragua with their literacy campaigns; the establishment of the

Institute of Cultural Action in Geneva in 1971; a brief return to Chile after Salvador Allende was assassinated in 1973, provoking General Pinochet to declare Freire a subversive; participating in literacy work in São Tomé and Príncipe from 1975 to 1979; his brief visit to Brazil under a political amnesty in 1979; and his final return to Brazil to teach at the Pontifiçia Universidade Catolica de São Paulo. Freire would go on to undertake literacy work in Australia, Italy, Angola, the Fiji Islands and numerous other countries throughout the world.

In São Paulo, Freire joined the socialist democratic party, Partido dos Trabalhadores (Workers' Party, or PT), which was formed in 1979. When the Workers' Party won the 1989 municipal elections in São Paulo, Mayor Luiza Erundina appointed Freire Municipal Secretariat of Education for São Paulo, a position he held until 1991. Under Freire's guidance, the Secretariat of Education set up a literacy programme for young people, MOVASP (Literacy Movement in the City of São Paulo) that contributed to strengthening popular movements and creating alliances between civil society and the state.

By linking the categories of history, politics, economics and class to the concepts of culture and power, Freire managed to develop both a language of critique and a language of hope that work conjointly and dialectically and which have proven successful in helping generations of disenfranchised peoples to liberate themselves. Freire's pedagogy of the oppressed involves not only a redistribution of material resources, but also a struggle over cultural meanings in relation to the multiple social locations of students and teachers and their position within the global division of labour.

Liberal progressives remain drawn to Freire's Christian humanism; Marxists and neo-Marxists to his revolutionary praxis and his history of working with revolutionary political regimes; left liberals to his critical utopianism; and even conservatives begrudgingly respect his stress on ethics. No doubt his work will continue to be debated by his followers – as selected aspects of his corpus are appropriated uncritically and decontextualised from his larger political project of struggling for the realisation of a truly socialist democracy – in order to make a more comfortable fit with various conflicting political agendas. Consequently, it is important to read Freire in the context of his entire corpus of works, from *Pedagogy of the Oppressed* to a recent reflection on this early work that he called *Pedagogy of Hope*, 1994.

Further reading

Gadotti, M. READING PAULO FREIRE, SUNY Press, 1994.
McLaren, P. and Lankshear, C. POLITICS OF LIBERATION: PATHS FROM FREIRE, Routledge, 1994.

McLaren, P. and Leonard, P. Paulo Freire: A Critical Encounter, Routledge, 1993.
Taylor, P. V. The Texts of Paulo Freire, Open University Press, 1993.
P.McL.

FREUD, Sigmund

Psychologist	born Moravia 1856–1939
Associated with	Psychoanalysis ■ Oedipus Complex ■ The Unconscious
Influences include	Brucke ■ Schopenhauer ■ Darwin
Shares common ground with	Jung ■ Fromm ■ Klein
Main works	The Interpretation of Dreams (1900) The Psychopathology of Everyday Life (1901) Three Essays on the Theory of Sexuality (1905)

SIGMUND FREUD ROSE to prominence in the first decade of the twentieth century as the father of psychoanalysis. He enrolled in medicine at the University of Vienna in 1872. Between 1876 and 1882 he studied the nervous systems of animals and humans under the supervision of Ernst Brucke. In 1885 he attended lectures on hypnotism by Jean Martin Charcot at Charcot's Pathological Laboratory in Paris. This solidified an interest in the unconscious which he had awoken through reading, *inter alia*, Schopenhauer, Nietzsche and Dostoevsky. He returned to Vienna and commenced medical practice upon patients with 'nervous diseases'. This specialism was seen to be situated on the frontiers of acceptable medical inquiry. Freud developed psychoanalysis against the general indifference or antipathy of established medical practitioners and in the context of virulent anti-Semitism. His success in apparently curing patients with severe psychological disorders, and his development of a theory of the mind, gradually won a devoted following. From the publication of his ground-breaking *The Interpretation of Dreams* until his death, Freud was the *paterfamilias* of the psychoanalytic movement.

He was the key figure in the professionalisation of psychoanalysis and attained worldwide acclaim as a major intellectual. With the rise of the Nazis he was forced to flee Vienna. He died in London at the outbreak of the Second World War.

Freud is a seminal, iconoclastic figure whose ideas exerted a profound influence upon the study of personality and human culture. His theory of psychodynamics divides the mind into three elements: the id, ego and super-ego. The id is located in the unconscious mind and follows the pleasure principle. That is, it seeks to gratify sexual and aggressive instincts. The sexual instinct is connected with a wider biocultural force which Freud called Eros; while aggression is connected with Thanatos, or a yearning for death. However, as Freud recognised in one of his last works, *Civilization and Its Discontents* (1939), human culture would be impossible if the id were allowed free rein. The ego develops as that part of the personality charged with the task of managing the id by conveying awareness of the real world. It operates under the reality principle and, in properly functioning human beings, ensures that the demands of the id are expressed in socially acceptable forms. The ego is governed by the super-ego. The super-ego operates as the conscience and emerges from the internalisation of the perceived standards of appropriate behaviour gleaned from one's parents.

Freud's theory is developmental and it identifies the Oedipus Complex as the crucial stage in the formation of the super-ego. The Oedipus Complex refers to the unconscious desire of little boys to kill the father and marry the mother. This desire is reconciled by recognising the threat that the father's physical power poses to the boy. The recognition of this threat is painful, but it leads to the internalisation of the perceived moral values of the father. Little girls have the opposite desire to marry the father and kill the mother. This is reconciled through the Electra Complex, though the term Oedipus Complex is usually used for both sexes.

Freud proposed that many adult neuroses have a physical basis in blocked sexuality. Through repression, sexuality is converted into anxiety. Anxiety may take the extreme forms of hysteria or neurosis through which the individual suffers a mental breakdown. Freud's superb case studies of 'Anna O', 'Little Hans', the 'Rat Man' and the 'Wolf Man' described in detail how repression was dealt with through denial, displacement, projection, transference, reaction-formation, sublimation and other defence mechanisms. However, repression is more commonly evident in slips of the tongue, forgetting people's names, and other parapraxes of everyday life.

Psychoanalytic practice locates repression through the technique of structured consultation. Free association is one method of exposing unconscious, bottled-up wishes, desires and anxieties. However, the 'royal road' to the unconscious is provided through the analysis of dreams. Freud believed that dreams are unconscious wish-fulfilments. He drew a distinction between the manifest and latent content of dreams. The manifest content generally distorted the latent content, but psychoanalytical probing is capable of unlocking the secrets of the dream world and curing neuroses.

Freud's insistence on the active operation of the unconscious in everyday life and his proposition that sexuality is the key to personality and culture are his most important legacies to cultural theory. Symbols and taboos are part of the human condition. Freud postulated a scientific method of decoding their true meaning. His later work on the psychology of religion (*Totem and Taboo* (1913), *Future of an Illusion* (1927), *Moses and Monotheism* (1938) argued that religion is a wish-fulfilling compensation for childhood weaknesses, while his essay on *Civilization and Its Discontents* (1939) explained many of the problems of civilisation in terms of the voluntary renunciation of our instinctual desires for sexual and aggressive gratification. He was criticised in his own lifetime for nurturing exaggerated hopes in the capacity of science to solve the problems of the human mind and human culture. Certainly, for all his sensitivity to symbolism, metaphor and repression in human relations there is an underlying conviction in the triumph of scientific method. His work has also been criticised by feminists for reproducing the values of patriarchal culture and legitimating the dependent status of women. Freud was certainly a man of his times and his work on female sexuality is unsatisfactory. However, the transformation in the balance of power between the sexes would probably have been impossible without his work on sexuality. He remains an indispensable figure in understanding the tracks of nineteenth- and twentieth-century Western culture.

Further reading

Gay, P. FREUD, Dent, 1988.
Roazen, P. FREUD AND HIS FOLLOWERS, Penguin 1971.
Wollheim, R. FREUD, Fontana, 1971.

C.R.

FROMM, Erich

Psychoanalyst/social philosopher	born Germany 1900–1980
Associated with	PSYCHOANALYSIS ■ CRITICAL THEORY
Influences include	FREUD ■ MARX
Shares common ground with	MARCUSE ■ REICH ■ HORNEY
Main works	THE FEAR OF FREEDOM (1942) THE SANE SOCIETY (1955) THE ART OF LOVING (1956)

B ORN INTO AN orthodox Jewish family, Erich Fromm studied philosophy, psychology and sociology at the universities of Frankfurt and Heidelberg under Karl Jaspers and Alfred Weber. He received psychoanalytic training in his mid-twenties and in 1930 became one of the first members of the Institute für Sozialforschung in Frankfurt – out of which emerged the Frankfurt School. Fromm remained a member of the Institute, teaching and researching in psychoanalysis, throughout the 1930s, during which time the school relocated to New York to escape the Nazi regime. He left the Institute in 1939 following disagreement over the principles and critical implications of Freudianism, thereafter developing a humanist position that was at odds with the 'negative dialectics' of the Frankfurt School.

Erich Fromm's work represents a lifelong attempt to marry psychoanalytical insights into the roots of human behaviour with Marxian social and political analysis. He can thus be seen as one of the most influential Freudo-Marxists, along with thinkers like Reich, Adorno, Horkheimer and Marcuse. In the early 1930s his synthesis drew on a fairly conventional interpretation of Freud which stressed the theory of libidinal drives and their modification in the family structure by the socio-economic conditions analysed in Marx's Historical Materialism. This 'Analytical Social Psychology' led to one of the Frankfurt School's most important collective project of the 1930s – the 'Studies on Authority and the Family'. However, from the mid-1930s Fromm began to criticise the Freudian stress on sexual drives, eventually substituting for these his own theory of 'humanistic drives' related to the cultural–existential needs of the whole person. This theory was presented in Fromm's first and perhaps most important book, *The Fear of Freedom*. Here he argued, via analyses of social–cultural formations from the Protestant Reformation through to the Nazi regime, that modern individuals try to escape from their existential freedom by placing themselves in relations of dependency on authoritarian structures.

The Fear of Freedom, along with *Man of Himself* (1946) and *The Sane Society*, were celebrated alongside texts by Karen Horney and Harry Stack Sullivan as major works in the emerging 'neo-Freudian' tradition of American psychoanalysis. However, they were rejected as 'revisionism' by more orthodox Freudians, including Fromm's erstwhile Frankfurt School colleagues. Both Horkheimer and Adorno denounced Fromm's abandonment of the libido theory, which they continued to view as the most radical political aspect of psychoanalysis. In the epilogue to his own reinterpretation of Freud, *Eros and Civilization* (1956), Herbert Marcuse attacked Fromm's 'neo-Freudian revisionism' and its associated humanism, as a retreat from the radical materialism of both Freud and Marx into a socially-conformist idealism and moralism. This attack led to a celebrated series of exchanges between Marcuse and Fromm (the 'Fromm–Marcuse debate') in the journal *Dissent* which helped define the cultural politics emerging in the early 1960s around the themes of critical theory, therapy and social/cultural revolution.

A broad ethical, socialist–humanism was to characterise Fromm's mature output. He drew particularly on Marx's early 'humanistic' writings to develop a wide-ranging critique of the alienation of the individual in modern capitalist societies and this critique gradually incorporated insights from other humanistic traditions in philosophy and religious thought, particularly Zen Buddhism. In a series of books he treated cultural–psychological themes such as consumerism, violence and destructiveness, personal identity, the roots of nationalism, and human love relations. Though never matching the theoretical sophistications of some of the other Critical Theorists, Fromm's contribution to the understanding of contemporary culture is perhaps best illustrated in these popular and accessible works which were to reach wide audiences (the best-selling *The Art of Loving* running to over 1.5 million English-language copies by 1970).

Further reading:

Funk, R. ERICH FROMM: THE COURAGE TO BE HUMAN, Continuum, 1982.
Jay, M. 'The Frankfurt School's Critique of Marxist Humanism', SOCIAL RESEARCH 39, No. 2, (1972), pp. 285–305.
Wiggershaus, R. THE FRANKFURT SCHOOL: ITS HISTORY, THEORY AND POLITICAL SIGNIFICANCE, Polity, 1995.

J.T.

FUKUYAMA, Francis

Political scientist	born USA 1953—
Associated with	END OF HISTORY
Influences include	HEGEL ▪ KOJÈVE ▪ NIETZSCHE ▪ WEBER, M
Shares common ground with	BELL ▪ BELLAH ▪ BERGER
Main works	'THE END OF HISTORY' (1989)
	THE END OF HISTORY AND THE LAST MAN (1992)
	TRUST: THE SOCIAL VIRTUES AND THE CREATION OF PROSPERITY (1995)
	'Women and the Evolution of World Politics' IN FOREIGN AFFAIRS (1998)

ORN IN MANHATTAN of Japanese parents, Fukuyama studied classics and then comparative history at Yale. He studied in Paris under Barthes and Derrida before moving to Harvard, where he specialised in Middle Eastern and Soviet politics. After a period working for the Rand Corporation, Fukuyama was appointed deputy director of the US State Department's planning staff under the Reagan Administration. He returned to the Rand Corporation as one of the world's most discussed thinkers – due mainly to a single article (later expanded into a Penguin/Viking book).

Fukuyama's 'The End of History' appeared in 1989 in the Washington journal *National Interest*. At the time, the author was a government policy worker. But such was the impact of his argument that Fukuyama became an instant world celebrity. Quite apart from the provocative title, the inspiration for which came from Kojève, the essay contained an intellectually interesting synthesis. Adapting Hegel's conception of history as a dialectical process, progressing towards some end-point, Fukuyama argued that the end of the cold war provided irrefutable proof of the superiority of capitalism and the liberal democracy in which it prospers. While Hegel's philosophy had been widely interpreted as anticipating a communist ideal, Fukuyama insisted that history had reached its culmination in a mature capitalism. The ascension of the USA was, he suggested, aided by technological power (specifically, micro-electronics) rather than military might.

Leftwing theorists had appropriated some of Hegel's views, but distorted his overall project by identifying Soviet communism as the ideal. Fukuyama placed great store in technological progress and believed that the accumulation of knowledge was itself a guiding influence on history. Inexorably, progress has been towards capitalism and liberal democracy. Fukuyama gives the example of technology undermining political systems when he writes of the American micro-electronics industry which precipitated the demise of the communist system.

In *Trust* Fukuyama switched his focus to the cultural characteristics – what he calls 'social capital' – of nations and their role in the productive process. He argues that a high degree of trust is essential to the kind of economic flexibility that promotes growth and cites the examples of Japan, China and other East Asian economies that have flourished at least in part through their cultural traditions. Fukuyama is careful to note the cultural differences between East Asian societies. Like Weber, he remained sensitive to the pivotal function of culturally-transmitted ideas in economic life.

In another work, 'Women and the evolution of world politics' (*Foreign Affairs* 77:5 (1998) pp. 24–40), Fukuyama marshalled the support of socio-biologists to suggest that underlying biologically grounded drives should be *contained* through the institutions, laws and norms allowed by market economics. 'Socialism, radical feminism, and other utopian schemes do not: they try to change nature' (p. 40). The surprising element of this argument is Fukuyama's willingness to compare human and primate behaviour, and extrapolate from one to the other. In a way, he suggests that his favoured liberal democracy is a natural accommodation. He also argues against social interpretations of gender differences and for a recognition of the ineluctable biological differences that may, in some circumstances, predispose women to be better political leaders.

'Take human and particularly male desire to dominate a status hierarchy, which people share with the primates. The advent of liberal democracy and modern capitalism does not eliminate that drive, but it opens up many more peaceful channels for satisfying it,' wrote Fukuyama, again underlining his commitment to the liberal democratic ideal championed in *The End of History*.

Further reading

Arthur, C. 'Has History Ended?', RADICAL PHILOSOPHY, 76, 1996.
Curtis, J. 'After History: Francis Fukuyama and His Critics', CANADIAN JOURNAL OF POLITICAL SCIENCE, 28: 3, 1995.
McCarney, J. 'Shaping Ends: Reflections on Fukuyama', NEW LEFT REVIEW, 203, 1993.
Udick, R. 'A Letter from History: Mills and Fukuyama', SOCIALIST REVIEW, 23: 4, 1993.

E.C.

GADAMER, Hans-Georg

Philosopher	born Germany 1900—
Associated with	HERMENEUTICS
Influences include	KANT ■ HEGEL ■ HUSSERL ■ HEIDEGGER
Shares common ground with	RICOEUR ■ RESCHER
Main works	TRUTH AND METHOD (1959)
	PHILOSOPHICAL HERMENEUTICS (1976)
	PHILOSOPHIC APPRENTICESHIPS (1985)

G ADAMER STUDIED IN Marburg and his teachers included Heidegger. He went on to hold positions at Marburg, Leipzig, Frankfurt and Heidelberg before retiring in 1968. Nine of ten volumes of his collected works have appeared, but the English translations of his total output do not yet encompass them.

For Gadamer, propositions and interpretations issue from their own 'hermeneutic situation'. Most of his cited work on hermeneutics occurred in his Heidelberg period (1949–1968), after having held the Rectorship at Leipzig after the Second World War. However, despite the influence of Heidegger, Gadamer's work was lucid and clear. He was against special philosophic language understood only by philosophers; and rather sought to view philosophy as a form of poetry.

Understanding, for Gadamer, is historically and linguistically mediated. There is, in short, a pre-understanding; and the Enlightenment was wrong to refuse prejudice, having as it were its own prejudice against prejudice. Nor can there be an 'empathy' created, from our own intellectual resources, for the traditional texts we interpret. We cannot recuperate the past and, to use the words of a later thinker, Edward Said, we are in danger of orientalising it, as well as the thought of other cultures.

Truth and Method criticised the positivism embedded in the methodologies of pure or natural sciences; nor is Gadamer himself an inventor of methodology for the social sciences. Yet social scientists have sought to apply his work to their own. The difficulty here is that Gadamer's own analysis is centred on written texts and even works of art. If philosophy was to be written as a form of poetry, then its subject matter often was poetry itself. The question this raises is whether hermeneutical understanding can extend beyond the results of actions of creation, to other social actions. The text as model, however, for actions beyond text, has continued to fascinate social scientists who see that action should be understood hermeneutically. Thus, although Gadamer never sought to create such a methodology, proto-methodologies are put forward in his name, and not always with the clarity he sought.

What Gadamer did see, based on the analysis of texts, in particular written texts, was a view of language that was, despite all apparent differences in languages or the incommensurability of language games, language having in fact a constitutive, mediating and integrative character that transcends itself and leads to new understanding. Gadamer emphasises both questions and answers. Thus any statement is an answer to a question and every question stems from a background knowledge, so every question is itself an answer. This mediation of understanding by pre-understandings is at the heart of his work. The need for hermeneutic understanding is to break through the cycle of questions that are answers, to come to a genuine speaking that is not a giving of prearranged signals. Gadamer wished to see the merging of linguistic circles, and for this to happen in full complexity. He did not relish the levelling of language in an industrial and advertising age to a technical sign-system involving labels and the names of technological techniques – the result, to use other vocabulary again, of a certain commodification of language itself.

For Gadamer, communication and true understanding is possible, since there is no captivity in language. Simultaneously, there is not necessarily a method in it either. The more we speak, and the more we speak to each other, the more possible becomes that moment when, by words, we suddenly 'know'. Dialogue becomes then infinite and its inner, true meanings at last made possible.

Gadamer is important at the close of the century because of a life's work that questions the assertive certainties that have led to extremities of barbarism. On the other hand, he is not a thinker who revels in fragmentary evidences of difference. In his world, prefiguring Habermas's 'ideal speech' (although he and Habermas have significant differences), deeper understandings, i.e. not dependent on pre-understandings, are desirable and possible. In this light, finally, the linguistic circles of the world suggest the possibility of something universal, a moment of art. What is more implicit here is that the moment of understanding is purely aesthetic. In the 21st century, Gadamer's work will be seen as a means of integrating the understandings and moments of the present, alongside linguistically-experimental writers like James Joyce and his moment of 'epiphany', and Walter Benjamin's interrogative Kabbalistic angel who dives deeply.

Further reading

Baynes, K., Bohman, J. and McCarthy, T. (eds.) AFTER PHILOSOPHY: END OR TRANSFORMATION?, MIT Press, 1987.
Misgeld, D. and Nicholson, G. (eds.) APPLIED HERMENEUTICS: HANS-GEORG GADAMER ON EDUCATION, POETRY AND HISTORY, SUNY Press, 1992.
S.C.

GALBRAITH, John Kenneth

Economist/social critic	born Canada 1908—
Associated with	KEYNESIANISM ▪ LIBERALISM ▪ SOCIAL DEMOCRACY
Influences include	KEYNES ▪ MILL ▪ SMITH, A. ▪ VEBLEN
Shares common ground with	GARNHAM ▪ MILLS ▪ WILLIAMS
Main works	THE AFFLUENT SOCIETY (1958) THE NEW INDUSTRIAL STATE (1967) THE CULTURE OF CONTENTMENT (1992)

G
ALBRAITH WAS PROFESSOR of Economics at Harvard and worked for the Democratic presidential administrations in the 1940s and 1960s. He was an adviser to John F. Kennedy and US Ambassador in India from 1961 to 1963. Galbraith has continued to write and speak influentially on questions of economics and social justice well into old age. Schooled in Keynesian economics, he took an unorthodox line on the costs of economic growth in the 1950s and 1960s and was a fierce critic of the neo-liberal economics and politics of the 1980s and 1990s.

It is unusual to include an economist in a book on cultural theory yet, rare amongst economists, Galbraith has always displayed a keen interest in the relations between culture, understood in the anthropological sense of ways of life, and political economy. In this regard he may be seen in line of succession from Adam Smith, the most frequently cited founder of modern economics.

Smith was a Professor of Moral Philosophy at Glasgow University in the eighteenth century. Although now seen as the prophet of free-market economics, Smith himself was actually concerned with ethics and social justice as well as with economic success, as is Galbraith. Other influences on Galbraith include Keynes, the theorist of state intervention in mid-twentieth century capitalist economies, and Veblen, an early figure of American economics whose *Theory of the Leisure Class* was a pioneering examination of consumer culture.

Galbraith's most famous book is *The Affluent Society*, written during the post-Second War boom in the USA and Western industrial societies generally. He raised questions about the social and cultural costs of rapid economic growth and pointed particularly to the coexistence of 'private affluence' and 'public squalor'. High wages and expanded consumption had not been accompanied by sufficient expenditure on the collective infrastructures and fabric of a civilised society. The American Dream was too individualistic and untrammelled capitalism created sharp inequalities, from great wealth to extreme poverty, in the most affluent society in the world and in the world at large.

In *The New Industrial State*, Galbraith discussed the newly formed 'technostructure', drawing attention to how knowledge workers were of increasing importance in modern corporate America. This is related in Galbraith's reasoning to the rise of a 'new class', which he viewed sanguinely in the 1960s as a much expanded middle-class stratum of managers and technocrats of one kind or another who were benefiting from higher levels of education and opportunity; and whose culture was that of a leisured consumption in which 'lifestyle' was of prime concern. Yet still there remained pockets of dire poverty and social exclusion even in the most favoured of societies, which, in Galbraith's view, the state should ameliorate, a view held much more commonly in European social democracies than in the USA.

Galbraith returned to the theme of majority affluence and minority poverty in the 1990s, most notably in *The Culture of Contentment*. The neo-liberal political economy of the Reaganite era had exacerbated the unjust trends that Galbraith had identified many years previously. A fully-fledged 'underclass' had been created, largely composed of racialised and migrant groups, who suffered from the reduction of public funding and social provision while still being functional to the 'culture of contentment', by which Galbraith meant the ways of life and taken-for-granted assumptions of the comfortable middle class. The underclass, when not unemployed, provides casual and low-paid labour in the service of the comparatively affluent, in effect, supporting their privileged lifestyles. On the other hand, the contented have become remarkably stingy. They have revolted against the taxation necessary for social amelioration, believing they were receiving their just rewards and seeing the underclass as the undeserving poor. American society was thus sharply divided, not only economically, but culturally. In these circumstances the contented and the underclass view one another with mutual incomprehension and hostility. In effect, Galbraith analysed the conditions which contributed to, for instance, the Los Angeles riots of 1992. His general argument was that poverty is produced by the well-off, not only in the USA but throughout the world in debt dependency. So, Galbraith, the liberal economist and pillar of the Democratic party establishment, was still making arguments about the cultural and political dimensions of social economy when many Marxist and post-Marxist social and cultural critics had turned their attention elsewhere to, for instance, the cultural resistances of shopping.

Further reading

Campbell, B. GOLIATH: BRITAIN'S DANGEROUS PLACES, Methuen, 1993.
Davis, M. CITY OF QUARTZ: EXCAVATING THE FUTURE IN LOS ANGELES, Verso, 1990.
Therborn, G. 'The Two-Thirds, One-Third Society' in S. Hall and M. Jacques (eds.), NEW TIMES: THE CHANGING FACE OF POLITICS IN THE 1990S, Lawrence & Wishart, 1989.

J.McG.

GARFINKEL, Harold

Sociologist	born USA 1917—
Associated with	ETHNOMETHODOLOGY ■ INDEXICALITY ■ PRACTICAL ACCOMPLISHMENT
Influences include	PARSONS ■ HUSSERL ■ SCHUTZ
Shares common ground with	CICOUREL ■ SACKS ■ GIDDENS
Main works	STUDIES IN ETHNOMETHODOLOGY (1967) 'The Conditions for a Successful Degradation Ceremony' AMERICAN JOURNAL OF SOCIOLOGY, 61 (1956), pp. 240–4 ETHNOMETHODOLOGICAL STUDIES OF WORK (1986)

T HE RESEARCH AND writings of Garfinkel have had a major impact on sociology and linguistics. A graduate student under Parsons at Havard's Department of Social Relations, and initially influenced by structural–functionalism, Garfinkel rejected the analytical subordination of the social actor involved in systems theory. His innovative, some would say 'revolutionary', view of social action – formulated mainly from his home base at the University of California at Los Angeles – sparked off the new movement in US and European sociology known as ethnomethodology. For a time this new movement made great waves and divided some sociology departments into warring camps: 'conventional sociology' and the new ethnomethodological viewpoint. In time the more extreme confrontational stances lessened, but Garfinkel's ethnomethodology has had a lasting influence on the ways sociologists view social research and social theory.

Influenced especially by the work of the social phenomenologist Schutz, Garfinkel's contention in *Studies in Ethnomethodology* was that conventional sociology had neglected the study of the reasoning procedures and social competence (the 'ethnomethods' or 'members' methods') possessed by ordinary members of society employed by them in the ordinary conduct of their everyday social lives. According to Garfinkel, the common-sense knowledge possessed by actors that conventional sociologists have simply taken for granted (used merely as a 'resource') must become the explicit 'topic' of research. Garfinkel's injunction is to regard each social event, including what we conventionally understand as 'facts', as 'practical accomplishments'.

In a well-known early paper, 'The conditions for a successful degradation ceremony', Garfinkel identified the communicative work required to transform a person's entire status and identity to something much lower. The guilty offender in a court trial, for example, is reduced to a degraded status as 'murderer' or 'thief'. According to Garfinkel, the existence of such ceremonies is in 'dialectical contrast' to, and above all demonstrates, the 'ultimately valued, routine orders of personnel and action' within society.

More generally, Garfinkel demonstrated the importance of 'members' methods' by analysing the outcome of informal 'experiments' in which he encouraged his students to act as lodgers in their own homes. According to Garfinkel, what these and similar socially disruptive 'breaching' experiments clearly demonstrate is the existence of the 'taken-for-granted (the 'tacit') assumptions' underlying social interaction and also the 'indexicality' (the possession of meaning only in context) and the essential incompleteness of members' 'accounts' of their social actions. This essential incompleteness of accounts was dubbed 'the et cetera principle' by Garfinkel. Accounts serve particular or 'occasioned' purposes and are always merely good enough for the purposes at hand. Along with the member's creative capacity, these features of members' accounts are seen as invalidating the naïve 'scientific' stance of much conventional sociology which is seen as treating the social actor merely as a 'cultural dope', taking surface accounts as 'literal' and in general underestimating the complexity of social reality. The attempt of conventional sociology to create a science of society merely from a surface analysis of social accounts as in social surveys or the scaling of attitudes is seen as misconceived.

A significant example of the application of the ethnomethodological viewpoint to a consideration of the research methodologies of orthodox sociological research is Cicourel's *Method and Measurement in Sociology* (1964). What this work provides is a thoroughgoing critical analysis (and for the most part a demolition) of the assumptions of much statistical and mathematical work in social science, in the light of the situated, judgemental and negotiated character of all social categorisation which ethnomethodological studies exhibited. With its attacks on the basis of 'official statistics' and its castigation of 'measurement by fiat', the book amounted to a root-and-branch critique of the assumptions of dominant survey and questionnaire-based sociologies and measurement scaling.

An especially significant sub-field of ethnomethodology is conversation analysis, especially the work of Emanuel Schegloff and Harvey Sacks. Making extensive use of the careful recording and detailed transcription of ordinary conversation, ethnomethodologists have sought to reveal the more universal recurring members' methods involved in talk, e.g. the organised pattern of 'openings' and closings' or of 'turn-taking'. Other significant areas of ethnomethodological research include studies of work.

In addition to the work of Cicourel and Sacks a large number of works adopting and disseminating a broadly ethnomethodological stance on theoretical or research issues and illustrating its widespread influence include Silverman (organisation analysis), Woolgar (sociology of science), Coulter (theory of mind) and Giddens (general theory). The influence of ethnomethodology has been especially potent in loosening the previous stranglehold on much sociological thought of the 'positivist' legacy of Durkheim (as well as Giddens, see also Douglas 1967). However, although ethnomethodology was at first vaunted as an 'alternative' to conventional sociology, the insights drawn from it have in many instances been incorporated into more mainstream approaches, notably in the work of Giddens and in new ways of undertaking social research.

Further reading

Cicourel, A. METHOD AND MEASUREMENT IN SOCIOLOGY, Free Press, 1964.
Douglas, J. THE SOCIAL MEANINGS OF SUICIDE, Princeton University Press, 1967.
Giddens, A. NEW RULES OF SOCIOLOGICAL METHOD, Hutchinson, 1976.
Heritage, J. GARFINKEL AND ETHNOMETHODOLOGY, Polity Press, 1984.

D.J.

GARNHAM, Nicholas

Political economist/media analyst	born England 1937
Associated with	MARXISM ▪ POLITICAL ECONOMY ▪ SOCIAL DEMOCRACY
Influences include	ADORNO ▪ HABERMAS ▪ WILLIAMS
Shares common ground with	BOURDIEU ▪ GOLDING AND MURDOCH ▪ MIEGE ▪ SCHILLER ▪ SMYTHE
Main works	'CONTRIBUTION TO A POLITICAL ECONOMY OF MASS-COMMUNICATION' (1979) AND 'PUBLIC POLICY AND THE CULTURAL INDUSTRIES' (1983), BOTH REPRINTED IN N. GARNHAM, CAPITALISM AND COMMUNICATION (1990) 'THE MEDIA AND THE PUBLIC SPHERE' (1986) REPRINTED IN C. CALHOUN (ED.), HABERMAS AND THE PUBLIC SPHERE (1992)

G arnham worked as a documentary film-maker for the BBC in the 1960s and wrote a book with the television presenter Joan Bakewell, *Television: The New Priesthood*, at that time, which was based on interviews with broadcasting professionals. He subsequently entered academia at what was then the Polytechnic of Central London (PCL; now Westminster University), and where he remains Professor and Director of the Centre for Communication and Information Studies. With colleagues at the PCL in 1979, Garnham founded the journal *Media, Culture and Society*, the leading media studies journal published in the UK and one of international renown. Garnham's most important writings are in essay form and were mainly published first in the journal which is so strongly associated with his particular version of the political economy of culture perspective. He has also been an activist on the left of the Labour Party, working on issues concerning media and cultural policy.

Unusually in Marxist media and cultural theory, Garnham has held to the base-superstructure model of classical Marxism. In his seminal 'Contribution to a Political Economy of Mass-Communication' Garnham spelt out the terms of his analytical framework explicitly in opposition to the then influential Althusserial/Lacanian theory propounded by the journal *Screen*. Although generally considered a form of Marxism, this theoretical formation had dispensed with economic analysis and was preoccupied with questions of ideology and subjectivity. Against that current of thought, Garnham sought to recover a more classically Marxist approach to the critical study of media and culture. According to him, the fundamental struggle for material survival has ontological priority over culture. Cultural production becomes possible when a surplus of wealth exists above that required to fulfil the basic bodily needs of food, protection and shelter.

Cultural production is itself material in two main senses: first, that it involves the making of artefacts and, second, because its organisational forms are shaped by the general economic processes and structures of the society. Further, cultural production is economically and socially significant for two main reasons. First, cultural institutions are themselves economic entities – publishing houses, television companies, and so on. Second, culture is the medium of social and economic reproduction. For example, News Corp operates capitalistically in two ways: first, in particular, because it is a profit-making firm and, second, because it performs an ideological role for capital and its social organisation in general.

Garnham sought to escape the accusation of functionalism by arguing that capitalist cultural production has contradictory features. As with all commodities, the cultural commodity has use value as well as exchange value and this is given particular force, in the case of cultural commodity, by its meaning-bearing properties. The cultural commodity, for instance, is comparatively easy to pirate: so there is constant pressure on capital valorisation in cultural industries which is only partly controlled by the laws of copyright. Again, in classically Marxist terms, Garnham was stressing the contradictions between the forces and relations of production and particularly how they are exacerbated by technological motivation. From a policy-oriented point of view, he has emphasised the importance of understanding how the cultural industries work and, hence, the strategic points of entry for social-democratic politics and regulation, such as subsidising small cultural businesses and facilitating the distribution of cultural products that challenge the prevailing ideologies of capitalist societies. Garnham is a realist in theory and a pragmatic reformist in politics.

In his later work, Garnham has defended the institution of public service broadcasting by relating its cultural and political role to the Habermasian notion of the public sphere. Contrary to postmodernist thought, he, like Habermas, has insisted upon the continuing relevance and incomplete realisation of the Enlightenment project of universal rationality and justice. As the powers of transnational media conglomerates grow and markets become increasingly globalised, Garnham has argued for an international public sphere in a way which recalls Kant's ideal of world citizenship. In spite of his professed materialism, then, Garnham has been seen as an idealist both epistemologically and ethically. However, similarly to Habermas, Garnham is no doubt quite well aware of his vulnerability on this count and self-conscious about the 'Pasculian bet' he places on the possibility of democratically accountable communications in a world ruled by 'market forces'.

Further reading

Golding, P. and Murdock, G. 'Culture, Communications and Political Economy', in J. Curran and M. Gurevitch (eds.), MASS MEDIA AND SOCIETY, 2nd edn, Arnold, 1996.
Miege, B. THE CAPITALIZATION OF CULTURAL PRODUCTION, International General, 1989.
Mosco, V. THE POLITICAL ECONOMY OF COMMUNICATION, Sage, 1996.

J.McG.

GATES, Henry Louis

Literary theorist	born USA 1950
Associated with	'RACE' ■ BLACK CULTURE
Influences include	DU BOIS ■ AFRICAN FOLKLORE
Shares common ground with	FOUCAULT ■ WEST ■ BAKER
Main works	BLACK LITERATURE AND LITERARY THEORY (ED., 1984)
	'RACE', WRITING AND DIFFERENCE (ED., 1985)
	THE SIGNIFYING MONKEY: A THEORY OF AFRICAN-AMERICAN LITERARY CRITICISM (1988)

HENRY LOUIS GATES Jnr. grew up in the time of American desegregation. He has degrees from Yale and Cambridge and is presently Chairman of African-American Studies at Harvard University.

Throughout his work, Gates's aim has been to expose the prejudicial nature of the literary tradition. He sees the literary canon (which is mainly male and Western) and the pedagogy which it supports as a mechanism for political control. Gates proposes that literacy is the determining factor on matters such as acknowledged access to Reason and History, and, as a result, to fully-fledged membership of humankind. He defines literacy as

income-dependent and therefore an emblem that links economic subordination to racial alienation.

From this position, he articulates the paradox of presenting a 'black self' in
a linguistic tradition where blackness is a figure of absence and negation.

He vehemently dismisses the current dominant modes of analysing texts
from the African diaspora. His criticism encompasses issues of 'perfectability'
in Western terms, and the notion that African texts are in some way the 'truth'
about African experience, rather than being local, specific and style-driven.
Instead, Gates proposes an appreciation of black literature that does not treat
the bodies of work solely in ethnographic or historical terms.

Gates is not only concerned with revealing how text-specific literary theory
is, but also in discerning how suitable it proves to be for an investigation of
texts from the African diaspora. Gates chronicles his own development from
having attempted mastery of the Western literary tradition, to his rejection of
it, for the most part, in favour of theories indigenous to black culture. He
allows black traditions (and, in particular, their vernacular forms) to speak for
themselves, rather than applying them to other less fitting and appropriated
modes of analysis.

He cites the signifyin(g) monkey in its various incarnations across the world
(including the African-American dozens game) as deriving from Èsù-Elégbára
and Legba in the mythology of the Yorubo and Fon respectively. This figure
offers mediation, but mainly through the use of tricks. In a series of myths
featuring a lion and the signifyin(g) monkey, the monkey undermines the lion's
hubris by exploiting his inability to read the figurative as anything other than
the literal. For Gates, this strategy can be used to redress an imbalance of
power and to clear and occupy its space.

Among its many meanings, signifyin(g) incorporates evading, eluding,
deriding without direct implication, employing linguistic dexterity as a means
of mastery, and a playing of repetition and reversal. It can be homage, pastiche
or improvisation, as well as mockery. Indeed the very nature of signifyin(g)
precludes any single or fixed meaning for the word. Instead, it hints at the
importance of multiplicity, open-endedness and the indeterminacy of position
and meaning. Signifyin(g) works to make the literal seem figurative (to dismantle harmful 'truth' fallacies) and to render the figurative literal (to com-
plicate and assault the canon). It produces endless signifiers for a signified,
extending the implications of the original to include what it sees as previously
having been wrongly excluded, rather than destroying meaning. It replaces
semantics with rhetoric.

By editing several anthologies, Gates has expressed the need for plurality in
critical attitudes towards 'race', rather than an all-encompassing agenda.
Perhaps the most acclaimed of these collections is *'Race', Writing and Difference*. By rendering 'race' in inverted commas, he insists that the concept is not
a priori, not an objective term of classification, but a trope of difference whose

application is distinctly arbitrary. 'Race' posits a false, generalised and pre-determined set of clauses that assumes a particular physically defined group to share certain 'metaphysical' characteristics.

Gates has not only worked to create a more responsive mode of examining texts from the African diaspora, but has also brought to a wider audience within the Western literary tradition edited selections of these works, including an anthology of slave narratives.

Further reading

Cox, S. 'The Two Liberalisms', AMERICAN LITERARY HISTORY 6: 3, Fall, 1994, pp. 453–66.

K.D.

GEERTZ, Clifford

Cultural anthropologist	born USA 1923—
Associated with	ETHNOGRAPHY ▪ HERMENEUTICS ▪ SEMIOTICS
Influences include	MALINOWSKI ▪ RYLE ▪ WEBER
Shares common ground with	GIDDENS ▪ GOFFMAN ▪ WILLIS
Main works	THE INTERPRETATION OF CULTURES (1973) LOCAL KNOWLEDGE (1983) WORKS AND LIVES (1988)

GEERTZ WAS TRAINED as an anthropologist at Harvard and taught at the University of Chicago before moving to Princeton, where he is Professor of Social Science in the Institute of Advanced Study. He conducted fieldwork in South-East Asia, most notably in Bali, Indonesia in the 1960s, and has written influentially on the methodology of ethnographic research.

To appreciate the significance of Geertz, it is useful to see his work in contrast to that of Claude Lévi-Strauss, the French structural anthropologist. Geertz characterises his own approach as semiotic but not structuralist, by which he means that cultural anthropology is concerned with the interpretation of signifying practices and symbolic process in specific contexts, not with reducing signs to a universal system of signification, as in Lévi-Strauss's reduction of myth to sets of binary opposition. In comparison with Lévi-Strauss, Geertz is radically particularist and contextualist. Also, unlike structural anthropology, Geertzian cultural anthropology situates interpretation in relation to everyday understandings that may be more or less self-conscious. In this sense, Geertz is in line of descent from the classical anthropologist, Bronislaw Malinowski, author of *Argonauts of the Western Pacific* (1922). Malinowski argued famously that the task of the anthropologist was to interpret the world 'from the native's point of view'. Following this injunction, Geertz is interested in exploring the particularities of cultural difference and their representation, rather than seeking underlying utilities that can be modelled with mathematical precision; and, in that regard, can be seen as the precursor of post-structuralist and postmodern anthropology.

To understand culture as it is lived, according to Geertz, requires in-depth fieldwork in the classical tradition of anthropology. The aim of ethnographic interpretation is to produce 'thick description', in the philosopher Gilbert Ryle's phrase. Geertz's most celebrated ethnography is of cockfighting in Bali, which he reads as a form of 'deep play', in Jeremy Bentham's term, and that it has little practical utility but functions symbolically to articulate masculine identity in the double meaning of cocks in contest with one another. Seen in the context of Indonesia's traditional male culture, the cockfight has a comparable function to performances of, say, Shakespeare's *Macbeth* in traditional Western culture, argues Geertz.

A problem arises concerning the validity or artfulness of any ethnographic account. Research findings are communicated in written form, in anthropological essays and monographs, and occasionally in audio-visual media. They are texts that deploy narrative and metaophorical devices and are never simply 'objective' records of actions and events. Vincent Crampanzo (in *Writing Culture*) has read Geertz's essay on the Balinese cockfight from this 'writing culture' perspective. He notes that the very title of the essay, 'Deep Play', echoes the title of a notorious pornographic film, *Deep Throat*, released around the time the essay was written. Also, in the essay, Geertz constructs for himself the stereotypical role of cultural naïf who eventually wins acceptance within an exotic culture through a rite of passage and, hence, privileged access to obscure knowledge. Moreover, he gives a certain cultural authority to the cockfight by likening it to Western dramatic art. In the end, what Geertz has produced is an artful fiction, in Crampanzo's estimation.

The 'writing culture' perspective deliberately undermines the 'scientific' status of ethnography and, in a typically post-structuralist move, treats it exclusively as a textual form in an inter-textual web of significations, rather than as a representation of a reality beyond the text. Geertz himself is not at all naïve, however, about the mediation of writing. In answer to his own question, 'What does the ethnographer do?', he says 'writes'. And he has emphasised the value of literary theory for anthropology and the social sciences generally. The issue at stake, then, between Geertz and more radical proponents of the 'writing culture' perspective, is whether a self-consciousness about writing and textual artifice brings a further dimension of reflexivity to what is, in any case, a necessarily reflexive practice, or whether it makes ethnographic fieldwork redundant since, ultimately, it results in no more than another kind of fiction. This exemplifies a fundamental tension between realist and conventionalist epistemology: and, although Geertz would tend to regard himself as a conventionalist and a relativist, in fact, he may more accurately be viewed as a realist.

Further reading

Atkinson, P. THE ETHNOGRAPHIC IMAGINATION: TEXTUAL CONSTRUCTIONS OF REALITY, Routledge, 1990.
Clifford, J. and Marcus, G. (eds.) WRITING CULTURE: THE POETICS AND POLITICS OF ETHNOGRAPHY, University of California Press, 1986.
Seidman, S. (ed.) THE POSTMODERN TURN: NEW PERSPECTIVES ON SOCIAL THEORY, Cambridge University Press, 1994.

J.McG.

GELLNER, Ernest

Anthropologist/philosopher/social theorist	born France 1925–1995
Associated with	NATIONALISM ■ CRITICAL RATIONALISM
Influences include	TURNER ■ POPPER ■ WITTGENSTEIN ■ MALINOWSKI
Shares common ground with	KUHN ■ ANDERSON ■ RUSSELL ■ FRAZER
Main works	WORDS AND THINGS: A CRITICAL ACCOUNT OF LINGUISTIC PHILOSOPHY AND A STUDY IN IDEOLOGY (1959) NATIONS AND NATIONALISM (1983) ENCOUNTERS WITH NATIONALISM (1994) CONDITIONS OF LIBERTY: CIVIL SOCIETY AND ITS RIVALS (1994)

ALTHOUGH BORN IN Paris in 1925, Ernest Gellner's parents were Czech and he was brought up in Prague. He completed his schooling in England after his family emigrated in 1938, and won a scholarship to Balliol College at the University of Oxford. His studies were interrupted by his decision to enlist in the Czech Armoured Brigade in 1944, and he did not complete his degree in Politics, Philosophy and Economics until 1949. Accepting a teaching position at the London School of Economics, Gellner taught there for 35 years, becoming a Professor of Philosophy in 1962. He then accepted a Chair in Social Anthropology at the University of Cambridge in 1984 where he stayed until 1993. Taking advantage of the political transformation of Eastern Europe, Gellner returned to Prague to help establish the Centre for the Study of Nationalism at the Central European University, where he was research director. Although suffering from osteoporosis, he remained an active academic until his sudden death in 1995.

Ernest Gellner was a nonconformist intellectual who not only excelled in critical writing in a number of disciplines – chiefly philosophy, anthropology and the social sciences – but used his publications to challenge accepted orthodoxies and debunk leading contemporary thinkers. Among his chief targets were relativism, accepted accounts of nationalism, and, in his later years, psychoanalysis and postmodernism; and among the theorists he tackled were

Clifford Geertz, Edward Said, Tom Nairn and Perry Anderson. Gellner's contribution can best be described as displacing conventional tenets of social and cultural inquiry and inserting rigorous propositions that drew on philosophical principles, acknowledged social embeddedness and recognised cultural specificity in positive ways. Thus, while he was unrestrained in his criticisms of the views of others, his own analyses attempted to do justice to grounded social and political dynamics.

Gellner was an extraordinarily prolific thinker and writer, with over twenty books to his name and countless articles, chapters, press pieces and other publications. Hall and Jarvie (1992) have argued that not only did Gellner write on a diversity of topics, but he attempted to develop 'a single line of thought that unites problems and ideas around which the academy has put artificial disciplinary boundaries'. This was the notion that society was more important for the understanding of phenomena than culture or individuals. Thus he argued that ideas were formed by society and that resources belonged to society. As such, his thinking countered contemporary dominant approaches. Indeed, he characterised people as three types: fundamentalists, relativists and 'Enlightenment Puritans', placing himself in the latter category, and launching scathing (though often humorous) attacks on the former.

Gellner's first book, *Words and Things*, brought him to immediate attention and notoriety. The book attacked the idealism which marked Oxford linguistic philosophy. This was the first of a number of works on problems in philosophy, language, reason, rationality and ethics. Other publications included *Thought and Change* (1965), *The Devil in Modern Philosophy* (1974), *Legitimation of Belief* (1974), *Plough, Sword and Book: The Structure of Human History* (1988), *The Psychoanalytic Movement* (1985), *Reason and Culture: The Historic Role of Rationality and Rationalism* (1992) and *Postmodernism, Reason and Religion* (1992).

As an anthropologist, his fieldwork among the Berbers in Morocco formed the basis of *Saints of the Atlas* (1969). This was not only an ethnographic study of the holy men but an incisive (though contentious) analysis of the role they played in maintaining the peace between the shepherds' seasonal herding and rustlers. He used his analysis of the micro-politics of Berber life to extrapolate on the Berbers' rejection of the modern Moroccan state and its political system. This work led to a lifelong interest in the culture and politics of North Africa, Arab culture and Islam. Other publications included *Arabs and Berbers: From the Tribe to Nation in North Africa* (edited with C. Micaud, 1973) and *Muslim Society* (1982). More generally, his interest in political anthropology, the role of government and the state, and the nature of the polity informed other books, such as *Contemporary Thought and Politics* (1974), *Patrons and Clients in Mediterranean Societies* (with J. Waterbury, 1978) *Culture, Identity and Politics* (1987) and *Anthropology and Politics: Revolutions in the Sacred Grove* (1995). His 1994 book, *Conditions of Liberty: Civil Society and its Rivals*, addressed the rebirth of the idea of civil society in post-communist and post-modernist times.

Best known were Gellner's thoughts on nationalism. His books *Nations and Nationalism* and *Encounters with Nationalism* remain key texts for students. He argued that nationalism was an historical political form associated with pre-modern societies and that modernisation would supplant it in new states. Thus he believed that nationalism was a passing phase, and that ethnic nationalism played a benign role in modernisation. Reflecting his interest in Islam and nationalism, he argued that Islam in modern states was a highly disciplined and single-minded facilitator of modernisation that replaced nationalism. While the dissolution of Eastern Europe and continuing unrest in the Middle East led him to modify some of his views, he maintained his central thesis.

Gellner also maintained an engaged and combative interest in social science theory and methodology, as evidenced in his publications *Spectacles and Predicaments: Essays in Social Theory* (1980) and *Relativism and the Social Sciences* (1985). Perhaps the most succinct and accessible overview of his work can be found in *Cause and Meaning in the Social Sciences* (1973).

The significance of Gellner's mulfarious contributions to shaking up the academy can be glimpsed in Hall and Jarvie's *The Transition to Modernity: Essays on Power, Wealth and Belief*, where leading writers tackle the implications of Gellner's writings on power, wealth and belief. Above all, he was committed to challenging ideas that seemed right but were proved wrong.

Further reading

Gellner, E. Cause and Meaning in the Social Sciences, Routledge & Kegan Paul, 1973.

Hall, J. and Jarvie, I.C. (eds.) The Transition to Modernity: Essays on Power, Wealth and Belief, Cambridge University Press, 1992.

Ignatieff, M. 'Conditions of Liberty – Civil Society and its Rivals: E. Gellner', Foreign Affairs 74: 2 (1995), pp. 128–36.

Periwal, S. (ed.) Notions of Nationalism introduction by E. Gellner, Central European University Press and Oxford University Press, 1995.

J.C.

GIDDENS, Anthony

Social theorist/sociologist	born England 1938—
Associated with	STRUCTURAL THEORY ▪ HERMENEUTICS ▪ SOCIAL DEMOCRACY
Influences include	DURKHEIM ▪ MARX ▪ WEBER
Shares common ground with	BAUMAN ▪ BECK ▪ BOURDIEU ▪ HABERMAS
Main works	NEW RULES OF SOCIOLOGICAL METHOD (1976) THE CONSTITUTION OF SOCIETY (1984) THE CONSEQUENCES OF MODERNITY (1990) MODERNITY AND SELF-IDENTITY (1991)

GIDDENS WAS BORN in London and studied at the University of Hull. He lectured at the University of Leicester, Simon Fraser University, Vancouver and The University of California at Los Angeles before taking up an appointment at Cambridge towards the end of the 1960s and where he subsequently became Professor of Sociology. He is now Director of the London School of Economics. With James Curran, he founded the academic publishing house, Polity, during the 1980s. In Britain, where public intellectuals are little recognised, at least in comparison with, say, France, Germany or the USA, Giddens has established an unusual presence as both an internationally famous social theorist and, latterly, something of an ideologist for 'New Labour' politics. With the possible exception of Herbert Spencer, Giddens is arguably the greatest British-born sociologist, the author of a distinctive framework of concepts that he calls 'structuration theory'.

In the early part of his career, Giddens gained a reputation for being an excellent interpreter of classical social theory and he took part in the general turn against functionalism and positivism in sociology. Steeped in the writings of Durkheim, Marx and Weber, Giddens contributed to the development of sophisticated theorising and the generally theoretical caste of latter-day British sociology. He read widely in French and German and was able to speak with extraordinary clarity on the various strands of modern social thought, particularly the hermeneutic and critical theory traditions. His own standing as an original social theorist is, however, a matter of some controversy. Giddens is prolific at coining new terminology, but whether or not his theorising resolves what he calls 'central problems in social theory' is in dispute. Some think his work is an eclectic amalgam of ideas of no more than descriptive value, whereas others believe he has produced a general theory that has powerful explanatory force.

Structuration theory aims to overcome the dualism between agency and structure. According to Giddens, structure is the product of agency and constitutes rules and resources through which agency is reproduced. There is, then, a perpetual process of structuration going on. In order to formulate this dynamic notion of structure, Giddens distinguishes it from systemic constraints on action; structure, for him, is enabling rather than constraining. In his *New Rules of Sociological Method*, Giddens defined the appropriate epistemology of social research as a 'double hermeneutic' whereby the meaning frames of theory and everyday life are in dialectical relation. However, in *The Constitution of Society*, Giddens also insisted that his theorising is primarily ontological rather than epistemological in purpose. He is making claims about how social life works, not simply prescribing how to study it. Yet, clearly Giddens does favour an approach to social research that is strongly inflected by attention to the symbolic mediation and, hence, cultural determination of agency and structure. And, influenced by time-geography, Giddens insists on the need always to analyse the time–space coordinates of structuration processes.

Giddens's trilogy, including *The Transformation of Intimacy* (1992) in addition to *The Consequences of Modernity* and *Modernity and Self-Identity*, has made his work more immediately relevant to cultural theory. This is so, in the first instance, because *The Consequences of Modernity* represents one of the most convincing theoretical critiques of postmodernist assumptions. He rejects the claim made by Lyotard and others that there is a shift occurring from modernity to postmodernity. Instead, Giddens argues that modernity is becoming accentuated and extended, particularly through globalisation: the juggernaut of modernity rolls on in a simultaneously frightening and exhilarating manner. Moreover, he has argued that much of what is misinterpreted as 'postmodern' is, in fact, indicative of 'detraditionalisation', the elimination of the final vestiges of pre-modernity. Interestingly, Giddens extends his analysis of the transformation of world society, modernisation and globalisation to an examination of how the late modern self and its intimate relations are being transformed.

The late modern self is a reflexive project, according to Giddens, no longer so restrained by tradition and in a state of constant reinvention. Existential anxiety and ontological security coexist on the terrain of everyday life. Uncertainty haunts our actions and, in this sense, manifests the radical doubt of post-traditional knowledge, yet a sense of stability that is produced by the routines of daily existence enables us to go on in a more or less predictable manner. The coexistence of contrary forces, in this and other instances, is characteristic of Giddens's thought and is also represented by his political conviction that in many respects the opposition between Left and Right has become blurred and, to a significant extent, transcended in the high or late modern world.

Further reading

Beck, U., Giddens, A. and Lash, S. REFLEXIVE MODERNIZATION, Polity, 1994.
Bryant, C. and Jary, D. (eds.) GIDDENS'S THEORY OF STRUCTURATION, Routledge, 1991.
Craib, I. ANTHONY GIDDENS, Routledge, 1992.
Heelas, P., Lash, S. and Morris, P. (eds.) DETRADITIONALIZATION, Blackwell, 1996.

J.McG.

GIDE, André

Novelist/essayist/dramatist	born France 1869–1951
Associated with	PEDERASTY ■ INVERTS
Influences include	PLATO ■ VON GOETHE ■ DE GOURMONT
Shares common ground with	ELLIS ■ FOUCAULT
Main works	CORYDON (1924)
	LES FAUX-MONNAYEURS (1926)
	SI LE GRAIN NE MEURT (1926)

A SICKLY, ONLY CHILD brought up in an atmosphere of strict Protestant morality and female authority, André Gide developed constrasting streaks of puritanism and libertinism. In his early twenties he travelled to Algeria, where he shook off his guilt and made uncomplicated love with boys for the first time. Although he later married a cousin, the marriage was never consummated. Gide was co-founder and active editor of the journal *La Nouvelle Revue Française*. He was awarded the Nobel Prize for Literature in 1947.

Although now best known as a novelist, Gide was an engaged political commentator. He was severely critical of French colonialism in two works, *Voyage au Congo* (1927) and *Le Retour du Tchad* (1928). He violated leftist orthodoxies by publicising his disillusionment with Stalinism in *Retour de l'U.R.S.S.* (1936). His major statement on sexuality was *Corydon* (1924), which Gide regarded as his most important book. It consists of four 'Socratic' dialogues on the topic of male homosexuality.

The book's protagonist, Corydon, argues that male homosexuality is no sickness, nor is it unnatural. Indeed, it may well be a signal of good health and harmony with nature. Distinguishing between physiological processes, governed by the concept of nature, and permissible behaviour, governed by morality, he argues that homosexuality as a condition should be discussed dispassionately, as if by a natural historian. Noting that most animal species indulge in homosexual behaviour, he asserts the independence of reproduction and sexual pleasure.

The weakness of the ethological approach is that it does not answer Christian objections to serial sexual enjoyment: promiscuity is too much like the animals, too natural by far. Gide does not respond to such arguments. He is more concerned to oppose the imposition of a medical model on homosexuality. This is why Corydon acknowledges, but states the wish to move on from, the theoretical positions of Richard von Krafft-Ebing and Albert Moll.

Having established the place of homosexuality in nature, Corydon argues that its occurrence in human behaviour is to the same extent natural. Nor does this suggest a remnant of some pre-civilised, brutish habit: for homosexuality is capable of acting as a dynamo to the most refined of civilisations. In this reference back to Greece – as in his use of the dialogue form – Gide shows that he has much in common with conventional homosexual classicists of the late nineteenth century. Indeed, where Gide fails as a Modernist in his theorisation of homosexuality is in his refusal to defend either adult men who desire adult men or 'inverts' – passive effeminates. He is content to consign the latter to the medical realm, as being diseased.

The 'Socratic' form enforces an association between modern male love and ancient Greek pederasty. This equation, particularly common in French culture since the Enlightenment, was dismissed as sloppy and anachronistic by Michel Foucault in *L'Usage des plaisirs* (1984), the second volume of his history of sexuality. Moreover, *Corydon* presents sexology in its purest form, untainted by psychoanalysis.

In a note dated November 1922, added to his preface to the 1924 edition of *Corydon*, Gide dismisses the position of Marcel Proust, his contemporary, whose novel *Sodome et Gomorrhe* was published in 1921. Proust subscribed to Magnus Hirschfeld's theory of the 'third sex', which, in Gide's opinion, only dealt with 'inversion, effeminacy and sodomy'. Gide's defence is of pederasty, which has nothing to do with effeminacy in either partner. He seems to have taken exception to Proust's greatest character, the Baron de Charlus, a haughty and effeminate queen who turns out, in *Le Temps Retrouvé*, also to be a practising masochist.

The novelist Marcel Jouhandeau re-examined and updated Gide's themes in his essay *Ces messieurs: Corydon résumé et augmenté* (1951). This involvement of homosexual novelists in the theorisation of homosexuality is a striking characteristic of French culture. The tradition has continued more recently in Tony Duvert's *L'Enfant au masculin* (1980), a pugnacious defence of paedophilia, and in Hervé Guibert's fictionalised accounts of his dialogues with Michel Foucault.

Further reading

Apter, E. ANDRÉ GIDE AND THE CODES OF HOMOSEXUALITY, ANMA Libri & Co., 1987.
Pollard, P. ANDRÉ GIDE: HOMOSEXUAL MORALIST, Yale University Press, 1991.
Stambolian, G. and Marks, E. (eds.) HOMOSEXUALITIES AND FRENCH LITERATURE, Cornell University Press, 1979.

G.W.

GOFFMAN, Erving

Sociologist	born Canada 1922–1982
Associated with	DRAMATURGICAL PERSPECTIVE ■ INTERACTION RITUAL
Influences include	DURKHEIM ■ SIMMEL ■ MEAD
Shares common ground with	BLUMER ■ GARFINKEL ■ SARTRE
Main works	THE PRESENTATION OF SELF IN EVERYDAY LIFE (1956) ASYLUMS: ESSAYS ON THE SOCIAL SITUATION OF MENTAL PATIENTS AND OTHER INMATES (1961) INTERACTION RITUAL: ESSAYS ON FACE-TO-FACE BEHAVIOUR (1967)

G OFFMAN'S JEWISH FAMILY moved from Russia to Canada at the end of the nineteenth century; his father was a tailor. After school in Winnipeg he started a chemistry degree at Manitoba. This was interrupted by the war, and Goffman joined the staff at the National Film Board of Canada. He returned to university and graduated in sociology in 1945 from Toronto. He then took a doctorate at Chicago University based on fieldwork in the Shetland Islands. After completing his Ph.D. in 1953, he did fieldwork of a different sort as a ward orderly in an asylum at Bethesda, Washington, DC, details of which appear in various places in his publications. In 1957 he worked at the University of California at Berkeley, as a sociologist; in 1968 he moved to Pennsylvania, where he worked closely with sociolinguists until his early death in 1982.

Goffman preferred the term 'micro-sociology' for his studies, which were almost always at the level of small institutions or small-scale interactions, or the latter in the institutional frame. His style of analysis was to refuse to see culture or institution as a structure which could be used as a grid for behaviour. Interested in social role, structure and organisation, these were never simple givens but always in play with the selves, identities and actions of individuals. Thus at the beginning of his famous analysis of total institutions in his book *Asylums: Essays on the Social Situation of Mental Patients and Other Inmates* he stresses that in the ritual passage from outside to inside, what the institution does is not to aim for 'cultural victory' but to maintain a tension between the two worlds as an object of 'strategic leverage'. The process of entry is nevertheless marked by conscious or unconscious rituals of passage, which act to alter beliefs concerning self and significant others, but not as a complete reprogramming, as is often believed. The social world of interactions, though sanctioned by rules and beliefs, gives rise to discrepancies and behaviours that are out of place, sometimes spectacularly so. Goffman is thus involved in an analysis which sees individuals aware of playing with their own identities and social positions, even in the mode and degree of involvement in their role or situation. Out of the forms of involvement and styles of social interaction are developed idioms of a culture: either within an institution or as informal encounters. Looking at parents with children on a merry-go-round he notes parents act with a different style of enjoyment and involvement: looking at people playing games, he notes that taken too seriously, there is no fun.

In his analysis of institutional life the many kinds of interactions are situated within the framework of the social divisions and functions of the staff–inmate relationship. In a long analysis he investigated the underlife of such places as mental hospitals. He suggested that there were only a limited number of ways of surviving, and they are all based on the same procedures which in normal times go to make up acceptable interaction, except here they change their form and are out of place. It is then that secondary adjustments arise in an underlife: activities through which the inmates establish a distance from their institutionally allotted roles. Goffman thus reverses expectations and uses these examples in return as an explanation of the normal world of the self: the self is not something defined in relation to a fixed social point, or a total form of involvement in which selflessness is absolute. The culture of ritual transition creates stable social forms, but identities are often dependent on there being cracks in the cultural edifice.

Goffman's work has been widely influential. The main criticism of his work is that, by remaining at the level of micro-analysis, he provides a picture of relatively unchanging societies, or a picture of overworlds and underworlds which are universal and timeless.

Further reading

Burns, T. ERVING GOFFMAN, Routledge, 1992.
Drew, P. and Wootton, A. (eds.) ERVING GOFFMAN: EXPLORING THE INTERACTIONAL ORDER, Polity, 1988.
Manning, P. ERVING GOFFMAN, Polity, 1992.

M.G.

GOLDMANN, Lucien

Literary historian/social theorist	born Romania 1913–1970
Associated with	HUMANISM ■ WESTERN MARXISM ■ STRUCTURALISM
Influences include	LUKÁCS ■ PASCAL ■ PIAGET
Shares common ground with	EAGLETON ■ GORZ ■ WILLIAMS
Main works	THE HUMAN SCIENCES AND PHILOSOPHY (1952, 1966) THE HIDDEN GOD (1955) TOWARDS A SOCIOLOGY OF THE NOVEL (1964) CULTURAL CREATION IN MODERN SOCIETY (1971)

Goldmann was born in Bucharest and studied law at its university. He studied philosophy in Vienna, where he was introduced to the work of his most important influence, Georg Lukács; and law, political science and literature in Paris. During the 1940s, Goldmann worked as a research assistant for the psychologist Jean Piaget in Geneva. He taught and researched in Paris throughout the 1950s and became director of a research centre on the sociology of literature at the Free University in Brussels in 1961. He was a non-aligned Marxist, passionately opposed to Stalinism, a supporter of the student revolts of 1968 and an enthusiastic advocate of worker self-management on the Yugoslavian model.

In certain respects, Goldmann is a characteristic figure of the Western Marxist tradition, which is documented by Perry Anderson in *Considerations on Western Marxism* (1976). In politics this tradition represented a comparatively libertarian and democratic alternative to Soviet communism. And, philosophically, it was sparked off by the recovery of the Hegelian aspects of Marxism and the humanism of the young Marx, initiated particularly by Lukács's *History and Class Consciousness* (1923), the book which shaped Goldmann's perspective on the human sciences and the sociology of culture. The key methodological concept in the Lukácsian current of thought was totality, enabling the understanding of social forces as parts of a complex and dialectical whole. The totalising quality of such humanistic Marxism may be further illustrated by Goldmann's argument in *The Human Sciences and Philosophy* that the intellectual superiority of Marxism lay in its capacity to account for the historical genesis of other philosophies. In that sense,

Marxism could be seen as a history of history, a philosophy of philosophy and a sociology of sociology. It was not a closed intellectual system and dogmatically opposed to other theories, but was critical of their partial vision and capable of absorbing their insights into a more comprehensive means of making sense of the dynamics of culture and society.

Goldmann called his own methodology 'genetic structuralism', which analyses structure but in a more processual, diachronic fashion than the synchronic procedures of classical structuralism. He was interested in examining how mental structures of a collective kind are related to social and historical structures. His concept of the collective subject is an idealisation of the historically significant group and the potential and limits of its view of the world. Goldmann distinguished between mere ideology and world-view. Most philosophising and cultural creation reflect the fragmented ideologies of groups in conflict and struggle, whereas world-views transcend the partiality of ideology and articulate a more profound sense of history. For Goldmann, such world-views are present in great works of art and is what makes them great, especially literature. He was not interested in lesser works.

His study of the Jansenist thought of Blaise Pascal, its correspondence with the dramatic structures of Racine, and their mutual relationship of homology with the social position and philosophical disposition of the *noblesse de robe* in seventeenth-century France, *The Hidden God*, is the most sophisticated application of the genetic structuralist method. The *noblesse de robe* were caught in a difficult and, indeed, impossible position between the aristocracy and monarchy, on the one hand, and the rising bourgeoisie on the other. As state functionaries, they were dependent upon the king and the *noblesse de coeur* (aristocracy) for their livelihood and thus, in effect, tied to a dying regime, yet they could not make common cause with modernising forces. Their view of the world was tragic. They were trapped socially, and spiritual transcendence was denied them, because they could see no necessary proof for the existence of a greater source of meaning, that is, God. Pascal, of course, famously wagered on the existence of God but, rather like Calvinism, Jansenism found little comfort in faith.

The tragic vision of seventeenth-century Jansenism was profound, in Goldmann's estimation, because in some sense it understood the limits of the *ancien régime* and, in a curious way, anticipated the wager of revolutionary socialism, that a form of social transcendence was imaginable and, Goldmann hoped, achievable. Wherever he looked, however, Goldmann discovered tragic visions. He agreed with the neo-Marxist position that the proletariat had, under organised capitalism, ceased to be the potential source of revolution. Modern capitalism had stabilised and reified consciousness predominated, meaning that the fate of human beings was experienced as under the control of economic laws and systemic processes beyond their control. Goldmann found the literary correlative for reification and commodity fetishism in the *nouveau roman* of Alain Robbe-Grillet, where subjectivity is eliminated and the object world dominates (*Towards a Sociology of the Novel*).

Goldmann's theses on the relations between literature and society were bold and striking, yet the very methodological principle to which he adhered, totalisation, became a limitation and actually a straitjacket for literary–sociological analysis, certainly in comparison with the particularising approaches of post-structuralism.

Further reading

Cohen, M. THE WAGER OF LUCIEN GOLDMANN: TRAGEDY, DIALECTICS AND A HIDDEN GOD, Princeton University Press, 1994.
Glucksmann, M. 'Lucien Goldmann: Marxist or Humanist?', NEW LEFT REVIEW, 56 (1969).
Mellor, A. 'The Hidden Method: Lucien Goldmann and the Sociology of Literature', WORKING PAPERS IN CULTURAL STUDIES, 4, Birmingham, 1973.
Williams, R. 'Literature and Sociology: In Memory of Lucien Goldmann', in R. Williams, PROBLEMS IN MATERIALISM AND CULTURE, Verso, 1980.

J.McG.

GOMBRICH, Ernst H.

Art historian	born Austria 1909—
Associated with	FORMALISM
Influences include	KANT ▪ FREUD ▪ FIEDLER
Shares common ground with	POPPER ▪ LORENZ ▪ PANOFSKY
Main works	THE STORY OF ART (1950)
	ART AND ILLUSION (1960)
	THE SENSE OF ORDER: A STUDY IN THE PSYCHOLOGY
	OF DECORATIVE ART (1979)

GOMBRICH WAS BORN in Vienna in 1909. His mother was an accomplished pianist and circulated in the social circles of Arnold Schoenberg, Sigmund Freud and Gustav Mahler. His father was a lawyer, whose thriving practice was irrevocably disrupted with the onset of the First World War. So devastated was Vienna after the war that the young Ernst Gombrich was sent to Sweden for nine months in 1920 to avoid starvation.

His family condoned his eventual decision to study art history, a new discipline at the University of Vienna, not because the family considered it a promising venture, but because at the time they were not sure any venture was promising in post-war Vienna. Gombrich's doctoral thesis was on Giulio Romano, a prodigious student of Raphaello, who served as architect and decorator of the Palazzo del Tè in Mantova, Italy. Gombrich argued that the Palazzo represented the architectural equivalent of the paintings of El Greco and Tintoretto, thereby supporting the legitimacy of a distinct 'period' of art history, in this case the 'mannerist' period, distinguished by ambiguities and distortions of high Renaissance themes.

Gombrich's interest and respect for Renaissance art, especially that of the fifteenth century, never subsided. For much of his career, he was associated with the Aby Warburg Institute. The Institute, which was founded in Hamburg by its namesake, was devoted to tracking the influence of the classical world on the Renaissance. Gombrich, in fact, produced a long intellectual biography of Warburg.

Gombrich's first publication, which he claimed to have completed in six weeks, was a children's history of the world. It proved to be a very successful venture, and served to reinforce Gombrich's commitment to simple, clear writing. The commitment certainly carried over to his most famous venture, *The Story of Art*, which has become the pre-eminent introductory text to art history. There are certainly deficiencies in the volume. Photography was added as an afterthought in later editions, and film is not treated as an art form. However, it is difficult to typecast Gombrich as a snob. He eschews distinctions between 'high' and 'low' art, and his text explores non-Western artistic traditions.

Clearly, however, it is the Western tradition that is of most interest to Gombrich. In fact, to the Western tradition is owed the existence of art history itself. Egyptian and Byzantine art, for example, cannot claim a 'history', according to Gombrich, since those epochs placed no value on innovation or progress. The intention of the artist, rather, was to preserve, as well as possible, the conventions and images of the past, so as to maintain the purity of sacred images. Renaissance art, on the other hand, like the science that surrounded it, valued experimentation and innovation. Renaissance artists tried to outdo each other through stylistic and representational 'surprises'. Art history, for Gombrich, traces the development of these surprises.

This concern with the intention and inclinations of the artist was developed in Gombrich's later work, especially *Art and Illusion*, where he applied philosophical and psychological principles to the creation of art. The Impressionists, in their attempt to paint 'what they saw' were doomed at the outset. Following Kant, Gombrich argued that all products which were subject to the mediation of the human brain, including art, could never hope to represent reality. The depiction of nature in art is always preceded by thought, which cannot replicate nature. Ironically, stiff Egyptian art may be the most 'natural' of all, since it was more concerned with the depiction of thought than of nature, and thought is what is unavoidable in humans. The attempt to depict three-dimensional nature in two dimensions is not a closer approach to nature, but a more difficult and complex demand on thought and ingenuity.

Periods of art, then, represent ways of thinking. Artists carry certain established repertories and hypotheses regarding the purpose of art, which Gombrich called schemata, and they work to express those purposes as effectively as possible. Thus, Gombrich could make statements about the quality of various artworks within its identified schema.

Further reading

Gorak, J. THE MAKING OF THE MODERN CANON: GENESIS AND CRISIS OF A LITERARY IDEA, Athlone, 1991.
Richmond, S. AESTHETIC CRITERIA: GOMBRICH AND THE PHILOSOPHIES OF SCIENCE OF POPPER AND POLANYI, Rodopi, 1994.
Woodfield, R. 'Gombrich, Formalism and the Descriptions of Works of Art', BRITISH JOURNAL OF AESTHETICS, 34: 2 (April 1994), pp. 134–45.

T.J.L.

GORZ, André

Sociologist/philosopher	born Austria 1924—
Associated with	EXISTENTIALISM ■ MARXISM ■ VOLUNTARISM
Influences include	MARX ■ SARTRE ■ ADORNO
Shares common ground with	ILLICH ■ MARCUSE ■ BAHRO
Main works	FONDEMENTS POUR UNE MORALE (1977)
	FAREWELL TO THE WORKING CLASS (1980)
	PATHS TO PARADISE (1983)
	CRITIQUE OF ECONOMIC REASON (1988)
	CAPITALISM, SOCIALISM, ECOLOGY (1994)

REVISIONIST MARXIST, UTOPIAN visionary, anarcho-socialist, André Gorz cuts a peculiar figure in modern philosophy and sociology. He was born in Vienna of a Christian mother and a Jewish father. He suffered from the rise of anti-Semitism in the 1930s and dealt with it by repressing his Jewish roots and embracing Aryan culture. He soon repudiated his decision. He studied at the University of Lausanne, but immersed himself in French thinkers, notably Sartre. Gorz embraced French culture and the French language as a way of avoiding what he took to be the cultural paucity of his surroundings in Switzerland and his past in Vienna. His childhood and adolescence were apparently dominated by the desire to repress and reject many aspects of his experience in family life, community relations and national culture. France, or more specifically Paris, became his affirmation of identity.

In the late 1940s Gorz moved to Paris, where he commenced work on his first major study, *Fondements pour une morale* and wrote articles for a leftist weekly. He eventually became economics editor for *Les Temps Modernes* and wrote articles for the socialist weekly, *Le Nouvel Observateur*. His training as a journalist impressed upon him the value of concrete analysis. Marx eclipsed Sartre in his theoretical outlook and, from the 1950s, Gorz began to wrestle with conditions of capitalist oppression and strategies for socialist transformation. Changes in the division of labour, the promise of freedom offered by technological innovation and productivity gains, and his criticism of market rationality, emerged as pivotal themes in his work. Since the late 1970s, he has written extensively about ecology and the political consequences and opportunities of environmental attrition.

Gorz may not be the most original Marxist revisionist in the post-war period, but he is certainly one of the most indefatigable. He remains committed to emancipatory socialism, but he is critical of both statist and social-democratic welfarist models. Gorz learnt enough from Sartre to hold that the real challenge for leftist politics and social thought is to devise an approach to socialism which transcends both the commodity form and the industrial–bureaucratic machine. The fight for freedom and resistance to 'the system' are seminal themes in his work. Gorz distinguishes between heteronomous and autonomous spheres in industrial society. The heteronomous sphere refers to the requirements placed on the individual to gain paid labour, to marry, to deal with state administration and services, to learn how to use the transport system and, in short, to succumb to all of the routine requirements for participation in industrial civilisation. Gorz criticises the heteronomous sphere on the grounds that it is not the product of the voluntary co-operation of its members. He does not deny that autonomous experience is possible within the interstices of the heteronomous order. But he does propose that autonomy in these conditions will be fleeting. The goal of socialist liberation is to overcome heteronomy with autonomy so that individuals can determine the course of their lives and take responsibility for their actions.

Prima facie, Gorz's political commitment to increase autonomy may seem strange, for the foundation of his philosophical approach is that we are all free. Our freedom enables us to recognise structural constraints and to take steps to transcend them. Again, the legacy of Sartre is evident. Gorz argues that the economic productivity of capitalism has outpaced the central civil and moral categories devised under early capitalism to manage motivation and order. We face two choices. We have the freedom to pursue our individual ends selfishly. But this brings manifest social and ecological problems. Technology has replaced workers, leading to mass unemployment, and the pursuit of economic rationality has corroded the ecosystem. Moreover, pursuing individual ends simply reinforces the heteronomous sphere. We do not work for ourselves, but for the economic objectives of the system. The alternative choice is to reduce working hours and allow individuals to develop freely and fully. Gorz's 'politics of time' is designed to accomplish this purpose. He proposes that working hours should be reduced. Wage losses would be cancelled out by an indirect income levied from a new tax on consumption. Workers would not experience a decline in income, but their non-work time would be dramatically increased. Liberated time would be spent in developing individual creative faculties and developing voluntary, co-operative services such as child-care co-ops, shared transport and help for the elderly and disabled.

Gorz shrugs off criticism that his politics of time is impractical and that his concept of autonomy is utopian. He maintains that the failure to seek liberation from work and the expansion of autonomy simply conspires with the heteronomous order and the mutilation of life. Even so, he resembles a sort of post-industrial Rousseau who is so intoxicated with the repressed potential for good in people that he refuses to recognise the bad. The sphere of autonomy may promote mutuality, co-operation and solidarity, but without any 'external' regulating system, it might also lead to selfishness, venality and a Hobbesian war of 'all against all'.

Further reading

Frankel, B. THE POST INDUSTRIAL UTOPIANS, Polity, 1987.
Hyman, R. 'André Gorz and the Disappearing Proletariat', in R. Miliband and J. Saville (eds.), THE SOCIALIST REGISTER, Merlin, 1983.
Lodziak, C. and Tatman, J. ANDRÉ GORZ: A CRITICAL INTRODUCTION, Pluto, 1997.

C.R.

GRAMSCI, Antonio

Revolutionary socialist/political theorist	born Sardinia 1891–1937
Associated with	CULTURAL POPULISM ∎ HEGEMONY THEORY ∎ WESTERN MARXISM
Influences include	CROCE ∎ LENIN ∎ MARX
Shares common ground with	ALTHUSSER ∎ HALL ∎ WILLIAMS
Main works	ANTONIO GRAMSCI: SELECTIONS FROM POLITICAL WRITINGS (1977) SELECTIONS FROM THE PRISON NOTEBOOKS OF ANTONIO GRAMSCI (1971) ANTONIO GRAMSCI: SELECTIONS FROM CULTURAL WRITINGS (1985) (ALL THESE TEXTS ARE MAJOR SELECTIONS IN ENGLISH TRANSLATION FROM GRAMSCI'S EARLY POLITICAL AND CULTURAL WRITINGS AND HIS PRISON NOTEBOOKS, WRITTEN IN THE 1920S AND 1930S, AND WHOSE PUBLICATION IN ITALY ONLY BEGAN FROM THE 1940S.)

A S A YOUNG MAN, Gramsci settled in the industrial city of Turin in northern Italy, first as a student, then as a journalist and politician. He edited *Ordine Nuovo* (New Order) and rose to prominence in the Italian Socialist Party (PSI) during the factory occupations of 1920, which represented, for Gramsci, the prefiguration of workers' self-management in the coming socialist society. When the PSI ended the occupations by making a deal with the bosses, Gramsci became part of a faction that broke away and founded the Italian Communist Party (PCI), which he led from 1924 until his imprisonment by Mussolini's fascist regime in 1926. His immunity as a deputy in the Italian parliament was flouted and he remained in prison until, terminally ill, he was released a fortnight before his death in 1937. The prosecutor at his trial echoed Mussolini when he said: 'We must stop this brain from functioning for twenty years.' That they failed to do, since Gramsci spent his time making copious notes on culture and politics, which became of major influence on Western Marxist theory and strategy after they were smuggled out of prison and eventually published several years later.

Gramsci's key contribution to cultural and political theory is the concept of hegemony, derived from Lenin but which he developed into a much more complex tool of analysis. Lenin's version of hegemony became 'the dictatorship of the proletariat'. Gramsci broadened the notion of hegemony to refer to social leadership in general and used it to analyse how capitalist forces secured and maintained their command over subordinate groups, including liberal democratic and fascist regimes as well as in actual and potential forms of socialist governance. In a period of political defeat for the Left, Gramsci sought to analyse how capitalism had fought off the challenge of revolutionary socialism and how a popular counter-hegemony might be built, especially in political cultures with stronger traditions of democracy than had pertained in the unusual conditions of Russia, where the Bolshevik revolution had occurred. For instance, in Italy, the division between the modern industrial North and the pre-modern conditions of the rural South was of determinate significance, as was the enormous sway of the Roman Catholic church. His reflections on these matters were echoed many years later in the failed PCI strategy of the 1970s, 'the historic compromise' between communism and Catholicism. Gramsci, however, would probably not have disapproved of that strategy.

In his political and cultural reasoning, Gramsci used a military metaphor by distinguishing between 'war of manoeuvre' and 'war of position'. The Bolshevik revolution was a war of manoeuvre, a sudden assault on the crumbling power of the Czarist state. In Western democratic conditions, however, Gramsci recommended that a bid for state power must normally be prepared by what might turn out to be a very protracted war of position, staking out territory and forging alliances in civil society that would constitute a bloc of support, a consensus with deep roots. Achieving social leadership, in this sense, was more than simply winning elections. Gramsci was interested in how the balance of power in society shifted, including economic, political and cultural shifts, sometimes almost imperceptibly over time. Hegemony was about winning consent, framing problems and offering solutions that were sufficiently in touch with popular sentiments so as to command widespread support.

To understand the deep, almost glacial movements of social power, it is necessary to have a sophisticated grasp of culture at various levels, from everyday common-sense and popular forms to abstract philosophy and technical reasoning. The role of intellectuals in this is vital. Gramsci argued that everyone is an intellectual, but only some have the social function of intellectual. In this respect, he distinguished between 'traditional' and 'organic' intellectuals. Traditional intellectuals are the inheritors of the clerisy, for example, certain kinds of humanistic academic. Under modern, secular conditions, organic intellectuals are more significant than traditional intellectuals. A whole stratum of bureaucrats, managers, scientists and technicians have arisen with crucial tasks of social organisation, whether in the state or private sectors. In classical Marxist terms, these groups were seen as the functionaries of capital and the bourgeoisie, whereas oppositional intellectuals, communist party cadres and so forth, were considered the organic intellectuals of the proletariat. In a more complex view, however, one more closely attuned to the complexities of later modern societies, made up not only of fragmented class relations but also gendered relations and diverse ethnicities, the struggles are not so simply delineated. Yet, there is no doubt that a continual tussle takes place throughout the various social institutions, workplaces, households, cultural and media organisations, between contrasting ideas and senses of identity. The subtlety and flexibility of Gramsci's style of reasoning, then, still greatly illuminates 'the battle for hearts and minds'; and has been demonstrated by innumerable studies of social power and cultural struggle.

Further reading

Davidson, A. Antonio Gramsci: Towards an Intellectual Biography, Merlin, 1977.
Laclau, E. and Mouffe, C. Hegemony and Socialist Strategy: Towards a Radical Democratic Politics, Verso, 1985.
Showstack Sassoon, A. Gramsci's Politics, 2nd edn, Croom Helm, 1987.

J.McG.

GREENBERG, Clement

Art critic	born USA 1909—
Associated with	MODERNISM ■ ABSTRACT EXPRESSIONISM ■ AVANT-GARDE
Influences include	KANT ■ ELIOT ■ RUSKIN
Shares common ground with	ADORNO ■ JOYCE ■ ROSENBERG
Main works	THE COLLECTED ESSAYS AND CRITICISM (4 VOLS., ED. J. O'BRIAN, 1986–93) THE PRACTICE AND THEORY OF INDIVIDUAL PSYCHOLOGY (1924) UNDERSTANDING HUMAN NATURE (1927)

C LEMENT GREENBERG'S CAREER was to a great extent occupied with exposing the stupefying qualities of twentieth-century popular culture, and with extolling the power of modernist art as an antidote. During idle periods as a US customs official, Greenberg wrote essays on culture and art. As his reputation as a talented cultural analyst spread, Greenberg's opinions were soon being solicited by journals such as *Nation*, *New Leader* and *Partisan Review*, of which the latter published his famous article, 'Avant Garde and Kitsch', in 1939.

Greenberg lamented modern society's affection for the simplistic and saccharine artistic expressions of 'kitsch'. Kitsch, according to Greenberg, is related to the demands of advanced capitalism for a pliable yet literate workforce. According to Greenberg, accompanying the essential working-class literacy comes a desire to challenge and divert these new intellectual skills. Such a desire, however, threatens the workplace constraints of money, time and regimentation. The working class could not be allowed the aesthetic distractions available to the leisured class. Kitsch, for Greenberg, satisfies the diversionary interests of the newly literate without unleashing the more inquisitive and eccentric aspects of sophisticated artistry. In kitsch, the quest for the completely new is exchanged for the cute presentation of 'new twists' on old themes. The potentially disruptive intellectual development of the working class is diverted into art that employs formulas and mechanisms that parallel the rigidified intelligence needed in the workplace. Kitsch is cute, while avoiding the more contemplative and unsettling power of beauty.

How can the opiating effects of kitsch be overcome? The solution rests with modernism and the avant-garde. For Greenberg, there is such a paucity of stimulating and edifying references in the everyday world that good art must 'detach' itself from concerns of content and focus more energetically on consideration of form. And for Greenberg, the appropriate forms in the contemporary situation involve purity and limited accessibility. Because society is so arid and superficial, any art with the promise of edification can no longer seek validation in that society. Good art, instead, finds validation within itself, within forms and structures that pertain to the medium itself. If purity, originality and depth cannot be found in the everyday world, modernism will see to it that such concepts can at least be retained in artworks.

It is no surprise that Greenberg admires the work of Jackson Pollock. Pollock purged his painting of the corrupting influences of the external elements, including elements of other artistic media. Sculptural shading was replaced by pure, unnatural colour. Subtle sculptural curves were replaced by prominent, linear brush strokes. And geometric shapes, conforming to the dimensions of the canvas ('grid'), replaced natural and literary images. Greenberg's and Pollock's modernism represents a self-contained universe, unwilling to admit extraneous, diverting clutter.

Opposed to the lower forms like kitsch, Greenberg refers to the avant-garde as 'high' art. Modernist art cannot be appreciated 'without effort'. Because it is so tenuously connected to the contented present, it demands extrication from the easy chair of mindless consumption. Yet the extrication is crucial, given the paucity of other sources of stimulation. In fact, Greenberg burdens modernist art with the responsibility for puncturing the stupor of modern society. Needless to say, this cannot be an easy task for a movement so consciously dedicated to detachment from the cares of the given world.

Further reading

Clarke, D. 'The All-Over Image: Meaning in Abstract Art', JOURNAL OF AMERICAN STUDIES, 27:3 December 1993, pp. 355–76.
Decter, J. *et al.* 'The Greenberg Effect: Comments by Younger Artists, Critics and Curators', ARTS MAGAZINE, 64:4 December 1989, pp. 58–63.
Kuspit, D. CLEMENT GREENBERG, ART CRITIC, University of Wisconsin Press, 1979.
Rubenfeld, Florence CLEMENT GREENBERG: A LIFE, Scribner, 1997.

T.J.L.

GREER, Germaine

Feminist/writer	born Australia 1939—
Associated with	SECOND-WAVE FEMINISM ■ WOMEN'S LIBERATION
Influences include	DE BEAUVOIR
Shares common ground with	MILLET ■ FRIEDAN ■ FIGGS ■ FIRESTONE
Main works	THE FEMALE EUNUCH (1969)
	SEX AND DESTINY: THE POLITICS OF HUMAN FERTILITY (1984)
	THE CHANGE: WOMEN, AGEING AND THE MENOPAUSE (1991)

GREER WAS BORN and educated in Melbourne, Australia. She completed a BA at the University of Melbourne (1959), an MA at Sydney University (1963) and a Ph.D. at the University of Cambridge (1968). She began her career as a lecturer and journalist, occasional actor and television presenter. She rose to international prominence with the publication of *The Female Eunuch*, which was translated into twelve languages and considered a seminal text of the Women's Liberation Movement. More than any other figure of the time, Greer is attributed with popularising feminism worldwide. Greer is currently an unofficial fellow of Newnham College, Cambridge, while remaining a regular and often controversial contributor to the *Sunday Times*.

In *The Female Eunuch*, Greer analysed the condition of being female and demonstrated that femininity and the assumptions surrounding women's inferiority were a patriarchal construct which effectively enslaved women. The title of the book refers to her argument that women's sexuality has been repressed and denied. She detailed how women had been constructed and portrayed throughout literature, history and popular culture as 'symbolically castrated'. Freudian psychologists have theorised the development of the female sexual identity as predicated on lack (specifically the lack of a penis or sexual organ); the vagina itself had been virtually non-existent in sexual imagery up to that time and, concomitant with this symbolic castration, women were portrayed as also lacking sexual feelings and passions. As a result women's cultural status was equivalent to that of a female version of the castrated eunuch.

Through the book, Greer exhorted women to regain their sexuality and claim the right to assert their own sexual expression, take an active role in sexual activities and strive for equality in sexual relations. Until they did this, the relations between the sexes would remain predicated on unequal power relations, with women cast in the role of the passive recipient of the male sado-masochistic desires. Such uneven sexual relations must necessarily lead to misunderstanding and conflict, if not open hostility, between the sexes.

Greer firmly believed that women, in their passive acceptance of patriarchal constructions of femininity, were as much to blame as patriarchy itself for their situation. The solution was consciousness-raising through which women could free themselves from patriarchal and sexual restraints (which she believed imprisoned men as well as women), and effect a transformation of sexual relations. Not surprisingly, the so-called 'malestream' press tended to denigrate *The Female Eunuch* and, by extension, the Women's Liberation Movement, as advocating sexual licentiousness for women. Some feminists criticised *The Female Eunuch* for its lack of theoretical rigour.

Although *The Female Eunuch* became synonymous with the Women's Liberation Movement, Greer has maintained her distance from the organised women's movement and her relationship with feminism has been stormy. With the publication of *Sex and Destiny: The Politics of Human Fertility*, Greer once again ignited controversy. The book was seen by some feminists as a betrayal of feminism for championing the significance of mothering in women's lives and advocating a return to the extended family. Her later book, *The Change: Women, Ageing and the Menopause*, an exploration of 200 years of the cultural management of menopause, its treatment and medical theories associated with it, created more controversy. Greer argued that women needed to mentally prepare for menopause and grieve for the 'death of their womb' before they could move on.

Greer's journey from *The Female Eunuch* through to *The Change: Women, Ageing and the Menopause* can be seen as reflecting the developments and maturation of feminism itself. There is, however, another Greer often obscured by her flamboyant personality and confrontationist style. In *The Obstacle Race: The Fortunes of Women Painters and their Work* (1979), she has explored the work of previously ignored female painters in order to recover the history of women painters. In a similar project, Greer has also written about women poets (see *Kissing the Rod: An Anthology of* 17th Century Women's Verse, 1989 and *Slip-shod Sibyls: Recognition, Rejection and the Woman Poet*, 1995). In addition, Greer is a recognised Shakespearean scholar.

Her other works include *The Madwoman's Underclothes: Essays and Occasional Writings* (1986), an anthology of her newspaper and magazine essays (some previously unpublished); and *Daddy, We Hardly Knew You* (1989), an emotional and sensitive story of her search for her father's real identity beneath the subterfuge identity he had created for himself.

Further reading

Lovell, T. (ed.) BRITISH FEMINIST THOUGHT: A READER, Blackwell, 1990.
Raymond, M.E. 'Germaine Greer', in P. Kester-Shelton, FEMINIST WRITERS, St James Press, 1996.
Scneir, M. (ed.) THE VINTAGE BOOK OF FEMINISM: THE ESSENTIAL WRITINGS OF THE CONTEMPORARY WOMEN'S MOVEMENT, Vintage, 1995.

G.C.

GROSZ, Elizabeth

Philosopher/feminist theorist	born Australia
Associated with	FEMINIST EPISTEMOLOGIES ▪ PHILOSOPHY ▪ POST-STRUCTURALISM
Influences include	NIETZSCHE ▪ DELEUZE ▪ GUATTARI ▪ SPINOZA
Shares common ground with	GATENS ▪ LINGIS ▪ BUTLER
Main works	SEXUAL SUBVERSIONS: THREE FRENCH FEMINISTS (1990) VOLATILE BODIES: TOWARD A CORPOREAL FEMINISM (1994) SPACE, TIME AND PERVERSION: ESSAYS ON THE POLITICS OF THE BODY (1995)

ELIZABETH GROSZ IS currently Director of the Institute for Critical and Cultural Studies at Monash University, Australia. Her work engages with the connections across feminist philosophies of the body, deconstruction and post-structuralist configurations of thinking. Psychoanalysis provided the arena for her work on the interrelationships between the biological and the psychical. However, moving through an insightful study of psychoanalysis, phenomenology and neurophysiology, Grosz's work has provided new formations for contemporary feminist epistemologies of the body and subjectivity, by engaging with the philosophies of Nietzsche, Spinoza and Deleuze and Guaratti.

In line with much post-structuralist and anti-Cartesian thinking, Grosz's work seeks to explore and provide an affirmative understanding of the body which might prove useful for feminist epistemologies and for rethinking materiality. Thus, various issues in feminist theory, including women's subjectivities, experiences, desires and pleasures, may be reconceived in corporeal terms through newly configured theoretical paradigms. Providing a feminist philosophy of the body which endeavours to break away from dichotomous views of subjectivity, Grosz articulates an understanding of 'embodied subjectivity'. As a transformational philosophy, her work has encouraged retheorised conceptions of sexual specificity, sexed subjectivity and corporeality.

This has been of prominent importance to a feminist arena in a so-called 'post-feminist' era and as a consequence, to feminist cultural theories. If contemporary feminism is to question political, ethical, personal and social accounts of the 'self', Grosz's work provides new discourses through which to analyse the cultural zones between our 'selves', 'bodies' and the cultural formations and spaces with which we integrate. As a project for feminisms, her work has been valuable in rethinking the states of the 'body' within the mind/body dualism of Western metaphysical thought. Much of this work has come from Grosz's engagement with the writings of Spinoza, Foucault and the more recent work of Deleuze and Guattari and Alphonso Lingis. An anti-psychoanalytic version of desire then, Grosz would argue, is affirmative, not abyssal. She writes: 'Desire does not create permanent multiplicities, it experiments, producing ever-new alignments, linkages and connections, making things. It is fundamentally nomadic not teleological, meandering, creative, non-repetitive, proliferate, unpredictable' (Grosz 1994: 168).

Grosz draws on Deleuzian ideas of the body as 'assemblage' and 'text' to theorise the spaces between ourselves, our bodies and cultural forms, practices and formations: from cityscapes and architecture to fashion, perversion and the taboo. Her more recent interest in human materiality and its congruence with both organic and inorganic matter has encouraged her to move into molecular science and enquiry into a materialism that questions physicalism. As a result, her current work is taking her into evolutionary theory, molecular biology and the life sciences, moving beyond a feminist agenda of the corporeal.

Further reading

Grosz, E. JACQUES LACAN: A FEMINIST INTRODUCTION, Routledge, 1990.
Grosz, E. 'A Thousand Tiny Sexes: Feminism and Rhizomatics', in C. Boundas and D. Olkowski (eds.), GILLES DELEUZE AND THE THEATER OF PHILOSOPHY, Routledge, 1994.
Grosz, E. SPACE, TIME AND PERVERSION: ESSAYS ON THE POLITICS OF THE BODY, Routledge, 1995.

B.K.

GUATTARI, Félix

Psychoanalyst/philosopher	born France 1930–1992
Associated with	SCHIZO-ANALYSIS ■ DETERRITORIALISATION
Influences include	HEGEL ■ SPINOZA ■ LAING
Shares common ground with	DELEUZE ■ FOUCAULT ■ CHATELET
Main works	PSYCHANALYSE ET TRANSVERSALITÉ (1972) CAPITALISME ET SCHIZOPHRÉNIE (WITH GILLES DELEUZE, 1972, TRANS. CAPITALISM AND SCHIZOPHRENIA)
	VOL. 1: L'ANTI-OEDIPE (1972, TRANS. ANTI-OEDIPUS)
	VOL. 2: MILLE PLATEAUX (1980, TRANS. A THOUSAND PLATEAUX)

T HE KEYWORD IN the life of Félix Guattari was mobility. Growing up in a working-class suburb of north-west Paris, Guattari was briefly a student of pharmacy before turning his attention to philosophy, psychiatry and psychoanalysis. In 1953 he joined the psychiatrist Jean Oury in setting up, in a restored château near Blois, the clinic of La Borde, where he was to work for well-nigh forty years. Influenced by the so-called school of 'anti-psychiatry' associated with such figures as R.D. Laing, Guattari resisted all forms of coercive therapy or incarceration. He and his collaborators aimed to create an open environment in which patients were encouraged to participate in the collective activities of the clinic. Guattari always spent more time at La Borde than in Paris, and it was there that he died suddenly of a heart attack in 1992.

Given the left-wing sympathies of Guattari, La Borde also became the gathering point for militants of various causes. A member of the French Community Party after the war, Guattari was expelled from the party following divergences from party policy. However, he championed a succession of radical causes, and gained increased prominence during the May 1968 riots in Paris. One commentator has remarked that Guattari was a 'widower of 1968', and Guattari himself admitted in 1986 that, while the 1960s represented for him 'a seemingly endless spring', the 1980s were 'one long winter'.

Nevertheless, Guattari never lost his appetite for radical political campaigning. He supported a succession of causes, including homosexual equality and the feminist movement. In later years, he joined the Green Party, and spoke out vigorously on a range of ecological issues. An indefatigable 'founder', Guattari set up many study and research groupings, including CERFI (Centre d'Études et de Recherches sur le Fonctionnement des Institutions). He was also a founder of the journal *Recherches*.

Moreover, the 1970s were to constitute in many ways the decisive decade of his life. It was then that he collaborated with the philosopher Gilles Deleuze to produce one of the literary bombshells of the post-war period: *L'Anti-Oedipe*. Long disillusioned with the Freudian and Lacanian schools, Guattari here used his psychoanalytic expertise to join with Deleuze in denouncing what they saw as the sclerosis and reductionism of Oedipal discourse. Resisting the imposition of a triangular familial template, Deleuze and Guattari argued for a 'schizo-analysis' which recognised the multiple and polyvalent forces of desire, in a 'deterritorialisation' which was unshackled from the oedipal paradigm. In the second volume of *Capitalisme et Schizophrénie – Mille Plateaux –* they developed the argument further, exploring process and event in preference to being and activity.

Guattari was a conspicuous figure in left-wing intellectual circles, particularly from 1968 onwards. Prolific in speech and writing, he enjoyed the role of '*agent provocateur*', and was always conscious of a pedagogical vocation within psychoanalysis and political debate. Nevertheless, although his solo output contains eight books and many articles, it is mainly for his remarkable collaboration with Gilles Deleuze that he gained widespread attention. Although their interaction remained for many years on a fairly formal basis, their productive partnership sprang from what Jean Oury has called 'a sort of "dialectic" of friendship'. Both brought very particular specialisms and insights, and Guattari once remarked that, while he was the 'conceptual commando', Deleuze could add to their intellectual artillery the heavy weaponry of philosophy. Guattari has sometimes been criticised for appearing to be a 'touche-à-tout' (jack-of-all-trades). However, his consistent left-wing convictions and boundless energy ensured that all his activities bore the stamp of commitment. Moreover, within that nomadic flux which seems destined to be termed 'Deleuzian', multiplicity is a positive value, an alternative to the stranglehold of reification.

Further reading

Bogue, R. DELEUZE AND GUATTARI, Routledge, 1989.
Genoski, G. (ed.) THE GUATTARI READER, Blackwell, 1996.
Goodchild, P. DELEUZE AND GUATTARI: AN INTRODUCTION TO THE POLITICS OF DESIRE, Sage, 1996.

M.B.

HABERMAS, Jürgen

Philosopher	born Germany 1929—
Associated with	THE FRANKFURT SCHOOL
Influences include	HEGEL ∎ MARX ∎ WEBER
Shares common ground with	HORKHEIMER ∎ ADORNO ∎ MARCUSE
Main works	THEORIE DES KOMMUNIKATIVEN HANDELNS, 2 VOLS., 1981, 1985, TRANS. THE THEORY OF COMMUNICATIVE ACTION, 2 VOLS., (1981, 1987) LEGITIMATIONSPROBLEME IM SPÄTKAPITALISMUS (1973) TRANS. LEGITIMATION CRISIS, 1973) TOWARD A RATIONAL SOCIETY (1970)

HABERMAS GAINED HIS Ph.D. from the University of Bonn in 1954 and his *Habilitation* (a high-level postdoctoral degree) in 1961 from the University of Marburg. In 1964 he became Professor of Philosophy at the University of Frankfurt. He became Director of the Max Planck Institute in 1971. In 1981, he returned to Frankfurt as Professor of Philosophy.

First-generation Frankfurt School thinkers like Herbert Marcuse, Max Horkheimer and Theodor Adorno savaged the mentality of the Enlightenment for its repressiveness. Marcuse's *exposé* of 'technological rationality', *One-Dimensional Man*, is an epitaph to a species that has sacrificed all but the most remote possibility of reconciliation with internal and external nature to the obscene and gratuitous domination of science.

For Habermas, who inherits the analytical priorities of his Frankfurt predecessors, the problems with science and technology stem more from successes than deficiencies. He is not so much concerned with the exploitative character of science as that science is intruding into considerations where it is unqualified.

Scientific thinking, according to Habermas, is fundamentally instrumental. Science may be crucial to the implementation of the good life, but it lacks the equipment to consider and debate specifications. Because science has been so successful, and because of its posture as pure and objective, it has been allowed to intrude into non-instrumental discussions. But this leads to the unconsidered and authoritative (authoritarian) imposition of science's implicit values – prediction, replication, control. The good life becomes the scientific life.

In this sense, then, even Marx succumbs to positivism. The superiority of socialism is demonstrated scientifically. But this means that scientific priorities will be transported unscathed into the socialist alternative. Socialism is touted as more efficient without a thorough exploration of the origin and value of the concept of efficiency.

Where Adorno and Marcuse would demand more of science, that it link its instrumentality to a receptive and instructive nature, Habermas accuses his teachers of romanticism, and argues that human emancipation can and must come to terms with an exploitative relationship with nature. That this appears to be a concession, however, is vitiated by Habermas's insistence that human beings' relations amongst themselves promote different values and priorities, and that the wandering instrumentality of science can be given its appropriate identity by this other sphere.

Although he altered specifics over his writings, Habermas has consistently examined the realm of human communication. He argues that before any hierarchical, specialised and instrumental concept of science, there is human investment in forms of communication that are shared by all participants, and in which participants can exchange ideas amongst themselves as co-operative and reflective equals. Habermas pays special attention to the development of this kind of communication in the bourgeois era. In coffee houses and new periodicals, Habermas traces the growth of egalitarian communication and of the free and equal citizenship rights that are sought as a result. But Habermas is far from presenting this development in meliorist terms. On the contary, the critical bite to his argument is that contemporary advertising, public relations, mass media and popular leisure forms produce the 'refeudalisation' of the public sphere by manipulating and distorting communication. In this respect,

Habermas's criticism is reminiscent of Adorno and Horkheimer's denunciation of the 'culture industry'.

Science can distinguish itself only after the 'public sphere' is established and maintained. Science, which is only instrumental, is ultimately dependent for values accrued in this sphere. When science intrudes into the realm of communication and asserts exploitation and control in intersubjective relations, the result is loss of meaning, anomie and psychopathologies, according to Habermas. Habermas is not surprised or particularly depressed, then, that emancipatory energy is not forthcoming from the proletariat and others who are considered 'scientifically' more qualified to lead. Those who merely insist on a more efficient delivery of the goods are vulnerable to co-optation or distraction. Instead, Habermas detects a deeper alienation amongst those who are outside the instrumentalities altogether. It is one thing to demand that the system deliver the goods. It is yet another to demand a deep accounting of the entire delivery system. Those on the outside are more likely to see the need for free and equal participation in undistorted communication. Feminism, not the labour movement, then, is presently a more promising source of a more balanced, human perspective.

Further reading

Alford, C.F. SCIENCE AND THE REVENGE OF NATURE: MARCUSE AND HABERMAS, University Presses of Florida, 1985.
Braaten, J. HABERMAS'S CRITICAL THEORY OF SOCIETY, SUNY Press, 1991.
Roderick, R. HABERMAS AND THE FOUNDATIONS OF CRITICAL THEORY, St Martin's Press, 1986.

T.J.L.

HALL, Stuart

Cultural theorist/sociologist	born Jamaica 1932—
Associated with	CULTURALISM ■ HEGEMONY THEORY ■ STRUCTURALISM
Influences include	ALTHUSSER ■ ECO ■ FOUCAULT ■ GRAMSCI ■ HOGGART ■ LACLAU ■ WILLIAMS
Shares common ground with	EAGLETON ■ GILROY ■ JAMESON
Main works	POLICING THE CRISIS (WITH CHAS CRITCHER, TONY JEFFERSON, JOHN CLARKE AND BRIAN ROBERTS, 1978) 'CULTURAL STUDIES: TWO PARADIGMS' (1980) 'ENCODING/DECODING' (1980) 'THE REDISCOVERY OF 'IDEOLOGY': RETURN OF THE REPRESSED IN MEDIA STUDIES' (1982) 'MINIMAL SELVES' (1987) THE HARD ROAD TO RENEWAL (1988)

H ALL LEFT THE Caribbean with a Rhodes scholarship to study English at Oxford in the early 1950s. His organisational capacities quickly came to the fore when he edited *New Left Review* at the end of that decade. For a while he taught English in secondary modern schools in London, from which experience came his co-authored book, with Paddy Whannel, *The Popular Arts*, 1964 an early guide to media studies. In 1964 he took up a fellowship at the newly formed Centre for Contemporary Cultural Studies at the University of Birmingham, under the leadership of Richard Hoggart, whom he was eventually to succeed as Director. He moved on from Birmingham to a professorship in sociology at the Open University, where he remained until his retirement in 1997. Alongside a busy academic career, Hall has been a leading thinker on the left of British politics, from his early involvement with the New Left through his association with *Marxism Today* in the 1980s and the 'New Times' thesis. He coined the term 'Thatcherism', the emergence and significance of which he had already identified before Margaret Thatcher's first election victory in a *Marxism Today* article, 'The Great Moving Right Show' (1978). In his later work, Hall has been increasingly preoccupied with questions of identity, especially black identity in the context of Afro-Caribbean Britishness. He wrote and presented a brilliant BBC documentary series on the Caribbean, *Redemption Song*, in 1991.

Hall is a great synthesiser and extremely alert to symptoms of intellectual and social change. He has been able to apply sophisticated reasoning with speed and aplomb to current events and shifting mores. Some of his best writing is in the form of extended journalism. Hall's work has been extremely diverse and his position in constant revision. Among his most enduring themes, however, is how everyday life has been transformed under consumer capitalism, in such a way, in fact, that traditionally left-wing assumptions about class and politics have to be discarded. He has persistently called for fresh thinking and, to this end, Hall has seized upon new currents of thought, the continental Marxism that came into Britain to a significant extent through *New Left Review* during the 1960s and 1970s, and the latterly more fashionable strands of post-structuralism and identity politics. In the 1970s he created a neo-Gramscian synthesis which framed the main concerns of cultural studies for several years. Under his charismatic tutelage, what was later named in retrospect and from outside 'the Birmingham School' was made up of an exceptionally talented generation of postgraduate students, many of whom were to emerge as leading figures of cultural studies in their own right. The dynamic encoding/decoding model of media communication and its application to television audience research is a notable contribution of Hall and his followers during the 1970s. Hall's departure from Birmingham around 1980 led to the demise of the Birmingham School both institutionally and, more diffusely, in terms of intellectual and political direction. Hall's own position has since then become increasingly post-structuralist and is particularly influenced by Foucault and the culture, in Gilroy's phrase, of 'the Black Atlantic'.

In his most influential work, Hall's principal purpose was to produce a form of non-economist Marxism, drawing on Althusser and Gramsci, to the extent that he only rarely paid attention to the economic determinations of social and cultural change, the main exception being the 'New Times' thesis on post-Fordism. Instead, he has typically emphasised the role of ideology, not as 'false ideas' but as lived practices, and hegemonic principles of leadership in the struggle for social power. Hall stresses the role of popular culture in politics and, in the 1980s, he placed great emphasis on the tension between the 'authoritarian populism' of Thatcherite politics and the 'popular–democratic' politics of alternative and oppositional forces. His work during this period, including the collaborative publication, *Policing the Crisis*, a study of the 1970s 'mugging' panic as the harbinger of law and order solution to social crisis in Britain, particularly demonstrated the enduring relevance of Gramsci's thought to contemporary cultural and political analyses.

The collapse of Eastern European communism coincided rather curiously with the virtual discarding of Marxism in much cultural studies, which was, by the 1990s, a very marked feature of Hall's work. His turn towards identity politics and its theorisation reflects the general drift of thought in the field of study that he played a major role in mapping out. It also seems to have a very personal dimension in that Hall's own sense of black identity was not apparently a prominent feature of his thinking when he was more avowedly Marxist.

Further reading

Jacques, M. and Hall, S. (eds.) NEW TIMES: THE CHANGING FACE OF POLITICS IN THE 1990S, Lawrence & Wishart, 1989.
Morley, D. and Chen, K-H. (eds.) STUART HALL: CRITICIAL DIALOGUES IN CULTURAL STUDIES, Routledge, 1996.
J.McG.

HARAWAY, Donna

Scientist, socialist feminist	born USA 1944—
Associated with	SOCIALIST FEMINISM ▪ SCIENCE ▪ PARTIAL PERSPECTIVES
Influences include	HUME ▪ MARX ▪ NIETZSCHE
Shares common ground with	KUHN ▪ HARTSOCK ▪ HARDING
Main works	CRYSTALS, FABRICS AND FIELDS: METAPHORS OF ORGANICISM IN TWENTIETH CENTURY DEVELOPMENTAL BIOLOGY (1976)
	PRIMATE VISIONS: GENDER, RACE, AND NATURE IN THE WORLD OF MODERN SCIENCE (1989)
	SIMIANS, CYBORGS, AND WOMEN: THE REINVENTION OF NATURE (1991)

H ARAWAY TRAINED AS a biologist, and her cultural commentaries retain her interest and expertise in science. In fact, her concerns about feminism parallel her concerns about science. She sees that science is very much a high-stakes battlefield over competing priorities and perspectives, where money, prestige and position are often more effective weapons than expertise or ingenuity. Yet she would also like to think that her interest in science is something more than involvement in a political campaign. Discovering a cure for AIDS must be more meaningful than the arrival at a benchmark, the importance of which is derived completely from the self-serving priorities of the contemporary scientific hierarchy. This tension between relativism and progress has informed her investigations of contemporary culture and feminism in particular.

Postmodernism has allowed feminists to expose the thorough instrumentality and bias of purportedly neutral scientific and social constructs. Contemporary hierarchical systems can be justified only within their own 'texts', and they thus lose their status as anything more important. But, of course, this nonchalance about things considered true or valuable or progressive can have a devastating effect on commitments to feminism also, since the claim can be made that feminism too is no more than one competing text among many.

Yet amidst this apparent anarchy of competing claims and perspectives, Haraway discovers a guiding principle. She argues that since 'partial perspective' is all one can achieve, we can reject perspectives with more ambitious claims and instead embrace perspectives that recognise their inherent limitations and solicit the input, influence and proliferation of alternative perspectives. Haraway rejects the perspectives that attempt the 'God trick'. These perspectives issue from sectors of power, where knowledge systems seem more comprehensive. The comprehensiveness is illusory, however, because it is only brute force, manipulation and denial that resist other equally informative perspectives. Those who attempt the God trick are attracted to the idea of the 'disembodied gaze' – a way of looking at things as though at the controls of a video game, where viewers manipulate characters and objects while they themselves remain unrestricted by spatial or corporeal restraints. The God trick fails, however, because those corporeal 'restraints' are unavoidable aspects of human existence.

Not surprisingly, Haraway looks for advice to those who have been subjugated, because the God trick is unavailable to them and because they recognise it and resist it. For those who embrace situated knowledges and partial perspectives, the 'disembodied gaze' is replaced by vision that is constantly aware and reminded of the traits of the viewer and the perspective of the view – that is, reminded that no single perspective is complete.

To be honest to her prescription, then, Haraway must be critical of a good deal of feminism, especially that which is associated with 'identity politics'. In fact, she takes issue with the entire distinction between sex and gender, arguing that even morphological distinctions based on sexual traits are constructs of a partial perspective that privileges human sexuality. Haraway is not content with her identity as a 'woman'. She prefers to contemplate multiple identities, many of them having nothing to do with a distinction (either biological or social) between men and women. In her now famous 'Cyborg Manifesto', Haraway argues that the boundaries between animal, human and machine are breaking down. Biotechnology, virtual reality and computer simulation indiscriminately employ components from heretofore discrete sectors of animal, machine and human. Haraway sees herself as a fluid amalgam of animal, human and machine. She identifies with the 'chimponaut', HAM, and she contemplates carrying a hybrid foetus.

Further reading

Barns, Ian 'Post-Fordist People, FUTURES, 23: 9 (November 1991), pp. 895–914.
Dery, Marc ESCAPE VELOCITY: CYBERCULTURE AT THE END OF THE CENTURY, Hodder and Stoughton, 1996.
Prins, Baukje 'The Ethics of Hybrid Subjects: Feminist Constructivism According to Donna Haraway', SCIENCE, TECHNOLOGY, AND HUMAN VALUES, 20: 3 (Summer 1995), pp. 352–67.

T.J.L.

HARVEY, David

Urban geographer/political economist	born England 1935—
Associated with	CULTURAL GEOGRAPHY ▪ POLITICAL ECONOMY ▪ POSTMODERNISM ▪ REGULATION SCHOOL
Influences include	HEIDEGGER ▪ JAMESON ▪ JENCKS ▪ LEFEBVRE
Shares common ground with	CASTELLS ▪ DAVIS ▪ MASSEY ▪ SOJA ▪ VIRILIO ▪ ZUKIN
Main works	SOCIAL JUSTICE AND THE CITY (1973) THE LIMITS TO CAPITAL (1982) THE CONDITION OF POSTMODERNITY (1989)

D AVID HARVEY IS the leading British figure in Marxist and postmodern geography. However, he worked mainly in the USA, at Johns Hopkins University in Baltimore, as part of 'the brain drain'. In the late 1980s, Harvey returned to England for a few years to take up the Halford Mackinder Professorship in Geography at Oxford. His early *Social Justice and the City* (1973) signalled a break in his work from what he came to regard as a liberal geography to one inspired by classical Marxism, so that spatial analysis was informed by historically materialist categories. He later described his position, in *The Condition of Postmodernity* (1989), as 'historical–materialist geography'.

Since the 1970s, geography, which had until then hardly been a cutting-edge social science, entered an immensely fertile and mutual exchange with some of the most advanced thinking in social and cultural theory. Henri Lefebvre, the French urban sociologist, was a key inspiration for this encounter between Theory with a capital T and human geography. His *The Production of Space* (1974) made important distinctions between the physical, social and cultural constructions of space. The work of Manuel Castells also raised significant political questions about the social transformations of urban space, and the hugely influential Michel Foucault had, in his theory of discursive formations, placed great stress on the relations of space and power. These and other similar strands of thought had a considerable impact in both cultural theory and human geography.

Harvey's use of political economy in human and urban geography has been extremely technical and difficult for non-specialists to understand. This is particularly so of much of the reasoning in *The Limits to Capital* (1982). However, that changed with the publication of *The Condition of Postmodernity* in 1989, a book which Harvey himself has likened to Graham Greene's 'entertainments' in comparison with his serious novels. In spite of what he says, *The Condition of Postmodernity* is by no means a simple book. It combines Marxist political economy, urban geography and architectural, film and postmodern theory to produce a materialist account of the cultural contours, understood socially and spatially, of the present day. Harvey sees the shift into postmodernity as largely generated by economic developments in Western economies, precipitated by the OPEC oil crisis of 1973. The solution to the economic crisis thus sparked off was a switch in the mode of accumulation, from the rigidities of Fordism and state regulation into a flexible mode, which was identified by the regulation school of political economy as post-Fordism. In Harvey's account, this has been associated with the postmodernisation of culture. Postmodernism is not, then, to be seen first and foremost as an epistemological condition or an aesthetic trend. Rather, the postmodern is a social and spatial condition resulting from the collapse of Fordism, which, as Gramsci had argued, was not only a set of economic arrangements but a culture of social relations brought about by organised capitalism. Some have argued that post-Fordist capitalism is 'disorganised'. That is not, however, Harvey's opinion. For him the post-Fordist and postmodernist complex *is* organised, only differently from Fordism. With the over-accumulation and pressure on capitalism in the West, rapid processes of destruction and reconstruction took place. Old industrial areas went into sudden decline and urban dereliction. Western capital became even more spatially mobile than in the past. The postmodernisation of the city, in urban design and forms of consumption led by 'the new cultural intermediaries', has frequently been promoted as the solution to deindustrialisation and has been a prominent feature of Western urban and cultural policies.

Similarly to Paul Virilio, Harvey stresses the sheer speed of postmodern capitalism and culture. His notion of 'time–space compression' refers to the instantaneous communication of money and messages which is facilitated by information technologies and satellites. International financial markets operate, as Castells has argued, in a single time-frame, and events like the fall of the Berlin Wall are watched on television around the world as they happen. These processes are frequently cited as evidence of a ubiquitous 'globalisation' process whereby local and national differences are being obliterated. While not disputing that such a trend is to a significant extent occurring, Harvey qualifies the light-headed and neo-McLuhanite 'global village' thesis by pointing to the complex relations between space and place, the interconnectedness of globality and locality, in effect, the dialectical interplay of countervailing forces which produce new and dynamic spatial configurations.

Further reading

Castells, M. 'European Cities, the Informational Society, and the Global Economy', NEW LEFT REVIEW, 204, 1994.
Ellin, N. POSTMODERN URBANISM, Blackwell, 1996.
Massey, D. SPACE, PLACE AND GENDER, Polity, 1994.
Soja, E. POSTMODERN GEOGRAPHIES: THE REASSERTION OF SPACE IN CRITICAL SOCIAL THEORY, Verso, 1989.

J.McG.

HEGEL, Georg Wilhelm Friedrich

Philosopher	born Germany 1770–1831
Associated with	IDEALISM ■ DIALECTICS ■ GEIST
Influences include	KANT ■ GOETHE ■ SCHELLING
Shares common ground with	MARX ■ KOYEVE ■ LACAN
Main works	PHENOMENOLOGY OF SPIRIT (1977)
	PHENOMENOLOGY OF MIND (1967)
	THE PHILOSOPHY OF RIGHT (1964)

HEGEL WAS ONE of Germany's foremost Idealist philosophers. His ideas were to occupy Western philosophical thought for the greater part of the nineteenth century. Although direct references to his work have declined since then, his legacy has lived on through a highly influential set of lectures on his *Phenomenology of Spirit*, given by Alexandre Kojève in Paris between 1933 and 1939. These seminars were attended by an impressive list of twentieth-century thinkers; Lacan, Sartre, Bataille, Lévinas and Merleau-Ponty, to mention but a few.

Hegel's work was, in part, a reaction to that of his German predecessor, Kant. Kant argues that there exists an unknowable but essential aspect of the world; the realm of 'things-in-themselves'. Hegel contended, however, that appearance and essence are in fact intrinsically linked and not, as Kant had argued, alienated from each other. Instead, Hegel put forward the idea that all reality and truths are available as knowledge. Such knowledge, according to Hegel, can be appropriated from the phenomenological world by virtue of the ideas that we, as human beings, have about that world. The process within which we ultimately get to know reality is one that is fundamental to Hegel's philosophy; that of the dialectic.

Although the dialectic can be posited as a theoretical model; as a hypothetical movement between a thesis, its antithesis and finally, their synthesis, Hegel regarded his dialectic to be epistemologically essential; positing the workings of the universe as being necessarily dialectical.

According to Hegel the universe is a hierarchical and organic entity; with lower life-forms such as algae and bacteria being at the bottom, and human consciousness being at the top; however, all levels of this universe are intrinsically linked. The human ability to abstract truths from the world means that it is the only form of 'being' that can be truly free from the confines of the physical, the universe being infinitely accessible through the medium of human thought.

A way in which the teleology of the world can be observed is to regard it as a 'progress in the consciousness of freedom'. According to Hegel, the consciousness of any historical epoch is expressed above all in its intellectual and theological concerns and developments, religion and philosophy being an arena where 'a people defines for itself what it holds to be true . . . . Religion is a people's consciouness of what is, of its highest being.' Thereby advances in abstract thought, in religious conceptions and philosophical ideas, correspond with social and political freedom.

Hegel thought that the individual needs the state in order to acquire the system for freedom; that in order for that individual to be 'free' it has to have certain codes and frameworks to live by. He argues in *Philosophy of Right* that such a state is 'based on need'. There is, therefore, no freedom obtainable from 'outside' the state but only self-determination considered through the social and moral frameworks within. As any nation-state is a historical entity it moves, through dialectical motion, to a synthesis; or a state of absolute being. Governments may fall, but this is all part of the slow eradication of all that is unnecessary. Each state or nation has a 'spirit'; a mind of the people, or *Geist*. Any history, therefore, is a record of that spirit's progress; of its maturity and decline. But history as a whole forms a rational pattern; each mind of a people is a link in a chain in the progress of the 'world spirit'; the climax of which will be the absolute 'world mind'. The world, therefore, according to Hegel, is one large thinking organism.

For Hegel the thought of a nation manifests itself within its particular cultural artefacts and discourses. Man's ability to transform, to 'work upon' the world, means that he can know it completely. Hegel insists that art is not just a means of expressing or evoking feeling, but is a way of that society apprehending knowledge about itself and the world in a visual format; visually transforming the world for its own epistemological purposes. Religion, for example, offers the paradigm of the 'Holy Ghost' (or an equivalent) so that a nation can realise and visualise its own 'spirit'.

Hegel's notion of the dialectic was adopted, in part, by Marx as a way of revealing the 'growth' and collapse of social systems. Like Hegel, Marx interprets world history as a dialectical progression, but adopts a materialist stance. Marx comprehended 'material as the essence, as the self-validating essence of humanity'. Hegel's dialectic, therefore, was adapted by Marx to include productive forces. Marx's 'dialectical materialism' was further developed, distorted and elaborated by Lenin, Stalin and other Soviet thinkers.

Further reading

Beiser, F.C. THE CAMBRIDGE COMPANION TO HEGEL, Cambridge University Press, 1993.
Butler, J. SUBJECTS OF DESIRE, Columbia University Press, 1987.
Kojève, A. INTRODUCTION TO THE READING OF HEGEL, Cornell University Press, 1969.

J.S.C.

HEIDEGGER, Martin

Philosopher	born Germany 1889–1976
Associated with	EXISTENTIALISM ■ DASEIN
Influences include	KIERKEGAARD ■ HUSSERL ■ HEGEL
Shares common ground with	SARTRE ■ RORTY ■ DERRIDA
Main works	BEING AND TIME (1962)
	MARTIN HEIDEGGER: BASIC WRITINGS (1993)
	THE BASIC PROBLEMS OF PHENOMENOLOGY (1988)

HEIDEGGER WAS THE son of a Catholic sexton. After becoming a novice in a Jesuit Order, he went on to teach at Marlburg; eventually he replaced his former teacher, Husserl, at Freiburg-im-Bresgau in 1928. Although Heidegger was later to turn away from Husserl's theories on phenomenology, it could be argued that his influence is always present in his work.

Heidegger was to produce theories which were to revolutionise French humanist thought. Following in the footsteps of the Danish philosopher Søren Kierkegaard, the 'father of existentialism', Heidegger's main concern was that of the human subject, and its existence in the world. Kierkegaard's influence was to permeate both Husserl's and Heidegger's writings, and went on to be the basis of existentialism.

Heidegger's main philosophical treatise was *Being and Time*, first published in 1927. This work marks the introduction of Heidegger's now famous concept of *Dasein*. In this text Heidegger explains how human beings have an immediate experience and knowledge of the world, which cannot be examined by any preconceived epistemological or logical constructions.

Heidegger's work revolves around this notion of *Dasein*; a particular type of existence which was essentially human in character. *Dasein* according to Heidegger, is what separates human beings from the innate, phenomenological world. However, a characteristic of *Dasein* is the constant anxiety about the future; an awareness of the imminence of death, and the necessity of choice. Death is an important issue within this notion of *Dasein*, because not only is it possible for human beings to conceptualise their own 'cessation of being', but time itself can be seen as the move-towards-death. As a counteraction to this anxiety, human beings distract themselves by immersing themselves in routine and trivialities.

Heidegger, however, offers an alternative way to exist; an 'authentic' life within which death is faced head-on and freedom is exercised in a creative manner. Man must, according to Heidegger, begin to conceive the world in terms of utility and choice; as an arena where objects are always available for human activity. This 'authentic' self, therefore, is an entity which conceives of itself, and the world, in terms of potentiality and action. Characterised by its orientation towards the future, it entails the constant necessity for choice. Every choice is understood as the exclusion of an alternative, through which the 'nothingness' aspect of existence is expressed. Time therefore is significant in terms of unrealised and unrealisable possibilities. From this revelation, however, stem guilt and anxiety; as the recognition of the infiniteness of choice, and the finiteness of allotted time. This acceptance of 'nothingness', therefore, is the acceptance of the human condition; of *Dasein*.

According to Heidegger, *Dasein* relates the potentiality of objective world to man's authentic nature; reconnecting him with the 'Being' of particular, useful objects. Being, according to Heidegger, is always present and is always available to man if he would only 'open' himself up to it. A possible way of doing this is outlined in his article, *The Origin of the Work of Art*. In this article Heidegger posits the Van Gogh painting *Boots* as the site for the possible disclosure of Being. This is made possible through the displayed utility of the depicted object(s); and indeed in the utility of the work of art itself. Heidegger states that 'Some particular being, a pair of peasant's shoes, comes into the work to stand in the light of its Being. The Being of beings comes into the steadiness of its shining. The essence of art would then be this: the truth of beings setting itself to work. Art, therefore, can reveal truths about the world. *Dasein* can reveal the connectedness between Being and being; between existence and utility. However, according to Heidegger, the truth is often concealed and denied; as the acceptance of the truth would be the wholesale acceptance of death and 'nothingness'. As the world is constitutive of objects that are utilisable and accessible for purposive action, the portrayal of such potential for action is what Heidegger asks for in art; action and knowledge being inseparably related.

Heidegger's notion of *Dasein* was seen as a preliminary phase in a project investigating the type of existence particular to human beings, and his legacy has been extended by existentialist, post-structuralist and deconstructive theorists. Twentieth-century thinkers who owe a debt to Heidegger include Sartre, Merleau Ponty, Gadamer, Arendt, Foucault, Bourdieu, Derrida, Taylor and Rorty.

Heidegger's pragmatic approach to the world, however, fits uneasily with his argument against mass industrialisation and culture. Heidegger abhorred cultural 'vulgarity' and applauded Hitler's call for a 'true culture'. This affiliation with Hitler's National Socialism means that his work is considered, by some, to be tarnished; and can often be overlooked. The argument about how to approach his work therefore still rumbles on.

Further reading

Dreyfus, H.L. and Hall, H. HEIDEGGER: A CRITICAL READER, Blackwell, 1992.
Neske, G. and Kettering, E. (eds.) MARTIN HEIDEGGER AND NATIONAL SOCIALISM, Paragon, 1990.
Rockmore, T. HEIDEGGER AND FRENCH PHILOSOPHY, Routledge, 1995.
J.S.C.

HELLER, Agnes

Philosopher	born Hungary 1929—
Associated with	DESTINY ■ SELF-DETERMINATION ■ MULTIPLE LOGICS
Influences include	LUKÁCS ■ WEBER ■ KANT
Shares common ground with	CASTORIADIS ■ HABERMAS ■ DERRIDA
Main works	A PHILOSOPHY OF MORALS (1990) A PHILOSOPHY OF HISTORY IN FRAGMENTS (1993) AN ETHICS OF PERSONALITY (1996)

H ELLER EMERGED FROM the Budapest circle of left-wing scholars headed by Lukács. Her work has been dominated by a search to find a non-relativistic moral philosophy that is congruent with the 'contingency', pluralism' and 'multiple logics' of modernity and postmodernity. Her thought has been influenced by Lukács's Marxist revisionism, which sought to find a moral–aesthetic totality in a world of fragments, and Weber's neo-Kantian account of modernity (as a world composed of incommensurable value-spheres). Heller's life was buffeted by the see-saw of totalitarian repression and intermittent liberalisation that characterised mid-century Central Europe. Her father died in Auschwitz in 1944. After a precocious start to an academic career, the fall-out from the Hungarian Revolution (1956) saw her removed from her university life by official proscription. The subsequent loosening of the regime resulted in her appointment to a senior research post in the Hungarian Academy in 1963. The toleration of dissenting intellectuals was reversed after the Soviet invasion in 1968, and she was dismissed from her Academy post in 1973.

Heller and her husband Fernec Feher (1933–94), and other members of the Budapest School (a group of like-minded socialist intellectuals who had been connected with Lukács), were forced out of Hungary in 1977. Heller became Senior Lecturer, later Reader, in Sociology at La Trobe University (Melbourne, Australia). In 1985 she became Professor of Philosophy in the Graduate Center of the New School for Social Research in New York. Today she is Hannah Ardendt Professor of Philosophy at the New School and a Professor at Elte Eszteikai, Budapest.

Heller is fascinated by the question: How can individuals achieve 'human wholeness' in the contemporary world without sacrificing the differential logics, contingency and moral–aesthetic pluralism of modern life? Her answer is to appeal to a special kind of moral autonomy. Morally autonomous personalities display a kind of wholeness, integrity and consistency in their actions, despite the generalised fragmentation, inauthenticity and inconsistency of modern existence.

Moral autonomy requires making a choice of oneself – namely, choosing one's destiny, abandoning oneself to that destiny, making choices and decisions in light of that destiny and accepting and loving that destiny. Amongst all the possibilities and competing 'truths' of modern life, the individual – by making this existential choice – turns their own 'personal' truth into a kind of necessity. This 'truth' (their destiny) propels them – to action, to creativity in work, to causes and relationships. As seekers of their own destiny, morally autonomous personalities are not determined by social custom, institutional imperatives, background, circumstances, desire for recognition or public opinion. They are self-determining, not heteronomous. Yet the self-determining person is neither anomic or empty. Self-determination means, first, accepting one's own nature (talents, powers and infirmities, strengths and weaknesses of character), and taking that nature into account in one's action and choices. Second, it means being able to make and keep promises (i.e. self-imposed obligations). Third, it means that, although contemporary culture is fragmentary and highly pluralised, the self-determining person approaches what is 'true for me' (in art, philosophy, religion, etc.) with intensity, devotion and intellectual love. The autonomous person can still be edified or shaken by subjective truth – rather than cynically shopping around in the supermarket of discourses, looking for the next big thing. Fourth, self-determination means acting consistently and persistently to achieve one's destiny. The self- determined person is guided by a sense of being 'true to oneself'. He or she never lies in or with his or her work, and does not betray his or her own destiny. That is to say, amid all life's contingencies, he or she has a strong sense of destination, and, in pursing that destination, he or she is reliable and constant. As such, the autonomous person has an aura of trustworthiness, and others have confidence in such a personality.

Self-determination is control over one's own actions and choices, not mastery over others. The morally autonomous person, while not bound by social custom or public opinion, observes a few universal norms – norms that oblige the autonomous personality to respect the moral autonomy of others. Readiness to suffer wrong rather than cause it, preference for reciprocal (symmetrical) instead of non-reciprocal relationships, preparedness never to treat others as mere means, etc., help the autonomous personality to respect and facilitate the moral autonomy of others. Thus, when moderns make an existential choice of themselves (their destiny), they do not simply choose a cause or calling to which they will devote their life's energies. Rather, they choose themselves as (good) persons who care for the autonomy of all human beings, and who act as if all human beings were morally autonomous personalities.

Further reading

Burnheim, J. (ed.) THE SOCIAL PHILOSOPHY OF AGNES HELLER, Rodopi, 1994.
Habermas, J. THE PHILOSOPHICAL DISCOURSE OF MODERNITY, Polity, 1987.
Murphy, P. 'Agnes Heller', in P. Beilharz (ed.), SOCIAL THEORY: A GUIDE TO CENTRAL THINKERS, Allen & Unwin, 1991.

P.M.

HJELMSLEV, Louis Trolle

Linguist	born Denmark 1899–1965
Associated with	GLOSSEMATICS
Influences include	BADOUIN ▪ KRUSZEWSKI ▪ MAUSS
Shares common ground with	SAUSSURE ▪ BARTHES ▪ ULDALL
Main works	PROLEGOMENA TO A THEORY OF LANGUAGE (1953)
	LANGUAGE: AN INTRODUCTION (1970)

HJELMSLEV SPENT MOST of his professional career at the University of Copenhagen, where he taught comparative linguistics and collaborated with Hans Jørgen Uldall, with whom he pioneered a style of analysis know as glossematics. The term became linked with the Copenhagen School of Linguistics.

Hjelmslev's approach to the study of language bears similarities to the structural theories of Saussure and, later, Jakobson: all stressed the independent status of language as a formal structure of rules and conventions that should be analysed without reference to either semantics (i.e. meaning) or phonetics (sound). Language was to be treated as a 'self-sufficient totality, a structure *sui generis*'; its most interesting aspect lay in 'the relational patterns of language'.

Language was a distinct symbolic system and should be compared with other nonlinguistic symbolic systems. It was not to be viewed as a conveyor of thought, belief, knowledge or emotion; nor was it to be conceived as in commerce with an external reality; it should not be seen as a means to anything. The approach became known as glossematics (glosseme = feature of language that carries meaning and does not consist of smaller meaningful units). Language, in other words, was to be studied in its own right.

In his best-known work, *Prolegomena to a Theory of Language*, Hjelmslev argued that language is a sign system and a process of realisation. These equate roughly to what Saussure called *langue* and *parole*. Hjelmslev's understanding of signs is that they have meaning only in relation to each other: signs are intelligible in a context of other signs. It would be nonsense to talk of a sign in isolation: in fact, Hjelmslev avoided exactly that by invoking the concept of sign-functions, 'a dependence', as he calls it. Signs depend on each other for their meaning and these meanings can be actualised only in context. Again, the comparisons with Saussure are apparent: the relationship between the signifier and the signified suggests that the sign's relationship to any physical or nonphysical entity cannot be assumed. Hjelmslev writes of 'expression' and 'content', the relationship between which is fluid – this is the sign function.

Much of Hjelmslev's work is devoted to the detailed elaboration of the formal structure of language and, to this end, he developed his own technical vocabulary. Two terms deserve further explication here: denotation and connotation. The former refers to the area of expression or content. 'This is Janet. This is John', for example, denotes a boy and a girl. The same two sentences connote something different: something typical of a child's elementary reading book, perhaps; it evokes the context of children being introduced to reading. What happens here is that the expression and content taken together become another expression which refers to another content. Later writers, such as Barthes and Eco, included denotations and connotations in their semiotic analyses. Others who have been influenced by Hjelmslev's immanent theory of language include Derrida and Todorov. The effort that unifies such theorists is to develop a semiotic framework for language, a formal system that makes metaphysical references redundant.

Further reading

Harris, Zellig S. STRUCTURAL LINGUISTICS, University of Chicago Press, 1951.
Lepschy, Giulio, A SURVEY OF STRUCTURAL LINGUISTICS, Faber & Faber, 1970.
Malmberg, Bertil STRUCTURAL LINGUISTICS AND COMMUNICATION, Springer-Verlag, 1976.

E.C.

HOGGART, Richard

Literary critic/cultural analyst	born England 1918—
Associated with	CULTURALISM ▪ PRACTICAL CRITICISM ▪ SOCIAL DEMOCRACY
Influences include	ARNOLD ▪ LEAVIS ▪ TAWNEY
Shares common ground with	HALL ▪ THOMPSON ▪ WILLIAMS
Main works	THE USES OF LITERACY (1957) SPEAKING TO EACH OTHER (2 VOLS.,1970) THE WAY WE LIVE NOW (1995)

H OGGART WAS BORN in Leeds, England and studied at Leeds Boys' Grammar School and the University of Leeds. He served in North Africa during the Second World War. After the war he was employed in the Adult Education Department of Hull University from whence he moved to the English department at Leicester in 1959. As Professor of English at the University of Birmingham he set up the Centre for Contemporary Cultural Studies (CCCS) in 1964. He then became Assistant Director of UNESCO in Paris and returned to England in the 1970s to his final job before retiring, Warden of Goldsmiths' College, London. Hoggart also held a number of important positions in public service, including membership of the Pilkington Committee on broadcasting in the early 1960s and Deputy Chair of the Arts Council of Great Britain in the 1970s.

Hoggart's significance is as much defined by his own personal trajectory and institutional roles as by his ideas. He has, in fact, written a three-volume autobiography. His working-class background was made legendary by his most celebrated book, *The Uses of Literacy.* He is the archetypal 'scholarship boy' who achieved upward social mobility by means of educational success and the acquisition of 'Culture'. Although not peculiar to Britain, the type that he represents carries a distinctive Britishness or, rather, Englishness, redolent of a society where fine distinctions of class have been exceptionally pronounced. In the late 1950s and early 1960s, when Hoggart became famous, the fate of the traditional working class in an 'affluent society' was, arguably, the most debated cultural and social issue in the UK; and, of course, Hoggart was a major contributor to such debate. In many ways, he actually defined the terms of debate.

The Uses of Literacy is divided into two parts: the first deals with the 'traditional' working class, drawing particularly upon Hoggart's own childhood experience in the working-class districts of Chapeltown and Hunslet in Leeds; the second part is a critical reading of modern 'mass culture', popular fiction and magazines, and the everyday jukebox and café culture of the young. Hoggart discerned a decline in 'authenticity', that the older culture, crude and straitened though it may have been, was at least an urban culture of the people rather than a manufactured 'mass culture' imported from the USA. In effect, he was reiterating the theme of 'Americanisation' which, in the UK context, had originated in the nineteenth-century writings of J.S. Mill and Matthew Arnold. This placed him in a liberal tradition of thought rather than a strictly conservative one, although in retrospect his nostalgia and sweeping criticisms of contemporary popular culture have been much criticised as the latter. His perspective, however, was not so negative about present trends. Hoggart was concerned with distinguishing between 'the processed' and 'the lived' in popular culture; and he believed that it was vital to make discriminations in this regard concerning contemporary popular culture. He was thus applying a Leavisite critical principle to the field of mass and popular culture, not simply distinguishing between it and 'serious' culture. Hoggart was also very much concerned, from this point of view, with media and cultural policy. He was an advocate of a more discriminating popular culture in broadcasting and the arts, to be secured by public organisations like the BBC and the Arts Council.

Hoggart's founding of the Centre for Contemporary Cultural Studies at Birmingham contributed greatly to identifying popular culture as a legitimate object of university research and education. Very soon, however, Hoggart's perspective of discrimination was overtaken by the currents of continental theory flowing into British intellectual life from the 1960s onwards. When he departed from Birmingham for UNESCO the original intention may have been eventually to return, yet it was his at first temporary and then permanent successor as director of CCCS, Stuart Hall, who gave the most distinctive leadership to the development of cultural studies in Britain. Hoggart was clearly disgruntled by the sharp leftward and theoreticist swerve of cultural studies and, in the 1970s, he also became very hostile to the generalised populism of the cultural Left in Britain.

As the critical radicalism of cultural studies diminished during the 1980s, Hoggart re-emerged in very much his old social-democratic position as someone prepared to question the cultural consequences of Thatcherism and the adaptations it had brought about. His book, *The Way We Live Now*, demonstrated, sometimes biliously, how Hoggart had retained a critical eye that is, on occasion, impressive in its insights.

Further reading

Critcher, C. 'SOCIOLOGY, CULTURAL STUDIES AND THE POST-WAR WORKING CLASS', in J. Clarke, C. Critcher and R. Johnson, WORKING-CLASS CULTURE: STUDIES IN HISTORY AND THEORY, Hutchinson, 1979.

Hoggart, R. A LOCAL HABITATION: LIFE AND TIMES 1918–1940, Chatto & Windus, 1988.

Hoggart, R. A SORT OF CLOWNING: LIFE AND TIMES 1940–1959, Chatto & Windus, 1990.

Hoggart, R. AN IMAGINED LIFE: LIFE AND TIMES, 1959–1991, Chatto & Windus, 1992.

J.McG.

HOMANS, George Caspar

Sociologist	born USA 1910–1990
Associated with	HUMAN GROUP ■ SOCIAL EXCHANGE
Influences include	HENDERSON ■ SKINNER
Shares common ground with	LEWIN ■ BLAU
Main works	THE HUMAN GROUP (1950)
	SOCIAL BEHAVIOUR: ITS ELEMENTARY FORMS (1960, 1974)
	COMING TO MY SENSES (1984)

HOMANS STUDIED ENGLISH and later history at Harvard, where he became a Junior Fellow along with Conrad Arensberg, B.F. Skinner and William Foote Whyte. His introduction to theoretical sociology came via L.J. Henderson and his work on Pareto. At the same time he became familiar with research methodology through Elton Mayo and the Hawthorne Experiments: Mayo also introduced him to the interviewing skills required in psychotherapy and in the analysis of interpersonal relations. After service in the Second World War, during which he commanded a destroyer, Homans returned to Harvard to teach sociology for the rest of his career.

Homans's contribution to the understanding of culture needs to be judged against his aim of bringing some intellectual order to the 'familiar chaos' of social life. His most prestigious attempt came in *The Human Group*, although this was not his favourite work. His objective was a synthesis of existing knowledge about a particular area of social life – those small primary groups characterised by purposeful association and relatively frequent face-to-face interaction. This 'most familiar thing in the world' and 'most immediate social experience' for everyone was a neglected part of sociology; but it offered nonetheless the best possibility of establishing usable generalisation about social behaviour.

In developing what Robert Merton called 'a model of sociological analysis', Homans focused on three classes of variables – interaction, sentiment and activity. These basic concepts would cover all aspects of social organisation and be applicable to all concrete instances within his field of study. Together they provided a framework within which hypotheses about the functioning of groups might be advanced and tested. Activity is what persons do as members of a group; sentiments are all the internal states (emotions, feelings, and so on) each member has about what the group does; interaction is a unit of behaviour set in train by a relationship between one member and another. To these Homans added the norms or codes of behaviour adopted, consciously or unconsciously, by the group. Finally, the phenomena of group behaviour were to be treated not in isolation, but linked to their environments via the concept of an external system which may affect the group's behaviour or its capacity for survival.

The five studies which provided Homans with his empirical material were mostly well-known but diverse (they included, for example, the Bank Wiring Room study from the Hawthorne Experiments and Whyte's *Street Corner Society*). These are described and analysed to test a sequence of more than fifty hypotheses. In the first set, data from the Bank Wiring Room are applied to test the relationship between his three major variables. Successive sections deal with (i) interpersonal evaluation as a type of sentiment; (ii) the relation between three persons in terms of activity, sentiment and interaction; (iii) liking and disliking; (iv) leadership; and (v) social disintegration.

Homans's studies with *The Human Group* rested on the accessibility of these procedures, combined with the richness of the material on which he could draw. His sincerity and lucidity of exposition, together with his focus on clearly delineated examples, formed a refreshing contrast to the less tangible aspects and inconclusive sonorities of grand theory. For these reasons the publication of *The Human Group* suggested some sort of paradigm shift for sociology in the 1950s. However, Homans's subsequent work moved away from the group towards the analysis of social interaction as a form of exchange.

In *Social Behaviour: Its Elementary Forms* Homans set his sights on a theory of a higher order – one which would account for the actual behaviour of individuals in direct contact with one another. The emphasis was on elementary, sub-institutional face-to-face behaviour and the central propositions were directly related to those of behavioural psychology and elementary economics. Social life was to be understood in terms of the exchange of behaviour, tangible or intangible. For evidence Homans was initially dependent on laboratory studies in animal psychology. The close association with Skinner and operant conditioning disturbed his critics and reinforced charges of banality and reductionism, but Homans attracted growing support for his position that psychological generalisations are important components of sociological analysis. One result is that later models of human interaction have become more sophisticated but *The Human Group* remains Homans's most memorable work. Although his standing as a theorist continues to be controversial, he remains unique in his commitment to the formulation of an explicit theory of human behaviour as it exists at any level.

Further reading

Hamblin, Robert L. and Kunkel, John H. Behavioural Theory in Sociology; Essays in Honor of George C. Homans, Transaction Books, 1977.
Hare, A. Paul 'The Significance of the Human Group', in George C. Homans, The Human Group, Transaction Books, 1992.
Turk, H. and Simpson, Richard L. Institutions and Social Exchange: The Sociologies of Talcott Parsons and George C. Homans, Bobbs-Merill, 1970.
J.H.S.

hooks, bell
(pseudonym for Gloria Watkins)

Literary critic	born USA 1952—
Associated with	BLACK FEMINISM ■ ANTI-PATRIARCHY
Influences include	MORRISON ■ FREIRE
Shares common ground with	MORRISON ■ DAVIS ■ WEST
Main works	AIN'T I A WOMAN: BLACK WOMEN AND FEMINISM (1981)
	BREAKING BREAD: INSURGENT BLACK INTELLECTUAL LIFE (WITH CORNEL WEST, 1991)
	OUTLAW CULTURE: RESISTING REPRESENTATIONS (1994)

h OOKS'S BLACK FEMINIST thought, style of writing and mode of self-pre-
sentation originate in her experience of growing up in the American
South in the 1950s and 1960s. In what she calls her 'dysfunctional
family' she first encountered the abuses of patriarchy around which much of
her early work revolves; in Kentucky she was confronted with the everyday
humiliations and violations of white racism. Yet Southern African-American
culture also provided her with strong black female role-models and modes of
resistance, embedded in the speech of the black community, in the church, and
in a segregated education system which fostered the growth of self-esteem and
critical thinking. Moving away from home and into higher education, she
rediscovered these aspects of an autonomous black culture in the work of
Toni Morrison, about which she wrote her MA dissertation.

As a student, hooks began to develop her path-breaking critique of 'white
supremacist capitalist patriarchy', a key phrase in her theoretical vocabulary.
At Stanford she felt alienated and excluded from a Women's Movement which
was predominantly white, middle-class and – as she saw it – anti-men and anti-
family; her first book, *Ain't I a Woman*, was written when she was just 19 years
old. *Ain't I a Woman* mounted a stringent two-pronged attack on both (white)
feminism and patriarchy, including black men's oppression of black women,
from the nineteenth century through to the 1970s.

An important part of hooks's project there and since has been to challenge
cultural institutions such as academia and publishing itself, by defying scholarly convention in the use of a pseudonym (her great-grandmother's name)

printed in lower case, and the absence of footnotes and academic jargon in her early work. Characteristic is her use of the phrase 'feminist movement' without the definite article in order to emphasise feminism as a mode of activism, a dynamic process of transformation rather than an organisational entity.

hooks's polemical, deliberately non-academic style in *Ain't I a Woman* has evolved into an interventionist, relentlessly critical but above all politically committed stance in more recent collections of essays, which address topics as diverse as popular cinema, rap music, the spiritual legacy of Malcolm X, black folk culture and the practice of teaching as a black woman at Yale. She is a prolific writer with eclectic interests, and she often employs the autobiographical voice both to enhance the accessibility of her work, and as a pedagogical strategy demonstrating that intellectual work is not confined to the academy but addresses the living culture – of the streets and screen as well as the library.

In that, and every other sense bell hooks is first and foremost a public intellectual. Her critical practice – in teaching as in writing – consistently analyses the intersection of race, class, gender and sexual orientation in culture and politics. hooks has held academic positions in African-American Studies and Women's Studies at Oberlin College and Yale; she is currently Distinguished Professor of English at City College, New York. Her book *Teaching to Transgress: Education as the Practice of Freedom* (1994) pays tribute to her early education in the American South and celebrates the work of the Brazilian educationalist Paolo Freire, with whom she shares her belief in the liberatory potential of education in the political as well as the personal sense. More recent work on popular culture, postmodernity and the spirituality of the African-American folk tradition in *Black Looks: Race and Representation* (1992), *Yearning: Race, Gender and Cultural Politics* (1990) and *Outlaw Culture: Resisting Representations* has been highly influential in the field of Cultural Studies. In *Breaking Bread*, a collection of conversations with Cornel West, hooks articulates her distinctive vision of the importance of intellectual work: 'When intellectual work emerges from a concern with radical social and political change, when that work is directed to the needs of the people, it brings us into greater solidarity and community. It is fundamentally life-enhancing.'

Further reading

Collins, Patricia Hill BLACK FEMINIST THOUGHT: KNOWLEDGE, CONSCIOUSNESS AND THE POLITICS OF EMPOWERMENT, Routledge, 1991.
Davis, Angela WOMEN, RACE AND CLASS, Women's Press, 1982.
James, Stanlie M. and Busia, Abena P.A. (eds.) THEORIZING BLACK FEMINISMS: THE VISIONARY PRAGMATISM OF BLACK WOMEN, Routledge, 1993.

M.L.

HORKHEIMER, Max

Philosopher	born Germany, 1895–1973
Associated with	THE FRANKFURT SCHOOL ■ CULTURE INDUSTRY ■ INSTRUMENTAL REASON
Influences include	KANT ■ HEGEL ■ MARX
Shares common ground with	LUKÁCS ■ ADORNO ■ BENJAMIN
Main works	ECLIPSE OF REASON (1947) DIALEKTIK DER AUFKLÄRUNG (1944 TRANS. DIALECTIC OF ENLIGHTENMENT, 1972) KRITISCHE THEORIE (2 VOLS., 1968, TRANS. CRITICAL THEORY, 1972)

MORE THAN ANY other individual, Max Horkheimer is associated with the development and notoriety of the Institute for Social Research, a Marxist think-tank which was founded in 1923, and of which Horkheimer became Director in 1930. Because of its association with the University of Frankfurt, Horkheimer and his associates (Theodor Adorno, Walter Benjamin, Erich Fromm, Leo Lowenthal, Herbert Marcuse, Franz Neumann and Friedrich Pollock, among others) came to be known as the Frankfurt School. Repulsed by the rise of fascism in Germany, the Institute moved to Geneva in 1933, and to New York a year later. In 1950, Horkheimer and the Institute returned to Frankfurt.

Horkheimer examined the concept of reason in society. He demonstrated that, contrary to its common associations with expanded consciousness and access to the exotic, reason has undergone an insidious narrowing – to the point that to 'be reasonable' is to be susceptible to the most banal and repugnant of behaviours and beliefs. Hardly an anomaly, fascism was a quintessential example of the perversion of reason to fit the instrumentalities of the political structure.

Despite the patina of purity, reason has a vast history of serving and promoting the domination of nature, including the human beings that inhabit nature. The character of Odysseus, for instance, 'confronts' the prevailing myths that maintain the mystery and majesty of natural forces. Odysseus, instead of revering gods, makes deals with them. With the help of his crew (in Freudian terms, the brother clan) he overcomes the allure of the sirens, and thus his sensuality, through a repressive concentration on cleverness and industriousness.

According to Horkheimer, the domination of nature, and reason's participation in it, is reinforced in the modern era by Freud and Kant, both of whom appear resigned to the irreconcilability of practical human activity and the 'pure', natural elements which rumble inscrutably beneath the practical. Kant held that unmediated understanding was simply inaccessible, while Freud held that human nature contained certain repugnant drives whose liberation would threaten the fabric of civilisation. In either case, Odysseus is justified in forsaking the pursuit of impractical inclinations.

This attitude was a constant frustration for Horkheimer, who believed that reason has been systematically victim to a perversion which ever more effectively distances it from a reconciliation with natural or normative interests. Perhaps most culpable is science. Initially, science was a partisan tool to combat the inefficiency of revelation. Science served an array of bourgeois values. But eventually, science itself became a value. Under positivism, science is 'purified' to represent an appropriate existential model, thus obscuring the instrumentality and domination inimical to Enlightenment science. Human imagination, autonomy, and sensuality have been sacrificed to a harsh and clinical manipulation of nature – all in the name of reason.

And if 'scientific' rationality were not enough to sap imagination and eccentricity, the 'culture industry' of mass society could finish the job. Horkheimer was devastated by the extent to which advanced capitalism reinforced its priorities in the distractions of its participants. Cultural artefacts are subjected to a formula through which the audience can always predict the outcome – be it the next note in a jazz 'improvisation', or the denouement of this week's instalment of a favourite soap opera. The formula simultaneously offers escape and reinforcement. The escape is in its kitschiness, for the formula allows only simple and predictable variations on a theme, ensuring a suffocating comfort to the recipient. Yet the formula reinforces themes of repetitiveness and strict organisation which are carried to the workplace by conditioned participants.

Horkheimer began his philosophical career as one who wanted to adjust the focus of Marxism in the light of a materially distracted proletariat and a more ideologically potent state. As his career progressed, his depiction of the difficulties changed from formidable to monumental. There seemed always to be more sophisticated techniques to eviscerate human beings – along with fewer vantage-points from which to witness the evisceration.

Further reading

Held, David INTRODUCTION TO CRITICAL THEORY, University of California Press, 1980.
Jay, Martin THE DIALECTICAL IMAGINATION: A HISTORY OF THE FRANKFURT SCHOOL OF SOCIAL RESEARCH, 1923–1950, Little, Brown, 1973.
O'Neill, John (ed.) ON CRITICAL THEORY, Seabury Press, 1976.

T.J.L.

ILLICH, Ivan

Ascetic theorist	born Austria, 1926—
Associated with	TECHNOLOGY ▪ ENERGY ▪ HEALTH ▪ LITERACY ▪ SCHOOLING
Influences include	KOHR ▪ POLANYI ▪ DUMONT
Shares common ground with	SCHUMACHER ▪ McLUHAN ▪ ELLUL
Main works	TOOLS FOR CONVIVIALITY (1973) MEDICAL NEMESIS (1976) GENDER (1982) IN THE VINEYARD OF THE TEXT (1993)

IVAN ILLICH FIRST arrived in the USA in 1951 as a young priest seeking refuge from an impending career in the papal bureaucracy. Already holding advanced degrees in crystallography (Florence), philosophy and theology (Gregorian University) and history (Salzburg), he originally intended to pursue postdoctoral studies at Princeton University on Albert the Great's work in alchemy. However, after learning of the difficulties that Puerto Rican immigrants were experiencing in being accepted as full members of New York's Roman Catholic community, Illich requested and received assignment to serve these people in Incarnation Parish. In 1956, after having seen his efforts culminate in the first celebration of San Juan's Day, Illich was reassigned to the Catholic University at Ponce, where he served as Vice-Rector. While working in Puerto Rico, Illich established a Spanish language institute for training North American priests and others involved with Puerto Rican communities in the USA. He also conducted a series of workshops and seminars on the Church's role in international development and the growing trend of soliciting volunteers from rich countries to assist people in poor countries along the path of development. Many of Illich's writings, as well as the activities that would later engage him at the Center for Intercultural Documentation (CIDOC) in Cuernavaca, Mexico, developed from his reflections on these themes.

Though his open opposition to the Church's missionary role in international development eventually provoked Vatican authorities to summon Illich to Rome, to respond to an inquiry into his activities at CIDOC, an action that prompted Illich to resign from the public ministry, we cannot fully grasp his unique approach to cultural theory without understanding the centrality of certain Christian traditions in his writings. Foremost among these traditions is the practice of ascesis, including the cultivation of the inner senses that are rooted in the heart. 'For a full millennium,' Illich argues, 'the Church cultivated a balanced tradition of study and reflection . . . . The habits of the heart and the cultivation of its virtues are peripherals to the pursuit of higher learning today . . . . I want to argue for the possibility of a new complimentarity between critical and ascetical learning.' This complimentarity is ever present in Illich's own writings. On the critical side of learning, Illich is an historian. But the techniques of history he employs are guided by the ascetic imperative of clearing one's ground for spiritual as well as intellectual insight.

Herein lies the pedagogical value of Illich's writings. Engaging those writings in the spirit in which they were written entails the practice of critical asceticism. Reading Illich well demands that we join him in a disciplined state of altered awareness. His use of history produces this condition of altered awareness by transporting us back in cultural space and time to a place far removed from the certainties of the world in which we feel at home. For Illich, that place resides in the texts of twelfth-century Western civilisation, which he identifies as a crucial hinge period in which we can 'observe the emergence of many of those assumptions which, by going unexamined, have turned into today's certainties (our epoch specific, *a priori* forms of perception)'. Becoming familiar with the mental topology of this foreign world prepares us for a re-entry to our modern world that sparks awareness of how radically the present differs from the past. But reading Illich delivers us into more than a mere intellectual awareness of the cultural differences between worlds separated by nearly nine centuries of history. It can also foster an ascetic awareness that provokes in us, as it does in Illich, an almost unbearable anguish when confronting the certainties of our modern world. It is this anguish that leads Illich to renounce and abstain from such certainties.

Illich's dismantling of traditional education in *Deschooling Society* (Penguin, 1976) and his stinging attack on the medical profession *Disabling Professions* (Boyars, 1977) revealed the sharpness of his analysis when turning on mainstream institutions.

Further reading

Cayley, D. Ivan Illich: In Conversation, House of Anans, 1992.
Dumont, L. From Mandeville to Marx: The Genesis and Triumph of Economic Ideology, University of Chicago Press, 1977.
Gabbard, D.A. Silencing Ivan Illich: A Foucauldian Analysis of Intellectual Exclusion, Austin & Winfield, 1993.

D.A.G.

IRIGARAY, Luce

Philosopher, linguist/psychoanalyst	born Belgium 1932—
Associated with	WOMAN-AS-SUBJECT ▪ TWO LIPS
Influences include	FREUD ▪ LACAN ▪ DERRIDA ▪ LÉVINAS ▪ HEGEL ▪ NIETZSCHE ▪ HEIDEGGER ▪ MARX
Shares common ground with	LACAN ▪ DERRIDA
Main works	SPECULUM DE L'AUTRE FEMME (1974 TRANS. SPECULUM OF THE OTHER WOMAN 1985)
	CE SEXE QUI N'EST PAS UN (1977 TRANS. THIS SEX WHICH IS NOT ONE, 1985)
	AMANTE MARINE. DE FRIEDRICH NIETZSCHE (1980 TRANS. MARINE LOVER FREDERICH NIETZSCHE, 1991)
	L'OUBLI DE L'AIR CHEZ MARTIN HEIDEGGER (1983)
	ETHIQUE DE LA DIFFÉRENCE SEXUELLE (1984 TRANS. AN ETHICS OF SEXUAL DIFFERENCE)
	SEXES ET PARENTES (1987 TRANS. SEXES AND GENEALOGIES, 1993)

BEFORE RECEIVING A Master's degree in philosophy and literature from the University of Louvain, Irigaray was a schoolteacher in Brussels. In 1961 she received a Master's degree in psychology, and in 1962 a diploma in psychopathology. Further academic work followed in France, with a doctoral degree in linguistics in 1968 and in 1974 a doctorate in philosophy. Irigaray is a psychoanalyst and was 'effectively in charge' (Whitford 1991: 6) of the Department of Psychoanalysis at Vincennes. Jacques Lacan was her mentor and she attended his seminars at the École Normale Supérieure.

Biography is a philosophical issue for Irigaray, and a matter of sexual politics. Her refusal of biographical publicity is a strategy to avoid a trap that besieges brilliant women writers. Personal interpretations are made of them as women, and the political, creative and artistic seriousness of their philosophical texts is elided. 'Ecce Mulier?' (in Burgard, *Nietzsche and the Feminine* (Virginia University Press, 1994)) is a mimetic essay by Irigaray of Nietzsche's autobiographical Ecce Homo in which she makes a direct claim to the significance of herself as a woman philosopher who creates 'without submitting to the masculine order'.

Like Nietzsche, she creates a fantastical philosophical genealogy. Her texts create a symbolic position for women in culture and elaborate sexual difference as the major philosophical issue of our age. The paradigm of women as other, derelict of symbolisation, is constituted through phallic violence that threatens both the autonomy of women and the viability of life. A shift towards sexual difference in culture would signify a new balance, bringing forth a revaluation of the feminine and respect for fecundity.

Texts such as *Thinking the Difference* (1994), *Je Tu Nous* (1993) and *I Love to You* (1996) are infused with urgency for change to counteract the nihilistic destruction of nuclear arms and the relentless exploitation of the earth, and of women in late global capitalism. Irigaray's styles vary from lyrical and poetic to political and didactic, and her published work includes complex written texts, collections of lectures and papers.

Soon after the publication of *Speculum de l'autre femme*, Irigaray was expelled from Vincennes for her unacceptable political and feminist critique of psychoanalysis. In *Speculum* Irigaray engages psychoanalysis, philosophy and linguistics for the purpose of showing the operations of patriarchy to structure the exclusion of women. Psychoanalysis is employed in two ways: as constitutive of the impoverishment of women, and, as a discourse of the unconscious, to provide access to the passions which are the material of creativity. *Speculum* is a critique of the Lacanian theory of the mirror image in the formation of male subjectivity and a critique of the symbolic significance of the phallus. The Freudian/Lacanian phallogocentric narrative describes the female as lacking a phallus and therefore castrated.

No symbolic signification is attributed to the female sex. She is imaged as a 'hole' or 'lack', opposed, in this binary economy, to the male subject as other, or object. She has no identity of her own. The symbolic violence of this repression is that she has no language with which to represent herself. It is Irigaray's contention, then, that the feminine must be represented in the symbolic to achieve identity and to be valued in culture. Engaging the Heideggarian notion of language as the 'house' of subjectivity, Irigaray proposes that language which represents the feminine will build a (symbolic) 'home' for women. This will bring the possibility of women becoming subjects, and create a place/position for women in culture.

Patriarchal culture is not only deprived of women as partners in the creation of society, it is in debt to the feminine because it is constructed on the unacknowledged contribution of women, in particular, the mother who gives birth. Irigaray describes patriarchy as 'an exclusive respect for the genealogy of sons and fathers and the competition between brothers' (Whitford 1991: 174). Symbolisation of the genealogies of women and representation of the mother–daughter relationship are further conditions for identity that is linked to the ability to speak as women.

Irigaray's texts are devoted to the possibilities of 'women-becoming-subjects,' and to 'an ethics of sexual difference'. Lévinas's ethics of the face-to-face relation premised on absolute alterity provides her with the means to theorise sexual difference and to propose language of ethical exchange. The relationship between the sexes in an economy of sexual difference will have to be mediated, not by the distancing and repressive violence of opposition, but by processes that engage both the proximity of relationship and the incommensurability between the two subjects of sexual difference.

For consideration of such mediation Irigaray explores feminine models such as a placental economy, mucosity, fluidity. Angels also function for her as mediators. In ethical exchanges across sexual difference each might be other for the other, a fluid distribution of otherness in contrast to otherness as fixed to 'woman'. She employs metaphors of fluidity to signify the mobility that is necessary to the restructuring of the relations between the sexes.

Irigaray has been criticised as essentialist. These criticisms are largely misreadings of her references to the female body as a means to articulate women's specificity. Her symbolisations of the female body constitute a philosophical critique of rationality which has excluded the body. She employs Nietzsche's *oeuvre* for the inclusion of the body in philosophical discourse – the body, not as essential, but as a cultural production. Irigaray's referencing to bodies is always morphological, symbolic representations of the body which are not confined to the maternal, but which symbolise the importance of language and new forms of mediation, necessary to women becoming subjects. She has become known for the symbol of two lips for women – one representing the site of female genealogy, the possibility of representing the mother–daughter relationship, and the other, the site of language (of the feminine). With this symbol she seeks to confound sexual identity premised on male sexual functioning and its appropriations in the symbolic.

The notion of divinity for women is an example of Irigaray's mimetic strategy for constituting women-as-subjects. Male subjectivity is guaranteed by the Father-God who creates by the Word. A differently conceptualised notion of the divine will be necessary for female subjectivity. For women, the mother–dauthter relationship is divine, as is the task of creating female subjectivity. A notion of the divine for women provides an ideal, a necessary 'third term' that functions against the dangerous fusion of the mother–daughter relationship, that prevents autonomy.

Irigaray problematises feminist aspirations to equality – the desire to be the same as men does nothing to shift the binary structure of dominating, destructive power, nor to engage desire referenced to the feminine. The achievement of equality may bring some necessary, though unstable gains, but they will mean that women are implicated in the reproduction of patriarchy, in its varied guises. Sexual difference will constitute a fecund relation between the sexes, and is the condition for ongoing cultural regeneration.

Further reading

Burke, C., Schor, N. and Whitford, M. (eds.) ENGAGING WITH IRIGARAY, Columbia University Press, 1994.
Grosz, Elizabeth SEXUAL SUBVERSIONS, Allen & Unwin, 1989.
Whitford, Margaret LUCE IRIGARAY: PHILOSOPHY IN THE FEMININE, Routledge, 1991.
B.M.

JAKOBSON, Roman

Linguist	born Russia 1896–1982
Associated with	STRUCTURALISM ■ STRUCTURAL LINGUISTICS ■ RELATIONAL INVARIANTS
Influences include	SHKLOVSKY ■ TYNYANOV ■ SAUSSURE ■ PEIRCE
Shares common ground with	TRUBETSKOY ■ LÉVI-STRAUSS ■ WELLECK ■ MUKAROVSKY
Main works	KINDERSPRACHE APHASIE UND ALLGEMEINE LAUTGESETZE (1941, TRANS. CHILD LANGUAGE, APHASIA AND PHONOLOGICAL UNIVERSALS) FUNDAMENTAL OF LANGUAGE (WITH MORRIS HALLE, 1956) SELECTED WRITINGS, VOLS I–VII (1962–86) SIX LECTURES ON SOUND AND MEANING (1978)

S ON OF A CHEMICAL engineer and industrialist, Jakobson gained his first degree from Moscow University and his doctorate from the University of Prague. Between 1933 and 1939, he taught at Masaryk University, but was forced to leave Czechoslovakia during the Nazi occupation. After a period in Scandinavia, he became a professor, first at Harvard, then at the Massachusetts Institute of Technology.

Jakobson's influence extends far beyond his own specific area of study – wide as that area was. While he was principally concerned with language and prosecuted research aimed at producing a theory of speech acquisition, his work has been differently interpreted by a variety of scholars. His most celebrated interpreter is Lévi-Strauss, who wished to translate Jakobson's conception of a universal pattern by which all humans acquire language into a theory of how human minds are universally structured. Althusser was similarly inspired by Jakobson's concept of structuralism. Many more contemporary cultural theorists have been influenced by Jakobson's structuralist approach, which itself extended and developed the work of Russian Formalists, like Shklovsky (who studied the formal structure of literary works), Saussure and Hjelmslev. The uniting thread between them is their focus on the relations between linguistic phenomena rather than sounds or utterances themselves. The relations between sounds in particular contexts are what constitute meaning and give significance to speech acts. Language is a functional system.

There exist what Jakobson calls 'relational invariants': any linguistic system in the world is based on an opposition of two logical contradictories. For example, present: *table*; absent: *not-a-table*; present: *blue*; absent: *not-blue*. It is a universal requirement that we classify, in this binary manner, all sounds being reduced to oppositions (this binary coding was used by Lévi-Strauss as an analogy for the way the mind processes phenomena). While Saussure argued that language is arbitrary at the level of the signified (as well as the signifier) and that each native language divides up in different ways, Jakobson insisted that there are close links between the two parts of the sign. The implication of this is that language is a system not of fixed essences, but of changing forms, between constituent units which themselves are constituted by the differences that mark them off from other related units. In other words, without difference, there can be no meaning. John Sturrock, in his *Structuralism and Since*, states that it would be possible, if rudimentary, to 'differentiate the entire contents of the universe by means of a two-term code or language, as being either *bing* or *bong* perhaps. But without the introduction of that small phonetic difference between the two vowel sounds, we can have no viable language at all.' In this respect Jakobson's role in the development of contemporary semiology is apparent.

Jakobson was interested in applying his theory to linguistic pathologies. In *Child Language, Aphasia and Phonological Universals* he confronted aphasia – the loss of speech or understanding of language. Jakobson notes that some aphasiacs cannot differentiate vertically, or paradigmatically, and cannot identify likenesses between similar-sounding words, such as beer and hear. Those who cannot separate horizontally, or syntagmatically, have problems combining units of language at higher levels of complexity. These are the two basic dimensions of language: similarity (metaphor) and contiguity (metonymy). To understand the way the forms of aphasia affect the language function means we are able to understand how a breakdown occurs in the faculty of selection and substitution, *or* in the combination and contextualisation. In the first case, the person lacks ability at a metalinguistic level, while in the second, he or she cannot maintain the hierarchy of linguistic units.

In short, the entire linguistic activity gravitates around the two axes of selection and combination. The structure and function of the brain are reflected in the two types of discourse: poetry and prose.

Poetics were an abiding interest of Jakobson's, and he formulated a classificatory system that integrated poetry and poetic function into the speech event and the specific role in language and poetry. Critics of such Formalism argued that leaving no room for the aesthetics of poetry robbed the artform of all meaning. Jakobson was interested in how meaning is possible rather than its content.

Further reading

Bredin, Hugh 'Roman Jakobson on Metaphor and Metonymy', PHILOSOPHY AND LITERATURE, 8: 1, 1984.
Holenstein, Elmar ROMAN JAKOBSON'S APPROACH TO LANGUAGE, Indiana State University Press, 1974.
Sturrock, John (ed.) STRUCTURALISM AND SINCE: FROM LÉVI-STRAUSS TO DERRIDA, Oxford University Press, 1979.

E.C.

JAMES, Cyril Lionel Robert

Historian/political analyst	born Trinidad 1901–1989
Associated with	MARXISM ■ PAN-AFRICANISM ■ BLACK HISTORY ■ POLITICS OF CULTURE
Influences include	MARX ■ TROTSKY ■ HEGEL
Shares common ground with	NKRUMAH ■ WALTER RODNEY ■ FANON ■ WILLIAMS ■ E.P. THOMPSON
Main works	THE BLACK JACOBINS (1938/1963) BEYOND A BOUNDARY (1963) THE FUTURE IN THE PRESENT (SELECTED WRITINGS) (1977)

C.L.R. JAMES'S LIFE exemplifies the intellectual and physical journeyings of what Paul Gilroy has called the Black Atlantic. He lived for 30 years in the Caribbean, 15 in the USA, and most of the rest of his life in Britain, but was a frequent traveller, especially to Africa, not least because of his long involvement in the pan-African movement. His work unites concerns from all the countries and continents which his interests spanned, and he managed to be involved on numerous fronts simultaneously: for instance, after his arrival in Britain in 1932 he was writing a biography of the West Indian independence leader Cipriani, reporting on cricket for the *Manchester Guardian*, working with the radical Independent Labour Party, gathering material for *The Black Jacobins* and completing his novel *Minty Alley*.

E.P. Thompson said that the key to James's enquiring mind was 'his proper appreciation of the game of cricket', and *Beyond a Boundary*, James's classic study of cricket as a social, cultural and political practice remains one of his best known works. The book typifies James's concern with popular cultural forms neglected by academic analysts, as well as his desire to provide fully historicised accounts of them and their wider implications. His mocking, allusive question, 'What do they know of cricket that only cricket know?' prefaces his demonstration of the role of 'apolitical' sporting activity in colonial and post-colonial political and cultural relations, the complex way in which the same 'game' could involve powerfully hegemonic and counter-hegemonic – even utopian – elements, and the relation of all this to the capitalist system.

James's ability to provide a significantly different perspective is also exemplified in *The Black Jacobins*, his history of the slave rebellion in San Domingo – later Haiti – in the 1790s, and the creation of the first black republic. This founding example of what later came to be called 'history from below' anticipates E.P. Thompson by a whole generation. The book's difference consists not simply in the fact that it is a radical history of black people (perhaps the first of its kind), nor that it overturns cherished European historical myths, but that it shows black people as the active and principled creators of the circumstances of their own history, rather than its passive victims. Further, while it illustrates the way in which the masses can make history, it also shows how the periphery can determine the decisions of the centre, so that at certain moments it is the actions of the masses in San Domingo which are responsible for the behaviour of the revolutionary masses in Paris.

For someone with so deep and unswerving a belief in the potential of the masses, James was also, disconcertingly, a believer in 'the great artist', and the 'essentially individual' nature of artistic production. At the same time, he insisted that the conditions of possibility for the production of culture were socially and historically formed, and that, in a way which exactly paralleled what Fanon was writing at that moment, the creation of a national consciousness was essential for the improvement of the quality of cultural output. (Fanon would not, however, have shared James's faith in the 'supreme artist' and his or her influence on national consciousness.) Even the disregarded forms of popular culture such as calypso produce their own important artists, however, and James wrote about the calypsonian Mighty Sparrow as perhaps the first artist to represent all of the West Indies. A particular problem facing artists in the Caribbean is the need to work with, and eventually through, languages and cultural forms which not only do not belong to them, but are the 'property' of the former colonial masters. Despite that colonial history, however, James was adamant that Western culture was part of the heritage of Third World peoples, and was not simply to be discarded. Beyond the European, it is world culture which is the ultimate heritage, nothing less than which was appropriate to the internationalism which found its differing expression in James's Marxism and pan-Africanism.

Further reading

Buhle, Paul (ed.) C.L.R. JAMES: HIS LIFE AND WORK, Allison & Busby, 1986.
Buhle, Paul C.L.R. JAMES: THE ARTIST AS REVOLUTIONARY, Verso, 1988.
Robinson, Cedric J. BLACK MARXISM, Zed, 1983.

P.W.

JAMES, William

Psychologist/philosopher	born USA 1842–1910
Associated with	PRAGMATISM ▪ STREAM OF CONSCIOUSNESS ▪ JAMES–LANGE THEORY OF EMOTION
Influences include	BERGSON ▪ FECHNER ▪ HEGEL
Shares common ground with	HUSSERL ▪ LANGE ▪ DEWEY
Main works	PRAGMATISM: A NEW NAME FOR OLD WAYS OF THINKING (1907) THE PRINCIPLES OF PSYCHOLOGY (2 vols., 1890) THE VARIETIES OF RELIGIOUS EXPERIENCE (1902) 'DOES CONSCIOUSNESS EXIST?', in ESSAYS AND RADICAL EMPIRICISM (1912)

BROTHER OF NOVELIST Henry James, William James had an education comprising a series of journeys through Europe accompanied by a private tutor. After studing art, he transferred to Harvard, where he became a medical student and earned his MD in 1869. He returned to Europe regularly, usually for convalescence: James was prone to illness for most of his life. As much of his illness was thought to be psychosomatic, James may have gained important insights into the nature of abnormal psychological states. Taking up a teaching position at Harvard in 1875, he lectured in anatomy, physiology and, later, philosophy. He retired in 1907.

James's *The Principles of Psychology* is a seminal work in the strongest sense of the term: it led to entire schools of philosophical, psychological and sociological thought based on the foundations of what he intended to be a natural-scientific approach to the then young discipline of psychology. In Europe, theorists such as Wundt and Vygotsky had already begun to promote an experimental approach to studying the human mind; and the application of associationist principles led to claims from Pavlov, Haidenhain and Ludwig at around the time of James's writing. Like these early psychologists and physiologists (the distinction was hardly relevant), James was at pains to exclude as far as possible non-observable phenomena. But whereas associationists conceived of a physical basis for thought (ideas being like atoms linked by associations, themselves arising from practical experiences), James argued that thought is a stream of consciousness. He included such phenomena as thought and feelings in his definition of consciousness – subjective states, reference to which would have earned Pavlov's assistants dismissal from his laboratories.

Ideas have practical utility, argued James, acknowledging Peirce as the key influence on his concept of pragmatism. There is no value, nor even significance for concepts beyond what future consequences they lead to. Such notions as intrinsic meaning and truth are quite irrelevant. Darwin's influence is apparent: the instrumental value of ideas is judged according to whether they assist us in our adaptation to practical reality. If they do have utility, they will enable us to change that reality to suit our purposes. In *The Will to Believe* (1897), James himself called this theory radical empiricism; at its heart is the contention that meaning is a sum of the consequences that follow on from a state of affairs signified by the concept or proposition. Ideas are anticipations of future events.

Possibly even more radical was James's answer to the question 'Does consciousness exist?' No: consciousness is merely a function of an underlying process called pure experience. Consciousness is always consciousness *of* events in our experience.

His collaboration with Danish physician/psychologist Carl Georg Lange produced the James–Lange Theory of Emotion, which stated that the physical response of an arousal precedes the sensation and appearance of emotion. In other words, our emotions are experienced because of a bodily change, such as an increased heart rate and an adrenalin rush. The famous example of this is the 'See the bear, then run and *then* feel afraid.' This reverses the usual approach to emotional experience and situates the source as the interaction between the central nervous system and the material environment. Emotion is a product of this interaction, not a cause of it.

As one might anticipate, existentialists of the day, particularly Sartre, objected to this somewhat mechanistic account. For Sartre, James misunderstood emotion, which is not just a response, but a 'lived experience'. Similarly, the body is not only a physical entity in which changes can be induced, but a phenomenon that is humanly experienced, 'lived'.

James's work on consciousness was a stimulus to G. H. Mead and hence to the school of thought that became symbolic interactionism. James was intrigued by the peculiar duality involved in thinking: when we think about ourselves, who is doing the thinking? We think about ourselves as objects, someone whom we know; yet there is also a subject doing the knowing. 'For shortness we may call one the *Me* and the other the *I*', wrote James. The division coincides with what James considered a crucial stage in the development of consciousness, namely when we become sensitive to the opinions of others. Mead was later to call this 'taking the attitude of the other', meaning that a child recognises a certain attitude in someone else, understands its meaning and then learns to take it him or herself. In James's perspective, the child arrives at the point where he or she is able to imagine what other people are thinking and feeling. Vicariously, the child takes part in others' cognitive and affective activity, placing him or herself in their position. Schellenberg (below) shows how James's framework for theorising the self fits well with more recent work by both proponents and critics of symbolic interactionism, although his view of the link between self and society provided only a beginning for more sociological interpretations.

Further reading

Leary, D.E. 'William James and the Art of Human Understanding', AMERICAN PSYCHOLOGIST, 47: 2, 1992.
Schellenberg, J.A. 'William James and Symbolic Interactionism', PERSONALITY AND SOCIAL PSYCHOLOGY BULLETIN, 16: 4, 1990.
Taylor, E. WILLIAM JAMES ON CONSCIOUSNESS BEYOND THE MARGIN, Princeton University Press, 1996.
Taylor, E. and Wozniak, R. (eds.) PURE EXPERIENCE: THE RESPONSE TO WILLIAM JAMES, Routledge, 1996.

E.C.

JAMESON, Fredric

Cultural critic	born USA 1934—
Associated with	CRITICAL THEORY ■ HERMENEUTICS ■ POSTMODERNISM ■ WESTERN MARXISM
Influences include	ADORNO ■ ALTHUSSER ■ AUERBACH ■ BAUDRILLARD ■ LUKÁCS ■ SARTRE
Shares common ground with	EAGLETON ■ HALL ■ HARVEY ■ KELLNER ■ WILLIAMS
Main works	MARXISM AND FORM (1971) THE POLITICAL UNCONSCIOUS (1981) POSTMODERNISM, OR, THE CULTURAL LOGIC OF LATE CAPITALISM (1991) THE GEOPOLITICAL AESTHETIC (1992)

J AMESON IS THE leading Marxist cultural critic in the USA. In a period when it is often said that Marxism has finally been eclipsed not only politically, with the collapse of Marxist–Leninist regimes, but also theoretically because it has been superseded by the varieties of post-structuralist thought, Jameson has held firm to the tradition of a creative Marxism which he has done so much himself to illuminate in books like *Marxism and Form*. His approach has been to synthesise the materialist conception of history with the insights of other traditions, especially theories inspired by structural linguistics, facilitated by his own literary and linguistic education. Jameson's academic position as a Professor of Comparative Literature derives, in the first instance, from French scholarship and his early work on Sartre in the 1950s, and whose formative influence persists through the various developments of Jameson's theorising since then. Jameson has taught at the University of California (including Santa Cruz and San Diego), Yale and Duke.

Whereas structuralism freezes time and places language at the heart of cultural analysis, for Marxism, it is history, understood as deep structures and processes, that is fundamental. So, when it comes, for instance, to making sense of postmodernism, the analysis and interpretation of signs in relation to signs is not enough. They must be understood in relation to something else, and in Jameson's classical Marxist reasoning, that means in relation to the dynamics of capital. A subtle reading of textual symptoms is necessary, however, to reveal the 'political unconscious' of cultural history.

As he argued famously in his *New Left Review* essay of 1984, which gave its title to Jameson's subsequent book-length analysis of the contemporary condition, postmodernism is 'the cultural logic of late-capitalism'. Postmodern culture is curiously 'depthless'. This is not only a characteristic of, say, television advertising's seductive and empty recycling of images, Las Vegas architecture, where façade is all there is, and retro-style pastiche in cinema, but of 'Theory' itself. The depth of materialism to which Jameson subscribes contrasts sharply with the intellectual surfing so typical of French theory and its followers. To take the obvious example, Baudrillard not only identifies the reduction of everything to signs; he actually reduces everything to signs himself.

Postmodernism is the culture of capitalism in the age of information technology and globalisation, according to Jameson. It is an inherently anomic culture in which it is difficult for individuals to sustain a coherent sense of self and find a satisfactory orientation. Sense of place is dislocated and social and spatial confusion endemic. If the diagnosis is correct then the remedy, in terms of cultural politics, is an aesthetic of 'cognitive mapping', an idea which Jameson derives from Kevin Lynch's *The Image of the City* (1960). As well as invoking a Lukácsian call for a new kind of realism, the idea of cognitive mapping is representative of the spatial turn in cultural theory and owes much to cultural geography. It is not surprising, then, that the title of Jameson's book after *Postmodernism* should have been *The Geopolitical Aesthetic*. This text combines the stress of spatiality with another strand of Jameson's work, his film criticism. He looks at both First and Third World cinema and Jameson proceeds according to what he describes as 'an unsystematic mapping or scanning of the world system itself'.

The ambition of Jameson's work is breathtaking in its scope. His writings are replete with striking insights. However, he is also frequently criticised for excessive totalisation, of being far too willing to make overarching connections between very disparate phenomena. While it is true that sometimes Jameson's totalising approach is unconvincing, his refusal to relinquish the project of a global sense-making is in many ways admirable. He is without doubt one of the few truly great cultural theorists of the late twentieth century.

Further reading

Dowling, W. JAMESON, ALTHUSSER, MARX: AN INTRODUCTION TO THE POLITICAL UNCONSCIOUS, Methuen, 1984.
Harvey, D. THE CONDITION OF POSTMODERNITY, Blackwell, 1989.
Kellner, D. (ed.) POSTMODERNISM/JAMESON/CRITIQUE, Maisonneuve, 1989.

J.McG.

JENCKS, Charles Alexander

Architectural historian/critic	born USA 1939—
Associated with	POSTMODERN ARCHITECTURE ■ URBAN SPACE
Influences include	NIETZSCHE ■ VENTURI ■ LORENZ
Shares common ground with	JACOBS ■ LYOTARD ■ EISENMANN ■ VENTURI AND SCOTT-BROWN ■ NEWMAN
Main works	MODERN MOVEMENTS IN ARCHITECTURE (1973, 1985)
	THE LANGUAGE OF POST-MODERN ARCHITECTURE (1977)
	WHAT IS POST-MODERNISM? (1986, 1996)
	THE ARCHITECTURE OF THE JUMPING UNIVERSE (1995)

HAVING STUDIED UNDER some of the key figures in post-war development of Modernist architecture, architectural historiography and cultural theory (e.g. Siegfried Gideon and Reyner Banham), Charles Jencks found his reputation during the mid-1970s as a controversial populariser and theorist of the phenomenon of 'postmodernism' in American architecture and urban design. His position is staged largely in terms of an irreverent criticism of the prevailing academic orthodoxy of Modernist design developed in the architecture and design departments at the Illinois Institute of Technology and at Harvard University; the places to which leading European Modernists (Gropius and Mies van der Rohe) were invited during the late 1930s in order to establish the tradition of design pedagogy that had been instituted at the Bauhaus.

Concerned at the condition of urban environments perceivably betrayed by the bureaucratic arrogance of Modernist design and planning dogma, he has been keen to promote a notion of the remedial social effect of a postmodern architecture. His main argument advocates the development of a witting, intellectually light, suggestive, adaptable, legible and easily influenced architectural grammar. He has sought to promote and defend the causes of a number of like-minded architects and, like others, has taken inspiration from the inventive vernacularity of the commercial architecture of Las Vegas. A justifying tenet of this recourse, one shared by influential urban critics like Robert Venturi, Jane Jacobs and Oscar Newman, lies in the belief that an architectural iconography derived from popular cultural imagery could do much to alleviate the characterlessness of some urban environments, promote a sense of social coherence and community and even reduce crime.

His central strategy has been the reappraisal of the forms of architectural history which seem devised to validate the inevitability of Modernist architectural pactice by derogating large areas of previous architectural practice. Most clearly outlined in *Modern Movements in Architecture*, he has proposed a view of architectural history comprised in a plurality of discontinuous traditions as opposed to the apparently dominating view of a singularly appropriate, international style, with its indisputable 'masters', canonical buildings and emerging concepts (concerning historical progress, transcendent architectural values and honesty in the *functionalist* expression of materials and construction). More recently, he has augmented this view with reference to the 'chaos-theory' of Konrad Lorenz, to forward a conception of human history proceeding by a series of 'jumps' that come as a result of unpredicatable conjunctures, and has drawn on metaphors of cultural diaspora in support of this. Seeing the problem of architecture as a broadly based cultural one, Jencks has also been instrumental in setting up interdisciplinary working groups. Regarding this, his work has been linked to philosophical and literary 'deconstruction'. Whilst relevant, this project and his own have since developed in different directions.

Jencks maintains that the Modernist cultural-historical model ignores not only certain buildings but also important intellectual aspects of some of the architects it most reveres. He has offered a rereading of Le Corbusier in this regard which emphasises poetically anthropomorphic features in his work. This manoeuvre itself hints at Jencks's own theatrical, rhetorical ability. He famously proclaimed the occasion of the demolition of a New Jersey block of public housing in 1979 as the final demise of the Modernist project. He has also highlighted the relationship of Mies van der Rohe and Le Corbusier to totalitarian regimes in order to challenge the unquestioning awe in which these figures have been held.

Jencks insists on the ambiguous, double-codedness of the architecture he supports. The recent use by architects of the classical tradition in a variety of ironic, humorous and earnest ways has been useful here. It has also been useful for him to distinguish postmodern from late modern practices; the latter representing a category of serious continuations of Modernist tradition and its cultural perspectives which, nevertheless, also represents a semiotic resource for a postmodern design sensibility to play with. Such generalisations and a poetic recourse to the device of the extreme *longue durée* of human civilisation, as deployed by Gideon (note Jencks's recent interest in cosmology), have led to accusations that he has presented theories of radical cultural rupture in the same way as some Modernist historians have. It should be noted too that his faith in postmodernism's potential for positive sociocultural reform is not entirely removed from notions of 'architectural determinism' put forward earlier by some Modernists. Given his liking for ironic gestures, however, these could equally legitimately be seen as purposeful restagings of key cultural-historical concepts.

Further reading

Caygill, H. 'Architectural Postmodernism: The Retreat of an Avant-Garde?', in R. Boyne and A. Rattansi (eds.), POSTMODERNISM AND SOCIETY, Macmillan, 1990.
Harvey, D. THE CONDITION OF POSTMODERNITY, Blackwell, 1990.
Rose, G. 'Architecture to Philosophy: The Postmodern Complicity', THEORY, CULTURE AND SOCIETY, 5: 2–3, 1988.
Venturi, R. *et al.* COMPLEXITY AND CONTRADICTION IN ARCHITECTURE, Architectural Press, 1966.

R.S.

JUNG, Carl Gustav

Psychoanalyst	born Switzerland 1875–1961
Associated with	DREAM ANALYSIS ■ PERSONALITY TYPES ■ COLLECTIVE UNCONSCIOUS ■ ARCHETYPES
Influences include	FREUD ■ NIETZSCHE ■ HAECKEL
Shares common ground with	FREUD ■ ROGERS ■ ADLER
Main works	MEMORIES, DREAMS, REFLECTIONS (1963) MODERN MAN IN SEARCH OF A SOUL (1933) CIVILISATION IN TRANSITION (1964)

CARL JUNG WAS born in Kesswil, a quiet backwater of Switzerland, where his father was a pastor of the Swiss Reformed Church. He was educated in Basle and studied medicine at the university there from which he graduated in joint first place in 1900. He worked initially at a mental hospital in Zurich and lectured at the University of Zurich. His work led to him meeting Freud in 1907 in Vienna. This meeting led to a strong collaborative working relationship and to Jung becoming President of the International Psycho-analytical Association from 1910 to 1914. After breaking with Freud in 1913, Jung followed his own interests. His collaboration with the National Socialists in the 1930s led to subsequent accusation of Nazi sympathies. He died in 1961.

Many of the concepts which Jung developed in his work have become part of everyday speech to such an extent that people use the concepts without being aware of their origins. An example of this is Jung's work in the development and identification of personality types. In this work he laid the foundations of psychometric testing as developed by Eysenck and his concepts of extraversion and introversion have entered common vocabulary. Other work led to his formulation of the concept of the collective unconscious as an impersonal substratum of memory underlying the personal unconscious and common to everyone. In this respect it can be likened to a form of racial memory which is independent of an individual's own experiences. As part of this concept of the collective unconscious Jung introduced the idea of archetypes which can be used to explain individual behaviour and which form the basis of much of the work of Joseph Campbell. These archetypes are claimed by Jung to provide the source of our attitudes and hence an explanation for our individual behaviour, but it is difficult to define in practice just what an archetype is.

For Jung, as for Freud, a basic part of his analytical process was based upon dream analysis, and he published extensively on this topic. Jung also considered and defined the process of individuation as the path to individual self-knowledge. According to Jung everyone has an innate desire to achieve this self-realisation, and the prevention of this through external influences (from other people in close contact with the individual or from societal pressures) is the root cause of an individual's dysfunctional behaviour. According to Jung an individual's personality can also be described in terms of the persona and shadow: the persona representing the mask which mediates between an individual and the world and the shadow representing that part of the personality which the individual will not allow him or herself to express. An individual also has both a masculine and a feminine side, labelled animus and anima. For a man the masculine side (animus) is resident in the conscious mind with the anima being present in the unconscious, while for a woman the reverse is the case.

In his later career Jung became extremely interested in and knowledgeable concerning the religions, myths and rituals of primitive societies and, as a result, after his break with Freud, he became more concerned with the interpretation of society rather than individual psychology. He used concepts from within these myths and the concepts from his own psychological work for his analysis, viewing societal development as a continuing battle between good and evil. In his later years Jung also became interested in the paranormal and in flying saucers. Much of his later work has a mystical aspect to it and this aspect of his work has led to a resurgence in popularity in Jungian psychology in recent years amongst alternative communities. Indeed the psychology of Jung provides much of the foundations of 'New Age' psychology and spirituality.

Further reading

McLynn, F. Carl Gustav Jung, Bantam, 1996.
Noll, R. The Jung Cult, Fontana, 1996.
Singer, J. Boundaries of the Soul, Prism Press, 1994.
D.E.A.C.

KAUTSKY, Karl Johann

Socialist/social theorist	born Czechoslovakia 1854–1938
Associated with	Marxism ■ Social Democracy
Influences include	Marx ■ Engels ■ More
Shares common ground with	Gramsci ■ Tawney
Main works	The Materialist Conception of History (1927)
	The Social Revolution (1902)
	The Agrarian Question (1899)

ALTHOUGH BORN IN Prague, Kautsky became a student in Vienna where he joined the Social Democratic Party. After moving to Stuttgart in 1882 he launched the socialist review, *Die Neu Zeit*, which he edited until 1917. After moving to London in 1885 he became private secretary to Engels. He supported pacifism during the First World War and opposed Bolshevism and the Russian Revolution. He refused to join the German Communist Party and after the Bolshevik victory he settled in Vienna. In 1934 he became a naturalised citizen of Czechoslovakia, but fled to the Netherlands in 1938 after the German annexation of Austria and just before the invasion of Czechoslovakia. He died in Amsterdam.

Although Kautsky was one of the leading exponents of Marxism at the turn of the century, he has generally been reviled by subsequent Communist writers, and was a particular target for hatred by Lenin and Trotsky because of his opposition to the Bolshevik Revolution and the creation of the Soviet state. It has generally been accepted therefore that Kautsky was a renegade Marxist, although previously considered to be a distinguished theoretician. As a consequence he has largely been ignored by history until a recent resurgence of interest in his theory. Indeed, until recently, some of his major works have not been translated into English. Furthermore, in 1929 Korsch argued that Kautsky had never really understood anything about Marxism either before or after he became a 'renegade'.

Kautsky's work was concerned throughout his career with the relationship between democracy and socialism. He based his arguments upon a recognition that uniform processes operate in nature and society, but that whereas plants adapt only passively and animals actively, humans adapt through the creation of artificial organs and structures. He viewed human nature as a set of social drives adapting to changes in the environment, and his focus was upon humans *en masse* rather than upon any concern with individual behaviour. His view of the role of the state therefore necessitated a central bureaucracy set within a political democracy, as an essential instrument for ascertaining the will of its citizens. In his earlier writing he talked about a socialist revolution and the dictatorship of the proletariat but only within the context of free elections, respect for civil liberties and a parliamentary democracy. His analysis of the relationship between society and the state therefore has more in common with social democracy than with Lenin's analysis, and his break with Communism can be seen to be inevitable.

Kautsky argued that the idea of direct democracy was doomed to failure in a society dominated by large-scale modern industry. He maintained that central planning was insufficient for co-ordination of the state and the economy, and that although the administrative apparatus constructed by the bourgeoisie could be used for their socio-political ends, it could not be replaced by any anti-bureaucratic state form of organisation. He viewed the centralised machine of the Soviet state as leading to the inevitable creation of a despotic political system and that such a system was doomed to failure. It is perhaps significant therefore that the collapse of the Soviet style of state has occurred at the same time as a resurgence of interest in and a re-evaluation of Kautsky's work.

Kautsky believed that there were no objective limits to the operation and perpetuation of capitalism and that socialism therefore could not arise through the inevitable collapse of capitalism, or through revolution, but only as an expression of the will of the people for a different social order, and that political democracy was a necessary and decisive condition for the growth of socialism. In this respect he deviated from Marxist ideology, questioned some of the central tenets of Marx's work and inevitably came into conflict with other Marxist theorists. Kautsky's work therefore can be considered as a synthesis of Marxist theory, social Darwinism and liberalism and this synthesis is the core of his work which has led to its recent re-evaluation.

Further reading

Anderson, P. ARGUMENTS WITHIN ENGLISH MARXISM, New Left Books, 1980.
Kautsky, J. 'J.A. Schumpeter and Karl Kautsky: Parallel Theories of Imperialism', MIDWEST JOURNAL OF POLITICAL SCIENCE, 5, 1961, pp. 101–28.
Salvadori, M. KARL KAUTSKY AND THE SOCIALIST REVOLUTION 1880–1938, trans. J. Rothschild, Verso, 1979.

D.E.A.C.

KEYNES, John Maynard

Economist	born England 1883–1946
Associated with	MACRO-ECONOMICS
Influences include	MARSHALL ■ MOORE ■ PIGOU
Shares common ground with	MALTHUS ■ HICKS ■ GEORGE
Main works	ECONOMIC CONSEQUENCES OF THE PEACE (1919)
	A TREATISE ON MONEY (1930)
	THE GENERAL THEORY OF EMPLOYMENT, INTEREST AND MONEY (1936)

JOHN MAYNARD KEYNES was born in Cambridge where his father, John Neville, was a fellow of Pembroke College and his mother, Florence (one of the first students at Newnham College), would complete a term of office as mayor. Keynes was educated at Eton, as a colleger, and then completed a degree in mathematics at Cambridge. In the following year he stayed on at Cambridge, studying economics under Marshall and also coming second in the Civil Service examination. His working life was primarily split between teaching at Cambridge and working for the Treasury.

Keynes's life and work were greatly affected by the times in which he was living. He was born in the late Victorian era and would live through the two world wars and the economic depression which separated them. These events were to inspire his greatest works. Following the outbreak of the First World

War he was employed by the Treasury, and by the time of the Paris Peace Conference he was the principal Treasury representative. He resigned this position before the agreement was finalised as he could not accept the high reparation terms which were being suggested. In response he wrote *Economic Consequences of the Peace*, which was not only an economic analysis but also a plea for greater restraint in the treatment of Germany. This work catapulted Keynes to fame.

His other great work concentrated on the British experience of high unemployment in the period between the wars. Keynes departed from the orthodoxy of the time in suggesting that an economy could reach a stable equilibrium below full employment. This changed the role of governments as it signified that it would be possible to tackle unemployment with appropriate public policy. Keynes suggested that the government should invest in public works to stimulate employment, something previously not considered worthwhile as it was believed that public investment replaced private investment and would therefore have no overall impact.

Keynes was not a socialist although he did have sympathies with certain of their ideas. However he could not agree with the class basis for socialism as he was very much 'on the side of the educated bourgeoisie'. Through his theories he attempted to set a public policy which would allow state interference to the extent that it would provide the correct framework within which there would be private enterprise. This would be a reformed capitalism which would be an alternative to a socialist state and a fully *laissez-faire* economy.

Keynes's economic work and life were greatly influenced by his membership of the Apostles, an élite philosophical group at Cambridge, and also the Bloomsbury group. Victorian Christian values were being replaced and Keynes placed importance on a system of ethics and conduct. He drew from G.E. Moore, the philosopher and older member of the Apostles, the value of personal relationships and the enjoyment of beautiful objects. The memberships of these groups are possibly the basis for Keynes's actions as a philanthropist, builder of the Cambridge Arts Theatre and as Chairman of the Arts Council.

As well as the work already mentioned Keynes was also a prolific journalist, chairman of several organisations (most notably the National Mutual Life Insurance Company), enjoyed a successful career in finance and formulated the British views concerning the economic reconstruction to follow the Second World War. He was the leading British representative at the Bretton Woods conference in 1944 and was influential in the founding of the International Monetary Fund. His analysis has generally been implemented by economic policy-makers throughout the world following the Second World War. Although the late 1970s saw a trend away from Keynesian economics and towards monetarist policies, this may be reversed in the 1990s as concern grows over continued high levels of unemployment. Possibly the most visible legacy that Keynes has left is the now common use of national income accounting and the acceptance that economic management is a crucial activity of governments in advanced capitalist economies.

Further reading

Moggridge, D.E. KEYNES, Macmillan, 1993.
Skidelsky, R. KEYNES, Oxford University Press, 1996.
Stewart, M. KEYNES AND AFTER, Penguin, 1972.
S.M.C.

KIERKEGAARD, Søren Aabye

Philosopher/theologist	born Denmark 1813–1855
Associated with	EXISTENTIALISM ■ THEOLOGY ■ LITERARY THEORY
Influences include	HEGEL ■ SOCRATES ■ LESSING
Shares common ground with	BLANCHOT ■ LÉVINAS ■ DERRIDA
Main works	EITHER/OR (1843) PHILOSOPHICAL FRAGMENTS (1844) CONCLUDING UNSCIENTIFIC POSTSCRIPT (1846)

S ØREN KIERKEGAARD ENROLLED at the University of Copenhagen in 1830. In 1841 he defended his thesis: *The Concept of Irony with Constant Reference to Socrates.* When published two years later, this text marked the inception of an astonishingly prolific period. From 1843 until his death in 1855, a romantically and religiously inspired Kierkegaard authored an extensive collection of papers and journals as well as more than thirty volumes, many of which were published pseudonymously.

Since a great deal of Kierkegaard's work was crafted to analyse and revitalise Christian faith, he has often been associated with theological discourse. Yet his work crosses the boundaries of philosophy, theology, psychology, literary criticism, devotional literature and fiction.

Kierkegaard's work continues to impact the course of contemporary cultural theory, even though the last of his texts was written over a century ago, for they address a very timely, if not timeless concern: the volatile relationship between subjectivity and the unspeakable encounter with difference. Central to Kierkegaard's approach to subjectivity, the concept of God as a figuration of the unknown and unknowable carries one of the most pressing questions of Kierkegaard's *oeuvre*: faith.

For Kierkegaard, Christian faith is not a matter of regurgitating church dogma, but an individual's constantly renewed and unspeakable subjective passion. One's very selfhood relies on the negative freedom imparted by the irony of uncertainty that makes faith possible, on its intimate relationship to the unknown and unknowable other. An infinite abstract negativity, irony is the freedom of 'sheer possibility'. It drives the 'random coming apart, the chance disconnections of *words* and letters from any semantically determined context' (Agacinski 1988: 27).

As Maurice Blanchot insists, Kierkegaard develops indirect communication – that is, irony and its extensions as pseudonymity, paradox and silence – because of the structural impossibility of communication. Kierkegaard's indirect communication, a constantly reiterated tribute to and mourning for this failure, demonstrates the impossibility of revealing the truth of otherness in the medium of language. It addresses the experience of paradox which is the source of a thinker's passion, the supreme paradox of all thought: 'the attempt to discover something that thought cannot think . . . the limit to which the Reason repeatedly comes . . . the absolutely different' (*Philosophical Fragments*).

Insofar as Kierkegaard's indirect communication delivers the immediacy of paradox, it serves as the rhetorical and epistemological tool with which he sustains a polemic against the widespread influence of Hegel during the 'golden age' of Denmark's intellectual and artistic activity (to which of course, Kierkegaard himself contributed). To clarify, while Kierkegaard greatly admired Hegel, he had grave reservations about Hegelianism's self-inflated claim to system that produces absolute knowledge. Hegel would have been the greatest thinker who ever lived, said Kierkegaard, if only he had regarded his system as a thought-experiment. Instead he purported to have reached the truth, and so rendered himself comical.

For Kierkegaard, Hegel's massive myopic system takes insufficient account of the individual and the unknown, the otherness through which irony constitutes subjectivity. And so, taking his example from Socrates' skilled exercise of irony, Kierkegaard wielded his indirect communication to make conventionally accepted forms of knowledge and value untenable. His became the 'art of taking away', and 'making difficult' since he thought his audience suffered from too much comfort and knowledge rather than too little. This attention to paradox, to the incommensurable failings of reason that foreground humankind's encounter with absurdity, serves as the cornerstone of many existentially informed literatures.

Further reading

Agacinski, S. APARTE: CONCEPTIONS AND DEATHS OF SØREN KIERKEGAARD, trans. Kevin Newmark, Florida State University Press, 1988.
Fenves, P. CHATTER: LANGUAGE AND HISTORY IN KIERKEGAARD, Stanford University Press, 1993.

O.C.

KOJÈVE, Alexandre

Philosopher	born Russia 1902–1968
Associated with	HEGELIANISM ■ MARXISM ■ PSYCHOANALYSIS
Influences include	HEGEL ■ MARX ■ HEIDEGGER
Shares common ground with	HEGEL ■ FUKUYAMA
Main work	INTRODUCTION TO THE READING OF HEGEL (1947)

A LEXANDRE KOJÈVE HAS had a profound, if largely unacknowledged, effect on contemporary cultural theory. His role in modern intellectual and cultural history is pivotal to an understanding of historicity and the dialectic, the political and the aesthetic, negativity, and, most importantly, Desire and the desire of the Other. Indirectly, he has left an indelible mark on the thinking of a generation of French and French-based thinkers, including Julia Kristeva and the *Tel Quel* group as a whole, on Michel Foucault, Jacques Derrida and Jean Baudrillard. Likewise, he has been instrumental in producing the conditions of possibility for the emergence of phenomenology, Lacanianism and post-Lacanian psychoanalysis and certain kinds of feminism. He is one of the great-grandfathers of structuralism and post-structuralism.

But how did this indirect effect belie a more direct influence? Kojève came to Paris in 1928. As an assistant to Alexandre Koyré, he began to teach in the division of religious sciences at the École Pratique des Hautes Études. Kojève is best known for his lectures on Hegel's *The Phenomenology of Spirit* which took place at the École between 1933 and 1939. These lectures did not appear in print until Raymond Queneau's notes of Kojève's oral presentations were edited together as *Introduction à la lecture de Hegel* (parts of which have been translated as *Introduction to the Reading of Hegel*) in 1947. These lectures on Hegel, along with the first complete French translation of Hegel's *Phénoménologie de l'esprit* by Jean Hyppolite in 1939 and Jean Wahl's interest in the young Hegel in 1929, herald an idiosyncratic and speculative resurgence of Hegelianism in France at this time, with an anthropological and Marxist bent which thus concretised Hegel's philosophy. Kojève lectures were attended by a number of his elders and contemporaries who were, or went on to become, the most important French thinkers of their generation and were instrumental in building the edifice of French critical theory. His audience included the likes of Raymond Aron, Georges Bataille, Henry Corbin, Jean Desanti, R.P. Fessard, Aron Gurwitsch, Jean Hyppolite, Pierre Klossowski, Alexandre Koyré, Jacques Lacan, Maurice Merleau-Ponty, Raymond Queneau, Patrick Waldberg, Eric Weil and occasionally André Breton, Emmanuel Lévinas and perhaps Jean-Paul Sartre.

It was Kojève who taught a generation of French intellectuals how to return to, read and interpret a text. This politics of pedagogy is well explained by Elisabeth Roudinesco in *Jacques Lacan & Co.: A History of Psychoanalysis in France 1925–1985* (University of Chicago Press, 1990) 'It was not by chance that Lacan discovered in Kojève's discourse the wherewithal to effect a new interpretation of an original body of thought. At Kojève's side, he learnt how to make Freud's text say what it does not say.' Similarly, a more immediate account of the explosive revelations of Kojève's teaching comes from Bataille: 'From '33 (I think) to '39 I attended the course that Alexandre Kojève devoted to the analysis of *La Phénoménologie de l'esprit* (an inspired analysis, measuring up to the book: How many times were Queneau and I staggered as we left the small room – staggered, stunned) . . . Kojève's course broke me, crushed me, killed me ten times over' [*OC*, vol VI, p. 416].

The other 'rightist' genealogy which has emerged from this Kojèvian or neo-Hegelian tradition is part of a very different history in which Kojève went on to become a high official in the French Ministry of Economic Affairs and was involved in the early stages of organising the European Union and GATT. Following his friendship with Leo Strauss and the work of Strauss's disciple Allan Bloom, this story culminates with the welcoming liberal fanfare that could be heard in certain quarters following the fall of Communism in Eastern Europe and its aftermath, heralding the final victory of capitalism's world domination. These are the same celebrations that greeted the academic and popular success of Francis Fukuyama's *The End of History and the Last Man* (1992).

Although these two trajectories cannot be dissociated – it was, after all, Kojève who gave us the notion of 'the End of History' – his French rather than American legacy should be remembered in this context. When we engage with

Hegel in the thought of post-structuralism, the writing of postmodernism and the structures of feeling which permeate our present condition we are, almost without exception, engaging with Alexandre Kojève. The influence that he has had on affecting the ways in which we have come to understand the production of culture and cultural theory is immeasurable.

Further reading

Auffret, Dominique ALEXANDRE KOJÈVE: LA PHILOSOPHIE, L'ÉTAT, LA FIN DE L'HISTORIE, Bernard Grasset, 1990.
Butler, Judith P. SUBJECTS OF DESIRE: HEGELIAN REFLECTIONS IN TWENTIETH-CENTURY FRANCE, Cornell University Press, 1987.
Roth, Michael S. KNOWING AND HISTORY: APPROPRIATIONS OF HEGEL IN TWENTIETH-CENTURY FRANCE, Cornell University Press, 1988.
M.S.

KRACAUER, Siegfried

Sociologist/cultural theorist	born Germany 1889–1966
Associated with	MASS CULTURE ■ ALIENATION ■ URBAN EXPERIENCE
Main influences	MARX ■ SIMMEL ■ LUKÁCS
Shares common ground with	BENJAMIN ■ BLOCH ■ ADORNO
Main works	THEORY OF FILM (1960) HISTORY (1969) THE MASS ORNAMENT: WEIMAR ESSAYS (1995)

K RACAUER BELONGS TO the generation of German cultural critics who found inspiration in the distinctive life-forms of the metropolis and the new electronic means of mass communication. He trained as an architect in Munich and moved to Berlin, where he studied sociology under

Georg Simmel. In 1921 he joined the *Frankfurter Zeitung* where he worked as a journalist. He eventually became cultural correspondent.

In the Weimar years, Kracauer mainly wrote about film and the culture of consumption. His style mirrored that of Simmel. He believed that the superficial, throwaway aspects of mass culture provided the best evidence of the character of the times. The 'daydreams' of society, reflected in advertising images, film, leisure pastimes and the desire to travel, were the window to society's soul. He called spatial images the 'hieroglyphics' of social reality. He argued that modern culture is increasingly emptied of meaning. Essential inner needs are deprived by 'the cult of distraction' in which consciousness is absorbed in a stream of passing superficial obsessions and preoccupations produced by capitalist technological innovation and the culture industry. The individual suffers from a loss of meaning in the world and longs for something to fill the empty intellectual void of daily life. Like Simmel, he perceived the increasing haste and hurry in the modern world as a symptom of denying the fundamental lack of meaning. Modern culture requires people to be busy, but it encourages collective amnesia about the key questions relating to the purpose of life. Collective amnesia is fuelled by the glamour of ever-new distractions. History is forgotten in the glare of endless technological and cultural novelty. By fragmenting our attention, modern culture prevents us from reflecting on the relationship between the individual and the totality. Modern men and women are cut off from any higher meaning or significance. The sense of homelessness is compounded by the erosion of religious belief through science, and increased social and geographical mobility.

Kracauer's first full-length reflection on the vacuity of rational–bureaucratic culture is *The Detective Novel* (1922–25). Divided into sections ('psychology', 'Hotel Lobby', 'Detective', 'Police', 'Criminal', 'Confession', 'Trial' and 'End'), the book underlines Kracauer's belief that everyday life has collapsed into a series of empty set-pieces. He argues that modern culture is a metronomic order of skin-deep profundity. The characters in detective novels are analysed as fragmentary social actors who no longer recognise a moral universe of binding laws. Instead they live by the contingency and opportunity afforded by rational–legal rationality. They are trapped in a labyrinth which is seemingly beyond their power to control. Solutions are momentary, and fail to address the pervasive sense of meaninglessness and helplessness caused by the wider system of living.

It is a position that Kracauer develops in his essays on consumer culture. Notably, in respect of his discussion of the mathematical choreography of dancing girls in the dance craze in Weimar Germany, which he regards as an extension of the Taylorist routines learnt in the workplace; and also in his analysis of travel as motivated by the desire to accumulate fleeting experience through constant movement as opposed to the classical desire to arrive. His discussion of white-collar workers drew direct parallels between the isolation, rootlessness and general sense of insecurity and the increasing popularity of conspicuous consumption, café society, dance halls and cabarets. He argued that leisure performs a compensatory function in modern culture. At the same time, modern culture constantly promises individuals more than it can deliver. The more that leisure is presented as an escape from work, the more leisure takes on the characteristics of work. Cultural spectacle replaces religion and constitutes a new form of domination rather than a sphere of free and spontaneous expression. Individuals become increasingly enmeshed in a fantasy world in which 'superficial manifestations' of culture hide the essential emptiness of life.

With the rise of the Nazis, Kracauer fled Germany. He first moved to France and in 1940 emigrated to the USA, where he could study the 'distraction factories' of Hollywood at first hand, and was awarded a Guggenheim fellowship to prepare a history of German film. *From Caligari to Hitler* was published in 1947. During the 1940s and 1950s Kracauer was a senior member of the Bureau of Applied Social Research at Columbia University.

In the USA Kracauer was known mainly as a theorist of film. He consolidated his reputation in 1960 with the publication of his influential *Theory of Film*, which was critically recognised as 'the bible of neo-realism'. Kracauer treated film as an extension of his earlier analysis of mass culture. Adorno and Horkheimer's thesis of the culture industry held that Hollywood film produced docility and conformity. In contrast, Kracauer argued that Hollywood movies expose cultural disintegration rather than masking it. Like Benjamin, he assigned a revelatory potential to popular culture. He advocated politically 'concerned' cinema as a way of exposing the contradictions in the social and economic structure.

Kracauer portrayed modern culture as wrapped in the painted veil of fantasy and delusion. The culture industry recognised fantasy as the only meaningful form of belonging. Yet he resisted the pessimistic conclusions of the Frankfurt School. He asserted that cultivating a sense of history and forcing social and economic contradictions to their extreme, through film and other cultural forms, are paths to redemption.

Further reading

Frisby, D. FRAGMENTS OF MODERNITY, Polity, 1985.
Jay, M. 'The Extraterritorial Life of Siegfried Kracauer,' SALMAGUNDI, 31/32 (1975/76), pp. 49–106.
Levin, T. 'Introduction', in S. Kracauer, THE MASS ORNAMENT: WEIMAR ESSAYS, Harvard University Press, 1995, pp. 1–30.

C.R.

KRISTEVA, Julia

Philosopher/psychoanalyst	born Bulgaria 1941—
Associated with	SEMANALYSIS ■ SEMIOTICS ■ FEMINISM
Influences include	HEGEL ■ BARTHES ■ LACAN
Shares common ground with	BARTHES ■ DERRIDA ■ IRIGARAY
Main works	LA RÉVOLUTION DU LANGAGE POÉTIQUE, trans. REVOLUTION IN POETIC LANGUAGE (1984)
	POWERS OF HORROR (1982)
	STRANGERS TO OURSELVES (1991)

WITH A UNIQUE scholarly background in Marxist thought, Russian Formalism (Bakhtin) and Hegelian negativity, Julia Kristeva stormed on to the Parisian intellectual scene in 1965. Her emigration was ensured by a scholarship to study with Lucian Goldman and Roland Barthes at L'École Pratique des Hautes Études. At this time Kristeva became involved with an avant-garde intellectual group and published a series of articles in their journal, *Tel Quel*. After writing two books, *Semeiotiké: Recherches pour une semanalyse* and *Le Texte du roman*, in which she develops her theory of semanalysis, Kristeva received her doctoral degree in 1973 with the defence of *La Révolution du langage poétique*, published in 1974. Since this time she has held a Chair in Linguistics at the University of Paris VII, with visiting appointments at Columbia University in New York, and is also a practising psychoanalyst in Paris. Kristeva's contribution to the study of culture is immense: through a complex interweaving of materialist theories of language, a critical reconfiguration of Jacques Lacan's psychoanalytic theories, and thorough interrogations of various cultural archives, she has provided a new understanding of the production and functionings of the subject, art and society within contemporary cultural life.

In her early work, whilst engaging with Russian Formalism and linguistics, Kristeva was able to bring together a definitive critique of structuralism and its scientific basis. As a result of this engagement, she puts forth an alternative critical apparatus known as semanalysis. Semanalysis 'jolt[s] . . . [and] carrie[s] theoretical thought to an intensity of white heat that set[s] categories and concepts ablaze – sparing not even discourse itself. *Semanalysis* . . . meets [this] requirement to describe the signifying phenomenon . . . while analyzing, criticizing, and dissolving "phenomenon", "meaning" and "signifier".'

Semanalysis as a means of setting categories and concepts ablaze has been an ongoing concern for Kristeva. In *Revolution in Poetic Language*, she presents a radical reconfiguration of the phenomenological and psychoanalytic subject through a critical semanalysis of the avant-garde in modern literature. Here Kristeva puts forth her notion of the 'subject on trial'; a dialectical subject which is psychically divided and in a constant state of production, of becoming. As such, the subject is at times able to articulate a revolutionary art practice through a radical re-engagement with its own subjectivity. This complex weaving of artistic production and subject formation is fundamental to Kristeva's understanding of culture and remains an ongoing concern in all her later work.

Kristeva then went on to write a series of texts on contemporary cultural maladies. *Powers of Horror* explores the notion of abjection through a close and critical reading of the Bible and the work of Céline. Kristeva's notion of abjection has become an invaluable concept for a series of contemporary discourses including feminism, literary theory, philosophy and ethics. *Black Sun* (1992) provides a semanalysis of the symptomatology of depression and melancholia which belies all linguistic meaning in our culture through a rigorous reading of the philosophical, psychoanalytic and theological aspects of Hans Holbein's painting *The Body of the Dead Christ in the Tomb*, along with the work of Nerval, Dostoevsky and Duras. *Tales of Love* (1989) offers an insightful exploration of the theory of love, desire and the subject within the Western philosophical tradition. *New Maladies of the Soul* (1995) focuses on the new illnesses produced from contemporary culture's dependence on the psychoanalytic couch for relief from everyday anxieties. While *Strangers to Ourselves* identifies the foreigner as a concept within both a national context and as a function within the subject itself.

Kristeva's *oeuvre* incorporates a series of fascinating and critical engagements with contemporary cultural debates by a philosopher, psychoanalyst and thinker who is deeply committed to these issues. Her importance and influence can be felt thoughout a variety of cultural analyses including feminist theory, cultural studies, sociology, linguistics, philosophy, psychoanalysis, ethics and theology.

Further reading

Coward, R. and Ellis, J. LANGUAGE AND MATERIALISM: DEVELOPMENTS IN SEMIOLOGY AND THE THEORY OF THE SUBJECT, Routledge, 1977.
Fletcher, J. and Benjamin, A. (eds.) ABJECTION, MELANCHOLIA AND LOVE, Routledge, 1990.
Oliver, K. READING KRISTEVA: UNRAVELING THE DOUBLE-BIND, Indiana University Press, 1993.

J.M.

KUHN, Thomas S.

Philosopher of science	born USA 1922–1996
Associated with	PARADIGM ■ SCIENTIFIC REVOLUTIONS ■ NORMAL SCIENCE
Influences include	WITTGENSTEIN ■ CONANT ■ BACHELARD
Shares common ground with	FEYERABEND ■ KOESTLER
Main works	THE COPERNICAN REVOLUTION (1957) THE STRUCTURE OF SCIENTIFIC REVOLUTIONS (1962) THE ESSENTIAL TENSION (1977)

K UHN STUDIED PHYSICS at Harvard and taught at the universities of California and Princeton before moving to the Massachusetts Institute of Technology in 1972, 10 years after the publication of his main work.

The Structure of Scientific Revolutions offered not only a new interpretation of the history of science, but a new theory of knowledge complete with its own lexicon. Kuhn used terms like 'normal science', 'incommensurability' and, most famously, 'paradigms' to explain that the progress of science was not in fact 'progress' at all, but a series of sudden, unexpected lurches in which old epistemological assumptions were discarded and new ones embraced. In moving from one paradigm to another, conceptions of the world, ways of understanding it and guides to further investigation of it were exchanged. As Kuhn put it, 'one conceptual world view is replaced by another'.

The paradigm is a key concept for Kuhn. Other writers have essayed similar ideas. For example, Mannheim's *Weltanschauung*, Wittgenstein's 'forms of life', Foucault's *episteme* and Althusser's *problématique* all suggest an enclosure or framework of knowledge; this was in stark contrast to rationalist conceptions of truth as corresponding to an independent reality. By conceiving of a regulating formation of rules and agreements that governs what can be defined as knowledge, each writer approached truth (and, by implication, falsity) as relative and changeable rather than absolute and fixed. The world is experienced and investigated according to the principles of a particular historical epoch. Kuhn's early research into the history of physics alerted him to the striking differences in conceptions of motion and matter through history: Aristotelian physics, he concluded, were not simply bad Newtonian physics; they were based on entirely different conceptions of the world.

From this observation, he fashioned a general theory of science, arguing that the paradigm embodies all scientific knowledge and practice during particular periods of history. The paradigm sets limits as to what might reasonably be asked about the world and so determines the patterns research makes. 'Puzzle-solving' is how Kuhn described the activities of scientists, whose criteria of accuracy, standards of measurement and interpretations of observations were all determined by the parameters of the paradigm – and were thus amenable to change. Problems, or puzzles, beget new problems, all of which may be investigated during the practice of what Kuhn called 'normal science'.

Normal science is a creative form of puzzle-solving and might be seen as a mark of the practitioners' ingenuity rather than a test of the truth of the paradigm. In this respect, he challenged the hypothetico-deductive conception of Karl Popper, who theorised that science proceeded through a process of conjecture (theory) and refutation (attempts to disprove it); in this way verisimilitude – or an approximation to objective knowledge – is approached and improved. For Kuhn, there is no objective knowledge, only a consensus about what is called 'truth'. The resemblance to Wittgenstein is clear: puzzle-solving bears strong comparison with Wittgenstein's 'language games'.

As long as the consensus holds, normal science is uneventful. But occasionally long periods of calm are interrupted after a build-up of what Kuhn called anomalies. These arise when experimental results continue to resist explanation in terms of the accepted paradigm. For instance, anomalies were introduced into a geocentric explanation of the universe (predicated on the conception of the earth at its centre) by successive pieces of research that seemed to indicate a heliocentric system. Once these had accumulated, a period of crisis followed and this eventually undermined the credibility of the old paradigm.

Many theorists of science may have agreed with Kuhn up to this stage, but it is Kuhn's understanding of the nature of the change to the heliocentric system that distinguished him. He argued that something like a *Gestalt* switch took place in which scientists suddenly abandoned previously held assumptions and perceptions and appropriated an entirely new consciousness of the world. Lavoisier's 'discovery' of oxygen caused believers in phlogiston – the element thought to cause combustion – to desert old theories. Galileo's supposed experiments with wood and lead balls dropped from the Tower of Pisa disarmed adherents of the Aristotelean theory that bodies fell at a speed proportional to their weight. In these and other historical instances, if and when enough scientists effected a change, a paradigm shift was said to occur and a new 'normal science' replaced the old. For Kuhn, this was not an orderly process, but a warrantable revolution: everything changed, including conceptual apparatuses, experimental methods and criteria of accuracy.

A similar cycle then begins, with puzzle-solving yielding anomalies, then crises and another paradigm shift. Scientific knowledge, on this account, is discontinuous: it does not progress in any sense apart from the paradigm's own definition of 'progress', which may vary from one paradigm to another. Whatever progress is made in science derives from agreements as to what constitutes an advance in scientific knowledge. This challenges theories of science based on its proximity to truth: for Kuhn, truth is culturally mediated and specific to its own paradigm.

While the import of Kuhn's conclusion was colossal, critics noted a looseness in his concepts. They wished for greater precision in his definition of paradigm, for example. Kuhn addressed this in a volume edited by Lakatos and Musgrave, but, in the process, scaled down some of his grander claims. His concept of incommensurability also riled critics: how was it possible to equate or even compare paradigms if their epistemological foundations were so radically different? Cynics even questioned Kuhn's authority to foist his theories of science on the world, turning his own conclusions on him. Presumably, Kuhn was working within a particular paradigm and his claims to truth were limited by this fact, they argued.

Further reading

Barnes, Barry T.S. KUHN AND SOCIAL SCIENCE, Macmillan, 1982.
Gutting, Gary (ed.) PARADIGMS AND REVOLUTIONS: APPRAISALS AND APPLICATIONS OF THOMAS KUHN'S PHILOSOPHY OF SCIENCE, University of Notre Dame Press, 1980.
Lakatos, Imre and Musgrave, Alan (eds.) CRITICISM AND THE GROWTH OF KNOWLEDGE, Cambridge University Press, 1970.

E.C.

LACAN, Jacques

Psychoanalyst	born France 1901–1981
Associated with	STRUCTURALISM ▪ MIRROR STAGE ▪ IMAGINARY
Influences include	HEGEL ▪ FREUD ▪ SAUSSURE
Shares common ground with	LÉVI-STRAUSS ▪ ALTHUSSER ▪ ZIZEK
Main works	THE LANGUAGE OF THE SELF (1956) ECRITS (1966) THE FOUR FUNDAMENTAL CONCEPTS OF PSYCHOANALYSIS (1973)

L ACAN WAS BORN into a prosperous family in Paris and was educated at a Catholic college, before studying medicine and psychiatry. From 1927 he received clinical training in the main psychiatric hospital in Paris, Sainte-Anne, and his doctorate, on paranoia, was awarded in 1932. He joined the French Psychoanalytic Society in 1934, worked in a military hospital in Paris during the war, and learnt Chinese. Lacan was greatly in demand as a psychoanalyst. In 1951 the Psychoanalytic Society objected to his unconventionally short analytic sessions, and from this period on Lacan was involved in many disputes within French and international psychoanalytic circles. Eventually, in 1964, he founded the École Freudienne de Paris and in 1974, Le Champ Freudienne at the University at Vincennes (Paris), even though he was not a member of its staff. In 1980 he dissolved the École Freudienne and established La Cause Freudienne in its place. He died a year later.

Lacan's contribution to cultural theory lies in his persistent updating and reworking of Freudian principles, particularly in his insistence that it is through an attendance to language and linguistic structures (as theorised via Saussure and Jakobson) that the structures of the unconscious are to be understood. Lacan's writing in the 1930s, subsequently developed for 20 years after the war, opposed the dominant ego-centred interpretations of Freud by arguing that the individual is alienated in language and that psychological maturation is not reducible to organic development. Lacan's work identifies a topography of the self: its registers of the Symbolic, Imaginary and Real. The Symptom is a fourth order which arises from the interpenetration of the other orders. Lacan theorises need through the concept of desire which is mediated in language by others. Lacan suggested that each individual between six and eighteen months encountered the mirror, an imaginary representation in which an identification with a total visual self, enabling the subject to pass through a stage in which the body is not experienced as an independently articulated being. From 1953 Lacan developed a theory of the symbolic order which stressed the movement of the subject into language, a pre-established order external to the subject. It is in this order that the law of the father functions, and through it the unconscious is formed.

This brief outline of Lacan's analysis understates its great complexity, but it does show something of its elusiveness. Indeed much of Lacan's writing is opaque, and many of the terms are left undefined or obscure as a deliberate strategy which forces the reader to treat them as algebraic signs. His work has been controversial. In particular the apparently harmonic nature of some of the formulations has been questions, notably, for example, in Derrida's essay on Lacan's reading of Poe's story. Surprisingly Lacan has been influential on feminist theory, perhaps because he sees male sexuality as perverse, for Woman becomes a symptom through fetishisation, while the feminine position can be read as leading to a particularisation, subversive of closure through the symbolic (Patriarchy).

Further reading

Grosz, E. JACQUES LACAN: A FEMINIST READING, Routledge, 1990.
Muller, J. and Richardson, W. (eds.) THE PURLOINED POE: LACAN, DERRIDA, AND PSYCHOANALYTIC READING, Johns Hopkins University Press, 1988.
Zizek, S. ENJOY YOUR SYMPTOM! JACQUES LACAN IN HOLLYWOOD AND OUT, Routledge, 1992.

M.G.

LAING, Ronald David

Psychoanalyst	born Scotland 1927–1989
Associated with	SCHIZOPHRENIA ▪ LIBERATION ▪ PSYCHOTIC VOYAGE
Influences include	KIERKEGAARD ▪ BUBER ▪ SARTRE
Shares common ground with	BATESON ▪ STACK SULLIVAN ▪ SZASZ
Main works	THE DIVIDED SELF (1960) SANITY, MADNESS AND THE FAMILY (WITH ESTERSON, 1964) THE POLITICS OF EXPERIENCE (1967)

LAING WAS AN emblematic figure of 1960s counter-culture and his reputation and readership diminished when the 1960s sense of exhilarating experimentation and the confrontational questioning of limits came to an end. Yet his ideas on the meaning of madness, therapies of treating mentally disturbed people and the politics of the family have an enduring importance. As a person he was not easily brushed aside, and the same is true of his best ideas.

He studied medicine at Glasgow University, graduating in 1951. After university he gained clinical experience in neurosurgery before his national service with the Royal Army Medical Corps. After his discharge Laing worked at the Gartnavel Royal Mental Hospital and the Southern General Hospital in Glasgow. It was during this period that he wrote *The Divided Self*. In this book he introduced his concept of 'ontological insecurity'. For most people, he argued, physical birth is followed by gaining an existential sense of personal integrity and independent reality. But if this does not happen it may be difficult to establish a sense of ontological security. Individuals in this condition encounter problems in recognising themselves or the situations around them as real. They become preoccupied with finding ways of trying to be real in order to acquire a sense of identity. The ontologically insecure person is prone to fears of 'engulfment', 'implosion' and 'petrification'. Engulfment is the fear of being overwhelmed by strong emotions, so safety is sought in isolation. Implosion is the fear that the fragile state of the world will collapse at any moment, so one must be always aware of impending disaster and extinction. Petrification is the fear that others have the power to turn one to stone, so treating others as 'things' becomes the safest way to protect oneself.

These fears are managed through a series of defence mechanisms which are designed to protect the 'inner' self by presenting a front to the world. This process of managing fear divides the individual between a mind and a body. The inner self becomes disconnected from the worldly front shown to others and loses itself in fantasy. Because it never addresses, or is addressed by, the external world, it sees itself as essentially lost or destroyed. The attraction of being destroyed is that one is eternally safe. Schizophrenics are buried people who conceal themselves behind an elaborate and exhausting façade of fragmentary states of being.

Laing argued that these states of 'chaotic non-identity' seem bizarre and irrational to the outside world. The inner self conducts an internal dialogue which has coherence. But it can only be comprehended by another once one understands the aetiology of the divisions within the self. The psychoanalytic task is to treat the behaviour of the mentally disturbed person as communicating something about the buried self. This requires the psychoanalyst to empathise with the patient's behaviour and try to see the external world through their eyes. This therapeutic method was against the depersonalisation of much psychoanalytic writing and practice.

Laing continued his training at the Tavistock Clinic in London before going on to private practice in the same city. His writings on mental illness now turned to the role of the family. Drawing on interviews with families with schizophrenics among their members, Laing argued provocatively that the family engenders mental illness. He described subtle techniques of emotional blackmail between parents and children in which violence masqueraded as love.

These arguments caught the spirit of the times and turned Laing into a much sought-after public figure. His work on the role of the family in mental illness was the basis of Ken Loach's film *Family Life*. He experimented with LSD and other mind-expanding drugs and became a figurehead of the permissive society and his criticism of the destructive effect of family life naturally expanded to condemn the management of normality in the whole of society.

Bureaucratic capitalism, over-specialisation, over-professionalisation and the impersonality of big city life combined to make ontological insecurity a generalised experience. In his most extreme moments, Laing argued that society was turning everyone mad. Moreover, he popularised from his therapeutic methods with schizophrenics and recommended that everyone should be in touch with their madness in order to understand it better.

One of the attractions of Laing was his refusal to be an armchair theorist and his willingness to become involved in testing his ideas in real life. In 1965, together with like-minded critical psychiatrists, he founded the Philadelphia Association. It took its name from the Greek for brotherly love and its motto from the Book of Revelations: 'I have set before thee an open door, and no man can shut it.' The Association opened a destructured therapeutic centre at Kingsley Hall in the East End of London. Here they accepted mentally disturbed patients and allowed them to experience their symptoms as a psychotic voyage of self-discovery. Laing also participated in the *Dialectics of Liberation* conference in London in 1967 which brought together figures from revolutionary politics, radical philosophy, sociology, psychiatry and the broader New Left and psychedelic movements to debate liberation politics. In the same year, Laing published the immensely popular *The Politics of Experience*. This semipoetic and concise book depicted a beserk world in which freedom and fulfilment were permanently mocked by omnipresent commodification, brutalisation and irrationality. Together with the exquisite and highly successful meditation on double binds, *Knots*, which he published in 1970, it confirmed Laing's reputation as a radical critic *nonpareil*.

The last 19 years of Laing's life were beset with increasing personal and professional difficulties. He discovered Eastern mysticism on a retreat to India. Upon his return to Britain he bewildered many of his followers by recanting that he was ever part of the 'anti-psychiatry' movement or that the family is an inherently violent institution. He became interested in rebirthing therapy and continued to practise and write about mental illness. But he bitterly sensed that his moment had passed, and he damaged his reputation by alchol-induced, rambling and incoherent public lectures and an ill-conceived truculence against public critics of his views. He was even given 12 months' conditional discharge for hurling a bottle of wine through the window of the Bhagwan Rajneesh Centre near his Hampstead home. 'Orange wankers', he is alleged to have called them.

Yet Laing's application of existentialist and phenomenlogical ideas to the positivist world of psychiatry was immensely and positively destabilising and has left its mark. Since his death his work has been reassessed by professionals and the indifference and impatience that was displayed to him in many professional quarters in the last decade and a half of his life is beginning to thaw. Beyond this his argumentative, combative, poetical style of humanism was hugely seductive for readers who experienced life as a series of frustrating limits. Laing is probably a flawed role-model for intellectuals of any cast to follow; but isn't every diamond?

Further reading

Clay, J. R.D. LAING: A DIVIDED SELF, Hodder & Stoughton, 1996.
Evans, R. R.D. LAING: THE MAN AND HIS IDEAS, Dutton, 1976.
Mullan, B. MAD TO BE NORMAL: CONVERSATIONS WITH R.D. LAING, Free Association Books, 1995.

C.R.

LAKATOS, Imre

Philosopher of science	born Hungary 1922–1974
Associated with	REFUTATION ■ ANOMALIES
Influences include	MILL ■ POPPER ■ QUINE
Shares common ground with	KUHN ■ QUINE ■ FEYERABEND
Main works	CRITICISM AND THE GROWTH OF KNOWLEDGE (1970) PROOFS AND REFUTATIONS (1976) THE METHODOLOGY OF SCIENTIFIC RESEARCH PROGRAMMES (1978)

LAKATOS EMIGRATED FROM Hungary after the suppression of the 1956 uprising and settled in the UK. In 1960 he took a post at the London School of Economics and became a professor there in 1969. Lakatos combined work in the philosophy of science with a parallel interest in the philosophy of mathematical discovery (which he suggested was more informal and creative than was commonly presumed). His relatively early death at 52 left a truncated body of work made up mainly of essays and papers. Though his ideas have been influential in the social sciences, at his death his perspective on research was still being refined, leaving its full implications to be developed by others.

Lakatos was concerned to formulate an account of advances in science which recognised that theories developed not only through a process of trial and error, the comparison of theory and evidence suggested by Karl Popper, but also through the juxtaposition of competing theories themselves. Most famously Lakatos suggested that: 'It is not that we propose a theory and Nature may shout NO; rather, we propose a maze of theories, and Nature may shout INCONSISTENT' (1970: 130). Thus, like Thomas Kuhn before him, Lakatos suggested that there were groups of theories which shared a world-view (Kuhn's paradigms), and within these groups acceptable procedures would govern the perception of rational argument. These groups of theories, which he referred to as research programmes, together produce a multifaceted picture of the field with which they are concerned around a set of core presumptions.

These research programmes shape and form the landscape upon which particular theories develop by implying certain positive and negative heuristics. The negative heuristic of the programme refers to the central core of the research programme which is accepted as given by its constituent theories, and is not subject to further research. The positive heuristic of the programme is the 'protective belt' of theoretical accounts that flow from the acceptance of the core. This protective belt is where anomalies may appear and where different theories may come into tension with each other. Importantly, Lakatos adopts a version of the 'Duhem–Quine' thesis which suggests that theories do not necessarily fail by being compared to apparently inconsistent 'facts'. This comparison will encourage the seemingly anomalous theory to reach out to find facts which would support it. Thus inconsistent theories may be held within the research programme until new facts emerge, dissolving the point of inconsistency.

It is this issue of theories seeking new facts, rather than facts falsifying theories which is at the centre of Lakatos's critique of Popper's methodology of conjecture and refutation. Lakatos's arguments in this regard lie on a line of development between Thomas Kuhn and Paul Feyerabend. Lakatos recognised within Kuhn the implicit position that within paradigms anomalies could remain until either new facts or new theories emerged to account for them. But Lakatos did not take this insight to its logical conclusion, stopping short of the Feyerabendian notion that 'anything goes', that within a research programme the only real test for theoretical insight is consistency (where the research programme itself proposes such criteria).

Within the field of cultural studies, the notion of research programmes (the acceptance of certain core elements alongside the parallel acknowledgement that theoretical anomalies may be held without difficulty) supports a theoretical pluralism, or eclecticism. Where the very issue of the recognition of salient 'facts' is itself a matter for debate (counterfactually and ontologically), the proposition of research programmes rather than formal scientific theorising allows for the cross-reading of insights while accepting that apparent inconsistencies may not be fatal to a particular argument. Lakatos's notion of a research programme is essentially permissive in that it allows for the emergence of inconsistency as part of a research programme's development, rather than seeing such inconsistency as immediately fatal for the overall programme.

Further reading

Archer, M. CULTURE AND AGENCY, Cambridge University Press, 1988.
Hollis, M. and Lukes, M. (eds.) RATIONALITY AND RELATIVISM, Blackwell, 1982.
Lakatos, I. 'Falsification and the Methodology of Scientific Research Programmes', in Lakatos, I. and Musgrave, A. (eds.), CRITICISM AND THE GROWTH OF KNOWLEDGE, Cambridge University Press, 1970.

C.M.

LASCH, Christopher

Historian	born USA 1932–1994
Associated with	NARCISSISM
Influences include	GOODMAN ▪ MARCUSE ▪ MILLS
Shares common ground with	MARIN ▪ SCHUR ▪ SENNETT
Main works	THE AGONY OF THE AMERICAN LEFT (1968)
	THE CULTURE OF NARCISSISM (1979)
	THE TRUE AND ONLY HEAVEN (1991)

PROFESSOR OF HISTORY at Northwestern University (1966–70) and, later, the University of Rochester, Lasch is best known for his best-selling *The Culture of Narcissism*, a critique of the narcissism he saw all about him in the North America of the 1970s. While he shared many of the concerns of his neo-Marxist counterparts, he retained a cynicism about the possibility of enduringly benign political positions – which is why he left no coherent doctrine in his wake.

Lasch's 1960s analysis of the New Left allowed little room for the kind of optimism he believed posed a threat to genuine radicalism. The 'agony' of the left was in its spurning of theory, or, to be more specific, in its (for him, unwarranted) expectation that theory would emerge spontaneously from the daily struggle of the working class.

The *Haven in a Heartless World* Lasch wrote of was the nuclear family, an institution he defended as both a mediator between social conditions and individual experiences and a shaper of perceptions of the world. Lasch abhorred the invasion of the market-place into family life. His defence – even celebration – of the family in this book, together with his earlier work, earned him the reputation of a reactionary. This is unfair: Lasch sought change, but was cynical of any movement promoting change with an ideal in mind. In his view, the social world did not 'progress' – he documented why in a later book.

A similar cynicism pervades his later work, which challenged both capitalism and its critics. Lasch's engagement with the work of English Marxists E.P. Thompson and Raymond Williams exposed him to 'a sympathetic account, not just of the economic hardships imposed by capitalism, but of the way in which capitalism thwarted the need for joy in work, stable connections, family life, a sense of place, and a sense of historical continuity'.

In focusing on the devaluation of the personal realm, he aligned himself with Schur, Sennett and, to a more limited extent, Riesman, all of whom analysed self-centredness and the spurning of collectivities. 'This self-absorption defines the moral climate of contemporary society', wrote Lasch. 'The conquest of nature and the search for new frontiers have given way to the search for self-fulfilment.'

Social questions, on Lasch's account, were recast as personal ones, so that solutions to fundamental issues of the day were sought, yet never found, in the pursuit of individual self-fulfilment.

Lasch revisited the site of his earlier critique in 1991 with his formidable *The True and Only Heaven*, in which he chronicled the development of theories of progress. Earlier, he had reviewed radical movements that drew sustenance from the myth of a golden age. In the later work, he turned on both Left and Right, exposing their common conviction in the desirability of economic and technical development. Both were premised on some vision of the 'good life'.

The book also contains an arguably more forceful critique of consumer society than that of *Narcissism*. Having traced the roots of capitalism to the scientific revolution of the seventeenth century (rather than the Protestant Ethic, as Weber had suggested), Lasch showed how it generated the promise of universal abundance. No limit to productive capacity was envisioned. Yet the universalistic pretensions have been shown to be exactly that – pretensions; and the material largesse enjoyed by only a privileged few has become widely diffused thanks to the predominantly US-owned mass media. By showing off its wealth, the West has both advertised a vision of progress, yet mocked the majority of the world's population which cannot share in it.

Published posthumously, *The Revolt of the Elites and the Betrayal of Democracy* targeted the symmetry between the élite attitudes of Left and Right. Managerial and professional élites are not so much a ruling class, but have managed to separate themselves from the community. 'They have more in common with their counterparts in Brussels or Hong Kong than with the masses of Americans not yet plugged into the network of global communications.'

Often misinterpreted as an onslaught on the Left, Lasch's work is actually a thoroughgoing critique of all political groups that have advanced a vision of progress toward some perfect end state. Lasch's alternatives were tentative and unsatisfactory: a culture that can accept limits, that can respect nature and can, in many ways, return to a more traditional, familial approach.

Further reading

Lasch, C. HAVEN IN A HEARTLESS WORLD, Basic Books, 1977.
Lasch, C. THE REVOLT OF THE ELITES AND THE BETRAYAL OF DEMOCRACY, Norton, 1995.
Shannon, C. CONSPICUOUS CRITICISMS, Johns Hopkins University Press, 1996.

E.C.

LASKI, Harold

Political Philosopher	Born England 1893–1950
Associated with	FABIAN SOCIALISM ▪ LIBERTY
Influences include	PROUDHON ▪ MARX ▪ THE WEBBS ▪ MILL
Shares common ground with	TAWNEY
Main works	THE GRAMMAR OF POLITICS (1925)
	LIBERTY IN THE MODERN STATE (1930)
	DEMOCRACY IN CRISIS (1931)
	REFLECTIONS ON THE REVOLUTION OF OUR TIME (1943)
	AMERICAN DEMOCRACY (1948)

L ASKI WAS BORN into a wealthy Jewish business family in Manchester. He graduated in history, worked in journalism, then took up teaching positions at McGill and Harvard and, later, the London School of Economics, where he was a professor of political science until his death. He was also a key figure in the Labour Party and his political affiliations led to his friendship with President Roosevelt.

Laski's contribution to cultural studies stems from his critiques of government and socialism. His early books were pluralist in that they were highly critical of the capitalist state, arguing that it served only to benefit the forces of capital. As an alternative he argued for a socialism based on increasing the power of other groups such as trade unions, while decentralising, federalising and democratising government in order to bring it closer to people's lives. He then pursued a line of enquiry in *The Grammar of Politics*, which marked a departure from pluralism towards a more statist, Fabian socialism that was characteristic of the Webbs.

In 1930 Laski published *Liberty in the Modern State*, which was essentially a libertarian text in which he argued for the importance of intellectual freedom, enquiry and dissent against the Establishment, whom he viewed as censoring ideas.

Laski's intellectual position changed dramatically in 1931 in response to the fall of the minority Labour Administration, after the Prime Minister Ramsay MacDonald left the Party to form a national government. This critical event spurred him to write the seminal *Democracy in Crisis* in which he adopted a Marxist position and contended that there could no longer be any compromise between capitalism and socialism. He argued that in order to undermine capitalism it was necessary to take control of industry. Moreover, he predicted that once socialist parties started to win general elections then capitalism's dedication to democracy would steadily diminish. Indeed, he predicted that the Establishment would use every means to maintain their position of power.

Throughout the 1930s, Laski made constant warnings about the threats to mankind from Fascism, and argued that depressed capitalist societies were inextricably linked to the emergence of Fascism. However, Laski was absolutely unequivocal in his support of democracy, and equally emphatic in his rejection of extra-parliamentary action, indeed, he argued for a transformation to socialism through winning elections.

This is the uniqueness of Laski's position in that he advocated Marxism combined with a commitment to democracy, freedom and tolerance; for him, these values were absolutely fundamental to a socialist society. This led Orwell to describe Laski as 'a socialist by allegiance and a liberal by temperament'.

Laski was fascinated by Soviet Russia, and unlike many others on the Left, he condemned the oppression of the Stalinist regime. However, he also saw Russia as being the harbinger of a new world. He expounded these views in *Reflections on the Revolution of Our Time*, arguing that socialism provided people with positive freedoms, that is, opportunities from the state, as opposed to the negative freedoms of capitalism, whereby the state protects individuals' rights and property.

The last major work completed by Laski was *American Democracy*, which was a *tour de force* on American society. He stated that the dominant values in American society were those of business and economic individualism. Polemically, he contended that for as long as this was the case it constrained the potential of the USA to be a beacon, as it had once been, for freedom and hope.

The historian Beloff described the inter-war years as 'The Age of Laski', whilst A.J.P. Taylor argued that Laski 'had remade English Social Democracy', and stated that he was one of the few men that helped make the world a different place.

Further reading

Kramnick, I. and Sheerman, B. HAROLD LASKI: A LIFE ON THE LEFT, Hamish Hamilton 1993.
Martin, K. HAROLD LASKI: A BIOGRAPHY, Jonathan Cape, 1969.
Taylor A.J.P. FROM THE BOER WAR TO THE COLD WAR, Penguin, 1996.
Zylstra, B. FROM PLURALISM TO COLLECTIVISM: THE DEVELOPMENT OF HAROLD LASKI'S POLITICAL THOUGHT, Van Goreum & Co. 1968.

C.C.

LATOUR, Bruno

Anthropologist/philosopher	born France 1947—
Associated with	ACTOR–NETWORK THEORY ■ NONMODERN CONSTITUTION ■ TRANSLATION ■ PURIFICATION
Influences include	TOURNIER ■ SERRES ■ GREIMAS
Shares common ground with	CALLON ■ LAW ■ HARAWAY
Main works	SCIENCE IN ACTION (1987) THE PASTEURIZATION OF FRANCE (2 VOLS., 1988) WE HAVE NEVER BEEN MODERN (1993) ARAMIS, OR THE LOVE OF TECHNOLOGY (1996)

BRUNO LATOUR TRAINED in anthropology and philosophy, gaining a doctorate from the University of Tours in 1974, and developing a special interest in the history and sociology of science. He is an important influence within the cross-disciplinary work of science and technology studies (STS), especially as one of the most significant theoreticians of actor–network theory (ANT). Since 1991 he has been Professor at the Centre de Sociologie de l'Innovation, École Nationale Supérieure des Mines, in Paris, and has also held posts at the Faculty of Law in Abidjan, the Conservatoire National des Arts et Métiers, the University of California at San Diego and the University of Melbourne. He was awarded the Bernal Prize of the Society for Social Studies of Science in 1992.

Latour's early work can be described as an anthropology of scientific practice. In *Laboratory Life* (written with Steve Woolgar, 1986) and *Science in Action*, Latour discussed the worlds of scientists, developing some of the ideas that were later to be built into actor–network theory: that the process of doing science involves mediating between, for example, scientific literatures, laboratories, and the institutional connections between science, the state and society. His field-work in laboratories at the Salk Institute in California, where he observed Guillemin's work on brain peptides (reported in *Laboratory Life*) discussed, among other things, the forms of conversation between scientists, and the role of paperwork and publishing as 'texts' with a specific role in constructing and concretising scientific 'facts'.

Combining insights from this anthropological approach with those from the history of science, the sociology of scientific knowledge (SSK) and the social construction of technology (SCOT), Latour and his contemporaries began to theorise science and technology as networks of heterogenous associations.

Within the SCOT perspective, the identification of so-called relevant social groups (RSGs) was already pointing towards this; these are the different groups of people with an interest in a piece of technology (inventors/designers, manufacturers, retailers and end-users), all of whom have a stake in the technology turning out a particular way. The negotiation between these groups directs the trajectory that technology takes until its form stabilises in a way that more or less suits all RSGs.

Perhaps the most significant step taken by actor–network theory has been the inclusion of non-humans – referred to by Latour as the missing masses of sociology – in the process of network building. Alongside all the RSGs, then, are an assortment of non-human actors (particles, components, machines). Collapsing the distinction between the human and the non-human has, for Latour, implications which reach far beyond those of STS; it also questions the distinctions between nature and culture (a theme central to *We Have Never Been Modern*). Stress is thus placed not on differentiating between categories, but instead upon investigating the links between them – an *as*sociology. This has led to comparisons between Latour and other 'associationist', 'non-representational' or 'materialist–semiotic' theorists, including Haraway (hybrids/cyborgs), Serres (quasi-objects), Deleuze and Guattari (assemblages/flows), and Foucault (power as relational/effects).

Subsequent explorations of ANT (by Latour himself, along with writers such as Michel Callon, John Law and Shirley Strum) have created a theoretical framework for understanding the complex processes involved in the building and sustaining of such networks from a flexible set of heterogenous elements, both human and non-human, from the sub-atomic to the macro-social. This includes the ways in which actors are enrolled (by other actors) into a common project, and the work of translation, displacement and black-boxing, which together function to render the network stable and durable (by, for example, controlling the amounts and kinds of information circulating between actors and other mediating nodes, called intermediaries). Key accounts include Latour's studies of Pasteur and of the Aramis transport system, and Callon's work on scallop fishing and on the French electric car. Also important is work by Latour and Strum on baboons, which they describe as living in a pure ethnomethodological society: interaction is society, and society is interaction. This raises the question of what has made human society more durable and stable than the decaying, performative interactions of simians. The answer comes from the delegation by humans of some activities to non-human materialities (such as tools). These non-humans become social partners with humans, helping to stabilise society in a set of heterogenous associations beyond pure interaction. As Latour puts it, technology is society made durable.

Aside from its impacts within STS and cultural studies of science and technology, ANT has been significant in many other disciplines, including organisation studies, social psychology and geography. Indeed, part of

Latour's aim in writing *We Have Never Been Modern* was to introduce ANT to a broader audience, stressing its relevance for understanding the project of modernity itself. Here Latour designates two key practices which embody being 'modern'; these are translation (the creation of hybrids of nature and culture) and purification (the construction of distinct ontological zones, one for humans [culture] and one for non-humans [nature]). Hybrids of nature and culture proliferate in modernity (examples include the hole in the ozone layer, where chemicals, industry, politics and ecology are intermixed), and yet are simultaneously disavowed by the rigidity of the nature/culture or human/non-human binary. Assessing the thinking of so-called premoderns, moderns and postmoderns, *We Have Never Been Modern* calls for a patching-together of nature, society, science and technology in a 'non-modern constitution' that will continue the proliferation of (albeit different) hybrids or networks without seeking to purify and dichotomise.

Further reading

Michael, Mike CONSTRUCTING IDENTITIES, Sage, 1996.
Murdoch, Jonathan 'Towards a Geography of Heterogenous Associations', PROGRESS IN HUMAN GEOGRAPHY, 21: 3 (1997).
Woolgar, Steve 'Science and Technology Studies and the Renewal of Social theory', in Stephen Turner (ed.), SOCIAL THEORY AND SOCIOLOGY, Blackwell, 1996.

D.B.

LAZARSFELD, Paul

Social scientist	born Austria 1901–1976
Associated with	SURVEY RESEARCH
Influences include	MARX ▪ WEBER ▪ ADLER
Shares common ground with	LYND ▪ ADORNO ▪ FESTINGER
Main works	THE PEOPLE'S CHOICE (WITH BERNARD BERELSON AND HAZEL GAUDET, 1944) VOTING (WITH BERNARD BERELSON AND WILLIAM MCPHEE, 1954) 'THE SOCIOLOGY OF EMPIRICAL SOCIAL RESEARCH', AMERICAN SOCIOLOGICAL REVIEW, 27 (1962), pp. 757–67

PAUL LAZARSFELD IS best known for his work in techniques of quantitative research. He adapted the survey research method, first employed in marketing, to concerns of the social sciences. He is credited with introducing the panel technique to academic concerns, which involves interviewing the same individuals over a period of time in order to track attitude shifts. New methodologies can inspire new substantive insights, however, and Lazarsfeld has disrupted traditional notions of political and social behaviour.

Lazarsfeld's scholarly interests developed out of a confluence of personal and historical factors. As a student in Vienna following the First World War, he was enamoured of Marx, and thus preferred to study the proclivities of working-class individuals over the intricacies of institutions considered to be moribund and secondary. Also, the Austro-Marxist preference for electoral over more militant strategies prompted Lazarsfeld to hone his mathematical and psychological training at the University of Vienna to concerns of voter sensitivities. Lazarsfeld was pleased to find that the survey questionnaire elicited intimate details of individual behaviour, and that the responses could be subjected to rigorous statistical tests. And, of course, Lazarsfeld's research was later facilitated by the availability and development of computers.

Lazarsfeld went to the USA in 1933. As director of the Office of Radio Research, first at Princeton and later at Columbia University, Lazarsfeld's commission was to track the social and cultural ramifications of the growing distribution of radios amongst the American population. Radios, and technology in general, were being accused of disrupting traditional community bonds. The result, according to some, was a disintegration of community in favour of independent, detached family units huddled around their own receivers; or, according to others, the new technologies were producing a mass culture, where distinctive community and individual identities were sacrificed to an innocuous and narcotic common denominator. Lazarsfeld's research, however, led him to conclude that neither scenario obtained. Instead, most citizens depended upon 'opinion leaders' – trusted and respected friends and associates – to sort, interpret and transmit social and political information. This 'two-step flow of communication' thus mitigated the forces of social disintegration or homogenisation purportedly associated with technology.

Lazarsfeld's commitment to 'immersion and quantification' was also disruptive of common notions of political behaviour. Prior to his investigations, pragmatic discussions of American citizens were tainted with theoretical biases. Since democracy called for informed participation in the system, democratic citizens were therefore thought to provide it. What Lazarsfeld discovered, however, was that he could predict political behaviour on the basis of variables which were hardly political. His Index of Political Predispositions consisted of the variables socio-economic status (income, education, occupation and subjective social class), region of residence (North or South, urban or rural) and religion; and he consistently found that he could predict voting behaviour better with this index than by asking respondents questions on specific political issues.

He also found that it was quite difficult to disabuse citizens of what little specific political knowledge they retained. The forces of selective perception and selective retention obstructed exposure to political information that was contrary to held concepts. Campaigns only reinforced prior attitudes, but could do little to change them. And for those who might seem most vulnerable to propaganda or other political persuasion, the 'independents', they did not seem interested or attentive to any political information. The notion of the non-aligned, issue-oriented independent voter was debunked; the most informed citizens belonged to political parties, and the depth of the political knowledge terminated in a vague appreciation of very general party philosophy. In the USA, at least, democratic citizenship had not lived up to its ideals.

Further reading

Glock, Charles Y. (ed.) SURVEY RESEARCH IN THE SOCIAL SCIENCES, Russell Sage Foundation, 1967.
Kendall, Patricia L. (ed.) THE VARIED SOCIOLOGY OF PAUL LAZARSFELD, Columbia University Press, 1982.
Mills, C. Wright 'Abstract Empiricism', in Paul F. Lazarsfeld (ed.), QUALITATIVE ANALYSIS: HISTORICAL AND CRITICAL ESSAYS, Allyn & Bacon, 1972.

T.J.L.

LE CORBUSIER,
Charles-Edouard Jeannert

Architect	born France 1887–1965
Associated with	RADIANT CITY ■ URBAN PLANNING ■ RATIONAL HUMANISM
Influences include	ANCIENT GREEKS ■ CÉZANNE ■ PICASSO
Shares common ground with	LLOYD WRIGHT ■ JENCKS ■ HARVEY
Main works	TOWARDS A NEW ARCHITECTURE (1923) THE RADIANT CITY (1967) CONCERNING TOWN PLANNING (1947)

L E CORBUSIER WAS not only the leading Modernist architect, he was the most important theorist of Modernist architecture. He believed that architectural design and urban planning must follow rational principles in order to maximise the opportunities for human creativity. He famously defined the home as 'a machine for living in' and argued that urban planning should follow a time budget which assumed that individuals required eight hours for work, eight hours for recreation and eight hours for sleep. His rationalism found no place for tradition or nostalgia. He was not interested in buildings or urban designs which tried to blend in with existing conditions. Instead he favoured designs which worked from a clean slate. For example, his controversial scheme for the rebuilding of Paris in the 1920s demanded that existing buildings and transport routes should be razed to the ground and replaced with functional, gridlike street patterns, skyscrapers and multi-lane highways to facilitate ease of movement. The form of cities should be determined by function. Hence they should be composed of dedicated, zoned areas for work, recreation, education and other functions necessary for healthy urban–industrial life.

His aesthetic ideas were heavily influenced by cubism and particularly the paintings of Cézanne, Picasso, Gris, Derrain, Matisse and Braque. He saw these as distilling the beauty of the mechanical age and sought to translate their aesthetic codes on to the arena of building blocks, mortar and glass. The challenge he set himself was to ally these aesthetic values with the values of nature. This underlay his concept of 'the radiant city' in which natural light, space and airiness would be assimilated as part of the structure of buildings and cities. He was also deeply influenced by the sense of proportion and geometric designs of the Ancient Greeks. He was impressed by the building philosophy of the Ancient Greeks which viewed buildings as a precise and coherent *ensemble* of architectural parts, which are designed to relate organically with the outside world. From them he also borrowed the practice of using white as the principal colour in his building designs. Indeed, he saw himself as the architect of the 'White World' which would be built around clarity and precision and which would leave the 'Brown World' of clutter, muddle and ambiguity behind.

Le Corbusier's early designs were geometric, with the cube acting as the central planning motif. It is no exaggeraton to say that at this time he was wedded to the cube as the fundamental principle of Modernist design. He developed the cube to accommodate a rich range of inflections – corkscrew stairs, cylinders on the roof, elegant ramps and handrails. Around the cube he constructed triangular and circular shapes. All of these, he claimed, are design elements which are comfortable to the eye and deliver rest and harmony. The driving force hebind his work at this time is the imagination of the mind rather than the senses.

His post-war designs make greater use of glass and steel. The *Unité d'habitation* development in Marseilles (1952–60) was designed like a town in which the frame relates to the whole rather than the parts. The relationship of every part is mathematically precise. The design uses elements from peasant buildings with geometric, machine forms. Admirers regard it to be the perfect realisation of Le Corbusier's rational humanism. If that is the case, his designs for Chandigarh, the Punjab capital, are a close rival. This massive undertaking applied Le Corbusier's familiar design ideas drawn from cubism and the Ancient Greeks and combined them with impeccable sensitivity to the natural and cultural conditions of India. Chandigarh enlarges his vision of designing buildings to establish an organic, harmonious, balanced presence which enables human interaction rather than dwarfs it. 'Architecture', wrote Le Corbusier, 'is the unending sum of positive gestures. The whole and the details are one.' Chandigarh was the most extensive design that he devised to embody this philosophy. His post-war work is usually understood to be moving away from the mind as the driving force of design towards a new appreciation of the senses in producing harmony and balance.

Le Corbusier's significance as the leading symbol of Modernist design principles was arguably more important than the buildings he designed. Rightly or wrongly, he is seen as the father of the rational, geometric, unsentimental urban planning philosophy of the post-war period. As such, he is a figure who is lamented as much as he is praised. Critics revile him as an architectural despot who pushed through absolutist rationalist planning principles over any respect for traditional order and history. His designs are attacked for ignoring the needs of real people and reproducing his view of the rational requirements for comfortable living in the Modern Age. Despite his professed humanism, his designs are frequently upbraided for their anti-humanist consequences. Against this, his admirers point to the technical breakthroughs he made in the use of glass and steel as essential principles of design; his awareness of the relation of light and nature in the construction of builings; and his eagerness to positively embrace the technical breakthroughs in velocity and movement in urban planning. His theoretical writings and buildings constitute a benchmark for Modernist design and they have been important in the development of postmodernist sensibility.

Further reading

Gardiner, S. LE CORBUSIER, Fontana, 1974.
Hervé, L. LE CORBUSIER: THE ARTIST, AND WRITER, Thames & Hudson, 1957.
Jordan, R. LE CORBUSIER, Dent, 1972.

C.R.

LEACH, Edmund Ronald

Social anthropologist	born England 1910–1989
Associated with	POLITICAL ANTHROPOLOGY ■ STRUCTURALISM ■ KINSHIP ■ ANTHROPOLOGY OF CULTURE
Influences include	MALINOWSKI ■ FIRTH
Shares common ground with	LÉVI–STRAUSS ■ FORTES ■ GOODY
Main works	POLITICAL SYSTEMS OF HIGHLAND BURMA (1954) RETHINKING ANTHROPOLOGY (1961) SOCIAL ANTHROPOLOGY (1982)

E DMUND LEACH WAS an important force in British anthropology because he challenged the accepted structural functionalist orthodoxy and introduced the English-speaking world to the then controversial theory of structuralism, especially through the works of Claude Lévi-Strauss (see his *Claude Lévi-Strauss*, 1970). Applying this method, Leach rewrote anthropological approaches to the study of kinship in part by relating it to the study of myth, symbols and communication. Rather than seeing the organisation of social life as concrete and distinct from cultural forms, Leach adopted the structuralist view that institutional forms embodied principles and contradictions of the symbolic realm. In addition to the empirical contributions from his extensive fieldwork studies (in Burma, China, Sri Lanka, Kurdistan, Botel Tobago, Sarawak, India and Nepal), Leach formalised a new structuralist-based mode of analysis for social anthropology. This has become the basis of contemporary anthropological method.

His approach is best outlined in what he called his 'arrogant' challenge to the discipline, *Rethinking Anthropology*, and his subsequent text, *Social Anthropology*. He questioned whether anthropology had achieved its aim of making comparative analyses of social structures, arguing that it had degenerated into mere 'impeccably detailed historical ethnographies of particular peoples'. He proposed that rather than a concern with comparison, anthropologists should approach explanations of patterns of social phenomena as mathematical patterns from which one could derive generalisations. Thus he explored social relations as systems of relations and exchanges rather than by attributing psychological explanations.

Edmund Leach was born in Sidmouth, England, and studied mathematics and engineering at Cambridge University. He enrolled in anthropology for his graduate studies at the London School of Economics where he subsequently taught between 1947 and 1953. It was during this period that he wrote his first major work, *Political Systems of Highland Burma*. From 1957 he was attached to Cambridge University, becoming a professor in 1972 and Provost of King's College from 1966 to 1979.

The importance of Leach's study of Burmese political structures was that it set the terms of political anthropology. The study explored the interrelationships between ideal models and political action, and placed this in the context of Burmese history. Leach argued that there were two competing models of social structure (the *gumsa* and the *gumlao*) which were in an oscillating equilibrium. This was a dramatic departure from preceding mechanical accounts of political processes in preliterate societies. It also challenged the assumptions of functionalism.

At Cambridge, Leach was a colleague of the products of the Malinowski and Radcliffe-Brown functionalist school, in particular, Meyer Fortes and Jack Goody. Most controversial was Leach's analysis of myth and symbolic systems as well as the parallels he drew between preliterate and literate forms of cultural organisation. The intellectual exchanges between these forceful characters reinvigorated anthropological debate at Cambridge and attracted a new generation of young, gifted anthropologists who over time developed a distinctive approach to the discipline.

Leach is perhaps best known for expounding on the views of Lévi-Strauss and adapting them for an Anglophile audience. In addition to his study of Lévi-Strauss, Leach further developed his version of structuralist analysis and applied it to a range of phenomena from kinship structures, to symbolic systems, to biblical myths. A clear explanation of his method can be found in *Structuralist Interpretations of Biblical Myth* (1983) (co-authored with D. Alan Laycock) and in the edited collection *The Structural Study of Myth and Totemism* (1967).

In addition to his best-known works, Leach published prolifically on a range of topics, and his papers have been donated to King's College Library in Cambridge for the use of scholars (see Hugh-Jones 1989). Apart from those mentioned, other major publications by Leach included *Pul Eliya: A Village in Ceylon: A Study of Land Tenure and Kinship* (1961), *Genesis as Myth, and Other Essays* (1969), and *Culture and Communication* (1976).

Leach had considerable success in bringing social anthropology to a wider audience, for example through his (the first) Malinowski Memorial Lecture at the London School of Economics in 1959 (republished as the introductory chapter to his *Rethinking Anthropology*, 1961), his BBC Reith lectures in 1967 (published as *A Runaway World?*, 1968), his Munro Lectures for the University of Edinburgh (published as *Custom, Law, and Terrorist Violence*, 1977); and his audio recording for the Open University (*The Role of Myth in Society*, 1972).

The work of Edmund Leach constituted a turning-point in British social anthropology, with its theoretically refined and informed approach to field-work and empirical studies as well as its radical reconceptualisation of the conceptual and analytical basis of anthropological thinking. Although primarily recognised for his contributions to anthropology, Leach's legacy has informed the Anglophile versions of structuralism that emerged during the 1970s and 1980s across the humanities.

Further reading

Firth, **Raymond** 'Foreword' to POLITICAL SYSTEMS OF HIGHLAND BURMA, 2nd edn, Beacon, 1965.
Hugh-Jones, **Stephen** EDMUND LEACH 1910–1989: A MEMOIR, King's College, Cambridge, 1989.
Leach, **Edmund** CULTURE AND COMMUNICATION: THE LOGIC BY WHICH SYMBOLS ARE CONNECTED: AN INTRODUCTION TO THE USE OF STRUCTURALIST ANALYSIS IN SOCIAL ANTHROPOLOGY, Cambridge University Press, 1976.

J.C.

LEFEBVRE, Henri

Philosopher/sociologist	born France 1901–1991
Associated with	EVERYDAY LIFE ▪ URBANISM ▪ SPACE
Influences include	MARX ▪ NIETZSCHE
Shares common ground with	HARVEY ▪ FOUCAULT
Main works	CRITIQUE OF EVERYDAY LIFE, Vol 1 (1991)
	THE PRODUCTION OF SPACE (1991)
	WRITING ON CITIES (1996)

HENRI LEFEBVRE ONCE remarked that 'our tragic period hides from itself the tragedy it lives'. Yet his lifelong study of tragic modernity was animated by a self-professed utopianism combined with an attention to concrete political and cultural practices. Born in the French Pyrenees, and returning to the region as a member of the Resistance during the Second World War, Lefebvre used this experience as the basis for a series of inquiries into rural societies. As student, teacher and one-time taxi driver in Paris, Lefebvre turned the same critical eye to the city and to processes of urbanisation. As a member of the French Communist Party from 1928–1958, Lefebvre investigated the conditions of daily existence under capitalism, and, in the immediate post-war period, brought the concept of everyday life into the lexicon of Western Marxism.

Lefebvre wrote more than fifty books, addressing issues in philosophy, history, Marxism, the everyday, city, the state, time and space. Through associations with members of the Dadaist and Surrealist movements, and the Situationist International, Lefebvre articulated a commitment to the radical potential in art, poetry, spectacle and direct participation of 'users' in cultural and political practice. Lefebvre's involvement with the 1968 Rebellion served to sharpen his integrated analyses of urban spaces and revolutionary practice under late capitalism. At the same time, he tended to operate as a critical, marginal or excluded voice in relation to political and artistic groups. His interest in capital's incursions into everyday life, and his refusal to be bound to an economistic Marxism, caused him to be marginalised in conventional Party circles. His continued interest in questions of agency and historicity resulted in a mutual antagonism between Lefebvre and the structuralists. His adherence to Marxist analyses as a part of any radical cultural critique and practice caused his marginalisation in post-Marxist and post-structuralist configurations. As a result, Lefebvre has been dubbed a 'nomadic' thinker, and is frequently ignored in intellectual histories of the foregoing movements.

Lefebvre argued that in the post-war period, everyday life was colonised by the operations of commodity and state capitalism. Moreover, the post-war 'survival of capitalism' was achieved through the production of space. Urbanism is the literal and figurative replacement for industrialism in the spatial settlement of late capitalism. Urbanism may still refer to the city, but also beyond the city, or to the process whereby spatial arrangements sustain capital on both the local and global scales. Lefebvre's development of the term 'abstract space' refers to that space produced and consumed to the exigencies of capital. This is a space that creates an illusion of homogeneity, of the suppression of difference or resistance.

Lefebvre was critical of Foucault, whom he accused of being too preoccupied with the peripheries of power to mount a systematic critique of capitalism. However, Lefebvre and Foucault share an understanding of the instrumental orchestration of space in modern power configurations. Moreover, both thinkers note the role of the body in the everyday organisation of capitalist spatialities *and* as a site of resistance. It is at the level of the body and lived experience that abstract space is subverted. Therefore, the radical critique of everyday life comes from within. What Lefebvre variously termed the 'struggle for the city', the 'right to the city', 'the right to urban life', could not be separated from his utopian vision of human agency and heterogeneity as expressed through the 'lived space' of the body.

Lefebvre's key contributions to theories of everyday life, urbanisation and space must be understood as part of a life project in which all three concepts were integrated with increasing complexity across a much larger (and still largely untranslated) *oeuvre*. Among anglophone readers, his studies have had a particular influence on cultural theorists, social geographers and post-modern thinkers with an interest in the cultural geographies of capitalism. More recently, Lefebvre's emphasis on the profound relations between space, the body and the constitution of subjectivity have been explored in conjunction with Freudian and Lacanian propositions.

Finally, and in terms of cultural politics, Lefebvre is perhaps more relevant today than ever before. Recent upsurges in user-participation movements, 'reclaim the city' groups and developments in direct action and carnival politics evoke the Lefebvrian vision that the transformation of the world will not be achieved without a profound reworking of everyday cultural and spatial practice.

Further reading

Gregory, D. GEOGRAPHICAL IMAGINATIONS, Blackwell, 1994.
Pile, S. THE BODY AND THE CITY: PSYCHOANALYSIS, SPACE AND SUBJECTIVITY, Routledge, 1996.

Soja, E. THIRDSPACE: JOURNEY TO LOS ANGELES AND OTHER REAL-AND-IMAGINED PLACES, Blackwell, 1996.

A.K.

LENIN, Vladimir

Politician/social theorist	born Russia 1870–1924
Associated with	MARXISM ■ BOLSHEVISM
Influences include	MARX ■ ENGELS ■ PLEKHANOV
Shares common ground with	TROTSKY ■ BUKHARIN ■ GRAMSCI
Main works	THE DEVELOPMENT OF CAPITALISM IN RUSSIA (1899)
	IMPERIALISM, THE HIGHEST STAGE OF CAPITALISM (1916)
	STATE AND REVOLUTION (1917)

LENIN'S FATHER WAS a school inspector, his mother a daughter of a surgeon. In 1887 his elder brother Alexander (Sasha), who had translated Marx, was hanged for plotting to assassinate Tsar Alexander III. In 1887 Lenin began a law degree at Kazan University, but by the end of December was expelled for participation in a demonstration. He was allowed to restart in 1888, but again his studies were disrupted. He finally took a course as an external student and qualified in 1891. Lenin travelled widely in Europe and was active in revolutionary circles in Russia. Arrested in 1895 and in 1897, he was sentenced, without trial, to three years in Siberia. In the Russian Social Democratic Party, Lenin led the Bolshevik faction and developed a conception of the revolution in a country with a large peasant sector undergoing a rapid socio-economic revolution. After the defeat of the 1905 revolution, the Bolsheviks came to power in 1917; Lenin was the effective leader of the revolutionary forces until his death in 1924.

Lenin adopted the view that Russia was undergoing a capitalist economic transition from Plekhanov, but he drew different political conclusions. Lenin argued against what he called economism, that politics necessarily follows the interests of the dominant economic class stage by stage. In opposition to this, Lenin argued that the specific features of the Russian Revolution meant that the growing bourgeoisie would rather ally itself to the aristocracy than form themselves into a revolutionary force, since if a revolution was provoked its initiative might pass into other hands. Lenin thus conceived the revolution as passing through a number of stages, and thought, in opposition to the Mensheviks, that a 'party of a new type' (the Bolsheviks) could lead each of these in a permanent revolutionary transition. Eventually, having succeeded in winning political power in 1917, and having started the economic 'transition to communism', he reflected at the end of his life on the need for a further deep cultural revolution in order to complete and maintain the revolutionary process. Ideas of cultural revolution in the communist movement largely derived their inspiration from Lenin's last writings on the stages of the transition from capitalism to communism.

Lenin's writings, which cover all aspects of Russian social life, also contain specific contributions on cultural practices such as his articles on Tolstoy written between 1908 and 1911. Often dismissed as no higher than journalese, writers in the structural Marxist tradition, notably Macherey, have argued that they develop analysis based on the theory of social contradiction in complex social transitions. Lenin's articles on Tolstoy were written in the immediate aftermath of the failed 1905 revolution, and in a period of retreat for the revolutionary movement. They are an attempt to show both the weakness of Tolstoy's vision, and at the same time to show that this vision revealed key features of the culture of peasant life in Russia in the period between 1861 (the ending of feudal serfdom) and the 1905 revolution. For Lenin, the political position of the peasantry oscillated between periods of considerable protest and acquiescence. The 1905 revolution was a turning-point, from Lenin's point of view, since it marked the end of the era in which the peasant revolt was the leading form of protest in Russia. Henceforth, in Lenin's view, the newly emerging urban working class was to take this role, and the whole character of peasant revolt was thus revealed to be highly ambiguous. For, on the one hand, the peasants fought against the newly structured estates, while on the other hand their objectives tended to crystallise around proprietorial demands for landownership. For Lenin, 'The era is characterised, then, not by real conflicts but by a fundamental collusion which depends on a latent contradiction' (Macherey 1978: 112). The specific character of Tolstoy's project was the construction by a member of the Russian aristocracy of an ideology of the peasant masses. Or rather, Tolstoy's writings are a particular encounter with peasant ideology in a vision which discounted the importance and significance of the rise of the new Russian bourgeoisie and modern industrial proletarians. Tolstoy's work, and we could take this as a general formula of his cultural analysis, is for Lenin, the mirror of the revolution, its reflection, and its expression. Tolstoy's view of the revolution is partial for a number of reasons: it is partisan, it is explicitly perspectival, and because of the complexity of the process Tolstoy catches only aspects of it: but these aspects, according to Lenin, focus on the pain of the rapid destruction of peasant patriarchal Russia, and in this analysis can be found the reasons for the failure of the revolution. Thus for Lenin, literature does not reflect and express directly the experience of social life: this expression is mediated by encounters with ideologies and contradictions which arise from it.

This reading of Lenin by Macherey was widely influential in literary criticism with the emergence of structural Marxism, in such authors as Terry Eagleton and Jonathan Dollimore. It forms an important point of reference for cultural analysis as a component aspect of political intervention.

Further reading

Bennett, T. FORMALISM AND MARXISM, Methuen, 1979.
Macherey, P. A THEORY OF LITERARY PRODUCTION, Routledge, 1978.
M.G.

LÉVI-STRAUSS, Claude

Social anthropologist	born Belgium 1908–1996
Associated with	STRUCTURALISM ■ KINSHIP ■ MYTHOLOGY
Influences include	ROUSSEAU ■ DURKHEIM ■ MAUSS ■ JAKOBSON
Shares common ground with	BOAS ■ RADCLIFFE-BROWN ■ LEACH ■ GELLNER
Main works	THE ELEMENTARY STRUCTURES OF KINSHIP, STRUCTURAL ANTHROPOLOGY (1949, TRANS. 1969) THE SAVAGE MIND (1962, TRANS. 1966) TRISTES TROPIQUES (1955, TRANS. 1973) MYTHOLOGIQUES I-IV (1964, 1966, 1968, 1971, TRANS. 1969, 1981)

THE SOCIAL ANTHROPOLOGIST, Claude Lévi-Strauss, has had a profound impact on approaches to, and theories of, culture across a range of social sciences and humanities. During his long academic career, he conducted several ethnographic expeditions in Brazil. These informed his work throughout his life and exposed him to anglophone anthropology and ethnography as well as structural linguistics. He secured a Chair in Paris in 1958, which he held until his retirement in 1982. His chief legacy was establishing structuralist approaches to cultural analysis that became the forerunners of deconstructionist and postmodern approaches. This major shift in theorising and analysing culture meant that the writings of Lévi-Strauss attracted considerable controversy as well as acclaim.

Perhaps the key to his work was the fact that he was a self-trained anthropologist who eschewed conventional theories and methodologies. Although he acknowledged the work of certain anthropologists as formative influences, in particular Emile Durkheim, Marcel Mauss, Franz Boas and Alfred Radcliffe-Brown, his thinking was equally inflected by his keen interest in geology, Marxism and psychoanalysis. The vehicle for his distinctive approach was his interest in structural linguistics, especially the work of Roman Jakobson and Ferdinand de Saussure.

Lévi-Strauss was a prolific writer who addressed a variety of anthropological and cultural topics in innovative and provocative ways. Analytically, he always emphasised the structural basis of social life which, he argued, derived from a set of rules and binary oppositions. These shaped the interplay of social relationships and cultural forms. Rejecting the individualist basis of other forms of social analysis, Lévi-Strauss argued that social life could be reduced to a few key principles of organisation from which cultural patterns were configured and reproduced. He applied this approach to the anthropological trinity of kinship, classification and mythology to turn conventional theories on their head. For example, in analysing kinship, he abandoned the focus on relations of descent, instead proposing a theory of relationships of marital alliance. The central tenet of his approach was the idea of reciprocity (borrowed from Mauss), particularly identifying the exchange of women as the counterpoint to the incest prohibition.

Thus, the basis of his structural method was the identification of elementary rules of social order which generated all social relationships. By reducing social phenomena to key rules that regulate relationships and structures, Lévi-Strauss explicitly related the material aspects of culture (such as rules of kinship, rites of passage and spatial organisation) to symbolic realms (such as language, myths and art). For Lévi-Strauss, myths were systems of transformation which could be analysed in terms of relations of opposition, inversion, symmetry, substitution and permutation. In addition, Lévi-Strauss proposed that the diachronic (refracted over time and related) order of myths could be interpreted in terms of synchronic and paradigmatic elements.

The ideas of Lévi-Strauss were expounded in his doctoral thesis, *The Elementary Structures of Kinship*, *Structural Anthropology* (1958, trans. 1963), and the enormously influential *The Savage Mind*. But his most popular book was his semi-autobiographical *Tristes Tropiques*, which was a highly readable anthropological interpretation of, and reflection on, his experiences in Brazil to which he applied his structural method. Because he appeared to reduce social phenomena to structures of the mind (key oppositions and transformative properties), his ideas were rejected by some critics as either being essentialist (reducible to mental structures), reflective (mirroring social reality), or impossible to verify.

Lévi-Strauss endeavoured to tackle these criticisms in his major – and arguably most important – work, *Mythologiques*, which consisted of four volumes: *The Raw and the Cooked* (1964/1969), *From Honey to Ashes* (1967/1973), *The Origin of Table Manners* (1968/1978) and *The Naked Man* (1971/1981). This work elaborated the idea that mythical thought emanates from primitive thought; it drew on almost a thousand myths from 200 Amerindian groups to further develop his structural methodology to show that 'the structures of myths could be traced back to the structures of human thought' (d'Anglure 1996).

Without a doubt, Lévi-Strauss revolutionised the way in which social and cultural phenomena could be apprehended. His influence had endured for over half a century, beginning in France and Europe but belatedly receiving accolades in the English-speaking world. While the general influence of structuralism waned from the 1980s, it continued to underpin the development of new intellectual approaches and remains a major defining moment of the twentieth century.

Further reading

D'Anglure, Bernard Saladin 'Lévi-Strauss, Claude', in Alan Barnard and Jonathan Spencer (eds.), ENCYCLOPEDIA OF SOCIAL AND CULTURAL ANTHROPOLOGY, Routledge, 1996.
Leach, Edmund LÉVI-STRAUSS, Fontana, 1970.
Lévi-Strauss, Claude and Eribon, D. CONVERSATIONS WITH CLAUDE LÉVI-STRAUSS, University of Chicago Press, 1988, trans. 1991.
Sperber, Dan 'Claude Lévi-Strauss today', in ON ANTHROPOLOGICAL KNOWLEDGE, Cambridge University Press, 1985.

J.C.

LÉVINAS, Emmanuel

Philosopher	born Lithuania 1906—
Associated with	AUTRUI/THE OTHER ■ ALTERITY
Influences include	BERGSON ■ HEIDEGGER ■ HUSSERL ■ ROSENZWEIG
Shares common ground with	BLANCHOT ■ SARTRE ■ DERRIDA
Major works	EXISTENCE AND EXISTENTS (1947)
	TOTALITY AND INFINITY (1961)
	OTHERWISE THAN BEING: OR BEYOND ESSENCE (1974)

WHILE A STUDENT at the University of Strasbourg, Lévinas became influenced by Bergson's work on time and duration, the relevance of which was clearer to him after attended a course of lectures by Husserl at the University of Freiburg. He befriended Maurice Blanchot and took French citizenship. He was known as one of the leading authorities on Husserl. Following the conclusion of the Second World War, Lévinas became the director of the École Normale Israélite Orientale in Paris. His other academic appointments included the universities of Poitiers, Paris-Nanterre and the Sorbonne.

Writing after the Holocaust, Lévinas dedicated *Otherwise than Being: or Beyond Essence* to the 'memory of those closest among six million assassinated by the National Socialists, and of the millions on millions of all confessions and all nations, victims of the same hatred of the other man'. Lévinas's exposition of ethics as responsibility for the Other is the response to the suffering and murderous violence borne out of the metaphysical repression of the Other. He premises his ethics upon the notion of 'absolute alterity'.

Lévinas's ethics is a critique of the metaphysical determinations of subjectivity that have characterised Western philosophy, although he claims that his re-formed notion of subjectivity does not take him outside metaphysics, but reclaims the meaning of metaphysics. His reconceptualisation of metaphysics for ethics has been of considerable interest to both Derrida and Irigaray. Lévinas's notion of ethics is conceived as the particularity of relation to the Other. As such it constitutes a critique of the universality that has dominated philosophical investigations into the meaning of subjectivity and ethics. In his ethical philosophy, Lévinas refutes the supposed neutrality of the universal (unlike Irigaray, for its presumptions of masculinity) because neutrality has no face. It is non-specific and therefore does not engender desire, which is necessary to relationality. Lévinas's ethics is not governed by the binary terms of the universal opposed to the individual. Both of these terms are made to recede with the attention Lévinas gives to the particularity and the materiality of the ethical relation between the two.

Lévinas is critically concerned with the temporality of the ontological subject whom Heidegger, in particular, interpreted as existing in the finite time between being and nothingness, as Being. Lévinas terms this a being-for-the-self. Time, in this conception, is characterised as linear, governed by a chronology of past, present and future which is the continuum through which Being is conceptualised as unitary. In addition to time being one of the conditions of the subject, philosophy has been premised on the knowing subject (for whom Lévinas uses the term, 'the Same') who achieves knowing consciousness, unity and identity by objectifying the Other. Lévinas recognises in the notion of subjectivity the existence of a relationship which is antecedent to the constitution of subjectivity. (This could be crudely stated as 'I cannot be an I without an other'.)

Lévinas focuses on the Other who is anterior and necessary to the process of objectification, whom he brings forward as the Stranger to whom 'I' have absolute responsibility. This Other (capitalised to signify the ethical primacy accorded to the Other) is privileged as transcendent and not reducible to enclosure in the totalising binary structure of the Same. This is not a new relationship. It has existed since time immemorial. What is new to philosophy is the privilege accorded to the Other as the Stranger who, in the face-to-face encounter, presents 'me' with the opportunity to respond with hospitality rather than hostility. It is an approach of welcome rather than threat. This, for Lévinas, is being-for-the-other, or 'otherwise than being', who disturbs the knowing subject as the foundation of philosophy. For Lévinas, 'The absolutely other is not the other of a same, its other, in the heart of that supreme sameness that is being; it is other than being' (Lyotard, in Cohen 1986: 119).

Lévinas conceives of ethical subjectivity as time for the Other. This temporality is not the finite time of Being (for oneself). Responsibility for the Other is infinite. There is no limit to call of the Other which materialises in the face-to-face relation. The time, therefore, which governs ethical subjectivity is infinity: it is a relation of a future – proposed against the subject of ontology which is enclosed in the time of the present.

Lévinas confronts the singularity of the subject in philosophy by recognising that the subjectivity is conditional upon a preceding relation. The Other for Lévinas is conceived not as 'the other in me', or the other of the same. The Other for Lévinas becomes absolutely other, quite discreet. He describes this Otherness as alterity or absolute alterity. Alterity is that which is beyond the comprehension of the knowing subject; where the Other is recognised as excessive of my capacity to know or understand; who is more than my need of him or her. It is respect for alterity that constitutes an ethical relation.

The capacity to relate to absolute alterity requires a restructuring of subjectivity. In *Totality and Infinity* Lévinas argues for the capacity for alterity to derive from a separation within subjectivity; separation between egotistical need and transcendent desire. The necessity of satisfying human needs corresponds to the value of freedom – freedom is the condition which enables a person to meet their needs. Lévinas's effort to rethink subjectivity is addressed to the individual ontological subject ('the Same') as the subject premised on freedom (from responsibility for the 'Other'). In encountering the 'Other' the Same either reduced the other to the Same, that is, to its own understanding, which gives rise to the claims of universal, or commonality; or excludes that which is in excess of its own comprehension. The subject of freedom is the knowing subject of philosophy with its 'comprehensive claims to mastery' (Critchley 1992: 8). This freedom is necessary to the fulfilment of needs – material, bodily, human. Lévinas brings the body into philosophy by giving honour and celebration to the pleasures and satisfactions of materiality. They are necessities for sustaining life.

Alterity is both internal, an aspect of the separation within the subject, and external: as the one who comes and interrupts my freedom, the Stranger or neighbour who is Other and who '[puts into question my] spontaneity by the presence of the Other' (Lévinas 1961: 43). The 'me' or 'my' spontaneity is intended in the personal sense – it challenges generalisation and abstraction and engages responsibility that is embodied, material and personal. The Other is the face who appears as the Stranger, the Widow, the Orphan, to whom 'I', particularly 'I', have responsibility to respond. As a relation with one who is not my equal, it is an asymmetrical relation. It is not equal because the Other is given priority to the extent of 'taking the bread from my own mouth' for him or her. It is a relation with one who is near, with the proximity of calling me to respond; and far away, respected in their alterity, not grasped or possessed, so in that sense, exterior.

Further reading

Bernasconi, Robert and Critchley, Simon (eds.) RE-READING LÉVINAS, Indiana University Press, 1991.
Bernasconi, Robert and Wood, David (eds.) THE PROVOCATION OF LÉVINAS, Indiana University Press, 1991.
Cohen, Richard A. (ed.) FACE TO FACE WITH LÉVINAS, SUNY Press, 1986.
Critchley, Simon THE ETHICS OF DECONSTRUCTION: DERRIDA AND LÉVINAS, Blackwell, 1992.

B.M.

LEVY-BRUHL, Lucien

Philosopher/anthropologist	born France 1857–1939
Associated with	PRIMITIVE MENTALITY ■ MORAL PHILOSOPHY ■ RATIONALITY
Influences include	DURKHEIM ■ COMTE ■ TYLOR ■ FRAZER
Shares common ground with	EVANS-PRITCHARD ■ LÉVI-STRAUSS
Main works	LA MORALE ET LA SCIENCE DES MOEURS (1903; TRANS. ETHICS AND MORAL SCIENCE, 1905) LES FONCTIONS MENTALES DANS LES SOCIÉTÉS PRIMITIVES (1910, TRANS. HOW NATIVES THINK, 1926) LA MENTALITÉ PRIMITIVE (1922, TRANS. PRIMITIVE MENTALITY, 1923)

LEVY-BRUHL WAS a philosopher, anthropologist and sociologist who was especially interested in understanding how the mind of 'the primitive' worked. His theory of primitive mentality has been widely cited (and discredited), although some commentators have argued that Levy-Bruhl was misinterpreted and that his position bore many similarities to the recent structuralist arguments. Even in his own lifetime, he reworked many arguments which were posthumously published. While his work has been declared synonymous with 'colonialist' approaches to understanding indigenous peoples, many continuities between his work and contemporary anthropology can be found.

Levy-Bruhl was born in Paris and studied at the École Normale Supérieure. In 1904, he was appointed to the Chair in the History of Modern Philosophy at the Sorbonne. He was influenced by many thinkers but was always an original and eclectic intellectual who queried ideas and taken-for-granted arguments. For example, although he was influenced by Durkheim, especially his *Rules of Sociological Method*, he also questioned the rationalism implicit in Durkheim. His early work concentrated on moral philosophy (*Ethics and Moral Science*) and the work of French philosophers such as Comte (*The Philosophy of Auguste Comte*, 1903) and Jacobi (*La philosophie de Jacobi*, 1894). His interest was in understanding morality as a culturally specific and changing set of beliefs and propositions and not as universals. This was a radical departure from previous studies, which treated morals in absolute terms. Instead, Levy-Bruhl argued that morals were relative and arbitrary social constructs.

Levy-Bruhl then initiated his major work on theories of primitive mentality culminating in six books: *Primitive Mentality, How Natives Think, The Soul of the Primitive* (1928), *Primitives and the Supernatural* (1936), *La mythologie primitive* (1935) and *Expérience mystique et des symbols chez les primitifs* (1938). The focus of these works was the proposition that ways of thinking were variable and that this could be graphically demonstrated by the differences between the mentalities of 'primitive' and 'civilised' people. Using documentation from preliterate societies, Levy-Bruhl showed that patterns of thought differed in significant ways, rather than simply being more rudimentary. He emphasised the prelogical or superstitious elements pervading mental processes in preliterate societies. Thus while a mystical explanation may be offered to explain phenomena in primitive societies, a causal one is offered in civilised societies.

Because he was concerned to emphasise the differences in thought between primitive and civilised people, critics such as Mauss and Evans-Pritchard argued that he did not differentiate between different primitive peoples who might display distinct thought processes, and that he was exaggerating the degree of difference. Some argued that he was characterising primitive thought as a form of prelogical thought in contrast to the logical thought habits of civilised societies. Levy-Bruhl rejected this accusation, instead arguing that these were two structures of mentality which coexisted, although he maintained that their balance differed: the prelogical dominated among primitive people whereas logical thought dominated the mentality of civilised people.

Partly in response to criticism, Levy-Bruhl modified or, at least, elaborated his views in later writings which were published posthumously as *Les carnets de Lucien Levy-Bruhl* (1949). His revisions maintained his notion of prelogical thought but proposed that this was mediated by mystical thinking that could give the appearance of non-logical thinking. He also became interested in the transition between primitive and civilised mentalities and how multiple forms of mentality coexisted. While his ideas – or popular interpretations of his ideas – were discredited, some (e.g. Evans-Pritchard) have argued that more subtle interpretations of his ideas in France and Germany have meant that his ideas and legacy have been more positively received than the 'neglect and derision' he has attracted among English anthropologists. Thus, despite his own criticisms of Levy-Bruhl, Evans-Pritchard argues that Levy-Bruhl's work greatly stimulated ideas about preliterate mental processes by identifying 'a new set of problems' and restating other problems that remain to be solved. In other words, his ideas deserved revision rather than rejection.

In short, Levy-Bruhl raised issues about the nature of human mental processes and whether or not – and if so how – they differed between preliterate and literate societies. By positing qualitative differences between thought processes, he shifted the debate away from evolutionary accounts and prefigured the possibility of competing forms of rationality among different peoples. This approach influenced many contemporary and subsequent anthropologists, even if it were only to refute his arguments as in Evans-Pritchard's study of witchcraft among the Azande. In this sense, a more sympathetic reassessment

of Levy-Bruhl's contribution to anthropological debate and conceptual preoccupations seems warranted.

Further reading

Cazeneuve, Jean LUCIEN LEVY-BRUHL, trans. Peter Rivière, Blackwell, 1972.
Evans-Pritchard, Edward A HISTORY OF ANTHROPOLOGICAL THOUGHT, Faber &
Faber, 1981.
Lévi-Strauss, Claude THE SAVAGE MIND, University of Chicago Press, 1966.
Levy-Bruhl, Lucien THE 'SOUL' OF THE PRIMITIVE, foreword by E.E. Evans-
Pritchard; authorised translation of L'AME PRIMITIF (1927) by Lilian Clare,
Allen and Unwin, 1965.
Levy-Bruhl, Lucien THE NOTEBOOKS ON PRIMITIVE MENTALITY, preface by
Maurice Leenhardt; translation of LES CARNETS DE LUCIEN LEVY-BRUHL,
1949, by Peter Rivière, Blackwell, 1975.
J.C.

LEWIN, Kurt

Social psychologist	born Germany 1890–1947
Associated with	FIELD THEORY ■ GROUP DYNAMICS ■ LIFE SPACE
Influences include	CASSIRER ■ KÖHLER ■ WERTHEIMER
Shares common ground with	BALES ■ CARTWRIGHT ■ MAYO
Main works	PRINCIPLES OF TOPOLOGICAL PSYCHOLOGY (1936) RESOLVING SOCIAL CONFLICTS (1948) FIELD THEORY IN SOCIAL SCIENCE (1951)

L EWIN WAS BORN into a Jewish family in Prussia and, after studying at
the universities of Freiburg and Munich, completed his doctorate at
Berlin University in 1914. While at the Psychological Institute in

Berlin, he became influenced by the gestaltist theorists Köhler and Wertheimer. Fleeing from Nazi Germany to the USA in 1933, he became visiting professor at Stanford and at Cornell before taking up an appointment as Professor of Child Psychology in the Child Welfare Research Station of the State University of Iowa in 1935; here he began to focus on social processes influencing behaviour, work which led to his founding of the Research Center for Group Dynamics at the Massachusetts Institute of Technology in 1945. Later, he co-founded the Commission on Community Interrelations for the American Jewish Congress in New York; this reflected his growing concern with social change and the application of social psychology to solving social problems.

Lewin's highly original and seminal theory of personality was derived from gestalt psychology and his studies of the effect of unfinished tasks and satiation on human behaviour. Starting with the notion of perception as an act determined by the perceptual field, he fruitfully extended this to learning – conceived as the dynamic reorganisation and institution of a new order of behaviour. Behaviour is seen as a function of the person and a whole concrete situation, or a field of coexisting facts; these facts are understood, not as independent phenomena but as interdependent with personal perceptions. In his well-known formula, Lewin stressed that the task of psychology was to predict human behaviour as a joint function of the individual and his or her total social situation (or environment), including all significant other people. The totality of facts determining the behaviour of a person and his or her situation are conceived topologically as his or her psychological 'life space' or bounded field of perception.

The relations between the person and his or her situation are perceived as positions with spatial properties, influenced and mediated by the various groups to which an individual belongs. Behaviour is expressed in interpersonal terms related to topological notions of region, 'correctedness', separateness and boundaries.

In particular, field theory refers to the method of analysing causal relationships in the field which can be dichotomised into subjective and objective psychological elements, or facts. Lewin insisted that the determinants of human behaviour would have to be represented in mathematical terms if psychology were to become a rigorous discipline, permitting the understanding and prediction of behaviour. Accordingly, he devised a schema of vectors for geometrically representing symbolic formations and spatial relations of psychological facts. There are two elements in the vectors: 'topological space' and 'hodological space'. These facilitate the creation of pictures of unique individuals, each with their own 'self-awareness field'.

Topological space is a set of objects or points with definite relations to one another which may be divided into sub-wholes; these structures fit into 'regions' (areas with points) of distinguishable parts of the life space (or person), which may be open or closed elements of the psychological environment (present or contemplated activities rather than to the objective areas in which activities are linked). The most fundamental and central topological construct for Lewin was the 'life space', the psychological field, or total situation in which a person operates and which confronts the individual, determining their behaviour at any given moment of time, i.e. in ahistorical terms in line with his 'principle of contemporaneity'.

The person, or 'behaving self', in the psychological life space includes friends and relatives and his or her perceived relationship to them, as well as the individual's ability to get things done in certain ways plus any forces that might inhibit personal actions. Regions of the life space as a psychological fact are divided by boundaries which have several dimensions, such as nearness/ remoteness or firmness/weakness. Some boundaries are weaker or easier to cross than others, such as passing a qualifying test or examination, which can be firm and difficult. Deriving from these basic structures of the life space are Lewinian constructs of degree of differentation, centrality, path and psychological distance.

To encapsulate the more dynamic side of life space dealing with changing relations within the person as well as his or her psychological environment in moving from one region to another in the life space, Lewin invented a kind of geometry applicable to behaviour, to personality and to groups which he called 'hodological space'. Such movement has direction, dependent on the properties of the whole field, in following a pathway, the characteristics of which vary according to the situation.

Lewin is credited with pioneering experimental group psychology, specifically Group Dynamics. A small group consists of between three and five persons, every one of whom can recognise and react to every other as a distinct individual, and who are likely to manifest sustained interaction, perception of group membership, shared group goals, emotional relations and group norms. Lewin always understood his theoretical work as having practical utllity: his much-quoted research on different styles of leadership (autocratic, *laissez-faire*, and so on) has implications for industrial organisation, thus affirming his strong belief that 'there is nothing so practical as a good theory'.

Further reading

Marrow, A. THE PRACTICAL THEORIST: THE LIFE AND WORK OF KURT LEWIN, Teacher's College Press, 1977.
Martindale, D. NATURE AND TYPES OF SOCIOLOGICAL THEORY, Routledge & Kegan Paul, 1960.
Stivers, E. and Wheelan, S. (ed.) THE LEWIN LEGACY, Springer-Verlag, 1989.

G.P.

LIPSET, Seymour Martin

Political scientist/sociologist	born USA 1922—
Associated with	NATIONAL CHARACTER ▪ POLITICAL CULTURE
Influences include	TOCQUEVILLE ▪ WEBER ▪ TALCOTT PARSONS
Shares common ground with	RIESMAN ▪ BOORSTIN ▪ HARTZ
Main works	THE FIRST NEW NATION (1963)
	AGRARIAN SOCIALISM (1950)
	POLITICAL MAN (1960)

SEYMOUR MARTIN LIPSET is a student of democracy. In an era of subdivision among and within scholarly disciplines, his approach to studying democracy is decidedly synthetic. Historical, sociological and political perspectives are all employed; and although the USA is clearly featured in his investigations, comparisons with other democracies are frequently used to sharpen the focus on key systemic traits. Lipset is especially interested in comparisons of the USA and Canada, where he argues that the American revolutionary experience has profoundly distinguished the USA from a Canadian polity that otherwise has shared the conditions of American development.

For Lipset (as for John Stuart Mill), democracy is characterised by a balance of countervailing tendencies. On the other hand, Lipset recognises the proliferation of bureaucracies in complex social arrangements democratic or otherwise. With Weber, he is concerned about the potential for a society of vacuous automatons, uninterested and uneducated in the eclectic and ambiguous concerns of democratic citizenship. Lipset is troubled by the modern transition from inner to outer-directed citizenship, most effectively described in David Riesman's classic, *The Lonely Crowd*, 1950. Social interdependence, vocational specialisation and organisational efficiency have devalued idiosyncrasy and independence, replacing secure egos with conciliation and accommodation. Weber and Riesman, then, represent the forces of apathy, conformity and stability.

But Lipset is equally concerned with the countervailing forces of division and conflict. He is not completely unsympathetic to Marx's analysis of the disintegrative tendencies of class conflict, but unlike Marx (and with Tocqueville), he hopes to manage the antagonisms rather than eliminate them. In fact, the total elimination of class conflict threatens the system with deadly uniformity. Lipset also recognises the disruptive potential of an active, informed citizenry, and therefore he endorses the perspectives of Berelson and others articulated in *Voting* (1954), that a certain amount of apathy and simplicity can strengthen the fabric of democratic society. Lipset is similarly concerned with the polarising effect of religious beliefs.

What distinguishes democracies, according to Lipset, is that they are characterised by a delicate balancing of the forces of conformity and disintegration. Nations that fail at democracy are often victims of migration to one or the other. And nations that succeed are almost always nurtured by a strong, expanding economy. Consistent growth, perhaps more than any other factor, helps to maintain the balance. Healthy tensions persist among citizens with discrepancies in wealth and success, but the growth factor ensures that the discrepancies are fluid, and that classes (the elements of cleavage) are not impenetrable.

The balance is also maintained by a citizenry whose divisions are 'cross-cutting'. There are a healthy amount of Americans in the Democratic Party, for instance, who support traditionally conservative concepts like tax cuts, just as there are many anti-abortionists who support affirmative action. Thus, sharp disagreements on seemingly monumental issues provide needed cleavages and ensuing mobilisation and debate. However, because the alliances on any one issue are rarely replicated over the long term, broadly-based zealotry and intransigence can be avoided.

The USA has undergone a historical conditioning of balance. The disintegrative effects of revolution were balanced by strong, unifying leadership. The disruptive possibilities of religious fanaticism were moderated by an intimate memory that the revolution was fought to establish religious pluralism. But most importantly, the USA was imbued from its inception with the sometimes antagonistic values of equality and achievement. The forces for equality included the need for a revolutionary identity that did not replicate that of the coloniser, the relative absence of aristocratic and feudal vestiges in the new nation, and the popularity of liberalism at the time of the founding. Inspiring achievement was the ascension of capitalism, the ragged but receptive primitiveness of the environment, and the Calvinistic conception that 'good works' were the sign of chosenness. Equality fosters consensus and achievement promotes cleavage, and thus, for Lipset, deep national character traits reinforce the American inclination to democracy.

Further reading

Baer, Doug *et al.* 'The Values of Canadians and Americans: A Critical Analysis and Reassessment', SOCIAL FORCES, 68: 3 (March 1990), pp. 693–714.
Marks, Gary and Diamond, Larry (eds.) REEXAMINING DEMOCRACY: ESSAYS IN HONOR OF SEYMOUR MARTIN LIPSET, Sage, 1992.
Ogmundson, R. and Fisher, Lee 'Beyond Lipset and his Critics: An Initial Reformulation', CANADIAN REVIEW OF SOCIOLOGY AND ANTHROPOLOGY, 31: 2 (May 1994), pp. 196–200.

T.J.L.

LUHMANN, Niklas

Sociologist	born Germany 1927–1998
Associated with	AUTOPOIESIS ■ SYSTEMS ANALYSIS
Influences include	BERTALANFFY ■ PARSONS
Shares common ground with	HABERMAS ■ BUCKLEY ■ ALEXANDER
Main works	SOZIALE SYSTEME (1984, TRANS. SOCIAL SYSTEMS, 1995)
	THE DIFFERENTIATION OF SOCIETY (1982)
	THEORIE DER GESELLSCHAFT ODER SOZIALTECHNOLOGIE: WAS LEISTET DIE SYSTEMFORSCHUNG? (WITH JÜRGEN HABERMAS, 1971)

L UHMANN WAS BORN in Lüneburg. He studied and practised law (1954 to 1962) before receiving his Ph.D. in Sociology from the University of Münster in 1966. He was awarded his *Habilitation* (a high-level post-doctoral qualification) in the same year. He then took up a position in sociology at the University of Bielefield, where he remained until his retirement in 1993.

Luhmann's work in many ways parallels that of Habermas, though he has failed to attract a comparable following, possibly because of the complexity of his analysis and, almost certainly, the turgidness of his prose. Also, unlike Habermas, he has no conception of a redemption in modernity: for Luhmann, the project of modernity and the vectors of communication it has opened offer no hope for humanity.

In its broadest sense, Luhmann's contribution lies in the area called General Systems Theory, a style of analysis pioneered in the 1930s by Bertalanffy who saw its task as in (1) integrating concepts, laws and models from an array of disiplines and facilitating transfers from one to another; (2) developing theoretical models; (3) promoting the unity of the sciences. While Luhmann cannot be said to have followed the dictum exactly, he has been truer to the spirit of Parsons, whose functionist approach to social systems was to lead him to a grand model of society which was (as he saw it) adequate at all levels, from the individual to the entire social system.

Luhmann's work can be read as a response to Parsons's straightforward functionalism. Prior to 1984, Luhmann's work stayed within a Parsonian framework, itself a synthesis of Durkheim and Weber. Then, Luhmann began to question the notion of social action. There are, according to Luhmann, three levels of action: the interactional; the organisational; and the societal. Each level has a degree of autonomy from the others, having its own processes, methanics of change and laws. Yet the levels are related systematically because the 'structures' at the organisational and societal levels are produced, reproduced and transformed in and through the everyday structures of interpersonal contact, i.e. at the interactional level. Such interpersonal contacts, while having relative independence, are structured themselves by the limits set by the larger systems in which they take place.

Systems are, for Luhmann, processes of communication. He visualises a society as composed of communicative sub-systems, such as politics, the economy, law, education, and so on. These are – and this is a crucial element of Lumann's theory – autopoietically closed. This means that information is not transferred between systems, but is always internally constructed by a system according to its own differentiating binary code, for example, legal vs illegal in legal systems; truth vs falsity in science. The choice of the term 'autopoiesis' is in contrast with the word 'cybernetics', which suggests some degree of input and output or transfer of information; this is not possible for Luhmann. He believes that effects provided by political programmes cannot be regarded as genuine steering because they depend on the internal construction of differences by other systems according to their own codes. There must be an irreducible separation of systems.

Dislocations between systems can occur when one system encroaches on, or attempts to influence, control or steer the operations of another system. All information is specific to the system that generates and transmits it; systems can only ever be self-referential and self-governing. Even if steering (a term Luhmann favours) is aimed outside, that is, at the level of the environment, it can only be the system's own environment, which is constructed in terms of its own binary logic, or code. Political strategies inevitably fail or result in some form of dislocation because they are aimed at intervening in the affairs of other systems. This is why societies frequently generate expectations that cannot ever be fulfilled and why the political allocation of resources is rarely satisfactory, because they are the results of one system interfering with the running of another which has different binary codes that determine its own 'laws'.

Luhmann also writes in terms of structural differentiation at three levels of action: interactional, organisational and societal. Each of these constitutes an autopoietic system; they are integrated in the sense that the larger structures of the organisation and societal levels are produced, reproduced and transformed in and through the everyday structures of interpersonal interactions. Yet these interactions themselves are conducted in and limited by the structural framework in which they can take place.

Luhmann believes that the problems of modernity have arisen from the differentiation of the various systems and the often contradictory codes that govern each. While Luhmann is at pains to avoid the epithet 'functionalist', others see a Parsonian theory construction, or rather, reconstruction.

Further reading

King, Michael and Schütz, Anton, 'The Ambitious Modesty of Niklas Luhmann', JOURNAL OF LAW AND SOCIETY, 21 (1994), pp. 897–930.
Luhmann, Niklas, THE DIFFERENTIATION OF SOCIETY, Columbia University Press, 1982.
Luhmann, Niklas, 'The Autopoiesis of Social Systems', in F. Geyer and J. van der Zouwen (eds.), SOCIOCYBERNETIC PARADOXES, Sage, 1986.

E.C.

LUKÁCS, Gyorgy/Georg

Aesthetician/literary critic	born Hungary 1885–1971
Associated with	RATIONALISM ▪ STALINISM ▪ WESTERN MARXISM
Influences include	DILTHEY ▪ HEGEL ▪ SIMMEL ▪ SZABO
Shares common ground with	ADORNO ▪ BRECHT ▪ GOLDMANN
Main works	HISTORY AND CLASS CONSCIOUSNESS (1923) STUDIES IN EUROPEAN REALISM (1950) THE MEANING OF CONTEMPORARY REALISM (1958) THE SPECIFICITY OF THE AESTHETIC (1963)

MICHEL LOWY ONCE described Lukács's project from 1928 onwards as 'a consistent attempt to "reconcile" Stalinism with bourgeois democratic culture'. From the 1920s until the collapse of Soviet Communism in Central and Eastern Europe around 1990 there was no shortage of ideologues, intellectuals generally and academic placemen in particular, who were prepared to bend knowledge to the twists and turns of party policy. Few, if any, were as brilliant as Lukács. He can be seen as someone who merely squandered his talents in a forlorn cause or, more charitably, as a tragic figure caught up in the extraordinary rise and fall of political Marxism during the twentieth century.

Lukács was born in Budapest to a Jewish bourgeois family. His mother, an Austrian, had to learn Hungarian on marriage. The language of the Lukács household was, however, primarily German, which is important since Lukács was to become as much a figure of German intellectual culture as of a comparatively marginal Hungarian one. As a young man, Lukács joined Max Weber's circle in Heidelberg and was influenced especially by Simmel. Back in Hungary, in 1919, he briefly became Minister of Education in the short-lived Communist government of Béla Kun. He spent most of the 1930s and 1940s in Russia during the Nazi period of domination in Central Europe. Again, he held a ministerial post briefly in Hungary during 1956, this time as Minister of Culture under Imre Nagy's reform government, which was brutally crushed by the Soviet Union's troops by the end of the year. After a short exile in Romania, Lukács returned to Hungary in 1957 and was deprived of his university post. His official position improved towards the end of his life and he rejoined the Hungarian Communist Party shortly before his death.

Although Lukács wrote a great deal over a long lifetime, his importance and enduring significance was secured by an early book, *History and Class Consciousness*, which revived the Hegelian aspect of Marxism and was, amongst other things, a great influence on the cultural theorising of the Frankfurt School. Since Engels, Marxist philosophy had become scientific, positivistic and deterministic; and Marxist politics, following Lenin's example, had become voluntaristic and extremely simplistic about the relation between thought and action. Lukács challenged both the prevailing philosophical and political assumptions of 1920s Marxism by stressing the complex interrelations between theory and practice, in effect, the role of praxis. From this point of view, Marxism was not to be understood as a deterministic set of economic laws or, on the other hand, Bolshevik conspiracy. Lukács argued for the concept of totality in Marxist thought and the indivisibility of fact and value. He produced an ideological critique of scientism as a feature of the reified consciousness of capitalism, setting abstract forces above human action, and criticised an obsession with atomised 'facts' for failing to grasp holistic relations.

One of the major arguments of *History and Class Consciousness*, however, indicates how it was that Lukács was later to support, at least in the 1940s, a Stalinist politics. This is the distinction between actual and potential or imputed consciousness. It was rather convenient to find that the actual consciousness of the proletariat was not its 'real' consciousness: this had, instead, to be extrapolated from analysis of its position and interests in capitalist society by means of dialectical reasoning. Such an argument is not a million miles away from the Leninist and Stalinist assumption that the party knows best. yet, nonetheless, there is a trace of Luxemburg's counter-influence in the view that an adequate understanding of proletarian consciousness is vital to Marxist politics.

What appears to be so, in 'actual' consciousness or readily observable, does not provide sufficient understanding of what is happening in any situation, historical event or literary text, according to Lukács. The fundamental theoretical weakness of Lukács is that he transposed espistemology into aesthetics. His critiques of both nineteenth-century naturalism (Flaubert, Zola) and twentieth-century modernism (especially Kafka) can be understood in these terms. He took up a view espoused by Marx and Engels that the politically progressive and realistic is not a matter of conscious intention: hence, Balzac, the reactionary legitimist, could be compared favourably with Zola. One of Lukács's key ideas was to do with characterisation in the realist novel. Socially significant characters are 'types' who embody the experiences and world views of classes. A slide into subjectivism (Emma Bovary or K), while articulating a current sensibility, do not include within their characterisation a social explanation of their constitution. A writer like Thomas Mann, who continued to write in a nineteenth-century mode during the twentieth-century, was superior to writers who actually sought to be Marxist in their writing, such as Brecht, or who illuminated the existential condition of twentieth-century life, such as Kafka. Thus, Lukács spelt out in a sophisticated manner the great fallacy and disaster of Marxist aesthetics, that a realist epistemology can only appreciate an epistemologically realist aesthetic. It is a view which did damage to both art and a realist theory of knowledge, which, if Marxist philosophy is anything, it is that.

Further reading

Lichtheim, G. LUKÁCS, Fontana, 1970.
Lovell, T. PICTURES OF REALITY, British Film Institute, 1980.
Meszaros, I. LUKÁCS' CONCEPT OF DIALECTIC, Merlin, 1972.
J.McG.

LYND, Robert Staughton and Helen Merrell

Sociologists	Robert Lynd born USA 1892–1970; Helen Merrell born USA 1894–1982
Associated with	URBAN SOCIOLOGY ▪ COMMUNITY STUDIES ▪ ETHNOGRAPHY
Influences include	SIMMEL ▪ TOCQUEVILLE ▪ HEGEL ▪ SNOW
Shares common ground with	MERTON ▪ LAZARSFELD ▪ MILLS
Main works	MIDDLETOWN: A STUDY IN CONTEMPORARY AMERICAN CULTURE (1929, 1930, 1963) MIDDLETOWN IN TRANSITION: A STUDY IN CULTURAL CONFLICTS (1963)

THE LYNDS ARE best known for their joint work, especially their studies of the mythical American Midwest town, Middletown, but they have also been recognised for their individual contributions to the social sciences. Of the two, Helen Merrell Lynd was more productive and possessed a broader range of interests and intellectual knowledge, yet her husband is better known. Robert Lynd was born in New Albany, Indiana, and graduated from Princeton University in 1914, when he entered the publishing profession. Disillusioned with this, he undertook a Bachelor of Divinity at the Union Theological Seminary (1920–23). He taught at Columbia University until his retirement in 1965 and was important in attracting many of the most significant sociologists of the day to Columbia, including Paul Lazarsfeld, Robert Merton and C. W. Mills.

Helen Merrell was born in La Grange, Illinois, and developed an interest in Hegelian philosophy at Wellesley College from where she graduated in 1919. She completed an MA (1922) and Ph.D. (1944) in history at Columbia, and taught at the Sarah Lawrence College from 1929 to 1964.

In 1921, Robert married Helen Merrell, and jointly they embarked on a study of a small city for the Institute of Social and Religious Research. While the Church was only interested in ascertaining patterns of religious behaviour and the role of religion in daily life, the Lynds believed that a broader understanding of social dynamics was necessary. They pushed the boundaries of the church focus desired by the Institute, and produced their ground-breaking study of Muncie, Indiana. In reality the methodology and outcome was the first cultural anthropology of modern American life. Their study was published as the classic, *Middletown*, and it set the terms of urban and community studies for many years.

Despite their formal lack of training in sociology, Robert Lynd (but not Helen Merrell Lynd) was awarded a doctorate from Columbia University in 1931 in recognition of the Middletown study (after they had removed the parts of the manuscript authored by Helen). While Robert Lynd was accepted into the male academic fraternity of Columbia, Helen Merrell Lynd remained on the fringes. Robert Lynd was less interested in publishing than in his roles as a charismatic teacher, active colleague, engaged debater and social and political activist.

By contrast, Merrell Lynd has been described as a 'polymath' (by Irving Horowitz) with an expertise not only in sociology, but equally in history, psychology and philosophy. In addition to her joint and sole authored work, Merrell Lynd was an active educational reformer, and defender of intellectuals harassed by the 1950s McCarthy hearings. The latter perhaps hindered her acceptance into the academic world, despite widespread acclaim for her research and her brave political stance.

The Middletown study was based on research undertaken by the Lynds and their research assistants while they lived in the community of Muncie for eighteen months. Here they recorded, through a variety of sources, information on aspects of daily life, including work, domestic arrangements, socialisation, schooling, leisure (including one of the first studies of mass communication), religious habits and relations with the government. It was the first application of ethnographic method to contemporary society and set the terms of urban anthropology and cultural ethnography. The Lynds' study was characterised by thoroughness, attention to detail and breadth of interpretative vision. Their findings illuminated 'a generation of social science, the essence of the American way of life . . . [which] precisely and devastatingly delineated what the nation had become' (Horowitz 1979).

The research was strengthened by the decision to analyse and contrast two slices of Middletown life in 1890 and 1924, thus giving a dynamic framework for understanding how the nature of community life changed and adapted over time. Implicit in the study was a Marxist perspective based on a class analysis in which the Lynds argued that every aspect of social life could be explained by class position, which determined the roles and statuses occupied by individuals. More disturbing was their conclusion that the major economic upheavals in Middletown had not led to radical social change but to the community's retreat away from politics and towards a concern with the minutiae of everyday life. This became the leitmotif of subsequent studies of American urban and suburban life. The success of this approach was quickly realised, since it addressed and unpicked the impact of modernisation and suburbanisation on and in middle America. The publication of *Middletown* (incidentally sold as a trade, not an academic, book) was highly successful, and spurred debate and the development of urban sociology, community studies and American studies. In short, it became the model for subsequent studies for a generation.

Not satisfied with a single study, the Lynds returned to Middletown during the Depression to see how life had changed over the intervening decade. They used the opportunity to apply new perspectives to the data and to test new sociological methods. The result was *Middletown in Transition*. Their study mapped the decline in the importance of religion (secularisation), the worsening economic situation and its impact on employment and quality of life, and changing political mores. Middletown had become a community in crisis, marked by uncertainty and pessimism, with its community spirit and cohesion under pressure.

While this study also contributed significantly to the emergence of cultural anthropology and community studies, it led Robert Lynd to question the futility of intellectual inquiry that failed to change the social and political conditions. Such concerns were the subject of his sole-authored book, *Knowledge for What? The Place of Social Science in American Culture* (Princeton University Press, 1939). Increasingly he turned away from his own research towards building up sociological debate within Columbia, although in 1956 he wrote a major critique of Mills's *Power Elite* ('Power in the United States', *The Nation*, 182, pp. 408–11).

Robert Lynd's pessimism and political engagement were matched by Helen Merrell Lynd's interdisciplinary and nuanced approach to research, academia and politics. She was a gifted thinker and writer, as evidenced in her book, *England in the Eighteen-eighties: Towards a Social Basis for Freedom* (Oxford University Press, 1945), the product of her doctoral work. This was a study of England in the 1880s, and she related social conflicts and conditions to the class structure and to the failure of political processes to come to terms with democratic individualism. In a subsequent book, *On Shame and the Search for Identity* (Harcourt Brace, 1958), Helen Merrell Lynd questioned the theories of Sigmund Freud and Talcott Parsons for their inability to come to terms with the role of social values in shaping the formation of the self. Her explanation of the relationship between the individual and society rested on the role of shame (the failure to achieve) as the basis of modern social life. Other writings by Merrell Lynd were published in *Toward Discovery* (1965). Increasingly she became more interested in history and in adding a female perspective to social analysis.

The Lynds' seminal research on Middletown remains a central text in community studies and its methodologies are still being replicated today (e.g. Caplow *et al.* 1982). Despite critiques (e.g. Stein 1960), the value of their detailed ethnography and politicised conceptual framework is in stark contrast to the mechanical, over-theorised, apolitical character of much contemporary sociology.

Further reading

Degan, Mary Jo 'Helen Merrell Lynd (1896–1982)', in M. J. Degan (ed.), Women in Sociology. A Bio-bibliographical Sourcebook (Greenwood Press, 1991), pp. 273–9.

Horowitz, Irving Louis 'Lynd, Robert S. and Helen Merrell', International Encyclopaedia of the Social Sciences: Biographical Supplement, 18, ed. D. Sills (Free Press, 1979), pp. 471–7.

Robert S. Lynd, Special issue on the work of Robert S. Lynd, Journal of the History of Sociology, 2 (1978/80), pp. 1–131.

J.C.

LYOTARD, Jean-François

Philosopher/political and cultural theorist	born France 1924–1998
Associated with	POSTMODERNISM ■ POST-STRUCTURALISM
Influences include	FREUD ■ LACAN ■ NIETZSCHE ■ WITTGENSTEIN ■ KANT
Shares common ground with	DERRIDA ■ FOUCAULT
Main works	ECONOMIE LIBIDINALE (1974, TRANS. LIBIDINAL ECONOMY, 1993)
	LA CONDITION POSTMODERNE: RAPPORT SUR LE SAVOIR (1979, TRANS. THE POSTMODERN CONDITION: A REPORT ON KNOWLEDGE, 1984)
	LE DIFFEREND (1983, TRANS. THE DIFFEREND: PHRASES IN DISPUTE, 1988)
	POLITICAL WRITINGS, TRANS. BILL READINGS AND PAUL GIEMAN, FOREWORD AND NOTES BY BILL READINGS, (1993)

JEAN-FRANÇOIS LYOTARD was appointed Professor of Philosophy at the University of Paris VIII (Vincennes) in 1972 and also taught at the University of California at Irvine. He was a founding member of the International College of Philosophy (Paris) and an original member of the radical Marxist group *Socialisme ou barbarie*, being head of its Algerian section for 12 years, before turning away from Marxism to philosophy in the late 1960s.

Lyotard's turn to philosophy and away from the strict orthodoxy of radical Marxism is best represented in *Economie libidinale*, but it is with *The Postmodern Condition* that Lyotard achieved international recognition as a theorist of postmodernism. Postmodernism in Lyotard's terms involves a radical break with the dominant culture and aesthetic, a critique and reappraisal of the underlying values and assumptions of the culture of the Enlightenment, and a different mode of economic and social organisation. He states 'I will use the term *modern* to designate any science that legitimises itself with reference to a metadiscourse . . . making explicit appeal to some grand narrative, such as the dialectics of Spirit, the hermeneutics of meaning, the emancipation of the rational or working subject, or the creation of wealth' (1984: xxii). By contrast, he defines the 'postmodern condition' as an 'incredulity towards meta-narratives', that is, a suspicion of the grand discourses of legitimation which purport to justify our institutions and practices.

Lyotard's major working hypothesis is that the status of knowledge changes as societies enter the post-industrial era and cultures enter the postmodern age. He argues that a set of transformations since the end of the nineteenth century have altered the game rules for science, literature and the arts and that particularly since the 1950s the new technologies – all language-related developments (cybernetics, informatics, telematics, computer languages) – have significantly impacted upon the two principal functions of knowledge, research and teaching. Knowledge has become the principal force of production changing the composition of the workforce. Its availability and exchange as an international commodity has become the basis of national competition in the global information economy. The commercialisation of knowledge will continue to widen the gap between North and South and between nation-states and the information-rich multinationals, thereby raising new legal, ethical and political problems. More than ever, knowledge becomes a question of government and the problem of legitimation necessarily comes to the fore: who decides what is 'true' or 'scientific'?

Lyotard (following Wittgenstein) provides an answer in terms of a pluralistic reading of language-games (or discourses) to advance an attack on the conception of universal reason (or universal 'scientific' discourse), of the unity of language and of the subject. There is no one reason (or discourse), only *reasons* (or discourses in the plural), where no one form of reason (or discourse) takes precedence over others. Where Jürgen Habermas and Critical Theory emphasise a bifurcation of reason into its instrumental (positivistic) and moral–practical forms, Lyotard emphasises the (postmodern) multiplicity and proliferation of forms of reason, each defined by the rules which constitute particular discourses or language-games. Each of the various types of utterance – denotative, prescriptive, performative – comprises a language-game, with its own body of rules. The rules are irreducible and there exists an incommensurability among different games. Further, Lyotard argues that the rules do not have a bedrock justification, nor do they carry with them their own legitimation: they are, rather, the object of a contract, explicit or not, between players which gives rise to an 'agonistics' of language. In this situation, where knowledge and power are two sides of the same question, the decision-makers proceed on the assumption that there is commensurability among different language-games. Increasingly, Lyotard suggests the game of science has fallen under the sway of another game, technology, whose goal is not truth or justice, but rather optimal performance (or efficiency) in terms of the system.

Lyotard develops this philosophical position and its political implications in *The Differend*, where he argues 'that a universal rule of judgement between heterogeneous genres is lacking in general' (p. xi), or that 'There is no genre whose hegemony over others would be just' (p. 158). A *differend*, as Lyotard defines it, is 'a case of conflict, between (at least) two parties, that cannot be equitably resolved for lack of a rule of judgement applicable to both arguments' (p. xi). Where multiple parties are involved from a variety of genres or discourse, each with a different perspective or argument, as is the case in the modernity/postmodernity debate, it is, perhaps, no wonder that there is no one ruling or hegemonic genre, no overarching metadiscourse, language-game or metanarrative, and no rule of judgement applicable to all arguments.

Further reading

Benjamin, A. (ed.) JUDGING LYOTARD, Routledge, 1992.
Bennington, G. (ed.) LYOTARD: WRITING THE EVENT, Manchester University Press, 1988.
Peters, M. (ed.) EDUCATION AND THE POSTMODERN CONDITION, Bergin & Garvey, 1995.
Readings, B. ART AND POLITICS: INTRODUCING LYOTARD, Routledge, 1992.

M.P.

MacINTYRE, Alasdair

Philosopher	born Scotland 1929—
Associated with	ETHICS ■ MODERNITY ■ CAUSALITY
Influences include	ARISTOTLE ■ AQUINAS ■ MARX
Shares common ground with	RICOEUR ■ TAYLOR ■ LASCH
Main works	AGAINST THE SELF-IMAGES OF THE AGE (1971)
	AFTER VIRTUE: A STUDY IN MORAL THEORY (1981)
	WHOSE JUSTICE? WHOSE RATIONALITY? (1988)
	THREE RIVAL VERSIONS OF MORAL ENQUIRY (1990)

THE WORK OF MacIntyre is centrally concerned with morality and the basic social, cultural and historical changes which have shaped our theorising about ethics. In an early study, *A Short History of Ethics* (1966), he traced the development of theories about morality from the Greeks to the present by emphasising the continuities and epistemic breaks in philosophical discourse. This book followed several others on Marxism and Christianity, Hume, the Unconscious and an apparently bewildering oscillation in political, academic and religious affiliation. And more shifts were to come. In reviewing MacIntyre's collected essays in 1971, Ernest Gellner commented that 'to lose one religion is understandable, to lose two is tolerable, but to lose several is gross carelessness'. However, it is fairer to see this early phase of MacIntyre's work as exploratory, partly in examining the issue of causality (and hence the underpinnings of most social science), and partly in establishing a meta-structure for understanding his central preoccupation with ethics. Both of these concerns involve the relationship between belief and action. In *Against the Self-Images of the Age*, the issues were examined through a series of articles which owed much to MacIntyre's ongoing preoccupation at the time with Marxism, Christianity and social philosophy as it dealt with belief systems. Thus he addressed such figures as Tawney, Marx, Trotsky, Lenin, Lukács, Stalin and Goldmann but also psychoanalysis and theology as professions. All of these essays hinge on teasing out the relationship between cause and effect. Did Stalin do what he did because he was a Socialist? No. '[The] purges and the trials were necessary because the history of the Bolsheviks, including the history of their theoretical positions, had to be rewritten so that the true nature of socialism could be forgotten and the Stalinist redefinition could reign unchallenged in a society where not the working class but the bureaucracy ruled.' Thus what a sociologist should do, as he expresses it later in a critical piece on Peter Winch, is to 'begin by a characterisation of a society in its own terms', otherwise 'we shall be unable to identify the matter that requires explanation'. In a series of pieces on the conceptions of 'is', 'ought', 'action' and 'morals' in the second part of the book, MacIntyre provides the philosophical groundwork for a critique of social science as it is professed, and hence a critique of rationality as the explanation for action, and with it a critique of the concept of value-free analysis.

Against the Self-Images of the Age was a watershed in MacIntyre's work. If one task was to understand each culture in its own terms, and if another was to understand the epistemic ruptures which created different frames of moral enquiry, then surely another issue was to evaluate the different frames. When *After Virtue* was published in 1981 it included most of the familiar themes except that Aristotle, who had been a shadowy figure in the earlier work, now assumed prominence. Most major philosophers of the Enlightenment and beyond had concerned themselves with reinterpreting philosophy in conjunction with theology and the then-current state of knowledge (Kant, Hegel, Marx and Nietzsche being the most prominent) and the starting point was invariably the Greeks. But which Greeks? Unlike the others, MacIntyre chose Aristotle rather than Socrates, the pre-Socratics or Plato, in part because Aristotle's work synthesises that of his predecessors, in part because he is the only Western philosopher whose influence is found strongly in Christianity (Aquinas), Judaism (Maimonides) and Islam (Averroës) – and also, parenthetically, in Marxism through Althusser – but much more centrally because in Aritstotle the Virtues are integral to the wellbeing of the individual, not as means–ends, but as the central feature of being. With the introduction of the Virtues, MacIntyre poses the central issue of the relationship of ethics to human behaviour. His argument is that the Enlightenment – and hence the entire Modern project – was a reaction to Aristotelianism and that the notion of the good could only be grounded in either instrumentality or essentialism. Aristotle's centrality was that he grounded his theorising on the understanding of human practices, thus the connection between practical intelligence and the virtues of character. This allows MacIntyre to reposition his critique of contemporary society by indicating that it does not cohere as a society at all. Instrumental reason has fundamentally no morality which comes from internal sense of value, but operates largely on the premiss of personal independence based on objective dependence. In this MacIntyre's work operates as a search for the knowable, liveable and moral community. In his most recent two books, these concerns are developed in the context of justice and pedagogy. In both he argues that there is no such thing as a rationality which is not the rationality of some tradition, and tradition necessitates a vibrant intellectual community which can articulate its concerns. His critique of contemporary law and justice as well as of universities argues that to talk seriously about moral concerns we need to respect the strength of the three great systems of knowing – the Aristotelian/Thomistic, the Encyclopedic/Enlightenment, and the Nietzschean genealogical. In *Three Rival Versions of Moral Enquiry*, he calls for universities to be established which are wholly within one or other of these traditions so that they can act as competitive intellectual systems and at the same time be critics of the instrumental reason of liberal/capitalist society. MacIntyre is one of the most sophisticated critics of modernity and postmodernity alike.

Further reading

Levine, D.H. 'Sociology After MacIntyre', AMERICAN JOURNAL OF SOCIOLOGY, 89: 3 1983.
McMylor, Peter ALASDAIR MACINTYRE: CRITIC OF MODERNITY, Routledge, 1994.
Sedgwick, P. 'An Ethical Dance: A Review of Alasdair MacIntyre's AFTER VIRTUE, in Ralph Miliband and John Saville (eds.), SOCIALIST REGISTER, New Left Books, 1982.

I.D.

McLUHAN, Marshall

Media and cultural critic	born Canada 1911–1980
Associated with	GLOBAL VILLAGE ■ HOT AND COLD MEDIA ■ MEDIUM IS THE MESSAGE
Influences include	RICHARDS ■ LEAVIS ■ INNIS
Shares common ground with	BAUDRILLARD ■ VIRILIO ■ BENJAMIN
Main works	THE MECHANICAL BRIDE (1951) THE GUTENBERG GALAXY (1962) UNDERSTANDING MEDIA (1964)

M cLUHAN THEORISED ABOUT the media and popular culture, arguing that the media is the main influence on culture. He distinguished three basic technological innovations in the history of the media. First, the invention of the phonetic alphabet. This transformed the primordial condition of sensory balance between smell, touch, sight, taste and sound. After the alphabet, primitive mankind became fixated upon visual culture, and the written word increasingly came to shape the human understanding of the real world. The second stage occurred in the sixteenth century with the invention of movable type, when the printing press extended the rule of visual culture by vastly multiplying texts and reproductions. Understanding and appreciation became concentrated in the eye. The basic principle of the printing press was repeatability. This is also the basic principle of the industrialisation. The Gutenberg revolution, argued McLuhan, was the foundation of the Industrial Revolution. The third stage occurred in 1844 with the invention of the telegraph. McLuhan sees this as the start of the electronic revolution. He argues that electronic forms of communication have the potential to restore the primordial balance between the senses and revitalise mankind. Print media are visual, mechanical, sequential, centred, univocal; electronic media are tactile, organic, reactive and discontinuous. He argued that television should be understood as an extension of the human central nervous system.

In this connection, he distinguished between hot and cold media. A hot medium excludes audience participation by providing high-definition data to the senses. A photograph or a lecture is hot because it presupposes limited audience participation. A cold medium is the opposite. It includes audience participation by providing low-definition data for the senses. Recorded music or seminar discussions are cool, because they demand extensive participation and interaction. McLuhan contends that for most of the media age the overwhelming majority of technologies have been hot, fragmented and exclusive. However, he defines television as a cool medium because it is inclusive and stimulates audience participation. Television and the concomitant electronic revolution in mass communications results in the retribalisation of society around common data and stimuli. But it is a mistake to regard retribalisation as unifying mankind.

In a famous metaphor, he argued that omnipresence and simultaneity of the media created 'the global village' in which national barriers and distances of time and space are erased. Critics argue that McLuhan's metaphor is utopian and idealistic. Yet McLuhan himself countered that he never believed the global village would be a place of harmony and uniformity. The withering of national boundaries and distinctions of time and space enlarges diversity and division. The global village is the opposite of peace and harmony. It was from McLuhan's interest in the media as a form of communication that one of the most celebrated catch-phrases of the 1960s was born: 'the medium is the message'. In coining it, McLuhan wanted to question the traditional privilege awarded to content in determining meaning. He insisted that the electronic revolution will inevitably increase the importance of form in making meaning.

Besides television, McLuhan's work on the effect of the media on popular culture included the analysis of cartoons, comic strips and advertisements. He analysed these consistently as ways in which the scale and form of human association and action are shaped. He believed that the new media change not our thoughts but the structure of our world. This sounds deterministic. However, it is not, because McLuhan sees cool media displacing hot media. Essential to the notion of cool media are the concepts of ambivalence and interpretation. Cool media do not privilege any voice or point of view. Rather, they emphasise the moral and cultural relativism of viewpoints.

Although he was frequently asked to morally evaluate the changes that he detected, he refused. He saw himself as a scientist whose business is to impart, in an objective and impartial fashion, the facts. The closest he came to an evaluation of the electronic communications revolution was this:

There are grounds for both optimism and pessimism. The extensions of man's consciousness induced by the electric media could conceivably usher in the millennium, but it also holds the potential for realizing the Anti-Christ . . . . Cataclysmic environmental changes are, in and of themselves, morally neutral; it is how we see them that will determine their ultimate psychic and social consequences. If we refuse to see them at all, we will become their servants.

McLuhan was a deliberately cool thinker in that his style of communication was typically opaque and deliberately encouraged audience participation. Many of his ideas have been criticised for lacking anthropological or historical accuracy. For example, his account of the primordial balance of the sense is largely an act of conjecture. The links he makes between the Gutenberg and Industrial Revolutions are also questionable. Yet a torrent of suggestive and often quite brilliant ideas flow through his work making him an indispensable resource in the study of media and popular culture.

Further reading

Kroker, A. TECHNOLOGY AND THE CANADIAN MIND: INNIS/MCLUHAN/GRANT, Montreal University Press, 1984.
McLuhan, E. and Zingrone, F. (eds.) ESSENTIAL MCLUHAN, Routledge, 1997.
Miller, J. MCLUHAN, Fontana, 1971.

C.R.

MALINOWSKI, Bronislav Kaspar

Social anthropologist	born Poland 1884–1942
Associated with	FUNCTIONALISM ▪ ETHNOGRAPHY ▪ SEXUALITY AND ANTHROPOLOGY
Influences include	FRAZER ▪ WESTERMARCK ▪ SELIGMAN ▪ HADDON ▪ RIVERS
Shares common ground with	EVANS-PRITCHARD ▪ FIRTH ▪ RADCLIFFE-BROWN
Main works	ARGONAUTS OF THE WESTERN PACIFIC: AN ACCOUNT OF NATIVE ENTERPRISE AND ADVENTURE IN THE ARCHIPELAGOES OF MELANESIAN NEW GUINEA (1922) THE SEXUAL LIFE OF SAVAGES (1929) CORAL GARDENS AND THEIR MAGIC (1935) A SCIENTIFIC THEORY OF CULTURE AND OTHER ESSAYS (1944)

BRONSILAV MALINOWSKI WAS born in Cracow, Poland, where he studied. His Ph.D. (completed in 1908 through the Jagellonian University) was in physics and mathematics but he was influenced by Frazer's *The Golden Bough* and began to study language and folklore. He also became interested in the work of the Finnish anthropologist, Edward Westermarck, who studied sexual taboos and marriage, in particular, the function of the incest taboo. In 1910, Malinowski joined the London School of Economics with the intention of doing fieldwork on the culture of the Australian Aborigines. He was inspired by the 1898 expedition of Haddon and Rivers to the Torres Straits and by the extensive fieldwork of Seligman. These anthropologists were among the first to undertake first-hand empirical studies rather than relying on accounts of travellers, missionaries and government officials.

Malinowski was one of the first anthropologists to insist that every student should do an intensive fieldwork study as part of their training, a requirement that became standard but was controversial at the time. The significance of Malinowski was a combination of his efforts to professionalise anthropological fieldwork method, his ethnographic observations in the West Pacific, his reflections on the discipline of anthropology, and his interdisciplinary work on the relationship between anthropology and psychology, religion and ethics.

He obtained funding to do fieldwork on the Mailu in the West Pacific and the Trobriand Islands. As a skilled linguist, he quickly learned the languages of the peoples he studied; this gave him considerable advantages in his work. These studies were important because he was able to implement his systematic approach to ethnography and fieldwork as well as to experiment with techniques of photography and recording as an aid to fieldnotes. Malinowski became particularly interested in the role of magic and sorcery in these societies because the centrality of such beliefs to cultural life confounded the usual mechanical accounts of kinship and social behaviour.

The publication of his book *Argonauts of the Western Pacific* secured his position as a professional anthropologist and he was offered a readership in 1924, and the first chair in anthropology at the University of London in 1927. Malinowski was a somewhat controversial figure, a highly gifted and charismatic teacher, and a team player, but he also exacted the highest standards from students and colleagues which resulted in ambivalent relationships (see Firth 1957, Gluckman 1947). Nonetheless, his lectures and courses attracted many students, researchers and professionals in cognate fields. His students included Edward Evans-Pritchard, Raymond Firth, Meyer Fortes, and Edmund Leach. His years in London were highly productive and he researched and wrote on a range of topics. In 1938, he went to the USA and accepted a chair at Yale. He took the opportunity to initiate new fieldwork on the Zapotec of Oaxaca (with Julio de la Fuente), but died in 1942 before this work came to fruition.

Malinowski's approach to fieldwork was characterised both by his genuine interest in primitive cultures but also his linguistic abilities which enabled him to get close to his subjects in the field. He was among the first to live among the people he was studying (a situation which had advantages and disadvantages). By advocating the strategy of living among the natives and learning their language, he pioneered the method of participant observation which was to become a standard ethnographic technique. He also pre-empted the use of film to record customs. His best-known work, *Argonauts of the Western Pacific*, related the structure of institutions, customs and codes to the cultural tapestry of the community. He was especially concerned to 'grasp the native's point of view, his relation to life, to realise *his* vision of *his* world'. He argued that by achieving a more empathetic understanding of native peoples and 'realising human nature in a shape very distant and foreign to us, we shall have some light shed on our own'. Malinowski's analysis of Trobriand society was based on his explanation of *kula*, a system of exchange. In *Coral Gardens and Their Magic* his focus was on the role of magic as a way of dealing with the 'chaos of facts'. This was regarded as his most sophisticated and self-critical work. Subsequent work pursued the themes of anthropology and psychology by taking ethnographic material as evidence for his generalisations. This work was also informed by his interest in Freudian theory and especially the work of Ernest Jones. In many ways, his move to America signalled the end of one era of research and heralded a more abstract approach to the analysis of culture.

Malinowski was a prolific researcher and writer on a numerous topics: on the Trobriand Islands (*Argonauts of the Western Pacific*, *The Sexual Life of Savages in North-Western Melanesia* and *Coral Gardens and Their Magic*); on magic and primitive culture (*Crime and Custom in Savage Society*, 1926, *Myth in Primitive Psychology*, 1926, and *Foundations of Faith and Morals*, 1936); on psychology and anthropology (*The Father in Primitive Psychology*, 1927); and on the discipline of anthropology ('Anthropology', 13th edn. of the *Encyclopaedia Britannica*, 1926, and *A Scientific Theory of Culture, and Other Essays*, 1944).

Malinowski's contribution to anthropology has been the subject of some debate. Undoubtedly he was part of the emergence of the discipline of British anthropology as a distinctive and professional school, particularly through his emphasis on methodology and his insights on providing functional explanations of social phenomena. But his ideas were complex and changing (as opposed to those of, say, Radcliffe-Brown) and his influence on anthropological thinking was more his breadth of vision and his challenges to accepted wisdom. Above all, his efforts to work from the data of intensive fieldwork to make sense of culture by distilling information into explanations of cultural behaviour contributed to his legacy as one of the founders of modern anthropology.

Further reading

Firth, Raymond (ed.) MAN AND CULTURE: AN EVALUATION OF THE WORK OF BRONISLAV MALINOWSKI, Harper, 1957.

Gluckman, Max AN ANALYSIS OF THE SOCIOLOGICAL THEORIES OF BRONISLAV MALINOWSKI, Oxford University Press, 1947.

Leach, Edmund 'Frazer and Malinowski', ENCOUNTER, 25: 5 1965, pp. 24–36.

J.C.

MANNHEIM, Karl

Sociologist	born Hungary 1887–1947
Associated with	SOCIOLOGY OF CULTURE ■ SOCIOLOGY OF KNOWLEDGE ■ IDEOLOGY
Influences include	MARX ■ M. WEBER ■ HUSSERL
Shares common ground with	LUKÁCS ■ SCHELER ■ A. WEBER
Main works	IDEOLOGY AND UTOPIA (1929) ESSAYS ON THE SOCIOLOGY OF CULTURE (1956)

MANNHEIM STUDIED PHILOSOPHY at the University of Budapest, after which, from 1919, he lived in Heidelberg in Germany where he was in contact with the Weber circle. He became Professor of Sociology at Frankfurt in 1928. In 1933 he fled the new regime in Germany and, invited by Laski, took up a position at the London School of Economics, where he stayed for 10 years. He died in 1947, aged 53.

Mannheim tried to establish a sociology as a synthesis of the ideas of Marx and Max Weber. An early doctoral thesis on forms of conservative thought opened a field of study which rejected either ahistorical approaches to culture, or historical accounts of ideas or cultural forms detached from social context. He studied the social and historical contexts of intellectuals in relation to styles and mentalities of thought, a project defined as a cultural sociology. If this was Marxist he did not follow intellectuals like Lukács into the communist movement under the spell of a communist utopia and imminent proletarian revolution; and if it was Weberian, he did not follow Weberians into a rejection of modern planning systems as fatal to democracy and inherently bureaucratic. For Mannheim sociology could and should play a crucial role in the creation of new institutions within a democratic framework, and to play a role in the creation of new central values destined to replace traditional ones destroyed in the process of modernisation. Thus Mannheim sought to resolve problems posed by Marx and Max Weber by defining the key problems of democratic cultures and outlining solutions for them. It led to a famous encounter with T. S. Eliot (see Eliot's *Notes Towards a Definition of Culture*, 1944).

Mannheim is probably most famous for his analysis of ideologies and utopias, as an aspect of a more general sociology of knowledge. This sociology, he sometimes, rather naively, suggests, has become aware of the true nature of the congruence of ideas and social reality, whereas ideologies and utopias are forms of thought in which there is a clear incongruence between representation and the actual social and historical situation. He provides a brief analysis of the crucial emergence of the concept of ideology through Kant, Hegel and Marx, to suggest the crucial significance of the experience of the French Revolution on European forms of historical consciousness: the effect was to make possible a form of understanding where thought was no longer conceived as autonomous and subject to an imminent logic, but was relative to the social situation of groups and social forces in conflictual situations.

Ideologies and utopias are essentially transcendent of their real situations: they are not, and do not play the role of, adequate social science. Ideologies are conceived here as constellations which, though different from social reality and even function to distort it, are not realisable as projects. They pose ideals which are used to justify a set of current practices in the presence of social mechanisms which function more or less effectively to manage the contradiction between these ideals and reality. Utopias, on the other hand, transcend reality but are characterised by attempts to change this reality towards the ideal. Utopias are thus associated with social classes which are in the process of ascent, or in crisis. Even here, however, the demarcation between ideology and utopia is often not clear cut: in the case of the bourgeois demand for freedom the utopian and ideological elements are closely interwoven, as the demand for freedom produced a framework for a new constrained form of free labour.

Mannheim outlined a picture of the changing configurations of the 'utopian mentality' in Europe from the Middle Ages in terms of four ideal types. The first is what he called orgiastic chiliasm, and is a form of early modern rebellion in which millenarian ideas become expressed by oppressed, lower strata groups. His main example is the Anabaptist experience of a sudden and immediate break from historical time into religious ecstasy, a type of orgiastic revolution quite unknown in medieval times. The second type, that of liberal humanist utopias suggested by the inevitable workings of a law of perfection or progress, as expressed by Condorcet, for example, makes the utopian form internal to the logic of history as its destiny. The third type is what he calls the conservative idea, which comes into existence only as a 'counter utopia' as it arises out of social groups whose positions have become insecure. Here, strangely perhaps, he notes that this utopia is indeed congruous with reality, which it tries to reveal as a necessary 'is'. But the representation is in tension since the utopia is not experienced in any simple linear historical time. The experience of the present has now a very distinctively new aspect: the past is conserved, or as Mannheim says, as a 'virtually present' in this utopia. His example is the pietistic reawakening in Germany after the Napoleonic Wars: here neo-Gothic revivals and cultural nostalgia were used to stimulate an inner illumination, a soft and sweet sentimentalism. Mannheim contrasts this with his fourth type, that of modern Communism. The distinctive feature here is that, added to a conservation of the dimension of the past, the future too has a virtual existence in the present. This form is exemplified in the thought of Engels, and the decisive break between Marxism and the older anarchist tradition of Bakunin. This new utopianism is concrete, deterministic, teleological, and its aesthetic tends to become realist, reflecting the aspirations of a new rising class, the modern proletariat which regards history as a 'controllable phenomenon'. Again, for Mannheim these are ideal types, and in fact some admixtures do occur: Bolshevism has its chiliastic aspects. Mannheim speculated on a post-utopian form of thought in the social sciences which he thought would tend to become simply a 'series of discrete technical problems'. He raises the post-modern paradox that with the destruction of the utopian dimension society has 'the highest degree of rational mastery of existence, (but) is left without any ideals'.

Further reading

Frisby, D. THE ALIENATED MIND, Routledge, 1983.
Kettler, D., Meja, V. and Stehr, N. KARL MANNHEIM, Open University Press, 1984.
Woldring, H. KARL MANNHEIM, St. Martin's Press, 1987.

M.G.

MARCUSE, Herbert

Philosopher	born Germany 1896–1979
Associated with	LIBERATION ■ FALSE NEEDS ■ ALIENATION
Influences include	HEGEL ■ SCHILLER ■ MARX
Shares common ground with	ADORNO ■ HORKHEIMER ■ HABERMAS
Main works	ONE-DIMENSIONAL MAN: STUDIES IN THE IDEOLOGY OF ADVANCED INDUSTRIAL SOCIETY (1964)
	EROS AND CIVILIZATION: A PHILOSOPHICAL INQUIRY INTO FREUD (1955)
	THE AESTHETIC DIMENSION: TOWARD A CRITIQUE OF MARXIST AESTHETICS (1978)

HERBERT MARCUSE IS most famous for his involvement in the civil rights and anti-war movements of the 1960s. His name became synonymous with the 'New Left', a generation of Marxists who saw that the Soviet experiment was not working, and who saw material comforts in Western industrialised societies as diversionary. Angela Davis was perhaps Marcuse's most famous student during this period.

But there clearly endures a less sensational scholarly side to Marcuse that is more comfortable with Hegel than with hippies. Marcuse's philosophical quest was for a 'pacified existence', an existence wherein individuals are 'at peace', not only with external nature, but within themselves and with others. Unfortunately, however, pacification is an elusive goal, and its apprehension seems ever more difficult, given surrounding conditions.

In his masterpiece, *One-Dimensional Man*, Marcuse discusses the conditions which prevent a more benign relationship with external nature. He argues that Western civilisation has consistently maintained an adversary relationship with nature under which humans sought to dominate what they believed to be an inscrutable and hostile environment. In the model of Odysseus, humanity has employed its rational capacities to outwit nature. Science has been the primary instrument of that wit, and science has been very successful in exploiting the resources of nature.

However, a detached look at the relationship between science and nature reveals that the adversary posture may be outmoded. The challenge of survival in nature has been won, and there is a window to consider relationships other than domination. However, may forces militate against such a perspective, and even though the progress and challenge of subsistence are over, the paradigm of domination distracts its participants (willingly) from considering new challenges and new forms of progress. The distractions come in the form of 'false needs', obsolescent trinkets of consumption that keep individuals in a state of suspended animation, prevented from experiencing the exhilaration and reward of pursuing a transcendent quality or image. Science now supports this arrested development with its operational thinking, whereby ambiguities are rendered irrelevant and concepts are redefined to comport with processes in the existing system.

But escaping the paradigm of external nature is not the only obstacle to a pacified existence. According to Freud, there are aspects of internal, psychic nature which must be dominated and repressed. Civilisation itself depends upon holding certain inclinations in check. The human psyche is plagued with Thanatos, the death instinct, and all its subsidiary inclinations to destruction. However, Marcuse chooses to enhance the life instinct, or Eros, thus minimising instinctual liabilities without repression. The death instinct is powerful only because human sensuality and erotic fulfilment have been sacrificed to the construction of civilisation. Just as the domination paradigm is outmoded in terms of the relationship with external nature, so is the repression paradigm outmoded in terms of the relationship with one's self. Living in an environment no longer considered hostile, individuals may feel safer in allowing their natural sensual inclinations to surface.

So, if the conditions for pacification are within reach, what can jolt humanity from its one-dimensional, repressive trance? Marcuse believes that a radical enhancement of human imagination, through immersion in the aesthetic experience, may be the answer. On the psychic front, the aesthetic imagination can take primitive erotic impulses (the only kind that are allowed in contemporary society) and expand them, through sublimation, into multifarious and complex forms of expression. Freud notes that the root of Eros is the pursuit of 'ever greater unities', and Marcuse sees no reason why, in a complex erotic environment, medicine or engineering could not be perceived and experienced as an erotic experience. Likewise, the aesthetic imagination may be what is needed to see through the constriction of contemporary technology, and the renewed imagination might be better prepared to place technology under priorities other than those of maximum protection of vested interests.

Further reading

Bokina, John and Lukes, Timothy J. (eds.) MARCUSE: FROM NEW LEFT TO NEXT LEFT, University Press of Kansas, 1994.
Kellner, Douglas HERBERT MARCUSE AND THE CRISIS OF MARXISM, University of California Press, 1984.

Lukes, Timothy J. THE FLIGHT INTO INWARDNESS: AN EXPOSITION AND CRITIQUE OF HERBERT MARCUSE'S THEORY OF LIBERATIVE AESTHETICS, Associated University Presses, 1985.

T.J.L.

MARSHALL, Alfred

Economist	born England 1842–1924
Associated with	MICROECONOMICS ■ NEOCLASSICAL ECONOMICS
Influences include	SMITH ■ RICARDO ■ MILL
Shares common ground with	KEYNES ■ BENTHAM
Main works	PRINCIPLES OF ECONOMICS (1890)
	INDUSTRY AND TRADE (1919)

BORN IN WANDSWORTH, London, in 1842, Alfred Marshall was the outstanding Anglo-Saxon economist of his time. After reading mathematics at St John's College, University of Cambridge, Marshall stayed on at St John's originally to teach mathematics, though in the next few years he developed an interest in metaphysics, ethics and economics. He was appointed to a special lectureship in moral science at St John's in 1868, but soon turned to the study of political economy. In 1875, Marshall went to the USA to observe the effects of tariff protection. He returned to England to spend four years as Principal of the University College of Bristol. In 1881, he spent a year in Italy, and then returned to Bristol in 1882 as a professor. He then spent a brief time as a Fellow of Balliol College, University of Oxford. From 1885 to 1908 he taught political economy at Cambridge.

Marshall's career as an economist was shaped by two key factors: a strong religious background and an aptitude for mathematics. Prior to his undergraduate studies, Marshall had planned to become a member of the clergy. By the late 1860s he had chosen instead a career as a teacher–scholar in economics, though his religious views were still to play an important role in his work.

Marshall was a humanitarian, with a strong desire to improve the plight of the poor. Although, as we shall see, Marshall made significant contributions to economic theory, he always held that the purpose of theory was to help remedy practical problems. Indeed, he hoped that the study of economics would lead to an improvement in the wellbeing of society as a whole. He maintained a concern for social issues throughout his career, and contributed to the work of official commissions dealing with monetary questions, taxation and poverty.

Marshall is regarded as the father of neoclassical economics, a tradition which emerged towards the end of the nineteenth century. In contrast with the preceding classical and Marxist schools, neoclassical economics focused upon microeconomic rather than macroeconomic questions, and in particular was most concerned with the way in which competitive markets allocate resources between alternative uses.

Marshall's work made a very significant contribution to the neoclassical movement. His single most important achievement was to combine the classical economics of Smith and Ricardo with the mathematical marginal analysis of the neoclassical school, to provide an analytical framework which remains a relevant basis for understanding current economic theory. A key part of this framework related to the theory of prices. The classical economic view was embodied in Smith's argument that a product had two prices: its market price at which it changed hands, and its 'natural price' or 'value' which was based on the cost of production. Later, Jevons and others argued that it was demand, or more specifically, marginal utility, rather than supply which determined prices. Marshall combined these two views into a unified theory of price determination, in which prices were formed by the interactions between both demand and supply.

Marshall was keen to ensure that his work had practical relevance, and despite Marshall's mathematics training, and in sharp contrast with many neoclassical economists of the time, he recognised the importance of communicating economic findings in everyday language. Much of the mathematical support for his work was, therefore, presented only in footnotes or appendices. He also spent many years trying out his concepts on students and colleagues before publishing his work.

Marshall had very great influence on the following generation of economists, including John Maynard Keynes, his most gifted pupil at Cambridge. Much of his work still serves today as a framework for understanding microeconomics.

Further reading

Homan, P.T. ALFRED MARSHALL IN CONTEMPORARY ECONOMIC THOUGHT, Harper, 1928.
Keynes, J.M. ALFRED MARSHALL IN ESSAYS AND SKETCHES IN BIOGRAPHY, Meridian, 1956.
Pigou, A.C. (ed.), MEMORIALS OF ALFRED MARSHALL, Kelley & Millman, 1956.
Viner, J. 'Marshall's Economics in Relation to the Man and His Times', AMERICAN ECONOMIC REVIEW, 31 June 1941.

M.D.

MARX, Karl

Philosopher/social theorist	born Germany 1818–1883
Associated with	HISTORICAL MATERIALISM ■ DIALECTICAL MATERIALISM ■ REVOLUTION
Influences include	HEGEL ■ RICARDO ■ SAINT-SIMON
Shares common ground with	ENGELS ■ LENIN ■ GRAMSCI
Main works	THE GERMAN IDEOLOGY (WITH FRIEDRICH ENGELS, 1845)
	COMMUNIST MANIFESTO (WITH FRIEDRICH ENGELS, 1848)
	A CONTRIBUTION TO THE CRITIQUE OF POLITICAL ECONOMY (1859)

KARL MARX'S FATHER had turned from Judaism and assimilated into a Pietist community in Westphalia. Marx went through an intense Christian phase before going to Berlin to study law and philosophy, where he came into contact with the movement of 'young Hegelians'. He married in 1843, and moved to Paris where he encountered the debates of the utopian socialists. He met Friedrich Engels in the mid-1840s, with whom he struck up a lifelong intellectual partnership dedicated to scientific socialism.

The French government expelled Marx, who moved to Brussels, where he was expelled again. He moved on to London in 1849, where he spent the rest of his life working partly as a journalist but mainly as a writer supported by funds from Engels. His notoriety was renewed world-wide when he supported the Paris Commune in 1871, arguing that it was the realisation of his ideas of proletarian dictatorship.

Marx's writings have formed one of the most influential contributions to the social theory of culture, even though Marx wrote comparatively little on cultural analysis as such. Parts of an early study of the art of the Pietist 'awakening' in Germany were published, and have been called Marx's 'lost aesthetic' (Rose). And aspects of Marx's philosophy and social theory have been used as the starting point of many different schools of Marxist analysis. What they have in common is a theoretical framework which claims to be materialist, historical, and which makes the political and cultural class struggle arising from an economic infrastructure central to the analysis. There is, then, in the Marxist tradition, a tendency to reduce cultural to economic practice, and a number of different means of trying to prevent this have been elaborated in the major schools of Marxism. But crucial to Marxism is the view that modern society is dominated by a capitalist mode of production whose own logic produces the conditions for the rise to power of a bourgeois ruling class. This class reproduces its conditions of existence – the exploitation of an industrial proletariat of wage-earners – through a political state (a legal and armed repressive organisation) and through a system of ruling ideas and culture. This new socio-economic system, capitalism, produces in turn the agency, the proletariat, of a new revolution. This revolutionary process is not determined by progressive reason, or cultural evolution, which are super-structural features, but by contradictions arising in the economic, the material, basis of modern society.

In 1857 Marx wrote notes on the problem of art which simplified the issue: he posed the question in terms of the socio-technical conditions of art: is Greek art possible where there are self-acting mules? He noted that 'all mythology subdues, controls and fashions the forces of nature in the imagination; it disappears therefore when real control over these forces is established'. But Marx expressly notes that the real problem is not that of understanding Greek art in relation to its technology, but why this art still gives aesthetic pleasure and is still a 'standard and unattainable ideal'. This acknowledgement of the vitality of Greek art is a constant theme in Marx's notes on aesthetics: his lost aesthetic may well have been an attempt to try to show that the vitality of pagan forms continued into early Christianity. This analysis would then have been used to criticise the reactionary Pietist movement in art in Germany in the 1830s, particularly the neo-Gothic style of the Nazarenes headed by Peter Cornelius, by supporting the positions of Heine, Feuerbach and Bauer who developed a version of Hegelian Helenism. The critique of religion and of religious art was not, then, in Marx's writings an absolute one: there is an attempt, many times referred to, to stress the importance of the relative autonomy of aesthetics while at the same time indicating the political significance of particular aesthetic movements.

Further reading

Lifshitz, M. THE PHILOSOPHY OF ART OF KARL MARX, Pluto, 1973.
Nelson, C. and Grossberg, L. (eds.) MARXISM AND THE INTERPRETATION OF CULTURE, Macmillan, 1988.
Rose, M. MARX'S LOST AESTHETIC, Cambridge University Press, 1988.

M.G.

MAUSS, Marcel

Sociologist anthropologist	born France 1872–1950
Associated with	SOCIAL TOTALITY ▪ ETHNOLOGY ▪ SOCIOLOGY OF RELIGION ▪ HABITUS
Influences include	DURKHEIM ▪ MALINOWSKI ▪ KANT
Shares common ground with	LÉVI STRAUSS ▪ BOURDIEU ▪ DUMONT ▪ GRANET ▪ FEBVRE ▪ BLOCH
Main works	THE GIFT: THE FORM AND REASON FOR EXCHANGE IN ARCHAIC SOCIETIES (1925, TRANS. 1950, REPRINTED 1990) (ORIGINALLY PUBLISHED AS 'ESSAI SUR LE DON, FORME ET RAISON DE L'ÉCHANGE DANS LES SOCIÉTÉS ARCHAÏQUES', ANNÉE SOCIOLOGIQUE, NEW SERIES I (1925), PP. 30–186)
	'TECHNIQUES OF THE BODY', ECONOMY AND SOCIETY 2 (1973), PP. 70–88 (ORIGINALLY PUBLISHED AS 'LES TECHNIQUES DU CORPS', JOURNAL DE PSYCHOLOGIE NORMAL ET PATHOLOGIQUE, PARIS, ANNÉE XXXII (1935), PP. 271–93; REPRINTED IN SOCIOLOGIE ET ANTHROPOLOGIE, PRESSES UNIVERSITAIRES DE FRANCE, 1936)
	SOCIOLOGIE ET ANTHROPOLOGIE (2nd EDN, PRESSES UNIVERSITAIRES DE PARIS, 1960)

M ARCEL MAUSS WAS the nephew of Emile Durkheim and became his student then colleague and interpreter. Both exemplified the work of the French School of Sociology that is best remembered through its journal, *Année Sociologique*. Founded by Durkheim and Mauss, and largely edited by the latter, the journal was devoted to developing a distinctive approach to the analysis of social phenomena that was interdisciplinary and emphasised the collective basis of social life. The journal published the work of members of the school and appeared in three disjointed series. The interruptions were largely a consequence of the two world wars which decimated the school. Casualties from the First World War included Henri Hubert, André Durkheim, Robert Hertz, Antoine Bianconi, Georges Gelly, Maxime David and Jean Reynier. Durkheim himself died in 1917. The Second World War and Nazi occupation of Paris also resulted in the death of close friends and colleagues. In response, Mauss devoted himself to completing unfinished works of his colleagues with the consequences that his own publications were far less than his immensely fertile intellectual output could have achieved. Yet his legacy has survived in two ways: as the co-ordinator of the body of work associated with the *Année*; and through the long-term uptake of his major publications, in particular, *The Gift*.

Mauss was born in Epinal, France. He studied philosophy under Durkheim at Bordeaux and history of religion at the École Pratique des Hautes Études in Paris. In 1902, he accepted a Chair as Professor of Primitive Religion at the Ecole, where he remained throughout his career. In 1925, he co-founded (and co-directed) the Institut d'Ethnologie de l'Université de Paris, which simulated the development of fieldwork-based anthropology by young academics. Between 1931 and 1939 he also taught at the Collège de France. After the war, his productivity declined as a result of the traumas to his personal and professional life.

The figure of Mauss is important as the link between the sociology of Durkheim and contemporary French sociologists, such as Claude Lévi-Strauss, Pierre Bourdieu, Marcel Granet and Louis Dumont, as well as the historical approaches of Lucien Febvre and Marc Bloch (who founded the journal *Annales d'histoire économique et sociale* in 1929). In addition to being a sociologist, Mauss was an historian of religion and a mythologist. Although he adopted a similar approach to Durkheim, Mauss's analytic framework has been credited with being more supple, more appropriate to apply to empirical studies and more fruitful. The keynote of his approach was the notion of 'total social facts', that is, attempting to relate 'collective representations' (ways of thinking and acting) to fundamental characteristics of social organisation. Mauss is best known for a few important essays, although he wrote prolifically with other members of *Année* on a broad array of topics. His publications fall into two broad categories: major ethnological works on exchange, body techniques and the category of the person; and on social science methodology (see *Sociologie et anthropologie*; and 'Fragment d'un plan de sociologie generale descriptive', *Annales sociologiques*, Series A, 1934).

Mauss's most important work was his study of the gift as the basis of exchange in primitive societies (*The Gift*). This is still read by students of anthropology and has had a particular resonance in the field of economic anthropology. This work expands his idea of the total social fact by treating exchange as a symbolic system which could be deciphered in terms of the social relationships (alliances) that were inscribed within the process of gift giving and receiving. Mauss argued that the gift was a fundamental – if not universal – basis of social relationships in all societies. Forms of exchange were impor-tant less for the material value of the objects exchanged than for their work in cementing and ordering social relations. Thus gifts were more significant as group phenomena than as individual acts of giving, receiving and reciprocat-ing. He suggested that gifts were both symbols and expressions of social relations and thus their exchange was obligatory as the means of actualising group alliances – be they organisational, legal, religious, moral, mythological or aesthetic.

Related to this study was Mauss's work on magic (*A General Theory of Magic,* trans. R. Brain, Routledge, 1972; first published as 'Esquisse d'une théorie générale de la magie', *Année Sociologique*, 7, 1904) in which he argued that the importance of magic was understanding the power relations that underpinned the status of the magician, and that this was what enabled magic to be believed and to work. Mauss proposed that magic was not about collective misrecognition or mysticism but about the properties of the game of magic that structure its rules of operation. The magician assumes the powers associated with those operations, and can use that magic power legitimately or illegitimately. As with other work, Mauss perceived magical exchanges as a totality – as behavioural indicators of total social movements or activities. Simultaneously, in this work and others, Mauss drew on his prodigious knowledge of ethnographic material and placed it within his rigorous sociological method and contextual theories.

In a similar way, Mauss tackled the topic of sacrifice (Henri Hubert and Marcel Mauss, *Sacrifice and its Function*, trans. W.D. Halls, foreword by E. Evans-Pritchard, University of Chicago Press, 1968; first published as 'Essai sur la nature et la fonction du sacrifice', *Année Sociologique*, 2, 1899). They argued that sacrifice involved processes of sacralising and desacralising, in which the former directed the holy towards the person or object, and the latter away from a person or object. This pre-empted his work on the category of the person (*Une catégorie de l'esprit humain: la notion de personne, celle de 'moi'*, 1938; trans. M. Carrithers and S. Lukes and republished in 1985) and techniques of the body ('Les techniques du corps', *Journal de psychologie normal et pathologique*, 32, 1935; trans. B. Brewster and republished in 1973). Mauss proposed that the body should be understood not as a natural given but as the product of specific training in attributes, deportments and habits. He argued that body techniques were at once biological, sociological and psychological, and that their analysis must be able to apprehend these elements simultaneously. Accordingly, Mauss defined the person not as the locus of physical manifestations and individual psychology, but as a category of thought, and as the articulation of a particular culture's embodiment of law and morality. In this sense, the person was constituted by a set of roles (*personnages*) which were occupied and executed through the deportment and exercise of specific body techniques and attributes. As Carrithers has put it, the person was the incarnation of 'a fixed stock of roles'. While this view was and remained highly controversial at the time, because it conflicted with the psychologisation of individuals and social behaviour, Mauss's terms have persisted among some sociological approaches. His terms, persona and habitus have been taken up in recent sociological and cultural studies, particularly by Pierre Bourdieu.

Throughout his life, Mauss applied his knowledge of ethnology to problems of classification in anthropology and sociology (see, for example, Emile Durkheim and Marcel Mauss, *Primitive Classification*, trans. and ed. R. Needham, University of Chicago Press, 1963; first published as 'Quelques formes primitives de classification. Contribution à l'étude des réprésentations collectives', *Année Sociologique*, 6, 1903). In this work, Durkheim and Mauss sought to find correspondences between social and symbolic classifications (in time, space, class and status) among different preliterate societies. The existence of such relations raised the possibility that social organisation was as much the product of cognitive processes as physical arrangements.

Given his extraordinary breadth and depth of knowledge, the ideas of Mauss had a major influence on French anthropology and social science. For example, he taught ethnographic method to first generation of French anthropology students (see *Manuel d'ethnographie*, Payot, 1947). He also influenced many British anthropologists including Radcliffe-Brown, Malinowski, Evans-Pritchard and Firth. In addition to his academic activities, Mauss embraced the role of the public intellectual and became a well-known left-wing political activist and journalist for *L'Humanité*, advocating the emancipation of the human spirit.

The influence of Mauss has persisted and has informed recent French social science. Since English translations have become available, the ideas of Mauss have also had a significant impact on Anglophile post-structuralist perspectives in anthropology, cultural studies and cultural history; especially recent work on the body and the category of the person. He has influenced post-structuralist and post-Foucauldian intellectuals because he combines an ethnographic approach with a contextualisation that is historical, sociological and psychological. Indeed, it is arguable that Mauss succeeded in executing anthropology in its original intended form.

Further reading

Carrithers, Michael, Collins, Steven and Lukes, Steven THE CATEGORY OF THE PERSON, Cambridge University Press, 1985.
Evans-Pritchard, Edward A HISTORY OF ANTHROPOLOGICAL THOUGHT, Faber & Faber, 1981.
Fournier, Marcel MARCEL MAUSS: DURKHEIM'S NEPHEW, MARCEL MAUSS AND THE FRENCH SCHOOL OF SOCIOLOGY, Fayard, 1994.
Lévi-Strauss, Claude, INTRODUCTION TO THE WORK OF MARCEL MAUSS, Freeman, Barbara (trs.), Routledge & Kegan Paul, 1983, originally published as 'Introduction à l'oeuvre de Marcel Mauss', in Marcel Mauss, SOCIOLOGIE ET ANTHROPOLOGIE, Press Universitaires de France [1950] 2nd edn 1960.

J.C.

MEAD, Margaret

Cultural anthropologist	born USA 1901–1978
Associated with	GENDER ROLES ▪ CULTURAL CHANGE ▪ BIOLOGICAL–CULTURAL INFLUENCES
Influences include	BOAS ▪ BENEDICT ▪ RADCLIFFE-BROWN ▪ BATESON
Shares common ground with	TURNER ▪ GEERTZ
Main works	COMING OF AGE IN SAMOA (1928) MALE AND FEMALE: A STUDY OF THE SEXES IN A CHANGING WORLD (1949) CULTURE AND COMMITMENT: A STUDY OF THE GENERATION GAP (1970)

MARGARET MEAD is one of anthropology's most controversial figures who is best known for her well-publicised views on the sexual freedom of women in Polynesia. More generally, her work on the transition from childhood to adulthood, acquisition of gender roles, and rites of passage to sexuality was widely disseminated within academia and amongst the general public. She graduated from Barnard College in 1923 where she was taught by Franz Boas and Ruth Benedict, both of whom were lifelong influences on her work. She completed an MA in psychology in 1924 and a Ph.D. in anthropology in 1929. Central to Mead's career was the active encouragement she received from her family and mentors to excel educationally, and subsequently to enter a male-dominated profession which entailed undertaking fieldwork in remote places. As such, Mead became an important role-model for subsequent generations of American women.

Mead's anthropology was the product of extensive fieldwork in the South Pacific during which time she was attached to the American Museum of Natural History and, later, Columbia University. Throughout her career, she received many distinctions and awards; becoming president of the American Association for the Advancement of Science in 1975 (only the second woman to hold the position) and being elected to the National Academy of Sciences in the same year. As well as a prolific writer, Mead became a popular public speaker who related her fieldwork experiences to the challenges and crises of the modern world. Not only did she promote controversial views within academia (which have continued after her death) but she had a major influence on changing ideas about adolescence and sexuality. She has been described 'as a major second-generation link between Franz Boas, founder of American anthropology, and today's third and fourth generations of American cultural anthropologists' (Yans-McLaughlin 1988: 258) and, during the 1930s and 1940s, arguably the most famous anthropologist in the world.

Of her forty four published books, the best known is *Coming of Age in Samoa*, which argued that Samoan girls made an easy transition into adulthood because sex and sexuality were openly discussed and practised. At least, this has become the best-known element of Mead's work. In fact, the leitmotif of her fieldwork and publications was exploring complex patterns of interaction between biological and cultural determinants of behaviour, of which sexuality was just one facet. She was in essence a cultural relativist who argued that each culture could only be understood on its own terms and comprehended as a product of the interaction between biological and cultural factors that framed the particular patterning of society and lifestyle. She followed up her Samoan study with studies of the Arapesh, Mundugumor and Tchambuli in New Guinea, and fieldwork in Bali, which culminated in *Growing Up in New Guinea* (1930) and *Sex and Temperament in Three Primitive Societies* (1935). From this research, Mead proposed a schema of culturally defined temperamental expectations for men and women which formed the basis of her belief in the cultural variability of maleness and femaleness (*Male and Female*).

Lesser known is Mead's work during the Second World War when she was employed to apply her anthropological insights to improving the morale of American service personnel and citizens by developing their sense of national identity and responsibility. During this time, she backpedalled on her recognition of the biological determinants of culture in the light of Hitler's extreme theories and activities in this area.

In the post-war period, she resumed her fieldwork and publishing, increasingly relating her theories to contemporary American cultural issues such as the generation gap, educational opportunities for women, the legalisation of marijuana, and racism. She also reflected on the methodologies and relevance of anthropology for studying culture, especially promoting the work of Ruth Benedict (*Ruth Benedict*, 1974). She was especially concerned to sharpen the tools of cultural analysis employed by anthropologists, in particular, by improving the reliance on and validity of participant observation, and introducing techniques of visual anthropology. While this enhanced the accessibility of her work and created contemporary relevance with emerging fields of ethnographic studies and sociology, Mead was a somewhat controversial figure among anthropologists, some of whom accused her of impressionistic work that lacked rigour and scientific precision.

The greatest controversy exploded shortly after her death when Derek Freeman (1983) criticised her Samoan fieldwork. The basis of his criticisms was that Mead had done shoddy fieldwork and been too easily taken in by what informants had told her. In fact, he claimed, Samoan girls had mischievously told her lies and exaggerated their experiences and views, and Mead had been only too keen to believe them because their stories confirmed her theories.

On the contrary, Freeman argued that his own extensive fieldwork showed that, rather than exhibiting little conflict, aggression and sexual angst, Samoa had a high incidence of rape and that Samoans held extremely puritanical views about sex. Given the wide dissemination of Mead's ideas and their influence on contemporary notions of adolescence and sexuality, what might have been an arcane dispute between anthropologists became a *cause célèbre* (see Caton 1990). The dispute remains unresolved, though it has reignited the 'biology versus culture' debate, clouded the reputation of Mead, and contributed to a re-evaluation of the role of anthropologists in cross-cultural analysis. Nonetheless, Mead remains a major figure in anthropology who created new audiences for its methods and insights.

Further reading

Bateson, Mary WITH A DAUGHTER'S EYE: A MEMOIR OF MARGARET MEAD AND GREGORY BATESON, William Morrow, 1984.
Caton, Hiram THE SAMOA READER: ANTHROPOLOGISTS TAKE STOCK, University Press of America, 1990.
Freeman, Derek MARGARET MEAD AND SAMOA: THE MAKING AND UNMAKING OF AN ANTHROPOLOGICAL MYTH, Harvard University Press, 1983.
Mead, Margaret 'Introduction', in Joan Gordon (ed.), MARGARET MEAD: THE COMPLETE BIBLIOGRAPHY 1925–1975, Mouton, 1976, pp. 1–21.
Yans-McLaughan, Virginia 'Margaret Mead', in Ute Gacs, Aisha Khan, Jerrie McIntyre and Ruth Weinberg (eds.), WOMEN ANTHROPOLOGISTS: A BIOGRAPHICAL DICTIONARY, Greenwood Press, 1988, pp. 252–60.

J.C.

MERLEAU-PONTY, Maurice

Philosopher	born France 1908–1961
Associated with	PHENOMENOLOGY ■ *LEBENSWELT* ■ BODY
Influences include	HUSSERL ■ KOJÈVE ■ SAUSSURE
Shares common ground with	SARTRE ■ LÉVI-STRAUSS ■ LACAN
Main works	PHENOMENOLOGY OF PERCEPTION (1962)
	THE VISIBLE AND THE INVISIBLE (1968)
	THE PROSE OF THE WORLD (1974)

MERLEAU-PONTY CURRENTLY enjoys the reputation of being the most important French philosopher of phenomenology in the twentieth century. It is a status he has won from his rival Jean-Paul Sartre. Merleau-Ponty disagreed with Sartre's defence of hardline Communism in the Soviet Union. His current ascendancy is perhaps bound up with what many now see as a prescient and courageous stand against the authoritarianism of the French Left between the 1930s and 1950s.

Merleau-Ponty graduated in philosophy from the École Normale Supérieure in 1930. He was deeply influenced by Kojève's famous lectures on Hegel. This led to a discovery of the work of Husserl, who was the decisive influence on Merleau-Ponty's phenomenology. During the Second World War he fought in the infantry and was captured and tortured by the Nazis. Between 1945 and 1952 he worked on Sartre's journal *Les Temps Modernes*. In 1949 he was appointed to the Chair of Child Psychology at the Sorbonne and in 1952 he was elected to the Chair of Philosophy at the Collège de France. It was a post he retained until his sudden and early death in 1961.

Merleau-Ponty argued against positivism. He maintained that lived-in experience (the *Lebenswelt*) is the relevant context in which philosophy must operate. Following Husserl, he argued that phenomenology is the study of essences. The purpose of phenomenology is to articulate transcendental essences in human existence which have been obscured by the 'natural attitude'. The subversive aim of phenomenology is to reawaken knowledge of the life-world which has been lost or veiled in the obscurantism of scientific thought and practice and 'common sense'. Merleau-Ponty's battle-cry was to 'rediscover the strangeness of the world'.

Human perception is the sole means through which human beings can know themselves. *Contra* Sartre, Merleau-Ponty argued that there are important limits to freedom. The primary and most obvious limit is set by the human body. The body provides the *innate structure* in limiting human experience. In this connection, Merleau-Ponty argued against the Cartesian split between mind and body. Perception is always *embodied* and the natural attitude which separates the mind from the body is a fallacy. At the same time the body is not separated from the world but, on the contrary, is always situated in the world. He also recognised that culture and language impose limits on perception. In his later work, especially *The Prose of the World*, he follows Saussure in holding that language springs from a diacriticial relationship between signs. It is entirely consistent with his view of the embodied character of lived experience that he insisted that language must be viewed as enacted rather than the 'pre-given' crucible out of which meaning and interpretation flow. Merleau-Ponty privileges *parole* over *langue*.

Merleau-Ponty's methodology argued that the transcendental sphere could be opened to human consciousness by *bracketing* out the natural attitude. Bracketing revealed the relationship of the *cogito* in being in the world which is the basis of all philosophical 'essences'. *Cogito* is the capacity of each human subject to remove itself from involvement in the world and reflect upon the relationship between the self and the world. The later work also announces a new wariness in attributing intentionality to consciousness. Merleau-Ponty sees transcendental subjectivity as the Achilles heel of phenomenology. To correct it, he insists on the 'intentionality within being' which precedes consciousness. This practice does not reach back *à la* Husserl to subjective operations as the ultimate foundation of the world. Instead, it refuses to acknowledge consciousness as the foundation of the life-world.

Yet he has been criticised in this respect for engaging in little more than word magic. Critics have pointed out that in his philosophy incarnate consciousness behaves no differently from transcendent consciousness. In this way, Merleau-Ponty is attacked for restating the very idealism from which he claims to have departed.

Further reading

Burke, P. and van der Veken, J. (eds.) MERLEAU-PONTY IN CONTEMPORARY PERSPECTIVE, Academic Books, 1991.
Langer, M. MERLEAU-PONTY'S PHENOMENOLOGY OF PERCEPTION, Macmillan, 1989.
Schmidt, J. MAURICE MERLEAU-PONTY: BETWEEN PHENOMENOLOGY AND STRUCTURALISM, Macmillan, 1985.

C.R.

MERTON, Robert K.

Sociologist	born USA 1910—
Associated with	FUNCTIONALISM ■ THEORIES OF THE MIDDLE RANGE ■ SOCIOLOGY OF SCIENCE
Influences include	DURKHEIM ■ WEBER ■ PARSONS ■ THOMAS
Shares common ground with	LAZARSFELD ■ MILLS
Main works	SCIENCE, TECHNOLOGY AND SOCIETY IN SEVENTEENTH CENTURY ENGLAND (1935) SOCIAL THEORY AND SOCIAL STRUCTURE (1951) SOCIOLOGY OF SCIENCE (1973) CONTEMPORARY SOCIAL PROBLEMS (WITH ROBERT NISBET, 1973)

A STUDENT OF PARSONS at Harvard, Merton moved to Columbia in 1941 and became associated with the Bureau of Applied Social Research, or the Columbia School.

Merton's contribution falls into three areas: (1) sociology of science; (2) sociology of crime and deviance; (3) sociological theory. In his doctoral thesis, Merton revisited a theoretical terrain pioneered by Weber in his *Protestant Ethic and the Spirit of Capitalism*: how religious ideas are linked to areas of social activity. Weber had suggested a strong – some interpret it as causal – relationship between Protestant beliefs and the economic activity that gave rise to capitalism. Merton's painstaking research (including piecing together biographical details on scientists) highlighted a complimentarity between puritanical Protestant beliefs and science, which developed rapidly in the seventeenth century. The Protestant emphasis on scriptural interpretation by individuals, as opposed to the acceptance of dogma, was entirely congruent with the investigations and experimentations that underlay science and technology. In demonstrating that science and the knowledge it generates are products of historical conditions, Merton made arguably the first major contribution to what became known as the sociology of science.

His work on deviance acknowledged a debt to Durkheim, whose structural–functionalism was Merton's favoured theoretical framework. Merton argued that deviance is most likely to occur when there is a discrepancy between culturally prescribed goals and the legitimate means of obtaining them. 'Money has been consecrated as a value in itself,' observed Merton of North America's materialism in the 1940s. Americans were 'bombarded on every side by precepts which affirm the right or, often the duty of retaining the goal'. Those who were not equipped to attain the goal would experience 'strain' and so adapt other methods of achieving the goal. Merton's version of 'anomie theory' suggested five modes of adaptation, one of which he described as 'innovation': in this case, the goal of material success was accepted, but the legitimate means were abandoned in preference for illegitimate ones. So, theft might replace hard work as the means for achieving goals.

Merton's work on deviance was an example of what he called a 'theory of the middle range'. He had practised sociology amid an intellectual atmosphere dominated by Parsons's systems theory. Merton mistrusted the larger claims of such grand schemes, but was also uncomfortable for the atheoretical empiricism that lacked generalisability. His alternative was to examine aspects of society, always using functional analysis. Merton's work on bureaucracies modified the earlier work of Weber by empirically demonstrating the dysfunctional as well as functional aspects of the complex organisations that were dominating Western culture. For example, strict adherence to bureaucratic rules may lead to rigidity and inefficiency. According to Merton, some social functions are intended and recognised as such; these are known as manifest functions. Others are unintended and unrecognised; these are latent functions.

Perhaps the most enduring addition Merton made to our vocabulary was the self-fulfilling prophecy, which he introduced in an *Antioch Review* (vol. 13, 1948; reprinted in *Social Theory and Social Structure* and several other anthologies). Merton's seminal argument began with W.I. Thomas's proposition, 'If men define situations as real, they are real in their consequences.' Merton offered an example of North American whites who had genuinely-felt beliefs about the typical migrated black worker from the non-industrial South: 'Undisciplined in traditions of trade unionism and the art of collective bargaining . . . a traitor to the working class.' Whites saw these as 'cold hard facts' and acted on them, excluding blacks from unions so that the only way in which blacks could find work was as scab labour; this served to confirm the whites' original beliefs. 'The self-fulfilling prophecy is, in the beginning a *false* definition of the situation evoking a new behavior which makes the originally false conception come true', wrote Merton. The concept has had many applications, especially in the field of education. R. Rosenthal and L. Jacobson's *Pygmalion in the Classroom* (Holt, Rinehart & Winston, 1969) is a particularly telling study.

Further reading

Clark, J. Modgilla, C. and Modgilla, S. (eds.) ROBERT K. MERTON: CONSENSUS AND CONTROVERSY, Falmer, 1990.

Crother, Charles ROBERT K. MERTON, Ellis Horwood, 1987.
Mullan, Bob SOCIOLOGISTS ON SOCIOLOGY, 2nd edn, Avebury, 1996.

E.C.

MICHELS, Robert

Sociologist	born Germany 1876–1936
Associated with	ÉLITES ■ IRON LAW OF OLIGARCHY
Influences include	MACHIAVELLI ■ WEBER
Shares common ground with	MOSCA ■ PARETO
Main works	POLITICAL PARTIES (1911, TRANS. 1949)
	FIVE LECTURES ON POLITICAL SOCIOLOGY (1949)

AFTER A PERIOD of political activity in Germany, Michels pursued an academic career at the Universities of Basle, Turin and Perugia. He was made Professor of Economics at Perugia in 1928, his reputation already well established by his classic treatise, first published as *Zur Sociologie des Parteiwesens in der Modernen Demokratie*, 1925.

The book is in many ways a model of political sociology: Michels focused on the bureaucratisation of democratic societies. Like Weber, whom he knew, Michels believed the exponential growth in size and complexity of bureaucracy in all aspects of society would have far-reaching consequences. In the political sphere, he reasoned that the increasing remoteness or organisations would effectively exclude popular participation in the democratic process. Rank-and-file members of political organisations would find their influences diminishing as the genuine power became concentrated in the hands of a few. The few would converge towards an élite group and their interests would become virtually identical, so much so, that they would assist and support each other in maintaining their positions of power.

In time, Michels argued, élites within any complex political organisation would become less concerned with issues that affected the rest of society and more interested in the preservation of their own status. This depended on the relations of power remaining essentially the same. So, élites' primary objective became keeping the status quo intact. The apathy of non-élite groups hastened the concentration of power and served to remove any challenge to the privileges of the élite.

Michels believed that any complex organisation, regardless of political ideology or ostensible aims, would, in time, exhibit these kinds of oligarchic tendencies. Michels called it an 'iron law of oligarchy' and suggested its applications were everywhere. Trade or labour unions would eventually become conservative organisations, existing principally to preserve their own élite in the same way as overtly reactionary groups. Any organisation will produce its own oligarchs as its grows in size and complexity; change would always be resisted, no matter what political credo the organisation embraced.

As Weber had predicted a highly specialised division of skills and expertise, so Michels saw knowledge and skills being concentrated in the hands of specialists. Michels demonstrated how such groups typically deny access to such skills and expertise and so use them as resources to enhance and preserve their own positions of influence.

For Michels, there is an inevitability about these processes which make if difficult to be confident about the long-term benefits of fresh, radical programmes of reform: modernity has created a need for complex organisations, and with them come the kind of oligarchic tendencies that militate against genuine change. Michels raised the question of whether 'the domination of the elected over the electors, of the mandatories over the mandators, of the delegates over the delegators' would always obtain. His answer was derived from the lessons of both the German and Italian Socialist Parties; despite radical promises, both succumbed to the organisational imperatives to preserve and perpetuate themselves.

Michels's theory is often compared with those of Mosca and Pareto, both of whom agreed that élites will predominate in any social order where bureaucracies are the principal mode of organisation. All saw a contradiction in the demands of organisations and democracy. More broadly, all absorbed some aspect of the work of the fifteenth-century and sixteenth-century Florentine theorist Niccolò Machiavelli, who argued that any enduring constitution must balance monarchic, aristocratic and democratic elements: states produce order, but those in power lose their civic virtue and indulge in private passions. In Machiavelli's thought, liberty inevitably gives way to corruption. Michels nearly went so far as to endorse the inevitable: he showed no resistance to the rise of Fascism in his adopted Italy, presumably feeling that it mattered little which party was in power – all would generate élites which would, in turn, serve themselves rather than the rest of the society.

The almost fatalistic resignation with which Michels observed the rise of extreme reactionary politics has led some to describe him as a conservative theorist, rather than a theorist of conservatism. His theories were put to the test in the 1950s, most famously by Djilas (*The New Class*), who examined the state bureaucracy of Soviet states, and Mills (*The Power Élite*), who studied the interlocking interests of what he called the American military–industrial élite.

Further reading

Bottomore, Tom ELITES AND SOCIETY [1964], 2nd edn, Routledge, 1993.
May, J.D. 'Democracy, Organisation, Michels', AMERICAN POLITICAL SCIENCE REVIEW, 59 (1965).
Nye, Robert, A. THE ANTI-DEMOCRATIC SOURCES OF ÉLITE THEORY: PARETO, MOSCA, MICHELS, Sage, 1977.

E.C.

MILGRAM, Stanley

Social psychologist	born USA 1933–1984
Associated with	OBEDIENCE TO AUTHORITY ■ FAMILIAR STRANGERS
Influences include	ALLPORT ■ ASCH
Shares common ground with	ZIMBARDO ■ ADORNO
Main works	OBEDIENCE TO AUTHORITY (1963, 1965, 1974) THE EXPERIENCE OF LIVING IN CITIES (1970) PSYCHOLOGICAL MAPS (1972)

MILGRAM GREW UP in the Bronx and finally returned home in 1967 as Director of the Social Psychology Graduate Program at the Graduate Center of the City University of New York. The intervening years took him to Queen's College, where he graduated in political studies, Harvard University, where his Ph.D. was supervised by Gordon Allport, then to Princeton, New Jersey, where he worked for Solomon Asch; and on to Yale as Assistant Professor of Psychology before returning to Harvard in 1963.

Soon after his arrival at Harvard, he published the first in a series of experiments on blind obedience to authority. These were instantly controversial and have become probably the most important studies in social psychology. In his experiments, Milgram demonstrated the banality of evil where most ordinary people would obey instructions to inflict lethal (simulated) levels of electric shock.

The research ensured Milgram's place in history and its legacy is one that continues to provoke controversy. Participants took part in what was called a 'learning experiment', either as 'teacher' or a 'learner'. A group of teachers were told to administer electric shocks to another group. The deception was that the would-be recipients of the shocks were not wired up at all. The teachers knew nothing of this, but carried on regardless, presuming they were causing great distress to the recipients. Milgram suggested that humans are highly manipulable in the face of authority. Prior to the Milgram work, it had been supposed that the atrocities of the Second World War were the product of pathologies. Milgram argued that, given the 'right' circumstances, anyone is capable of performing the genocide of Nazi Germany.

The American Psychological Society's ethics committee launched an immediate inquiry (during which time his APA membership was suspended). Soon after his reinstatement to the APA, in 1965, the American Association for the Advancement of Science awarded him the prize for outstanding contribution to social psychological research. The full account of the experiments published in 1974 was nominated for a National Book Award. However, there was far more to Milgram than these experiments. He remains one of the great researchers in the social sciences who cared little for theory. He described the true source of his various and usually brilliant experiments as 'the texture of everyday life. They are imbued with a phenomenological outlook.' Milgram observed the world around him and asked questions that no one else had. Sometimes, as in the obedience studies, he asked the unthinkable and gave us answers we did not want to hear. It was Milgram who, long before the thirty eight silent witnesses to the Kitty Genovese murder, had identified the problem of unresponsive bystanders in emergency situations. However, he always believed 'a Pandora's box lies just beneath the surface of everyday life', and had a rare talent for finding it, against the expectations of others.

Perhaps a good example of this is *The Small World Problem* (1967), where he posted letters to people in distant cities, asking them to get a folder to a named target person, but only if they knew them personally. If they did not know the target personally they should pass it on to a personal acquaintance who might. He concluded that 'almost everyone in the United States is but a few removes from the President or Nelson Rockefeller'. In fact, on average, there were a mere five circles of acquaintance between them. This must be a message of hope for those with less ambitious needs to contact someone they do not know personally.

Another example is the norm violation research on the New York underground where, as Milgram observed, 'common sense suggests it would be impossible to obtain a seat on the subway simply by asking for it'. And yet almost seven out of ten travellers complied. Perhaps more interesting was Milgram's observation that few experimenters, himself included, were able to utter such a request, revealing the enormous inhibitory tendencies that usually control the breaching of social norms. Introspection and phenomenology provided a creative insight for Milgram into how individuals function in a social world. Apparently mundane events, such as the 'familiar stranger' whom we see almost every day on the station platform, were explored to show the curiously rich 'frozen relationship' which we enjoy with them. Social responsibilities lie dormant, awaiting a crisis, or perhaps only a new context to be activated. Related to this was Milgram's exploitation of an apparently equal mundane event – that of coming across a stamped and addressed envelope in the street. *The Lost Letter Technique* (1965) involved experiments dropping letters addressed to different organisations such as political parties to provide an unobtrusive measure of public support for these in the area.

New York inspired the seminal essay *The Experience of Living in Cities*, which ranged widely and, unusually for Milgram, attempted some organising theory to embrace the phenomena described. He demonstrated the marked differences between cities and towns in social behaviour elicited by requests for help, such as ringing doorbells to ask to use the householder's phone. Here and elsewhere his experiments were bold and elegantly simple. But how can people's experience of a city really be captured? What is the distinguishing 'urban atmosphere' of a particular city? Is it too evanescent to be reduced? Milgram thought not, and placed an advert in the *New York Times* asking people to describe accounts of typical *experiences* of different cities. Here the everyday narratives provided by people were factor-analysed to reveal the distinctive images which cities such as London and Paris enjoy. It was at this time that Milgram began to explore the psychological maps that people held of cities. This was a research endeavour which, with a Guggenheim fellowship grant, took Milgram to Paris (*Psychological Maps of Paris* (1976)), where he shared the excitement of the city communicated by his respondents through their maps.

Among Milgram's many interests – he was an accomplished amateur songwriter and inventor of games – was a passionate interest in photography. In his essay *The Image Freezing Machine* (1975), Milgram reflects that a photograph does not merely capture events. It creates them. Not the least of the creation is a relationship between the photographer and the photographed which, unsurprisingly, Milgram turned into yet another experiment to examine the social rules at work.

There is little doubt that, had Milgram lived to his expected years, an entry such as this might have been bristling with references to classic studies which might well rank as importantly as his studies on obedience. However, in all Milgram's work the same bold, elegantly simple, illuminating experiments stand out, and all of them reflect an insatiable curiosity about the individual in a social world about which he really cared.

Further reading

Milgram, S. THE INDIVIDUAL IN A SOCIAL WORLD, McGraw-Hill, 1977, 1992.
Milgram, S. 'Part 3: Perspectives on Obedience to Authority', JOURNAL OF SOCIAL ISSUES, 51 Fall, 1995.
Miller, A.G. THE OBEDIENCE EXPERIMENTS, Praeger, 1986.

G.Cu.

MILLETT, Kate

Literary critic	born USA 1934—
Associated with	SEXUAL POLITICS ■ WOMEN'S LIBERATION
Influences include	de BEAUVOIR ■ FRIEDAN
Shares common ground with	GREER ■ FIGGS ■ FIRESTONE
Main works	SEXUAL POLITICS (1970)
	FLYING (1974)
	SITA (1977)
	THE BASEMENT (1980)
	GOING TO IRAN (1982)
	POLITICS OF CRUELTY (1993)

KATE MILLETT WAS born in St Paul, Minnesota, and studied at the University of Minnesota; she took a first-class degree at St Hilda's College, Oxford and received a Ph.D. from Columbia. Initially a sculptor, then a member of the English Department at Barnard College, she was active in the 1960s civil rights movement and an early member of the National Organisation for Women (NOW). Her Ph.D. thesis became the world-wide best-selling book, *Sexual Politics*.

Millett's *Sexual Politics* (1970) was also a ground-breaking seminal text for the second wave of feminism in a number of significant ways. It provided a broad (though not rigorous) theoretical base for the early women's liberation movement, which until the publication of *Sexual Politics*, had lacked such a base. Additionally, it is considered by many to be the first book of academic feminist literary criticism with its detailed analysis, from an explicitly feminist viewpoint, of D.H. Lawrence, Henry Miller, Norman Mailer and Jean Genet, as well as considerations of numerous other writers including James Joyce, John Ruskin and Oscar Wilde.

In the preface to *Sexual Politics*, Millett states that she has attempted 'to formulate a systematic overview of patriarchy as a political institution', and her book is seen as offering one of the earliest attempts to provide an analysis of patriarchy which posits the source of women's oppression in patriarchy as opposed to a biological, essentialist account of women's oppression.

Millett's analysis of the sexual relationships between male and female in patriarchal society is illustrated through examples from the male literary canon. First, Millett argues that 'sex has a frequently neglected political aspect' (preface), and second, that sexual relationships are relationships of power relationships and therefore political. This analysis provided the basis of the slogan, 'The personal is political', one of the central tenets of second-wave feminism.

Sexual Politics also provided the founding moment in contemporary psychoanalytic feminism. Millett's scathing critique of Freudian psychology was taken up by many of the second wave feminists and led Juliet Michell, in *Psychoanalysis and Feminism*, to refute Millett's reading of Freud. This inflamed an ongoing controversy in feminism concerning the usefulness of Freudian analysis to the feminist movement, given that many feminists see psychoanalysis as inherently patriarchal.

Millett's book consists of three sections: sexual politics, historical background and the literary reflection. The first section provides examples of sexual politics and a theory of sexual politics. The second section provides an historical overview of the transformations 'in the traditional relationship between the sexes' in the nineteenth and twentieth centuries; it also examines the backlash by patriarchy against these transformations, which ultimately capped the gains made by the first-wave feminists. The final section illustrates Millett's arguments through a detailed examination of the work of various male authors.

Sexual Politics provided the basic theoretical approach that American feminists of the second wave initially followed, namely a broadly sociological approach and content analysis methodology to the analysis of literature, film and the mass media. This approach was predicated on reflection theory which posited that images created in literature, film or the mass media unproblematically mirrored the real world. Millett's analysis formed the basis for the work of other second-wave feminists (such as Shulamith Firestone) and she has remained active in fighting for women's rights. Her influence on second-wave feminism and her exposition of a radical feminism cannot be overlooked.

Millett has also published *The Prostitution Papers* (1971); her autobiography *Flying* (1974); the story of her love affair with another woman (*Sita*, 1977); *The Basement: Meditations on a human sacrifice* (1979), *Going to Iran* (1981), *The Loony-Bin Trip* (1990) and *The Politics of Cruelty* (1993). She has made a film concerning women, *Three Lives* (1971) and has also continued to pursue her interests in sculpture.

Further reading

Clough, Patricia Ticineto FEMINIST THOUGHT: DESIRE, POWER AND ACADEMIC DISCOURSE, Blackwell, 1994.
Moi, Toril SEXUAL TEXTUAL POLITICS: FEMINIST LITERARY THEORY, Routledge, 1985.
Tong, Rosemary FEMINIST THOUGHT: A COMPREHENSIVE INTRODUCTION, Westview Press, 1989.

G.C.

MILLS, Charles Wright

Sociologist	born USA 1917–1962
Associated with	POWER ■ ÉLITES ■ SOCIOLOGICAL IMAGINATION
Influences include	WEBER ■ VEBLEN ■ DEWEY
Shares common ground with	GOULDNER ■ MERTON ■ REISMAN
Main works	WHITE COLLAR (1951) THE POWER ÉLITE (1956) THE SOCIOLOGICAL IMAGINATION (1959)

MILLS WAS THE last populist sociologist. He wrote for the public, in the conviction that sociology must address public issues or lose its moral force. Raised in Texas, he studied philosophy at the

University of Texas at Austin, and in 1939 enrolled as a graduate student in sociology at the University of Wisconsin. Here he made two important friendships. One was with the head of department, the pragmatist and crusading liberal, Edward A. Ross. From Ross, Mills learnt the lesson that sociologists must be engaged in the events of the day and not flinch from speaking the truth. The other was with Hans Gerth. Gerth had been a student at the Frankfurt Institute of Social Research. He exposed Mills to European social thought, critical theory and comparative sociology. Mills was rejected for the war service because he suffered from hypertension. In 1941 he became assistant professor in sociology at the University of Maryland before moving to Columbia University in 1945. At Columbia he encountered some of the leading Ameican sociologists of the day: Robert Lynd, Robert MacIver, Paul Lazarsfeld and Robert Merton. Columbia also had links with *emigré* scholars from Germany, notably some of the exiled members of the Frankfurt School. However, the most formative influence on Mills at this time was his work with the Bureau for Applied Social Research. While attached to the Bureau, Mills became increasingly interested in the influence of the mass media in American society. He also began to accumulate data on power and stratification. However, Mills eventually became disenchanted with what he saw as the Bureau's over-reliance on statistical approaches and its tendency to under-theorise research data. In the last years of his life, Mills travelled extensively in Latin America and Europe. Ever the exponent of engaged sociology, he began to write about what he saw as the key problems of the time, notably the dangers of the Cold War and the poverty gap between the developed and underdeveloped world.

Mills was only 46 when he died. Yet his work encompasses the main themes that have haunted sociology in the post-war period. Three, in particular, stand out. First, the uses and abuses of power. *White Collar* and *The Power Elite* attack the complacency of post-war consumerism by starkly revealing the depth of alienation in American society and identifying the power élite as the root of social manipulation. Mills expressed the fear that a new corporatism had emerged to dominate American society: directed by the business, military, political and celebrity élite. He argued that their influence threatened to smother the free and open debate required for democracy to be meaningful.

Second, Mills sought to show how the private troubles of individual men and women relate to the social structure. The theme is present in one of his first books, *Character and Social Structure* (with Hans Gerth, 1953). But it is more perfectly realised in *The Sociological Imagination*. Mills argues that the capitalist and Communist models of modernisation are incapable of delivering genuine freedom or solidarity. He repeats his argument that the power élite manipulates the public and follows Weber, in pointing to the irrational consequences of bureaucratic organisation. Mills clearly had the sense that modernity was in the process of collapse. He even uses the term 'post-modernism' to decribe the emerging social and economic formation. But unlike the established postmodern authors of the present day, he defended reason as the most cherished value of the new self-questioning, contradictory epoch. The populist in Mills never allowed him to criticise society without inferring that a 'New Deal' was waiting around the corner, if only people had the courage to stand up for the truth.

Third, Mills commented on the relevance of sociology. He criticised Parsonian grand theory and the 'abstracted empiricism' practised by Lazarsfeld and his associates in the Bureau of Applied Social Research, for being out of touch with real life. Sociology, he contended, was retreating into the ivory tower. Its proper place is in the public arena.

In his lifetime Mills was criticised for lacking a sensibility to the nuances of social life. His scholarship was sometimes accused of cutting too many corners and resorting to soap-box oratory as a means of argument. Yet although many of his arguments have undoubtedly dated, the passion and challenges presented in his work remain relevant. For many sociologists, especially in the USA, he remains a model of radical, principled, pragmatic sociology.

Further reading

Eldridge J. C. WRIGHT MILLS, Tavistock, 1983.
Horowitz, I. C. WRIGHT MILLS: AN AMERICAN UTOPIAN, Macmillan, 1983.
Tilman, R. C. WRIGHT MILLS: A NATIVE RADICAL AND HIS AMERICAN INTELLECTUAL ROOTS, Penn. State University Press, 1984.

C.R.

MORRIS, William

Designer/poet/utopian socialist	born England 1834–1896
Associated with	MARXISM ■ ROMANTICISM ■ UTOPIANISM
Influences include	KINGSLEY ■ RUSKIN ■ MARX
Shares common ground with	BERGER ■ BRECHT ■ GORZ
Main works	THE EARTHLY PARADISE (1868–70)
	ART AND SOCIALISM (1884)
	USEFUL WORK VERSUS USELESS TOIL (1885)
	HOW WE LIVE NOW AND HOW WE MIGHT LIVE (1887)
	NEWS FROM NOWHERE (1890/91)

MORRIS, THE SON of a businessman, was educated at Malborough public school and Oxford. As a young man he became associated with the Pre-Raphaelite Brotherhood, who, as their name suggests, wanted to return to the more decorative art that preceded the realism of the high Renaissance. They were a later current of the English Romantic movement and its revolt against modern industrialism. Morris's early poetry, which made him famous with the Victorian bourgeoisie, is inspired by medievalism. And, in his maturity, he even imagined a future socialist utopia to be rather like a medieval 'golden age'. He was not alone in forging a link between Romanticism and socialism. An important influence on Morris, John Ruskin, the architecture and art critic, had already made this connection and is considered one of the founding figures of the British Labour movement. Although best known during his lifetime as a poet, Morris's longer-term significance was to be a designer and a theorist of art, socialism and the good life, which in certain respects antici-pated the ecological politics and 'new age' subculture of the present.

Morris & Co., owned and run by Morris himself, pioneered a greater simplicity and respect for nature and materials in design than was prevalent in Victorian design generally. Morris's famous and ubiquitous wallpaper and curtain designs, usually deploying flower motifs, have in the latter part of the twentieth century, however, been a popular feature of the turn against modern functionalism and are, in a sense, characteristic of an everyday postmodern taste. Morris sought to create ideal interiors in his houses, most notably Kelmscott Manor in Gloucestershire, which is now a museum of Morrisonian design. He also campaigned publicly on art, architecture and design issues. The Society for the Protection of Ancient Buildings was founded by Morris and he was a leading figure in the arts and crafts movement.

In his own practice Morris was an all-rounder: designer in several media, painter, poet, successful entrepreneur and socialist activist and thinker. He joined the Social Democratic Federation in 1883, one of the antecedents of the British Labour Party, and he edited the federation's journal, *Commonweal*, from 1885 to 1890. However, his own politics were rather more anarchistic than social democratic. On his conversion to socialism, he began a series of public lectures on art, work and socialism that were published in *Commonweal* and in pamphlets. In *Art and Socialism*, for instance, Morris made it clear that his view of socialism was essentially aesthetic, a sensuous self-making, not just a means of organising society. His conception of alienated labour under industrial capitalism was remarkably similar to the philosophical anthropology of the young Marx. In the factory system the worker is alienated from the product of his or her labour and exploited by the employer. A socialist revolution would end this state of affairs and return control over the labour process to the worker who would, thus, be able to take pride in the work produced. Morris believed that the creative potential of ordinary human beings was enormous, yet stunted by capitalism. In the future socialist society, however, human potential would be released. There would cease to be a distinction between art and work. Morris, in effect, envisaged a small workshop economy with systems of mutual exchange instead of the mediation of money. Industrial pollution would end and everyone would live in an Arcadian paradise of collaboration and self-realisation, as Morris described it in his utopian novel, set in the late twentieth century, *News from Nowhere*.

Morris articulated a sensibility which in terms of practical politics was throughly unrealistic yet, as a measure of wellbeing and inspiration for alternative practice, has an enduring appeal. E.P. Thompson, Morris's greatest biographer, valued his synthesis of Marxism and Romanticism. Now, the synthesis might be seen to represent the combination of Romantic socialism with the lifestyle alternatives of ecological radicalism.

Further reading

McCarthy, F. WILLIAM MORRIS: A LIFE FOR OUR TIME, Faber & Faber, 1994.
Thompson, E.P. WILLIAM MORRIS: ROMANTIC TO REVOLUTIONARY, 2nd edn, Merlin, 1977.
Thompson, P. THE WORK OF WILLIAM MORRIS, Quartet, 1977.
J.McG.

MUMFORD, Lewis

Historian/cultural critic	born USA 1895–1995
Associated with	CITY ■ CIVILISATION ■ UTOPIA
Influences include	GEDDES ■ HOWARD ■ SPENGLER
Shares common ground with	VERLEN ■ RUSKIN ■ SENNETT
Main works	TECHNICS AND CIVILISATION (1934)
	THE CITY IN HISTORY (1961)
	THE MYTH OF THE MACHINE (2 VOLS., 1967, 1970)

T HE PROMISE OF rationally combining the immense fruits of science and technology with humanism lay at the heart of Mumford's lifelong work. In his youth he was influenced by the urban-reform and town-planning ideas of Patrick Geddes and Ebenezer Howard. Strategically, Mumford saw the city as the distillation of civilisation. Practically, his experience of being born and raised in New York suggested that the city was out of control, dehumanising personal relationships and blighting the ecosystem. The city should be a boon to civilisation, but it was turning into an impediment.

For Mumford, the root of this brutalisation lay in technology. He divided the modern machine age into three stages, each defined by a particular mode of energy and technology: the ecotechnic, the paleotechnic and the neotechnic. The ecotechnic period stretched from the Middle Ages to the start of the Industrial Revolution. He characterised this as a time of slow technological expansion and rich cultural diversity. Economic value had not superseded political and civil values as the ruling standard of life. Perhaps Mumford exaggerates the benefits of the ecotechnic stage, for this was also a time in which human life was at risk from pestilence, disease and disharmony. Yet it is clear that he regards the ecotechnic stage as an exemplary period of balance between culture and economy.

This is succeeded by the paleotechnic stage in which science and technology dominate culture. The age of the Industrial Revolution debases human relations in the name of economic and technological progress. Mumford saw this as a period in which no limits were recognised to progress. But progress was narrowly defined by economic criteria.

The gap between the promise and achievements of technological revolution was the context in which Mumford believed his own thought was being formed. In it he saw the glimmers of the neotechnic stage in which rational planning principles would be redirected in the interests of freedom and social community. Mumford looked forward to the centralisation of city populations and the development of 'organic cities' in which the ideal of balanced human civilisation is realised. Without planning and intervention, Mumford argued that the growth of Megalopolis would mutate into Tyrannapolis, with gangster élites running affairs and, finally, Nekropolis, a city turned into a living grave filled with war, famine and disease.

Although Mumford later questioned the accuracy of this classification system, it remains the most helpful guide to his thoughts on the development of civilisation. His work traces the expansion of technology and science at the cost of culture and civilisation. Yet it never quite surrenders the belief that rational planning can introduce a new harmony into the midst of the modern city.

The City in History is a rich, scholarly work in which Mumford seeks to subtantiate some of his more speculative ideas. He argues that the original neolithic cities were ruled by feminine principles of reproduction, nurturing and planting. These were challenged by male principles of warriorship and control. Mumford locates the 'trauma of civilisation' in the pre-eminence of masculine values. In the Paleolithic period it led to the emergence of the 'hunter-chieftain' which Mumford identified as the forerunner of kingship. He draws a parallel between the emergence of hierarchical systems of power and the spread of machine-like organisation throughout the population. The Greek *polis* formed an historical exception. Mumford writes approvingly of the values of Greek civilisation. In common with the medieval city, he finds in the best aspects of the Greek city-states the model for the organic communities that he envisages in the neotechnic stage. The city of the Industrial Revolution is treated as a monument to bad planning and the worst effects of greed. Yet the wealth produced in this period suggested what could be accomplished through rational planning. Essentially, Mumford reiterates his ideal of the garden city in which work and recreation interconnect to strengthen the bonds of community.

Mumford's later work extends the metaphor of the machine to castigate industrial bureaucracy. The centralised powers of the state operate remorselessly to deaden city life and community spirit. In the urban redevelopment programme headed by Robert Moses in post-war New York, Mumford found the crystallisation of the bureaucratic 'megamachine'. He denounced Moses's multi-lane expressways and high-rise building projects for the poor for their insensitivity to human relations. The bureaucratic megamachine presented itself as irresistible and the consequences of its decisions as ultimately beneficial. It is founded on a 'pentagon of power': Power, that is energy; Productivity for the sake of Profit; Political control and Publicity. Mumford rejects this as the 'myth of the machine'. This foundation is adduced as an invincible and inevitable model for progressive human development. Against the submission to the pentagon of power, Mumford urged that autonomy and diversity must be celebrated.

Mumford's work has been criticised for its utopianism and failure to articulate a political programme capable of realising the organic cities of the future. His sociology is attacked for failing to pay enough attention to the opposition of interests that drive culture along. Yet his criticism of unregulated metropolitan growth, his sense that ecological and civilisational values were at risk from the mindless celebration of technology and science, remain powerful and prescient themes.

Further reading

Miller, D. LEWIS MUMFORD, Weidenfeld & Nicolson, 1989.
Novak, F. 'Lewis Mumford and the Reclamation of Human History', CLIO, February 1987, pp. 159–81.
Thomas, J. 'Lewis Mumford: Regionalist Historian', REVIEWS IN AMERICAN HISTORY, March 1988, pp. 158–72.
C.R.

MURRAY, Charles

Political/public policy	born USA 1944—
Associated with	UNDERCLASS ■ RACE ■ IQ
Influences include	NOZICK ■ JENSEN ■ EYSENCK
Shares common ground with	ETZIONI ■ HERRNSTEIN ■ WILSON
Main works	LOSING GROUND: AMERICAN SOCIAL POLICY 1950–1980 (1984)
	THE EMERGING BRITISH UNDERCLASS (1990)
	THE BELL CURVE: INTELLIGENCE AND CLASS STRUCTURE IN AMERICAN LIFE (1994)

CHARLES MURRAY WAS born and grew up in Newton, Iowa, USA. He studied for a History degree at Harvard and completed his doctorate at the Massachusetts Institute of Technology. After working at the Manhattan Institute for Public Policy Research during the 1980s, he became the Bradley Fellow at the influential American Enterprise Institute in Washington, DC in the early 1990s. During this period, his hard-edged critique of post-war public policy and 'underclass' thesis shook the political landscape in the USA and established his reputation as one of America's most important and notorious neo-conservative writers. Thanks to the patronage of Britain's *Sunday Times*, Murray's ideas crossed the Atlantic in the early 1990s, making a defining impact upon social policy debates in the UK. The incendiary views on race and intelligence expressed in *The Bell Curve* propelled Murray (and his co-author, the maverick Harvard psychologist Richard Herrnstein) to new levels of controversy, with the *New York Times* branding him 'the most dangerous conservative in America'.

In many industrial societies, a debate has been raging about whether the public's desire for state-provided welfare services can be reconciled with the electorate's demand for low levels of personal taxation. Policy makers and politicians have been forced to rethink the normative justifications for and social consequences of state intervention in the welfare arena. Sooner or later in the course of their deliberations, they have to consider Murray's underclass thesis. His starting point is that poor people (like everyone else) are rational, calculating individuals who must be defined not just by their objective condition but by their behaviour. He goes on to claim that the principles underpinning post-war social policies in the USA and UK have had a dramatic impact on the norms of behaviour and cultural values of those with low incomes. The stress on *rights* and *entitlements* embedded in welfare, educational, housing and medical policies fundamentally transformed the rewards and penalties – the rules and 'finer strokes' of the game – that governed the behaviour of the poor. These principles undermined the values of individual responsibility, self-reliance and self-restraint and obliterated the age-old distinction between the respectable/deserving and disreputable/non-deserving poor.

The poor were transformed into an homogeneous group, furnished with a 'vocabulary of excuses' (including the notion that they were victims) and encouraged to take advantage of an extensive network of cash benefits and welfare programmes. The result, according to Murray, was not the eradication of poverty and disadvantage but the creation in the USA of a largely, but not exclusively, black urban underclass culture characterised by pathological forms of behaviour, e.g. high rates of illegitimacy, family disintegration, illiteracy, drug addiction and petty crime, casual violence, voluntary withdrawal from the labour market and welfare dependency. This underclass has been allowed to reproduce itself at an alarming rate, producing run-down neighbourhoods of concentrated and intractable multiple social problems.

Murray argues that 'blinkered' policy makers must acknowledge that this is not a static situation: the dysfunctional values and forms of behaviour of the underclass have become the norm for a significant fraction of the population for two reasons. First, they have been passed on generationally and second, they are corrupting the mainstream values and webs of interaction of adjacent respectable, low-income neighbourhoods. For Murray, the pressing political task is to break the destabilising underclass culture by scrapping the entire welfare system and return to a situation where individuals are held morally and economically responsible for their actions. Since he views the proliferation of young single mothers supported by welfare payments as the source of the burgeoning underclass, he advocates the elimination of these incentives. He wants to make sure that lower-class young women think through the consequences of their actions: 'Are you going to engage in sex? If you get pregnant, are you going to carry that baby to term? If you carry that baby to term, are you going to give that baby up for adoption? At each of those steps there is a choice to be made' (*The Independent*, 9 March 1995).

The Bell Curve analyses the role of inherited intellectual capacity in exacerbating social inequalities in the USA. The book's starting point is the belief that people differ in IQ and high IQ, because of the cognitive–cultural capital it bestows on an individual, has an overwhelming bearing on life chances. America now has a prestigious and powerful IQ élite, a middle class of average IQ and an underclass of limited cognitive ability. 'Race' is significant, according to Murray and Herrnstein, because intelligence is unevenly distributed by ethnic group and a disproportionate number of African-Americans are located at the low IQ underclass end of the bell curve.

Critics accuse Murray of producing a crude cocktail of 'redneck' cultural reductionism and right-wing moral absolutism which stigmatised poor black communities and hardened the resolve of the Right to dismantle welfare and anti-discrimination programmes. His work on intelligence is also charged with providing a cloak of scientific respectability for those who believe that the low-IQ poor should be discouraged from 'breeding'.

Further reading

Jencks, C. RETHINKING SOCIAL POLICY, Harvard University Press, 1992.
Katz, M.B. THE UNDERCLASS DEBATE: VIEW FROM HISTORY, Princeton University Press, 1993.
Wilson, W.J. THE TRULY DISADVANTAGED: THE UNDERCLASS AND PUBLIC POLICY, Chicago University Press, 1987.
E.McL.

NISBET, Robert

Sociologist	born USA 1914–1996
Associated with	UNIT IDEAS ■ SOCIOLOGY AS AN ART FORM
Influences include	BURKE ■ TOCQUEVILLE ■ TÖNNIES
Shares common ground with	OAKESHOTT ■ BELLAH ■ BERGER
Main works	THE SOCIOLOGICAL TRADITION (1970)
	HISTORY OF THE IDEA OF PROGRESS (1980)
	A HISTORY OF SOCIOLOGICAL ANALYSIS (1979)

SON OF A Los Angeles lumberyard worker, Nisbet graduated from the University of California at Berkeley and taught at the University of California Riverside until 1972, when he moved to the University of Arizona. Two years later, he took up the Schweitzer Chair at Columbia. He ended his career as resident scholar at the American Enterprise Institute.

Nisbet's theorising fits into a conservative tradition that begins with Burke and runs through Tocqueville, Durkheim and, to a degree, Weber. This tradition was created by Burke's *Reflections on the Revolution in France* (1790), which countered the rationalist insistence on rebuilding entire societies in the spirit of innovation, as a break with the past; the present is never free from the past, Burke argued. Fundamental constituent parts of society, such as the state's legitimacy, are the product of traditions that stretch back several generations. Much of this informs Nisbet's work, particularly the work for which he is best known, *The Sociological Tradition*.

The book is a history of ideas, in this case the key ideas that informed the development of sociology in the nineteenth century. Nisbet believed there were five 'unit ideas', each with a linked antithesis, the conflict between which gave rise to a specific type of analysis of society, which became sociology. The five unit ideas and their antitheses were: community–society, authority–power, status–class, sacred–secular and alienation–progress.

Europe had experienced two large-scale social transformations: the French Revolution (1789) and the Industrial Revolution (late eighteenth/early nineteenth centuries). With the transformations had come secularisation, popular democracy and social egalitarianism. While such themes gave the appearance of progress, writers such as Tocqueville and Weber were drawn to more morbid conclusions about human alienation, the overpowering of community by mass society and the eclipse of religious values; in other words, their concern was with the possible consequences of the break-up of the old order and its replacement by modernity.

The prospect of social disorder led theorists to ponder the problem of how to restore some of the traditional properties that were threatened by the industrial and scientifc age. Nisbet believed that community, in particular, was uppermost in the minds of theorists, as the fragmentation of experience and the erosion of individuality were consequences of the transformation. The unit-ideas worked as what Nisbet called 'searchlights', illuminating areas of cultural life that were considered worthy of detailed examination.

As sociologist, Nisbet saw himself as part of the same tradition that sought to oppose the overbearing tyranny of large-scale bureaucracies and political administrations, at the same time upholding intermediate institutions such as the family, neighbourhood and his beloved community.

Nisbet's *History of the Idea of Progress* was an examination of the various theories based on the premise that humankind was advancing from some *ab origine* condition of primitiveness to some superior stage of being. Absent in all theories was empirical evidence. The belief in the inevitability of progress is not a product of modernity, argued Nisbet, but can be traced back to the beginnings of Western civilisation. It is also a durable belief. 'Our problem in this final part of the twentieth century is compounded by the fact that the dogma of progress is today strong in the official philosophies or religions of those nations which are the most formidable threats to Western culture and its historical moral and spiritual values', he wrote in *History of the Idea of Progress*, (Heineman, 1980).

Further reading

Dawe, Alan 'The Two Sociologies, in Kenneth Thompson and Jeremy Tunstall (eds.), SOCIOLOGICAL PERSPECTIVES, Penguin 1971.
Nisbet, Robert 'Sociology as an Art Form', PACIFIC SOCIOLOGICAL REVIEW, Fall 1962.
Nisbet, Robert 'Conservatism', in Tom Bottomore and Robert Nisbet (eds.), A HISTORY OF SOCIOLOGICAL ANALYSIS, Heinemann, 1979.

E.C.

PAGLIA, Camille

Art historian/cultural theorist	born USA 1947—
Associated with	COMPARATIVE LITERATURE ■ CULTURAL STUDIES ■ SEXUAL POLITICS
Influences include	FREUD ■ NIETZSCHE ■ SADE
Shares common ground with	BLOOM ■ MAFFESOLI
Main works	SEXUAL PERSONAE: FROM NEFERTITI TO EMILY DICKINSON (1990) SEX, ART AND AMERICAN CULTURE (1992) VAMPS AND TRAMPS (1994)

B RILLIANT INTELLECTUAL PROVOCATEUR, cantankerous anti-feminist, motormouth iconoclast, self-promoting mountebank, pop culture diva – all of these characterisations have been used to describe Camille Paglia. Born of Italian immigrant parents and educated at Yale under the guidance of Harold Bloom, Paglia laboured in relative obscurity until 1990 when her magnum opus, *Sexual Personae* – an encyclopaedic survey of literature and art from Antiquity to the end of the nineteenth century – became an unexpected best-seller. Subsequent publications employing themes to those articulated in *Sexual Personae* examine television, cinema and celebrity icons from Elizabeth Taylor to Madonna. Paglia's views on feminism, the academy, sex and date rape have stirred up considerable debate, making her one of the most controversial cultural critics to emerge in recent history.

Paglia identifies sex, violence and aggression as the major motivational inspirations for artistic creativity and human relationships. Drawing upon Nietzsche's reformulation of the Greek myths of the gods Apollo and Dionysus, Paglia argues that the defining characteristic of the entire history of Western civilisation has been the constant struggle between these two binary principles, the Apollonian and the Dionysian. The Dionysian represents the raw, brute, earth power or what she prefers to call the chthonian, and the Apollonian, the civilising force that continually fights to contain the pagan power of the Dionysian. In Paglia's narrative, the greatest cultural achievements have come from the quarrel with nature and constitute moments of Apollonian transcendence. Incorporating Sade's theory of nature and his satiric critique of Rousseau, Paglia claims that the great works of Western culture are actually efforts to subvert the 'daemonic' power of nature through the creation of an array of sexual personae or *masks*. According to Paglia, Western civilisation arose from the denial of the bodily, the elemental and the chthonian and created a nature which is manifest in the aggressively imagined forms of Western art and the sharp outlines of the Western personality. In short, the Apollonian impulse created civilisation as a way of containing the predatory energies inherent in human nature. She writes: 'Apollo makes the boundary lines that are civilisation but that lead to convention, constraint, oppression. Dionysus is energy unbound, mad, callous, destructive . . . Apollo is law, history, tradition' (1990:96).

Paglia applies her Apollonian/Dionysian metaphor to an examination of gender identities linking masculinity with culture and thus the Apollonian and femininity with nature and the Dionysian. For Paglia, the Apollonian is a masculine swerve away from the murkiness of female nature. Hence, contrary to most contemporary scholarship seeking to deconstruct the seeming 'natur-alness' of gender differences and the hierarchical valorisation of male/culture over female/nature, Paglia embarks on a philosophical journey back to biology and maintains that there are, in fact, radical and irreducible differences between the sexes. In many respects, her treatment of the culture/nature binary constitutes a critique of the constructionist position which has gained ascen-dancy in much feminist and cultural theory, since she asserts that sexual identities are products of biological differences that cannot be socialised out of existence.

As one might expect, the Apollonian/Dionysian framework also informs Paglia's theory of popular culture. While she credits the Apollonian impulse for the great works of Western culture, she argues that it is the repressed pagan tradition or Dionysian impulse which underscores many of the great media – rock music, film, advertising and other forms of contemporary popular culture. More specifically, Paglia's theory of television, which resonates with McLu-hanesque themes, borrows and translates from earlier popular split-brain localisation research that had suggested that the left and right hemispheres of the brain perform different functions and possess disparate cognitive skills. Rational, analytical and linear characteristics are commonly associated with the left or, in Paglia's terms, the Apollonian side of the brain while the right, or Dionysian hemisphere, is considered to be the realm of the intuitive and emotional. For Paglia, then, television and the visual images of popular culture, both of which are pagan, appeal to and activate the right hemisphere of the brain.

Paglia's insistence that the artefacts of Western civilisation and contemporary popular culture can be interpreted and understood by employing the Apollonian/Dionysian framework has been challenged for its reductionism and undialectical character. In addition, while Paglia has gained some notoriety for her condemnation of postmodernists, her championing of, and uncritical approach to, popular culture, shares some affinity with those strands of post-modernism that merely celebrate popular forms without any mediating critical analysis.

Further reading

hooks, bell, 'Camille Paglia: "Black" Pagan or White Colonizer?', in OUTLAW CULTURE, Routledge, 1994.
Maffesoli, Michel, THE SHADOW OF DIONYSUS: A CONTRIBUTION TO THE SOCIOLOGY OF THE ORGY, SUNY Press, 1993.
Walker, John, 'Seizing Power: Decadence And Transgression In Foucault And Paglia', POSTMODERN CULTURE, 5:1 September, 1994.
V.S.

PARETO, Vilfredo

Sociologist/economist	born France 1848–1923
Associated with	CIRCULATION OF ÉLITES ■ MACHIAVELLIANS ■ RESIDUES/DERIVATIVES
Influences include	MILL ■ SPENCER ■ WALRAS ■ PANTALEONI ■ SOREL
Shares common ground with	MOSCA ■ PARSONS ■ MICHELS ■ BOBBIO ■ ARON ■ SCHUMPETER
Main works	COURS D'ÉCONOMIE POLITIQUE (2 VOLS., 1896–97) LES SYSTÈMES SOCIALISTES (2 VOLS., 1901–02) TRATTATO DI SOCIOLOGIA GENERALE (1916)

PARETO WAS BORN in France in 1848 of an Italian father, who was exiled from Genoa for his Mazzinian opinions in the middle 1830s, and a French mother. Pareto's family lived in Italy from 1855, after Pareto's father was allowed to return to the country. As a young man Pareto studied engineering at the Turin Polytechnic. Subsequently he moved to Florence. Under the influence of the moderate conservatives of Tuscany he embarked on a period of intense political activity, publishing several articles supporting the ideas of free trade, universal suffrage, disarmament and republicanism. In those years he developed a strong antipathy towards politics which he viewed as a corrupt and evil expression of power. Despite his hostility towards a centralised and bureaucratic state Pareto supported the ideas of order, authority and hierarchy.

Pareto was extremely critical of all Italian governments following unification. In 1891 he withdrew from active participation in politics and business in order to devote himself to the studying of economics. One of his friends, the economist Maffeo Pantaleoni, introduced him to the market theories of Leon Walras, and in 1893 Pareto accepted the Chair of Political economy at Lausanne University, where he succeeded Walras. In 1896–97 he wrote his first book, *Cours d'économie politique*, in which he maintained that the study of the economy has to adopt the logical–empirical method of the natural sciences. Investigation into economics has to be schematic, with the aim of identifying elementary economic mechanisms. According to Pareto, therefore, the study of economics becomes similar to that of rational mechanics. The approach to the economy Pareto outlined in *Cours* originated a philosophy of social evolution; history is a cyclical sequence of events which shows that man is unchanging. With this view, Pareto was markedly different from the positivists of his time. He no longer believed in 'progress' and science.

The draconian repression of the Milan uprising in 1898 inspired *La Liberté économique et les événements d'Italie*, in which Pareto investigated the social, political and economic origin or unease in Italian society. At the same time the first doubts concerning the validity of free-trade ideas were sown in his mind. In his next book, *Les systèmes socialistes*, Pareto had become convinced that most human behaviour is inspired by irrational considerations, but this behaviour is cocooned in a veneer of false logic developed in order to satisfy a human craving for the security of having acted rationally. According to Pareto a more conclusive science than economics would need to be developed in order that a scientific understanding of society could be taken to a higher level. Finally he realised that pure economic analysis was incapable of explaining human behaviour. Richard Bellamy stated that Pareto's 'sociology became the inverted image of his economics – describing the pursuit of self-interest by irrational rather than rational means' (1987:22).

In 1916, after two decades of investigation into human behaviour, Pareto wrote the *Trattato di sociologia generale*, aiming to illuminate the true actions as 'logical' and 'non-logical'. The first category of actions are 'logically related to an end, not only in respect to the person performing them, but also for those who have a more extensive knowledge'. Therefore 'logical' actions are rare and can be identified mainly in the field of art and science. All other actions, which fail to adopt 'logical–experiemental' modes of reasoning, are, according to Pareto, 'non-logical'. The most significant part of the *Trattato* is devoted to the analysis of the 'non-logical' actions that determine the majority of human actions and are the outcome of a 'non-rational' state of mind. Therefore 'non-logical' actions are the result of the complex interplay of emotions and interest. Behind all human behaviour lie ambiguous emotions, inclinations and psychological drives that operate on a subconscious level. In the field of 'non-logical' actions, Pareto distinguishes between what he called 'residues', that is, the uniform psychological basis underlying social action, and 'derivates', that is, rationalisations advanced by social participants as justifications of their social actions. The aim of social scientists is to discern the residues and the derivations made by the social actor. Pareto identified 52 residues that he divided into six classes.

In the *Trattato* Pareto holds that all societies are governed by an élite. The entire story of humanity is marked by élites that govern by using force and cunning and, in periods of decadence, are deposed by other élites that usually, at that particular moment, act with a pretence of defending the interest of the working class, the proletariat or any exploited group. Yet when the new élite is in power it establishes a society whose features are very different from those promised before gaining power. History, in Pareto's view, is a cemetery of aristocracies.

Pareto's theory of the élite is associated with the work of Gaetano Mosca. The two scholars are considered founding fathers of this theory, although Pareto is considered as having a more scientific approach. Yet the main distinction between the two thinkers is ideological. Mosca's concept of a 'political class' is that of a moderate conservative, while Pareto's is classical liberal.

Pareto has been accused of supporting Fascism; in fact, he welcomed the new regime in Italy mainly because it proved the prevision of his sociological studies. He also considered Mussolini to be a statesman of the first rank. However, Pareto's appreciation of Fascism cannot be generalised and judged on the opinions he expressed at the end of 1922 and early 1923. Pareto in fact died in 1923 when Fascism, although it governed the country with the use of violence, was not yet the totalitarian dictatorship in place after the middle 1920s. It is impossible to say whether Pareto, with his liberal background, would have continued to support Fascism even after individual freedom in Italy became increasingly limited and the state the main and only actor in political life.

Further reading

Aron, R. MAIN CURRENTS IN SOCIOLOGICAL THOUGHT, Penguin, 1970.
Bellamy, R. MODERN ITALIAN SOCIAL THEORY, Polity, 1987.
Nye, R.A. THE ANTI-DEMOCRATIC SOURCES OF ELITE THEORY: PARETO, MOSCA, MICHELS, Sage, 1977.
Powers, C.H. VILFREDO PARETO, Sage, 1987.

P.T.

PARSONS, Talcott

Sociologist	born USA 1902–1979
Associated with	SOCIAL SYSTEM THEORY
Influences include	DURKHEIM ■ WEBER ■ FREUD
Shares common ground with	MERTON ■ SHILS ■ ALEXANDER
Main works	THE STRUCTURE OF SOCIAL ACTION (1937)
	THE SOCIAL SYSTEM (1951)
	SOCIETIES (1966)

TALCOTT PARSONS BECAME the dominant American social theorist of the 1950s and 1960s. His father was a Congregational Minister and President of a minor college. Parsons took a degree at Amherst in 1924 and then travelled to Europe, where he studied at the London School of Economics and then at Heidelberg where he encountered the Weber study circle and completed his doctoral thesis. On returning to the USA he took a position as instructor at Harvard University. He was eventually promoted to the Chair of Sociology at Harvard in 1944 and taught there until his death in 1979.

In his famous *The Structure of Social Action* Parsons attempted to show that the positivistic cultural and social theories of the nineteenth centuries, particularly those of Comte and Spencer, had been surpassed by modern writing in France, Germany and Italy: the work of Durkheim, Weber and Pareto, arising independently of each other, had revolutionised the field of social sciences. His new synthesis of these writings would produce an empirically grounded sociological framework which would be unlikely to undergo any further radical modification. His basic idea was that positivist and determinist theory had given way to a consensus around a theory of action as the basis of sociology. In the years following, he added the names of Freud and of Marx to the founding influences of this synthesis. The central idea in Parsons's work was to identify the specific features of the social system from the cultural system, and Parsons's main contribution to cultural theory is to have made this demarcation and to have analysed the relation between the two systems.

Parsons suggests that the social system is best conceived as the site of institutions and institutional processes, defined in terms of networks of roles and statuses governed by norms (regulating function) and values (underpinning meaning and choice). Cultural elements are institutionalised into the social system, and are internalised into the personality system, as independent levels of analysis. For the sociologist therefore the specific domain of study is the working of the social system and the interrelation of this system with culture and personality as external categories. In his work on social systems Parsons tries to identify the universal requirements of social systems, their forms of crystallisation around necessary functions, and their forms of structural change and differentiation. Much of this discussion is at a very high level of analytic abstraction, but it is clear that the social system in this conceptualisation does not work on its own in isolation from the other two systems, and that the sociologist is forced to go beyond the social system in his analyses.

Parsons refused to follow Mannheim, however, in trying to generate a sociology of culture in which knowledge and other cultural phenomena were to be treated on equal terms. He noted that his position was closer to that of Weber, and the maintenance of a strict separation between empirical knowledge, expressive symbolism and style, motivational values, and grounds for the evaluation of meaning and action, which together go to make up the specific characteristics of cultural systems. For Parsons the problem of ideology is one which arises in the analysis of the social institutionalisation of cultural meaning, and is strictly parallel to the analysis of the internalisation of culture in the personality – the process of rationalisation. Yet the sociology of knowledge cannot be divorced from a more general consideration of the interpenetration of the social and cultural orders.

Parsons goes further against Mannheim in suggesting that the key problem of analysing 'ideological strain' in society, and even of explaining the prevalence of ideology more generally, is really a problem of the continuously changing nature of modern societies as they readjust and reintegrate in response to changes in technology and other subsystem developments. For Parsons, these ideological stresses do not reflect a problem of integration at the highest level of core institutionalised values. In effect, here Parsons's thought is not empirical, but attempts to provide a clarification of theoretical terminology and conceptualisation. And this leads to more precision in asking questions: under what conditions does successful institutionalisation occur, and what are the main problems which arise when this process is incomplete or partially successful?

C. Wright Mills argued that Parsons's analysis was both too abstract to be useful (an abstract empiricism) and, when illustrations were provided, they were no better than those of common sense. Whether this is true or not (the present writer thinks not), Parsons established the dominant sociological framework between the 1940s and 1960s and it was to reaction against this body of theory, even by his own students, that much recent cultural theory owes its richness, sophistication and depth.

Further reading

Mills, C. Wright THE SOCIOLOGICAL IMAGINATION, Oxford University Press, 1959.

Munch, R. and Smelser, N. (eds.), THEORY OF CULTURE, University of California Press, 1992.

M.G.

PEIRCE, Charles Sanders

Philosopher/scientist	born USA 1839–1914
Associated with	PRAGMATISM ▪ SEMIOTIC ▪ OBJECTIVE IDEALISM
Influences include	JONATHON EDWARDS ▪ DUNS SCOTUS ▪ HEGEL
Shares common ground with	WITTGENSTEIN ▪ SAUSSURE
Main works	SOME CONSEQUENCES OF FOUR INCAPACITIES (1868) THE FIXATION OF BELIEF (1877) HOW TO MAKE OUR IDEAS CLEAR (1878)

C HARLES SANDERS PEIRCE graduated from Harvard in 1859 an expert in natural science, mathematics, logic and philosophy. He spent most of his life employed by the US Coast and Geodetic Survey since his rather short-lived academic career as lecturer in logic at Johns Hopkins University lasted only for approximately five years. Peirce was once considered a less than prolific writer, since, during his lifetime, he published only one book. However, more than ten thousand pages in scholarly journals, popular periodicals, and so on may be attributed to him. This massive *oeuvre* is being prepared for publication by Indiana University Press in a thirty-volume collection entitled: *Writings of Charles S. Peirce.*

Although they were lifelong friends and William James attributed the foundations of pragmatism to Peirce, their work had very little in common. Peirce went so far as to use the term pragmatism to differentiate his work from the empiricism to which James's misunderstanding of Peircian pragmatism led. As opposed to Kant's subjective idealism, which argues that what is known of objects is contributed by the human beings who perceive them, objective idealism preserves Peirce's monism by holding that the world is constituted by an order which, although mental in character, is independent of the human mind.

Semiotic realism holds that thought or the sign relation is objectively real and can validly be used to understand nature because it possesses a real unity with nature. For, as opposed to materialists, in Peirce's schema 'meaning' and 'purpose' are real. They are not a *product* of human activity because no recognisably human activity is ever without them. Furthermore, all of our activity is meaningful and purposeful because of our special relationship to language. Thus the ultimate result of Peirce's belief that 'all thought whatsoever, is a sign, and is mostly of the nature of language' means that the study of language is the study of the mind in relation to the world and therefore of the world itself (Mounce 1997: 23).

According to Peirce, *signs* are a product of both an *object* and *interpretant*. Thus signification involves a triadic relationship, since for Peirce meaning is always to some extent intended and intentional relationships are always inherently triadic. This theory of signification differs from Rationalist and Empiricist conceptions of meaning because Peirce posits a relative rather than an absolute conception of knowledge. He locates the observer in the world and therefore requires that knowledge be acquired from a point of view.

Since the interpretant of a sign is always some further sign, meaning is always based on other signs. Meaning occurs relationally over time. And since it is and was always becoming, an original sign is logically inconceivable. An essentially practical enterprise, meaning is grasped by acquiring a *capacity* or *habit* in handling it. It is acquired only in practice.

Peirce's theory of signification is derived of the basic logical formula for any relationship to and in the world, including but not limited to meaning and consciousness. He writes of three categories. First (feeling) and Second (reaction) represent those elements in the world of chance and contingency; his category Third (habit), those elements of law and generality. In short, for Peirce pragmatism is not a philosophy of practical results but a method in logic. So much so, that the terms 'semiotic' and 'logic' may be considered synonymous. For if 'as Peirce held, all thinking is inference from signs and every sign relation possesses a quality of mentality or thirdness, then logic – the science of sound thinking – is the science of sign relations' (Hoopes 1991: 231).

Peirce holds a special position within the history of theory insofar as he contributes both as logician *and* metaphysician. Interested in the logic rather than the details of the universe, Peirce promotes an integrated view of human interaction with and in the world. Thus, the main concern of his metaphysical views is the problem of continuity and discontinuity. He affirms the reality of both, for his cosmology, based on contingency and possibility where existing regularities are recognised as contingent rather than ultimate, is much akin to the statistical real of quantum mechanics.

In cultural studies, Peirce's theory of semiotic has often been less favoured than Saussure's. It is presented as an alternative that was never taken up. Only recently has effort been made to understand the implications of Peirce's semiotic apart from those developed by Saussure. Richard Rorty, contemporary neo-pragmatist largely indebted to the work of William James and John Dewey, has declared that Peirce is associated with pragmatism in name only. However, recent work has uncovered many aspects of Peirce's work which show it to be an independent and complete from of pragmatism rather than a mere namesake or negligible influence.

Further reading

Hoopes, J. (ed.) PEIRCE ON SIGNS, University of North Carolina Press, 1991.
Mounce, H.O. THE TWO PRAGMATISMS: FROM PEIRCE to RORTY, Routledge, 1997.
O.C.

PIAGET, Jean

Psychologist	born Switzerland 1896–1980
Associated with	ADAPTATION ■ ASSIMILATION ■ GENETIC EPISTEMOLOGY
Influences include	BALDWIN ■ CLAPARÄDE ■ HEGEL ■ JANET ■ SIMON
Shares common ground with	CHOMSKY ■ HABERMAS ■ VYGOTSKY ■ DEWEY
Main works	THE LANGUAGE AND THOUGHT OF THE CHILD (1923) THE CHILD'S CONCEPTION OF THE WORLD (1926) THE MECHANISMS OF CONCEPTION (1961) THE DEVELOPMENT OF THOUGHT (1975)

BORN IN NEUCHÂTEL, Switzerland, Piaget received his doctorate for research on molluscs in 1918. In 1921 he became Director of Studies at the Jean-Jacques Rousseau Institute in Geneva, which had been founded by the psychologist Edouard Claparäde. Two years later, Piaget published his first psychology book, *The Language and Thought of the Child*. From 1940 to 1971, he held a Chair in Experimental Psychology at the University of Geneva. During his productive academic career, he revolutionised thinking about the development of children's knowledge-acquisition which, he argued, grew through qualitative changes in biological structures resulting from interaction with the environment.

Piaget's original intention was to unify biology and logic. It appears his early work on molluscs suggested to him that interaction with the environment can create change in biological structures. This formed the basis of his theory of cognitive development. His early psychological research comprised observation of his own three children. In contrast to theories that posited the idea of a cognitive development independent of the child's activity, Piaget proposed that children are active participants in their own development.

Throughout the development, changes in cognitive structure occurred. The structures themselves bear resemblance to a lift, each succeeding floor reaching a higher level of awareness and understanding. According to the *Oxford Companion of the Mind* (OUP, 1987), Piaget was drawn by Hegel's dialectic: he coined the term 'dialectical constructivism' to capture the toing-and-froing between the child's mental processes and the surrounding world encountered, newly acquired knowledge guiding the child's future investigations – and discoveries – of the world. Knowing is not a matter of data entering a blank mind, but an activity in which the human organism, through experience, makes sense of the environment.

There are two principal features of this process. *Assimilation* involves an incorporation of perceptual inputs into existing knowledge structures (the organism can only assimilate certain types of input just as, say, the digestive system can assimilate animal fats, but not metal – this is an oft-quoted simile); and *accommodation* describes the action of the environment on the mental structure. As new inputs from the environment destabilise the mind's organisation, so assimilation and accommodation restore equilibrium.

As the child develops, its cognitive structures change from the 'instinctual' through the 'sensorimotor' to the operational structure of adult thought, and Piaget maintained that these three forms of cognitive arrangement represent different periods, or stages of knowing. Each stage has to be satisfactorily completed before the child can enter the next. This is because each is typified by distinct knowledge structures defining modes of thinking.

In the sensorimotor period, the child is unable to make any distinction between him or herself and the rest of the world and remains egocentric. In a much-quoted experiment, children were asked to describe what a model of a mountain range would look like from a different standpoint. They could not. Instinctually, children can suck, grasp and perform other basic behaviour. But, by the age of two, they can perform sophisticated mental tasks, such as separating objects from their own actions.

The second period (up to 13 years) is divided into two sub-phases, the pre-operational and concrete operational. An example of change here is 'irreversibility'. While the child at the pre-operational sub-phase is to some extent able to transform mentally the present state of things into some future state, he or she is unable yet to realise that the transformation he or she has brought about is reversible by a series of changes in the opposite direction. A four-year-old was asked: 'Do you have a brother?' and answered 'Yes, he's called Jim.' To the question 'Does Jim have a brother?' the reply was 'No!' The relationship was conceived as acting in one direction only: from the subject to the brother.

The final period is 'formal operational' and its most marked feature is the ability to think logically. Piaget observed that, while the concrete operational thinker is concerned to manipulate things even if he or she does this 'in the mind', the formal operational thinker has become able to manipulate propositions, or ideas. Piaget quoted the following problem: Edith is fairer than Susan. Edith is darker than Lily. Who is the darkest? This problem gives considerable difficulty to many 10-year-olds. Yet, if it were a question of arranging three dolls in serial order, the task would be easy for them. Once into the formal operational period, applying ideas to other ideas enables us to think abstractly, without need of actual experience. The stage is liberatory.

For Piaget, cognitive development is associated with a decentring process in which the child gradually moves away from a primitive concentration on its own immediate concerns towards an expanded awareness of the concerns of others. Something similar is the case with Habermas's concept of social evolution, which drew on Piaget's model. Small-scale traditional cultures are dominated by myth and particular modes of thought. In more advanced Western societies, Habermas notes 'post-conventional' cognitive domains, in which there are opportunities for argumentation and self-criticism.

Piaget described his theory of knowledge growth as a genetic epistemology, suggesting a basis in biological adaptation. As such, his view that language acquisition fits in with the structure of mind was at odds with the relativist views of Sapir and Whorf, for whom thought was a reflection of particular languages. Piaget also took issue with both the *tabula rasa* conception of behaviourists and the nativism of gestalt psychology. Chomsky's transformational theory of grammar, which shared some common ground with Piaget's, laid too much stress on innate characteristics. While Piaget was Kantian in his respect for the role of uniquely human cognitive filters in the acquisition of knowledge of the world, he did not consider these *a priori* structures, as fixed from birth, but rather arising in a long-evolving process of construction.

Further reading

Reed, E., Turiel, E. and Brown, T. (eds.) VALUES AND KNOWLEDGE: THE JEAN PIAGET SYMPOSIUM SERIES, Lawrence Erlbaum Associates, 1996.
Smith, L. NECESSARY KNOWLEDGE: PIAGETIAN PERSPECTIVES ON CONSTRUCTIVISM, Lawrence Erlbaum Associates, 1993.
Vidal, F. PIAGET BEFORE PIAGET, Harvard University Press, 1994.
Wadworth, B. J. PIAGET'S THEORY OF COGNITIVE DEVELOPMENT: FOUNDATIONS OF CONSTRUCTIVISM, Longman Publishing, 5th edn, 1996.

E.C.

POPPER, Karl R.

Philosopher	born Austria 1902–1994
Associated with	FALSIFIABILITY ▪ THE OPEN SOCIETY
Influences include	ADLER ▪ BACON ▪ DARWIN ▪ MILL
Shares common ground with	CARNAP ▪ LAKATOS ▪ TARSKI
Main works	THE OPEN SOCIETY AND ITS ENEMIES (1945)
	THE LOGIC OF SCIENTIFIC DISCOVERY (1959)
	CONJECTURES AND REFUTATIONS (1963)

SENIOR LECTURER IN Philosophy at Canterbury University, New Zealand until 1945 and Professor of Logic and Scientific Method at the London School of Economics, 1949–69, Popper held several other prestigious positions in a fertile academic career, much of which was spent in disputing the truth claims of positivism, defending what he called 'Open Society' and challenging determinist authoritarianism.

Popper's epistemology was set out in his first major work, *The Logic of Scientific Discovery*, in which he took issue with the Vienna Circle's proposal that the formal criterion of what should pass for scientific knowledge was verification. Vienna's logical positivists argued that, if a knowledge claim could not be verified empirically (i.e. deriving from sensory experience alone), then it was senseless and should be rejected as such.

Popper countered this by insisting that no amount of positive evidence in favour of a proposition was enough to constitute verification. Instead, he proposed that knowledge proceeds by setting up hypotheses and subjecting to every available attempt to falsify them. The emphasis was moved from corroboration to refutation. A theory was never more than conditional. If it were strong, efforts to falsify would fail; but it could never pass as truth. The title of Popper's 1963 book *Conjectures and Refutations* sums up the process by which scientific knowledge progresses.

Scientific conjectures are educated guesses: rational science is geared towards their elimination of wrong guesses. The kernel of the idea of valuing negative evidence is found in Francis Bacon and J.S. Mill, though Popper used it as a way of solving what David Hume had called the problem of induction. Induction involves accumulating and classifying particular pieces of information and generalising from the regularities these exhibit. This is what Popper called the 'bucket theory of mind': there is nothing in our intellect that has not entered through our senses (another phrase is the more familiar *tabula rasa*). For Popper, induction is untenable: drawing isolated fragments of empirically gathered evidence from the natural world and using these as the basis of universal knowledge has certain attractions; but it contains no guarantee that the world will not change in some drastic way in the future – rendering all knowledge worthless.

Popper's alternative was to proceed deductively, creating abstract frameworks of knowledge, then collapsing them into testable theories that could be subjected to the most stringent of challenges. The assumption underlying this was that the natual world lay outside our construction of it: an independent sphere that was open to human scrutiny. This is elaborated in *Objective Knowledge*, in which Popper writes of three worlds, the first of which (W1) is that of physical objects, the second (W2) comprising states of consciousness and the third (W3) filled with the contents of human thoughts. Knowledge in the 'I know' sense is in W2 but scientific knowledge is in W3. 'We are seekers of truth, but we are not its possessors', wrote Popper. There *is* such a thing as objective knowledge, but we can only approach it via the verisimilitude of our knowledge to truth. We can never actually know for certain.

Critics of Kantian leanings assailed Popper for his naïvety in proposing W3: scientific knowledge is the product of agreements, conventions and shared understandings; its correspondence to a 'natural world' is a matter of orthodoxy and such an orthodoxy is susceptible to sudden, transformative changes – what Kuhn called 'scientific revolutions'. Popper preferred the evolutionary metaphor: 'The growth of knowledge – or the learning process – is not a repetitive or a cumulative process but one of error-elimination. It is Darwinian selection, rather than Lamarckian instruction.'

The same mistrust of knowledge that purports to be certain informed Popper's political philosophy, much of which may be seen as a critique of Marx (and, to a lesser extent, Freud), whose blueprint for the reconstruction involved social laws of progress. Invoking so-called laws of social progress was near-tyranny for Popper. As inductivist philosophers had generalised from observations to laws, so social theorists had attempted to disclose laws of society. As a methodological individualist – and hence a reductionist – Popper rejected collectivist conceptions, especially those that entailed deterministic connotations of progress. All we understand about social processes must come from the 'actions, interactions, aims, hopes and thoughts of individual men'.

To theorise at a level above the individual is to expose 'the open society' to its enemies, ideologies and dogmatists. The society Popper favoured was rather like the science he found so enlightening: it advanced through the 'piecemeal' rejection of unsatisfactory or impracticable social programmes and their replacement by alternatives, themselves available to critical examination. Popper's term for this was 'social engineering'.

As might be expected with a body of work as vast in scope as Popper's, critics are plentiful: most criticisms revolve around his robust insistence on a hierarchy of knowledge at a time when scholarly consensus had moved to the acceptance of a plurality of knowledge, none enjoying privileged status over the others. Popper, as an absolutist, rejected such relativism: for him, there was but one truth and one science that could approach it.

Further reading

Corvi, Roberta INTRODUCTION TO THE THOUGHT OF KARL POPPER, trans. Patrick Camiller, Routledge, 1996.
O'Hear, Anthony (ed.) KARL POPPER: PHILOSOPHY AND POLITICS, Cambridge University Press, 1995.
Shearmur, Jeremy THE POLITICAL THOUGHT OF KARL POPPER, Routledge, 1996.

E.C.

PROPP, Vladimir

Cultural theorist/narratologist	born Russia 1895–1970
Associated with	NARRATOLOGY ■ RUSSIAN FORMALISM ■ FOLK CULTURE
Influences include	AFANAS'EV ■ SAUSSURE ■ SHKLOVSKY
Shares common ground with	LÉVI-STRAUSS ■ TODOROV ■ BARTHES
Main works	MORPHOLOGY OF THE FOLKTALE (1928) HISTORICAL ROOTS OF THE WONDERTALE (1946) PROBLEMS OF LAUGHTER AND THE COMIC (1976)

PROPP WAS BORN in St Petersburg and stayed there for most of his life, firstly as a student of languages and philology during the Revolution where he was a contemporary of Bakhtin, and subsequently as a teacher of folklore at the University of Leningrad. Propp's importance lies in his contribution to our understanding of both the importance and the function of narratives in culture – and in particular to debates around the possibility of universal, as opposed to culturally specific, accounts of narrative. In his most important work, *Morphology of the Folktale*, Propp's approach is uncompromisingly scientific. He referred to himself as an 'empiricist' and he considered the laws of narrative as accessible as those governing any other phenomena. Drawing on the scientific interest in the folktale which emerged in Russia during the mid-nineteenth century, Propp undertakes a detailed structural analysis of 100 tales from the collection of Afanas'ev. The central idea of the work is simple and has three strands: in spite of an abundance of variety of detail, the tales share one basic plot; this plot is constructed from thirty one 'functions' (the basic units of narrative which advance the plot) which occur in identical sequential order even though not every function is present in all the tales; and that seven recurring 'spheres of action' (which correspond approximately to 'characters') form the nucleus of all examples. Propp's final six functions are as follows:

XXV	A difficult task is proposed to the Hero
XXVI	The task is resolved
XXVII	The Hero is recognised
XXVIII	The false Hero or Villain is exposed
XXIX	The Hero is given a new appearance
XXX	The Villain is punished
XXXI	The Hero is married and ascends the throne

Besides the Hero and Villain, the remaining spheres of action are: donor (provider); helper; princess (sought-after person) and her father; dispatcher; and false hero.

The applicability of this formula to Western folktales is immediately apparent. It may also be extended to other narrative genres, such as chivalric romance or twentieth-century spy thrillers, and a Proppian analysis of the science-fiction narrative *Star Trek* is both fascinating and productive. The limits of such generalisations are immediately apparent, however, and the analysis of narratives of any sophistication (even those ending without narrative resolution) invariably demands a refinement of Propp's method. Commentators have widely criticised Propp's failure to address the cultural context of the tales and the way he ignores the problems of the extent to which their Russianness is a mediating factor on the structural principles which drive them. More recent narratologists (Greimas, Todorov, Barthes, Genette), by excavating at levels of structure deeper than Propp's linear analysis of plots and the surface character of his spheres of action, have approached a universal account of narrative far more closely. Propp's influence was constrained by his immersion in Soviet history. His interests in the formal aspects of narrative located him uncomfortably in relation to the demands of the socialist realism which dominated intellectual and aesthetic life during the Stalinist period. Propp was denounced for 'pro-Western sycophancy' on account of the proliferation of non-Soviet references in the Bibliography of *Historical Roots*. He acknowledged these shortcomings, apologised and survived in his academic post. Propp's consequent renunciation of Western sources isolated him from European structuralist work on narratology.

Morphology was not translated until 1958. Lévi-Strauss published a critique in 1960 which was critical of aspects of Propp's theoretical framework.

Further reading

Lévi-Strauss, C. STRUCTURAL ANTHROPOLOGY, Vol 2, trans. M. Layton, Allen Lane, 1977.
Liberman, A. (ed.) VLADIMIR PROPP: THEORY AND HISTORY OF FOLKLORE, Manchester University Press, 1984.
Mletinskij, E. 'A Structural–Typological Study of the Wondertale', GENRE 4, 1971, pp. 249–79.

B.A.

RADCLIFFE-BROWN,
Alfred Reginald

Social anthropologist	born England 1881–1955
Associated with	FUNCTIONALISM ▪ ETHNOGRAPHIC METHOD ▪ CHICAGO SCHOOL
Influences include	HADDON ▪ RIVERS ▪ DURKHEIM ▪ COMTE
Shares common ground with	MALINOWSKI ▪ FORTES ▪ FIRTH ▪ ELKIN
Main works	THE ANDAMAN ISLANDERS (1922)
	THE SOCIAL ORGANISATION OF AUSTRALIAN TRIBES (1931)
	METHOD IN SOCIAL ANTHROPOLOGY (1958)
	STRUCTURE AND FUNCTION IN PRIMITIVE SOCIETY (1961)

ALFRED RADCLIFFE-BROWN was born in Birmingham, England, and graduated in mental and moral sciences from Cambridge University in 1905. He was influenced by his lecturers Haddon and Rivers (to whom he dedicated his thesis and book on the Andaman Islanders) as well as a number of other philosophical, sociological and political figures. These included William Whewell and his theories of the philosophy of science, the philosophies of Comte, Montesquieu and Spencer, the communitarian views of Kropotkin and the sociological approaches of Durkheim, Henri Hubert, Marcel Mauss and Havelock Ellis. This mixture of influences shaped Radcliffe-Brown's desire to develop a research methodology that combined intensive and systematic fieldwork with the development of a rigorous theoretical framework.

Radcliffe-Brown expounded his programme early on and this structured his life's work. His aim was to apply the methods and principles of natural science to the study of society by: (1) treating social phenomena as natural facts which could be explained in terms of conditions and laws; (2) applying scientific method to ethnography; and (3) testing and verifying anthropological theories and interpretations against empirical data. Radcliffe-Brown was one of the progenitors of the theory of functionalism and explication of scientific anthropological method that came to characterise the British school of anthropology.

Unlike many of his colleagues, Radcliffe-Brown's career was conducted on the international stage and he rarely stayed anywhere for more than a few years. He held Chairs of Anthropology at Cape Town, Sydney, Chicago (1931–37) and Oxford (1937–46), in addition to visiting and other appointments at

Yenching (1935), São Paulo (1942–44), the Farouk I University of Alexandria (1947–49), the Rhodes University of South Africa (1951–54) and at the Universities of London, Birmingham and Manchester. This international reach and his brilliance as a teacher ensured that his ideas and theories had a major international impact on scholars and students alike. For example, he influenced the formation of the Chicago School of social anthropology and the emergence of anthropology in South Africa and Australia.

Radcliffe-Brown's own fieldwork was conducted in the Andaman Islands (1906–08) and north-west Australia (1910–12), although he also made extensive use of other fieldwork data in subsequent studies of kinship and social organisation. His book, *The Andaman Islanders*, was published the same year as Malinowski's *Argonauts of the Western Pacific*, but did not attract similar public acclaim. This disparate reception may have accounted for the rivalry between the two men that persisted throughout their careers. It is arguable that Radcliffe-Brown's book deserved more attention because, in addition to the ethnographic material and his analysis of myth and ceremony, Radcliffe-Brown also outlined his theoretical approach to anthropology that was to become the keynote of his work.

His essential theoretical position was that social structures could be understood as a system of relations of association in which social values were encoded in institutional arrangements. He therefore believed that it was possible to schematise the structural characteristics of societies in terms of typologies as the basis for explaining their social dynamics and capacity to adapt to social change. His focus on reducing social phenomena and cultural patterns to sets of relationships and abstract propositions meant that while his approach approximated the desire to achieve 'scientific' precision in analysis, the approach was regarded as sterile and unresponsive to the humanist-inspired approaches of anthropologists like Evans-Pritchard.

Although he was not a prolific publisher, a number of his works have had lasting effects both on the ethnographic literature and on debates about social anthropological theory. His *The Social Organisation of Australian Tribes* had a prodigious and lasting impact because of its ambitious and comprehensive attempt to catalogue an enormous amount of data on all of Aboriginal Australia, and the development of a typology of relationship systems based on this data. Even though his analysis has been somewhat discredited, this book has been cited in recent land-rights claims by indigenous Australians. Radcliffe-Brown also wrote on a wide range of other anthropological topics: totemism, primitive law, sanctions, patrilineal and matrilineal succession, taboo, joking relationships, religion, and political systems. Generous assessments of Radcliffe-Brown's work and legacy can be found in collections by his students (Eggan 1937; Fortes and Evans-Pritchard 1940; Radcliffe-Brown and Forde 1950).

Further reading

Eggan, Fred (ed.) SOCIAL ANTHROPOLOGY OF NORTH AMERICAN TRIBES, University of Chicago Press, 1937.

Fortes, Meyer ed. SOCIAL STRUCTURE: STUDIES PRESENTED TO A.R. RADCLIFFE-BROWN, Clarendon, 1949.

Fortes, Meyer and Evans-Pritchard, E. (eds.) AFRICAN POLITICAL SYSTEMS, Oxford University Press, 1940.

Radcliffe-Brown, A.R. and Forde, Daryll (eds.) AFRICAN SYSTEMS OF KINSHIP AND MARRIAGE, Oxford University Press, 1950.

J.C.

RAWLS, John

Political and moral theorist	born USA 1921—
Associated with	LIBERALISM ■ DISTRIBUTIVE JUSTICE
Influences include	LOCKE ■ MILL ■ KANT
Shares common ground with	HART ■ DWORKIN ■ NOZICK
Main works	A THEORY OF JUSTICE (1971)
	THE IDEA OF AN OVERLAPPING CONSENSUS (1987)
	POLITICAL LIBERALISM (1993)

ORN IN BALTIMORE in 1921, Rawls taught philosophy for over thirty years at Harvard University. In a series of essays he developed his framework for an egalitarian liberalism and provided a theoretical foundation for the political and ethical concepts that would dominate the latter part of the twentieth century. His ideas were first expressed in the essay *Justice as Fairness* (1958), which was developed in *Distributive Justice* (1967) and culminated in his major work *A Theory of Justice*.

The widely acclaimed and highly influential book placed Rawls alongside eminent writers such as Hart, Dworkin and Nozick. *A Theory of Justice* is a seminal treatise of relevance to political scientists, economists, philosophers and legal theorists alike. Set against a period of public disquiet concerning the role and justice of political and social institutions, the 1970s saw a revival of liberal ideas in political philosophy. Rawls's aim was to produce a new framework for his egalitarian liberalism based on contractarian political theory, and his work was to have a major impact on public policy and social theory.

Though Rawls's doctrine has strong roots in the works of Locke, Mill and Kant, he is identified as a social liberal. He developed a concept of social organisation based upon the classic liberal concerns for genuine freedom, equality and justice. Like Locke and Mill, Rawls believes that for government to be legitimate it must be democratic in principle. However, unlike Mill, Rawls is not a utilitarian, believing utilitarian concepts to be inadequate and incompatible with moral judgments.

In *A Theory of Justice* Rawls articulates his commitment to a just society, where justice means freedom and where individuals have a fair opportunity to pursue their objects and values. He provides a theory that rejects utilitarianism on the grounds that such principles undermine justice, and instead emphasises the priority of 'right over good'. He argues that all social arrangements require legitimacy and seeks to provide a theory to explain our reasoning about what constitutes justice. Rawls outlines and develops a number of key principles which must be satisfied if any given society is to be just. He uses a social contract model to discover the principles of social justice and to establish that there are key binding moral principles that all individuals would agree to.

Rawls imagines a group of individuals who are located in the 'original position' behind a '*veil of ignorance*'. These individuals must choose the principles for determining the principles of justice for that society. The individuals lack all knowledge about themselves. They do not know their class, status, sex, religion, intelligence or natural ability, although they are aware that these are features which will exist once the 'veil' is lifted. Rawls suggests that 'no one is in a position to tailor principles to his advantage' and that a 'maximin' strategy will apply, with all individuals ensuring that the least well off are put in the best position available. Rawls contends that two principles will derive from the 'original position':

First Principle – 'Each person is to have equal right to the most extensive total system of equal basic liberties compatible with a similar system of liberty for all.'
Second Principle – 'Social and economic inequalities are to be arranged so that they are both:
(a) to the greatest benefit of the least advantaged,
(b) attached to offices and positions open to all under conditions of fair equality and opportunity.'

The first principle of basic liberties has an underlying individualism and ensures that there are certain rights which must be respected and which cannot be surrendered on aggregate welfare grounds. The second 'difference' principle attempts to attain fairness through economic distribution. The model is expository and justificatory. It provides a more manageable analytic device and Rawls also believes that the resulting principles must be objective since any person who entered the *original position* would identify the same key principles.

A Theory of Justice has been subjected to rigorous criticism and assessment since its publication. Critics include Marxists, feminists, communitarians and social and liberal theorists. Though an appealing device, critics argue that the 'original position' is not altogether convincing. It is suggested that Rawls has simply created conditions to achieve his desired outcome, that the process is therefore subjective and inconsistent. The 'original position' fails to take account of the fact that man is in reality intolerant and cannot be abstracted from his material circumstances. As a result, many critics question the validity of Rawls's two principles.

In an effort to defend his theory of justice, Rawls responded to his critics in the article 'The Idea of an Overlapping Consensus' (1987) and in *Political Liberalism*. Rawls refines his thesis propounded in *A Theory of Justice* and suggests that although individuals will hold divergent conceptions of good, they are able to discover through an 'overlapping consensus' a shared belief as to the basic structure of a democratic society.

Further reading

Barry, B. THE LIBERAL THEORY OF JUSTICE: A CRITICAL EXAMINATION OF THE PRINCIPAL DOCTRINES IN A THEORY OF JUSTICE BY JOHN RAWLS, Oxford University Press, 1973.
Blocker, H. and Smith, E. JOHN RAWLS' THEORY OF SOCIAL JUSTICE, Ohio University Press, 1980.
Wolff, R. UNDERSTANDING RAWLS: A RECONSTRUCTION AND CRITIQUE OF A THEORY OF JUSTICE, Princeton University Press, 1977.

G.B.M.

REICH, Wilhelm

Psychologist	born Austria 1897–1957
Associated with	ORGONES ▪ SEXUAL POLITICS
Influences include	MARX ▪ FREUD
Shares common ground with	FOUCAULT ▪ GUATTARI
Main works	THE MASS PSYCHOLOGY OF FASCISM (TRANS., 1970)
	THE FUNCTION OF THE ORGASM (1927)
	CHARACTER-ANALYSIS (TRANS., 1970)

WILHELM REICH WAS a psychologist and an outstanding pupil of Freud, who exiled himself to the USA away from 'Fascist/Stalinist' Europe. An ardent socialist and advocate of sexual freedom, he proclaimed a cosmic unity of all energy and built a machine (the orgone accumulator) to concentrate energy on human beings.

The strength of Reich's analysis consists in showing how psychic repression depends on social repression. Since social repression needs psychic repression precisely in order to form docile subjects and to ensure the reproduction of the social formation, including its repressive structures. Reich's analysis of social repression is not based upon a conception of familial repression coextensive with civilisation – rather, it is civilisation that must be understood in terms of a social repression inherent to a given form of social production. Social repression acts upon desire – defined not as a 'lack' (see Lacan) or solely as needs and interests – only by the means of sexual repression. Of course the family is the agent of this psychic repression, in that it guarantees 'a mass psychological reproduction of the economic system of a society'. Thus the social repression of desire or sexual repression – that is, the *stasis* of libidinal energy – is that which actualises and engages desire in this reciprocal impasse, organised by the repressive society.

Reich was the first to raise the problem of the relationship between desire and the social field (and went further than Marcuse, who treats the problem lightly). This new 'materialist psychiatry' situated the problem in terms of desire, and was the first to reject the explanations of a summary Marxism which argued that the masses are fooled or mystified. However both Reich and psychoanalysis fail to determine just how desire is inserted into the economic infrastructure, the insertion of drives into social production. And ultimately it was this failure which left psychoanalysis as merely having the role of explaining the subjective, the negative, and the inhibited, without participating directly as a psychoanalysis engaged in the positivity of the revolutionary movement. Reich argues that it is better to depart in search of orgones, the vital and cosmic particles of desire, that fell to earth from space and on which a person's orgasmic energy partly depended.

Thus Reich concluded in favour of an intra-atomic cosmic energy – the orgone – generative of an electrical flux and carrying submicroscopic particles, the bions. This energy produced differences in potential or intensities distributed on the body considered from a molecular viewpoint, and was associated with a mechanics of fluids in this same body considered from a molar point of viewpoint. What defined the libido as sexuality was therefore the association of the two modes of operation, mechanical and electrical, in a sequence with two poles, molar and molecular (mechanical tension, electrical charge, mechanical relaxation). Reich thought he had thus overcome the alternative between *mechanism* and *vitalism*, since these functions, mechanical and electrical, existed in matter in general, but were combined in a particular sequence within the living. And above all he upheld the basic psychoanalytic truth, the supreme disavowel of which he was able to denounce Freud: the independence of sexuality with regard to reproduction, the subordination of progressive or repressive reproduction to sexuality as a cycle.

Obviously Reich's final theory is problematic when comparing sexuality with cosmic phenomena such as 'electrical storms', 'the blue colour of the sky and the blue-grey of atmospheric haze', the blue of the orgone, 'St. Elmo's fire, and the blueish formations [of] sunspot activity', fluids and flows, and matter and particles; but in the end this seems eminently more adequate than the reduction of sexuality to the pitiful 'little familial secret'. Reich remained steadfast in viewing libido as the core of Freudian theory. Justified by his ample clinical evidence of the existence of sexual energy, Reich was led, unlike Freud, to the laboratory and to the discovery of the 'libido' *in vitro*. In so doing, he inherited the criticism and stigmatisation that Freud had previously endured. But more than this, for with his discovery of a tangible, physical energy, Reich could not provide the same sort of appeasement that the world demanded and received from Freud. Freud capitulated (sublimation, death-instinct, and cultural theories) and gained fame; Reich died in prison.

Perhaps Reich did not go far enough in denouncing the way in which psychoanalysis joins forces with social repression, because he did not see that the tie linking psychoanalysis with capitalism is not merely ideological but depends directly on an economic mechanism.

Further reading

Meo, James D. Der Orgonakkumulator: Ein Handbuch, Zweitzavsendems, 1994.

Robinson, P. THE SEXUAL RADICALS, Maurice Temple Smith Ltd, 1970.
Rycroft, C. REICH, Collins, 1971.

N.L.

RICARDO, David

Economist/politician	born England 1772–1823
Associated with	VALUE AND DISTRIBUTION THEORY
Influences include	SMITH ■ MALTHUS ■ SAY
Shares common ground with	MARX ■ BENTHAM ■ MILL
Main works	AN ESSAY ON THE INFLUENCE OF A LOW PRICE CORN ON THE PROFITS OF STOCK (1815)
	PROPOSALS FOR AN ECONOMICAL AND SECURE CURRENCY (1816)
	PRINCIPLES OF POLITICAL ECONOMY (1817)

DAVID RICARDO WAS born in London. His family were Sephardic Jews who had emigrated from Holland in 1760. His father was a successful member of the stock exchange and Ricardo was to join him in business at the age of fourteen. Having been disconnected from his family, when he married the daughter of a Quaker, he continued as a broker and then a jobber on the Stock Exchange. By 1814 Ricardo had built up a substantial personal fortune and was able to retire and to concentrate his efforts on more academic pursuits. However, these were to be concentrated into a relatively short period as he died in 1823. He was also elected to the House of Commons in 1819.

Ricardo's interest in economics began when he read Adam Smith's *Wealth of Nations*. His major work, *Principles of Political Economy*, was in many ways a response to this work and the course of economics changed in two distinct ways as a result of his success. First, his methodology was extremely theoretical, without, however, preventing him using the theoretical results to suggest public policy, and second he redefined the scope of political economics as an inquiry into the laws of distribution of income.

The question of distribution of income between landlords, capitalists and labour was of primary concern to Ricardo. His theory therefore needed to explain the types of income that each of these sectors of the economy would receive (namely rent, interest, profit and wages). As he developed this theory it became apparent that this was not possible without first addressing the question of value. He proposed a labour theory of value which was later to be extended by Marx. However, Ricardo himself was to later admit that value did not uniquely depend upon the quantity of labour, as capital is also productive, but the implication remained that the quantity of labour was the key determinant.

Ricardo showed that there was a conflict between the landowners, capitalists and the proletariat. The Malthusian population theory was incorporated to suggest that the supply of labour would, in the long run, continually adjust so that the natural wage to labour would be at the subsistence level. Further, that over time population would increase, necessitating the agricultural use of less fertile land. Ricardo gave a clear exposition of the law of diminishing returns and introduced the theory of differential rent, which showed that as this less fertile land was used, so the landowners would benefit from higher rents. Thus the landowners' share of income would increase and consequently the profits to capitalists would fall. Ricardo perceived that this lowering of profits to capitalists would result in lower capital accumulation which, in turn, could lead the economy to a steady state. Practically, this was used to argue against the Corn Laws of the time which artificially set minimum prices for corn. Ricardo argued that the high price of corn resulted in high rent and therefore was accelerating the approach of the steady state. Further, he argued against tariffs on corn imports as their removal would put a temporary hold on the movement toward the steady state. Ricardo was strongly in favour of international free trade as it could benefit all countries and he showed this, most clearly, through the theory of comparative advantage.

Ricardo's theories became extremely powerful weapons in the struggle for power between the capitalists and the landlords. He was very much in favour of *laissez-faire* capitalism and defended, against Malthus, Say's law which states that there could not be under-consumption and unemployment. Further he believed work-relief schemes should be abolished as this merely deprived capital from those who best knew how to use it. Similarly, taxation should be kept to a minimum, and the poor laws scrapped as they interfered with the workings of the labour market. In retrospect, Keynes was to argue that the success of Ricardo and the domination of his theories was to handicap Western economics for over a century.

Further reading

Blaug, M. RICARDIAN ECONOMICS, Yale University Press, 1958.
Finkelstein, J. and Thimm, A.L. ECONOMISTS AND SOCIETY, Harper & Row, 1973, pp. 62–87.
Hollander, S. THE ECONOMICS OF DAVID RICARDO, University of Toronto Press, 1979.

S.M.C.

RIESMAN, David

Social scientist	born USA 1909—
Associated with	LONELY CROWD ■ OTHER-DIRECTEDNESS ■ AMERICAN SOCIAL CHARACTER
Influences include	TOCQUEVILLE ■ FROMM ■ HUGHES
Shares common ground with	MILLS ■ LASCH ■ FROMM
Main works	THE LONELY CROWD (1950) INDIVIDUALISM RECONSIDERED (1954) ON HIGHER EDUCATION (1980)

RIESMAN GRADUATED FROM Harvard University in 1931 with a degree in biochemical sciences. He went on to Harvard Law School, graduating in 1934. He worked in the law with the US Supreme Court before spending four years as Professor of Law at Buffalo University, and ending with a year as Deputy Assistant District Attorney of New York County.

During the Second World War Riesman studied psychoanalysis with Erich Fromm. Fromm exerted a major influence on Riesman's thought. He introduced him to the significance of Freud's work and impressed upon him the importance of the notion of social character. Shortly after the war, Riesman moved from psychoanalysis to the social sciences at the University of Chicago. He was taken under the wing of the department Chair, Everett Hughes, who turned Riesman towards sociology. Riesman never earned a Ph.D. in sociology, nor in any other discipline. He prefers to see himself as a social scientist working on the borderlines between disciplines rather than a specialist bound by the blinkers of his chosen specialism. Riesman also felt that sociology leaned too far to the left and wanted the space that interdisciplinary work afforded.

Riesman is best known for *The Lonely Crowd*, which he wrote with Nathan Glazer and Reuel Denney. The book was a huge success, selling over a million copies and establishing Riesman as a major commentator on culture. In 1958 he accepted the post of Henry Ford II Professor in Social Sciences (not sociology) at Harvard. He became emeritus in 1980.

The thesis that Riesman developed in *The Lonely Crowd* was bold and compelling. He argued that social character in the USA has been gradually transformed from tradition-directed to other-directed character. By 'other directedness' Riesman meant an orientation to social life which is closely tuned to the example and fashion set by the mass media. Television, advertising, public relations and marketing set the standards which the other-directed personality seeks to emulate. By the same token the standards of family and community life have an attenuated significance. Social mobility and the penetration of the media in mass society have the effect of tearing individuals from their places of origin and submitting them to a variety of seductive external influences. Riesman recognised that the cult heroes of consumer culture were no longer figures drawn from the local community and the sphere of production. Instead they were movie stars, pop idols, television presenters and sports personalities. The other-directed personality develops strong feelings of attachment to these distant role models. Although Riesman's argument is couched in American experience, he presents the American story as the future for all industrialising consumer cultures.

Riesman's argument was one of the first to present a view of the media and mass society which challenged the naïve progressive evolutionism of liberal analysis and the principled pessimism of the Frankfurt School. It refused to present the individual in mass society as caught between the Scylla of absolute freedom or the Charybdis of absolute control. Riesman's individual is a reflexive agent who is not only seduced by the myths of advertising and the mass media, but also sees through them.

Riesman's work after the 1960s moved on to the terrain of higher education. He presented the expansion of the university system as the triumph of the faculty over earlier controls. Professional academic standards and processes displaced the power of religious bodies, business-oriented boards of trustees, vigilante groups and powerful college and university presidents. There are echoes of Weber in this analysis. But Riesman does not quite draw out the same inferences for the disenchantment of the world that Weber did in his account of bureaucratisation and rationalisation. Although critical of many aspects of the modern university, Riesman defends higher education as a social benefit to be cherished against attack.

Less well known is Riesman's lifelong defence of maverick figures in social science. His interest in Thorstein Veblen and Alexis de Tocqueville was considered unfashionable at a time in which classical social theory was being redefined in terms of the legacies of Marx, Durkheim, Weber and the American schools of structural functionalism and symbolic interactionism. Riesman is attracted to Veblen, Tocqueville and Freud because their work insisted on an engagement with society. They saw themselves as social critics as well as social scientists, and this is also Riesman's self-image.

Riesman's work has been criticised for failing to distinguish adequately between inner-directedness and autonomy. His work lacks an empirical dimension so that his arguments about deep cultural change exist only at the level of ideas. His description of contemporary society as 'a lonely crowd' of individuals suggests a vision of transcendence. But this is never fully worked out in Riesman's work. He is clearly dissatisfied with many of the impersonal, status-driven features of contemporary consumer culture, but he fails to suggest convincing ways forward. The work on personality types and the omnipresence of the values of consumer culture is likely to endure. Several of the main themes in current debates about sign cultures and globalisation can be found in Riesman's work. In this respect, he is a neglected figure. Few sociologists working in the 1950s and 1960s were so prescient about the trends that a later generation came to label as 'postmodernism'.

Further reading

Gans, H.J. THE MAKING OF AMERICANS: ESSAYS IN HONOR OF DAVID RIESMAN, University of Pennsylvania Press, 1979.
Haskell, T.L. and Teichgrueber, R.F. THE CULTURE OF THE MARKET, Cambridge University Press, 1993.
Lipset, S.M. and Lowenthal, L. (eds.) CULTURE AND SOCIAL CHARACTER: THE WORK OF DAVID RIESMAN REVIEWED, The Free Press, 1961.

S.M.

RORTY, Richard

Philosopher/literary theorist	born USA 1931—
Associated with	PRAGMATISM ■ IRONY
Influences include	DEWEY ■ NIETZSCHE ■ WITTGENSTEIN
Shares common ground with	DERRIDA ■ DAVIDSON ■ BLOOM
Main works	PHILOSOPHY AND THE MIRROR OF NATURE (1979)
	CONSEQUENCES OF PRAGMATISM (1982)
	CONTINGENCY, IRONY, AND SOLIDARITY (1989)

RICHARD RORTY IS presently Kenan Professor of Humanities at the University of Virginia. Prior to this, he taught at Wellesley, and Princeton University, where he was Stuart Professor of Philosophy. Aside from his highly influential books, Rorty has also published extensively in literary magazines, academic journals and served as President of the Eastern Division of the American Philosophical Association. His decision to abandon a prominent post in philosophy for one in the field of humanities is reflective of his numerous writings.

A prominent critic of the Western philosophical tradition, Rorty believes that *Philosophy* needs to shed its scientific claims and proceed as a literary genre. Or as Rorty once wrote, 'the best hope for philosophy is not to practice Philosophy'. As a pragmatist and advocate of what has been termed the linguistic turn, Rorty urges that certain concepts which have tormented philosophical discourses for centuries such as: mind, soul, Reality, Truth, consciousness, and so on, ought to be regarded as elements of language. They should not be regarded as entries external to language or existing independently of human intervention. Thus, philosophers have treated these concepts in a non-contingent fashion by granting them intuitive or natural status.

In *Philosophy and the Mirror of Nature*, Rorty puts forth that Western metaphysics from Plato to Descartes should be forsaken. This assault on classical Realism and philosophical foundations holds that the problem of knowledge is created rather than innate. Descartes is targeted as the main villain. For Rorty, Descartes's distinction between the mind and body forces a division between the mind's understanding of the world. In order to dissolve this tradition, language should cease to be regarded as a medium between the self and the world. Drawing from Dewey, Rorty claims that language is analogous to the 'toolbox' metaphor so endearing to pragmatism. Under this rubric, language is regarded as a set of tools for contending with the world

rather than representing or mirroring the world. This move has special implications for philosophy and the study of culture.

If language is to function or be used in a non-representational manner, if it is
void of a foundation, then does a standard exist against which the long term
concern of truth can be measured? Rorty believes that the idea of an objective truth is illusory. The truth as 'out there' awaiting discovery is set aside.
Truth does not exist independently from human creation; we do not discover
truth, we create it. It is a quality/characteristic of our descriptions. Aligning
truth with language use, Rorty constitutes a literary/poetic culture where
narrative replaces 'hard scientific fact'.

In *Contingency, Irony, and Solidarity*, Rorty cites the Romantics as fully
understanding the importance of imagination and rhetoric over reason and
truth. Concerning persuasion, Rorty writes 'that a talent for speaking differently, rather than for arguing well, is the chief instrument of cultural change'.
It is this acknowledgement on behalf of Rorty that blurs his role as philosopher
and would seem to place him with cultural/literary theorists that stress polysemy, meaning instability, and the play of signifiers. It is with literature (and
Rorty utilises this term broadly to include film, music and television) that
progressive change is possible, that useless vocabularies give way to the more
useful.

Rather than look towards Theory or Philosophy as a grand system of
knowledge, we should turn towards literature as a new way of describing
our concerns. George Orwell's *Nineteen Eighty-Four* serves as an example.
Rorty regards Orwell as an ironist. As an ironist, Orwell's ability to 'redescribe'
totalitarianism directs our attention to details that may have been overlooked.
By 'redescribe' or 'rediscription' Rorty means that certain events or objects are
discussed in an unfamiliar, neologistic jargon to tempt readers into adopting
and expanding this new way of speaking rather than simply adopting and
extending old ways of questioning and speaking. This attitude is one that is
aware of its foundational lack, yet precisely due to this lacking, the ironist is
licensed to produce narratives without appealing to a conclusion.

Further reading

Hall, D.L. RICHARD RORTY: PROPHET AND POET OF THE NEW PRAGMATISM,
SUNY Press, 1994.
Malachowski, A. READING RORTY: MIRROR OF NATURE, Blackwell, 1990.
Wheeler, K.M. ROMANTICISM, PRAGMATISM AND DECONSTRUCTION, Blackwell,
1993.

R.G.

ROSTOW, Walt W.

Economist/historian	born USA 1916—
Associated with	STAGE THEORY ■ CONVERGENCE ■ INDUSTRIAL SOCIETY ■ TAKE-OFF
Influences include	MARSHALL ■ GROCE ■ PLATO
Shares common ground with	MARX ■ SCHUMPETER ■ PARSONS
Main works	THE PROCESS OF ECONOMIC GROWTH (1953) THE STAGES OF ECONOMIC GROWTH (1960) POLITICS AND THE STAGES OF GROWTH (1971)

A FTER EDUCATION AT Yale (BA and Ph.D.) and attendance at Oxford University, Walt Rostow taught at Columbia, Oxford, the Massachusetts Institute of Technology and then, for many years, as Professor of Economics and History at the University of Texas at Austin. During the most difficult times of the Cold War, he served in the US State Department and as a special assistant to Presidents Kennedy and Johnson. Although he is of far greater eloquence and sophisticated technique, much of the work of Rostow elaborates the simple and often single-minded stage theories of the proponents of economic development for the poor nations of the world. During the 1950s and 1960s the distinctions between underdevelopment and development seemed naked and unambiguous, and in essence could be defined as a contemporary version of an historical phenomenon – all rich nations had at some time been poor. At a time when the Cold War determined that blocks of poor regions were to be claimed for either democracy or Communism, the strident and elegant assertions of *The Stages of Economic Growth*, famous for its subtitle, presented transition as lengthy but understandable and attainable through five stages: 'It is possible to identify all societies in their economic dimensions, as lying within one of five categories: the traditional society, the pre-conditions for take-off into self-sustaining growth, the take-off, maturity, and the age of high mass consumption. These stages are not merely descriptive.' Within the Rostovian perspective, a study of history led to a choice of democracy and markets over Communism and planning, and his approach generally represented a restatement of conventional neoclassical economics but within an historical framework which explicitly acknowledged the causative and progressive work of dynamic international and social elements.

Although Rostow plainly draws upon a tradition of stage theory which includes the works of Gustav Schmoller, Bruno Hilderbrand and Friedrich

List, his contribution served to switch attention away from the metaphysics of stage development and its moral or racial dimensions, towards explicitly material interpretation, and away from narrow economism towards an explanation of economic development in terms of variables other than the direct components of growth itself. The approach was broadly outlined in *The Process of Economic Growth*, the first part of which applied these to issues of war, the terms of trade and public policy. In order to uncover historical processes behind the conventional variables of capital and labour, Rostow nominated the workings or differential presence of six propensities: to develop and nourish fundamenal science, to apply science to economic ends, to accept innovation, to seek material advance, to consume, and to have children. These were designed to reflect the underlying value system effective within society and differentiate degrees of success and failure in the economic development stakes.'

In effect, *The Stages of Economic Growth* and later work is a generalised historical application which posits the essential characteristics required of the proto-industrialising system, the vital role of an accelerated rate of effective investment during the fundamenal transition of 'take-off' (to the well known but now hotly contested level of 10 per cent of national income) and the notion of cultural convergence of all industrial systems in their maturity phase of high consumption. Rostow produces a stage theory which provides a direct mechanism of transition between and dynamics within phases and predicts a convergent, calm 'end of history' outcome.

Work during the 1970s was designed to test such claims, but professional historians have on the whole rejected Rostow's main mechanisms of transition and criticised the tendency to underplay the impacts of international or exogenous factors on national development. Although by far the best known of all the products of twentieth-century historians, the Rostovian schema has not accorded very coherently to the hisorical experiences of the century. The end of the Cold War and the collapse of the planned and centralised regimes is not unquestionably a victory for markets or a measure of global development and convergence: much of East Asian development appears to arrive from novel public–private institutional arrangements, whilst the great cases of Southern Asia, Africa and South America are hardly yet evidence of either successful transitions or of the relevance of a long period of sociocultural preconditioning.

Finally, Rostow's emphasis on the nation-state as either organisation or market does not sit comfortably with the shifts of power to the extremes of globalisation and localism. The Rostovian view might well persist because of the clarity with which it summarised and represented the high points of modernist developmental analysis, and the thrust it gave to a broad-based approach to historical interpretation and change.

Further reading

Adelman, I. and Taft Morris, C. SOCIETY, POLITICS AND ECONOMIC DEVELOP-MENT, Johns Hopkins University Press, 1967.
Kuznets, S. MODERN ECONOMIC GROWTH, Yale University Press, 1966.
Rostow, W.W. THE ECONOMICS OF TAKE-OFF INTO SUSTAINED GROWTH, International Economic Association, 1963.

I.I.

SAID, Edward

Literary theorist	born Palestine 1935—
Associated with	POST-COLONIALISM ■ ORIENTALISM ■ CONTRAPUNTAL READING
Influences include	GRAMSCI ■ ALTHUSSER ■ WILLIAMS ■ FOUCAULT
Shares common ground with	SPIVAK ■ BHABHA ■ SULERI
Main works	ORIENTALISM (1978) THE WORLD, THE TEXT, AND THE CRITIC (1983) MUSICAL ELABORATIONS (1991) CULTURE AND IMPERIALISM (1993) PEACE AND ITS DISCONTENTS (1996)

EDWARD SAID RECEIVED his BA from Princeton in 1957 and Harvard granted him an MA in 1960 and a Ph.D. in 1964, both in English. He has lectured at Harvard, Johns Hopkins and Yale. From 1989 to 1992 he held the Old Dominion Foundation Professorship in the Humanities at Columbia University where he now Chairs the doctoral programme in Comparative Literature. Said's expansion of Foucault's theories about the relationship between power and discourse led him to an examination of the relationships between discourse and imperialism. Because of his Arabic heritage, a childhood spent in Palestine and Egypt and his subsequent emigration to the USA he generally restricts his focus to an examination of American, English and French imperialism and literature of the cultures of the Near East and Palestine.

Said's cardinal work, *Orientalism*, reconfigures the historical contruction of European and Euro-American discourses about Near-East civilisations, cultures and peoples, by redefining such 'Oriental' studies within the context of Western imperialism. Orientalism, as Western studies of the East, can only begin to be understood when examined as a discourse, in Foucaultian terms. The European and American discourse of Orientalism, Said maintains, enables 'the enormous systematic discipline by which European culture was able to manage – and even produce – the Orient politically, sociologically, militarily, ideologically, scientifically, and imaginatively during the post-Enlightenment period'. The primary argument remains centred around the power relationships of such discourses relative to political agendas. No Western discourse, whether literary or scientific, about a nation, culture or people can be inert within the context of imperialism and colonisation because all participants maintain a vested interest in how the cultures of the East and the Near East come to be defined. Thus, Said argues, 'the history of Orientalism has both an internal consistency and a highly articulated set of relationships to the dominant culture surrounding it'. Literary and historical texts are constructed within these political contexts, creating a discourse about the East as the cultural 'other'.

The image of exiles who must 'voyage in' to their own indigenous spaces, in effect living as *émigrés* within their own culture, is inherent to the expansion of Said's theory in *The World, the Text, and the Critic*. The image of exile reveals the sense of expatriation, separation and displacement often felt by those caught between the discourse of the dominant culture and their own experience of history. Said argues that those critics with an *émigré*'s 'double vision' occupy a unique space wherein cultural arbitration can occur. From their exile, Said believes, comes the possibility of contrapuntal reading, a reading of the spaces between cultures where connections have occurred. The critic enables the exchange of cultural capital between dominant and indigenous peoples which, in turn, permits a coherent system of relationships to develop. In effect, the critic creates and facilitates a unification of disparate ideologies through a contrapuntal reading of the systems involved.

In more recent works, *Musical Elaborations* and *Culture and Imperialism*, Said analyses the way nineteenth-century European and American imperialism continues to authorise the unified world it constructed. As in music, contrapuntal relationships occur between the nations, cultures and politics of imperialism that provide a space wherein, as he argues in *Culture and Imperialism*, we can 'think through and interpret together experiences that are discrepant, each with its particular agenda and pace of development, its own internal formation, its internal coherence and system of external relationships, all of them co-existing and interacting with others'. Imperialism and subsequent colonisation create areas of connection between all the participants of imperialism, whether colonises or indigenous. He rejects the idea that the 'Orient' remained passive during or after the process of Western imperialism, asking instead for a contrapuntal reading of the discourse of imperialism.

Further reading

Bhabha, Homi K. (ed.) NATION AND NARRATION, Routledge, 1990.
McClintock, Anne *et al.* **(eds.)** DANGEROUS LIAISONS: GENDER, NATION AND POSTCOLONIAL PERSPECTIVES, University of Minnesota Press, 1997.
Said, Edward W. THE PEN AND THE SWORD: CONVERSATIONS WITH DAVID BARSAMIAN, Common Courage Press, 1994.

T.T.

SAPIR, Edward

Cultural linguist/anthropologist	born Germany 1884–1939
Associated with	LINGUISTIC RELATIVISM ■ SAPIR–WHORF HYPOTHESIS
Influences include	BOAS ■ BLOOMFIELD
Shares common ground with	WHORF ■ LOWIE ■ LAKOFF
Main works	LANGUAGE: AN INTRODUCTION TO THE STUDY OF SPEECH (1921)
	LETTERS FROM EDWARD SAPIR TO ROBERT LOWIE (1965)
	SELECTED WRITINGS OF EDWARD SAPIR IN LANGUAGE, CULTURE AND PERSONALITY (ED. DAVID G. MANDELBAUM, 1949)

S APIR WAS BORN in Lauenberg and migrated to the USA as a young child, where he grew up and was educated in New York. After graduating in 1904 from Columbia University, he remained there to undertake graduate work with Franz Boas who inspired him to pursue the links between anthropology and linguistics. This formative influence shaped his lifelong work, although he also investigated many other areas, including Semitic studies, and poetry. Sapir furthered his research on American Indian languages as chief anthropologist for the Geological Survey of Canada (1920–25), subsequently moving to the University of Chicago, and in 1931 accepting a Chair at Yale.

Sapir's work on the cultural and anthropological dimensions of language has contributed to developments in a number of fields: linguistic anthropology, formal descriptive linguistics, cultural anthropology, personality and culture, and cultural studies. He is best remembered for the Sapir–Whorf hypothesis which proposes that the structure of language influences how people perceive the world and think.

Sapir's chief intellectual contributions were in the areas of cultural anthropology and linguistics. He was a meticulous ethnographer and the undisputed expert on numerous American Indian languages and customs for, unlike other anthropologists, Sapir combined his interest in recording the complex of native languages with the principle underlying forms of social organisation. In addition to arguing for the linguistic basis of cultural practice, Sapir also questioned the dominant anthropological assumption that culture (of primitive peoples) was not universal and fixed but changing, along with its linguistic structure. This reasoning was to influence contemporary anthropology and subsequent generations of anthropologists and linguists. His work also provided a bridge for the emerging fields of sociolinguistics, structuralism and cultural studies.

Sapir wrote only one book, *Language*, but it has had a significant and lasting impact. A large number of his research papers were published in *Selected Writings* and continue to inspire researchers, while the privately published *Letters from Edward Sapir to Robert Lowie* provide a fascinating insight into his ethnography, conceptual developments and reflections on cultural anthropology.

The oft cited Sapir–Whorf hypothesis was developed by his student, Benjamin Lee Whorf, who credited his mentor with initiating the idea. The hypothesis investigated the ways in which language structured perception, speech and behaviour by determining and constraining what and how phenomena could be apprehended and comprehended. A commonly cited example is the two Hopi words for water, 'keyi', meaning water in a container, and 'pahe', meaning flowing or unconstrained water, a distinction which allowed for much greater precision (and abbreviation) in daily life. More dramatic examples were phrases or sentences in which the linguistic structure itself seemed to determine how people comprehended phenomena, depending on parts of speech used, order of words, emphasis on abstraction or sensation and long-winded versus shorthand references. Whorf's premature death in 1941 meant that he could not defend his hypothesis against criticisms of linguists such as Noam Chomsky who proposed linguistic universals. Nonetheless, the Sapir–

Whorf hypothesis resurfaced in the 1970s and enjoyed currency among emerging forms of interdisciplinary cultural analysis.

Sapir was a scholar with wide interests, as reflected in the entries he wrote for the 1932 edition of the *Encyclopaedia of the Social Sciences*, in which he covered 'Group', 'Custom', 'Dialect', 'Fashion', 'Language', 'Personality' and 'Symbolism'. These entries are notable for their incisive analysis of dominant theories and alternative postulations with enduring relevance for today. He also became increasingly interested in the links between personality and culture, shaping the development of this new area of psychology. Later, he initiated research in the area of Semitic studies, an interest fanned by the Fascist oppression of Jewish people in the 1930s. In the field of linguistics, Sapir developed phonemic theory which analysed the sounds of a language and the systematic patterns of sounds that are perceived by listeners. This recognition of language as behaviour structured by linguistic rules and selection made Sapir, along with Leonard Bloomfield, one of the founders of formal descriptive linguistics. In addition to this highly technical work, Sapir undertook research on historical and comparative linguistics, looking at linguistic changes over time (language drift), and tracing connections between Indo-European and Semitic languages.

Sapir achieved many distinctions: as an unparalleled ethnographer of American Indian languages, as founding figure of cultural linguistics (and its interdisciplinary spin-offs), and as a formative influence on contemporary humanities.

Further reading

Darnell, Regna EDWARD SAPIR: LINGUIST, ANTHROPOLOGIST, HUMANIST, University of California Press, 1990.
Koerner, Konrad EDWARD SAPIR: APPRAISALS OF HIS LIFE AND WORK, J. Benjamin Publishing Co., 1984.
Preston, Richard 'Edward Sapir's Anthropology: Style, Structure and Method', AMERICAN ANTHROPOLOGIST, New Series, 68, 1966, pp. 1105–28.

J.C.

SARTRE, Jean-Paul

Philosopher/dramatist/novelist	born France 1905–1980
Associated with	EXISTENTIALISM ■ PHENOMENOLOGY ■ WESTERN MARXISM
Influences include	HEIDEGGER ■ FLAUBERT ■ VOLTAIRE
Shares common ground with	BARTHES ■ CAMUS ■ de BEAUVOIR ■ GORZ ■ LEFEBVRE ■ LUKÁCS
Main works	BEING AND NOTHINGNESS (1943) CRITIQUE OF DIALECTICAL REASON (1960) BETWEEN EXISTENTIALISM AND MARXISM (1974)

SARTRE IS ONE of the greatest intellectuals of the twentieth century and, in many ways, the very epitome of the public intellectual, though perhaps, in this respect, a figure at the end of a tradition stretching back to Voltaire. However, he failed his École Normale Supérieure *aggrégation* (degree) at the first attempt in 1928. The following year Sartre passed it in first place. During the 1930s he taught in lycées and spent a year studying existential phenomenology in Germany. His first novel, *Nausea* (1938), brought Sartre instant fame. He wrote his first great philosophical treatise, *Being and Nothingness*, during the Second World War, partly when he was a prisoner of the Germans in the early 1940s. Sartre was associated with the French Resistance in the later part of the war and in the post-war period he emerged as one of the leading figures on the Left in France, editor of the journal *Les Temps Modernes*, named after Charlie Chaplin's film, and a fellow-traveller but never a member of the Communist Party. His seemingly apologetic relationship to Stalinism, however, led to a famous falling-out with Camus. Sartre wrote three further novels (the *Roads to Freedom* trilogy), but his greatest success as a writer was as a dramatist with a series of much acclaimed existentialist and political plays. He spent much of his time supporting oppressed minorities and radical causes, for instance, challenging anti-Semitism and homophobia, and making common cause with the Algerian war of independence and the student movement of the late 1960s.

In his early work, Sartre produced a radical individualist philosophy which was derived from elements of Heideggerian and Kierkegaardian thought. 'Man' [*sic*] was 'condemned' to freedom and, hence, was responsible for 'choosing' himself, for making original choices. Individuals, however, are adept at finding excuses which justify acting in 'bad faith'. That Sartre not only expressed his views in technical philosophy but also in novels and plays meant that he was able to capture and articulate a cultural mood that was evocative of the Bohemian quarters of the Left Bank of the Seine. Pale young men and women dressed in black, smoking Gauloises and discussing the meaning of it all in the Café Voltaire, with the Gallic jazz of Django Rheinhardt jangling in the background, became the clichéd image of existentialism internationally and had a widespread and powerful subcultural appeal by the 1950s.

Sartre himself, though, was not an idle poseur. He was, in fact, quite dour in his ethical and political commitments. His doctrine of a literature of 'extreme situations' placed enormous stress on the writer's engagement with current issues in a world of relative perspectives and where there was no consensual truth. As his thinking developed, Sartre sought increasingly to reconcile the existentialist 'ideology' with Marxism, which he came to regard as 'the most profound philosophy of our time'. His early existentialism identified how 'being-for-itself' strikes out into a world of 'being-in-itself', thus presenting a negation which is transformative. This dialectic was theorised at the level of the individual project and its encounter with 'the other' and the brute facticity of 'the practico-inert'. In his later philosophical writing, Sartre tried to redefine the individual project in collectivist and materialist terms so that class praxis, history and economic scarcity become key categories of an existentialised Marxism. For instance, in *The Critique of Dialectical Reason* he is concerned with how the seriality of everyday life and how individual and fragmented experience are overcome to produce 'the group-in-fusion'.

Sartre's preface to this book – also published separately in 1958 as *Question de Méthode* – is an important and neglected text in which Sartre formulated the 'progressive–regressive method' whereby structural explanation and situated interpretation should be combined to construct a dialectical mode of social and cultural analysis. His intention was to break with 'the dialectic without men' of orthodox Marxism by grasping 'the profundity of the lived'. In this he was influenced by Henri Lefebvre.

During the 1960s Sartre's existential Marxism became the main target of structuralist 'anti-humanism'. The ideas of, say, Althusser and Foucault, especially their more extreme pronouncements about structural determination and discursive formation, are not really intelligible without some understanding of the towering figure they were reacting against, namely Sartre. He, in response, criticised their dissolution of agency and, for instance, accused Foucault of replacing 'cinema with a magic lantern' in his historical researches. Foucault, on the other hand, saw Sartre as a hopelessly 'universal intellectual', committed to a redundant agenda of Enlightenment and unable to operate strategically in particular situations, which is ironic since Sartre had always placed great emphasis on situatedness. Foucault rightly identified Sartre's increasing irrelevance in the 1970s, his gesture politics and Maoist delusions, which is not the same, however, as saying that Foucault had solved the problem of agency that had preoccupied Sartre.

Further reading

Cohen-Solal, A. SARTRE: A LIFE, William Heinemann, 1987.
Laing, R.D. and Cooper, D. REASON AND VIOLENCE, Tavistock, 1964.
McGuigan, J. 'The Literary Sociology of Sartre', J. Routh and J. Wolff (eds.), THE SOCIOLOGY OF LITERATURE: THEORETICAL APPROACHES, University of Keele, 1977.
J.McG.

SAUSSURE, Ferdinand de

Linguistic theoretist	born Switzerland, 1857–1913
Associated with	STRUCTURAL LINGUISTICS ■ SIGNS
Influences include	MEILLET ■ HUMBOLDT ■ WHITNEY
Shares common ground with	JAKOBSON ■ LÉVI STRAUSS ■ PEIRCE ■ BARTHES
Main work	COURSE IN GENERAL LINGUISTICS (1983)

FERDINAND DE SAUSSURE was a Swiss linguist generally credited with having laid the basis for the science of linguistics. The bulk of his linguistic theory is contained in one volume, published after his death by two of his students. Entitled *Course in General Linguistics*, it is a work of reconstruction based largely on notes taken at his lectures. Hailed, when it first appeared, as a book of great importance, it went on in the 1960s to acquire the reputation of having effected something like a Copernican revolution in the social sciences.

Two main principles characterise Saussurean linguistics. The first principle establishes an opposition between language and speech (*langue* and *parole*), modelled on the Durkheimian distinction between the social and the individual. *Langue* is shown to be a 'social product' – and in this sense cultural – a treasure-house of signs of which individuals are the passive depositories. It is a code shared by members of a community, contrasted with *parole*, an individual act of externalising a code through different combinations of its elements. Saussure argues that *langue* is the proper object of linguistics.

The second principle relies on another opposition: between synchrony and diachrony. Diachrony refers to the historical development of a language. Saussure ignores it in favour of synchrony and in doing so fulfils a methodological commitment to ignore all external phenomena, leaving him to study language 'in itself for itself'. This marks him off from his predecessors, for whom thought *qua* logic precedes and imposes its forms on language. For Saussure, by contrast, language is an autonomous 'principle of organisation' and a closed system whose chief function is communication.

From these two principles there emerges a definition of language as a system of signs. Signs, for Saussure, have two components, a signifier or acoustic image, and a signified or concept. He characterises the relationship between the two as arbitrary and shows that the signified – roughly speaking, 'meaning' – depends on the totality of the sign-system to which it belongs. The signified is therefore a value – not a substance – defined as having either relations of equivalences with other terms (of exchange) or of differential oppositions. Language as a whole is thus conceptualised as a formal system of interrelated terms, Saussure comparing it alternately with algebra or with a game of chess.

Outside linguistics proper, Saussure's formalist approach to the study of language has had its greatest impact on the structuralist movement in philosophy and the social sciences. Thinkers as diverse in their interests as Derrida, Foucault, Barthes, Althusser and Lacan have benefited from his insights, even if it is, as in Derrida's case, to contest some of his conclusions. Lacan has exploited these insights in psychoanalysis, using language analysis to argue that 'the unconscious is structured like a language'. Barthes has extended them to semiotics as a study of sign-systems especially in the cultural field, where somebody like Baudrillard has sought inspiration in a by-product of Saussure's theory: the study of anagrams. Even Althusser, going against a tradition in Marxist theorising that eschews the ahistorical, succumbed to structuralism in an attempt to place Marxism on a scientific basis. But it is Lévi-Strauss who has made the fullest use of Saussure in his study of myths and kinship, viewing both of these as communication systems of the same order as language.

Further reading

Culler, J. SAUSSURE, Collins, 1976.
Holdcroft, D. SAUSSURE: SIGNS, SYSTEM AND ARBITRARINESS, Cambridge University Press, 1991.
Jameson, F. THE PRISON-HOUSE OF LANGUAGE, Princeton University Press, 1974

G.S.

SCHOPENHAUER, Arthur

Philosopher	born Germany 1788–1860
Associated with	THE WILL ▪ AESTHETICS ▪ VOLUNTARISM
Influences include	KANT ▪ BUDDHISM ▪ PLATO
Shares common ground with	BAKHTIN ▪ FREUD ▪ NIETZSCHE
Main works	THE WORLD AS WILL AND REPRESENTATION (1969)
	ON THE FREEDOM OF THE WILL (1960)
	PARERGA AND PARALIPOMENA (1974)

S CHOPENHAUER SPENT MUCH of his intellectual endeavour being antagonistic towards the rampant idealism of his academic counterparts. However, the somewhat eccentric nature of his work has meant that his theories are adaptable, and have been adopted by many other theoretical disciplines, including psychoanalysis and literary theory.

Although Schopenhauer's work was highly theoretical (his first work, *On the Fourfold Root of the Principle of Reason*, was based on a radical development of Kantian philosophy, and a reaction to the raging Hegelianism of his time) he was later to become one of the first philosophers to incorporate the problematic of the desiring human body into his work (later theorists to do so include Bakhtin, Kristeva and Freud).

The two main concepts used in Schopenhauer's work are the Will, and the Aesthetic. His notions of the Will, and the subject in torment, were later to be utilised by psychoanalytic theory (within concepts such as the Id, the unconsciousness and the alienated subject). The Will was conceived by Schopenhauer as the aimless and persistent desire which forms the root of all humanity and the basis of all phenomena (including all cultural frameworks and artefacts). The Will, according to Schopenhauer, causes a conflict between the body and the intellect; giving the subject the incessant, but indeterminable, feeling that it is alienated from itself. However, the intellect, in an effort to silence this discord, 're-creates' the world and projects back to itself the illusion of metaphysical prowess. This gives the impression that the subject, and its endeavours, are always above any desirous, Will-full origins. This constant cycle of denial and affirmation is possible, according to Schopenhauer, only through the creation of cultural systems (religious, moral, artistic).

Cultural systems therefore are conceived by, and maintained through, a false consciousness; the intellect thereby believing that it is representing itself, and the world just as they are, infinitely knowable and interpretable. However, according to Schopenhauer, such reductive systems cannot represent, in any real sense, the multiplicity of bodily desire and experience, or the transient nature of the phenomenological world.

This antagonistic relationship between body and intellect means that interpretation of such cultural systems can lead to unforeseen difficulty. As Schopenhauer states, 'the intellect remains so much excluded from the real resolutions and secret decisions of its own will that sometimes it can only get to know them, like those of a stranger, by spying out and taking unawares: and it must surprise the will in the act of expressing itself, in order merely to discover its real intentions'.

The use of humour and comedy are, for Schopenhauer, the most effective device for 'surprising of the will'; as at the basis of any humour is a discrepancy between 'high' words and concepts, and their low meaning (e.g. double entendres, political satire). In Schopenhauer's theory, therefore, humour is posited as cultural and political subversion; a resolution which was later maintained by Bakhtin in his theory of the carnival.

History also constitutes a disparity between intellect and experience; as Schopenhauer believed that history only serves as a record of death, despair and wretchedness. The social and academic valorisation of historical events deny the misery usually inflicted on the silent majority by the victorious minority. This romantic and idealistic aspect of social memory never ceased to sicken Schopenhauer. Nevertheless, his theories, however unpopular at the time, later attracted major literary figures such as Tolstoy, Conrad, Proust and Mann.

However, Schopenhauer offers a chance of a momentary escape from the incessant Will, but not in an unproblematic way. Paradoxically, the only way of achieving this release, according to him, is through the aesthetic appreciation of art. Art is conceived as the only cultural artefact through and by which man may escape subjection to the will; by disinterested and non-subjective aesthetic contemplation. It is interesting to note, however, that this only includes the visual arts, as Schopenhauer proclaimed that music was the manifestation of pure Will. This notion of the aesthetic again corresponds, in part, to Freud's theory of the pre-Oedipal; basking in a subliminal and oceanic state of subject-less pleasure. It also reveals the influence of Buddhist philosophy on Schopenhauer's work.

Further reading

Eagleton, T. THE IDEOLOGY OF THE SUBLIME, Blackwell, 1990.
Hamlyn, D.W. SCHOPENHAUER: THE ARGUMENTS OF THE PHILOSOPHERS, Routledge, 1980.
Janaway, C. SELF AND WORLD IN SCHOPENHAUER'S PHILOSOPHY, Clarendon, 1989.
J.S.C.

SCHUMACHER, Ernst 'Fritz'

Economist/conservationist	born Germany, 1911–1977
Associated with	ECOLOGY ■ INTERMEDIATE TECHNOLOGY ■ META-ECONOMICS
Influences include	AQUINAS ■ JAMES ■ TAWNEY
Shares common ground with	GUENON ■ PIEPER ■ WARD
Main works	SMALL IS BEAUTIFUL (1973) THE AGE OF PLENTY (1975) A GUIDE FOR THE PERPLEXED (1977)

GERMAN-BORN SCHUMACHER first went to England in 1930 as one of the first German Rhodes Scholars after the First World War to study economics at New College, Oxford. He spent much of the 1930s studying and working in Britain and the USA, where he taught economics at Columbia University. In 1937, he left Nazi Germany to settle in England. Following brief internment in 1943 he published work in international economics as well as working out policies for full employment. His desire for real practical experience of applied economic problems led him to become economic adviser to the British Control Commission (1946–50). After becoming adviser to the recently nationalised British Coal Board in 1950 he increasingly concerned himself with conservation matters and ecological problems of waste disposal arising from nuclear energy. A visit to Burma in 1955 sparked his interest in developing countries and what he calls 'Buddhist Economics' as well as intermediate technology, leading to his foundation of the Intermediate Technology Group in Britain (1965) and his advice being sought by many overseas governments.

Schumacher's central ideas on economics and economic development are encapsulated in his essays in *Small is Beautiful*, which broadly refer to the modern world, resources, the Third World and organisation and ownership. With regard to the first sections, his principal concern is with production in the rich countries which, in his view, fail to recognise the distinction between income and capital in relationship to the world's natural resources ('natural capital') – especially as consumers and legatees of the fossil or 'income fuels' since 1945 (following the unique quantitative growth in industrial production in the Western world).

He also highlights a unique and simultaneous qualitative leap with regard to the artificial products, e.g. fertilisers, of scientists and technologists which, in bulk, have a potentially dangerous ecological impact, i.e. pollution, which threatens civilisation and life itself. There is a growing consciousness that human industrial processes have produced an entirely new social and cultural situation whereby the rich countries are very rapidly using up and damaging a certain kind of finite and irreplaceable natural capital asset, namely 'the tolerance margins which benign nature always provided'.

Schumacher also presciently warned (pre-3 Mile Island and Chernobyl disasters) that even the seeming solution of nuclear energy in industrialised societies, with its attendant hazards of storing radioactive waste, only ostensibly solves one problem by shifting it to another sphere.

He further points up the social costs 'eating into the very substance of industrial man' – what he calls 'human substance' – as the third element of irreplaceable capital which is at risk in the industrial system by consuming the very basis on which it has been erected. Whilst higher living standards might bring benefits under capitalism through competition and efficiency, Schumacher argues that this is at the expense of the social costs of debasing human culture.

With regard to Third World countries and solutions to their special needs for economic development as well as economic organisation and ownership, Schumacher's striking idea of 'intermediate technology' is associated with the possibility of evolving a new lifestyle and 'alternative society' designed for peace and permanence. This would entail forms of non-violent or 'self-help' technology – 'technology with a human face' – appropriate for 'labour surplus societies' in the Third World. New forms of partnership between management and workers or new forms of common ownership would emerge. This contrasts with the 'idolatry of giantism' exemplified by large-scale industrial firms and cities which, in their regard of land and people as mere 'factors of production, lead to mass unemployment and poverty. It also contrasts with the 'super-technology' of developed societies.

Schumacher sees regionalism (the geographical distribution of population) as the most important problem on the agenda of the larger developing countries in the second half of the twentieth century. In the smaller developing countries there is also the need for the development of an entirely new system of thought based on attention to people rather than goods: 'Production by the masses rather than mass production'.

His ideas prompted the US government subsequently to set up a \$20 million fund for research into alternative technologies (e.g. solar energy, wind power) and this idea has unquestionably changed the direction of thought about economic development. Despite this political initiative, the practical implementation of such a radical new direction of thought has proved far from easy, given the dominance of large-scale capitalist multinational corporations in the global economy today.

Despite his ideas spawning the new sub-discipline of Environmental Economics, Schumacher's insistence that what he calls 'meta-economics' – with its qualitative non-economic values emphasize and recognition of the existence of 'goods' which never appear in the market – is a necessary preliminary before any such economic analysis begins, has largely fallen on deaf ears. For him such total suppression of qualitative cultural and social distinctions, whilst facilitating economic theorising, at the same time makes it totally sterile. Meta-economics, in dealing dually with humans and the environment, confirms that economics as a cultural artefact must derive its aims and objects from what Schumacher calls 'a study of man' and that 'it must derive at least part of its methodology from a study of nature'.

Further reading

Douthwaite, R. SHORT CIRCUIT, Resurgence Books, 1996.
Willoughby, K.W. TECHNOLOGY CHOICE: A CRITIQUE OF THE APPROPRIATE TECHNOLOGY MOVEMENT, IT Publications, 1990.
Wood, B. ALIAS PAPA: A LIFE OF FRITZ SCHUMACHER, Cape, 1984.

G.P.

SCHUMPETER, Joseph

Economist	born Austria 1883–1950
Associated with	CREATIVE DESTRUCTION ■ DEMOCRATIC ÉLITISM ■ ENTREPRENEUR
Influences include	MARX ■ WALRAS ■ WEBER
Shares common ground with	DAHL ■ DJILAS ■ GALBRAITH ■ LIPSET
Main works	CAPITALISM, SOCIALISM, AND DEMOCRACY (1942) IMPERIALISM AND SOCIAL CLASSES (1951) HISTORY OF ECONOMIC ANALYSIS (1954)

S CHUMPETER WAS BORN into a cloth manufacturer's family in what was then the Austro-Hungarian Empire. On his mother's remarriage in 1893 he moved to Vienna, attending the élite grammar school, where his interest in sociology and philosophy was kindled. In 1901, he enrolled at the University of Vienna as a law student (despite his predilection for economics, which he simultaneously took courses in). On attaining a doctorate in law in 1906 he travelled in Europe, returning to Austria to lecture in political economy at his old university and later at the University of Czernowitz in Romania. Following his appointment as Economics Professor at Graz University (1911–14), he was exchange professor at Columbia University in 1913. After a brief political excursion as Austrian Finance Minister in 1919, he resigned to become chairman of a private bank in 1921 which failed in 1924, leaving him penniless. In 1925, Schumpeter accepted the Chair in Public Finance at Bonn University in Germany where he taught and researched until 1932. Turned down for a prestigious Chair in Berlin in that year, he accepted the post of Professor of Economics at Harvard which he occupied until his death.

Strongly influenced by the broad-based Austrian School of Economics, from the 1920s Schumpeter proposed a new and original way of looking at the science of economics. His first major work, *The Theory of Economic Development* (1912), broke with all previous static or equilibrium theories of capitalist economic development by explaining its fluctuations as part of a coherent dynamic and endogenous process, i.e. they are inherent in the economy. This 'Schumpeterian system', as it came to be known, was a pioneering study which, whilst showing affinities with Marxian economic theory, was less concerned with historical stages and inner contradictions of capitalist economic adjustments than in discovering what causes the movement away from or destruction of economic equilibrium.

The key to this process is the central significance of the entrepreneurial function and its disturbance of the equilibrium which is at the heart of economic development. The Schumpeterian 'entrepreneur' differs from the traditionalist 'static producer' in continuously looking for and applying new combinations of products and means of production as the human agent of economic change and development. The financing of such projects requires the particular role of the banking system, and the creation of credit, which provide the entrepreneur with the means to switch productive forces from their old use into innovative employments.

In his later work on *Business Cycles* (1939), Schumpeter applied a unique mixture of theoretical, historical, quantitative and comparative techniques to explain economic growth and fluctuations in the USA, Germany and the UK, focusing on *innovations* as the independent endogenous variable that causes economic life to go through a number of cycles. Fleshing out his theory with historical material, based on economic cycles of varying duration, he identifies external and internal factors generating booms and recessions in the economic process of capitalism; these represent cyclical fluctuations away from economic equilibrium.

Schumpeterian change proceeds through a dialectic process of advances and setbacks with the combinations of overinvestment, overproduction and credit expansion caused by the inrush of less gifted imitators of successful innovations; this leads to a downturn in prices, profits and investment associated with economic recession. This, in Schumpeter's view, is a healthy phase of economic restructuring that paves the way for a new burst of innovations and an upturn in an entirely new business cycle. What later he was to term 'a perennial gale of creative destruction' is therefore a competitive process essential to the dynamic character of a private enterprise economy which, in Schumpeter's words, is: 'The process of industrial mutation that incessantly revolutionizes the economic structure from within, incessantly destroying the old one, incessantly creating a new one'.

Evidence of this process can be seen in the post-Second World War global economy in which new 'sunrise' industries (electronics, computers) have displaced former leading 'sunset' industries (coal, steel) as the prime movers of post-industrial societies.

From the late 1930s, Schumpeter turned his fertile mind to relating economic phenomena to the larger political and sociocultural contexts, employing as his touchstone an analysis of Marxian sociology in relation to his own discussion of socialism and class theory. His most famous work, *Capitalism, Socialism, and Democracy* (translated into sixteen languages), along with the works of Dahl and Lipset, constitute what became known as the 'revisionist' or 'procedural' theory of democracy. He anticipated the public choice theories of the 1980s, reducing democracy to its bare essentials of a 'theory of competitive leadership' in which the maximisation of individual welfare of politicians as entrepreneurs and bureaucrats plays an essential role.

He saw the electoral process of Western democracies in terms of the market-place in which élite parties, like firms, compete with one another periodically for the support of voters, who are the consumers, and politicians and bureaucrats who are the producers of public goods and services. The influence of Weber and Michels is further evident in Schumpeter's modified form of the theory of 'democractic élitism' in his subscribing to the limits of democratic participation and his rejection of such unrealistic tenets of the classical theory of democracy as 'the common good' and the 'will of the people', which he dismissed as manufactured by political leaders.

Further reading

März, Eduard JOSEPH SCHUMPETER: SCHOLAR, TEACHER AND POLITICIAN, Yale University Press, 1991.
McKee, David SCHUMPETER AND THE POLITICAL ECONOMY OF CHANGE, Praeger, 1991.
Swedberg, Richard JOSEPH A. SCHUMPETER: HIS LIFE AND WORK, Polity 1991.

G.P.

SIMMEL, Georg

Sociolist/philosopher	born Germany, 1858–1918
Associated with	FORMS ■ MODERNISM ■ DYAD/TRIAD
Influences include	KANT ■ SCHOPENHAUER ■ NIETZSCHE
Shares common ground with	PARK ■ BENJAMIN ■ GOFFMAN ■ COSER
Main works	THE PHILOSOPHY OF MONEY (1900)
	SOCIOLOGY (1908)
	PHILOSOPHICAL CULTURE (1911)

SIMMEL WAS BORN in Berlin. In 1876 he enrolled at the University of Berlin where he began by studying history under Theodor Mommsen and psychology under Moritz Lazarus. However, the direction of his thought moved inexorably towards social philosophy. In 1881 he received his doctorate for a study of Kant. Further work on Kant and the obligatory public presentation led to his appointment as a lecturer at Berlin University. He continued his interest in philosophy with popular lectures on moral philosophy, history and philosophy and the philosophy of pessimism. But he was increasingly attracted to sociology. He began to publish on social differentiation and the boundaries of sociological enquiry. However, his sociological work was always strongly informed by philosophy, and Simmel himself objected to being known only for his sociology. Simmel's attempts to gain a Chair in Berlin were obstructed by anti-Semitism. He was not made a full professor until 1914 when he obtained a Chair of Philosophy at Strasbourg University. Simmel regarded the move from the cultural stimulation of Berlin to be a calamity. His intellectual productivity continued with studies on philosophy and history, Rembrandt and modern culture. However, to his friends he complained of growing mental and physical exhaustion. He died of liver cancer in 1918.

It is a pity that Simmel first became associated in the English-speaking world with formal sociology. The main conduit of his ideas in America was Albion Small and the Chicago School circle. Their interest in Simmel reflects their own twin concerns to produce a sociological understanding of the city and to establish sociology on a firm footing within the Academy. They drew heavily on Simmel's conceptual distinctions in *Sociology* regarding group and social life, dyad and triad, sociability and form and content. The result was that Simmel's significance as one of the first theorists to grasp the contradictory cultural currents of modernity was lost for over half a century.

Simmel's *magnum opus* is *The Philosophy of Money*. This labyrinthine, multifaceted and compelling study takes money as the key metaphor of modernity. In the instability, reactivity and circulation of value, Simmel found the perfect parallel to represent the polymorphous, restless, uncertain, fragmented character of modern social relations. Simmel's method emphasises the reciprocal interactivity of social relations. He argued that society should be studied as 'a web of interactions'. This is not achieved through conventional sociological devices such as questionnaires, interviews and focus groups. Instead Simmel attempts to distil philosophically the essence of the times. This involved developing sensibilities to the social which are quasi-artistic in form and content. Frisby (1981) calls Simmel's approach 'sociological impressionism' and this captures the quasi-artistic, highly refined and, in many ways, inimitable approach that Simmel developed. His conception of modernity recognises new forms of social cohesion. Money makes relations between people impersonal and anonymous, but it also releases them from paying back in friendships or favours. In this sense they are freer. This impersonal aspect was thought to be inevitable. Hence Lukács and other critics objected to the proposition that it would always remain, regardless of whether the system was capitalist or socialist.

Simmel's early fame in the USA rested upon his work on the formal categories of sociological analysis and the dynamics of social forms. Formal sociology, he argued, deals with the universal, abstract, recurring features of social life. He devised a number of concepts to encapsulate these forms. Dyad relationships, involving two parties, and triad relations, involving three parties, correlate with contrasting forms of social interaction. He argued that policies of divide and rule were compatible with triad relations, but harder to achieve in dyads owing to the 'peculiar closeness' of two compared with three. He also argued that the stranger introduces a distinct dynamic into group relations. The stranger is situated on the margin; he or she signifies a degree of remoteness from the values of the group; and he or she disturbs established relationships of proximity in the group. Simmel's work on sociological categorisation and classification was attractive to early American sociologists because it promised a scientific basis for studying urban space and urban forms. But it does not follow that it is the most durable part of his work.

The most interesting parts of his analysis concentrate on the new forms of agitation and disturbance associated with rapid urban–industrial expansion. He presented modern culture as dense and changeable. The characteristic personality types that emerge from these positions are the *neurasthenic* and *blasé* personalities. Neurasthenic types live in a condition of heightened anxiety and regard the metropolis as a tumult of shocks and collisions. Blasé types develop a sense of casual indifference and find it difficult to commit to others and general society.

Simmel was a virtuoso sociologist. Who else would write about the cultural significance of 'the adventure', 'the ruin', the 'Berlin Trade Exhibition', the 'picture frame' and the 'stranger'? During his life, his style of 'sociological impressionism' was imitated but rarely equalled. This deepens the irony of associating Simmel with formal sociology. Only in a very superficial sense is it correct to claim that his work conforms to a system. The reason why there has been no Simmelian School to speak of, is precisely because it is so difficult to systematise his thought or match the power of his insights. The growing interest in postmodernity during the 1980s led to a revival of interest in Simmel's work.

Further reading

Frisby, D. SOCIOLOGICAL IMPRESSIONISM: A REASSESSMENT OF GEORG SIMMEL'S SOCIAL THEORY, Free Press, 1981.
Levine, D. (ed.) GEORG SIMMEL ON INDIVIDUALITY AND SOCIAL FORMS, University of Chicago Press, 1971.
Wolff, K. THE SOCIOLOGY OF GEORG SIMMEL, Heinemann, 1950.

C.R.

SKINNER, Burrhus Frederic

Psychologist	born USA 1904–1990
Associated with	RADICAL BEHAVIOURISM ■ OPERANT CONDITIONING ■ SKINNER BOX
Influences include	PAVLOV ■ CROZIER ■ WATSON ■ THORNDIKE ■ HOMANS
Shares common ground with	BANDURA ■ HULL ■ HERRNSTEIN, EYSENCK
Main works	THE BEHAVIOUR OF ORGANISMS (1938) VERBAL BEHAVIOUR (1957) WALDEN TWO (1948) BEYOND FREEDOM AND DIGNITY (1971)

SKINNER RECEIVED HIS MA from Harvard in 1930 and his Ph.D. a year later. At Harvard, he worked as an instructor, research fellow, associate professor, full professor and, after his retirement in 1974, emeritus professor.

During his professional career, Skinner established radical behaviourism as the dominant research-oriented psychology in the USA and paved the way for a miscellany of therapies based on his theories of learning. He also wrote philosophically about the need to reconceptualise cherished notions about our own essential humanity. And, perhaps most controversially, expressed (in the form of a novel) his vision of a new utopia (or, for some, dystopia) in which behaviourist principles would guide everything.

While it is appealing to see Skinner's work extending that of Pavlov, Watson and Thorndike, he added new dimensions to behaviourist theory, replacing the simplistic cause-and-effect mechanism which was the source of learning in classical conditioning with the idea of an *operant*. Skinner shared with Pavlov the importance of classical stimulus-response connection in explaining various reflexive-type behaviours as responses to neutral stimuli in the environment, but rejected Pavlov's passive conception of the organism. For Skinner, organisms were active.

If an organism performs a piece of behaviour and is positively reinforced, then the likelihood is that it will repeat the behaviour in similar situations. Punishment of the behaviour will deter its repetition. The potency of rewards and punishments in social life has been widely explored from ancient Greek scholars to twentieth century anthropologists, like Mauss and Malinowski. Before Skinner, Thorndike had investigated the concept experimentally, though only with kittens: he built a 'puzzle box' comprising chambers, entry to which involved pulling strings or pushing levers. Hungry cats were confined in a chamber, food lay outside and the animals were left to fathom their ways out. They were forced to learn the appropriate combination of levers and strings that let them escape to the food. After trial and error, the cats discarded behaviour that produced nothing and repeated behaviour that led to the rewarding food. In other words, they learned to pull the rights strings and push the right levers and their learned behavior was conditioned.

Skinner extrapolated from this research to human beings: if cats could be conditioned to behave in certain ways, then so could humans. Reinforce desired behaviour with rewards and humans could live in a more desirable society. Skinner's innovation was that he visualized a society in which the positively reinforced behaviour is repeated and this in turn produces consequences that yield even more desirable behaviour in the future. Responses to stimuli themselves become stimuli – the consequences themselves become stimuli, or, in Skinner's term, operants.

The efficacy of positive reinforcement was stressed by Skinner. Punishment, on the other hand, was discouraged. Desired behaviour can be elicited by positive reinforcement. After his often astounding experiments with non-humans (teaching pigeons to play ping-pong, rats to perform complicated tasks), he outlined his plans for a community in which humans would be subject to rigorous conditioning programmes. Their behaviour would be perfectly aligned with the patterns favoured by the community, which was called

Walden Two. Plasticity is of paramount importance to Skinner: even the most complex human behaviour is amenable to manipulation. Skinner uses the idea of chaining behaviours together to produce complex patterns.

In Skinner's utopian (for him, at least) society, planning is based on technologies of behaviour and nothing is left to chance. Skinner's veiled warnings about leaving the future to chance or what he calls 'biased control' are manifested in his account of a world in which punishment is a thing of the past. Once we have knowledge of the precise contingencies that produce desired behaviour, we plan by arranging environments in such a way as to reward that behaviour.

His *Beyond Freedom and Dignity* extended his approach, this time by arguing that the hallowed human notions in the title are illusory: we are already controlled in some way by environmental factors, so the fact that we regard ourselves as having both freedom and dignity is at the outcome of a (probably unplanned) conditioning. Of course, one obvious objection to Skinner's world was how to prevent a power-holder monopolizing the keys to reinforcement. Skinner's leader was benign; but there is no built-in guarantee that it would remain that way.

Skinner set in motion an enduring research tradition in American psychology and, in sociology, social exchange theory accepted many of Skinner's propositions (Homans and Skinner worked together at Harvard). Many have despaired at what they consider to be the dehumanising reductionism implied by such research. Skinner's 'ratomorphic' conception of the human, in which all reference to human uniqueness is either elided or denied, is seen as overly mechanical and, as Chomsky and others have pointed out, too convenient an instrument for those who wish to find ways of enshrining the status quo.

Further reading

Nye, R. THE LEGACY OF B.F. SKINNER: CONCEPTS AND PERSPECTIVES, CONTROVERSIES AND MISUNDERSTANDINGS, Brooks/Cole Publishing, 1992.
Prilleletensky, I. 'On the Social Legacy of B.F. Skinner', THEORY AND PSYCHOLOGY, 4: 1 1994.
Todd, J. and Morris, E. MODERN PERSPECTIVES ON B. F. SKINNER AND CONTEMPORARY BEHAVIORISM, Greenwood Press, 1995.
Wiener, D.N. B. F. SKINNER: BENIGN ANARCHIST, Allyn & Bacon, 1996.

E.C.

SMITH, Bernard

Art historian	born Australia 1916—
Associated with	CULTURAL TRAFFIC ▪ CULTURAL RECYCLING ▪ CIVILISATION
Main influences	MARX ▪ TOYNBEE ▪ GOMBRICH
Shares common ground with	GRAMSCI ▪ SAID ▪ BOURDIEU
Main works	EUROPEAN VISION AND THE SOUTH PACIFIC (1960) AUSTRALIAN PAINTING (1962) MODERNISM'S HISTORY (1998)

BERNARD SMITH IS conventionally described as Australia's leading art historian. He is more usefully viewed as a cultural historian or a social theorist of the Antipodes. The distinction between 'Australia' indicates a *place*, the Antipodes suggests a relationship. While Smith's major area of activity has been art history, the impact of his thinking has powerfully influenced work in other areas, from Pacific history and anthropology to cultural studies and sociology.

Smith was born in Sydney. In the 1930s he encountered surrealism and joined the Sydney Teachers' Branch of the Communist Party. Marx was a major influence, alongside Toynbee into the 1940s; the Bible remained a residually powerful influence from his childhood, as he remembers in *The Boy Adeodatus: The Portrait of a Lucky Young Bastard* (1984). He published his first history of Australian art, *Place, Taste and Tradition* in 1945; already it pointed inward to geography, botany and landscape, and outward, to European eyes and continental art-styles, to the world system of imperialism. This work took Smith to the centre, to the Warburg Institute over the cusp of the 1950s. There he made contact with and was influenced by Charles Mitchell, Rudolf Wittkower and Ernst Gombrich, and he worked on the basis of his greatest book, *European Vision and the South Pacific*. This is a remarkable study which in many ways anticipates the work of Edward Said. The difference is that Smith's thinking rests on the idea of cultural traffic within the asymmetrical relations of the world system. In order to understand 'Australian art' you need to understand British and French art; but more, and *per contra*, in order to really understand, say, the English Enlightenment, you need first to know about the great expeditions to the South Land. The experiences of the voyages of Cook, and Banks and the Forsters therefore became formative for the path of English natural and social sciences. These tensions between experience and imagination are pursued further in *Imagining the Pacific* (1993).

From Marx and Toynbee, Smith develops the sense that all cultures are ghosted by their past, by past memories or by imported fictions such as orientalism. Smith's sensitivity to the idea of *cultural traffic* across nations or cultures goes together with the idea of *cultural recycling*, or what others call the invention of tradition. Pastoralism, utopianism, romanticism, primitivism – in Australia, aboriginalisms – are all constituent parts of modernity, for modernity cannot generate its own consciousness out of nothing. Smith can therefore be understood as a civilisational thinker, for he relies not only on detailed case study but also on comparison and argument about period styles. This places him especially well to theorise the postmodern, in turn, as a combination of new, but also modern and non-modern cultures. These issues are pushed further in his major study of the twentieth century, *Modernism's History*.

Alongside Said, in contemporary writing, Smith might be compared to Bourdieu or to Gramsci. Like Bourdieu he has a primary interest in art as a social institution, in its commodification and in the non-commodity, status-based claims of artists to romantic autonomy. The parallel with Gramsci is perhaps more locational; like the Sardinian, Smith is a cultural Marxist of peripheral vision, one for whom the Southern Question is central as well as peripheral. But more, just as Gramsci's Marxism is deeply formed by the specificity of his location, so does Smith's project combine European, local and synthetic ways of thinking.

Smith's most widely influential book is *Australian Painting* (1962; 1991 edition co-authored with Terry Smith). He has also produced two volumes of essays, *The Death of the Artist as Hero* (1988) and *The Critic as Advocate* (1989) and has published widely on English and French expeditions into the Pacific, most notably his three volumes on the art of Cook's voyages (with Rüdiger Joppien, 1985–87).

Further reading

Beilharz, P. 'Bernard Smith: Imagining the Antipodes', THESIS ELEVEN, 38 (1994).
Beilharz, P. IMAGINING THE ANTIPODES: CULTURE, THEORY AND THE VISUAL IN THE WORK OF BERNARD SMITH, Cambridge University Press, 1997.
Smith, B. 'Modern and Postmodern', THESIS ELEVEN, 38 (1994).

P.Be.

SONTAG, Susan

Literary critic	born USA 1933—
Associated with	METAPHOR ■ AESTHETICS ■ MODERNISM
Influences include	GOODMAN ■ BENJAMIN ■ BARTHES
Shares common ground with	JAMESON ■ EAGLETON ■ LASCH
Main works	STYLES OF RADICAL WILL (1969) UNDER THE SIGN OF SATURN (1980) ILLNESS AS METAPHOR (1978)

S ONTAG'S WORK STRADDLES *fin de siècle* apprehension that modernism is exhausted with the intimation that culture and society are moving into a new condition of postmodernity. Her scholarly work never declares affiliation to postmodernism, although her 'Notes on Camp' comes pretty close. However, in her fiction, notably *The Volcano Lover* (1992), she displays a fascination with ambivalence, multilateralism and contingency. Most commentators regard these as the defining traits of postmodernist sensibility.

Sontag stands in a tradition of popularising aesthetics which reaches back to Arnold and Ruskin. Her immediate reference group was 'The New York Intellectuals' who, between the depression years of the 1930s and the onset of the 1960s, dominated American criticism. Writers like Irving Howe, Clement Greenberg, Dwight MacDonald and Lionel Trilling sought to establish the canons of taste which separated High Culture from Mass Culture and the avant garde from kitsch. Their work was inspired by a Leftish reformism. Yet they occupied the high ground. For example, they lamented the 'homogenizing effect' of mass culture and championed avant garde art as the highest distillation of critical culture.

Sontag's first writings attack this tradition. She rejects the New York Intellectuals for their elitism and she refutes their epistemology. Following Nietzsche, she argues that there are no facts: only interpretations. Sontag denies that print culture possesses inherent cultural superiority and urges a new openness to explore the potential offered by experimental art. The critical response from Howe and his associates was swift and largely dismissive. They painted Sontag as a glamorous hothead, more concerned with self-publicity than making a cultural contribution. The condescending tone grated with the rising critical cultures of the 1960s.

For some years, they embraced Sontag as a counter-culture heroine. This is a misreading that Sontag has found it hard to bury. To some degree she has contributed to the interpretation by continuing to experiment with a variety of aesthetic forms, including film, television and drama, as well as novels and *belles lettres*. This openness to experimentation was seen by many to solidify her counter-cultural credentials. In fact, Sontag has never been very interested in forms of collective consciousness, let alone the consciousness of the counter-culture.

At the heart of her work is a passionate interest in self-consciousness. Her readings of Barthes, Benjamin, Bataille, Canetti, E.M. Cioran, Riefensthal, Seyberberg and Artaud, as well as her acclaimed study, *Illness as Metaphor*, and her controversial studies of pornography and Aids, are all linked by a fascination with the effect of extreme situations upon self-consciousness. Sontag's work explores how art, aesthetics and self-consciousness in extremity (e.g. life-threatening illness) can operate as methods of negating the myths of modernism and achieving transcendence.

All of this is delivered in an adamantine self-reflexive style which seems calculated to militate against identification. Reading Sontag sometimes gives one the impression that her audience consists of a collection of social isolates with over-articulate, self-cancelling vocabularies. Certainly, the greatest weakness of her work is the absence of a tangible political dimension. Above all, Sontag sees herself as an independent writer and in this, she reproduces the critical tradition of American individualism more faithfully than perhaps she would wish to acknowledge. In general, her political statements have been few and far between. It is surely paradoxical that one of the leading female American writers of her generation has never written at length about her relationship to feminism.

Moreover, her reputation in the counter-culture suffered a blow in 1982 when she appeared to recant New Left values to a meeting organised by the American left in support of the Polish Solidarity movement. Perhaps Sontag intended the speech to emphasise her intellectual independence, but it was widely seen, perhaps unfairly, as a turn to the Right. Significantly, her most public political involvement has been with PEN (Poets, Playwrights, Editors, Essayists and Novelists) – an organisation dedicated to issues of human rights, censorship and freedom of expression. Once again, the role of self-consciousness, and the capacity of art and aesthetics, to negate repression, seems to be Sontag's natural home.

Further reading

Barnham, R. 'Speaking Itself: Susan Sontag's Town Hall Address,' QUARTERLY JOURNAL OF SPEECH, August 1989, pp. 259–76.
Kennedy, L. SUSAN SONTAG: MIND AS PASSION, Manchester University Press, 1995.
McRobbie, A. 'The Modernist Style of Susan Sontag', FEMINIST REVIEW, 37, 1991.

C.R.

SOROKIN, Pitirim

Sociologist	born Russia 1889–1968
Associated with	INTEGRALISM ■ IDEATIONAL CULTURE ■ IDEALISTIC CULTURE
Influences include	VICO ■ HEGEL ■ MARX
Shares common ground with	TOYNBEE ■ KROEBER ■ MANNHEIM
Main works	THE CRISIS OF OUR AGE (1941) MAN AND SOCIETY IN CALAMITY (1942)

PITIRIM SOROKIN WAS born amongst peasants in the north of Russia on 21 January 1889. His life in Russia was not a smooth or convenient one. He was imprisoned three times for anti-tsarist activities, and three times for anti-communist activities. In between, he served as minister in Kerensky's cabinet and was a member of the Constituent Assembly. After his third arrest by the Communist authorities, in 1922, he was deported to Berlin. In 1923, he went to the USA to lecture on the Russian Revolution, and in 1930 he became the first Chair of Sociology at Harvard University. From 1949 until his retirement ten years later, Sorokin directed the Harvard Research Center in Creative Altruism. His published works cover such diverse areas as rural sociology, the causes of war and revolution, comparative criminology, the component of greed and altruism, philosophy of science and human sexuality.

Sorokin is best known, however for his analysis of social change, and his apparently eclectic interests are almost always tied in some way to this concern. He studied social change as a self-described 'integralist', whereby societies are studied under the widest possible lens using multiple methodologies, albeit with an eye toward isolating powerful, general explanatory principles. Ethics, economics, politics, family dynamics and the fine arts are all considered as important causes and indicators of a society's identity. Sorokin is not distracted by simple structural discrepancies, however. The integralist approach helps him see through surface distinctions, like those between Fascism and Communism, to identify shared characteristics. In fact, Sorokin reduces cultural multiplicity into three fundamental supersystems. Cultures are for the most part either ideational, sensate or idealistic.

Ideational culture focuses on other-worldly, spiritual interpretations of reality. Western medieval culture, for example, produced art and architecture that glorifies God at the expense of human autonomy and agency. Science, philosophy, ethics, law and family were all inspired and guided by a distrust of the sensory world and a submission to a supersensory supreme being. Authorship of things beautiful or edifying was attributed to God, and punishment for evil would take place after death.

Sensate cultures, on the other hand, eschew the spiritual in favour of the tangible. Art and architecture, like that of the Greco-Roman period from the third century BC to the fourth century AD, celebrate human wit and excess. Noble and transcendent subject matter is replaced by graphic depictions of the quotidian. Science, law, ethics and politics attend properties that can be substantiated in the physical world. Evil is punished with physical pain or deprivation, and spiritual concerns are considered irrelevant, unreliable and unimportant.

Idealistic cultures participate in characteristics of the other two, and not surprisingly, then, are preferred by Sorokin, whose own methodology is driven by the integration of diverse elements. Like fifth-century Athens, idealistic cultures acknowledge the empirical world yet focus on its nobler aspects. Human concerns are considered within transcendent values, and the human physique, although often employed, is depicted in ideal rather than pedestrian form. In Nietzschean terms, the Dionysian is balanced by the Apollonian.

For Sorokin, the twentieth century represents the exhaustion of a 400-year-old sensate phase. So much has the focus been on the tangible that culture has succumbed to the surface. Cultures are growing bored with hollow sensual diversions that are ultimately unsatisfying. Disconnected sensual variety is leading to a sense of chaos, and the technical means of producing that variety are eclipsing the former aesthetic priorities. The culture is in a negative phase, rebelling against the limitations of the sensate supersystem. In the artistic world, impressionism (the outer limit of the sensate) has given way to modernism, which disrupts and challenges happy sensual reception. Cubism imposes depth on that which has been depicted superficially. And the political counterparts of modernism – Fascism and Communism – rebel against the alienation of appetite. Modernism, Fascism and Communism will fail, however, because of their fundamental negativity. Cubism retains the sensate for its content, and is thus destined to crave depth only in the material world. Likewise, the critiques of Communism and Fascism address the inadequacies of the capitalist material world without offering a genuine spiritual alternative. Thus, Western civilisation awaits a more genuine ideational or idealistic identity.

Further reading

Allen, Philip J. PITIRIM A. SOROKIN IN REVIEW, Duke University Press, 1963.
Cowell, Frank HISTORY, CIVILISATION, AND CULTURE: AN INTRODUCTION TO THE HISTORICAL AND SOCIAL PHILOSOPHY OF PITIRIM A. SOROKIN, Beacon Press, 1952.
Pronovost, Giles 'The Sociological Study of Time: Historical Landmarks', CURRENT SOCIOLOGY, 37 (Winter 1989), pp. 4–19.

T.J.L.

SPENCER, Herbert

Philosopher/sociologist	born England 1820–1903
Associated with	EVOLUTIONARY SOCIOLOGY
Influences include	COMTE ■ MILL ■ DARWIN
Shares common ground with	DURKHEIM ■ PARSONS
Main works	SOCIAL STATICS (1851)
	THE STUDY OF SOCIOLOGY (1873)
	THE PRINCIPLES OF SOCIOLOGY (1876–96)

HERBERT SPENCER WAS privately tutored, first by his father in Derby, and then by his uncle in Bath. In 1837 he trained to become an engineer for the London and Birmingham Railway. In 1841 he returned to Derby to contribute to nonconformist journals, and in 1848 he became a sub-editor on *The Economist* in London. In 1853 his uncle died, leaving him a substantial inheritance, and Spencer left his job to become a freelance writer. He began an enormously ambitious programme of writing in the later part of the nineteenth century through a form whereby readers paid an advanced subscription to the programme, which he then fulfilled chapter by chapter, a regime he came to regard as a form of slavery. He died in 1903, having seen his writings become widely influential across the world.

Spencer's work resides on early commitments to individualism and social equality, and yet paradoxically he attempted to develop a sociology in a way which closely parallels the strategy of August Comte. Yet where Comte based his sociology on the theory of the inevitable antagonism between theology and science, Spencer tried to argue there was no such antagonism. Spencer's mature writing tries to establish a new method and first philosophy (1862) and a subsequent analysis of biology, psychology, sociology and ethics, a project taking some forty years of continuously sustained work. His work is guided by the idea that there is a general law of nature which can be seen in every aspect of existence: the evolutionary law of growth in complexity and hetero-geneity, but equally in equilibration and equilibrium. In the life sciences evolution produces eras of ascent, but also decline. His sociology attempts to chart the forms of increasing social complexity and is led to arguments of social over cultural causation that were influential particularly on the Durkheimian school in France.

Spencer developed the idea that in the first human cultures fetishism was not a primary but a secondary feature, since from the evidence, all primitives could distinguish between the animate and the inanimate (Comte thought otherwise).

The motor for cultural development comes from the social interpretation and meaning of death, which is the site of powerful emotional ceremonies which establish through ritual and taboo the basic separation of sacred and profane objects. All mythologies are ways of moralising the effects of fetish worship derived from funereal ritual and the vivid experience of ghosts and spirits. It is from this source, the experiential response to mortality, that the idea of a god is evolved in the context of the complexity of the social groups concerned. All such bodies, and corporations such as the priesthood, are subject to the law of differentiation. The emergence of the sciences does not destroy religion, it makes its knowledge relative. Indeed, modern science generates its own specifically religious attitudes to nature, which leads to an ultimate form of religion beyond the angry gods of warrior societies.

The key element in Spencer's relation to culture is his suggestion that between social structure and cultural ideas the productive milieu is that of ceremonial which always takes precedence over representations even in political, legal and civil affairs. The central social control is always established over ceremonial observance in the first instance. Ceremony does not originate in conscious symbolisation, or in law. Thus the first rulers in all aspects and areas of society are the masters of ceremony. The original ceremonial practices disappear only insofar as more detailed and elaborate rules are evolved and adopted. It is on this basis that Spencer provides a detailed sociology of the culture of such objects as trophies, presents, titles of address, badges and fashion. This sociology of culture is rarely cited today; one sociologist who recognised its significance was Goffman.

Further reading

Turner, J. HERBERT SPENCER, Sage, 1985.
Taylor, M. MEN VERSUS THE STATE, Clarendon, 1992.
M.G.

SPENDER, Dale

Feminist researcher	born Australia 1943—
Associated with	FEMINIST ■ LINGUISTICS
Influences include	DE BEAUVOIR
Shares common ground with	LAKOFF ■ SWIFT ■ MILLER ■ KRAMARAE
Main works	MAN MADE LANGUAGE (1980)
	WOMEN OF IDEAS: AND WHAT MEN HAVE DONE TO THEM (1982)
	MOTHERS OF THE NOVEL: 100 GOOD WOMEN WRITERS BEFORE JANE AUSTIN (1986)
	THE WRITING OR THE SEX (1989)
	NATTERING ON THE NET (1995)

I N A CAREER spanning over thirty-five years, Dale Spender has been a secondary school teacher, researcher, writer and media performer. She is a prolific writer with over thirty books to her name. She has been involved in numerous ventures aimed at increasing opportunities for publishing material by and about women, for example, as a founding editor of Pandora Press and the Athene Series; commissioning editor of Penguin's Australian Women's Library; associate editor of the Great Women Series International; founding and consulting editor, *Women's Studies International Quarterly*; co-originator of WIKED (Women's International Knowledge: Education and Data), an international database on women; and founding member of Women, Information Technology and Scholarship (WITS). She has had considerable media exposure internationally. Most recently she has been involved in developing gender equity policies for the electronic age and consulting in the field of information and communications technology.

In her internationally accumulated *Man Made Language*, Spender placed the study of language on the feminist agenda. She argued that language is shaped and largely controlled by men as the dominant sex in patriarchal society and thus reflects their world-view. Women, denied access to public life, have not had the same opportunities to shape language. Women are further disadvantaged by the sexist nature and bias of naming in general, evident in language, and the negative connotations ascribed to words associated with women. Men's control of language works to silence women by excluding their experience and knowledge. Linguistic usage therefore contributes to the oppression and subordination of women and is instrumental in the perpetuation of patriarchy.

Spender subjects the education system to scrutiny in *Invisible Women* (1982), revealing the inherent gender bias of the system which, as with language, has been largely controlled by (white) men. She launches a similar attack in her edited anthology, *Men's Studies Modified* (1981), where she refutes male paradigms of apolitical, objective knowledge. She argues that the academic curriculum should be designated as 'men's studies' given that academia takes the male world-view as the norm, omitting women's knowledge or relegating it to an inferior status. Women are excluded from the production of knowledge, further contributing to their oppression.

Elaborating on this theme, her *Women of Ideas* focused on the exclusion of women from the literary canon. In a related book, *Mothers of the Novel*, Spender demonstrates that throughout the eighteenth century, the majority of novels published were written by women, a fact not reflected in the male-dominated literary canon. The omission of so much women's work from the literary canon, Spender argues, amounts to patriarchal censorship. In her edited anthology, *Feminist Theorists: Three Centuries of Women's Intellectual Traditions*, 1983, she argues that women theorists have been excluded in a similar way from the realm of intellectual theory.

More recent publications include *Nattering on the Net*, where Spender offers a feminist perspective on the implications of the Internet, computer and new communication technologies for women, literature, education, publishing, the print media, the library, readers and authors. She sounds a warning to women that they cannot afford to allow themselves to be marginalised by these new technologies which are currently male dominated. Cyberspace, the Internet and computer technologies are the locus of future power in society and women must join in or risk being disadvantaged, as they were following the print revolution.

All her works emphasise gender bias and inequities, justified by the exclusion of women from historical accounts. Much of work can be seen as an attempt to reclaim women's history. Despite her enthusiasm for her topics and commitment to feminism, Spender has been a controversial figure among feminists and women scholars. She has attracted criticism for her deterministic approach, dogmatism, populism and, at times, less than rigorous theoretical methodology. Nonetheless, she has contributed to debates about gender in areas of education, literature, linguistics and media which set the agenda for the early second-wave feminists and provided the basis for other researchers to build upon.

Other books by Spender include *There's Always Been a Women's Movement in This Century* (1983), *Time and Tide Wait for No Man* (1984), *For the Record: The Making and Meaning of Feminist Knowledge* (1985) and *Dymphna Cusack: Politics and the Pen* (1995).

Further reading

Black, Maria and Coward, Rosalind 'Linguistic, Social and Sexual Relations: a Review of Dale Spender's *Man Made Language*', SCREEN EDUCATION, 39 (Summer 1981), pp. 69–85.
Grinnan, Jeanne 'Dale Spender', in FEMINIST WRITERS, St James Press, 1996.
McKluskie, Kate 'Women's Language and Literature: a Problem in Women's Studies', FEMINIST REVIEW, 14 (June 1983).
G.C.

SPIVAK, Gayatri Chakravorty

Feminist literary theorist/cultural critic	born India 1942—
Associated with	POSTCOLONIALISM ■ SUBALTERN
Influences include	DE MAN ■ MARX ■ DERRIDA
Shares common ground with	BHABHA ■ DERRIDA ■ HARAWAY
Main works	'TRANSLATOR'S PREFACE' TO J. DERRIDA, OF GRAMMATOLOGY (1976)
	IN OTHER WORLDS: ESSAYS IN CULTURAL POLITICS (1987)
	THE POST-COLONIAL CRITIC: INTERVIEWS, STRATEGIES, DIALOGUES (1990)

GAYATRI CHAKRAVORTY SPIVAK is Avalon Foundation Professor in the Humanities in the Department of English and Comparative Literature at Columbia University in New York. She was born in Calcutta, excelled at English in the universities of Calcutta, Cornell and Cambridge, and has published extensively in the fields of literary criticism and cultural politics. Her preferred writing style is the long essay for academic journals, and her articles, interviews and papers have been collected together to form books organised around various themes, including *Outside in the Teaching Machine* (1993).

Spivak does still describe her academic self as belonging to the discipline of literary studies, but her own production transcends traditional conceptions of what literary studies is about and can do. For Spivak's work is as involved with philosophy, linguistics, economics and anthropology, for instance, as it is with literature. In fact, Spivak's engagement with the concerns of the humanities is formidable, and she commands just as comprehensive a knowledge of political, militaristic and economic activities ('global capitalism') around the world as she does of literature.

Perhaps Spivak is best known for her feminist lessons in archival readings and her work on the subaltern, as in 'The Rani of Sirmur: An Essay in Reading the Archives' and 'Can the Subaltern Speak? Speculations on Widow-Sacrifice' (both 1985). These works confront the silencing of marginalised sections of society. They do so with a view to drawing attention to and hence moving towards the eradication of the invisible, entirely exploited and exploitable, groups and positions in the world. Perhaps the paradigm-case of such a position is that traditionally occupied by Indian wives – a position on the margins of complex power networks of domination, subordination and exploitation in terms of gender, ethnicity and alterity. Yet her work is not limited to the academy, and she is involved with such other projects as the 'rearticulating' of NATO, women's groups in Bangladesh, and also the Council For Foreign Relations, which, since 1952, has been a key tool of the US government in the dissemination of (usually right-wing, imperialist) informations.

Spivak's relationship to the power networks that facilitate her own speaking, her own empowerment and her object of study (those that cannot 'speak' and are 'spoken' by others) constitutes the working-through of a set of positions and problematics that is famously intricate and exhaustive. Spivak herself is aware that at times the complexity of her work will exclude a certain readership by being 'too' academic. To circumvent as much of this unavoidable censorship as possible, she uses various writing and speaking styles appropriate to different situations.

In terms of purely academic criteria, Spivak contributes to our understanding of culture through the ever-vigilant engagement with the three major paradigms of cultural studies: psychoanalysis, Marxism and deconstruction. Whilst it is common for a theorist to work predominantly under the rubric of one of these three (among various others), Spivak never shies away from a responsibility to confront that 'constitutive contradiction' which is an integral yet effaced structuring aspect of psychoanalysis, deconstruction and Marxism, and their relationships. It is, of course, a paradox that it is a deconstructive perspective which facilitates any such working at the margins, at the limits, of these theoretical trajectories. Spivak regularly cites Derrida as being a central inspiration and continuing point of reference within her work. But Spivak cannot be classified as being merely a deconstructionist, for her work never falters from a sophisticated feminist imperative.

Because of the level of rigour that feminism demands in terms of the theorisation of identity and cultural power, Spivak's achievement is not only in the single field of feminism, but is also evident as a thorough interrogation of the methods, assumptions, exclusions and effacements permeating the humanities. She has argued that feminist theory is not just a sub-section of the humanities faculty, but that it is rather to be held up as a model from which we should derive codes of practice and methodological imperatives. It can be said with certainty that whilst there are many who claim deconstruction has few practical political uses, it is no coincidence that Spivak's feminist work is imbricated in Derridean deconstruction and that very few of the critics of deconstruction would today deny the political efficacy of deconstruction in the sphere of practical feminist politics.

Further reading

Ashcroft, B. Griffiths, G. Tiffin, H. (eds.) THE POST-COLONIAL STUDIES READER, Routledge, 1994.
Bhabha, H. THE LOCATION OF CULTURE, Routledge, 1993.
McRobbie, A. POSTMODERNISM AND POPULAR CULTURE, Routledge, 1994.

P.B.

STRAUSS, Anselm

Sociologist	born USA 1916–1996
Associated with	GROUNDED THEORY ■ SYMBOLIC INTERACTION
Influences include	DEWEY ■ MEAD ■ THOMAS ■ PEIRCE
Shares common ground with	BLUMER ■ BECKER ■ GOFFMAN
Main works	MIRRORS AND MASKS: THE SEARCH FOR IDENTITY (1959) AWARENESS OF DYING (1965) THE DISCOVERY OF GROUNDED THEORY (WITH BARNEY GLASER, 1967)

ORN IN NEW YORK, Strauss studied at the University of Virginia, before moving to the University of Chicago for his master's and doctoral degrees. He later returned to Chicago before becoming Director of Research at the Michael Reese Hospital and, in 1960, moved to the University of California to teach on the doctoral programme in nursing.

Strauss's contribution is in two main areas: research methods and medical sociology. The combination of these resulted in the seminal *The Discovery of Grounded Theory*, in which he and Barney Glaser – both influenced by earlier pragmatists – utilised Peirce's creative or abductive reasoning. Theory, argued Glaser and Strauss, should not be formulated abstractly then applied to the empirical world for testing. Rather, it should be discovered through practical experience. Criticised for its inductivism, grounded theory involved researchers in long, often painstaking and detailed observations, piecing together fragments in the expectation that theory would emerge in the process. Ideas crystallise into theories. While this may appear to encourage empiricism, Strauss remained mindful that theory's most useful resource, experience, was itself – to use one of Strauss's favoured terms – a negotiated phenomenon, sensitive to context, researchers' expectations and a complex of other factors that mitigated against the possibility of any type of 'direct' observation.

The book became a standard for qualitative research, though, over time, the very term 'grounded theory' became synonomous with any technique that began without suppositions. Like Goffman, Strauss's name was a watchword for research that spurned theoretical generalisations and inclined towards the microanalysis of actual situations. And also like Goffman, he ventured into psychiatric institutions: Strauss was specifically concerned with how psychiatric ideologies sustain both the institutions and the treatment that is provided for patients. This was one of several studies in medical settings. He was a member of the research team that prepared the famous *Boys in White* study in 1961.

With Glaser, Strauss undertook a non-medical study of chronically, often terminally ill patients. Consistent with symbolic interactionist approaches, the study focused on the subjective experience of being ill, how subjects negotiated their illness and how members of their families, and institutions, respond. Extending this with two studies in the mid-1960s, Strauss explored what he called (in the title of one of his books) *The Awareness of Dying*. The research suggested that, like other experiences, such an awareness is influenced by all manner of agencies and situations; as such, the awareness is a context rather than a dawning. Strauss used the phrase 'dying trajectories' to capture the way in which social processes affect the patient's recognition of death.

Most of Strauss's work has theoretical implications, though *Mirrors and Masks* perhaps best explicates his position, particularly on the importance of naming, categorising and conferring identities and statuses. While the presence of Mead is never far away, Strauss believed much symbolic interactionism too idealistic – ungrounded. His commitment to the accumulation of copious data was, in a sense, a counter to this. He was known for enjoining his co-researcher to discard nothing. 'Don't throw anything away,' he bade his followers, 'that's what some people should listen to – their own experience.' The affinities with Goffman are again clear; but similar criticisms surface. Strauss's method was considered interesting but too intuitive to be replicated; and the results of his research too context-specific to be generalisable.

Strauss's attempts to remedy this led him away from his earlier position and in a collaborative book with Juliet Corbin, *Basics of Qualitative Research*, he produced a new technique for coding qualitative materials, a procedure derived from a close reading of data. Glaser made public his disagreement with what he considered a betrayal of grounded theory.

Further reading

Conrad, Peter and Bury, Mike 'Anselm Strauss and the Sociological Study of Chronic Illness', SOCIOLOGY OF HEALTH AND ILLNESS, 19: 3, 1997, pp. 373–6.
Strauss, Anselm SOCIAL PSYCHOLOGY, Dryden, 1949.
Strauss, Anselm and Corbin, Juliet BASICS OF QUALITATIVE RESEARCH: GROUNDED THEORY, PROCEDURES AND TECHNIQUES, Sage, 1990.

E.C.

TAWNEY, Richard Henry

Economic historian/socialist	born India 1880–1962
Associated with	ENGLISH SOCIALISM ■ EQUALITY ■ CRITIQUE OF CAPITALISM
Influences include	WEBER ■ LASKI ■ COBBETT
Shares common ground with	MARSHALL ■ ORWELL ■ KAUTSKY
Main works	THE ACQUISITIVE SOCIETY (1926) RELIGION AND THE RISE OF CAPITALISM (1926) EQUALITY (1920)

ALTHOUGH BORN IN Calcutta, Tawney was educated at Rugby and Balliol College, Oxford. After a spell of social work at Toynbee Hall in the East End of London he became involved in the Workers' Educational Association as tutor (from 1905) and president (1928–44). He was severely wounded during the battle of the Somme (1916). As a lifelong Christian he was heavily influenced by the Christian Socialist movement of the early twentieth century. He became Professor of Economic History at the University of London (1931–49). He was married to one of Lord Beveridge's sisters from 1909 until her death in 1958.

Tawney was regarded as a source of wisdom by the Labour Party from the First World War until his death, when Gaitskell described him as 'the best man I have ever known'. As a moralist, Tawney had a vision of society embodying a set of ideals which he pursued politically and personally throughout his life. His life and vision have, however, been dismissed by MacIntyre as a monument to the impotence of ideals'.

Tawney's work is based upon Weber's thesis that individualism and worldliness, when associated with the doctrines of Calvinism and Puritanism, were the moral engines which fuelled capitalist development. Unlike Weber, however, he considered that there was a two-way causal interaction between religion and economics. He raised fundamental questions concerning the morality of twentieth-century social institutions as vehicles for fomenting a desire for the acquisition of material possessions, and as part of the societal mechanism for sustaining capitalist development. He viewed capitalism as anti-Christian in the way in which it converted economic means into overriding ends, basing his conception of the social order upon the morality of the New Testament. He considered that adverse circumstances can destroy good conduct if an individual, acting in isolation and without societal support, was too weak to combat their effects.

For Tawney socialism was an ethical philosophy, concerned with the quality of life rather than the possession of goods, and this implied a society which valued public welfare above private display. The important aspect of human beings therefore was not individual differences in income and circumstances but rather the common bond of humanity which united them. As a consequence, his philosophy was concerned with reducing individual differences to their proper place of insignificance and this led to his concern with capitalist exploitation of the working class. He rejected Marxism and considered that socialism was only possible as an extension of political democracy. He likewise rejected Liberalism and considered that socialism was not the antithesis of democracy but rather its extension into spheres of life which had previously been excluded. Thus Tawney viewed the ideal society as nurturing people and being nurtured by a moral outlook amongst ordinary people in the traditions of ethical socialism. He considered that state intervention was necessary to bring about this conception of society.

He joined the Fabian Society in 1906 and the Labour Party in 1909 but rejected both the prevalent Marxist stance and a concern with institutional arrangements for effecting change, arguing instead that moral relationships were of supreme importance. In this respect Tawney echoed the sentiments of the nineteenth-century Arts and Crafts movement. He believed that both religious and political thoughts, as expressed by their respective proponents, could influence belief and conduct and help alter economic conditions.

Tawney's socialism was centred on people, and he believed that socialism as a mode of social organisation could produce good people while good people could sustain socialist relationships. The relationship between people and society was therefore a complex and changing interaction. His arguments implied state intervention to manage the economy in the public interest and to provide protection for the individual against the excesses of capitalism, and he was concerned with a fair distribution of wealth rather than continuing growth as the basis for a socialist society. These arguments found ready favour with the socialist outlook of the Labour Party of the time and this helps to explain his lasting influence.

Further reading

Dennis, N. and Halsey, A. ENGLISH ETHICAL SOCIALISM, Clarendon, 1988.
Vincent, A. MODERN POLITICAL IDEOLOGIES, Blackwell, 1992.
Wright, A. BRITISH SOCIALISM, Longman, 1983.

D.E.A.C.

THOMPSON, Edward Palmer

Historian and political activist	born England 1924–1993
Associated with	HISTORY FROM BELOW ■ MORAL ECONOMY ■ WORKING CLASS
Influences include	MARX ■ BRAUDEL ■ MORRIS
Shares common ground with	WILLIAMS ■ HOBSBAWM
Main works	THE MAKING OF THE ENGLISH WORKING CLASS (1963) WHIGS AND HUNTERS: THE ORIGIN OF THE BLACK ACT (1975) CUSTOMS IN COMMON (1991)

EDUCATED AT KINGSWOOD, the Methodist boarding school, and Corpus Christi College, Cambridge, Thompson was called up in 1942, and served in North Africa and Italy, leading a tank squadron in the battle of Cassino. He returned to Cambridge in 1945 to complete his degree, led a large British brigade of volunteers in the reconstruction of the Samac–Sarajevo railway in Yugoslavia in 1947, and moved to West Yorkshire in 1948, where he taught in adult education until 1965. Following the enormous success of his second book *The Making of the English Working Class*, he was appointed to a Readership at the University of Warwick in 1965, where he founded the Centre for the Study of Social History. Thompson resigned in 1972 following a showdown with the university authorities over civil liberties. From then until his death from cancer in 1993 he worked as an independent writer and lecturer. He was a key figure in the international peace movement throughout the 1980s.

Thompson's distinctive and important contribution to cultural studies arose from his determination as a historian to rescue from oblivion those lives (the majority) whom historical study routinely ignored, and write what would become known as 'history from below'. This meant going far beyond the orthodox sources of historical scholarship, and examining such areas as criminal and judiciary activity, religion and superstition, customary and ritual activity and popular forms of political protest such as food riots. (If these areas are nowadays routinely examined by social and cultural historians, it is largely as a result of Thompson's work and that of a small number of his contemporaries). Because much of what was examined was mass or collective activity of various kinds, this sort of historical research needed to develop new forms of analysis. Thompson drew on the idea of *mentalité* from the French *Annales* writers, and developed his own idea of 'moral economy', the system(s) and sources from which mass activity and thought derived its motivation and sense of moral authority. His work drew on a wide range of cultural sources, including popular and literary materials, and he was especially interested in drawing on areas such as 'custom' – a term which in earlier centuries, he argued, 'was used to carry much of what is now carried by the word "culture;"' (*Customs in Common*, p. 2).

One reason why the scholarly results of this historical work, especially *The Making of the English Working Class*, have been so influential in cultural studies, is that cultural studies itself, as Stuart Hall has argued, came out of tests which were to some extent works of 'recovery', especially Richard Hoggart's *The Uses of Literacy* and Raymond Williams's *Culture and Society*. The processes of 'reading' working-class culture, and of what Hall calls 'the "culture-and-society" mode of reflection', were initiated in these two texts in the 1950s. *The Making of the English Working Class*, though it came a little later and was apparently working in a different discipline, belongs decisively, as Hall says, to the same 'moment' in which cultural studies emerged as a 'distinctive problematic': 'in its foregrounding of the questions of culture, consciousness and experience, and its accent on agency, it also made a decisive break: with a certain kind of technological evolutionism, with a reductive economism and an organisational determinism. Between them, these three books constituted the *caesura* out of which – among other things – "Cultural Studies" emerged' ('Cultural Studies: Two Paradigms', in R. Collins *et al.*, *Media, Culture and Society*, Sage, 1986, pp. 33–48, at pp. 33–4). Hall is careful to avoid suggesting that these were *founding* texts of cultural studies; rather, they were a part of the process which made cultural studies possible. The range of practices developed by Thompson (and indeed by Williams) and the new modes of analysis they developed as a response to the inadequacy for their purposes of most existing models and methods, showed the need for a new academic discipline, and fed important ideas into its early development. Thompson's work also had other important implications for cultural studies, not least in its concern with the totality of 'social being' and 'social consciousness', and with ideas of what comprises 'culture' (Hall's essay is illuminating on both topics).

The work Thompson and his fellow-historians produced at Warwick, notably the collection *Albion's Fatal Tree* (ed. D. Hay *et al.*, Allen Lane, 1975), overturned traditional ways of looking at the eighteenth-century and the history of the law, previously two of the most traditional and conservative areas for historical study. Thompson's own *Whigs and Hunters* (also 1975), working in the same general area, brilliantly uncovered a history of cultural resistance lurking in the forests of eighteenth-century England, hidden in the administrative undergrowth of Walpole's Game Laws. A series of major essays on customary activities and rights, on the 'moral economy' of the crowd, and on 'Time, Work-Discipline and Industrial Capitalism', collected (together with some later work on ritual activity) in *Customs in Common*, followed the same pattern of unearthing highly significant cultural and historical phenomena, typcially from hitherto disparaged, overlooked, or poorly understood areas of cultural history.

Framing this extraordinary series of rediscoveries, rewritings, and re-representings, are two books which rescue, not a neglected underclass, but two of the most thoroughly canonised of modern cultural figures, William Morris (*William Morris: Romantic to Revolutionary*, 1955, revised edition Merlin, 1977), and William Blake (*Witness Against the Beast: William Blake and the Moral Law*, Cambridge University Press, 1993). The veneer of post-humous literary respectability is stripped away from both writers, in order to reveal the thoroughly radical and challenging ideas that it had artfully concealed in their writings. Thompson's greatest art was this ability to cut through appearances and masks of all kinds, to reveal the meanings and potential meanings they concealed, and to relate them to larger developments. His great strength, inherited from the English dissenting and radical traditions, was never to accept received opinions, received readings, received cultural truths, however persuasive and respectable they might seem, without thoroughly challenging and testing them in this way.

Further reading

Butler, M. *et al.* 'E.P. Thompson and the Uses of History: Samples from the History Workshop conference of July 1994', HISTORY WORKSHOP JOURNAL, 39, Spring 1995, pp. 71–135.

Hobsbawm, E.J. 'Edward Palmer Thompson, 1924–1993', PROCEEDINGS OF THE BRITISH ACADEMY, 90, 1996, pp. 521–39.

Kaye, H.J. and McLelland, K. (eds.) E.P. THOMPSON: CRITICAL PERSPECTIVES Cambridge University Press, 1990.

J.G.

TOCQUEVILLE, Alexis de

Sociologist/political theorist	born France 1805–1859
Associated with	LIBERTY ▪ DEMOCRACY ▪ REVOLUTION
Influences include	MONTESQUIEU ▪ ROUSSEAU ▪ HOBBES
Shares common ground with	MILL ▪ WEBER ▪ LOCKE
Main works	DEMOCRACY IN AMERICA (1835, 1840) THE OLD REGIME AND THE FRENCH REVOLUTION (1856) RECOLLECTIONS (1893)

TOCQUEVILLE WAS BORN into an aristocratic family which had been decimated by the French Revolution. His parents escaped the guillotine but endured several months in prison, which was to have a lasting effect on them both. Tocqueville's first formal education was from the Royal College of Metz at the age of 16. In 1827 he became a junior magistrate in Versailles where his father was Prefect, but he was to be disappointed by this career. In 1831 he visited America primarily to study the penitentiary system; however it is from this trip that Tocqueville gained his insights into the American form of government which was to be the basis of democracy in America. In 1839 he was elected to the French government where his roles included an involvement in drafting a new constitution (in 1848) and a brief period as Foreign Minister in 1849. He abandoned public life in 1851 following Louis Napoleon's *coup d'état* and died in 1859.

Tocqueville distanced himself from his aristocratic background as he saw the movement towards democracy and the levelling of social ranks in Western societies as irresistible. However, at the same time, he was concerned by the impact that this movement would have, especially as there also appeared to be a corresponding decline in the values and culture on which liberty had previously been based. Democracy, for Tocqueville, was the belief that all individuals were socially equal and that liberty was their birthright. However, democracy was not a panacea, and it would bring with it risks to society. One such risk would be its impact on the arts, philosophy and cultural aspects of society. Tocqueville believed it unlikely that a society such as the democracy present in America would produce art and literature of the standard previously seen as they would become trades and hence attempt to conform to mass opinion. The result would be mediocrity.

Of even greater importance was the threat to liberty that democracy itself actually posed. Specifically within democracy there is a tendency towards centralisation and individualism. The centralisation of power robs individuals of involvement in and responsibility for the welfare of society which, in turn, leads to a society where individuals, or families, become increasingly isolated and motivated by their own material wellbeing. A democratic society could deteriorate into a tyranny of the majority, who would abuse their position to oppress the minority. *Democracy in America* analyses the American political system and its evolution in an attempt to understand how this system appeared to succeed in creating a liberal democratic society. It was hoped that the lessons learnt would help achieve a liberal democracy in France.

Tocqueville saw the success of the American system to depend upon three key aspects. First, and foremost, there were the customs, manners and beliefs on which American society was based. Second, there were its laws; and finally, the size of America and its lack of neighbours required diplomatic consideration. The American system had been successful in ensuring against centralisation and individualism, specifically through its pluralism. There was a combined spirit of religion and liberty which underpinned society and was probably a legacy of the first Puritan immigrants. Additionally, there were important roles for local government, which fostered experience of self-government, and voluntary organisations which ensured that there were intermediary bodies between the individual and the centralised government. These conditions, Tocqueville argued, halted the movement toward an individualistic society.

Tocqueville's work has had a wide influence in both sociology and political thought. This influence appears to have increased in the twentieth century as his concerns for society appear to have been confirmed. The dangers of an all-powerful state and the harm to society if individuals become 'alienated' within it are issues which are still considered today. Throughout his work possibly the most important argument is the need for individuals to associate with each other and for them to understand their duties as citizens to the society in which they live.

Further reading

Aron, R. Main Currents in Sociological Thought, Vol. 1, Weidenfeld & Nicolson, 1968, pp. 181–232.
Jardin, A. Tocqueville, Peter Halban, 1988.
Siedentop, L. Tocqueville, Oxford University Press, 1994.
S.M.C.

TODD, Emmanuel

Historian	born France 1951—
Associated with	FAMILY GAZE ▪ IDEOLOGY ▪ NEW HISTORY
Main influences	LE PLAY ▪ SIEGFRIED ▪ BRAUDEL
Shares common ground with	LASLETT ▪ MACFARLANE ▪ STONE
Main works	THE EXPLANATION OF IDEOLOGY (1983)
	THE CAUSES OF PROGRESS (1984)
	THE INVENTION OF EUROPE (1990)

SON OF THE journalist, television interviewer and novelist Olivier Todd, Emmanuel Todd is a graduate of the Institute of Politics, Paris. His doctoral thesis, in historical anthropology at the University of Cambridge, compared peasant communities in three eighteenth-century European countries. Between 1977 and 1984, Todd was literary critic of *Le Monde*. Since 1984 he has been Head of Archives at the National Institute of Demographic Studies, Paris.

Todd's key argument is that the culture and politics of societies are determined by the prevailing family form. His theories of development and political behaviour are based upon the empirical work of many anthropologists and demographers. The interpretation of history, development and politics to which they give rise are controversial.

The Cambridge Group for the History of Population and Social Structure, studying the Industrial Revolution in Europe, found that family form is a precondition rather than a consequence of important social and economic developments. Todd has spelled out the implications of this, proposing that economic development, politics and culture are functions of family form. From his early work in French electoral sociology Todd posited, in *L'Invention de La France*, a relationship between family form and voting patterns. He went on to theorise a correlation between family form and ideological systems in *The Explanation of Ideology*, which found that ideologies correspond to sets of attitudes determined by family form, which has predisposed adherents of those ideologies to particular kinds of doctrines; indeed ideologies spread only so far as the geographical diffusion of the family forms with which they have affinity. Far from being determinants of behaviour they are reflections of it. In *The Causes of Progress* he found that family form rather than economics accounts for the rate of industrial development of a given society, and in particular that societies in which women have higher status have greater potential for socio-economic development.

Todd assigns all known human families to seven broad categories, distinguished by the position of women, modes of marriage and inheritance, the respective roles of mother and father, the hierarchy of siblings, expression of authority and exogamy/endogamy. These differences have implications, for they determine the values of the individuals and the groups to which they belong. While the concrete day-to-day operations of these values is left to the micro-studies, the proof of their importance lies in the correlations between family form and social phenomena; it is these correlations that prove the primacy of those values generated by family form and suggest a challenging determinism in human affairs. As his own précis in *L'Invention de L'Europe* (pp. 11–12) puts it:

The fundamental values of liberty or authority, equality or inequality which stimulate, organise and guide the movement of modernity are rooted in the original soil of the family, that primordial substratum whose traces are found at every stage of European progress. The diversity of family systems allows us to explain both the plurality of relations – according to region – to the protestant reformation and the French revolution, the numerous varieties of socialism and nationalism in the 20th century, and the unequal capacities of the different geographical areas as to literacy, industrialisation, dechristianisation and contraception.

Even if determinism is rejected, Todd's 'family gaze' has many implications. Economic and geographical factors are relegated to a secondary role in determining how societies will develop and female emancipation is seen to be a precondition of economic progress. Culture, especially such causal factors as 'protestantism' or 'secularism', are seen as functions of family-form demography, which also helps to explain how societies superficially as different from each other as Japan and East-Coast USA have similar development patterns. Where they are based upon assumptions about economic and geographical preconditions, development policies need rethinking. Moreover, race is rendered irrelevant in considering development, because family form does not respect racial boundaries. As to politics, even when institutions look similar, such as in, say, Italy and the UK, the reality conforms to the tendency of the dominant family form.

Todd has received scant attention in the Anglophone world. This is perhaps because his generalisations seem far-fetched and his determinism unpalatable both to those wedded to traditional political economy approaches and to those of cultural studies and the 'argumentative turn'. Yet the failure of the Academy to explain why particular religious or political ideas and institutions take root where they do is a reason for us to pay attention to Todd, who offers insights to development economists, public policy specialists and students of history and culture alike.

Further reading

Hall, J.A. 'Review', CONTEMPORARY SOCIOLOGY 17: 6, 1989.
Revel, J.F. 'Todd's Originality', ENCOUNTER, 64 February 1985.
Townsend, C. 'Recent, Relative and Rational', PHILOSOPHY, 8–14 January 1988.
H.d.B.

TURNER, Bryan Stanley

Sociologist	born England 1945—
Associated with	BODY ■ CITIZENSHIP ■ MODERNITY
Influences include	NIETZSCHE ■ WEBER ■ FOUCAULT
Shares common ground with	BOURDIEU ■ SAID ■ RORTY
Main works	THE BODY AND SOCIETY (1984)
	WEBER AND ISLAM (1974)
	FOR WEBER: ESSAYS ON THE SOCIOLOGY OF FATE 2ND EDN, 1996)

T URNER'S PROLIFIC OUTPUT has sometimes led to the charge that he is profligate with his gifts. He has made original contributions to social theory, the body, medical power, ideology, citizenship, human rights, the sociology of religion, Islam, modernity and postmodernity. In the post-war Anglophone sociological tradition, only Giddens has made a comparable contribution. Yet while until recently, Giddens situated his work in the elaboration of 'structuration theory', Turner has chosen to work in the classical tradition of macro-sociology, historical sociology and comparative research.

The response to the daunting array of his research interests has been allowed to obscure the nucleus that informs all his work. In fact, Turner's work is organised around an interrogation of what he calls 'the normative institutions of coercion', e.g. religion, medicine and the law. Hence, the interest in Weber/ Islam and religion, Foucault/body/medicine and law/citizenship. He is interested in how 'normality' and 'pathology' are classified. He relates this to the professionalisation of society, notably the rise of the medical and legal professions; the centralisation of power in the hands of the state; and the secularisation of society. It amounts to perhaps the most imaginative combination of Weberian and Foucauldian traditions that we currently have at our disposal.

Against the relativism of post-structuralist and postmodern theory, Turner sees the human body as fundamental to morality. He offers the frailty of the human body, and the precariousness of existence, as the basis for a new approach to human rights and citizenship, based in the recognition of universal conditions. Nowadays, the idea of universalism is unfashionable in some circles. Yet it shows the moral seriousness in Turner's thought which has always refused to succumb to the rhetoric of relativism. Turner is interested in a practical engagement with the problems of citizenship. But of course, he is aware of the charges made against Enlightenment forms of universalism and pragmatism. Turner's pursuit of the normative consequences of the body in the construction of theories of citizenship and models of human rights dismisses essentialist notions of humanism. Rather, it is founded in the practical considerations of what follows in all cultures from being born helpless, from ageing and eventually dying. He uses historical and comparative methods consistently to support and advance his analysis. The body situates us in a field of rights and responsibilities. Of course these vary historically and cross-culturally. The task of citizenship studies and theories of human rights is to extrapolate just, democratic methods of managing this situation.

Turner was educated at the University of Leeds where he did doctoral research on Methodism. He has held academic lectureships in the UK at the universities of Lancaster and Aberdeen and was Professor of Sociology at Essex. He has also held Professorships in Sociology at the Universities of Flinders (South Australia) and Utrecht. Until 1998 he was Dean of Humanities in the Faculty of Arts, Deakin University. He is currently Professor of Sociology at the University of Cambridge. It is a career of some considerable physical restlessness, although his intellectual concerns have remained quite stable. From his doctoral work on religion to his latest writing on the body, citizenship and globalisation he has been concerned to explore how knowledge and power shape human capacities, opportunities and life-chances.

Recently, Turner's work has taken a more empirical turn. It is as if he is now intent on testing some of the theoretical formulations made in earlier work. He is developing his interest in citizenship through an empirical study of voluntary associations and the welfare state; a trans-national study of post-war generations; and a study of love, intimacy and ageing.

This has hardly led to the abandonment of his theoretical concerns. He continues to make important contributions to historical sociology. Recent studies include evaluations of the work of Weber, Durkheim, Mannheim, Lowith, Parsons, Ludwig Klages, Baudrillard and Lyotard. He is also developing his work on the body, citizenship, ideology, Islam and globalisation. He was one of the founding members of *Theory, Culture and Society*; and he is foundation editor of the new journal *Citizenship Studies*.

A criticism of Turner's work is that it has ignored the utopian opportunities offered by modernity. Turner does not reject Marx *tout court*, but his writings on class and ideology do not pull their punches in exposing the weaknesses in Marxist thought. Similarly, Turner's response to feminism is one of qualified support. He clearly supports the feminist attack on the unequal, prejudicial character of male culture. Yet at the same time, he insists that the recognition of formal equality before the law is not negligible and has had a tangible effect in weakening male power. His work on the body, citizenship and love suggests that a pivotal crisis in modernity is the crisis of male authority. This is likely to become a more prominent theme in his future work, which is already committed to exploring love and intimacy. At the heart of his sociology is a concern with the practical and moral possibilities of sociology in acting upon the world.

Further reading

Bilton, T., Webster, A., Stanworth, M. and Sheard, K. (eds.) INTRODUCTORY SOCIOLOGY, Macmillan, 1996.

Fardon, R. 'Interview with Bryan Turner', in B.S. Turner, REGULATING BODIES, Routledge, 1993.

Petersen, A. and Bunton, R. (eds.) FOUCAULT, HEALTH AND MEDICINE, Routledge, 1997.

C.R.

TZARA, Tristan

Poet	born Romania 1896–1963
Associated with	DADAISM ▪ SURREALISM
Influences include	NIETZSCHE ▪ BRETON
Shares common ground with	HANS ARP ▪ MARCEL DUCHAMP ▪ FRANCIS PICABIA
Main works	OEUVRES COMPLÈTES (3 VOLS., 1975–91)
	LAMPISTERIES, PRÉCÉDÉES DE SEPT MANIFESTES DADA (1963) TRANS. SEVEN DADA MANIFESTOS AND LAMPISTERIES (1977)
	L'HOMME APPROXIMATIF (1931) TRANS. APPROXIMATE MAN (1973)

I N A COLLECTION devoted to cultural theory, Tristan Tzara is most aptly remembered as an inventor of Dada. That is not to say that a more purely biographical study should ignore his stormy association with surrealism and André Breton, who on at least two famous occasions accosted Tzara during public recitation. Nor should one neglect Tzara's post-Second World War migration to Communism and more tendentious forms of artistic expression. But surrealism and socialist realism can be described conceptually with purer advocates. Dadaism cannot.

There are debates on the origin of the term 'Dada', along with its intended meaning. What is clear, however, is that the term, like the movement it represents, is irreverent. It cannot be accidental that the movement was born in a Zurich café (Café Voltaire, 1 Spiegelgasse) during the conflagration of the First World War. A multinational band of refugee artists reinforced a shared bewilderment regarding the maintenance of aesthetic 'business as usual' while the world was collapsing all around. In fact, the Dadaists came to reject the concept of beauty detached from reality. Purity, depth and originality seemed absurd artistic ideals in a world of filth, duplicity and mundane instrumentality. Art which remained committed to such concepts was necessarily delusional, hypocritical and diversionary.

Dada hoped to expose high art and its bourgeois patrons by mocking them. The transcendent muse of poetry was displaced by nonsense poems whose verses were chosen out of a hat. Deep aesthetic contemplation was replaced by simultaneous poetry, spontaneous screamings in different languages delivered all at the same time. An erudite language was replaced by sound poems, where Tzara and his cohorts attempted to avoid any sounds that even approximated words. The Dadaists felt horribly restricted by high culture and language, and they wanted to break its spell by mocking its pretensions.

Expressions of supposed 'spiritual autonomy' were rendered mechanistic and banal. Dadaist painter Marcel Duchamp depicted bourgeois individuals as machines in many of his works. The bachelors, for example, in '*The Bride Stripped Bare by her Bachelors, Even*', were represented by a paddlewheel, a grinder and an assortment of metallic funnels. Sexuality, romance and creativity were exposed as the simple products of cultural robotics. There was, then, a serious element to the apparent silliness.

If Dada were serious, however, it could not be admitted. Such would have been a concession to the status quo. A serious Dada is one open to analysis and rational debate – and thus to the repugnant paradigm. So when asked about the ability of Dada to inform praxis, Tzara replies: 'Dada is a dog – a compass – the lining of the stomach – neither new nor a nude Japanese girl – a gasometer of jangled feelings – Dada is brutal and doesn't go in for propaganda – Dada is a quantity of life in transparent, effortless and gyratory transformation.' (*Seven Dada Manifestos and Lampisteries*, p. 43).

If there are any limitations to Tzara's iconoclastic approach, it would be that Dadaism may be less disruptive and radical than it seems or intends. Despite the disconcerting reordering of images, Dadaism still relies on common elements of bourgeois existence. No matter how radically the dictionary is assaulted, its use as a medium still condemns the artist to use common words. And as shocking as obscenity might be, it is nevertheless easily understood by the audience, and is hardly transcendent. Thus, it is not surprising that Dadaists, including Tzara, eventually left the fray to engage in political and artistic ventures that were more independent of the given.

Further reading

Bigsby, C.W.E. DADA AND SURREALISM, Methuen, 1972.
Erickson, John D. DADA: PERFORMANCE, POETRY, AND ART, Twayne, 1984.
Peterson, Elmer TRISTAN TZARA: DADA AND SURRATIONAL THEORIST, Rutgers University Press, 1971.

T.J.L.

VEBLEN, Thorstein

Economist/sociologist	born USA 1857–1929
Associated with	INSTITUTIONAL ECONOMICS ■ CONSPICUOUS CONSUMPTION ■ LEISURE CLASS
Influences include	MEAD ■ JAMES
Shares common ground with	DEWEY ■ MILLS ■ COMMONS
Main works	THEORY OF THE LEISURE CLASS (1899) THE THEORY OF BUSINESS ENTERPRISE (1904) THE ENGINEERS AND THE PRICE SYSTEM (1921)

THORSTEIN VEBLEN was a first-generation American; his parents were Norwegian immigrant farmers who settled in the predominantly Scandinavian-inhabited Lutheran farming community of Wato, Wisconsin. He was educated at Carleton College, Johns Hopkins and Yale, receiving a doctorate in economics in 1884. He was then unemployed for seven years, which he spent working on the farms of relatives. He eventually obtained a tutoring position at Cornell University but his agnosticism, persistent womanising and personal idiosyncrasies meant that he was unable to secure a permanent position at any university and he drifted from one university to another. Although his fame and his reputation as an original thinker grew with his publications, he was unable to achieve academic success. He eventually retired to California where he lived in isolation until his death.

Veblen was both an economist and a social critic, presenting a powerful critique of American capitalism which he regarded as both predatory and parasitic. As the founder of an approach which became known as Institutional Economics he concentrated not upon the factors of production as explanation for societal wealth creation, as was the norm among economists at that time, but rather upon consumption as the driving force behind economic development. He created the phrase 'conspicuous consumption', arguing that the lifestyle of the richest part of society, the so-called 'Leisure class', was based upon an overt show of wealth through their consumption, and that this led to consumption of wealth being the dominant force in society as the rest of that society sought to emulate the leisure class. He was fiercely critical of this model of social practice and his hope was that eventually both the leisure class and modern corporate power would be replaced by the rule of engineers. By this means he hoped that the instinct for workmanship and craftsmanship would provide a stimulus for individual growth.

For Veblen the economy had to be comprehended in holistic terms as an evolving process. It consisted of a complex set of institutions, a set of habits and thoughts, and as an arena of conflict. His critique was based upon a rejection of the rationality principle of conventional economics which, he argued, could not explain the evolutionary nature of the economy and the changing institutional and power structures of society. Mainstream economics had become, he argued, little more than a subtle defence of existing institutions and power structures, designed to maintain the status quo. Veblen's critique distinguished between industrial and pecuniary considerations, arguing that business had a tendency to sabotage production through its dedication to profit making. He believed that there was evolutionary process in society which transcended the market and constructed an evolutionary theory of value based upon the habits of social life.

He viewed institutions as legitimised vehicles for perpetuating the power of the dominant class and described social progress as a contest between the progressive drive of technology and industrialisation and the retarding force of established institutions. At the same time he created the concept of the business cycle, which he blamed upon financial institutions. Veblen was not surprised by the world war which started in 1914, regarding it as inevitable that capitalism should lead to war. He traced the origins of the war to Germany's late industrialisation and its lack of a democratic political tradition. For him industrialisation and democratic processes were the unique forces of social progress.

Although Veblen gained a reputation as an economic and social theorist during his lifetime, it is not surprising that his ideas did not meet with universal acceptance, given his criticisms of the dominant groups of society. Thus Institutional Economics remained a school of thought of little perceived relevance until a revival of interest in the role of institutions was promoted through the Austrian School in the 1970s. This has led to a resurgence of interest in Veblen's work and to the creation of the New Institutionalist School of Economics.

Further reading

David, A. 'Thorstein Veblen', in D. Sills (ed.) INTERNATIONAL ENCYCLOPAEDIA OF THE SOCIAL SCIENCES, 16, Macmillan, 1968.
Tilman R. THORSTEIN VEBLEN AND HIS CRITICS 1891–1963, Princeton University Press, 1992.
Tilman, R. THORSTEIN VEBLEN AND CURRENT SOCIAL THEORY, Princeton University Press, 1995.

D.E.A.C.

VIRILIO, Paul

Urban philosopher/cultural theorist	born France 1932—
Associated with	ARCHITECTURE ■ SPEED POLITICS ■ WAR ■ TECHNOLOGY
Influences include	HEIDEGGER ■ FOUCAULT ■ DELEUZE ■ GUATTARI
Shares common ground with	DELEUZE ■ GUATTARI ■ BAUDRILLARD ■ KROKER ■ HARVEY
Main works	SPEED AND POLITICS: AN ESSAY ON DROMOLOGY (1986) WAR AND CINEMA: THE LOGISTICS OF PERCEPTION (1989) OPEN SKY (1997)

ALTHOUGH VIRILIO BEGAN his career as an artist in stained glass, in 1958 he turned to philosophical and cultural questions relating to urban and military space from the perspective of a committed Christian and political activist. With Claude Parent, he founded the 'Architecture Principie' group and the review of the same name in 1963. However, Virilio's active political militancy during the events of May 1968 led to an irreparable break with Parent. In 1969 Virilio was nominated Professor at the École Spéciale d'Architecture in Paris, becoming its Director in 1975 and its President in 1990. Since the 1970s he has not only organised exhibitions on the themes of war, urbanism, media and democracy, but has also been a member of the editorial staff and a contributor to a variety of influential periodicals, including *Libération* and *Les Temps Modernes*. Virilio's writings earned him the 'National Award for Criticims' in 1987, while his political activities currently involve, amongst others, membership of the High Committee for the Housing of Disadvantaged People.

The cultural significance of Virilio's work flows from his early architectural and photographic inquiries, documented in *Bunker Archeology* (1994), into the 'Atlantic Wall' – the 1,500 German bunkers constructed during the Second World War along the coastline of France to prevent an Allied invasion. The Wall inspired Virilio to develop 'the war model' of urban space, speed, power, military force and disappearance. Accordingly, in *The Function of the Oblique* (1996), Virilio and Parent outline their efforts to initiate an urban regime based on the theory of the 'oblique function', which while founded on uneven planes and bodily disorientation, nevertheless resulted in the construction of the

Church of Sainte-Bernadette du Banlay at Nevers in 1966. Virilio's later writings on 'The overexposed city', 'Improbable architecture' and 'Critical space' are contained in *The Lost Dimension* (1991). In *Speed and Politics*, an essay on 'dromology' – the compulsive logic of speed – Virilio suggests that successive technological revolutions imply both the disappearance of geographical space and a new cultural politics of real time. *Pure War* (1983), by contrast, is a book-length interview with Virilio, and, in the same manner as *War and Cinema* (1989), and *Popular Defense and Ecological Struggles* (1990), it discusses the use by the military of cinematic technologies of perception, 'Pure power' – the enforcement of surrender without engagement – and the case for 'Revolutionary resistance' to war. In recent works, such as *The Aesthetics of Disappearance* (1991), *The Vision Machine* (1994), *The Art of the Motor* (1995) and *Open Sky* (1997), Virilio argues that postmodern culture is characterised by a new 'disappearance aesthetic'. Indeed, he claims that this aesthetic is the source of the crisis of cinematic images, a crisis which is presently obliterating the distinction between our mental images and the virtual images generated by the new information and communications technologies of perception, such as surveillance cameras, virtual reality and cyberspace.

Any critical evaluation of Virilio's work must recognise that it allows for a Foucauldian conception of power. It is a Nietzchean–Deleuzian philosophy of *forces* rather than a Hegelian–Marxian philosophy of subjects. Nevertheless, Virilio's writings are in fact largely derived from his own biographical, religious and intellectual experiences. Moreover, he often seems unaware (or worse, uninterested) in other cultural theorists. For instance, Virilio appears to be oblivious of 'cyberfeminist' debates about the body, technology and cultural identity. His writings would therefore benefit greatly from a sustained engagement with such authors. Assessing the impact of Virilio's work is difficult because it is only recently that it has come to be recognised by other cultural theorists for what it is: unique. For his writings have, almost without exception, anticipated, rather than complied with, later cultural and theoretical developments. It is for these reasons, then, that his work is now being avidly read by growing numbers of cultural theorists, architects, political scientists, military historians and digital artisans.

Further reading

Armitage, J. 'Accelerated Aesthetics: Paul Virilio's *The Vision Machine*', in C. Blake and L. Blake (eds.) ANGELAKI, 2: 1, 1997, pp. 199–209.
Der Derian, J. (ed.) THE PAUL VIRILIO READER, Blackwell, 1998.
Kroker, A. 'Paul Virilio: The Postmodern Body as War Machine', in THE POSSESSED INDIVIDUAL: TECHNOLOGY AND POSTMODERNITY, Macmillan, 1992.

J.A.

VYGOTSKY, Lev Semyonovich

Psychologist	born Russia 1896–1934
Associated with	THEORY OF INNER SPEECH
Influences include	BEKHTEREV ■ PAVLOV ■ MARX
Shares common ground with	BRUNER ■ PIAGET ■ MEAD ■ WUNDT
Main works	THOUGHT AND LANGUAGE (1934)
	MIND IS SOCIETY (1978)
	'PLAY AND ITS ROLE IN THE MENTAL DEVELOPMENT
	OF THE CHILD', SOCIAL PSYCHOLOGY, 3: 5 (1933)

VYGOTSKY WAS A student of history and philosophy at the Shaniavkii Moscow universities, graduating in 1917. He taught at Gomel, Belorussia and later became a professor at Moscow University. Vygotsky insisted that there was a particular relationship between the human mind and the social context. As such, much of his work – especially his early work – was in reaction to the research of Pavlov, who had bridged the philosophical tradition of associationism and empirical research, and Bekhterev, whose reflexology minimised differences between human beings and other animals.

While Pavlov believed that what he called the 'higher nervous activity' of humans could be conceptualised with the same terms as those of other living organisms, Vygotsky insisted that consciousness, being a uniquely human attribute, needed to be analysed separately. Ironically, in rejecting introspection as a legitimate scientific technique, he veered towards the behaviourist methods prefigured by Pavlov. All Vygotsky's work was done in controlled laboratory settings which he believed to be appropriate to explaining behaviour, as opposed to just describing it. Two types of action which may be behaviourally identical may have quite different origins and features. Describing them would leave the analysis at what Vygotsky called the phenotypic level; but he wished to delve into what he regarded as the genotypic level.

For Vygotsky, the key characteristic of the human mind is the propensity to use signs as memory aids. His efforts were geared towards discovering the process by which children develop the ability to construct and utilise signs and tools, the former being internalised reconstructions of the latter. The mind is a type of internal reconstruction of a world outside. He believed the construction process proceeded in three phases;

1 In this phase, wrote Vygotsky: 'an operation that critically represents an external activity is reconstructed and begins to occur internally'. Words begin to express the child's relationship with the world of objects outside him or her.

2 Words are used by adults to communicate or convey to the child the relationship words have with things; in Vygotsky's words, 'an interpersonal relationship is transformed into an intrapersonal one'.

3 This is a transformative phase in which words become intrinsically meaningful to the child: this means that words become tools that help people to control 'lower functions'. Words acquire abstract meanings.

Vygotsky emphasised the role of play, that is, action subordinated to meaning. He meant by this that we regulate action with rules which we then obey. The act of obeying them facilitates play. As the child grows up, rules become a more important feature of his or her social landscape, especially in play activities.

He also worked on the development of written language in children, believing that writing should be taught as if it were as natural a process as speech. These functions become enmeshed in a 'complex dialectical process, characterised by periodicity, unevenness and the development of different functions'. Vygotsky's concept of inner speech as a transformative ability was instantiated in the oft-quoted example of the young boy who breaks the crayon he is drawing with, says 'broken' and proceeds to draw a broken car.

Coming to prominence in the wake of the Russian Revolution, Vygotsky saw much of his work as an attempt to shape a psychology that was compatible with Marxist theory. Many of his mental concepts are drawn from economic theory. For example, one of his basic arguments is that humans use signs as psychic tools signs; the signs themselves are the products of previous activity and, as such are a mental equivalent of a means of production – produced through engagement with the outside, material world of things. Cognitive processes are in no way separable from changing material contexts. With Wundt, he paved the way for an alternative conception of psychology than that of associationists (later, behaviourists), one based on the relationship between higher developmental processes and social circumstances.

Further reading

Smolka, A-L., de Goes, M-C. and Pino, A. '(In)determinacy and the Semiotic Constitution of Subjectivity', in A. Fogel, M. Lyra and J. Valsiner (eds.) DYNAMICS AND INDETERMINISM IN DEVELOPMENTAL AND SOCIAL PROCESSES, Lawrence Erlbaum Associates, 1997.

Tolman, C., Cherry, F., Van Hezewijk, R. and Lubek, I. (eds.) PROBLEMS OF THEORETICAL PSYCHOLOGY, Captus Books, 1996.

'Vygotsky's Cultural–Developmental Theory of Human Development: An

International Perspective', Special issue of ANTHROPOLOGY AND EDUCATION QUARTERLY, 26: 4, 1995.

E.C.

WALKER, Alice

Cultural commentator	born USA 1944—
Associated with	WOMANISM ▪ BLACK FEMINISM
Influences include	HURSTON ▪ KING
Shares common ground with	MORRISON ▪ HOOKS
Main works	MERIDIAN (1976)
	THE COLOR PURPLE (1982)
	IN SEARCH OF OUR MOTHERS' GARDENS (1983)

D AUGHTER OF BLACK Georgia sharecroppers, Walker obtained a scholarship to Spelman College, and then Sarah Lawrence. After working in Civil Rights and visiting Africa, she began to write poetry, then novels and essays. The Pulitzer Prize-winning *The Color Purple* secured her international acclaim.

Walker's cultural theorising is rarely original. Her stress on the importance of securing a 'black perspective' upon society and culture – possessing a continuity with past black culture and disseminating through the establishment of viable sociocultural role-models – is well rehearsed. Zora Neale Hurston's writing and her research into black folklore in the 1920s is one clear precursor. Walker's main statement of these ideas can be found within *In Search of Our Mothers' Gardens* (*ISOMG*), a collection of essays and reviews spanning 1966–82. Her accompanying insistence on the importance of stimulating emancipatory momentum for black women in particular, given their acute repression under the combined effect of racism, sexism and class oppression, is again well foreshadowed (Hurston can again be named). Similarly, when Walker stresses the importance for women of finding space in which to write, Virginia Woolf has anticipated her.

It is, however, part of Walker's project to draw openly upon an eclectic list of sources, redefining perspectives supplied by not only a wide variety of past and present black role-models (including, besides Hurston, Phillis Wheatley, Sojourner Truth, Nella Larsen, Gwendolyn Brooks, Rebecca Cox Jackson, Paule Marshall, Bessie Smith, Billie Holiday, Nina Simone and Aretha Franklin) but also white influences (such as Kate Chopin, Flannery O'Connor, Muriel Rukeyser and Carson McCullers) and male writers (such as Frederick Douglass, W.E.B. DuBois, Langston Hughes, Jean Toomer, Martin Luther King and William Faulkner). This diverse and incomplete list, which indicates the roots of her theories, repeatedly names women famous for the strength of their personality, and helps explain why Walker's version of black feminism, 'womanism', places stress on audacity, courage and strength. But it is also syncretistic – a reminder that 'womanism' emphasises non-separatism. Walker's formulation of womanism (evolved between 1981 and 1983; the label is original) is again largely derivative, drawing upon pre-existing strands of black feminism, even if its metaphysical stress on the central importance of universalism and animism when defining womanist communal enterprise provides a (theoretically unconvincing) means of differentiation. Her determined fusing of past theories and approaches when delineating a liberatory and emancipatory model was, however, uniquely inclusive when it appeared.

Her evolving list of black forebears is dominated by creative women working in a variety of popular cultural mediums. This is attributable to the insistently high valuation Walker places (again, not originally) upon the central importance of examining a variety of cultural forms when exploring the parameters of a black female perspective. This helps explain the repeated presentation of domestic art in her writings: gardening, cookery, clothes-making, and, especially, quilt making. Yet again this last emphasis is unoriginal, but a cameo version of central motifs in her theorising emerges in Walker's insistence on how, made up of scraps of material possessing their own 'herstories', quilts have inherent continuity with the past, serve as a channel of inclusive and uncensorable creative expression, and possess practical as well as aesthetic domestic functions. Additionally, however, Walker views quilts as 'telling' (extended) family stories (combining her*story* and artistic design), and in this respect her ideas incorporate a more original line of argument. This places a high valuation on the role of storytelling in securing cultural and social definition: for individuals, for communities, but especially for blacks and above all for black women, given the centrality of oral transmission in black culture. This allies her argument, independently, with the more or less congruently evolving theories of cultural psychologists, such as Jerome Bruner, Michael Cole, Bradd Shore and R.A. Shweder, turning to social anthropology to reconsider methods of studying the 'mind'. Walker's writing shows a lively sense of the way in which, as cultural psychology also suggests, we live in a sea of stories and either learn or do not learn to recognise how stories' narrative modes construct and interpret – functioning as tools of the mind for making sense both of and in the world. Walker calls it 'learning how to check out stories' (*ISOMG*); the requirement is to resist passive reflection of 'someone else's literary or social fantasy' ('Coming in from the Cold', *Living by the Word* [1988]).

Accordingly, Walker tells stories to convey her theories: about the relationship between pornography and black patriarchal oppression ('Porn' and 'Take Back the Night'), about the need for tradition and the penalties for lacking it ('Fanu'), about how black women have moved from being 'suspended' in history to making a space for themselves (*ISOMG*) – to name just three. This is a repeated pattern in her work: her theories are explained/explored as and through stories, in their own right/write. Thus it is possible to view her writing as theory in practice. For example, *Meridian* and *The Color Purple* combine to serve a narrative exploration of the shifting continuities between Civil Rights campaigns in the 1950s, the experience of black women in the period stretching from the mid-1890s to near the end of the Second World War, and, behind both stories, slavery and its narratives. The structure of *The Color Purple*, in particular, implicitly aligns itself with cultural psychology's theories: by inverting 'normal' narrative hierarchies, black women's stories are brought to the fore, and other histories (both 'white' history, such as the two world wars, and 'black' history, such as the impact of DuBois, Garvey and 1920s Harlem) ironically become only the unobtrusive quilting stitches counterpointing the vivid, womanist story-patches. Even more polemically and overtly, Tashi (a compulsive storyteller) and the other characters in *Possessing the Secret of Joy* (1992) learn to confront not only the taboo status of clitoridectomy and infibulation but also the way, 'telling of the suffering [is] itself taboo'. The story itself thereby fractures that taboo: the novel, and (in 1993) *Warrior Mark's* 'true life' stories alongside it, thereby become praxis – formal demonstrations of narrative's powers.

Walker's significance thus primarily resides in the ways she anecdotalises and thereby fundamentally popularises well- or recently established theories of black sociocultural experience and beds them in narratives that exemplify how they ultimately circulate in an ocean of contending stories, where they must work for attention lest they be neglected, like so much other black heritage needing anthropological rescue. Emblematically, it was Walker who both discovered Hurston's 'lost' grave and tells the story of how she did it: first by tracing stories, then turning them to 'Everyday Use'.

Further reading

Bloom, Harold Alice Walker: Modern Critical Views, Chelsea House, 1990.
Gates, Henry, Louis Jr. and Appiah, K.A. (eds.) Alice Walker: Critical Perspectives Past and Present, Amistad Press, 1993.

R.J.E.

WALLERSTEIN, Immanuel

Sociologist	born USA 1930—
Associated with	WORLD-SYSTEM ANALYSIS ▪ CORE/PERIPHERY ▪ HISTORICAL SOCIOLOGY
Influences include	BRAUDEL ▪ MARX ▪ POLANYI ▪ MILLS ▪ SCHUMPETER
Shares common ground with	FRANK ▪ ARRIGHI ▪ AMIN
Main works	THE MODERN WORLD-SYSTEM (3 VOLS., 1974, 1980, 1988) THE CAPITALIST WORLD-ECONOMY (1979) UNTHINKING SOCIAL SCIENCE (1991) AFTER LIBERALISM (1995)

IMMANUEL WALLERSTEIN STUDIED initially at Columbia University, New York, gaining his Ph.D. in 1959. His early career was as an Africanist but he came to realise that Africa's problems could never be resolved without recourse to what he came to refer to as 'the modern world-system'. His response was to analyse world history, particularly from the sixteenth century, when he considers the 'world-system' to have originated. This was how he came to influence and be influenced by the French historian of the *Annales* school, Fernand Braudel, who also sees the sixteenth century as the beginning of the rise of the West and therefore a major turning-point in world history.

Since 1976 Wallerstein has been Distinguished Professor of Sociology at the State University of New York at Binghampton and also Director of the Fernand Braudel Center for the Study of Economies, Historical Systems and Civilisations. With the publication of *The Capitalist World-Economy* he described himself trained as a social scientist, politically committed and regarding open polemics as a necessary part of his scholarly activity. He eschews the idea that there is a theory of the world-system and instead emphasises that the Fernand Braudel Centre exists for the interpretation of world history using 'world-system analysis' as a heuristic device.

It was Wallerstein's *The Modern World-System* which arguably has had the greatest impact upon the academic world. Probably more than any other book, this has been instrumental in bringing sociology back into contact with the detail of history after a lengthy period tending towards a historical theorising. Even in terms of the sociology of development, Wallerstein, more than Gunder Frank, uses detailed historical evidence to make his case. The book is a masterful account of those developments which resulted in the concentration of capitalist economic power in north-western Europe during the sixteenth century. In Wallerstein's terms this amounts to the creation of a 'European world-economy' precisely because north-western Europe began to dominate other areas economically. In Eastern Europe this brought about a 'second serfdom' amongst its grain-producing peasantry and to the West there was the beginning of the Atlantic slave trade and the establishment of plantation agriculture in the colonised Americas.

Basically Wallerstein contrasts this 'world-system' based upon expanding European capitalist economics with 'world-empires' such as that of the Romans or the successive Islamic empires with which Christian Europe competed. Furthermore he employs the terms 'core', 'semi-periphery' and 'periphery' to describe relationships within the world-system, and this is essentially Wallerstein's approach to global social inequality. Thus north-western Europe is seen as the successful 'core' of the developing capitalist world-economy. The 'periphery' consists of areas touched upon by these developments, that is Eastern Europe, the Americas and other parts of the world colonised and exploited by Europeans. The Mediterranean area, including the Portuguese and Spanish states which actually pioneered European maritime expansionism, form merely a 'semi-periphery' because they lacked the capacity to develop capitalist institutions as effective as those of north-western Europe.

The first volume of *The Modern World-System* was followed by a second which covers seventeenth- and early eighteenth-century Mercantilism and the further consolidation of the European capitalist world-economy. In 1988 a third volume was added tracing 'the second era of great expansion of the capitalist world-economy' during the Industrial Revolution. In this work Wallerstein outlines periods when specific geographic 'cores' enjoyed hegemonic control. First there is the case of the Dutch United Provinces roughly between 1620 and 1672, then the UK as a modern nation-state between 1885 and 1873, and then the USA as a contemporary 'superpower' from 1945 to 1967. These are speculative assertions, as Wallerstein admits, but they illustrate a conceptual principle in terms of which an 'agro-industrial edge' over competition is achieved first, then a 'commercial edge' and finally a 'financial edge'. These are seen as consecutive but overlapping periods and it is the overlap between the initial period of 'agro-industrial edge' and the final period of 'financial edge' which Wallerstein sees specifically as the 'economic position of hegemonic power'.

Wallerstein's work has led to the establishment of a sub-discipline in sociology and cognate disciplines, particularly in North America. This comprises scholars who work under the broad aegis of 'world-system analysis' applying its principles to socio-economic studies over the full span of world history.

Further reading

Shannon, Thomas R. An Introduction to the World-System Perspective, Westview, 1989.
So, Alvin Y. Social Change and Development: Modernisation, Dependency and World Systems, Sage, 1990.
Spybey, Tony World-System Analysis, Sage, 1998.

T.S.

WEBER, Max

Sociologist/economist	born Germany, 1864–1920
Associated with	Verstehende Sociology ∎ Ideal types ∎ Rationalisation
Influences include	Marx ∎ Nietzsche ∎ Rickert
Shares common ground with	Horkheimer ∎ Adorno ∎ Habermas
Main works	'Objectivity' in Social Science and Social Policy (1904)
	The Protestant Ethic and the Spirit of Capitalism (1904/5, revised 1920)
	Economy and Society: An Outline of Interpretive Sociology (1922)

Born in Erfurt, Weber studied law at the universities of Heidelberg, Göttingen and Berlin, completing his doctoral thesis on the history of trading companies during the Middle Ages in 1889. In 1894 he was appointed Professor in Economics at Freiburg, and two years later accepted a Chair at Heidelberg, but retired from teaching for nearly five years following a nervous breakdown in 1898. In 1903 he joined the editorship of the influential social science journal *Archiv für Sozialwissenschaft und Sozialpolitik* (Archive for Social Science and Social Policy), and in the following years published extensively on the methodology of social and cultural science, the sociology of religion, economics, politics and law. These wide-ranging studies subsequently formed the groundwork of *Economy and Society*, a vast work of interpretative sociology which Weber was unable to complete before his death from pneumonia in June 1920.

In his essay *'Objectivity' in the Social Sciences* (1904) Weber defines culture as 'a finite segment of the meaningless infinity of the world process, a segment on which human beings confer meaning and significance'. This complex statement infers that all knowledge is perspectival, and that history becomes culture only insofar as we assign significance to it and relate it to particular value ideas. Culture is thus said to exist as a sphere of value-conflict or disagreement, and on this basis Weber argues that cultural science cannot proceed through formulation of universal laws, but through causal imputation of individual phenomena. Weber here draws on Windelband's distinction between nomothetic and idiographic knowledge to distinguish between the natural and social sciences. The former, he argues, studies physical events, explaining them through reference to universal laws, whilst the latter studies social action and seeks to understand its causes through gaining an empathetic understanding of the 'inner states' of the social actors involved. In view of this, Weber argues that explanation in the social sciences, unlike that in the natural sciences, must be adequate both at the levels of *causation* and *meaning*. Weber notes, however, that scientific knowledge is itself a product of culture, and as such represents a possible and not a natural way of depicting the world. In the light of this, he maintains a distinction between the facts and values of cultural science through the introduction of 'ideal-type' concepts. These concepts are analytical constructs that enable a logical rather than subjective interpretation of irrationality in social action, thereby allowing an objective understanding of the real causes of cultural history.

Weber's *Sociology of Religion* offers a powerful account of the influence of culture on the direction of historical development. *The Protestant Work Ethic and the Spirit of Capitalism*, Weber's best known and most controversial work, posits an affinity between the rise of 'this-worldly asceticism' and the development of capitalism. Although Weber recognises that 'No economic ethic has ever been determined solely by religion', this work makes a connection between the early capitalistic rationalisation of Western culture and the austere work ethic or 'calling' of the Puritan sects. Weber notes, however, that capitalism, once established, no longer needs the support of asceticism, for its highly mechanised and bureaucratic system of production requires no form of spiritual legitimation. Weber argues that disenchantment of religious legitimation leads to insoluble conflict between and within the life-orders and value-spheres of modern culture: the religious, economic, political, aesthetic, erotic and intellectual. For Weber, the rationalisation of Western culture is thus a tragic process, for although capitalist rationality heightens the calculability of social action, this very process inaugurates an irreconcilable struggle between values, heightens the impersonality of social relations, reduces value-rationality to instrumental rationality, and thereby reduces the scope for individual initiative and personal fulfilment.

A number of critics, in particular Georg Lukács, have connected Weber's call for 'value-free' methodology to the rise of Fascism in Germany, whilst others, in particular Herbert Marcuse, have attacked Weber for defending the instrumental rationality of capitalist relations and placing culture above economics as a determinant of social change. These criticisms are not entirely unfounded, but have generally failed to locate Weber's political views within the particular historical context of post-Bismarckian Germany, and have overlooked his deep concern for the fate of individuality and creativity within bureaucratic, rationalised Western culture.

Weber's work has left a lasting impression on social and cultural science. His interpretative methodology, in particular his theory of concept formation, is still employed by many sociologists and cultural theorists today. Recent interest in Weber's work, however, has tended to centre on his account of the rise of rationalism in the West, an account which has been developed by critical theorists such as Adorno, Horkheimer and Habermas, and which continues to influence contemporary debates over the nature and trajectory of modern and postmodern culture.

Further reading

Lash, S. and Whimster, S. (eds.), MAX WEBER, RATIONALITY AND MODERNITY, Allen & Unwin, 1987.

Scaff, L. FLEEING THE IRON CAGE: CULTURE, POLITICS AND MODERNITY IN THE THOUGHT OF MAX WEBER, University of California Press, 1991.

Turner, C. MODERNITY AND POLITICS IN THE WORK OF MAX WEBER, Routledge, 1992.

N.G.

WHORF, Benjamin Lee

Anthropologist	born USA 1897–1941
Associated with	LINGUISTIC DETERMINISM ■ LINGUISTIC RELATIVISM
Influences include	VON HUMBOLDT
Shares common ground with	SAPIR ■ CHOMSKY
Main works	LANGUAGES, THOUGHT AND REALITY (1956) COLLECTED PAPERS ON METALINGUISTICS (1949)

IN CONTRAST TO his theories, which were extraordinary and provocative, Whorf himself led an uneventful life, mostly working as a risk assessor for an insurance company in Hartford, Connecticut. His only degree was in chemical engineering (from the Massachusetts Institute of Technology), and he specialised in risk-assessment in the chemical industry. While his theories were based on the languages of American Indians in Mexico, he remained based in New England, taking up a position at Yale in 1937. His insurance work allowed him sufficient time to complete detailed library study on languages and he had developed an outline of his ideas when he met the more experienced scholar, Edward Sapir, who helped him formalise his theory, which became known as linguistic determinism.

The conception of language as a determinant of thought was approached in some eighteenth- and nineteenth-century philosophies. Those of Karl Wilhelm Von Humboldt, the German naturalist, can be singled out. At the turn of the nineteenth century, Von Humboldt travelled from his native Germany to East Asia, and later the South Sea Islands. His traveller's reports hinted at the possibility that language, far from reflecting particular cultures' images of the universe, actually ordered them. Whorf's study of the indigenous languages of Mexico, especially the Nahuatl (Aztec) and Maya, had inclined him to a similar view. Added to this was the recognition that, despite a bewildering range of differences, there were still commonalities – features that could be found in many other languages, including Hebrew, which he had also studied comprehensively.

After meeting Sapir, he focused his work on the Hopi culture. Hopi language bore similarity to the Nahuatl. The research proved to be revelatory: in Hopi, Whorf found that language operated at a conceptual level, structuring perceptions and understandings of time and space and thus of the entire cosmos. Hopi thought and, by implication, culture, was a function of the language in use. The Hopi language made no distinction between past and present: it recognised only becoming. Whorf argued that the Standard Average European (or SAE, as he called them) languages articulate time and space as linear, moving in a particular direction. Western science, of course, reflects this.

For Hopi, language has no equivalent to the SAE time/space linearity, but has a quite difference dichotomy between the manifest and the unmanifest. The former refers to both present and past, as they are revealed to the human senses. The latter refers to the purely mental and the future. According to Whorf, the Hopi Indians' conception of the world is structured by the language. Science, at least that developed in the West, is not possible without the linearity implicit in SAE concepts of time and space.

While the insight was accepted as valuable, Whorf's contention – as proposed in the Sapir–Whorf hypothesis – went further: it identified language as the governing factor in thought formation. Put simply: we cannot think without language. Sapir had earlier argued that linguistic categories strongly influence habitual thought, though, it seems, Whorf's input cemented the relationship. Objectors argued that, while there was certainly a relationship between thought and language, Whorf had exaggerated the power of language as a determinant and so rendered the relationship mechanical.

Further reading

Fabrega, H. 'Language, Culture and the Neurobiology of Pain: A Theoretical Exploration', BEHAVIORAL NEUROLOGY, 2: 4, 1989.
Gumperz, J and Levinson S. (eds.) RETHINKING LINGUISTIC RELATIVITY, Cambridge University Press, 1996.
Smith, M. 'Linguistic Relativity: On Hypotheses and Confusions', COMMUNICATION AND COGNITION, 29: 1, 1996.

E.C.

WILLIAMS, Raymond

Cultural theorist/literary critic	born Wales 1921–1988
Associated with	CULTURAL MATERIALISM ■ SOCIAL DEMOCRACY ■ WESTERN MARXISM
Influences include	BAKHTIN/VOLOSINOV ■ LEAVIS ■ GRAMSCI ■ TAWNEY
Shares common ground with	EAGLETON ■ GARNHAM ■ HALL
Main works	CULTURE AND SOCIETY 1780–1950 (1958) THE LONG REVOLUTION (1961) TELEVISION, TECHNOLOGY AND CULTURAL FORM (1974) PROBLEMS IN MATERIALISM AND CULTURE (1980) TOWARDS 2000 (1983)

WILLIAMS CAME FROM a working-class background in rural Wales and went to Cambridge to study English at the beginning of the Second World War. During the war he was a tank commander. In the 1950s he worked for Oxford University's adult education delegacy. Then, he returned to Cambridge and was made Professor of Drama there in the early 1970s. Williams was the leading cultural theorist of the British New Left and he put together the 1968 *May Day Manifesto*, a characteristic publication of the time. Throughout his life Williams was associated with a series of left-wing interventions in culture and politics from a broadly Marxist perspective, However, his own theorising, although it has an affinity with Marxism, is actually quite distinctive and draws upon much more varied traditions of radical democracy and cultural critique. Williams was the one genuinely original cultural theorist working in Britain during the second half of the twentieth century. His work is of comparable stature to French theorists such as Barthes, yet it is rarely appreciated as such even in Britain.

In an empiricist culture where, for example, literary analysis was seen 'innocently' as just practical criticism of canonised texts, Williams in some isolation commenced upon a scheme of work during the 1950s of an unusually theoretical and programmatic kind, which is represented by his two early classics, *Culture and Society* and *The Long Revolution*. He formulated a 'theory of culture as the study of relationships in a whole way of life'. In effect, he was producing a sociology in a literary idiom that was initially derived from the English tradition of criticism. Working on the borders of disciplinarity and schools of thought, Williams began to make connections across disparate

phenomena and to frame urgent issues at a comparatively high level of theoretical abstraction in such a way that influenced the thinking of a generation
and in a manner that became so deeply ingrained in cultural studies as to be
barely understood by its exponents. This is why it is difficult to reflect upon
and fully appreciate Williams's work as a body of theory. So much of what he
had to say is now simply taken for granted. For example, his original notion of
'the selective tradition' indicated how in any society there is a constant construction of its historical culture through selection of past texts and artefacts
to value and study. The selective tradition represents current preoccupations at
least as much if not more than a 'real' past. Another key concept of Williams is
'structure of feeling', which is meant to refer to the sensibility of a generation,
its socially reflexive experience articulated in cultural forms, although the
concept is often misused and trivialised in reference to something like a set
of attitudes.

With the rush of theorising in the 1970s, Williams found it incumbent upon
himself to clarify his own position. This he named cultural materialism, 'the
analysis of all forms of signification . . . within the actual means and conditions of their production'. Williams defined his general position in the context
of a critique of the base and superstructure model of classical Marxism and in
a relationship of affinity to Gramsci's theory of hegemony. He not only
disagreed with economic reductionism but made the crucial argument that
cultural production should itself be understood materially in both its industrial
setting and signifying practices. His conception of cultural industry, then, is a
non-pejorative one in contrast to that of Adorno and Horkheimer, yet not
confined to economic and organisational analysis. It is necessary to have a
cultural analysis of cultural production. This should be understood as a
determinate moment in a circuit, including the practices of cultural consumption. In most cultural theory, however, production in the materialist sense of
making something is neglected in favour of exclusively textual and reception
analysis.

Williams's hugely influential and very wise critique of technological determinism in communications media and his analytical emphasis on a combination of determinations in bringing about innovation and transformation is a
good illustration of the subtlety of his perspective on cultural production and
social change. He was interested in how technological media, particularly
television, are inscribed in the textures of everyday life, resulting in, for
example, the emergence of a pattern of 'mobile privatisation' which has contradictory features. In his later work, Williams developed a keen interest in
ecological politics and processes of globalisation and localisation, identifying
trends that have since become of focal concern in cultural analysis. His *Towards
2000* extended and internationalised the approach that was initiated by *The
Long Revolution*. By the 1990s, Williams was being widely and opportunisti-
cally dismissed as passé: his work, it was said, had been superseded by various
schools of thought, post-structuralism, and so forth. This hasty judgement is

very largely explicable in terms of the decline of belief in socialism and the feasibility of a 'common culture', even of the open and creative kinds espoused by Williams. The fact is, however, that the problems he addressed remain of critical significance and, no doubt, Williams's pioneering work will continue to be an available source of inspiration for the future development of cultural analysis.

Further reading

Eldridge, J. and Eldridge, L. RAYMOND WILLIAMS: MAKING CONNECTIONS, Routledge, 1994.
Inglis, F. RAYMOND WILLIAMS, Routledge, 1995.
McGuigan, J. 'Reaching for Control: Raymond Williams on Mass Communication and Popular Culture', in W.J. Morgan and P. Preston (eds.), RAYMOND WILLIAMS: POLITICS, EDUCATION, LETTERS, Macmillan, 1993.

J.McG.

WILLIS, Paul

Cultural analyst/ethnographer	Born England 1945—
Associated with	CULTURAL POPULISM ■ ETHNOGRAPHY ■ HEGEMONY THEORY
Influences include	GRAMSCI ■ MARX ■ WILLIAMS
Shares common ground with	BOURDIEU ■ FISKE ■ GEERTZ ■ HALL ■ HOGGART
Main works	LEARNING TO LABOUR (1978) PROFANE CULTURE (1978) COMMON CULTURE (1990)

PAUL WILLIS WAS a postgraduate student and fellow at the University of Birmingham's now defunct Centre for Contemporary Cultural Studies in the 1970s. He is one of the leading and most original figures of the erstwhile 'Birmingham School' and marked out a particular space for himself as its chief exponent of ethnographic research practice. Willis is now a professor at his home-town university of Wolverhampton in the English Midlands.

The theoretical importance of Willis's work may be understood in terms of Glaser and Strauss's 'grounded theory'. Although hugely informed by Marxist thought in particular, Willis does not simply 'apply' theory in his empirical research. Instead, he is inventive in theorising the meaning and significance of ethnographic findings. His early work, however, does exemplify some of the key theoretical assumptions of the Birmingham School in its heyday, especially concerning ritualised resistance to the norms of late capitalism. The key site of such resistance was deemed to be youth subculture, theorised as particular styles of 'magical solution', in Phil Cohen's term, to the problems of class and generational experience on the terrain of consumer culture. Willis's own doctoral thesis, published as *Profane Culture*, a comparison of working-class biker and middle-class hippy cultures in the late 1960s and early 1970s, is fairly typical of Birmingham School subcultural analysis. In their different class-based ways, these subcultures saw through and issued messages of resistance to capitalist culture.

Willis's most brilliant study, *Learning to Labour*, one of the 'classics' of British cultural studies, produced an almost tragic reading of youth cultural resistance. In the period immediately preceding mass youth unemployment in Britain, Willis set himself the problem of explaining why working-class boys, in particular, end up in unrewarding working-class jobs. The comprehensive educational system was supposed to give everyone an equal opportunity, yet innumerable studies had shown that children from middle-class backgrounds tended to be educational successes whereas the disadvantages of most working-class children were not ameliorated by education. The general theoretical issue was that of social and cultural reproduction which, in sociological analysis, was either treated empirically and in a policy-orientated perspective as a demographic phenomenon, or explained at a high level of theoretical abstraction, as in the problematic of reproduction in the writings of Althusserians and Bourdieuans. Willis was sceptical of deterministic and structural accounts, although he did not disagree with them in general terms. He wanted to examine, however, the level of cultural agency at which reproduction worked. To this purpose, he conducted a small-scale ethographic study of secondary-school students in Wolverhampton, mainly through in-depth interviews and discussions. Willis focused particularly upon 'the lads', whom he found to have a penetrating insight into their actual conditions of existence and life prospects. They knew only too well that 'meritocracy' did not work and that they were destined for lower-paid manual work. Hence, they rebelled at school and refused to bow down to the duplicitous authority of the educational system. Yet, in so doing, in their very acts of classroom and class resistance, typically limited by racism and sexism, they ensured class reproduction and their own particular fates within it.

The effect of such research, in spite of its experimental subtleties, was largely to confirm the grinding structural power of inegalitarian social and cultural reproduction. As British cultural studies developed, however, that critical message became much less pronounced and more positive emphasis was placed instead upon resistant activities, not in challenging the system but in creating a measure of autonomy to live within it. Willis's theoretical text, *Common Culture*, reporting on the Calouste Gulbenkian research on art and young people which he directed in the late 1980s, reflected the uncritical populist drift of British cultural studies during the 1980s. Young people's use of capitalist cultural commoditites displayed their 'symbolic creativity', their active meaning-making modes of consumption. Mass-market texts and products had no inherent meaning but were made to mean through the 'grounded aesthetics' of everyday consuming practices. So, for example, the significance of television advertistments addressed to the young was not to be seen as consumer manipulation but, rather, as supplying aesthetic materials for popular judgement. The problem with this position was not that it valued the use of mass-popular culture but that it gave a one-dimensional and essentially consumptionist account which ignored the relations between ideology, culture and capitalism at the actual point of production and it closed off serious consideration of issued to do with cultural value.

Further reading

Alasuutari, P. RESEARCHING CULTURE: QUALITATIVE METHOD AND CULTURAL STUDIES, Sage, 1995.
Jefferson, T. (ed.) RESISTANCE THROUGH RITUALS, Hutchinson, 1976.
McGuigan, J. CULTURAL POPULISM, Routledge, 1992.

J.McG.

WINCH, Peter

Philosopher	born England 1926–1997
Associated with	CONCEPTUAL ANALYSIS
Influences include	WITTGENSTEIN ∎ RYLE ∎ AUSTIN
Shares common ground with	BERGER ∎ CICOUREL ∎ STRAUSS
Main works	THE IDEA OF A SOCIAL SCIENCE AND ITS RELATION TO PHILOSOPHY (1958)
	TRYING TO MAKE SENSE (1987)
	THE JUST BALANCE (1989)

W INCH READ PHILOSOPHY, Politics and Economics at St Edmund Hall, Oxford, then took the Oxford B.Phil. degree, which would have exposed him to the kind of philosophy espoused by the likes of Gilbert Ryle and J.L. Austin: ordinary language philosophy, sometimes known as linguistic analysis, which was influential in British philosophical circles after the war. This style of analysis tried to reconcile the apparent conflict between everyday wisdom and philosophical theories or scientific findings through the treatment of our use of language.

Winch, however, found a much more profound influence in the work of Ludwig Wittgenstein, who died in 1951, but whose thesis, *Philosophical Investigations*, was not published in English until 1953. Winch was clearly affected by this and Wittgenstein's earlier *Tractatus* (first published in journal form in 1921), which consisted of a puzzling series of maxims with little in the way of supportive reasoning and no evidence at all. Language, argued Wittgenstein, contains propositions that are collages of facts of which the world is constructed. The 'facts' themselves must exist in a form that is comprehensible – they must allow themselves to be articulated or expressed.

Wittgenstein later issued a completely different philosophy in which language is absolutely central and meaning derives from its use in specific contexts. The earlier idea of language as a kind of calculus with atomic elements was abandoned in favour of a more sophisticated understanding of language as a stream of ways in which we make sense: 'language games' suggested that we come together in rule-bounded discourses. On this account, there is no world that language describes; rather, language use makes the world possible.

This is the theme that influenced Winch and, in 1958, he published what was to be a seminal monograph, *The Idea of a Social Science and its Relation to Philosophy*. In this, Winch proposed a form of idealism in which concepts structure experience. This struck at the Popperian model of social science which rested on the testing of hypotheses with ever-more stringent quantitative techniques. The premise of much social science, according to Winch, assumed that there was an objective world available to our senses and that we should strive towards developing procedures to measure this world. In contrast, Wittgenstein had already demonstrated that the world is not divorced from our sense-making processes: specifically the language we use to talk about the world. For Winch, this was the way forward for social science: to investigate its own epistemological bases rather than push forward with empirical enquiry.

Winch's slim book had a dramatic effect and reoriented much social research. It might be maintained that the reverberations of his thesis were felt in the phenomenological movements that affected the social sciences in general, but sociology in particular in the 1970s. Winch's advice that any worthwhile study of society 'must be philosophical in character' was heeded by a generation of sociologists whose enthusiasm for conceptual analysis became apparent in the various studies of 'everyday life'.

Investigations of the things people say and do, which were characteristic of ethnomethodology, were unquestionably influenced by Winch's injunctions to ground social-scientific work in particulars rather than pitch at high levels of generality. In this sense, Winch's work compares with that of, for example, Peter Berger, Anselm Strauss and other social scientists who, in some way, fell under Wittgenstein's – sometimes unacknowledged – spell.

But perhaps even longer lasting is the effect of Winch's rendering of Wittgenstein's ideas of rules. While it has been tempting for social scientists to explain human behaviour in terms of the human propensity to follow rules, Wittgenstein and Winch argued that no course of action can be determined by rules because any course for action could be said to accord with the rule. In other words, rules, and the application of the concepts in them, depend on taken-for-granted customs and practices: the notion of meaning is explained in terms of its use.

Further reading

Block, Irving (ed.) PERSPECTIVES ON THE PHILOSOPHY OF WITTGENSTEIN, Blackwell, 1981.
Kenny, Anthony THE LEGACY OF WITTGENSTEIN, Blackwell, 1984.
Schatzki, Theodore R. SOCIAL PRACTICES: A WITTGENSTEINIAN APPROACH TO HUMAN ACTIVITY AND THE SOCIAL, Cambridge University Press, 1996.

E.C.

WITTGENSTEIN, Ludwig

Philosopher	born Austria, 1889–1951
Associated with	LOGICISM ■ ORDINARY LANGUAGE PHILOSOPHY ■ LANGUAGE GAMES
Influences include	RUSSELL ■ FREGE ■ SCHOPENHAUER ■ KRAUS
Shares common ground with	VIENNA CIRCLE ■ HEIDEGGER
Main works	LOGISCHPHILOSOPHISCHE ABHANDLUNG (1921, TRANS. TRACTATUS LOGICO-PHILOSOPHICUS) PHILOSOPHISCHE UNTERSUCHUNGEN (1953, TRANS. PHILOSOPHICAL INVESTIGATIONS) ÜBER GEWISSHEIT (1969, TRANS. ON CERTAINTY) VERMISCHTE BEMERKUNGEN (1977, TRANS. CULTURE AND VALUE)

LUDWIG WITTGENSTEIN, THE youngest of eight children, was born into a wealthy family of Jewish extraction and he grew up in the rarefied intellectual milieu of *fin de siècle* Viennese modernism, where artists like Gustav Mahler and Gustav Klimt were regular visitors to the family mansion. In a note he records in 1931 he lists the influences upon his thinking as Boltzman, Hertz, Schopenhauer, Frege, Russell, Kraus, Loos, Weininger, Spengler, and Sraffa.

From his Viennese background he inherited a strong scepticism towards traditional philosophy, cultural pessimism, the critique of language and culture, an appreciation of Austrian music and poetry (Bruckner, Grillparzer, Labor, Lenau), his concern for style, a belief in the inexpressible (or mystical), a deep ethical and aesthestic sense and an ascetic individualism. He first studied engineering and later, at the age of eighteen, aeronautics at Manchester. His thinking turned to the philosophy of mathematics and on the advice of Frege, whom he met briefly in 1911, he went to study the foundations of logic and mathematics under Bertrand Russell at Cambridge. The First World War interrupted his work with Russell. He served in the Austrian army and, while a prisoner of war, completed his *magnum opus*, the *Tractatus Logico-Philosophicus*, in which he thought that he had solved all the problems of philosophy. In the years 1920–26 he worked as a primary school teacher, returning to philosophical work under Ramsey's persuasion and making contact with members of the Vienna Circle, whom he greatly influenced, before returning to Cambridge, where he succeeded Moore as Professor of Philosophy in 1939. It was during the period 1936 to 1948 that Wittgenstein composed the first part of *Philosophical Investigations*, which was published posthumously. He resigned his Chair in 1947, dying of cancer four years later.

Wittgenstein's literary legacy comprises seventy eight manuscripts, thirty four typescripts and eight dictations he made to colleagues or pupils. Much of his work has been published in edited collections posthumously. Wittgenstein is certainly one of the greatest philosophers of the twentieth century. His work in philosophy of language, philosophy of logic and mathematics, philosophical psychology and on the role of philosophy itself, has not only shaped the trajectory of contemporary philosophy but also greatly influenced the intellectual culture of modern times.

The *Tractatus* comprises seven major propositions, beginning 'The world is all that is the case' and ending 'What we cannot speak thereof we must remain silent', arranged in a numbered sequence, with sub-propositions, etc., in an elaborate structure which stylistically and 'architecturally' reinforces and reflects its subject matter. It has the same austere beauty as the mansion Wittgenstein designed for his sister. The *Tractatus* analyses the logical form of a proposition or sentence positing a picture theory of meaning according to which a fact-stating sentence (or *sätze*) represents the world (truly or falsely) by picturing or mirroring a state of affairs. There is a strict isomorphism between the structure of an atomic sentence and the structure of state of affairs it depicts. All sentences which are not atomic sentences or truth-functional composites are consigned to the realm of nonsense, that is, only fact-stating or 'scientific' sentences can be true or false and are therefore meaningful: all other sentences (for example, those in ethics and aesthetics) are, strictly speaking, meaningless or nonsense, including those of the *Tractatus* itself, which Wittgenstein asserts can be *shewn* but not said. As well as the doctrine of logical form the *Tractatus* has a 'mystical', romantic and ethical side, strongly influenced by Schopenhauer. By plotting the limits of (scientific) language Wittgenstein is leaving room for ethics. In the latter part he devotes himself to questions of the 'I', the subject, the will ('*The limits of my language* mean the limits of my world', 5.6; 'The subject does not belong to the world, but is rather a limit of the world, 5.632).

While Wittgenstein had formally given up philosophy after completing the *Tractatus*, in the ensuing period he continued to read philosophy-related works, including those of Freud. His experience as a schoolteacher renewed his interest to how children *learned* language. It was during this period that he came to question his earlier logically pristine conception of language and, in particular, the underlying idea that the meaning of a word is the thing it stands for. (From the mid-1930s Wittgenstein also renewed his interest in the foundations of mathematics.) The *Investigations* espouses, by contrast, a pragmatic view of language in which 'meaning is use' and must be learned. Against his earlier view Wittgenstein maintains that there is no common logical form even for descriptive sentences: the fact is that there are many different kinds of sentence (orders, demands, questions, etc.) which take their meaning from the everyday actions and social activities – 'language-games' – comprising a culture or 'form of life'. Language is learned as the child is initiated into a form of life: that is, it is learned practically. Running through the *Investigations* is also an attack upon Cartesian subjectivity conceived as a doctrine of 'inner sense' and a foundation for language; that words have meaning by virtue of naming inner states and that the subject has privileged access to these states. Wittgenstein's famous private language argument indicates that inner states or experiences stand in need of external and public criteria.

Philosophy consists in 'assembling reminders' rather than building a theory; its method is purely descriptive and as a kind of therapy helps us to overcome our bewitchment by language. Wittgenstein's style reflects his interest in promoting a shift in understanding or solving 'grammatical' puzzles (which reflect deep disquietudes in our cultural life): aphorism (after Lichtenberg, Schopenhauer and Nietzsche), metaphor, analogy, little sketches and diagrams, make up his philosophical repertoire.

Further reading

Hacker, P.M.S. WITTGENSTEIN'S PLACE IN TWENTIETH-CENTURY ANALYTIC PHILOSOPHY, Blackwell, 1996.
Janik, A. and Toulmin, S. WITTGENSTEIN'S VIENNA, Simon & Schuster, 1973.
Monk, R. LUDWIG WITTGENSTEIN: THE DUTY OF GENIUS, Cape, 1990.

M.P.

WOLLSTONECRAFT, Mary

Social theorist	born England, 1759–1797
Associated with	RATIONALISM ■ FEMINISM ■ RIGHTS
Influences include	ROUSSEAU ■ PRICE ■ SMITH
Shares common ground with	PAINE ■ GODWIN ■ DE BEAUVOIR
Main works	A VINDICATION OF THE RIGHTS OF WOMAN (1792)
	AN HISTORICAL AND MORAL VIEW OF THE FRENCH REVOLUTION (1794)
	LETTERS WRITTEN DURING A SHORT RESIDENCE IN SWEDEN, NORWAY AND DENMARK (1796)

MARY WOLLSTONECRAFT CAME from a family of declining gentlemen-farmers, her education informal and intermittent. She left home at 19, and earned a living as a companion, by needlework, by starting up a small school, or as a governess, which she did in 1786. In the following year her *Thoughts on the Education of Daughters* was published and she was also dismissed from her post. Her first novel, *Mary, A Fiction* was published in 1788, and she began to earn her living translating from French and German. Encouraged by her publisher, Joseph Johnson, she began to write prolifically in an increasingly radical milieu of political and religious dissent where she met Paine, Price and Henri Fuseli. She was an active participant in the debate which began in 1789 with the fall of the Bastille, around the significance of the French Revolution, and was one of the first to respond to Burke's conservative reaction. The work she is best known for, *A Vindication of the Rights of Woman*, was a contribution to the process of widening the scope of the revolutionary process, and as soon as it was written she went alone to Paris to see what was happening for herself. Her writings on the revolution reveal a series of new apprehensions, and her personal life became complicated as for security she registered herself as the wife of an American (Imlay), by whom she had an illegitimate child. She returned to London in early 1795, but left for Sweden on a business mission for Imlay later in that year. She finally broke with Imlay and secretly married William Godwin, with whom she had her second child (Mary, later Mary Shelley) in August 1797. She died 10 days after the birth. Her posthumous autobiographical novel, *The Wrongs of Woman*, was published in 1798.

Despite Wollstonecraft's lack of systematic education her writings reveal a brilliant mind and imagination, and a wide culture in literature and languages. Her contribution is an original theory of the paradoxes of gender relations in the democratic revolution, including its cultural dimensions. Her theory is constructed out of a critique of the Enlightenment writings of Locke, Rousseau, Adam Smith and the influence of religious dissent from Richard Price. The key terms of her theory are reason, power, virtue and sex. She adopts and develops the idea that where power hierarchies develop in institutions or society more generally an inevitable process of corruption begins unless there are rational explanations available to legitimise the structure of inequalities produced. Appeal to tradition or mystical rights was insufficient in an age of reason, and she pushed this idea further than most could tolerate – into the domestic sphere and to gender relations more broadly.

The key assumptions of her position were that, first, the capacity to acquire and produce knowledge was the same for men and women. Second, that reason was the necessary basis for the acquisition of virtue. And third, that the emancipation of women depended on ending the exclusion of women from acquiring and applying reason. These ideas, she argued, were simply a necessary consequence of the modern revolution, which showed that social progress was a result of the growth of the powers of reason across all aspects of society, from the Church, the monarchy, the armed forces, the economy, and also to gender roles in the family and society, an effect of the growing self-awareness of the people in their struggle against feudal authorities and relations. She saw this struggle from a Puritan perspective as one concerning the connection between reason and virtue. While the results of the segregation of the sexes permitted men to develop reason, a necessary condition for the production of active virtue, women could attain virtue only by remaining sexually pure, a passive and negative virtue. Given male sexual demand, women found themselves, however, the object of flattery and coquetry. Cut off from real political and economic power, women could nevertheless locate another power, but one identical in form to that of a parasitic élite. Her radical theory thus concluded that as an effect of the feudal divisions of gender relations, women constituted themselves as a variant form of an aristocracy, and as such became corrupted by its power dynamics. The revolution in modern citizenship, according to Wollstonecraft, had to be completed by a revolution in sexual manners, a sexual desegregation, and the development of a new culture of the sexes based not on seductiveness and flattery, but on friendship and reason. Thus her cultural critique was aimed at the image of women produced in the Enlightenment as the 'weaker sex', as possessing a 'fair defect' in their nature. Such views, she argued, were caught in a power game which rested on the maintenance of pseudo-chivalrous gender relations around a passive and irrational sexual aristocracy, a condition which necessitated the exclusion of women from society and modern citizenship more generally.

Wollstonecraft's remarkable theory is similar in its main argument with that of Simone de Beauvoir, written under very different conditions 150 years later. More recent feminism of sexual liberation rejected her analysis as exhibiting a negative attitude to sexual pleasure. More recent writing has taken interest in the complexity of her life, her cultural theory and styles of writing.

Further reading

Kelly, G. REVOLUTIONARY FEMINISM: THE MIND AND CAREER OF MARY WOLLSTONECRAFT, Macmillan, 1990.
Sapiro, V. A VINDICATION OF POLITICAL VIRTUE, University of Chicago Press, 1992.
M.G.

WRIGHT, Erik Olin

Marxist sociologist	born USA 1947—
Associated with	CLASS ANALYSIS ■ ANALYTICAL MARXISM
Influences include	MARX ■ ROEMER ■ BURAWOY
Shares common ground with	BOWLES ■ COHEN ■ ELSTER ■ PRZEWORSKI
Main works	CLASSES (1985) INTERROGATING INEQUALITY (1994) CLASS COUNTS (1997)

I N A WORLD of post-Marxisms, Erik Olin Wright, Professor of Sociology at the University of Wisconsin, Madison, stands out for his continuing commitment to Marxist social science. Unlike others who originated in this intellectual tradition but subsequently abandoned it, Wright has worked stubbornly towards its reconstruction. This project has resulted in an accumulating body of work on social class analysis and, more recently, on what has become known as 'Analytical Marxism'. While his work has not been explicitly concerned with the subject of culture, he has influenced a number of other writers by showing that it is still possible to undertake a credible Marxist analysis of capitalism at the end of the twentieth century.

Wright's first major work, *Class, Crisis and the State*, launched him into the forefront of Marxist scholarship. In it, he sought to fit Marxist theory to the realities of late twentieth-century capitalist societies, notably to the problem presented by the growth of the 'middle classes'. He resolved this by arguing that professionals, managers and others occupied 'contradictory locations' in a system of class relations which was defined in terms of domination in the labour process.

This interest in questions of class analysis became a preoccupation which resulted in the International Project on Class Structure and Class Consciousness which he has led since 1978. This project, which was guided by Wright's belief that the validity of Marxist theories could be established by empirical evidence, began as a survey of the USA, Italy and Sweden and has since included some sixteen countries, ranging across Western and Eastern Europe, North America and the Asia-Pacific rim. This collaborative project has culminated in the publication of the widely praised *Class Counts*.

Though Wright's approach to class has always been critical of the failure of 'bourgeois social science' to capture the dynamics of class relationships, he has, however, also displayed a willingness to use the statistical techniques of its practitioners. This development, which has marked him out as the pioneering figure of 'multivariate Marxism', brought him to the attention of a number of leading 'bourgeois' sociologists with whom he has engaged in a series of long-running debates over social stratification.

During the course of these debates he revised his approach to class analysis. His new approach, which appeared initially in *Classes*, and was subsequently elaborated in *Class Counts*, was heavily influenced by John Roemer's incorporation of rational choice arguments into Marxism. Wright now contends that class relations only emerge out of the property relations that accrue from the possession of three types of assets: assets in the means of production, skill assets, and what he terms 'organization assets'. This change not only brought further criticism from his non-Marxist opponents, it also attracted criticism from a new quarter: traditional Marxists who believed that his innovations were diluting Marx's original insights.

This development should, however, be viewed in the context of Wright's increasing involvement in the emergence of 'Analytical Marxism' since the mid-1980s. This intellectual current is the work of a small network of leading international scholars such as G.A. Cohen, Jon Elster, Adam Przeworski and John Roemer who all define their work, at least, partly as an engagement with that of others in the group. Their most distinctive feature as a theoretical tendency is the use of rational choice arguments to show that macro-level events and conditions can be explained by micro-level behaviour. For this reason, they are sometimes known as 'Rational Choice Marxists'.

Since this group forms one of Wright's key intellectual reference points, and since it clearly lies within the Marxist community, there may be some justification in the claims by non-Marxist sociologists to the effect that not only does he ignore their criticisms, his work is also characterised by too much abstract and too little engagement with social reality.

Further reading

Mills, C. 'Rational Choice Marxism and Social Class Boundaries', RATIONALITY AND SOCIETY, 6: 2, 1994, pp. 218–42.
Rose, D. and Marshall, G. 'Constructing the (W)right Classes', SOCIOLOGY, 20: 3, 1986, pp. 440–55.
Wright, E.O. *et al.* THE DEBATE ON CLASSES, Verso, 1989.

P.McG.

WUNDT, Wilhelm

Psychologist	born Germany 1832–1920
Associated with	APPERCEPTION ■ CREATIVE SYNTHESIS ■ VÖLKERPSYCHOLOGIE
Influences include	LEIBNIZ ■ KANT ■ HERBART ■ VON HELMHOLTZ
Shares common ground with	SWEDENBORG ■ ROMANES ■ VYGOTSKY ■ MALINOWSKI ■ ALLPORT
Main works	PRINCIPLES OF PHYSIOLOGICAL PSYCHOLOGY (1897) FOLK PSYCHOLOGY (10 VOLS. 1900–20) THE LANGUAGE OF GESTURES (1973)

MEDICALLY TRAINED AT the University of Tübingen, Wundt moved to the University of Heidelberg where he was awarded his doctorate in 1855. His early research was in the area of sensory and neural physiology, though he later became involved in psychological experimentation. Taking up a position as Professor of Philosophy at Leipzig in 1875, he set up facilities for laboratory-based studies in physiological psychology. This initiative earned him the epithet 'father of experimental psychology' – though, in fact, a large part of his corpus was devoted to historical and philosophical as well as experimental explorations of the human mind; this was reflected in the journal *Philosophische Studien*, which he edited.

Like many of his contemporaries, Wundt was influenced by associationism, at least the applied branches of this subject (which later became behaviourist psychology). But Wundt's critique of the conditioning process of associationism was that learning involves more than a mechanical stimulus-response connection: there is what he called a creative synthesis at work, in which a combination of mental components gives rise to new emergent properties, not contained in the components themselves. Here was a recognition of: (1) the possibility of free will and (2) the structural character of the human mind. The aim of Wundt's version of structural analysis was to study conscious processes and to delineate as precisely as possible how mental components connect and combine with each other to produce new qualities.

Wundt's term 'apperception' (*vide* Leibniz, Kant and, later, Herbart) described the emergent process through which mental activity creates something completely new. The activity involved in this process contrasted with the *tabula rasa* passivity suggested by the associationist conception of the human mind. Wundt's term to describe the workings of the structure-building was the 'law of psychic resultants'. Herbart's work was influential not so much as in positing a plurality of things that possess in themselves absolute existence apart from apperception by the human mind, but in the attempt to formulate a quantifiable process through which new events, objects or ideas are assimilated into existing stocks of knowledge.

The controlled laboratory experiments involved painstaking documentation of experiences, such as sensations, which were classified in terms of, for example, their modality, intensity and duration. Sensations were central to Wundt's research and in this endeavour, he used introspection as a method. Feelings were plotted in terms of pleasure–displeasure, tension–relaxation and excitement–depression measures. Wundt's reputation was founded on this detailed statistical approach, though he was critical of psychologies that limited their studies to such laboratory-based research. He accepted that important findings on the specifics of simple behaviour could be discovered; but human conduct was patterned and, as such, remained susceptible to the shaping influences of culture and social institutions.

To understand the full complexity of human behaviour, psychology should take account of historical and social variables that extended beyond the scope of any individual. This approach to study was what Wundt called *Völkerpsychologie*, which equates to what today would be called social psychology, albeit with more comparative and historical material than might be allowed in most contemporary studies. One area that Wundt anticipated in his 10-volume work *Völkerpsychologie* was that of linguistics. Wundt contrasted the sensory-motor level of linguistic performance with higher, more abstract cognitive levels.

His *magnum opus* was less well received than his work on physiological psychology and later developments ensured that he would remain best known for his early work. In moving away from the experimental approach and trying to induce voluntarism into his model, he found little favour with psychologists, who were occupied in establishing the study of the mind as a legitimate science. While they warmed to his pioneering laboratory work, his later theories veered too far away from the positivist orientations that experimental psychology elected to adopt.

Further reading

Benjamin, L. (ed.) A HISTORY OF PSYCHOLOGY: ORIGINAL SOURCES AND CONTEMPORARY RESEARCH, McGraw-Hill, 1997.
Blumenthal, A.L. 'A Reappraisal of Wilhelm Wundt', AMERICAN PSYCHOLOGIST, 30, 1975.
Bringmann, W.G. (ed.) WUNDT STUDIES: A CENTENNIAL COLLECTION, Hogrefe, 1980.

E.C.

ZIŽEK, Slavoj

Philosopher/cultural theorist	born Slovenia 1949—
Associated with	PSYCHOANALYSIS ■ IDEOLOGY ■ THEORY OF THE SUBJECT AND ANTAGONISM
Influences include	LACAN ■ ALTHUSSER ■ HEGEL ■ KANT
Shares common ground with	LACLAU AND MOUFFE ■ JAMESON ■ COPJEC
Main works	THE SUBLIME OBJECT OF IDEOLOGY (1989)
	LOOKING AWRY (1991)
	FOR THEY KNOW NOT WHAT THEY DO (1991)
	ENJOY YOUR SYMPTOM! (1992)
	TARRYING WITH THE NEGATIVE (1993)
	METASTASES OF ENJOYMENT (1994)
	THE PLAGUE OF FANTASIES (1997)

HAVING STUDIED PHILOSOPHY in Ljubljana, Zižek turned to the discipline of psychoanalysis at the Université Paris-VIII in the early 1980s. Since that time he has developed a characteristic intellectual project which combines psychoanalysis and philosophy with the study of contemporary culture and politics. In Ljubljana, Zižek has sought to develop this project through the Institute for Social Sciences, where he is a Senior Researcher, and the Society for Theoretical Psychoanalysis, of which he is the founder and president. Zižek's opposition to totalitarianism and racism (in both their left- and right-wing variants) is well known, and, during the 1980s, he was not only politically active in the alternative movement in Slovenia but also stood as a candidate for the presidency of the Republic of Slovenia in the first multi-party elections in 1990.

Following the 'new school' of French psychoanalysis, led by Jacques-Alain Miller, Zižek lays emphasis on the later Lacan. In particular, he stresses the centrality of that which cannot be represented – the Real – and the underlying forces of trauma and enjoyment. In contrast to postmodern celebrations of difference, Zižek affirms that all identification is driven by the need to escape falling into the traumatic void at the centre of every identity (the eternal 'who am I?'). This void is the subject (the 'barred S': $) which all structures of identification attempt to fill out. When these structures fail (as in, for example, the loss of a partner) the result is traumatic dislocation in which the individual reverts to subject and falls into the Real of $ (s/he 'falls apart').

From this perspective, the traditional approach to ideology, as false consciousness and illusion, is turned on its head. Ideology does not distort or conceal an underlying positive reality (human nature, class interests, etc.). On the contrary, the mark of ideology is that it attempts to conceal an existential void and the traumatic knowledge that it cannot be filled out. What ideology offers, in fact, is the construction of social reality itself as a way to escape the horrifying condition of lack in the Real.

While particular ideologies have a characteristic content, their universal function is to provide a symbolic coherence and sense of solidity against the distorting presence of an eternally corrosive Real. In this way, ideology subsists in the fantasy of mastering the Real by providing straw enemies – 'fictional' embodiments of the Real – which 'if only they could be eliminated' would enable social harmony to be realised and the circuit of enjoyment to be completed. In short, society is impossible and the Other is made responsible for this original 'crime'. In Nazi discourse, for example, it is the Jews who are made responsible for stealing German enjoyment and preventing harmony (thereby denying the *immanent* impossibility of such harmony). The central paradox, therefore, is that what is concealed by imputing to the other the theft of enjoyment is that we never possessed what was allegedly stolen from us.

Zižek's project is strongly characterised by an attempt to place Lacanian categories within an Hegelian–Marxist framework. In consequence, he has tended to neglect alternative possibilities of developing Lacanian categories within post-Hegelian and/or post-Marxist contexts where there is greater emphasis on deconstruction and articulatory practices. This is particularly apparent with reference to the political terrain. In *Tarrying with the Negative*, for example, Zižek tends to present contemporary politics in terms of opposing ideological formations attempting a total concealment of the Lacanian lack: an exclusionary liberal–democratic capitalism, on the one hand, and nationalist closure, on the other. The way to break this deadlock, he argues, is to develop more inclusivist forms of universalism of the type we find in ecologism. From a deconstructive perspective, however, it is clear that between lack and its total concealment there are wider subversive possibilities than Zižek appears willing to allow. Instead of absolutist displacement, deconstruction enables us to approach nationalism and liberal–democratic capitalism as undecidable constructions which are subvertible through political practices which strive to deepen and expand the democratic and universalist dimensions in each formation. In this way, a radical politics may be constituted which is 'aware' of the Lacanian lack (aware of its own impossibility) and thereby endeavours only a *strategic* concealment of it. The fundamental contribution of Zižek has been his reconceptualisation of the terrain of ideology and reality in terms of its Lacanian fantasy structure.

Further reading

Eliot, A. SOCIAL THEORY AND PSYCHOANALYSIS IN TRANSITION, Blackwell, 1992.
Stavrakakis, Y. 'Green Fantasy and the Real of Nature: Elements of a Lacanian Critique of Green Ideological Discourse', JOURNAL FOR THE PSYCHOANALYSIS OF CULTURE AND SOCIETY, 2: 1, Spring 1997, pp. 123–32.

G.D.